An Explanatory Guide to the

ENGLISH LAW OF TORTS

An Explanatory Guide to the

ENGLISH LAW OF TORTS

by

PETER KAYE, LL.M, Ph.D, AKC (LOND.)
of Gray's Inn, *Barrister*

Morgan Bruce Professor of European Law and Legal Process
at the University of Wales Swansea, United Kingdom
and
Guest Professor of Common Law at the
University of Trier, Germany

Barry Rose Law Publishers Ltd
Chichester, England

ISBN 1 872328 53 9 paperback

ISBN 1 872328 28 8 casebound

Works by the same Author

Civil Jurisdiction and Enforcement of Foreign Judgments under the Brussels Convention (1987, Butterworths, London)

The Private International Law of Tort and Product Liability (1991, Dartmouth Publishing, Aldershot)

The New Private International Law of Contract of the European Union and the Rome Contracts Convention (1993, Dartmouth Publishing, Aldershot)

International Contracts (1993, Barry Rose, Chichester)

Damages for Personal Injuries. A European Perspective, ed. with F. Holding (1993, John Wiley & Sons, Chichester)

Methods of Execution of Orders and Judgments in Europe, ed. (1996, John Wiley & Sons, Chichester)

Published by
Barry Rose Law Publishers Ltd
Chichester, England

Printed by BPC Wheatons Ltd, Exeter, Devon

This publication is printed on Acid Free Paper

Contents

To Fred, Janet and Sallyann Holding

Preface

This is a book originally conceived and written for foreign lawyers and foreign law students - principally those who are non-native English speakers. For this reason, the essential task was perceived to be one of providing clarity and simplicity in respect of language and explanation of fundamental principles and policies. The need to avoid unnecessarily elaborate detail at the expense of comprehensibility was seen to be paramount.

Such are the book's admittedly very modest aims. In particular, it does not seek to evaluate nor to analyse in any particular depth the integrity and internal functioning of the English tort law mechanism. This role is happily left to the impressive array of standard student textbooks, of which there are currently some excellent examples. Odious though it may be to select from the totality of the latter, the author has been greatly assisted by accounts of the law of tort provided by the following works, in no particular order of merit, to which further reference is made at the end of each chapter: Brazier, M., *Street on Torts,* 9th ed., 1993 (Butterworth & Co., London); Fleming, J.C., *The Law of Torts,* 8th ed., 1992 (The Law Book Company, Sydney); Hepple, B.A. and Matthews, M.H., *Tort: Cases and Materials,* 4th ed., 1991 (Butterworth & Co.); Heuston, R.F.V. and Buckley, R.A., *Salmond and Heuston on the Law of Torts,* 20th ed., 1992 (Sweet & Maxwell, London); Howarth, D., *Textbook on Torts,*

1995 (Butterworth & Co., London); Jones, M.A., *Textbook on Torts*, 4th ed., 1993 (Blackstone, London); Rogers, W.V.H., *Winfield and Jolowicz on Tort*, 14th ed., 1994 (Sweet & Maxwell); Weir, T., *A Casebook on Torts*, 7th ed., 1992 (Sweet & Maxwell, London).

One of the objects of the present relatively minor contribution is to inform and to assist readers to access and better comprehend the law in greater detail as presented in the preceding and other standard works on tort and to assist in their use and usefulness. It may therefore be used as a companion to the leading accounts rather than necessarily as a substitute therefor. Nevertheless, readers who merely require a basic, yet comprehensive, explanation of the main principles of the subject may feel satisfied with this work alone.

The publishers made the point that the book's aims, method and content seemed as valid for the needs of *English* law students as for those of foreign students and lawyers who wished to familiarize themselves with English torts law. From this it was impossible to dissent. Accordingly, the title now reflects its general mission to provide an introductory, explanatory guide for *all* who seek to learn of the English law of torts.

The book contains few, if any, revolutionary thoughts or processes. The presentation and structure, generally, is hardly different from that of many of the standard works. The author, however, allowed himself one small *eccentricity* with respect to the structure of ch.5 which deals with establishment of the *duty of care* in the tort of *negligence*. The accepted test for the existence of such duty is commonly called the *three-stage test*, consisting of *i.* reasonable foreseeability of harm to the plaintiff from the defendant's actions, and *ii.* proximity of relationship between plaintiff and defendant, and *iii.* fair, just and reasonable as a matter of juridical policy for duty of care to be held to exist (see ch.5). However, the author is yet unconvinced that outside the specific areas of recovery of damages for *nervous shock* and for *pure economic loss through negligent misstatement*, the concept of stage-2 'proximity' has the slightest genuinely independent existence from stage-3 juridical policy - and even in the preceding two areas themselves, it remains to be proved that whatever function it is which *is said* to be performed by 'proximity', cannot equally be discharged by the juridical policy stage itself, alongside the anti-generalization device of incremental development through the cases. Thus, the sense in which 'proximity' is a requirement in nervous shock, it will be seen, is physical - in time and space - and familial - closeness of domestic relationships - between plaintiff and defendant's victim; while, in the case of pure economic loss from misstatements and advice, liability is largely through proximity of relations in a contractual setting or the like. Naturally, it is comforting for those concerned about legal certainties, for liability which is held to exist in particular factual situations and categories thereafter to be justified on the ground of 'proximity'. But actually to go further and to assert that those decisions were reached *because of* the existence of 'proximity', frankly, strains credulity, and, more importantly, leads almost inevitably to the additional conclusion that proximity exists both generally and independently as a criterion for the duty of care in negligence (see *supra*), required to be satisfied in *all* cases if liability is to be established, not just in nervous shock and pure economic loss: so, a careless motor car driver who knocks down a pedestrian will be liable if the victim's and the driver's mutual legal relations are sufficiently *proximate*. This resulting formulation is plainly a nonsense and entirely circular. The driver should of course only be held liable if he ought to have foreseen that he would injure the victim and if it is considered by the court to be fair, just and reasonable in all the circumstances that he should compensate the injured party. To be sure, there is little to be criticized in the attempt to develop the law on nervous shock and recovery for pure economic loss incrementally, by reference to specific types of situation as they appear before the courts; but then to try to vest the process with a greater degree of validity and to suggest a higher level of certainty, through the attachment to the procedure of the generalized, pseudo-scientific label 'proximity', is to risk seriously distorting the underlying and otherwise broadly acceptable doctrinal principles worked out in those cases.

For the reasons preceding, therefore, it was decided to structure the presentation of duty of care in the form of a different three-stage *process,* namely: *i.* reasonable foreseeability (conforming to the orthodox stage-1); *ii.* juridical policy, *incorporating proximity* (being stages 3 and 2, respectively, of the orthodox three-stage test, *supra*); and *iii.* public policy grounds against existence of a duty of care, of which the application is nowhere denied. This is the book's sole *deviation.* Sacrilege indeed. If it is successfully established that 'proximity' - *assuming a responsibility towards* (see *Swinney v. Chief Constable of Northumbria Police* (1996) *The Times,* March 28, CA) - means anything other than that it is fair, just and reasonable as a matter of juridical policy for the defendant *to be treated by the law* as having so assumed a responsibility towards the plaintiff, the author will be pleased to review his schema.

There are a number of persons who, consciously or unconsciously, assisted the author in the preparation of this work and whose contribution deserves to be recorded here.

In the first place, the author's gratitude is extended to current and former students on the Foreign Law and Language Programme at the University of Trier, the answers to a number of whose probing questions have found their way into the text at various points.

Secondly, the author's thanks are due to colleagues at Trier who have made the author's association with the Faculty wholly stimulating and fulfilling, in particular, to Professors von Hoffmann, Robbers and Schulze (the latter now of the University of Münster).

Thirdly, the author is grateful to members of the administrative section of the Law Faculty at Trier, in particular to Herr Meyer, Frau Goergen and Frau Schmidt, who have enabled the author to function to some extent.

Fourthly, the author thanks colleagues at the University of Wales Swansea for making available their expertise on the law of tort on a number of occasions, in particular Jane Lawson, LL.M. (Cantab.), LL.B. (Wales), Solicitor, Lecturer in Law, and Ruth Redmond-Cooper, LL.M. (Bristol), LL.B. (Kent), Lic. en droit (Paris XI), Visiting Research Fellow, and is grateful too to head of department Professor Jenny Levin for her consistent support.

Finally, the author wishes to express his appreciation to

his colleague, legal anthropologist and personal injuries law reformer Frederick Holding, whose infectious enthusiasm for his subject achieved the remarkable feat of converting, partially, a previously unmitigated commercial private international lawyer into a willing - though wholly insignificant - contributor to the personal injuries debate. Holding made two main propositions which he has since sought to expound: (1) that law and medicine had moved apart at an unacceptable rate since the initial structuring of the British welfare system and that efforts were required to be made without further delay in order to achieve a more effective balance; and (2) that lawyers and doctors ought to collaborate with others involved in long-term support of severely injured brain or spinal patients, in order to provide a holistic care system, appropriately funded by the law and correspondingly targeted by the medical support team. For the specific purpose of promoting such inter-professional collaboration, Holding co-founded with the author the journal *Personal Injury Law and Medical Review* (Barry Rose, Chichester), which subsequently became *Personal Injury* (John Wiley and Sons, Chichester) and continues its progress to this day under the general editorship of Fred Holding.

It remains to state that the law has sought to be incorporated as far as possible up to December 1995, although, thanks to the publishers' generosity, it has also proved practicable to include a number of further developments beyond that date. Such mistakes as exist in the text are the author's alone.

April 1996
Trier
Peter Kaye

Glossary of English Legal Terms and Abbreviations

AC	Appeal Cases Law Reports
Act	Legislation passed by Parliament
All ER	All England Law Reports
ALR	Australian Law Reports
Appellant	Party who brings an appeal
Bill	Proposed legislation
CCR	County Court Rules
Ch	Chancery Law Reports
County courts	Local courts of inferior jurisdiction
Court of Appeal	Appellate court from the High Court
Defendant	Party against whom a court action is brought
DLR	Dominion Law Reports
EG	Estates Gazette (journal)
EHRR	European Human Rights Law Reports
FSR	Fleet Street Reports
High Court	Court of first instance for cases over a certain value
House of Lords	Highest court in England and Wales
IRLR	Industrial Relations Law Reports
J	Judge of the High Court

LGR	Local Government Law Reports
LJ	Judge (Lord Justice) of the Court of Appeal
Lord	Judge of the House of Lords
NI	Northern Ireland Reports
NLJ	New Law Journal
NZLR	New Zealand Law Reports
P	Probate Law Reports
Plaintiff	Party by whom a court action is brought
QB/KB	Queen's/King's Bench Law Reports
Respondent	Party against whom an appeal is brought
RPC	Reports of Patent, Design and Trade Mark Cases
RSC	Rules of the Supreme Court
RTR	Road Traffic Reports
Tortfeasor	Person who commits a tort
Tortious	Relating to tort liability
WLR	Weekly Law Reports

Table of Cases

Table of Statutes

Pending Statutes

European Legislation

Court Rules

PART I

Chapter 1

Introduction

Those who seek to study the English Law of Torts are entrants to a world of caves and swirling pools where shafts of light belie reality and risk deceiving all but the most observant of travellers.

Policies - social and economic - vie with law, language and logic at times to lead the way into new, dimly lit passageways from which return is difficult and progress oft interrupted.

The guides are Judges, frequently replaced, responding to an ever-changing landscape, undoing the past, tying up the future.

Pity the poor diarist who must chronicle these voyages in the annals of legal posterity for those who seek to follow.

This book is one such account.

It is common to present English tort law as a series of sufficiently separate categories of tort liability, each the subject of particular rules and requirements for the establishment of the cause of action, yet frequently possessed of related features and common doctrine, and always reflecting the overriding characteristic of tort as:

the imposition of non-criminal legal responsibility upon the person by the state, non-dependent upon parties' contractual agreement.

The present work does not form an exception to the practice described and is divided into parts which are devoted to those generally recognized distinct areas of liability in tort. It will further come to be appreciated that the general areas themselves will sometimes contain internal divisions, separate torts, nonetheless possessed of legal characteristics or objectives so related as to merit common classification within a single general category.

The following are some of the major torts which form part of the overall treatment of the subject in this book:

Negligence

At the present day the tort of negligence, Judge-made law, enjoys the highest profile. It is the most general of torts, consisting of any conduct of a person, which fails to satisfy the standard of care towards another set by the law and which, as a consequence, causes personal injuries to the victim or damages his property or even, in some circumstances, harms a person financially and economically.

Inevitably, because of the potential width of liability under this tort, the main issues and difficulties will concern its precise scope of application and where to draw the boundaries in a fair and civilized society.

Occupier's Liability

Those who inhabit property have a duty towards others

whom they invite to visit them in those premises - and even towards uninvited guests, in the eyes of the law - to take certain steps to try to ensure that the visitor is safe and remains uninjured. Because of the particular sensitivity over balancing rights of hosts and guests in a just manner, the legislator stepped in in order to regulate the position, although it still remains for the courts to dispense justice within the statutory framework.

Strict Liability Torts

Sometimes policy dictates that a certain situation is so dangerous or liability so socially and economically desirable that a party ought to be held legally responsible in tort regardless of personal fault. He will thus be said to be "strictly liable".

Protection of the Person

The old tort of *Trespass against the Person* exists as a specially tailored form of liability where a person is physically interfered with. Nowadays, of course, much of its scope will be covered by the younger tort of negligence where the latter's requirements are satisfied. But there will still be some situations where negligence is unable to be established, in which event trespass will remain available if its own conditions of application are fulfilled.

Economic Torts

In a free society, there is great pressure to leave businessmen and industrialists alone, to survive or fall according to market forces. Notwithstanding this underlying spirit of abstentionism, the law has deemed it necessary to intervene on certain occasions of *Intimidation* or *Conspiracy* or *Inducement of Breach of Contract* in order to protect some sort of concept of the fair and orderly conduct of industrial and commercial relations in society. Certain behaviour is considered to be so unacceptable in its nature and effects that the law of tort has to step in in order to protect the economic position of the victim.

Land

What people do on their land, or from their land, touches deep psychological roots, individually and collectively, within society. Home, family, enjoyment: fundamental human aspirations. Not surprisingly, the law seeks to protect these interests through a series of provisions ranging from the old tort of *Trespass to Land* through to the broader liability in *Nuisance.*

Reputation

Society would be in turmoil if people were allowed to lie about each other publicly, with no legal remedy for the victim. The tort of *Defamation,* with others, attempts to strike a balance, not always easy, between the public interest in free speech and freedom to criticize on the one hand, and the individual citizen's reasonable desire for privacy on the other.

Defences

Against the preceding torts there exists a number of general defences which seek to take account of the needs of justice in particular circumstances where liability would otherwise be imposed. For example, the law may consider that there was *Consent* to the tort by the victim, or *Contributory Negligence* on his part, or that a contractual *Liability Exclusion Clause* or notice applied.

Remedies

The object of legal proceedings in tort is to obtain compensation in the form of financial damages, or an injunction which is a court order to prevent a threatened wrong or continuation of an existing state of affairs amounting to tort.

Such is the subject matter of this book.

The English Law of Torts is an example of the common law at its most active and dynamic, both historically and in the present era. It is certainly not the product of an isolated exercise in rigid academic analysis and systematization, but instead almost a living and breathing body of law, regularly changing in order to reflect transition in the surrounding social, political and economic environment: a fascinating object of comparative study and application, with either of which aims, it is hoped, this explanatory book will go some way to assist.

Further reading:

Brazier, *Street on Torts*, 9th ed, 1993 (Butterworth & Co., London): ch.1.
Fleming, J.G., *The Law of Torts*, 8th ed, 1992 (The Law Book Company, Sydney): ch.1.
Howarth, D., *Textbook on Tort*, 1995 (Butterworth & Co., London): ch.1.
Jones, M.A., *Textbook on Torts*, 4th ed, 1993 (Blackstone, London): ch.1.
Markesinis, B.S. & Deakin, S.F., *Tort Law*, 3rd ed, 1994 (Clarendon Press, Oxford): ch.1.
Rogers, W.V.H., *Winfield and Jolowicz on Tort*, 14th ed, 1994 (Sweet & Maxwell, London): chs.1 & 2.
Stanton, K.M., *The Modern Law of Tort*, 1994 (The Law Book Company, Sydney): chs.1 & 2.

PART II

Chapter 2

Nature and Development of the English Law of Torts

1. The General Features of "Tort"

Tort, from the Latin *tortus,* and taken into medieval law-French in England, means "twisted" ... "wrong".

It describes the body of judicial and legislative doctrine in the common law to provide a civil remedy for wrongs through the courts. Tort is principally to be distinguished from:

- criminal offences, and
- contract.

For commission of a crime, the penalty is payment of a fine to the state, or imprisonment - as a *punishment.* The main remedy for tort is *compensation,* paid by the defendant, the "tortfeasor", to the victim for the damage he has suffered as a result of the tortfeasor's "tortious" behaviour. Alternatively, the court may order measures preventing further loss from the tort, for example, an injunction.

Contracts come from an *agreement* between parties, whereas the duty in tort is imposed by the law irrespective of parties' desires, either as a societal obligation, or partly as punishment, or simply in order to give effect to the judicial concept of justice.

However, tort shares with crime the feature of state imposition of liability, and with contract the element of compensation as a remedy.

Furthermore, the same situation can give rise to both criminal proceedings and to those in tort: in the case of dangerous driving, for example, which causes injuries to people on or near the road, the victims can sue for damages in tort and the police may bring criminal proceedings against the driver; and a plaintiff may sue in both contract and tort in the alternative, for example, where a carelessly driven train crashes and consequently fails to carry out the contract to transport a passenger to his destination and also causes him to suffer personal injuries at the same time (see generally, *Henderson v. Merrett Syndicates Ltd* [1994] 3 All ER 506, pp.533 and 534, HL, and *Holt v. Payne Skillington (a Firm) and Another* (1995) *The Times,* December 22, CA), although certain case law suggests that in commercial cases, if there is a contract, this should form the basis of the action (see *Tai Hing Cotton Mill Ltd v. Lui Chong Hing Bank Ltd* [1985] 2 All ER 947). Damages may be more favourable and liability easier to establish in contract than in tort, which frequently requires fault to be proven; but commencement of time limitation for court actions to be brought can be better for a plaintiff in tort than in contract where date of breach rather than subsequent damage may instead be referred to for the purpose (see *Aiken v. Stewart Wrightson Members Agency Ltd* [1995] 1 WLR 1281 - although the plaintiff cannot sue in tort in order to escape from a contractual liability-exclusion clause, *ibid.* and *infra* Chapters

5 and 29).

So the preceding are some of the features of tort and its position relative to other areas of law.

2. Terminology

We frequently speak of the English law of *torts* in the plural, rather than using the singular term *tort* to describe this area of legal jurisprudence and doctrine, because, traditionally, there has been no *single* principle of tortious liability in English law - certainly nothing to compare with Germany's Article 823(1) of the *Bürgerliches Gesetzbuch* or Article 1382 of the French Civil Code - although, in recent times, certain academic commentators have sought to extract and to present a common law of *obligations* from the combined corpus of rules in the English law of tort and contract, and the most important English tort of *negligence,* only established by the courts as recently as 1932, has gone a long way towards creating a *general principle of liability for wrongful acts,* possibly capable of being transferred to other, separate areas of tort liability.

The historical reason for the existence of distinct torts in England is that tort is centrally bound up with the very development of English law itself by the courts of common law in the middle ages through the *writ system.* Each complaint would only receive a remedy if the facts could be fitted into an *existing* formal category - called a *form of action* - for which a remedy had *previously* been provided, or if the courts were willing to *extend* an existing form of action to cover similar, though not identical, facts. In this way, different tortious situations were provided with a remedy, from *trespass to land* to *assault and battery* (that is, trespass *to the person*). Broader *economic* interests received the protection of the law at a later stage, and contracts themselves only later became enforceable, as trade and commerce developed, through the action of *assumpsit* - trespass *against a promise.* As a result, at the present day we have separate torts, with different names and governed by varying principles. For example:

(a) some can only be committed if the defendant *intended* the wrong to take place (for example, various forms of trespass to the person), whereas others merely require negligence in their commission (for example, occupiers' liability), while there are those which do not require any fault at all on the part of the defendant for them to be committed, called torts of strict liability (for example, employers' liability for the torts of employees); and

(b) whereas some torts cannot be committed unless damage was caused (for example, negligence), others are regarded as sufficiently serious as to create liability even without proof of damage (for example, trespass to land).

3. Consequential Difficulties

The major problem for students of the law of tort is that because of its long development through the cases, it is not always easy to understand the reasoning and the policy behind some of the judgments, where these were motivated more by the Judges' commendable desire to do justice in the individual cases before them, in the ever-changing social, economic and ethical environment of the time, than by any great attachment to a coherent theory of tort doctrine in the particular area in question.

Thus, although in recent times Judges have made considerable advances in their efforts to produce an orderly and cohesive explanation for past and developing principles of English tort law, traditionally, on the whole, it has been left to academic lawyers to try to detect consistent lines of thought behind the cases and any likely future trends, and to present their findings to students of law in what is, hopefully, a rational and intelligible manner.

The present work, therefore, it is both trusted and intended, may provide a further - if only small and unworthy - contribution to the process as described, in particular for those readers who approach the English law of tort as that of a foreign legal system rather than as part of their own, and whether as the subject of academic comparison with their native law or as being possibly applicable to the international dispute with which they find themselves to be concerned as practitioners.

Further reading:

Fleming, J.G., *The Law of Torts*, 8th ed, 1992 (The Law Book Company, Sydney): chs.1 & 20.

Heuston, R.V.F. and Buckley, R.A., *Salmond and Heuston on The Law of Torts*, 20th ed, 1992 (Sweet & Maxwell, London): chs.1, 2 & 3.

Jones, M.A., *Textbook on Torts*, 4th ed, 1993 (Blackstone, London): ch.1.

PART III

Chapter 3

Parties to Tort Actions

1. Parties Who Can Sue in Tort

Anyone may sue in tort, including children who are minors (suing through their "next friend"). Children who are born disabled are even able to sue for negligence taking place prior to their birth, under the Congenital Disabilities (Civil Liability) Act 1976 (although they cannot bring a "wrongful life" claim on the ground that they ought to have been aborted: *McKay v. Essex Area Health Authority* [1982] QB 1166).

Husbands and wives can sue each other in tort, subject to certain restraints.

2. Parties Who Can Be Sued in Tort

(i) The Crown

The Crown Proceedings Act 1947 removed the Crown's previous common law immunity from suit in tort for the acts of its servants. The defendant is the relevant minister, or the Attorney-General if none. However, the Queen personally cannot be sued in tort (nor may the armed forces for death or injury on duty).

(ii) Companies

Companies are legal persons and can sue or be sued in tort and are vicariously liable for acts of employees in the course of employment, as well as being primarily liable for acts of the persons in charge of the company (*Lennard's Carrying Co. v. Asiatic Petroleum Co. Ltd* [1915] AC 705).

(iii) Unincorporated Associations and Clubs

These lack legal personality and cannot therefore sue or be sued as such. Members must sue or be sued separately, or, more conveniently, in a representative action by or against one of them as representative of the others.

An exception to this incapacity are trade unions which can sue and be sued in their own name, by virtue of s.2(1)(c) of the Trade Union and Labour Relations Act 1974, although, they also enjoy certain immunities from suit in connexion with industrial action.

(iv) Minors

There is no minimum age for being sued in tort. Parents are not vicariously liable for their childrens' negligence, although they may be primarily liable for their own lack of care, as in *Newton v. Edgerley* [1959] 1 WLR 1031 where a father gave his 12-year-old son a rifle, which the boy then used to injure the plaintiff.

(v) Mentally Disordered Persons

This is not a defence if the tort merely requires an intention to commit it which was possessed by the insane defendant, even though he did not also understand it to be unlawful, as in the case of battery (*Morris v. Marsden* [1952] 1 All ER 925). Where negligence is concerned, liability depends upon the standard of care reasonably required to be shown by the mentally disordered defendant in relation to the particular activities involved.

(vi) Judges and Others

Judges, arbitrators and court witnesses cannot be sued for negligence arising out of the proceedings.

Further reading:

Brazier, *Street on Torts*, 9th ed, 1993 (Butterworth & Co., London): ch.31.
Heuston, R.V.F. and Buckley, R.A., *Salmond and Heuston on The Law of Torts*, 29th ed, 1992 (Sweet & Maxwell, London): ch.20.
Jones, M.A., *Textbook on Torts*, 4th ed, 1993 (Blackstone, London): ch.25.

PART IV

Chapter 4

Liability in the Tort of Negligence

Negligence is the most *general* of all English torts: *negligent behaviour leading to civil liability in tort.*

1. Introductory Remarks

"Negligence" is the most general of all torts. Broadly speaking, it consists of:

- *any* behaviour
- causing *damage* to another person
- for which the law provides a *remedy* under the tort of negligence on the ground that the person causing the damage did not take sufficient care in what he was doing.

A simple non-legal explanation would be: a failure to behave with sufficient care.

For example:

- a person drives his car too quickly around a bend in the road and crashes into a pedestrian;
- a person makes a meal for guests, with food which is

out-of-date and they all become ill;
- a person playing with a ball carelessly throws it in the direction of a passer-by who is struck on the head.

All of these are very different actions, but have one thing in common - one person injured another through the former's activities. If the law considers that the first person's behaviour fell below the legal standard required in the circumstances, he will be liable for negligence.

The tort of negligence, consisting of *any* activity carried out without sufficient care, should be distinguished from "negligence" as one element which may be required to exist in certain other torts. As will be seen, some of the other torts (for example, breach of statutory duty in certain instances) may be committed even if the defendant was neither intentional nor negligent (torts of "strict liability"); in others (for example, fraudulent deceit), mere negligent behaviour would not be enough and the defendant must be shown to have known of the harm; whereas, in certain torts (for example, nuisance), the negligence element of reasonable foreseeability of damage is a requirement rather than intention to cause loss.

For the tort of negligence to be committed, it is convenient to adopt an analysis requiring the following elements to be established:

1. existence of a *duty of care* towards the plaintiff
2. which has been *breached* by the defendant
3. causing *damage* to the plaintiff.

These may not be universally accepted criteria but are a

convenient starting point for legal consideration of the cases, because the tort of negligence is, predominantly, case law. There will be other issues too: causation - did the defendant's acts in breach of the duty of care in fact cause the damage; extent of loss - to what degree are the losses which occurred linked to the defendant's behaviour; defences - are there any factors which excuse the defendant's behaviour?

All such matters must be discussed in the course of considering the tort of negligence, which enjoys a primacy amongst torts through its generality. The tort of negligence is the closest English law comes to the more generalized German, and even more so, French, laws of tort.

Finally, it will not be lost sight of that many of the issues arising in the major tort of negligence, including:

- whether a duty of care is owed towards the plaintiff
- whether the standard expected of the defendant has been breached
- whether the line of causation between conduct and damage can be said to have been broken
- whether particular degrees of the resultant damage should be recoverable for

are largely devices of judicial policy for achieving a just and fair result in individual cases, having no fixed answers or meanings which naturally present themselves (see Lord Denning in *Lamb v. Camden LBC* [1981] QB 625, at p.636; and in *Spartan Steel & Alloys Ltd v. Martin & Co. (Contractors) Ltd* [1973] 1 QB 27, pp.36-37; and Lord Wilberforce in *McLoughlin v. O'Brian* [1982] 2 All ER 298, at p.303). In this situation, the English system of binding case precedent can be both a good thing, as providing consistency and stability in an uncertain world, and a problem, in that it sometimes makes it difficult for courts to reach the decision they wish to, without first claiming to have discovered subtle differences from the facts of previous cases.

2. Elements of the Tort of Negligence

It is the practice, both judicial and academic, to describe the tort of negligence in terms of a series of elements which have to be shown to be present in an individual case for liability to be held to exist. These elements are based upon an analysis of past court decisions and on particular commentators' views as to what should be considered to be the proper basis for liability in the tort of negligence. Not surprisingly, therefore, there may be differences of presentation, even of substance, between various writers' perception of the negligence tort, through such diverse interpretation of the common precedents-source and of the needs and moralities of an ever-changing modern society.

The following account of the elements required to constitute the tort of negligence represents, inevitably, a personal conception and analysis of the English law of negligence - although not too far removed, it is hoped, from the common core of precedent and principle habitually drawn upon by all others involved in enunciating the rules of the English law of negligence in tort.

Further reading:

Fleming, J.G., *The Law of Torts*, 8th ed, 1992 (The Law Book Company, Sydney): ch.6.
Howarth, D., *Textbook on Tort*, 1995 (Butterworth & Co., London): chs.2 and 3.
Jones, M.A., *Textbook on Torts*, 4th ed, 1993 (Blackstone, London): ch.2.
Stapleton, "Tort, Insurance and Ideology" (1995) *Modern Law Review* 820.

Chapter 5

Duty of Care

1. General Remarks

The defendant's duty of care is the first requirement for liability to be established in the tort of negligence: this is a duty to be careful that whatever it is a person - the defendant - is doing or in some cases even not doing, that behaviour does not cause harm to another - the plaintiff.

If the law prescribes that there is to be found such a duty in the circumstances of the individual case, the first stage of liability in the tort of negligence is satisfied.

But if there is held to be no such duty in the light of the facts, the tort of negligence cannot be established.

What, therefore, are the principles for demonstrating the existence of a duty of care in negligence?

How do we know when another person's behaviour towards us may be tortiously negligent?

The bad news is that there is no definite answer to this fundamentally important question such as will immediately inspire confidence in the actual or potential victim of the tort of negligence that his claim will be blessed with a successful outcome.

It is bad news, but not simply because of uncertainty surrounding the question of the existence, or not, of a duty of care on the facts of the case, capable of leading to liability. Such uncertainty is largely inevitable in any system which wishes to retain a mechanism for flexibility by refusing to incorporate a rigid and exhaustive list of defined cases in which a duty of care will be held to exist - an approach which would be dangerously restrictive, capable of producing injustice, and probably impossible to formulate and to foresee. To that extent, uncertainty is inevitable and pardonable.

What is more difficult to accept, however, under the English negligence-tort system, is the uncertainty which exists as to the very principles themselves which can be considered to govern the question of ascertaining the existence of a duty of care. This *primary,* and not merely *secondary*, uncertainty arises from two factors:

- in the first place, the statements of Judges as to the test for duty of care have on some occasions been lacking in precise terminological and analytical clarity, with the result that it can be extremely difficult for all those concerned with the practice or examination of legal doctrine in the area, to interpret their decisions in a clear and uniform manner and to conclude exactly what the Judges meant, and
- secondly, whatever it is precisely which the courts do intend, there is at least wide agreement amongst commentators that there has been an expressed and intended change of approach, or at least emphasis, during the last decade and a half, on the part of the Judges, which - even if felt to be entirely desirable and justified - does not amount to a positive influence in

favour of clarity of understanding and ease of practice.

Therein lie the current difficulties of the English tort of negligence: a largely inexplicable basis of liability and duty of care is said to have been replaced by a new and occasionally incomprehensible test of existence of such duty of care.

As a result, the tort of negligence may not appear to be the best advertisement for the benefits of having the English common law system of development through the cases - except to the extent of demonstrating the ability of courts, when faced with a difficult and imprecise set of principles from previous case law, to interpret the latter out of existence ... *even if this is from the frying pan into the fire (vom Regen in die Traufe)!*

Thus, given the inability of legislators to foresee all possible future fact situations or to generalize without automatically referring the matter back into the hands of the courts, if ever there was an occasion on which the relatively low status and influence of academic commentators within the English legal system was to be regretted, this is it. The Judges have done their best, but are frequently pinned down in their deliberations by the facts of the case, respect for their colleagues and predecessors, heavy workload and constraints of time, and possibly even in some cases, relative inexperience of theoretical enunciation and comprehensive scrutiny of juridical philosophy. Assuredly, the English Bar and judiciary are a quite stunning source of sometimes awesome talent and ability. Yet, occasionally, it requires academic skills and detachment from the restrictions of actual case litigation, to develop a workable and cohesive formulation for the governance of legal principle in a particular area. Duty of care in negligence-tort liability is one such sphere, it is believed. Unfortunately, however, there is no developed tradition or general inclination within the English common law system for *doctrine* to be accorded such influence and significance.

Commentators are, therefore, simply left with the prospect of:

- describing, as best they can, the manner in which the law of negligence has been developed by the English courts, and
- attempting to decide what, if anything, it all means, and
- venturing to suggest how the overall position can at all be improved.

Above all, to understand where the tort of negligence is now, it is necessary to examine where it *was* in previous times.

2. Stages of Judicial Development of the Tort of Negligence

a. Early restrictive "categories" of negligence - duty of care held to exist only in defined situations

Before 1932, there was no general law of negligence in the United Kingdom.

In line with the traditional procedural development of

English law through specific-fact categories of legal liability, there was simply a number of set situations in which the court had held a duty of care to exist: for example, possession of inherently dangerous objects causing damage; and bailment (custody of another person's property) carelessly carried out.

This lack of general legal regulation and a developed system of recompense for negligent activities sat well with nineteenth century English attitudes of *laissez-faire* and individualism against the protective intervention of the state. If the victim of negligence could not bring himself within one of the recognized factual categories, or, alternatively, base his action upon existence of some contractual relationship between himself and the "tortfeasor", he would then have no claim in negligence upon which to rely.

b. Donoghue v. Stevenson (1932): the start of a general law of negligence, incorporating a reasonable foreseeability requirement

The first third of the twentieth century saw a major change in social attitudes and legal and economic conditions in England.

The serious economic effects of the first world war; the desire for greater social equality between classes and sexes; the advances in science and medicine, making proof of connexion between acts and subsequent damage easier to obtain. All of these influences meant that in the area of negligent damage, the old individualism and abstentionism of the previous century seemed outmoded and insufficient for a modernized industrial society. The law itself had been released from its former procedural chains by the reforms of the late nineteenth century, which meant that courts would now feel the more able to respond to the changed social atmosphere and expectations through development of the law of negligence.

This occurred in 1932 in the famous case of *Donoghue v. Stevenson* [1932] AC 562, in which the highest English court (albeit, by a simple majority) laid the foundation of the modern English law of negligence by generalizing the negligence liability on the basis of the reasonable foreseeability requirement. In that case, on a late August day in 1928, Mrs Donoghue went into a café in Scotland with a friend for a refreshing ice cream and a bottle of ginger beer, which the friend purchased. Some of the ginger beer was poured into Mrs Donoghue's glass which she drank. When the remainder of the contents of the bottle was emptied into Mrs Donoghue's glass, a decomposed snail which had previously been residing in the bottle floated out. Mrs Donoghue, far from being impressed with the additional flavour which this watery deposit might possibly have added, alleged that she had suffered shock and gastro-enteritis sickness and claimed £500 damages from Stevenson, the manufacturer of the ginger beer, for his negligence in failing to take sufficient care to ensure that harmful objects were not to be found in the bottles containing the product.

Why, it might immediately be wondered, did Mrs Donoghue decide to sue the manufacturer rather than the café owner, and in negligence?

The answer is simple: she could not sue the café itself for breach of contract, because it was her friend who had made the contract with the café to purchase the ginger beer, not Mrs Donoghue. Therefore, in accordance with the English doctrine of "privity of contract", a third party in Mrs Donoghue's position, for whose benefit two other people had concluded a contract, would not be permitted to enforce that contract nor to sue for its breach (see *Tweddle v. Atkinson* (1861) 1 B & S 393). Nor, presumably, could Mrs Donoghue have sued her friend or the café itself for negligent breach of duty with very great prospects of success in the circumstances, given their quite understandable inability to divine whatever else might be contained in a sealed bottle of ginger beer apart from the liquid itself (see *infra,* pp.417-419).

Furthermore, it was clear that if this action was going to succeed, the courts would have to be prepared to develop the law of negligence beyond its previously strictly confined specific categories of liability, since this was not a case of bailment or damage from dangerous objects or vehicles. Accordingly, the effect of the House of Lords' judgment was to do precisely this: the old constraints were departed from and the foundation of the modern, generalized new English law of negligence was laid.

The House of Lords held by a majority of three to two that the manufacturer of the ginger beer owed a duty of care towards the ultimate consumer of the product in the position of the plaintiff to take sufficient care to ensure that no injury was caused by it to the plaintiff and that this duty had been broken - although, as it happens, the case was settled for £100, because the defendant manufacturer died before the case was able to be proceeded with in order to assess the evidence, the judgment being limited to the preliminary point of law of existence of a duty of care. It will never be known for sure, therefore, whether the object that slithered from the bottle really was a snail and, even if it was, whether it had caused Mrs Donoghue's stomach upset.

For the majority, Lord Atkin attempted to formulate a general rule of negligence which would both attract within the net of legal liability the generality of acts of human beings which might be said to fall below the accepted standard of behaviour to be expected of them, but at the same time set reasonable limits to those expectations which might otherwise place intolerable burdens and risks upon the ordinary conduct of human intercourse, the concern of the dissenting minority in the House of Lords. Thus, a moral right had to be distinguished from a narrower legal right and the mechanism for placing limits upon the former had to be incorporated within any such formulation of legal principle, or else people might become too frightened to engage in business or other activities for fear that they would incur legal liability. Lord Atkin, therefore, expressed the ruling as follows [1932] AC 562, at p.580):

> "The rule that you are to love your neighbour becomes in law, you must not injure your neighbour; and the lawyer's question, who is my neighbour? receives a restricted reply. You must take reasonable care to avoid acts or omissions which you can reasonably foresee would be likely to injure your neighbour. Who, then, in law is my neighbour? The answer seems to be - persons who are so closely and directly affected by my act that I ought reasonably to have them in contemplation as

> being so affected when I am directing my mind to the acts or omissions which are called in question."

This was the starting point of the modern English law of negligence - the *neighbour principle*.

What the principle amounts to is this: that, of the sum total of human activities actually giving rise to damage to another person, *only those which it ought reasonably to have been foreseen would cause damage to the plaintiff* will be able to give rise to a duty of care in negligence towards the plaintiff.

Reasonable foreseeability that a person in the position of the plaintiff would suffer damage, as the basis of a duty of care: although, it should immediately be added at this stage that even if reasonable foreseeability were to be held to exist according to this test, this would only be the *first* step in establishing liability, because, as will be seen below, in the first place, even if the damage was reasonably foreseeable on the facts, existence of the duty of care nevertheless ultimately remains a question of law for a court to decide upon as a matter of policy, and its judgment may be to find against admission of the duty in a particular situation, as a matter of judicial or public policy, and secondly, again as will later be seen, although the court might decide that there was a duty of care, nonetheless, for liability then to be imposed:

- the defendant must also be shown to have broken the duty which he is under, by failing to take reasonable care to perform it (people cannot be expected to go to *any* lengths and expense to fulfil this duty, only to

take *reasonable* measures), and furthermore
- even if such breach of the duty can be shown, it may be that the *extent* or *type* of damage suffered by the foreseeable victim was itself unforeseeable, in which case there will be limits to the defendant's liability.

These preceding additional requirements can in fact be seen in Lord Atkin's formulation ... take *reasonable* care (standard) ... which you can *reasonably* foresee (policy), just as existence of the duty of care itself is there similarly prescribed ... you ought *reasonably* (policy) to have them in contemplation.

Such, then, is the test for existence of a duty of care in negligence according to Lord Atkin in *Donoghue v. Stevenson:* reasonable foreseeability that someone would suffer damage from the defendant's activities, and reasonable foreseeability that the victim would be, or at least include, the plaintiff.

The truth of course about this test is that it is substantially lacking in any meaningful objectivity, for the simple reason that it is impossible to prove that damage to the plaintiff should or should not reasonably have been foreseen in a particular case.

Consequently, except in those situations in which it has been held that for some juridical or public policy reason, as a matter of law, a duty of care cannot be found to exist, the decision upon whether a duty of care was owed or not is really one upon which the conscience of the individual Judge, as to whether it is right for the plaintiff to obtain a remedy or not, can have a significant effect (which itself may vary from one Judge hearing a case to another): so that one is led to ask whether in certain proceedings the result would have been any different had the Judge simply been instructed to reach the decision on existence of duty of care which he considered to be right, proper and just, regardless of any consideration of whether it had been reasonably foreseen that the plaintiff would have suffered damage?

For who can say what is reasonably foreseeable?

Let us suppose that a man who recently left prison after serving a sentence for stealing the belongings of several old and seriously ill hospital patients is driving a car at twice the maximum speed limit, along what is usually a quiet street with very few pedestrians. A group of orphaned children is being taken on a day's outing to the city, paid for by a local charity and through collections at a number of schools in the area. The children's teacher decides to take them through the normally quiet street. The children are struck by the man's car and half of them are killed. The remainder will be in wheelchairs for the rest of their lives. The police say that they are unable to bring criminal proceedings against the man, because the higher criminal standard of proof cannot be satisfied.

Are we to expect a Judge in a negligence action brought on behalf of the victims to take the view that this former prisoner ought reasonably to have foreseen that there might have been a group of children walking down a normally very quiet street, who might have been injured by his car driven at excessive speed?

Suppose now that the facts were different. This time the person driving at excessive speed is a nurse who has heard on her car radio that there has been a train crash at the local station and who wishes to see if there is any way in which she can help the injured. The victim whom she knocks down in the usually quiet street with no pedestrians is a mercenary soldier who has taken part in the massacre of civilians in several third world countries engaged in war with neighbouring states. At the time of the collision, the mercenary had taken the quiet street in order to evade the local police who wanted to question him about his activities abroad.

As the Judge, should one conclude that the defendant ought reasonably to have foreseen that the plaintiff might have been walking along a street which was widely known as an area where, usually, there were no pedestrians from one day to another?

In truth, in either example, one can answer in whichever way one chooses, depending upon the result one seeks to achieve in terms of a perceived just outcome to the case. If liability is believed to be desirable, damage to the plaintiff was reasonably foreseeable and a duty of care exists; not so if liability is sought to be avoided.

"Reasonable" foreseeability, therefore, in the *Donoghue v. Stevenson* development, merely encompasses the Judge's own covert policy conviction as to the justice of the case on its facts, and provides a measure of - at least, terminological - reassurance for those who may be troubled at the thought of a Judge's individual discretion and subjective view of justice in the imposition of tort liability for negligence.

At the end of it all, however, what is most important to be understood in all of this is that Lord Atkin's statement in *Donoghue v. Stevenson* was capable of achieving two things at the same time:

- first, to *admit* a general duty of care in the tort of negligence from that time onwards (*You must take*

reasonable "care" not to injure your neighbour), but
- secondly, to *limit* that duty to where its operation is believed to be appropriate in the individual case (*persons ... I ought "reasonably" to have ... in contemplation ...*).

This meant that later courts would be able to adopt either a *broad* or a *narrow* approach towards the application of Lord Atkin's statement, according to whether they wished to extend or to control the development of the tort of negligence. If their inclination was:

(i) to develop the law, in applying the principle to the facts they would place greater emphasis upon the first part of the principle, imposing the duty of care through a finding of reasonable foreseeability; but

(ii) if they wished instead to restrict the law's development, then they would:
   - in applying principle to the facts of the case, place greater emphasis on the second part of the statement and possibly find against reasonable foreseeability of harm to the plaintiff, and furthermore
   - importantly, they could also quite justifiably claim that Lord Atkin's statement, although constituting part of the test for existence of the duty of care, was not the *sole* requirement: that it merely stated whether a duty of care *could* exist, not that it *did* exist, which ultimately was an issue of law for courts to decide upon. So, even if damage to the victim was inescapably

> foreseeable on the facts, it was still a matter of law for courts to pronounce upon whether in the situation a duty of care could or could not arise as a matter of judicial or public policy.

This tension between potentially conflicting elements of the negligence principle - enabling and restrictive - is not exclusive to English law. For example, although Lord Atkin's statement may at first sight seem more complex than the corresponding provisions of the civil law, it would be incorrect to conclude from this that there were not similar conflicts in the latter. Take, for example, German and French tort laws:

Article 823(1)	Bürgerliches Gesetzbuch
	Wer vorsätzlich oder fahrlässig das Leben, den Körper, die Gesundheit, die Freiheit, das Eigentum oder ein sonstiges Recht eines anderen widerrechtlich verletzt, ist dem anderen zum Ersatze des daraus entstehenden Schadens verpflichtet.
Article 1382	Code Civil
	Tout fait quelconque de l'homme, qui cause à autrui un dommage, oblige celui par la faute duquel il est arrivé, à le réparer.

Article 1383 Code Civil

Chacun est responsable du dommage qu'il a causé non seulement par son fait, mais encore par sa négilgence ou par son imprudence.

Notwithstanding that these provisions of German and French law may appear to be far less restrictive than Lord Atkin's formulation, the fact is that concepts of *Verletzung* and *causation* contained in those rules have enabled German and French courts also to apply policy restrictions upon liability thereunder through finding absence of causation - a break in the *lien de causation* between act and damage.

So, to sum up on the state of the law as it came to be formulated as at the date of the decision in *Donoghue v. Stevenson,* in order for a duty of care in negligence liability to be established, two conditions had to be satisfied:

(i) in accordance with *Donoghue v. Stevenson* itself, harm to the plaintiff from the defendant's activities had to be reasonably foreseeable, itself a covert matter of judicial policy on the facts and justice of an individual case, but

(ii) even if this were to be so, the case in question should not be one in which the courts considered, as an overt matter of policy, that a duty of care should not be held to exist in the type of situation in question (details of which are dealt with below).

What of later developments?

How did the courts apply the new generalized law of

negligence and its reasonable-foreseeability criterion, subject to the negative operation of general policy, through the cases?

This we are about to see.

c. Decisions Post-Donoghue v. Stevenson

It will not be a cause of great surprise for it to be said that following *Donoghue v. Stevenson,* there occurred much judicial comment and legal juxtapositioning with regard to the reasonable foreseeability condition for duty of care - although, equally, there have been some very significant developments concerning cases in which, whatever the position on foreseeability, a duty of care may be held not to exist as a matter of policy.

It is proposed now to deal with each of these spheres constituting the two main elements of duty of care as they developed in the aftermath of *Donoghue v. Stevenson:* the reasonable foreseeability requirement, with its covert policy element contained in the concept of "reasonableness" of foreseeability, and overt policy grounds for refusing to find a duty of care notwithstanding foreseeability on the facts.

(i) The reasonable foreseeability requirement

There are two main stages of case law development so far as reasonable foreseeability is concerned: (i) the period immediately following *Donoghue v. Stevenson* up until the 1980s, in particular, the 1970s, and (ii) the 1980s, up to the present.

The 1960s and 1970s

This was the period in which Lord Atkin's formulation of the duty of care in *Donoghue v. Stevenson* was given its broadest interpretation and application.

Major emphasis was placed by the courts upon the feature of Lord Atkin's test which sought to impose the duty to take reasonable care: and the potentially negative covert policy control mechanism within the test of reasonable foreseeability of damage to the victim, together with any independent overt policy against existence of the duty notwithstanding foreseeability, on grounds of juridical or public policy, was accorded the lesser importance.

This was not surprising, given the atmosphere in England at that time. These were the decades of modern socialist government, and the spirit of the times was one of state interventionism with comprehensive power and support for labour and membership of society: plaintiffs' times.

It was possible to demonstrate that virtually any misfortune arising from a defendant's behaviour could reasonably have been foreseen. In the case of *Home Office v. Dorset Yacht Co. Ltd* [1970] AC 1004, 1027, Lord Reid indicated in the House of Lords that Lord Atkin's speech in *Donoghue v. Stevenson* ought to apply so as to uphold a duty of care unless there was justification for exclusion, which almost seemed to say that reasonable foreseeability should be found unless proved otherwise - that is, that there was a presumption of reasonable foreseeability. Manufacturers would have to have serious talks with their insurers and ensure that their processes were safe in the new legal environment. For example, in the case of *Grant v. Australian Knitting Mills* [1936] AC 85, the manufacturer of a pair of woollen underpants was held to be under a duty of care towards an ultimate consumer who suffered an uncomfortable skin complaint from chemicals used in the manufacturing process, even though it was estimated that only one person in five million would suffer in this way. It should reasonably have been foreseen.

The highpoint of this period of development of concentrating predominantly upon the foreseeability issue, liberally applied, almost to the exclusion of other intrinsic and extrinsic policy controls, was the decision of the House of Lords in *Anns v. Merton London Borough Council* [1978] AC 728, in which Lord Wilberforce (pp.751-2) clearly confirmed that liability was no longer dependent upon whether the dispute fell within a set of facts in which a duty of care had previously been held to exist and that foreseeability would *prima facie* give rise to a duty of care - although, ironically, in his use of language to enunciate such a principle, he actually sowed the seeds which facilitated a subsequent judicial retreat from the very liberal approach which he himself had advocated. In summary, Lord Wilberforce explained that for a duty of care to arise:

- first, there had to be reasonable foreseeability of damage to the plaintiff on the part of the defendant arising from a sufficient relationship of proximity between them, so as to give rise *prima facie* to a duty of care; and
- secondly, if this was so, for the duty to be imposed, there had to be no factors negativing or limiting the scope or extent of the duty or class of persons to whom it may be owed.

This is commonly referred to as the "two-stage" test for duty of care in *Anns*:

- reasonable foreseeability, and
- no other factors of social, economic or other policy reducing or eliminating the duty.

In the later case of *Curran v. Northern Ireland Co-ownership Housing Association Ltd* [1987] 2 All ER 13, at p.17, Lord Bridge referred to the *Anns* case as the "high-water mark" of the generalization of the law of negligence, away from the previous system of specific categories of liability, and transforming Lord Atkin's neighbour principle in *Donoghue v. Stevenson* into one of "general application from which a duty of care may always be derived unless there are clear countervailing considerations to exclude it." Duty of care was in this way now extended into previously forbidden areas: for example, as will be seen, nervous shock (*McLoughlin v. O'Brian* [1983] 1 AC 410) and recovery for pure economic loss (*Junior Books v. Veitchi Co. Ltd* [1983] 1 AC 520).

The essence, then, of the *two-stage* test of duty of care in negligence was:

- liberal (covert policy) assessment of "reasonable" foreseeability whenever an element of doubt might exist, and
- subsidiary status for the residual power to find against duty of care for (overt) policy reasons notwithstanding foreseeability of loss to the plaintiff, confining such ground to known categories (see later).

The 1980s and beyond

This was the age of political conservativism - in particular, "Thatcherism" under the then Prime Minister, Mrs Margaret Thatcher. The old socialist slogans were thrown out. There was no such thing as *society*. Thenceforth, we were all *citizens*, engaged in the common pursuit of self-supporting individualism.

This changed social and political atmosphere also had repercussions in the judicial sphere within the United Kingdom. The almost limitless opportunities for compensation of victims under the previous two-stage test of foreseeability in duty of care in *Anns* seemed contrary to the new spirit of personal self-respect and self-sufficiency. Courts should not be called upon to support citizens every time they were unfortunate enough to fall victim to someone else's activities; and cases of compensation should be more strictly controlled - defendants' law - the irony being of course that a person who was seriously injured as a result of another's behaviour, for which compensation was held not to be able to be awarded by the courts, even where the defendant was insured, would then be all the more likely to have to call upon the social welfare provision of the state for financial support and sustenance than if he had received full damages from the defendant. Nevertheless, such was the new spirit of the times, and this led to what is frequently referred to as the "retreat from *Anns*", the high-water mark of the generalization of the duty of care.

The retreat consisted of a number of court decisions, in which the Judges made great efforts:

- generally to distance themselves from the expansive

spirit of Lord Wilberforce's *two-stage* test of duty of care in *Anns,* which had risked opening the "floodgates" to all sorts of negligence liability;

- again, generally, to replace the generality of approach in *Anns* by what is known as an *incremental,* restrictive step-by-step development, only admitting existence of a duty of care in circumstances which are similar to previous cases in which this had been held to be justified, a nostalgic throwback to the traditional development of English law;
- and more particularly, to upgrade the importance of the thitherto relatively subdued policy element, first, by showing greater reluctance to hold harm to have been reasonably foreseeable where there is no absolute clarity on the matter, thereby promoting the negative operation of the covert policy element in that test to a higher level, and secondly, even where damage to the plaintiff must, unquestionably, be held to have been reasonably foreseeable on the facts, by nevertheless making the overt judicial policy element, negativing existence of a duty of care notwithstanding foreseeability, forming the second stage of Lord Wilberforce's dual test in *Anns,* far more active and not restricted to public policy, and generally therefore treating foreseeability and policy as equal elements of duty of care rather than the former as presumptive.

How the courts achieved all this is of interest, because they appear to have converted the *Anns* two-stage test into a new *three-stage* process, by actually using the very words of Lord Wilberforce in *Anns,* in the time-honoured tradition of the common law to try to anchor any new doctrine firmly in the soft sea-bed of the past, for the sake of stability.

What the courts appear to have done may be summed up as three things:

i. **First,** there does seem to be a basic three-stage formula available for use in determining duty of care.

Various formulations of how the courts have applied the three-stage process for assessment of negligence duty of care are possible.

What may confidently be called the orthodox approach is to look for all of the following:

1. reasonable foreseeability of damage to the plaintiff; and
2. a sufficiently proximate relationship between the plaintiff and defendant; and
3. no juridical policy factors making it unjust and unreasonable for a duty of care to be imposed (see *Caparo Industries plc v. Dickman* [1990] 2 AC 605, pp.617-8, *per* Lord Bridge).

This is the standard "starting point" to any inquiry into duty of care in negligence at the present day (see *Elguzouli-Daf v. Commissioner of Police of the Metropolis* [1995] 2 WLR 173, p.184, *per* Morritt, LJ, and p.180, Steyn, LJ "... in so approaching the question we must consider the ultimate question from three perspectives, namely (a) the foreseeability of the harm that ensues, (b) the nature of the relationship between the parties, usually called the element of proximity, and (c) the question whether it is fair, just and reasonable that the law should impose a duty of care"; see too *X (Minors) v. Bedfordshire CC etc.* [1995] 3 All ER 353, p.371, *per* Lord Browne-Wilkinson; *Marc Rich & Co. v. Bishop Rock Marine Co. Ltd* [1995] 3 All ER 307, p.326, *per* Lord Steyn; and *Mulcahy v. Ministry of Defence* (1996) *The Times*, February 27, CA, *per* Neill, LJ).

However, the present writer finds this presentation from the judgments unhelpful and potentially misleading to the extent that it may be taken to suggest that there exists a greater difference between preceding stages one and two or, alternatively, two and three than is actually borne out by the facts, whereas, in reality, they can in fact be seen to cover the same ground - and in addition, it gives the appearance of ignoring the public policy category of absence of duty of care, which may have been central to Lord Wilberforce's second stage test in *Anns.* At the other extreme, however, some writers appear to treat the juridical policy category as no different from that of foreseeability, emphasizing the policy nature of a finding in favour of or against the latter, rather than the independent operation of negative policy against duty notwithstanding a finding of reasonable foreseeability - again, unacceptable, as confusing covert policy under reasonable foreseeability with overt policy operation beyond the greater limitations of such covert policy.

Accordingly, the following different structure of the three-stage *process* for duty of care, in the light of what the courts *have actually done* and may be expected to do, is here preferred for purposes of presentation and explanation:

- reasonable *foreseeability,* and

- *no social or other juridical policy* making it unfair, unjust and unreasonable to impose a duty of care on the ground of lack of proximity of relations, where the damage was foreseeable, and
- *no public policy* against duty of care.

The second of the preceding elements is most noteworthy. The courts appear to have translated the reference by Lord Wilberforce in *Anns* to required *proximity of relationship* between plaintiff and defendant as having to mean something *different* from his accompanying condition of *reasonable foreseeability of damage,* whereas, of course it is probable that Lord Wilberforce intended nothing of the sort and that reasonable foreseeability and relationship of proximity were meant to form part of a single foreseeability test (see, for example, Lord Slynn in *Spring v. Guardian Assurance plc* [1994] 3 All ER 129, HL, p.161, appearing to equate the two).

Nevertheless, courts have been able to employ the proximity concept in a very useful way, which is to say that what proximity should mean is that the parties are or are not in *such a relationship* as would, as a matter of *justice and policy,* make it *fair, just and reasonable* for a duty of care to be held to exist between them. This, it is submitted, is what the so-called "proximity requirement" ought to be taken to mean. Thus, in this manner, the courts may be taken effectively to have split the second element of Lord Wilberforce's two-stage test - the overt negative policy control - itself into two: (i) the now more active *general juridical policy and administration of justice* requirement that duty of care should be just and reasonable, and (ii) probably what was intended as the original meaning, as those highly restrictive cases in which, as a matter of *public policy* and protection of the state's processes and society's interests, a duty of care should not be imposed, for example, in the case of the police or barristers performing their functions.

Thus, in *Peabody Donation Fund v. Sir Lindsay Parkinson & Co. Ltd* [1984] 3 All ER 529, at p.534, Lord Keith said: "A relationship of proximity in Lord Atkins' sense must exist before any duty of care can arise, but the scope of the duty must depend on all the circumstances of the case ... In determining whether or not a duty to take care of particular scope was incumbent on a defendant it is material to take into consideration whether it is just and reasonable that it should be so." (A similar statement was made by Lord Bridge in *Caparo Industries plc v. Dickman* [1990] 1 All ER 568, at pp.573-4). Likewise, in *Elguzouli-Daf v. Commissioner of Police of the Metropolis* [1995] 2 WLR 173, CA, Steyn, LJ, who had previously pronounced it to be necessary to satisfy the three requirements of foreseeability, proximity and fair, just and reasonable imposition of a duty (p.180), subsequently conceded (p.183): "For my part the matter turns on a combination of the element of proximity and the question of whether it is fair, just and reasonable that the law should impose a duty of care. It does not seem to me that these considerations can sensibly be considered separately in this case: inevitably they shade into each other." (As it happened, the Court of Appeal in fact held that the defendant Crown Prosecution Service would not owe a duty of care over delays in proceeding with prosecutions in any event, on the ground that this would be contrary to public policy: see *infra*, p.228.) Further, in

West Wiltshire District Council v. Garland [1995] 2 WLR 439, concerning liability of auditors towards local council officers, Balcombe, LJ, stated that it would not be fair, just and reasonable to impose such a duty of care and that the "same result can be achieved by saying that in the circumstances ... there does not exist ... a relationship characterized by the law as one of "proximity" ... Whichever test be adopted, in the last resort it is a question of policy ..." (p.449).

What this splitting of the two-stage second element in *Anns* may be taken to mean, therefore, is that the new three-stage process in essence should consist of the following:

(i) reasonable foreseeability,
(ii) general juridical policy, making it just and reasonable to impose a duty of care, on grounds including the so-called "relationship of proximity", and
(iii) absence of any public policy negativing the duty.

All three requirements have to be satisfied for the duty of care to exist.

When Judges were faced with the need to check the further expansion of duty of care under Lord Wilberforce's original two-stage test in *Anns,* the splitting of overt *policy* considerations into elements two and three through separate reference to "proximity" as stage 2 under the orthodox presentation, and separate categorization of juridical policy as stage 3 thereunder, was perfectly understandable. Judges would have been very uncomfortable at possessing an open-ended discretion to deny existence of a duty of care notwithstanding foreseeability which, in effect, could have substantially neutralized the foreseeability element itself of the test. It is far more characteristic of the English legal system that the Judges should have chosen to hook the general overt policy discretion onto an identifiable concept such as *proximity of relationship,* conveniently found in Lord Wilberforce's speech in *Anns.* Nevertheless, such considerations should not be permitted to divert from the fact that the concept of "proximity" as an independent element is essentially meaningless and that the three-stage process, structured as put forward above, equating proximity and juridical policy in a single stage 2, with public policy brought in as stage 3, is, it is submitted, more helpful and realistic - at least as a matter of presentation.

It should immediately be cautioned, however, that not all commentators or Judges can be expected to agree with the formulation of the three-stage process as it is here preferred to be presented, and it remains common for the orthodox *i. foreseeability - ii. relationship of proximity - iii. juridical policy* division to be used (see, for example, *X (Minors) v. Bedfordshire County Council* [1995] 3 All ER 353, HL; and *Marc Rich & Co. AG v. Bishop Rock Marine Co. Ltd (The Nicholas H)* [1995] 3 All ER 307, HL). It is considered, nonetheless, that this approach makes little or no difference in practice, since "proximity" suggests no genuine additional criterion beyond the other two - other than in the special areas of liability for nervous shock and for economic loss arising from negligent misstatements or advice (see *infra*, p.67 *et seq.*) - and public policy must always be taken into account in any event. Accordingly, unless and until there is convincing evidence outside the preceding areas of nervous shock and negligent advice that "proximity" is given an independent role *generally* and in practice, this writer prefers to link it to fair, just and reasonable juridical policy as stage 2, on the ground that this corresponds with what actually happens. Perhaps courts will take into account the refinements of presentation here advocated and adopt the approach suggested, which seems to offer the advantage of a somewhat greater degree of clarity. In the meantime, the reader will patiently bear in mind the formal differences between the two possible formulations of the so-called three-stage test referred to - the standard approach and that which is here favoured. Lest it should be sought to be argued that *general* applicability of the proximity requirement was confirmed by the majority judgment of Lord Steyn in the House of Lords in *Marc Rich & Co. AG v. Bishop Rock Marine Co. Ltd (infra,* p.53), there were special reasons in that case why the Lords specifically dealt with proximity in the plaintiff cargo owners' action for negligence against the defendant who had negligently advised the shipowners on the safety of their ship which then sank, with the loss of the cargo: 1) the plaintiffs had argued that the *Caparo* stages 2 and 3 restrictions were only intended to apply to cases of economic loss, and not also to physical damage as was involved in the existing case, and, naturally, in rejecting this, Lord Steyn, for the majority in *Marc Rich,* was compelled to restate the proximity element as stage 2 and to demonstrate its application (pp.326-7) - while, Lord Lloyd, dissenting, though agreeing with the plaintiffs, nevertheless examined proximity in any event and concluded that it existed, on the rather curious technicality that according to English maritime law, ship and cargo were regarded as involved on a joint venture (p.318); but 2) when Lord Steyn actually came to assess proximity, he devoted one half of a sentence to it and *assumed* that it existed (p.332), and Lord Lloyd expressed the view that in physical damage cases "proximity very often goes without saying" (p.322) - and the remainder of the judgments was concerned with the fair, just and reasonable on juridical policy requirement (see *infra*, p.211); and 3) although the damage to the cargo was physical, the cause was that of negligent advice to another, the shipowner, so that the proximity cases on economic loss from misstatement or advice (*infra*) were not wholly unrelated (pp.317, 327, 333).

ii. **Secondly,** the overall attitude of the courts in applying the new approach is clearly going to be restrictive rather than expansive - incremental instead of unrestrictedly generalist. The task of establishing (a) reasonable foreseeability, (b) just and reasonable nature of an alleged duty on policy through "proximity", and (c) absence of public policy limitations, will clearly no longer be as easy to discharge; and courts will wish to be satisfied that new situations of duty of care are not too far removed from the pre-existing - leading some commentators to draw a parallel between the modern-day situation and that of restricted categories of negligence liability as it existed pre-1932. So, for example, in *Leigh & Sillavan Ltd v. Aliakman Shipping Company Ltd* [1986] 2 All ER 145, at p.153, Lord Brandon commented that the Wilberforce statement in *Anns* did not provide a universal test for duty of care in the tort of negligence; and in the Court of Appeal [1985] 2 All ER 44,

Oliver, LJ, at pp.57-8 also expressed a similar view that the *Anns* test was not a magic formula enabling courts to decide upon duty of care in all cases, nor should it be treated as giving courts a free hand to determine the limits in each case; in *Curran v. Northern Ireland Co-ownership Housing Association Ltd* [1987] 2 All ER 13, at p.17, Lord Bridge warned against acceptance of a general principle from which duty of care could be universally derived; and in *Yuen Kun-Yeu v. A-G of Hong Kong* [1987] 2 All ER 705, at p.710, delivering judgment for the Judicial Committee of the Privy Council, Lord Keith said: "Their Lordships venture to think that the two-stage test formulated by Lord Wilberforce for determining the existence of a duty of care in negligence has been elevated to a degree of importance greater than it merits, and greater perhaps than its author intended." Again, in *CBS Songs Ltd v. Amstrad Consumer Electronics plc* [1988] 2 All ER 484, p.497, Lord Templeman famously said that *Anns* had "put the floodgates on the jar" so that "a fashionable plaintiff alleges negligence." He went on: "The pleading assumes that we are all neighbours now, Pharisees and Samaritans alike, that foreseeability is a reflection of hindsight and that for every mischance in an accident-prone world someone solvent must be liable in damages." While, in *Rowling v. Takaro Properties Ltd* [1988] 1 All ER 163, at p.172, Lord Keith championed the incremental approach towards duty of care on a case-by-case basis, which was "of an intensely pragmatic character, well suited for gradual development but requiring most careful analysis"; and in *Caparo,* at p.582, Lord Roskill said that the incremental approach of specific categorization of liability was by far to be preferred to "wide generalizations which leave their practical application matters of difficulty and uncertainty."

A recent example of rejection of the two-stage test in favour of the incremental approach was *Ephraim v. Newham London Borough Council* (1993) 91 LGR 412, CA (*Current Law Yearbook,* 1993, Case 2044). The plaintiff tenant was injured in a fire in a house without proper fire escapes. The Court of Appeal held that it would not be fair, just and reasonable to hold the local housing authority, which advised the plaintiff of the accommodation, to be under a duty of care in negligence, even if injury were foreseeable, because the defendants had not yet had an opportunity to inspect the property. So, step-by-step, softly softly, is the new mantra.

iii. **Thirdly,** candour about the policy basis of decisions on duty of care. Although, on the one hand, the actual formulation of the second element of the current three-stage process as here presented - just and reasonable on policy (stage three under the orthodox approach) - as well as arguably also the first itself ("reasonable foreseeability"), is less than candid, as previously commented, in its linkage to the more objective-looking "proximity of relationship" condition (stage two under the orthodox three-stage test), on the other hand, the Judges themselves have in fact been refreshingly open and frank about the real nature of the test, as being founded upon nothing less than judicial discretion and *feel* for the just decision in many cases.

With regard to the foreseeability requirement, there will of course be certain instances in which damage to the plaintiff must, or conversely, could not possibly, have been "reasonably foreseen": and in those circumstances, policy clearly may not play a great part in the decision on reasonable foreseeability. Not so, however, where it is less certain and the waters are muddier and foreseeability could go either way - here policy matters and the Judges have admitted this.

Similarly, what is a relationship of "proximity" between plaintiff and defendant (the name here given to the second stage juridical policy - or independently to the second stage under the orthodox approach)? Does it add anything to first-stage reasonable foreseeability itself, when the latter is unattached from its true policy function? Clearly not (see *Caparo,* at p.803, Bingham, LJ). So, at least elements one and two of the orthodox three-stage test are arguably both vacuous in many cases and not distinct at all - not to mention stages 2 and 3 thereunder. This has been largely acknowledged by the Judges themselves. In *James McNaughton Papers Group Ltd v. Hicks Anderson & Co.* [1991] 1 All ER 134, at p.142, Neill, LJ, said that "fairness" was elusive and might be no more than one of the criteria by which proximity was to be judged; and in *Ravenscroft v. Rederiaktiebolaget Transatlantic* [1991] 3 All ER 73, at pp.84-5, Ward J commented that "proximity" required "such a relation between the parties as renders it fair, just and reasonable that liability be imposed ... the policy factors should now be considered as part and parcel of the relationship of proximity." Further, in the *Caparo* case, Lord Oliver said (at p.585): "Indeed, it is difficult to resist a conclusion that what have been treated as three separate requirements are, at least in most cases, in fact merely facets of the same thing, for in some cases the degree of foreseeability is such that it is from that alone that the requisite proximity can be deduced, whilst in others the absence of that essential relationship can most rationally be attributed simply to the court's view that it would not be fair and reasonable to hold the defendant responsible. 'Proximity' is, no doubt, a convenient expression as long as it is realized that it is no more than a label which embraces not a definable concept but merely a description of circumstances from which, pragmatically, the courts conclude that a duty of care exists." This is very English: judicial justice and discretion with - at least a terminological - safety-net against outrageously incorrect decisions. This is only made possible by the personal and professional ethic and extremely high social and juridical status of the English Judge.

Also in *Caparo*, at pp.581-2 (see too Lord Bridge, at p.547), Lord Roskill observed: "... it has now to be accepted that there is no simple formula or touchstone to which recourse can be had in order to provide in every case a ready answer to the questions whether, given certain facts, the law will or will not impose liability for negligence or, in cases where such liability can be shown to exist, determine the extent of that liability. Phrases such as 'foreseeability', 'proximity', 'neighbourhood', 'just and reasonable', 'fairness', 'voluntary acceptance of risk' or 'voluntary assumption of responsibility' will be found used from time to time in the different cases. But ... such phrases are not precise definitions. At best they are but labels or phrases descriptive of the very different factual situations which can exist in particular cases and which must be carefully examined in each case before it can be pragmatically determined whether a duty of care exists and, if so, what is the scope and extent of that duty" (note too May, J, at first instance in *Topp v. London Country Bus Ltd* [1993] 3 All ER 448, at p.460).

So, "proximity" it would seem, if not also "foreseeability", is just a label to reassure people. The tell-all term from Lord Roskill's speech above is "pragmatic" - usually itself synonymous with the widest possible discretion in the interests of justice. In this connexion too, the decision of the House of Lords in *Marc Rich & Co. AG v. Bishop Rock Marine Co. Ltd* [1995] 3 All ER 307, HL, may be noted. There Lord Steyn considered that although the so-called three-stage requirements were convenient and helpful approaches to the pragmatic question of whether a duty of care should be imposed in any given case, nevertheless, they were not to be treated as wholly separate and distinct elements, and whether the law did impose a duty in any particular circumstances *depended on those circumstances* (p.327). In those proceedings, the claim was brought by cargo owners against *inter alia* the defendant "classification society", which had arranged for a survey of the cargo-carrying ship, which subsequently sank, resulting in a loss of over six million dollars to the cargo owners. The House of Lords held by a majority of four to one that it would not be fair, just and reasonable to impose a duty of care in negligence upon the defendant classification society, which was a non-profit-making body, set up to promote the collective welfare and safety of life and property at sea. The majority rejected Lord Lloyd's interesting dissenting view that the so-called "retreat from *Anns*", which case had previously given pre-eminence to foreseeability, involved pure economic loss cases, whereas, in those involving physical damage, as here, the additional requirement of proximity very often went without saying and was necessarily also satisfied, whilst, where the facts cried out for the imposition of a duty of care, as they did here, it would require an exceptional case to refuse to impose a duty on the ground that it would not be fair, just and reasonable, *lest the law of negligence were to disintegrate into a series of isolated decisions without any coherent principle at all and the retreat from Anns turn into a rout* (p.322). Still the battle rages!

The preceding account principally placed the duty of care *foreseeability requirement* within its historical developmental context and in juxtaposition with policy as a criterion of duty of care. Foreseeability, it was seen, now forms merely an equal part of a three-stage test, of which the other two are largely negative policy elements of "proximity" and "fair, just and reasonable" - although, here preferred to be presented, more realistically it is believed, as stage 2 fair, just and reasonable on the basis of the perhaps more reassuring-sounding, yet largely meaningless, concept of proximity, and as stage 3 traditional public policy considerations; while foreseeability itself is now to be more restrictively applied than before and doubtless subject to significant covert policy considerations.

But the findings with regard to the functioning of *policy* itself must now also briefly be summarized in terms of the latter's historical development, for purposes of the treatment of the post-*Donoghue v. Stevenson* background to the current legal position, as in the case of foreseeability before that.

(ii) The policy requirement

It will be recalled that there has been a change so far as policy is concerned.

Policy started out under Lord Wilberforce's two-stage test in *Anns* in a very subsidiary way. Its main features were:

(i) it was liberally applied in a covert manner in assessment of whether foreseeability was "reasonable" under stage one if any doubts existed on the facts;

(ii) in its overt form under stage two, it was merely to be used to overturn what was almost the presumption of duty of care from the liberally applied first-stage reasonable foreseeability test, and was largely confined to categories in which, as a matter of public policy, it was considered inappropriate to impose a duty of care; for example, in certain circumstances in the case of the police.

Subsequently, however, as part of a new three-stage process for duty of care in *Caparo v. Dickman*, as here presented:

(i) **first**, the covert policy element of "reasonableness" of foreseeability under stage one, where facts could support either view, was to be more restrictively applied against foreseeability;

(ii) **secondly,** overt policy under the former stage two was split into a new:

- stage two (or stage three, under the orthodox presentation, to so-called stage-two "proximity"): a general judicial power to decide whether it would be just and reasonable, or not, to impose a duty of care in respect of that which in the circumstances of the case was compelled to be regarded as reasonably foreseeable harm to the plaintiff, whether chosen to be referred to instead as a "relationship of sufficient proximity" between plaintiff and defendant, or not, and
- stage three (or not separately mentioned at all under the orthodox presentation): the previous public policy categories of objection to duty of care, such as in the case of police or barristers; and

(iii) **thirdly**, policy - certainly under the fair, just and reasonable stage, not to mention stage one itself - would have a more dynamic (and negative) function and be on an equal footing with stage one foreseeability - whether masked in the guise of a "relationship of proximity", or openly, as an admitted policy decision by the Judges - and instead of the floodgates of liability being presumed by the courts to be wide open, duty of care would be developed on a more gradual and restrictive incremental approach, moving from one similar case to another - a development not unrelated, according to some observers, to the reduced availability and extremely high cost of liability insurance in recent years.

So there it was, following *Donoghue v. Stevenson*: elements of foreseeability and policy openly split and accorded equal importance.

3. Comment Upon Historical Development

The problem of formulating a rule for duty of care in negligence is one of balancing the not wholly reconcilable factors:

- on the one hand, that the variety of different fact situations in which one person's activities may cause damage to another is so infinite that it is impossible to draw up a complete list or to devise a formula providing a definite rule of application, and
- on the other hand, that there is a natural concern that litigants should be given some indication of what the court's decision might be prior to the proceedings or even prior to the activity causing damage.

How courts resolve this conflict was accurately explained by Lord Roskill in *Caparo* referred to above: they reach the decision which they believe to be just and reasonable on policy, but frame it in terms of "reasonableness of foreseeability" and "proximity of relationships". In truth, however, even if these *labels* were completely abandoned, the result might be exactly the same: damage was only reasonably foreseeable if the Judge says it was; the parties are only in as proximate a relationship as the Judge considers them to be. The only real control upon the Judge is the scrutiny of precedent in similar situations, which doubtless the Judge will be conscious of when reaching his decision.

In this way, therefore, English courts do appear to have found a "pragmatic" course to steer between the requirements of flexibility and certainty:

- judicial discretion is openly acknowledged as inevitable, even if presented in meaningless terms of reassurance; but
- the incremental approach becomes primarily not a tool of retrogressive and anti-compensatory, pro-defendant policy, but a necessary influence for stability and certainty of expectation in the administration of justice.

Judges, consequently, can continue to be as generous as they wish towards plaintiffs: but that generosity of spirit will not be carried out with total disregard to precedent.

It is submitted that the combination of broad judicial discretion on the part of high-status English Judges, together with their candour, far-sightedness and self-awareness, is a fairly impressive basis for a modern rule of duty of care in negligence and a handsome tribute to the quality and versatility of the highest Judges who have brought about this position in the course of the past 30 years.

4. The Current State of the Law on Duty of Care

Having thus looked at the historical development of the law so as to reach a conclusion as to the true nature of the process conducted before the English courts, it is now possible to review some of the legal data surrounding those elements making up the duty of care - foreseeability, proximity and juridical policy and discretion, and public policy - with perhaps a deeper understanding of their effects, functioning and overall contextual position than might otherwise have been the case.

i. Reasonable Foreseeability

(a) General: The unforeseen plaintiff

According to the precedents, it is insufficient for duty of care and liability to exist if injury to someone other than the plaintiff himself was reasonably foreseeable (*Caparo,* at p.599, *per* Lord Oliver).

The plaintiff must be the person, or at least within the class of persons, who is foreseeable as being likely to suffer harm, if he is to be able to recover compensation. There is said to be no duty of care towards the *unforeseeable plaintiff.*

An example usually cited is the American case of *Palsgraf v. Long Island Rail Road* (1928) 248 NY 339. A man was running to catch a train. The railway staff pushed him on board the train as it was moving out of the station. As a result, the man dropped the package he was carrying onto the station platform. It contained fireworks, which exploded, causing heavy metal scales to topple over onto the plaintiff, Mrs Palsgraf, who was standing some distance away on the platform. The New York Court of Appeals held that the defendant railroad company owed no duty of care to avoid injury to Mrs Palsgraf in the manner which had occurred.

Some injury to persons standing nearby would have been reasonably foreseeable from the manoeuvre of pushing a passenger onto a moving train. For example, someone might easily have been knocked over. But the possibility of a package containing fireworks, causing a set of metal scales to collapse upon someone standing away from the immediate scene could not reasonably have been foreseen. Liability to other potential victims was not sufficient to establish liability towards the plaintiff.

The standard English case demonstrating the principle is *Bourhill v. Young* [1943] AC 92, in which the defendant motor-cyclist negligently crashed into a car and was killed. The plaintiff, Mrs Bourhill, heard but did not see the accident from where she was standing, but shortly afterwards she saw the crash scene and some blood on the road. As a result, she suffered nervous shock and miscarried her baby with whom she was eight months pregnant. The House of Lords held that the defendant (through his estate) was not under a duty of care towards the plaintiff. Injury to people in the car or to other road users was reasonably foreseeable, but not also injury to a person in the position of the plaintiff who happened to witness the scene afterwards: "... John Young was certainly negligent in an issue between himself and the owner of the car which he ran into, but it is another question whether he was negligent *vis-à-vis* the appellant ... She cannot build upon a wrong to someone else. Her interest, which was in her own bodily security, was of a different order from the interest of the owner of the car" (p.108, *per* Lord Wright).

Clearly, it is possible to be critical of cases like this on the ground that on the facts, injury to the plaintiff should properly have been held to be reasonably foreseeable. But whether that view is supported or not is not the issue here. What is important is the principle that if injury to X was foreseeable, but not to Y, only X can recover, not Y. Y is an unforeseeable plaintiff to whom a duty of care is not owed.

(b) Rescuers

Since there is no legal duty to save another person from peril, the courts are favourably disposed to compensate people who are injured in an attempt to rescue others in a number of situations, on the optimistic ground that selfless acts by individuals to help others are reasonably foreseeable. Recovery has been allowed in the following types of cases:

(i) Against the person who placed the rescued person in danger

In *Haynes v. Harwood* [1935] 1 KB 146, the defendants left horses unattended in a street. They bolted when they were startled by a boy throwing stones, and the plaintiff was injured as he tried to stop the horses from galloping into a group of people. The court held the defendant liable towards the plaintiff. Horses left alone on a busy road may be disturbed; they could well rush off and injure people; and someone is likely to try to stop them. All of it is reasonably foreseeable. Again, in *Baker v. T.E. Hopkins & Son Ltd* [1959] 1 WLR 966, two workers who had been lowered down a well were experiencing breathing difficulties because of fumes which the defendant employer had negligently allowed to escape into the well. The plaintiff, a doctor, was lowered into the well in order to assist the men, but the rope became caught, and all three died. The Court of Appeal held the employers liable in negligence towards the plaintiff - it was reasonably foreseeable that someone would attempt to rescue the workers. As Cardozo, J famously said in the American case of *Wagner v. International Railway Co.* (1921) 133 NE 437 (232 NY 176, at p.180): "Danger invites rescue. The cry of distress is the summons to relief ... The wrong that imperils life is a wrong to the imperilled victim; it is a wrong also to his rescuer."

Given the nature of the rescue situation, there may be a number of possible defences open to the defendant, such as where the person to be rescued was already known to be dead. But these are dealt with later in connexion with defences against liability in tort. For the present, the important principle is that courts are prepared to regard rescue as foreseeable conduct.

(ii) Against a person placing himself in danger

If someone puts himself in a dangerous situation, the courts have held that he may be under a duty of care to anyone who tries to help him. Again, rescue is reasonably foreseeable; and, vitally, the duty towards a rescuer is independent, not reliant upon existence of a duty owed towards a person in danger. This was adjudged to be the case in *Videan v. British Transport Commission* [1963] 2 QB 650, 669, where the defendant railway was held to owe a duty of care towards a father who hurled himself onto a railway track in order to save his two-year old son, who was sitting there about to be struck by a railway trolley. As a matter of judicial policy, no such duty was owed to the son, who survived, because he was a trespasser, but it was reasonably foreseen that a person such as the father, who was killed, would try to rescue a person, even a trespasser, in the position of the son. Thus, in *Harrison v. British Railway Board* [1981] 3 All ER 675, a person tried to jump on board a moving train, and the plaintiff train guard was injured when he attempted to prevent the passenger from being hurt. It was held that the passenger owed a duty of care towards the plaintiff rescuer, having put himself in danger.

Naturally, this category of liability towards rescuers of oneself is more dubious and controversial. The midnight swimmer becomes responsible to conscientious members of the public who decide to rescue him. Perhaps this is a step too far for foreseeability.

(iii) Against a rescuer whose negligent rescue attempt creates a new danger leading to injury to a new rescuer

It seems that if rescuer 1 negligently creates a new risk in the course of his rescue attempt, and rescuer 2 is then injured, rescuer 1 will be under a duty of care towards rescuer 2. But if it is simply the case that rescuer 1 is not performing particularly well and is joined by rescuer 2 in order to relieve the person at risk from the *original* danger, rescuer 1 will not be liable towards rescuer 2. This was stated as a principle in the Canadian case of *Horsley v. MacLaren* [1971] 2 Lloyd's Rep. 410, in which a person fell off the defendant's boat, and both that person and a fellow passenger died when the latter made an unsuccessful rescue attempt, following the defendant's initial efforts to effect a rescue. The court said that for rescuer 1 to fall under a duty of care towards rescuer 2, the former must have placed the person at risk "in an apparent position of increased danger subsequent to and distinct from the danger to which he had been initially exposed by his accidental fall" - a new situation of peril. Commentators have quite rightly treated this statement of the rule as too technical and restrictive, in that rescuer 1 should also be able to be held independently liable towards rescuer 2, where the former increased the danger to the latter even if not also to the person to be rescued.

(c) The unborn child

After some uncertainty, it was finally established that, as a matter of reasonable foreseeability, a defendant can be under a duty of care for injuries to a child *en ventre sa mère* (*Burton v. Islington Health Authority* [1992] 3 All ER 883, CA). However, the old law has been replaced by the Congenital Disabilities (Civil Liability) Act 1976 in the case of births on or after July 22, 1976, which places the right of action on a statutory footing.

The interesting effect of s.1 of the Act is that the child suffering from a disability through the action of the defendant prior to or during the birth or even at the embryo-treatment stage, has a right of action if the defendant owed a duty of care towards the mother, even if the mother herself did not suffer injury - for example, the child, but not the mother, was affected by a drug - provided, however, that at least one of the parents was ignorant of the risk before the child was conceived.

In this way, the child in the womb is treated very much as though it were an injured part of the mother herself, so that issues of foreseeability in respect of damage to the child, which might involve difficult questions of evidence, are subsumed under that of actual or potential liability to the mother. If you hurt the child, you hurt the mother.

Fathers too can be defendants under the Act; but mothers themselves only in respect of negligent driving, where they will be subject to compulsory insurance.

As to types of injury which can be claimed for on the part of the child, the Act does not give a right of action for a *wrongful life claim:* that is, where a child is born disabled from natural causes, but claims a duty of care against the parents or doctors for allowing it to be born rather than having, or as the case may be, advising on an abortion. In *McKay v. Essex Area Health Authority* [1982] QB 1166, the Court of Appeal held that such a claim by a disabled child against her mother's doctors for failing to advise her mother of the risk to the child when her mother caught German measles during pregnancy, would be against public policy at common law which applied to the case, and that the action would also have been excluded had the Act applied.

On the other hand, it is possible for parents to bring a *wrongful birth* claim. In *Emeh v. Kensington and Chelsea and Westminster Area Health Authority* [1985] QB 1012, the Court of Appeal held that where a woman gave birth to a child after a negligent operation to be sterilized, the health authority was liable and under a duty of care to prevent foreseeable mental, physical and financial disadvantages.

Such, then, are some of the situations which may arise in connexion with the foreseeability requirement.

What of the next element in the three-stage process for duty of care in negligence, as here presented: juridical policy?

ii. Judicial Policy on Fair, Just and Reasonable Recovery and Proximity of Relationship Between Plaintiff and Defendant

1. *General*

The courts have held against recovery in a number of situations as a matter of judicial policy on fairness and reasonableness, including:

(1) where a person acquitted of a criminal offence in proceedings not amounting to (intentional) malicious prosecution nevertheless wishes to sue for negligent investigation, which would otherwise have attached considerable risk to the prosecution of crimes (*Calveley v. Chief Constable of the Merseyside Police* [1989] 1 All ER 1025);

(2) in certain circumstances, where the cause of action is, in essence, contractual, yet the victim of the breach of contract seeks to sue for negligence consisting in the breach rather than for breach of contract itself (*Greater Nottingham Co-operative Society Ltd v. Cementation Piling and Foundations Ltd* [1988] 2 All ER 971 - see *infra,* however, on the courts' subsequent change of approach in relation to such claims in tort, now permitted to co-exist with contract, subject to construction of the latter as exceeding or partially excluding the general duty of care in negligence);

(3) where a person injured is an unauthorized visitor - a trespasser (*Videan v. British Transport Commission* [1963] 2 QB 640).

2. *Nervous Shock*

The courts have traditionally been reluctant to compensate victims of "nervous shock", for two main reasons:

- first, because of doubts over genuineness of the condition and a fear of fraudulent claims and difficulties of proof, and
- secondly, in order to control a potentially enormous number of claims were the floodgates of liability to be opened in respect of nervous shock (see *Page v. Smith* [1995] 2 All ER 736, 759-760, HL, Lord Lloyd).

The law nevertheless has been able to develop, through advances in medical science and psychiatric evidence as to the nature of the condition and as a result of various legal controls which have been worked out alongside the provision made for a remedy. It is because these controls are a matter of legal policy rather than merely foreseeability (*Page v. Smith, supra*) that nervous shock is dealt with in this section.

A number of questions have to be answered therefore: what is nervous shock; when is it recoverable for in damages; what are the conditions for a successful claim?

Meaning of nervous shock

"Nervous shock", as it is understood and applied by the courts, is a recognizable psychiatric illness - damage to the mind. It may have any number of manifestations: nightmares, depression, shaking, tiredness, heart attack, pregnancy miscarriage, to name but a few possibilities. In

Page v. Smith (supra) it was considered to include the condition known as ME (myalgic encephalomyelitis) about which there had been some scepticism on the part of certain doctors (pp.754 and 756).

What it is not, however, is mere grief and emotional upset without any of the preceding characteristics (see *McLoughlin v. O'Brien* [1982] 2 All ER 298, at p.311; *Alcock v. Chief Constable of the South Yorkshire Police* [1991] 4 All ER 907, 925; *Page v. Smith,* pp.739, 756-7, 760). With regard to such simple grief and upset, the position is as follows:

(a) There is no duty of care - except that where a victim is killed, his relatives are able to claim damages for bereavement under the Fatal Accidents Act 1976, s.1A.

(b) But if there is some physical injury accompanying grief and distress to the plaintiff, the plaintiff *can* then also claim for the pain and suffering as "non-pecuniary" damages under general legal principle - all the more so where the mental anguish and emotional distress actually delayed physical recovery (*Kralj v. McGrath* [1986] 1 All ER 54, 62).

Conditions for recovery for nervous shock

Naturally too, "nervous shock" itself, where there are also physical injuries, or damage to the plaintiff's property (so the plaintiff is the "primary victim"), will be able to be claimed for without the restrictions on recovery referred to below, provided that - as will be seen in ch.7 on damages as a remedy - the nervous shock is not held to be too remote a loss on the facts of the case (*Pigney v. Pointer's*

Transport Services Ltd [1957] 1 WLR 1121). Thus, in *Owens v. Liverpool Corporation* [1938] 4 All ER 727, relatives in a funeral procession were able to recover for nervous shock when the car carrying the coffin crashed into another vehicle and the coffin fell out. Although, as will come to be appreciated from what follows, the result in this case may possibly now be regarded as suspect at first sight, since the deceased could hardly have been regarded as being "in danger" - the normal test for recovery in nervous shock (below) - it should, nonetheless, still be possible to uphold the decision on the ground that the shock might instead have been looked upon as being a mere additional head of damage under a main claim of physical damage to the coffin - or even to the corpse itself if the relatives could be considered to have a property right in it (see Appendix).

It would seem too, conversely, that where the plaintiff is able to establish damage from nervous shock, his damages will not be discounted to the extent of that part of his condition which can be attributed to the (itself otherwise irrecoverable) normal grief and suffering which would have been sustained in any event: this should avoid difficult psychiatric distinctions in the assessment of damages, and if the plaintiff's right of action for nervous shock were anyway to be substantiated, there would be no *floodgates* danger (*Vernon v. Bosley* (1996) *The Times,* April 4, CA).

The real problem arises, however, when nervous shock is the sole effect of the behaviour and there is no related physical injury or damage to property alongside it.

Is there to be recovery at law in such cases of pure nervous shock, where, as seen, there is none for mere grief and anguish unaccompanied by physical damage?

and anguish unaccompanied by physical damage?

On the basis of the cases, it may be that a distinction has to be drawn in certain respects for these purposes between:

- cases where the shock is suffered as a result of a fear of danger *to the plaintiff himself,* which is not so difficult to accept as reasonably justifying compensation, and
- shock from knowledge of danger caused by the defendant *to a third party* (sometimes called "ricochet" shock), which presents far greater policy difficulties, given the fragile nature of the human psyche and the infinite number of circumstances in which people may be affected by witnessing the misfortunes of others, especially, for example, if the event causing shock were to be filmed and shown on television. Liability might be owed to millions of people.

Each of these types of case will be looked at in turn.

Recovery for shock from danger to the plaintiff himself

One of the first cases in which liability for nervous shock was admitted was *Dulieu v. White* [1901] 2 KB 669, where a horse-drawn van smashed through the window of a bar. The plaintiff, who was cleaning glasses in the bar, was terrified and as a result of the shock, gave birth to her child prematurely. The court held the defendant liable, as being under a duty of care where the shock was one which arose from *a reasonable fear of immediate personal injury to oneself.* Nervous shock in such a case was clearly foreseeable.

As to what is meant by "reasonable fear", modern cases

have shown that this is to be assessed according to the plaintiff's reasonable perception of the danger at the time of the activity, and not on the basis of what was subsequently discovered to be the real nature of the threat.

An example of an unsuccessful attempt to rely upon the principle was *McFarlane v. E.E. Caledonia Ltd* [1994] 2 All ER 1, CA, in which the plaintiff sought to recover for nervous shock arising out of the Piper Alpha oil platform explosion, either through witnessing the death and suffering of others, or because of his alleged fears for his own safety at the time of the fire. The plaintiff was a painter who suffered psychiatric injury when he watched the fire from on board a boat 50 metres away. The Court of Appeal disallowed his claim: he was not sufficiently involved to qualify as a rescuer, and, following *Alcock v. Chief Constable of the South Yorkshire Police* [1991] 4 All ER 907, HL, (*infra*), a mere bystander, not involved with the victims through close ties of love and affection, could not plead nervous shock from witnessing their injuries (see *infra,* p.83). The plaintiff had also claimed damages for shock due to his alleged fear for *his own* safety (pleadings were amended to this effect after the judgment in *Alcock*). However, the Court of Appeal considered that in order to be held to be a participant in the disaster for such purposes, who could then be taken to have reasonably feared for his own safety, the plaintiff either has to be in the "actual area of danger created by the event, but escapes physical injury by chance or good fortune" (p.10), or although not actually in danger, nevertheless "because of the sudden and unexpected nature of the event he reasonably thinks that he is" (p.10) - neither of which was found to be satisfied in the case of the plaintiff on the facts and evidence available, so that his claim would fail.

Thus, as a matter of juridical policy, provided that the preceding alternative conditions are satisfied, courts *are* willing to permit recovery for nervous shock in this type of case, although of course, for such liability and duty of care to exist, the normal principle of reasonable foreseeability that the victim would suffer nervous shock must also be satisfied (*Alcock v. Chief Constable of the South Yorkshire Police* [1991] 4 All ER 907) so that, accordingly, it ought to be able to be concluded that there are two requirements:

1. the plaintiff's shock was caused by a reasonable fear for his own safety, and
2. this shock was reasonably foreseeable by the defendant, on normal principles of existence of duty of care.

However, as a result of the House of Lords' three to two majority decision in *Page v. Smith* [1995] 2 All ER 736, HL (Lords Lloyd, Ackner and Browne-Wilkinson in the majority), it would seem that the second of these two principles is not wholly accurate. Thus, according to the majority Judges in *Page v. Smith*, all that in fact requires to be shown for nervous shock to be recovered for in the circumstances of plaintiff's reasonable fear for his safety is that *physical injuries* to the plaintiff were reasonably foreseeable by the defendant, in which event the plaintiff can thereupon succeed in nervous shock, even though physical injuries did not actually occur, as was the position in *Page v. Smith* itself involving a car accident between on the part of the plaintiff. The plaintiff had previously suffered from ME (myalgic encephalomyelitis) and began to suffer severely again following the accident (although note that causation had not yet in fact been definitively settled in the case, p.768).

Consequently, for the first time, the House of Lords held that defendant's reasonable foreseeability of physical injury was enough for nervous shock (in agreement with the first instance Judge, but against the Court of Appeal's judgment), where the plaintiff was the "primary victim", himself involved in the accident - whereas in *Bourhill, McLoughlin* and *Alcock,* plaintiffs had been "secondary victims", not themselves at physical risk. This was said to be the simpler solution (p.758) and, in view of the different circumstances from those cases, not a radical departure from the authorities.

The basis for the majority's findings were the following:

(1) Policy control mechanisms on recovery - for example, that the plaintiff must be someone of normal fortitude (see *infra*) - were necessary in the case of secondary victims, in order to limit the number of potential claimants and so as not to open the door to multiple plaintiffs, but were quite out of place so far as primary victims were concerned (pp.759-760, 767). Furthermore, in the latter case, it would not matter if the mental illness was of a rare form; and the defendant would have to take the victim as he found him (pp.753-4, 760, 768 - the 'eggshell skull' principle, *infra*, p.311 *et seq.*, was therefore to be extended to eggshell *personalities*).

(2) If there were physical injuries, the court would then not also consider foreseeability of nervous shock before a

not also consider foreseeability of nervous shock before a duty of care could arise, so that if such actual, physical injuries were fortuitously absent, the legal situation should not alter. "In an age when medical knowledge is expanding fast, and psychiatric knowledge with it, it would not be sensible to commit the law to a distinction between physical and psychiatric injury, which may already seem somewhat artificial, and may soon be altogether outmoded. Nothing will be gained by treating them as different 'kinds' of personal injury, so as to require the application of different tests in law" (p.759, Lord Lloyd).

(3) Whereas it made sense to assess foreseeability of nervous shock itself *ex post facto* with hindsight in the case of secondary victims, in respect of whom it was the only type of injury to the plaintiff which was involved and which could not have been foreseen *ex ante* by the defendants - unaware of the extent and severity of the primary victim's physical injuries at that stage prior to their occurrence - this was neither logical nor just where primary victims themselves were plaintiffs (pp.759, 767). Thus, Lord Lloyd remarked (p.759):

> "... in nervous shock cases the circumstances of the accident or event must be viewed *ex post facto* ... This makes sense ... where the plaintiff is a secondary victim. For if you do not know the outcome of the accident or event, it is impossible to say whether the defendant should have foreseen injury by shock. It is necessary to take account of what happened in order to apply the test of reasonable foreseeability at all. But it makes no sense in the case of a primary victim. Liability for physical injury depends on what was reasonably foreseeable by

the defendant before the event. It could not be right that a negligent defendant should escape liability for psychiatric injury just because, though serious physical injury was foreseeable, it did not in fact transpire. Such a result in the case of a primary victim is neither necessary, logical nor just. To introduce hindsight into the trial of an ordinary running-down action would do the law no service."

(4) Bogus claims would be controlled by virtue of the very nature of nervous shock, which was required to be a recognizable psychiatric illness rather than mere fright (p.760). Furthermore, with regard to other controls on recoverability for nervous shock to secondary victims - proximity of relationship and of time and space and normal fortitude of the victim (see *infra*) - none of these mechanisms was required in the case of a primary victim, because since "liability depends on foreseeability of physical injury, there could be no question of the defendant finding himself liable to all the world ... [P]roximity of relationship cannot arise, and proximity in time and space goes without saying" (pp.760, 767).

(5) Statements in previous cases requiring foreseeability of nervous shock itself for a duty of care to arise all involved secondary victims, and the danger of any good phrases in those decisions was that these came to be "repeated so often and applied so uncritically that in the end it tends to distort the law" (p.764)! With primary victims - referring in particular to certain words of Denning, LJ in *King v. Phillips* [1953] 1 All ER 617 at p.623, which could be taken, incorrectly, to suggest that foreseeability of

nervous shock would be required in *all* cases, including those involving primary, not merely secondary, victims - once it was decided that physical injury was foreseeable, the defendant was then under a duty of care not to cause *injury* to the plaintiff and it made no difference whether injuries actually caused were physical or mental (*ibid.*).

To decide otherwise than the preceding, it was considered by Lord Lloyd, would be to take a step backwards in the law (p.768).

In the minority, Lord Keith and Lord Jauncey dissented (pp.741-2, 742-3 and 752), on the ground that the issue was purely one of defendant's reasonable foreseeability of nervous shock in the light of what had taken place in hindsight, whether the plaintiff was a primary victim as here or secondary as more usual (pp.747 and 748): should the defendant reasonably have foreseen that a person of normal fortitude would have suffered nervous shock had the defendant known that there would be a minor accident without physical injuries? - to which the answer should be no, on the facts (pp.742 and 751). In accordance with *The Wagon Mound (No.2)* [1967] 1 AC 617, injuries complained of had to be of the class or character which were reasonably foreseeable (pp.740 and 743). (Compare the view of Lord Ackner in the majority, who considered that if foreseeability of nervous shock *had* had to have been shown, even then this would have been foreseeable on the facts, p.742; see too Lord Lloyd, p.767).

It is submitted that Lords Keith and Jauncey were quite correct to dissent from the majority's finding. Nervous shock cases have invariably concerned "secondary victims", where foreseeability of nervous shock as the sole type of injury to the plaintiff involved is taken into account in assessment of *duty of care* and also incidentally settles the issue of *remoteness of type of damage* able to be claimed for (see below, ch.7). However, in the case of "primary victims", as in *Page v. Smith,* what the majority appeared to pay insufficient regard to was that:

1. whereas a *duty of care* in nervous shock might well be said to arise from mere foreseeability of any injury - including physical - without such foreseeability also being needed to be shown in respect of nervous shock itself,
2. nonetheless, in this sort of case, the court should have gone on to assess whether the particular type of injury which occurred - mental as opposed to physical - was reasonably foreseeable for purposes of *remoteness of damage* recoverability.

This is what Lord Jauncey seemed to wish to emphasize (pp.742-3 and 748) and that which the majority preferred to discount and to preoccupy themselves predominantly with duty of care foreseeability - normally perfectly safe in the case of secondary victims. This seems unfortunate, given that it was the majority itself which sought to draw the distinction in the first place between two different types of nervous shock victim - primary and secondary! Thus, note the comments of Lord Lloyd: "Since the defendant was admittedly under a duty of care not to cause the plaintiff foreseeable physical injury, it was unnecessary to ask whether he was under a separate duty of care not to cause foreseeable psychiatric injury" (p.758); "Once it is established that the defendant is under a duty of care to avoid causing personal injury to the plaintiff, it matters not whether the injury in fact sustained is physical, psychiatric or both ... it was enough to ask whether the defendant should have reasonably foreseen that the plaintiff might suffer physical injury as a result of the defendant's negligence, so as to bring him within the range of the defendant's duty of care" (p.761). Lord Browne-Wilkinson too reflected this approach: "... the defendant did owe a duty of care to prevent foreseeable damage, including psychiatric damage ... [O]nce such duty of care is established, the defendant must take the plaintiff as he finds him" (p.754).

However, it is true to say that the majority did not ignore remoteness entirely, and in fact, criticism of their decision cannot fully be sustained on this basis, for two reasons.

First, both Lord Lloyd and Lord Browne-Wilkinson (pp.753-4, 760, 768) indicated that different damage and injury would not be a bar to recovery, because of the "eggshell skull" - in this case, eggshell personality - exception to the normal remoteness of damage requirement that damage suffered should be that which was reasonably foreseeable for it to be recoverable (see *infra*, p.301 *et seq.*, on remoteness of damage): although it has to be said against this, that it is rather questionable whether that exception should properly be applicable to cases of this sort in which injury is, arguably, not of the same type - a principal requirement for remoteness (see *infra*) - rather than simply more serious than could reasonably have been foreseen - yet of the same type - by reason of the plaintiff's particular weakness and propensity to suffer a condition not normally likely to occur (*infra*, p.311).

Secondly, it is further possible for the majority's decision to be "saved" on the ground of their additional finding to the effect that physical and psychological injuries are no longer to be regarded as being of different *types* for purposes of damages in any event (see pp.754, 759, 761, 766, 767, 768). Yet, again, it has to be said, the view of this author is that even here, their reasoning is somewhat suspect in the context of liability for nervous shock. Is it truly correct to assert that foreseeability of physical injury *automatically* imports foreseeability of mental shock? Does every physical victim of a motor accident also suffer nervous shock? Of course not - the two effects are not the same. The test of equivalence or similitude for these purposes must surely be that of foreseeability - *and not the reverse*! Physical and psychiatric injuries *are* different for these purposes and should *not* be equated (see Lord Jauncey, p.743). In short, therefore, the present writer's criticism of *Page v. Smith* is not that the majority should not have found a duty of care to exist towards the plaintiff, on the ground of sufficiency of defendant's reasonable foreseeability of physical injury: but that they should not also then apparently have gone on to assume that the same process was possible for remoteness of damage and that all that was required to be established for nervous shock damage to be recoverable was that physical harm should had been reasonably foreseeable, irrespective of foreseeability of nervous shock itself.

Nevertheless, *Page v. Smith* is the law.

Where does this leave the older principle of *Dulieu v. White* above, requiring foreseeability of nervous shock? Does it have an independent function any more? The answer, it is believed, is yes. There may be circumstances where, conceivably, a "primary" victim may quite reasonably be foreseen as being likely to suffer nervous shock out of fear for their own physical safety, even though, from the defendant's standpoint, actual physical injuries were not in fact reasonably foreseeable. Such cases, it is submitted, would be covered by *Dulieu v. White* (notwithstanding Lord Lloyd's doubts as to whether the decision itself in that case was based upon actual foreseeability of shock as opposed to physical injury, p.762).

Recovery for shock from danger or injury to another person (plaintiff is the "secondary victim")

This is where most problems have arisen because of the potentially infinite number of cases in which liability may be sought to be imposed.

As a consequence of the latter, courts now seem to have moved to a position where:

- the basic principle of recovery is permitted on the ground of reasonable foreseeability,
- but subject to a number of additional restraints.

The main principles for recovery under a duty of care in nervous shock were laid down by the House of Lords in *Alcock v. Chief Constable of the South Yorkshire Police* [1991] 4 All ER 907, there building upon its earlier judgment in *McLoughlin v. O'Brian*[1982] 2 All ER 298.

The facts of these two cases, briefly, were as follows.

In *McLoughlin,* the plaintiff was told that her husband and three children had been in a road accident some two hours previously, caused by the defendant's negligence. When she went to the hospital, she discovered that one child had died and saw the other members of her family in a distressing state before they had been treated. The plaintiff suffered nervous shock and was held entitled to recover.

Alcock arose out of the disaster at the Hillsborough football stadium in 1989, at which 95 people were crushed to death and 400 injured through overcrowding on the terraces permitted by the defendants, the police. The horrifying events were shown live on television and the plaintiffs, who included parents, grandparents, spouses, uncles, brothers and in-laws, together with a fiancée and friends of some of the victims, claimed against the police for nervous shock. Although the police admitted negligence towards those killed and injured, they denied owing a duty of care towards third parties in respect of their nervous shock as a result of witnessing the after-effects of the disaster. The plaintiffs all lost their claims - some through absence of a sufficiently close relationship, the rest because of lack of proximity in time and space (see below). The police had no duty of care towards them.

As a result of the House of Lords' judgments in *Alcock,* therefore, it would seem that the following elements have to be satisfied - *in addition* to the usual requirements of reasonable foreseeability - before a claim by a third party for nervous shock may succeed:

(a) Existence of a sufficiently close relationship between the plaintiff and the injured person/person in danger.

What is a "sufficiently close" relationship in this context?

(i) Close ties of love and affection would normally be presumed to be sufficient (unless shown that the parties had fallen out) - plaintiffs who are parents, spouses or financées ought to qualify, but other relatives only subject to evidence (Lord Keith, p.914 - brotherhood was evidently not enough in *Alcock*).

(ii) Rescuers have traditionally been permitted to recover, even if total strangers. For example, rescuers were successful in *Chadwick v. British Railway Board* [1967] 1 WLR 912, where the rescuer saw terrible scenes at a train crash; and in *Wigg v. British Railways Board* (1986) 136 NLJ 446, where a train driver, who had gone to the assistance of a passenger who had fallen off a train which had started to move too soon, witnessed the passenger's death. As a result of this, courts have sometimes shown a willingness to classify people as "rescuers" where their status in this respect was open to question - for example, someone merely waving and shouting to warn a negligent driver that he would hit the victim - although, in *McFarlane v. EE Caledonia Ltd* [1994] 2 All ER 1, 13, the Court of Appeal declined to treat the plaintiff, who had suffered psychiatric injury after witnessing the fire on the Piper Alpha oil rig from a boat 50 metres away, as a rescuer, because he was never involved in the rescue operation beyond helping to move blankets with a view to preparing the heli-hanger to receive casualties and encountering and perhaps assisting two walking injured as they arrived on the boat. Presumably, technical justification for including rescuers within proximity of relationship would be that such a relationship is created in the short-term by virtue of the degree of

humanitarian dedication involved in the rescue activity.

(iii) Fellow employees. It is possible that sufficient closeness of ties may exist in such cases (*Dooley v. Cammell Laird & Co. Ltd* [1951] 1 Lloyd's Rep. 271 - crane driver, not at fault, drops load onto an area where others are working and suffers nervous shock even though no one is injured, able to recover). However, the position is subject to some doubt, and in *Robertson v. Forth Bridge Joint Board* (1995) *The Times,* April 13, the Scottish Court of Session held that, although in the case of employees, they would be finite in number so that claims would not be unlimited, nevertheless, they were not to be treated any differently from passive bystanders who were strangers but not employees - that is, in accordance with *Alcock,* as lacking the necessary close ties of love and affection between certain relations and closest friends. Thus, employees who witnessed one of their fellow workers being blown off the Forth Road Bridge where they were working, in a gust of wind, as a result of their employer's negligence, were unable to claim against the employer for their nervous shock, because they were outside the category of persons recognized in *Alcock* as being capable of bringing such an action.

(iv) Strangers and bystanders will not usually satisfy the proximity of relationship test (see *Bourhill v. Young* [1943] AC 92, in any event, as shown, considered an unforeseen plaintiff) - unless of course they become a rescuer! The House of Lords in *Alcock* took the policy decision that nervous shock on their part was not reasonably foreseeable. But they did not shut the door completely on this

(especially, according to Lord Oliver in *Alcock,* p.408E-F, where the plaintiff was himself involved as an active participant in the event injuring the victim, as opposed to his being a mere passive bystander). An accident might be so horrifying that even a stranger of normal sensitivities would be affected, as, for example, if a petrol tanker were to crash into a school and burst into flames (Lord Ackner, p.919; Lord Oliver, p.930; Lord Keith, p.914). The problem with this stance of course is that it is impossible to predict when the presumption against recovery and foreseeability would be overturned - no doubt, only in specific types of situation, as these are gradually and restrictively admitted as a matter of policy. Accordingly, in *McFarlane v. EE Caledonia Ltd* [1994] 2 All ER 1, 14, the Court of Appeal declined to accept this suggestion from *Alcock* as capable of arising in practice, if not also in principle: there had to be a sufficiently close tie of love and affection between plaintiff and victim. As to who is a stranger, and consequently the strength of the presumption against duty of care in such a case, this is a matter of degree (see Lord Bridge in *McLoughlin*). In *McLoughlin* the plaintiff was wife and mother and she recovered; in *Alcock,* some of the plaintiffs included brothers, grandparents and in-laws, and they did not.

Finally, in *Attia v. British Gas plc* [1987] 3 All ER 455, the Court of Appeal extended nervous shock to where the damage was done to property rather than to a third party in a relationship of proximity, there, a house burnt down as a result of negligent installation of central heating by the defendants. This seems like the sort of development which will need to be controlled as part of the general first stage reasonable foreseeability requirement: it is quite foreseeable that someone will suffer shock from seeing their house burning down, or, as the Court of Appeal itself envisaged, from seeing a lifetime's research or musical composition destroyed - yet, would the same apply to a cherished motor car, valuable necklace or sentimental picture? One imagines not.

So, proximity of relationship between plaintiff and victim is important.

(b) Proximity of plaintiff to the accident in time and space

(i) Sight. Clearly, if the plaintiff sees the danger to the victim, this should be sufficient. In *Alcock,* some of the Lords (and Nolan, LJ in the Court of Appeal) appeared to accept that a live televised report of a disaster could be equivalent to sight, or at least to the immediate aftermath (p.921). This was not so, however, in *Alcock* itself, because however distressing the pictures were, the actual faces of the victims had not been shown and identified. It might have been different had it been inevitable from the pictures that viewers' relatives were among the injured, as, for example, where a hot-air balloon carrying their children were to have burst into flames and fallen to the ground (Lord Ackner). As ever, however, even if the plaintiff is able to see what has happened, recovery is nonetheless also subject to the reasonable foreseeability requirement. Thus, in *King v. Phillips* [1953] 1 QB 429 a taxi driver negligently backed his vehicle over a small boy riding his bicycle near the taxi. The boy was not seriously injured, but his mother heard her son's cries of alarm and saw his bicycle under the

wheels of the taxi from a window 65 metres away and suffered nervous shock. The defendant taxi driver was held not liable to the mother: although she had heard and seen the accident, the court decided that it was not reasonably foreseeable that a plaintiff witnessing the events from that distance would be so affected. This is of course quite lacking in logic (unless it were to be argued that a reasonable person would never trust what he thought he had seen at a distance); but it may be that as a matter of policy the courts will draw this distinction between close-quarter sight or hearing - recoverable - and too distant - not recoverable - subsuming the difference under stage one reasonable foreseeability covert policy rather than stage two overt judicial policy because of the obvious logical defects under the latter (in fact in *Page v. Smith, supra,* Lord Lloyd actually commented that *King v. Phillips* would be decided differently nowadays on its facts, pp.763 and 768).

(ii) Hearing. Similarly, if the plaintiff heard the accident and realized what had happened, this should be enough. For example, where the plaintiff were to see an aeroplane carrying her spouse flying low over houses and a minute later hear a loud explosion, she would have witnessed the event with her own unaided senses. However, in *Bourhill v. Young* [1943] AC 92, a woman getting off a bus heard the sound of a crash 50 yards away, and miscarried her baby from shock after walking to the scene of the accident. She lost her claim for nervous shock *inter alia* because the victim was a total stranger (relationship requirement) and she was outside the area of impact (insufficient space proximity, even if in immediate time aftermath). The case has received

much criticism (she was also thought to have special sensitivity through being pregnant), although it has to be said that a plaintiff who walks to the scene of an accident, natural though this reaction may be, may not (unless he becomes a rescuer) be in quite the same position as one who appreciates the full horror of the accident from the sound alone.

(iii) Immediate aftermath. This has proved to be the most controversial requirement, applicable where the sight or hearing condition is unable to be satisfied. The plaintiff witnesses the effects of the accident some time after it has occurred and away from the scene. Thus, in *McLoughlin,* it was held that the plaintiff would succeed, as she had seen the effects of the accident in its *immediate aftermath,* which, on the facts, was two hours later. Obviously, it is difficult to define both *aftermath* and *immediate.* Presumably, *aftermath* refers to the condition of victims directly resulting from the negligent event itself, and *immediate* limits such effects to those which are most closely linked to such occurrence and prior to any significant transformation in the state, appearance and suffering of the victims. In *Alcock,* the House of Lords confirmed the immediate aftermath test, but held that the visit to the mortuary by the relatives of the dead in order to identify their bodies (rather than to comfort or rescue them) some eight hours after the disaster was either not the "aftermath", or at least not "immediate" (see Lord Ackner, at p.921 - although Lord Jauncey warned against having fixed rules as to the permitted purpose for viewing a victim). As in *McLoughlin,* it would seem that aftermath continues even when victims have been removed

to hospital, so long as they remain in substantially the same state as they were in at the time of the accident and have not been cleaned up or relieved (*Jaensch v. Coffey* (1984) 54 ALR 417; *Jones v. Wright* [1991] 3 All ER 88); and again, in *Attia v. British Gas* [1987] 3 All ER 455, a woman who returned home to find her house burning down owing to negligent installation of central heating was held to have suffered nervous shock in the immediate aftermath. It was their inability to fulfil the time and space proximity requirement, therefore, in *Alcock* which meant that even those relations and the fiancée who did satisfy the close ties of love and affection condition, would fail to recover for their nervous shock.

(iv) Communication by a third party. The House of Lords in *Alcock* was clear that this was insufficient. In *Hanbrook v. Stokes Bros* [1925] 1 KB 141, a mother saw a runaway lorry heading round a bend in the road where she had just left her three children on their way to school. She was very frightened at the time and when someone told her that there had been an injury to a child, she suffered nervous shock. The court held that the defendant lorry driver was liable if the plaintiff's shock was caused by what she saw rather than by what she was later told. Again, in *Guay v. Sun Publishing Co.* [1953] 4 DLR 577, a newspaper which published a false report of the deaths of the plaintiff's family was held not to be liable for nervous shock. Furthermore, even if a report is true, there is no duty to be sensitive over breaking the news (*Mount Isa Mines Ltd v. Pusey* (1970) 125 CLR 383). Some people have criticized the inability of close relatives to recover from a defendant for

nervous shock suffered on merely being told of the accident, as being unjust and illogical (see *Jaensch v. Coffey* (1984) 54 ALR 417, High Court of Australia). So it is. But if this extension were to be allowed, the integral policy limitations of proximity in time and space would be gone, and the top would assuredly be off the jar.

Thus, recovery for nervous shock in respect of another's injuries or danger requires:

- close ties of personal affection, presumed to exist in close family relationships, but not to do so with strangers (unless rescuers), and generally a matter of evidence, and
- personal, not hearsay, proximity to the event in time and space.

(c) Further conditions for recovery for nervous shock

There are three which are here worthy of mention.

First, the nervous shock must be caused by the horrific event - it is insufficient if the condition arises from subsequent efforts to care for the victim over a period of time (*Alcock,* p.918).

Secondly, recovery is only possible if it is reasonably foreseeable that a person of "normal" strength and sensitivity would have suffered nervous shock - the claim will not succeed if the plaintiff was unusually weak or likely to suffer psychiatric disorder (*McLoughlin*, p.309; *Page v. Smith, supra*). In *Brice v. Brown* [1984] 1 All ER 997, a woman described as "very neurotic" was unable to recover for nervous shock when she and her nine-year-old daughter were involved in a minor road accident with no serious physical injury, because a person of "normal" fortitude would not have suffered shock. However, the treatment of pregnancy by the House of Lords in *Bourhill v. Young* [1943] AC 92 as *abnormal* would probably be regarded as unacceptable at the present day.

Conversely, it is arguable that plaintiffs who belong to the professional rescue services, such as members of the fire brigade or ambulance service, should reasonably be expected to be *less* open to nervous shock than the ordinary citizen (although payments were made to firemen involved in the rescue of passengers in the 1992 King's Cross underground train station fire, and the successful train driver in *Wigg* had previous experience of accidents on the line).

Thirdly, the plaintiff's condition must arise from shock through danger or injuries caused by the defendant. This is different from the situation where the defendant's behaviour towards the plaintiff, without there being any danger or injuries directly leading to shock, nevertheless causes the plaintiff to suffer mental and psychiatric stress. In the latter circumstances, the controls on recovery for nervous shock do not apply. So, for example, an employee who suffers a nervous breakdown at work through lack of sufficient support from his employers may be able to recover damages from them for negligence (see *Walker v. Northumberland County Council* [1995] IRLR 35, (1994) NLJ 1659, Colman, J) - although, the precise limits and conditions for the latter liability itself have yet to be worked out in full (see Law Commission, *infra*).

It is impossible not to be sympathetic towards *the courts' nervous shock* at the prospects of opening the floodgates to liability of this nature. True, the consequent controls in the form of requirements of close proximity of relationship between plaintiff and victim, and of plaintiff to the event causing shock, in time and space, are made up of rather technical rules and distinctions of an incremental nature (largely developed from Lord Wilberforce's judgment in *McLoughlin* - the irony being that Lord Wilberforce appeared to be in the minority in *McLoughlin,* the other Lords wanting a less restrictive approach, based upon the general two-stage test of duty of care of Lord Wilberforce himself in *Anns*). But these policy mechanisms, together with the usual requirement of reasonable foreseeability, appear sufficiently broad and flexible to admit of decisions capable of leading to justice on the facts of the case. As is frequently so, the element of certainty can be provided through the operation of precedent to analogous situations.

Possible reform of nervous shock. Law Commission Consultation Paper No. 137

In 1995, the Law Commission published Consultation Paper No.137 concerning nervous shock called "Liability for Psychiatric Illness", in which it made provisional recommendations and solicited comment with a view to possible statutory reform.

The Law Commission initially refers to the strongly-held views on the topic: "On the one hand, there are those who are sceptical about the award of damages for psychiatric illness. They argue that such illness can easily be faked;

that, in any event, those who are suffering should be able "to pull themselves together"; and that, even if they cannot do so, there is no good reason why defendants and, through them, those who pay insurance premiums should pay for their inability to do so ... On the other hand, medical and legal experts working in the field, who are the people who most commonly encounter those complaining of psychiatric illness, have impressed upon us how life-shattering psychiatric illness can be and how, in many instances, it can be more debilitating than physical injuries" (para.1.9).

The Commission, following a review of the existing law (paras.2.1-2.55), thereafter proceeds to examine the medical background to the law, noting the modern medical recognition and classification of psychiatric disorders, in particular, post-traumatic stress disorder (paras.3.1-3.15).

Policy arguments for limiting recovery are then considered:

(1) Floodgates. Defendants are open to potentially very wide liability, especially where television is involved; and doctors and lawyers are all too willing to support such claims nowadays. Why should insurers and the public have to pay for this (paras.4.2-4.5)? However, the counter-argument is that medical classification is quite rigid and people are not always pleased to undergo court proceedings (para.4.6).

(2) Faked claims. The Law Commission notes that this charge has been discredited through the development of reliable testing (paras.4.7-4.9).

(3) Conflicting medical opinions. Again, the

Commission counters that courts are no less capable of weighing competing expert evidence than in other cases; and that psychiatrists are as consistent in their diagnoses as other physicians (para.4.10).

(4) Psychiatric illness is less serious than bodily injury. Discredited (para.4.11).

(5) Plaintiffs tend to be secondary victims and the law should therefore be all the more reluctant. The Commission suggests that this is merely the floodgates argument in a different form (paras.4.12 and 4.13).

Following this the Law Commission considers the possible options for reform and reaches provisional conclusions as follows:

(a) Liability for negligently inflicted psychiatric illness not arising from physical injury to the plaintiff should continue (para.5.3), as fulfilling a genuine social need (para.5.3).

(b) Liability should not be limited to psychiatric illness resulting from the plaintiff's fear for his own safety. Deserving cases, including rescuers, would otherwise be excluded (paras.5.4-5.6).

(c) Where the plaintiff suffered psychiatric illness as a result of danger or injuries caused by the defendant to someone other than the plaintiff: *(i)* the test should not purely be one of reasonable foreseeability, unrestricted by the conditions in *Alcock,* because this would be too uncertain and, in any event, under general negligence law, according to the three-stage test, foreseeability is but one element of liability and alone might risk opening the floodgates of nervous shock liability (paras.5.7-5.12); *(ii)* it is possible that the present law's exclusion of abnormally sensitive plaintiffs is too restrictive (para.5.13); *(iii)* a list of admissible "close" relationships, at least as rebuttable presumptions, could provide greater certainty - the issue then arises of who should be on the list (paras.5.14-5.19); but if there is to be no such list, it should be for the plaintiff to prove a close tie of love and affection to the primary victim (para.5.20); *(iv)* requirements of proximity to the accident in time and space and of perception by the plaintiff with his own unaided senses are too restrictive where it can be established that there is a close tie of love and affection between the plaintiff and the victim and should be abandoned in such circumstances (paras.5.21-5.27); *(v)* consideration should be given to whether recovery by mere bystanders should be excluded altogether, as in *McFarlane v. EE Caledonia Ltd (supra),* on the floodgates ground, or should the door be left open as in *Alcock* for where the accident is particularly horrific (paras.5.29-5.30); *(vi)* it required to be considered whether professional rescuers should be excluded from recovery or just find it more difficult to establish foreseeability as at present (paras.5.31-5.35); *(vii)* Lord Oliver's suggestion in *Alcock* (p.408) that people suffering nervous shock, through being led by the defendant to believe that they have caused an accident, should be able to recover, was approved of (paras.5.36-5.37); *(viii)* it needed to be examined whether nervous shock recovery should be limited as at present to cases where this was caused by a sudden shock rather than developing from normal grief or care of the victim (paras.5.38-5.39); the Law Commission assumed that damages recoverable for any nervous shock must at present be discounted to the extent of the element of normal mental grief *comprised in* these effects for which damages would not be awarded (para.5.38) - but a majority of the Court of Appeal has held in any event that such a discount should not take place, in *Vernon v. Bosley* (1996) *The Times,* April 4, CA; *(ix)* there should not be a threshold of sufficiently severe psychiatric illness as a new condition of recovery (paras.5.41-5.44); *(x)* in the absence of direct English authorities, it should be assessed whether the plaintiff ought to be barred from recovery where the defendant is also the primary victim of the injury, as in some foreign jurisdictions, as otherwise being contrary to principles of self-determination (paras.5.45-5.51); *(xi)* normal principles of causation should govern whether communication of true news about a primary victim should be taken to break the chain of causation from the defendant's negligence (para.5.52).

(d) *Attia v. British Gas plc (supra)* had allowed nervous shock to be recovered for in the case of foreseeable psychiatric illness consequent on damage to or fear for property, and the Law Commission provisionally found this persuasive (para.5.53). Where the property belonged to the plaintiff himself, the Law Commission considered that, as in the case of nervous shock from fears for the plaintiff's own physical safety, foreseeability should be the sole criterion (paras.5.55-5.56). However, when the fear is for the safety of someone else's property, there should be analogous further controls to those in the case of fear for another person's safety, for example, close attachment to the property (surely this should be *to the owner* of the property, or at least close attachment *of the owner* to the property!) and proximity in time and space to the danger or damaging event (even if these were to be scrapped in relation to persons themselves as primary victims in the course of the reforms) and retention of a requirement that the illness must have been shock-induced (para.5.54).

(e) It is uncertain whether there is a duty of care to communicate true bad news in a sensitive manner - possibly not (para.5.57). The Law Commission asks whether this is the correct approach and recites many arguments for and against, mostly the latter: floodgates, difficulty of determining whether nervous shock was caused by the communication or news communicated, freedom of speech and press, problems for police and medical professionals, risks of delays in and less frank reporting; and similar arguments apply, albeit with less force, even in the case of false reports (paras.5.57-5.59). The Law Commission provisionally takes the view that a duty of care should exist but may be limited to where the plaintiff has close ties of love and affection to the person injured or in danger.

(f) As seen earlier, in *Walker v. Northumberland* CC (1994) 144 NLJ 1659, [1995] IRLR 35, described by the Law Commission as a "landmark decision", a social worker was held to be entitled to damages for psychiatric illness caused by work-related stress. This would create no floodgates difficulties, because the plaintiff himself was the primary victim (and he was also entitled to damages for psychiatric illness for breach of contract, where psychiatric and phsyical injuries are treated alike) (para.5.61 - and *infra*). The Law Commission expects the law to develop by allowing claims by primary victims for psychiatric illness in a variety of situations: "We see no valid reason to object to such a development. More specifically, we see no good reason why the *Walker* case should be regarded as incorrectly decided. On the contrary, the reasoning of Colman, J. seems to us to constitute a logical and just application of the law on safety at work to psychiatric illness" (para.5.62). Their provisional conclusion, therefore, is that subject to standard defences, such as *volenti*, exclusion and illegality, there should be liability where an employer has negligently overburdened its employee with work, thereby foreseeably causing him or her to suffer a psychiatric illness (para.5.63).

(g) Finally, the Law Commission asks whether legal reforms should be carried out by legislation or left to the courts to develop the law incrementally, unhampered by an unduly rigid statutory framework? The problem with leaving matters to the courts is said to be that courts below the House of Lords are tied to *Alcock* and cannot, for example, relax the requirement of perception of the danger or injury to another in certain suggested circumstances such as where there is a close tie of love and affection between plaintiff and primary victim. Furthermore, the Law Commission points out, *Alcock* gave uncertain guidance on recovery by bystanders and from television shock; policy restrictions against opening floodgates are particularly well-suited to legislative control; Lords Oliver and Scarman called for legislation on secondary victims; and the experience of Australian jurisdictions (paras.5.64-5.68). Consequently, the Law Commission expresses its provisional view that legislation is required "in the central area where the defendant has negligently injured or imperilled someone other than the plaintiff and the plaintiff, as a result, has foreseeably suffered a psychiatric illness", although, it would not be sensible to attempt to codify in a comprehensive legislative scheme the *whole* of the law on negligently inflicted psychiatric illness (para.5.69). If legislation were to be introduced, it would be necessary to decide whether plaintiffs should be permitted to pursue their common law rights in the alternative - thereby avoiding legislative freezing of the law, yet possibly rendering the latter unnecessarily complex and uncertain (para.5.70).

3. *The Treatment of Pure Economic Loss*

The legal treatment of recovery for pure economic loss is intricately bound up with the overall development of the duty of care in negligence in recent years, in which the case law on economic loss has played a central role against a backdrop of changing political and social cultures of the 1970s and 1980s.

What is meant by "pure economic loss"?

It is financial damage to the plaintiff, unaccompanied by any physical injury to the plaintiff or damage to his property. The usual examples are where the defendant negligently cuts into an electricity cable supplying power to the plaintiff's business, which consequently has to shut down while the cable is repaired, resulting in loss of profits to the plaintiff; or where the defendant negligently advised the plaintiff to invest in an unsuccessful company - perhaps to become a "Lloyd's name". The sole loss to the plaintiff is economic. There is no other damage suffered by him. In these circumstances, English courts have traditionally experienced great difficulty in accepting the principle that plaintiffs should be entitled to recover whatever might have been their reasonably foreseeable economic loss, because of the potential for almost limitless liability. Who knows how many people would suffer from the electricity cut-off, and the amount of their losses? To admit unrestricted liability for pure economic loss could open the floodgates to claims, with unwelcome economic effects for insurers and manufacturers pricing products.

As a result of these fears over recovery for pure economic loss, the courts have now settled upon a very restrictive approach.

There is a distinction between their treatment of negligent *statements* and negligent *acts* - the latter is far more strict and recovery is only possible in a limited number of circumstances.

It should be made clear, however, before these two categories, statements and acts, are considered, that controls are only exercised in respect of claims for *pure* economic loss. Where the plaintiff has also suffered physical injury or damage to his property, he is then entitled to add on a claim for consequential financial loss, provided of course that this was foreseeable: for example, in addition to pain and suffering from personal injury, the plaintiff will also seek loss of earnings and hospital bills; and in addition to repairs to his car, he may claim the costs of hiring another vehicle (see *SCM (United Kingdom) Ltd v. W.J. Whittall & Sons Ltd* [1971] 1 QB 337).

In these cases of mixed financial and physical damage, normal rules (*infra*, ch.7) as to "remoteness" of recoverable losses will apply to the economic damage. For example, in *Meah v. McCreamer* [1986] 1 All ER 943, the plaintiff was imprisoned for life after committing a number of rapes following a personality change consequent upon personal injuries negligently caused by the defendant. The plaintiff included the financial compensation he had had to pay to the victims of the rape in his claim against the defendant, but the court held that this was too remote and unforeseeable a consequence of the defendant's negligence for the plaintiff to be permitted to recover.

a. Negligent Statements

(1) General

This is an area in which courts have been more prepared than in the case of negligent acts to accept that, subject to certain controls, there ought to be some provision made for recovery of pure economic loss - rather remarkable considering that negligent statements have a propensity to be even more widespread and unpredictable in their purely economic effects than negligent acts, the major consequences of which latter are frequently visible at some stage and easier to calculate. On the other hand, it is precisely *because* the control mechanism of so-called 'proximity of relationship' has been found to be feasible in relation to statements that restricted recovery for pure economic loss therefrom has been held to be possible. If you can control it, then you can grant it.

The discussion can be divided into three main stages in the development of the law:

i. Pre-Hedley Byrne (1964): no liability for unintentional harm from statements

There was no general liability for negligent misstatement causing economic loss - only where the parties stood in a 'fiduciary' relationship of trust and inequality, such as between lawyer and client, doctor and patient (*Nocton v. Lord Ashburton* [1964] AC 932), and in certain cases concerning the maritime carriage of cargo (*Morrison Steamship Co. Ltd v. Greystone Castle (Cargo Owners)* [1947] AC 265).

All that was available to a plaintiff before 1964 was the tort of *deceit;* and liability for deceit required the defendant to have made a false statement to the plaintiff *knowingly or recklessly,* and *intending* the plaintiff to act on it, which the plaintiff did, to his detriment. In other words: *fraud,* requiring a high standard of proof.

Thus, in *Derry v. Peek* (1889) 14 App Case 337, the House of Lords held that a statement which the maker honestly believed to be true, but which was not true as a result of his carelessness, did not amount to intentional deceit. Effectively then: no liability for mere negligent misstatements causing economic loss. Again, in *Candler v. Crane Christmas & Co.* [1951] 2 KB 164, accountants were held by the Court of Appeal to be under no duty of care in negligence towards clients or third parties who suffered loss through reliance upon carelessly prepared company accounts. Denning, LJ in the minority dissented, on the ground that there should have been a duty of care towards people relying upon the accounts.

ii. Hedley Byrne: liability for negligent misstatements on certain conditions

In *Hedley Byrne & Co. Ltd v. Heller & Partners Ltd* [1964] AC 465, the House of Lords introduced liability for pure economic loss arising from negligent misstatements and laid down the ground rules which were later to be elaborated upon as the law came to be developed. The plaintiffs were advertising agents and asked the defendant bankers for a financial reference in respect of a client. The reference was positive and in reliance upon it the plaintiffs incurred expenses on the client's behalf and eventually lost £17,000 when the client company failed. The plaintiffs alleged that the reference was negligent and that the defendants owed them a duty of care in respect of their -economic - loss. As it happened, the defendants were protected against possible liability by a disclaimer which they had attached to the reference. However, the House of Lords took the step of confirming *obiter* that in particular circumstances a duty of care would be held to exist in relation to a negligent misstatement causing economic loss. Lord Reid (at p.486) described the circumstances of liability in terms of there being a "special relationship" between the parties, meaning all those cases "where it is plain that the party seeking information or advice was trusting the other to exercise such degree of care as the circumstances required, where it was reasonable for him to do that, and where the other gave information or advice when he knew or ought to have known that the inquirer was relying on him." Lord Morris also spoke of the need for reasonable *reliance* upon the defendant's *skill, judgment or ability,* where the defendant provides information or advice which he knows or should know will be relied upon (at p.503). Lord Devlin indicated that the relationship would virtually be equivalent to contract in terms of *reliance* and *proximity* between the parties (pp.530-1).

In short, therefore, as a result of *Hedley Byrne,* negligence liability would now exist in respect of mere economic loss from statements where:

(i) these were *relied* upon by the plaintiff, and
(ii) the parties were *in such a relationship that it was reasonable* in the circumstances for the plaintiff so to have relied upon the defendant's advice.

An accountant would be liable for giving bad investment advice, whereas the owner of a bar might not; *vice versa* when it came to advice on horse racing. Specialist skills make it reasonable for the other party to rely on someone known to have specialist skills in the area in question upon whom it is reasonable so to rely.

iii. Post-Hedley Byrne: conditions for recovery

Not surprisingly, in the years which followed, the courts filled out the details surrounding the right to recovery of economic loss from negligent misstatements under the principle in *Hedley Byrne.*

One of the most significant decisions was *Caparo Industries plc v. Dickman* [1990] 1 All ER 568, where the House of Lords sought to revise the somewhat general previous statement of the law in *Hedley Byrne* in a way which would have the effect of more precisely locating the boundaries of liability. *Special relationship giving rise to reasonable reliance* in *Hedley Byrne* had seen the commencement of liability for negligent misstatement, but it remained a very vague criterion. In reality, it was probably a largely meaningless formula, enabling courts to adopt policy decisions as to when they considered that a duty of care should be held to exist on the facts - and the Lords' restatement of the law in *Caparo* was itself founded upon those same case authorities, so that little in essence may have changed.

In *Caparo* the Lords acknowledged the limitations of any attempt to apply a pre-set test to the question of liability, and realistically preferred the policy of applying a more stable and progressive incremental approach, based upon existing authorities in which duty of care had previously been held to exist, rather than a virtually open-ended general test of reasonable foreseeability and reliance. Lord Oliver's assessment of the duty in *Caparo* can, therefore, be treated as being as much a summary of the past, as instruction for the future.

The facts of *Caparo* were that the plaintiffs carried out a take-over of a company through the purchase of shares, and subsequently sued the defendant accountants, alleging that the plaintiffs had suffered financial loss through reliance upon the company accounts prepared by the defendants, who had negligently overvalued the shares. The House of Lords held that the defendants owed no duty of care to existing or potential shareholders who relied on their accounts in respect of the purchase of shares in the company in order to make a financial gain. The defendants' duty was limited to providing accurate information so that existing shareholders could exercise a proper control over corporate affairs. That was the purpose of the accounts.

Lord Oliver explained the limits of the duty laid down in *Hedley Byrne* (p.589):

1. advice must have been required for a specific or generally described *purpose,* expressly or impliedly *made known* to the adviser at the time;
2. the adviser *knows* expressly or inferentially that the

advice will be given for this *purpose* to the advisee individually or as a member of a class ("special relationship"), and
3. that the advice is likely to be acted on by the advisee *without independent advice* ("reliance"), and
4. this actually occurs, to the detriment of the advisee ("damage") (see too Lord Bridge, p.576 and Lord Jauncey, p.608).

There are, therefore, a number of elements in Lord Oliver's statement which stand out, some of which were subsequently referred to by Neill, LJ in *James McNaughton Papers Group Ltd v. Hicks Anderson & Co.* [1991] 1 All ER 134, at pp.144-5, following *Caparo*:

- the purpose of the advice should be *fixed*, specifically or by general description: advice to be used generally would not be sufficient for liability;
- *the purpose is known* to the adviser, or ought reasonably to have been known;
- the advice was *directed to the plaintiff* personally, or to a reasonably small-sized class to which the plaintiff belonged, and the adviser knew or ought reasonably to have known of this;
- the advisee reasonably *relied* on the information without taking independent advice, and the adviser knew or ought reasonably to have known of this.

On the one hand, these are considerable restrictions, based largely upon purpose, size of class to which the advisee belonged, relationship and relative knowledge and experience of the parties, reasonableness of reliance, and adviser's actual or constructive knowledge of these matters. Yet, on the other hand, they are clearly very broad directions, which raise many questions surrounding different circumstances of individual cases. Lord Oliver himself (p.587) commented that his list of conditions for duty of care was neither conclusive nor exclusive, and said that "circumstances may differ infinitely and, in a swiftly developing field of law, there can be no necessary assumption that those features which have served in one case to create the relationship between the plaintiff and the defendant on which liability depends will necessarily be determinative of liability in the different circumstances of another case" (see too Neill, LJ in *James McNaughton*).

The conclusion then from *Caparo* is fairly clear to state:

(a) in future, *Hedley Byrne* liability is to be carefully controlled;

(b) the decisions will be on a case to case ("incremental") basis;

(c) they should take place by reference - but not exclusively - to general criteria in Lord Oliver's statement, basically requiring:
- *limited purpose* of the advice to the advisee *personally* or as a *member of a small class*
- *reasonably relied* upon by the advisee without independent advice
- actually or reasonably *to the knowledge* of the maker of the statement; and

(d) the preceding criteria take into account past case

law, following *Hedley Byrne*. Thus, *reasonable reliance* is still there, and at least implicitly, the *expertise* of the adviser, albeit with new elaborations of specific purpose or class to which he belongs. However, it must be said that in the light of the *Caparo* re-formulation, previous case law examples of duty of care cannot automatically be assumed to be correct and are only so if consistent with the current approach and developed criteria. In other words, past cases can and should be looked at for help, but should always be treated with a degree of caution.

Accordingly, there are various cases which can be turned to - always cautiously - for elaboration on the conditions of liability, mostly concerning the element of "reasonable reliance" through appropriate relationship, and these may now be considered.

(2) Reasonable Reliance

The following standard case law may assist:

(a) *Social relationships.* Advice given socially is not usually held reasonably to be relied upon (*Howard Marine & Dredging Co. Ltd v. Ogden & Sons (Excavations) Ltd* [1978] QB 574). Do not always rely on what people tell you at parties. However, a duty of care will arise if it is made clear that serious reliance is nonetheless being placed and this is known. In *Chaudhry v. Prabhaker* [1988] 3 All ER 718, the plaintiff and defendant were friends and the plaintiff asked the defendant to find her a second-hand car which was in good condition and had not been in an accident. The defendant, who knew about cars but was not a mechanic, did so. The plaintiff sued him when she found out that the car was unroadworthy and had been in a serious crash. The Court of Appeal held the defendant liable for his negligent advice. He had claimed - albeit, in a social environment - to know what he was talking about, so that it was reasonable for the plaintiff to rely upon him in a matter as serious as car safety.

This again shows how "reasonable reliance" is able to be used by courts as a policy mechanism in order to reach the just solution on the facts.

(b) *The purpose of the statement.* This is a useful limiting device for the courts. In *Caparo,* it was considered that the purpose of the company's accounts was to assist the company, not potential shareholders, so that reliance by the latter would not be reasonable (p.593) - clearly, a policy decision to limit liability towards what would otherwise be potentially a very large class of people. In *Al-Nakib Investments (Jersey) Ltd v. Longcroft* [1990] 3 All ER 321, buyers of shares on the stock market were not owed a duty of care from reading a company's prospectus which had been issued solely to existing shareholders, inviting them to buy more shares (see, however, *Possfund Custodian Trustee Ltd and Parr v. Diamond* (1996) *The Times,* April 18, where Lightman, J held that prospectus liability towards purchasers of shares in the aftermarket was possible where reliance was intended by the publishers). Nor was there a duty towards a bank which lent money to a company after reading the auditor's report prepared for the company itself (*Al Saudi Banque v. Clark Pixley* [1989] 3 All ER 321).

(c) *Time of the statement.* Financial advisers to a company were held liable towards a take-over bidder in *Morgan Crucible Co. plc v. Hill Samuel Bank Ltd* [1991] 1 All ER 148, when they made statements about the company *after* the take-over process had begun, knowing these were likely to be relied upon.

(d) *Reasonableness of independent advice.* In *James McNaughton,* company auditors were not liable towards take-over bidders in respect of draft company accounts produced in the course of negotiations, because the plaintiffs would reasonably be expected not to act without consulting *their own* financial advisers. It might have been different if the plaintiffs had been private individuals rather than businessmen, who normally have their own advisers (Neill, LJ, at p.145). In *McCullagh v. Lane Fox* (1994) *The Times,* January 25, Colman, J in the High Court held defendant estate agents to be liable for orally misrepresenting the size of a piece of land to the plaintiff purchaser, because the defendants knew that the plaintiff did not intend to have the land independently surveyed and that the plaintiff would therefore rely upon their statement.

(e) *Reliance in fact.* If, as a fact, the plaintiff did not rely upon the defendant's statement, the defendant has no duty of care, even if it would have been reasonable for the plaintiff to rely on the defendant. In *JEB Fasteners Ltd v. Marks Bloom & Co.* [1983] 1 All ER 583, the plaintiff take-over bidders read the defendant auditors' negligent report on the company, but since the plaintiffs' reason for taking over the company was merely to obtain the services of two directors rather than the company itself, they were held not to have relied on the report, because they would have gone ahead with the take-over in any event even if they had known the truth about the company.

(f) *Adviser need not be in the business of giving advice.* Reliance can still be reasonable in these circumstances, if the adviser nevertheless may be expected to know what he is talking about. For example, in *Esso Petroleum Co. Ltd v. Marsdon* [1976] QB 801, the defendants were not professional advisers, but they knew about running a petrol filling station (the decision of the Judicial Committee of the Privy Council in *Mutual Life and Citizens Assurance Co. v. Evatt* [1971] AC 793, of persuasive authority, suggesting that the adviser must provide the information in the course of his business if he is to be liable, seemed to be disapproved of in *Esso Petroleum Co. Ltd v. Marsdon* and later in *Howard Marine and Dredging Co. v. A. Ogden and Sons (Excavations) Ltd* [1978] QB 574).

(g) *Plaintiff less knowledgeable than defendant.* Reliance would hardly be reasonable where both parties were equally experienced (*Wynston v. MacDonald* (1975)

DLR (3d) 527). However, it seems perfectly reasonable to rely upon an estate agent as to the size of a plot of land to be purchased when he knows that there is to be no independent survey (*McCullagh v. Lane Fox & Partners* (1994) *The Times,* January 25), or upon a local authority's advice that a child-minder is safe and reliable (*Harrison v. Surrey County Council* (1994) *The Times,* January 27), or upon a consulting engineer's advice as to construction of a factory chimney (*Pirelli v. Oscar Faber & Partners* [1983] 2 AC 1). Some commentators seek to draw a distinction between providing advice and merely passing on information, reliance being said to be reasonable in the former but not in the latter circumstance (especially if carried out in an informal manner) (*Royal Bank Trust Co. (Trinidad) Ltd v. Pampellonne* [1987] 1 Lloyd's Rep 218).

(h) *The contractual context in which a statement is made.* In *Smith v. Bush* [1989] 2 WLR 790, where a chimney collapsed following negligent valuation of a house, Lord Templeman, at p.798, referred to the relationship between the buyer of a house and the surveyor of the body lending money to the buyer to purchase the house, as being similar to contract - the buyer was funding the survey for the lender and the purpose of the survey was to enable the buyer to enter both a contract of loan with the lender and of purchase with the house seller. The implication seemed to be that the parties - plaintiff buyer/borrower and defendant surveyor - were just a small step away from having a contractual relationship. Accordingly, a duty of care in negligence was found to exist. On the other hand, if plaintiffs *do* have a contract with a third party (for example, the body lending the money to purchase the house), which actually seeks to settle what will happen if the defendant fails to act with sufficient care, the courts may be unwilling to hold that the adviser himself was expected by the parties to be under a duty of care in tort toward the plaintiff - quite the contrary, as in *Pacific Associates Inc. v. Baxter* [1989] 2 All ER 159, where the plaintiffs' contract of employment with their employer provided for the defendant consultant engineer to advise on and to supervise the work properly. It was held that the engineer had no duty of care in tort towards the plaintiffs. So *contractual context* can work both in favour of and against liability in tort. Not too little, but not too much if the plaintiff is to succeed (and certainly too, as a general principle it is now established that contractual existence will not automatically lead to exclusion of parallel liability in tort: see *Henderson v. Merrett Syndicates Ltd* and *White v. Jones, infra*). Furthermore, if liability is to exist, the purpose of the statement must principally be to enable the contract envisaged to proceed rather than having a different objective. Thus, in *Mariola Marine Corporation v. Lloyd's Register of Shipping, The Morning Watch* [1990] 1 Lloyd's Rep 547, the survey of a ship carried out by a Lloyd's surveyor was performed primarily in order to ensure safety at sea, so that the surveyor was held not to owe a duty of care towards the purchaser of the ship. The following diagrams serve to illustrate the possible effects described of contractual context upon existence or not of duty of care in negligence:

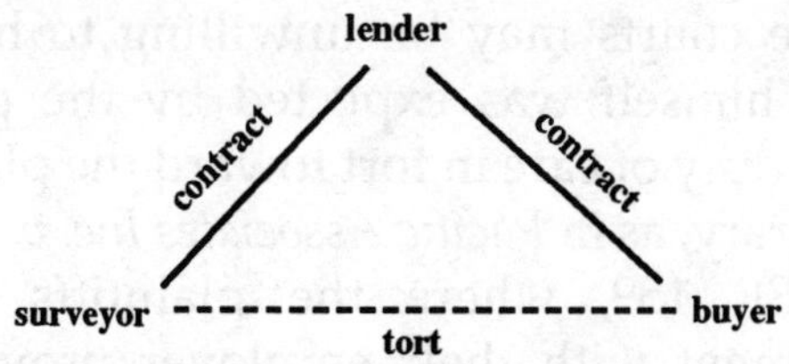

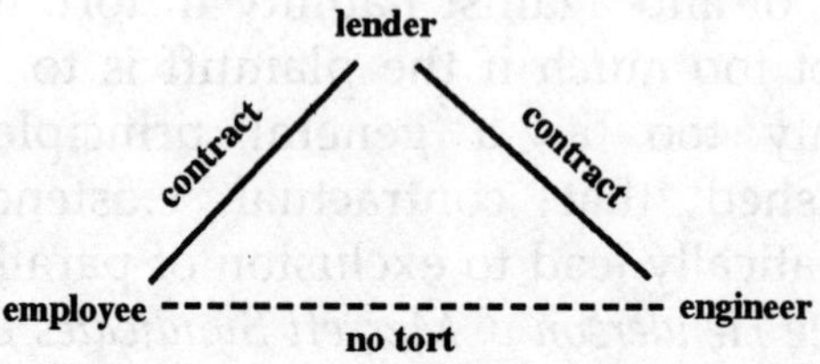

The preceding, therefore, are cases on "reasonable reliance" and "special relationship" requirements. What of judgments concerning the type and level of knowledge which is necessary?

(3) Knowledge of the Maker of the Statement

The maker need not have actual knowledge that his statement will reasonably be relied upon. It is sufficient if he ought reasonably to have known of this (*Beaumont v. Humberts* [1990] 49 EG 46).

However, if the maker does not intend his statement to be relied upon by certain people, it is then difficult to conclude that he ought reasonably to have known that it would be. Yet not impossible. For example, as previously noted, when people borrow money to buy a house, it is common for the lender to ask a surveyor to value the property as security for the loan, at the buyer's expense. The surveyor's report is not made available to the buyer, but many buyers assume from the lender's willingness to proceed that the surveyor's report on the house was positive. In *Smith v. Bush* [1989] 2 WLR 790, the House of Lords held that because of this, the surveyor owed a duty of care towards the buyer: even though the report was originally prepared for a different purpose, the surveyor should have known that the buyer was highly likely to rely on it in deciding whether to go ahead with the purchase, especially in view of the higher cost of a private survey, which would encourage the buyer to rely on the lender's survey. In *Yianni v. Edwin Evans & Sons* [1981] 3 All ER 592, it was said that only 15 per cent of house buyers had a private survey, and again, therefore, the buyer's reliance on the lender's surveyor was held to be reasonable and consequently reasonably foreseeable.

It must of course be added that whereas reasonable reliance will no doubt invariably be held to be reasonably foreseeable by the adviser, the reverse is not automatically so. Even if people do frequently rely on a statement, so that this is reasonably foreseeable, the reliance itself must still be reasonable for the duty of care to be held to exist. For example, in *Caparo* it was found that the purpose of company accounts was to assist the company itself and existing shareholders to exercise control, not to inform intending shareholders of the nature and value of their investment, so that reliance for the latter purpose would be unreasonable. Yet, clearly, such reliance is commonplace and consequently reasonably foreseeable. This may seem harsh towards the plaintiff, but the law must draw a policy line against recovery at some point.

Again, in *McCullagh v. Lane Fox and Partners Ltd* (1995) *The Times*, December 22, CA, the plaintiff purchased a house for nearly £900,000, which the defendant estate agents had negligently described as being almost one acre, instead of its actual size of ½ acre. Although the defendants' contract was with the seller for whom they acted, the plaintiff claimed damages against the defendants in tort under *Hedley Byrne* on the ground that he had relied upon the information which they provided, in deciding to proceed with the purchase of the property. The Court of Appeal held against the defendants' liability on this basis, for two reasons: 1) since the defendants had included a disclaimer of their liability in the particulars of the property drawn up for the seller, it was not reasonable for the plaintiff, an ordinary, intelligent member of the public, who had read these, to rely upon the details of the property provided by the defendants; and 2) two of the three Appeal Court Judges (Hobhouse, LJ and Sir Christopher Slade) also considered that this would have been the position in any event, even if there had been no such disclaimer - people buying expensive houses should carry out their own checks rather than automatically relying upon the accuracy of estate agents' particulars. Although this latter finding is somewhat debateable, the principle nonetheless is clear that reliance should not be unreasonable.

Furthermore, the defendant adviser's knowledge must be that the plaintiff non-addressee was *highly likely* to rely upon it. It is not sufficient if there was a *mere possibility*. Thus, in *Smith v. Bush,* Lord Griffiths remarked (at p.816) that it was only in cases where the adviser knew there to be "a high degree of probability" that some other identifiable person would act on the advice, that a duty of care would be imposed.

(4) Possible Extension of Hedley Byrne so as to Benefit Third Parties

There are two categories for discussion in this respect:

1. third party becomes object of defendant's assumption of responsibility; or
2. third party is intended beneficiary of defendant's assumption of responsibility to another.

1. Responsibility assumed towards third party who foreseeably relies upon the advice: Henderson v. Merrett Syndicates Ltd [1994] 3 All ER 506, HL

The plaintiffs in this case were "Lloyd's names" (investors in the insurance market with unlimited liability) who were members of syndicates which were managed by the defendant underwriting agents. The latter can be either *managing agents* or *members' agents*: the former carry out the reinsurance activities and pay claims, while the latter advise the names on choice of syndicates and give general information on investments. A managing agent alone would have no contract with the name: a member's agent would contract with the name and then sub-contract with the managing agent - here, the name is referred to as an *indirect name.* If the same agent was both managing and members' combined, the name would be a *direct name* (see Lord Goff in the House of Lords proceedings explaining these terms, at pp.511 and 539-541).

Which types of names and defendants were involved in *Henderson*?

The plaintiffs were either direct names, and the defendants combined members' agents and managing agents; or indirect names, and defendants both members' and managing agents. It was an implied term of the various agreements that managing agents would exercise due care and skill in conducting business for the names.

The plaintiffs sued the defendants for lack of care in carrying out their functions following heavy claims against the plaintiffs arising out of insured catastrophes, and they wished to establish a duty of care in the tort of negligence, not merely in contract, in order to take advantage of the more favourable limitation periods governing the former in the matter of accrual of the cause of action (see pp.515 and 525).

The central issues in the proceedings were:

(a) whether it was possible for a duty of care in tort to exist as between parties already bound by contractual relations, in respect of activities under the contract - the issue between the plaintiff direct names and the defendants who were combined members' agents and managing agents; and

(b) whether a duty of care arising from contractual performance between parties to the contract, here, the members' agents and managing agents, could be held to extend to a third party to the contract, here from managing agents to the plaintiff indirect names, and indeed notwithstanding the existence of the overall contractual structure between names and members' agents on the one hand and members' agents and managing agents on the other, omitting direct contractual relations between names and managing agents

- in either case, the damage claimed for amounting to pure economic loss?

As will be seen, the answer given by the House of Lords, through the leading judgment of Lord Goff, with whom the rest agreed (pp.510, 542 and 544), was that in both of the preceding cases a duty of care in negligence could exist.

What was the reasoning which Lord Goff employed in reaching these conclusions?

(1) Recovery by a second or third party for pure economic loss from misstatement

Lord Goff dealt initially with the central argument of managing agents that they were under no duty of care in tort towards plaintiff direct or indirect names because the loss claimed was purely economic - after which, if there were such a duty, he would deal with the other main issue (*supra*) which was that of whether contractual and tortious duties were capable of co-existence (p.518).

He examined the speeches of the Law Lords in *Hedley Byrne* (pp.518-520) and concluded that the factors underlying the imposition of negligence liability arising out of the direct relations between the parties in that case were

- *assumption of responsibility* by defendant towards plaintiff
- which the defendant knew or should have known that the plaintiff would *rely* upon (pp.520-1).

Thus, as to *Hedley Byrne,* Lord Goff explained: "We can see that it rests upon a relationship between the parties, which may be general or specific to the particular transaction, and which may or may not be contractual in nature. All of their Lordships spoke in terms of one party having assumed or undertaken a responsibility towards the other ... It follows, of course, that although, in the case of the provision of information and advice, reliance upon it by the other party will be necessary to establish a cause of action ... nevertheless there may be other circumstances in which there will be the necessary reliance to give rise to the application of the principle ... Since it has been submitted on behalf of the managing agents that no liability should attach to them in negligence in the present case because the only damage suffered by the names consists of pure economic loss, the question arises whether the principle in *Hedley Byrne* is capable of applying in the case of underwriting agents at Lloyd's who are managing agents ... I have no difficulty in concluding that the principle is indeed capable of such application ... there is in my opinion plainly an assumption of responsibility in the relevant sense by the managing agents towards the names in their syndicates. The managing agents have accepted the names as members of a syndicate under their management. They obviously hold themselves out as possessing a special expertise to advise the names on the suitability of risks to be underwritten; and on the circumstances in which, and the extent to which, reinsurance should be taken out and claims should be settled. The names, as the managing agents will know, placed implicit reliance on that expertise, in that they gave authority to the managing agents to bind them to contracts of insurance and reinsurance and to the settlement of claims. I can see no escape from the conclusion that, in these circumstances, *prima facie* a duty of care is owed in tort by the managing agents to such names. To me, it does not matter if one proceeds by way of analogy from the categories of relationship already recognized as falling within the principle in *Hedley Byrne* or by a straight application of the principle stated in the *Hedley Byrne* case itself. On either basis the conclusion is, in my opinion, clear. Furthermore, since the duty rests on the principle in *Hedley Byrne,* no problem arises from the fact that the loss suffered by the names is pure economic loss" (pp.520-2).

A broad principle indeed in relation to third parties suffering economic loss from negligent advice or misstatement provided *for another* - extracted from *Hedley Byrne,* itself concerned with liability towards the addressee of the advice or statement - namely, that if it was foreseeable that the third party would *rely upon* the advice or statement and in the circumstances the defendant could be taken to have *assumed a responsibility* towards the third party (or, it is submitted, *vice versa* - it does not seem to matter which, since the artificiality of the exercise is so glaring), the defendant is then under a duty of care towards the plaintiff third party (and there is also no further need to assess whether imposition of such duty is fair, just and reasonable, which it obviously is - *per* Lord Goff, p.521).

There is little point in attempting to rationalize this doctrine of responsibility and reliance as a genuine development of *Hedley Byrne* or not. Lord Goff's finding in this respect is almost akin to the following illustration: X says to Y "You recently hired out a motor car to my friend so that he could drive from London to York. I would like to drive from London to Edinburgh." Y replies, "Yes of course, here is a steering wheel." In other words, the steering wheel (responsibility and reliance) was essential to the functioning of the vehicle (*Hedley Byrne* liability) - but in no sense *exclusively* so and independently of the rest of the component parts, like brakes and engine.

Nevertheless, the fact is that this "development" now represents the unanimous ruling of the House of Lords (Lord Browne-Wilkinson, in his brief judgment, also referred to assumption of responsibility, pp.543-4).

Doubtless, the courts will *apply* the new principle carefully and incrementally; but its existence is not possible to deny. It is open to any third party who relied upon negligent advice of which he was not the addressee to argue that the reliance was reasonable and that the defendant assumed responsibility towards him - doubtless, two issues which will receive a common response from the court dealing with the matter.

Hedley Byrne: recovery of economic loss by the addressee of negligent advice or statement
Henderson: recovery of economic loss by a third party non-addressee, in circumstances of assumed responsibility and reliance.

Shortly too, below, it will be seen that the House of Lords, and in particular, Lord Goff, subsequently expanded the law on economic loss from misstatement or negligent advice even further in

White v. Jones: recovery of economic loss by a third party, in circumstances of *assumed responsibility* by the defendant, *even in the absence of any reliance by the third party,* if it was foreseeable that the third party stood to gain or to lose according to whether the defendant exercised reasonable care or not - although, on this occasion, the dissenting minority in the House of Lords was seriously troubled by Lord Goff's failure to provide a stable, rational and reliable basis for his recovery doctrine (see *infra*).

For the time being, however, it remains to draw attention to the other main issue in the judgment of Lord Goff in *Henderson* (following his finding, as a principle of contractual construction, that contractual discretion over performance is not necessarily inconsistent with imposition of a duty to exercise reasonable care and skill under the contract, at pp.522-3): this was the matter of whether, even if, as seen, a duty of care in economic loss could be owed by defendant managing agents towards the plaintiff third party names in respect of activities agreed between members' agents and managing agents, a duty of care in tort was in any event impossible towards both direct and indirect names, in the first case because of the existence of a contract between plaintiff direct names and defendant combined members' and managing agents, and in the second case because, although the plaintiff indirect names did not have a contract directly with the managing agents (only with the members' agents), nonetheless, they were part of a contractual chain or structure omitting such direct contractual relations between the two? Were contract and tort relations unable to co-exist?

> "All systems of law which recognise a law of contract and a law of tort ... have to solve the problem of the possibility of concurrent claims arising from breach of duty under the two rubrics of the law. Although there are variants, broadly speaking, two possible solutions present themselves: either to insist that the claimant should pursue his remedy in contract alone, or to allow him to choose which remedy he prefers."

So began Lord Goff's treatment of the issue (at p.523), whence he thereafter sought to educate his audience in the historical development of the law: France chose the exclusively contractual approach, Germany the optional course of concurrent remedies. In England, separation of obligations into contract and tort came with abolition of the forms of action in the nineteenth century, with no systematic studies of the consequences, due to the absence of significant law faculties in the universities until the latter part of the century (p.524). The issue certainly mattered - for reasons of limitation of actions, contribution between tortfeasors, remoteness of damage and service out of the jurisdiction (p.525). At first, England adopted the contract approach like the French: "This leads to the startling possibility that a client who has had the benefit of gratuitous advice from his solicitor may in this respect be better off than a client who has paid a fee" (p.525). Lord Goff then reviewed the case law and concluded that it was Oliver, J's judgment in *Midland Bank Trust Co. Ltd v. Hett Stubbs & Kemp (a Firm)* [1978] 3 All ER 571 - whose reasoning he approved and adopted - which first made the significant finding that a solicitor could be liable towards his client in either contract or negligence (p.527). This judgment, said Lord Goff, "broke the mould, in the sense that it undermined the view which was becoming settled that, where there is an alternative liability in tort, the claimant must pursue his remedy in contract alone" (p.530). Corresponding developments were being witnessed in Ireland, Canada, New Zealand, Australia and in the United States in favour of concurrent remedies (pp.530-1). He concluded on the matter: "... the law of tort is the general law, out of which the parties can, if they wish, contract; and, as Oliver, J demonstrated, the same assumption of responsibility may, and frequently does, occur in a contractual context. Approached as a matter of principle, therefore, it is right to attribute to that assumption of responsibility, together with its concomitant reliance, a tortious liability, and then to inquire whether or not that liability is excluded by the contract because the latter is inconsistent with it. This is the reasoning which Oliver, J as I understand it, found implicit, where not explicit, in the speeches in *Hedley Byrne*. With his conclusion I respectfully agree. But even if I am wrong in this, I am of the opinion that this House should now, if necessary, develop the principle of assumption of responsibility as stated in *Hedley Byrne* to its logical conclusion so as to make it clear that a tortious duty of care may arise not only in cases where the relevant services are rendered gratuitously, but also where they are rendered under a contract ... the common law is not antipathetic to concurrent liability, and ... there is no sound basis for a rule which automatically restricts the claimant to either a tortious or contractual remedy. The result may be untidy; but given that the tortious duty is imposed by the general law, and the contractual duty is attributable to the will of the parties, I do not find it objectionable that the claimant may be entitled to take advantage of the remedy which is most advantageous to him, subject only to ascertaining whether the tortious duty is so inconsistent with the applicable contract that, in accordance with ordinary principle, the parties must be taken to have agreed that the tortious remedy is to be limited or excluded ... in the present case liability can, and in my opinion should, be founded squarely on the principle established in *Hedley Byrne* itself, from which it follows that an assumption of responsibility coupled with the concomitant reliance may give rise to a tortious duty of care irrespective of whether there is a contractual relationship between the parties, and in consequence, unless his contract precludes him from doing so, the plaintiff, who has available to him concurrent remedies in contract and tort, may choose that remedy which appears to him to be the most advantageous" (pp.532-3).

Before that too, Lord Goff expressed his agreement (p.530) with Le Dain, J in the Canadian case of *Central Trust Co. v. Rafuse* (1986) 31 DLR (4th) 481 that concurrent liability in tort would not, however, be admitted, if its effect would be to permit the plaintiff to circumvent or escape a contractual exclusion or limitation of liability for the act or omission which would constitute the tort.

Lord Browne-Wilkinson added his own reasoning to that of Lord Goff: just as contractual duties would exist concurrently with *fiduciary* duties of trustees and agents and need not necessarily be co-extensive with the latter, so too with contract and tort (pp.543-4): "The existence of an underlying contract (eg, as between solicitor and client) does not automatically exclude the general duty of care which the law imposes on those who voluntarily assume to act for others. But the nature and terms of the contractual relationship between the parties will be determinative of the scope of the responsibility assumed and can, in some cases, exclude any assumption of legal responsibility to the plaintiff for whom the defendant has assumed to act. If the common law is not to become again manacled by 'clanking chains' (this time represented by causes, rather than forms, of action), it is in my judgment important not to exclude concepts of concurrent liability which the courts of equity have over the years handled without difficulty. I can see no good reason for holding that the existence of a contractual right is in all the circumstances inconsistent with the co-existence of another tortious right, provided that it is understood that the agreement of the parties evidenced by the contract can modify and shape the tortious duties which, in the absence of contract, would be applicable" (p.544).

On applying the preceding principles to the facts of the case, therefore, the House of Lords' conclusions were as follows.

In the actions by the plaintiff *direct* names who had a contract with defendant managing agents, contractual and tort duties were co-extensive and the plaintiff names could opt for either remedy against the defendants (p.533).

With regard to the plaintiff indirect names, there was no strong reason at all *on the facts* why the particular contractual chain involved should be held to be inconsistent with existence of assumption of responsibility in tort by defendant managing agents towards the plaintiffs - just as if they had also had a separate contract alongside that between the managing and members' agents (pp.533-4 "I ... cannot see why in principle a party should not assume responsibility to more than one person in respect of the same activity ... I can see no reason in principle why the two duties of care so arising should not be capable of co-existing", p.534). *However,* Lord Goff did go on to make the point that this may not *always* be so, and in many cases a contractual chain could prove inconsistent with an assumption of tort responsibility "which has the effect of, so to speak, short-circuiting the contractual structure so put in place by the parties" (p.534). Thus, Lord Goff signified his acceptance of the Court of Appeal's decision in *Simaan General Contracting Co. v. Pilkington Glass Ltd (No.2)* [1988] 1 All ER 791 (see *infra,* p.184), since there was "generally no assumption of responsibility by the sub-contractor or supplier direct to the building owner, the parties having so structured their relationship that it is inconsistent with any such assumption of responsibility" (p.534).

In summary, therefore, in the case of tortious liability for pure economic loss arising from a negligent statement or advice, following *Henderson:*

(a) third parties to the advice or statement can claim, if they can establish assumed responsibility and reliance;

(b) existence of a contract between parties, or, in the case of third party claimants, existence of a contractual chain or structure omitting direct contractual relations between plaintiff and defendant, is not automatically to be regarded as inconsistent with co-existence of duties in tort - and the latter may be co-extensive with any direct contractual duties, or greater, or lesser than these. It is all a matter of contractual construction as to existence and extent of otherwise independent (albeit related) duties in tort. The House of Lords thus held in favour of co-existence in the case of plaintiff Lloyd's names and defendant members' and managing agents in *Henderson,* in which event plaintiffs had the choice of proceeding either in contract or in tort, where possible against members' agents (and of course in tort alone against managing agents). However, it was also indicated by the Lords (see *supra*) that in building sub-contracting cases, it would be quite possible to view a chain of contracts between building owner and main contractor on the one hand, and main contractor and sub-contractor on the other, but with no direct contractual relations between building owner and sub-contractor, as being inconsistent with co-existence of a duty in tort owed by the latter to the former on the basis of assumed responsibility and reliance in respect of faulty work or materials, approving the decision in the earlier *Simaan* case concerning the recovery or not of economic loss from negligent *acts* (see *infra*).

In the end, it is uncertain whether the *Henderson rationalization* of *Hedley Byrne* will lead to a great expansion of liability for such economic loss. In the first place, any thought that the principle sounds the death-knell of the English principle of privity of contract, whereby a third party beneficiary under a contract (in *Henderson*, between defendant managing agents and the members' agents) is not permitted to enforce it (*Tweddle v. Atkinson* (1861) 1 B & S 393), should be discarded (see Lord Goff in *White v. Jones*, pp.709-710, *infra*, p.145 *et seq.*): there is an essential distinction between such *intention to benefit* a third party to the contract on the one hand, and an *assumption of tortious responsibility* towards him on the other. Secondly, where there is a contract between plaintiff and defendant, or if not, their relationship forms part of an overall contractual structure, the chances of concurrent tort responsibility *not* being held to be inconsistent with this (so that, for example, a plaintiff could take advantage of tort rules on remoteness of damage, or time limitation of actions under the Latent Damage Act 1986, or rights of contribution between joint tortfeasors) may not be so great. Accordingly, *Henderson* is again unlikely to be able to be used in order to enlarge liability significantly in the different area of economic loss from *acts* rather than statements, where legal development is even more restrictive than in the case of *Hedley Byrne* statements (see *infra,* p.173 *et seq.*). Furthermore, it may in any event even be the case, according to some commentators, that in practice the Goff explanation will be held to be applicable solely to "professional" defendants. As to the meaning of which scope-defining concept, if such is the position, it is almost inevitable that courts will proceed cautiously on a case-by-case incremental basis without propounding a general principle of classification - just and sensible, if not entirely in the interests of legal certainty for an initial period.

Henderson v. Merrett Syndicates Ltd was subsequently followed by the Court of Appeal in *Holt v. Payne Skillington (a Firm)* (1995) *The Times,* December 22, CA, where the plaintiffs sued the defendants, their solicitors and estate agents, who acted for them in the purchase of a property in Mayfair, London, in both contract and the tort of negligence. Referring to Lord Goff's judgment in *Henderson,* the court held that provided that the contract did not expressly nor impliedly limit the wider duty of care in tort to the more restricted contractual obligations of the defendants, there was no reason why a plaintiff should be prevented from proceeding on both, in the alternative. The duty of care in tort was imposed by law, whereas contractual obligations resulted from parties' intentions. As it happened, on the evidence it was found that the defendants were not liable in tort as having provided negligent advice.

In addition, in his dissenting judgment in the House of Lords in *Marc Rich & Co. AG v. Bishop Rock Marine Co. Ltd* (see *infra,* p.211), Lord Lloyd referred to *Henderson* as reaffirming the principle that the function of the law of tort was not limited to filling in gaps left by the law of contract and as rejecting an approach which treated the law of tort as supplementary to the law of contract, providing a tortious remedy only where there was no contract (p.315) - although, with the majority of Lords, Lord Steyn considered that since the plaintiff cargo owners were not even aware of the defendant surveyor's examination of the ship at the request of the shipowners, it was impossible to force the facts into even the most expansive view of the *Henderson* doctrine of voluntary assumption of responsibility on the part of the defendant (p.333).

A slightly different development of the issue in *Henderson* arose in the similar proceedings in *Aiken v. Stewart Wrightson Members Agency Ltd* [1995] 1 WLR 1281. Here too the plaintiff Lloyd's Names wished to sue their members' agents and the managing agents to whom the members' agents had delegated their functions in accordance with their contract with the plaintiffs. The managing agents had failed to effect proper reinsurance cover against calls for payment upon the plaintiffs and losses of £85 million were predicted. The problem for the plaintiffs was that in respect of their contractual action against the members' agents, the limitation period had expired - whereas the tort period for negligence would still run by virtue of s.14A of the Limitation Act 1980 concerning latent damage (see *infra,* ch.29). Following *Henderson,* the plaintiffs would have no difficulty in framing their action in tort rather than in contract in the circumstances and in asserting breach of a co-extensive duty of care in negligence, and Potter, J in the High Court readily acknowledged this (pp.1298-1300) - except of course where the effect would be to enable the plaintiff to circumvent a contractual liability-exclusion clause, p.1301 and see *infra*, ch.29). However, crucially, the plaintiffs wanted to do more than this: since the defendant members' agents' *contractual* duty towards the plaintiffs was considerably greater than what would otherwise be their duty of care towards the latter in tort - to use all care and skill *in obtaining reinsurance* and merely to exercise such care *in delegating* to managing agents, respectively - the plaintiffs sought to argue that the duty of care in tort would *necessarily* be co-existence with the greater degree of care required to be shown under the contract. This was different from the past cases, where it had been a matter of demonstrating that a tort duty could coexist with an equivalent contractual duty, or exceed the latter (see Potter, J at p.1300, and *supra, Holt v. Payne Skillington*).

Potter, J held that the law had not yet advanced to the point of accepting such automatic correlation between tort and higher contractual standard of care according to its terms (p.1301); for, whilst contractual existence would not preclude reliance upon a concurrent or alternative liability in tort, the two were independent (*ibid.*). Accordingly, the plaintiffs were in a position where the duty of care in tort upon which they relied against the defendant members' agents fell short of the specific obligation imposed by the express terms of the contract (*ibid.*). Their suit in tort, though not time-barred, would not avail them greatly.

The plaintiffs further tried to argue that the defendants' duty in tort was in fact *non-delegable* to the managing agents, so that the managing agents' negligence was also the defendants' own (p.1295). Potter, J rejected this line of argument as well (pp.1295 and 1304 - and see *infra,* ch.12).

One last point of interest relating to *Henderson* also arose in the *Aiken* case. In the plaintiffs' negligence action against the *managing agents* themselves in *Aiken,* the defendant managing agents denied that they owed a duty of care towards plaintiff Lloyd's Names who *subsequently* joined the plaintiffs' syndicate, after the original date upon which the defendants were engaged to conduct the plaintiffs' business affairs. Potter, J concluded that this was not an issue governed by the *Henderson* principle, since the question whether the defendants, employed by a third party (the members' agents), had nonetheless *assumed responsibility towards* and been *relied upon by* any other parties, within the terms of *Henderson,* "was no doubt the most appropriate and useful approach when considering the relationship between managing agents and their *existing* Names" (p.1308); but "when considering whether a duty of care admittedly owed by A to B [by defendants to existing Names] in respect of a particular transaction extends also to a third party C [subsequent Names], who suffers damage as a result of its negligent performance", the appropriate approach was said to be the ordinary procedure in *Donoghue v. Stevenson* as elaborated upon in *Caparo Industries plc v. Dickman* and adopted in *White v. Jones* in the Court of Appeal (*Ibid.*) (*Aiken* was decided before the House of Lords' decision in *White v. Jones* - see *infra*). Potter, J then adjudged that in fact the duty of care was owed by the defendants towards the plaintiffs on the normal foreseeability, proximity and fair, just and reasonable bases in *Caparo*: the defendants' duty was to the class of Lloyd's Names as it existed from time to time in the form of the syndicate as its collective client, and it was perfectly foreseeable and fair, just and reasonable that the duty of care should be owed to plaintiffs who were subsequent and not merely original members of the syndicate in these circumstances (pp.1308-1313) - Potter, J's tortuous efforts also to deal separately with "stage 2" *proximity* and "stage 3" *fair, just and reasonable* being somewhat excruciating in view of the artificiality of that distinction (see *ibid.*, pp.1309 and 1311).

It is submitted that *both* developments of liability towards third parties for their pure economic loss - that in *Henderson* and in *White v. Jones* in the House of Lords (see *infra*) - would in fact be satisfied on these facts. Both concern the *marketing* of special skills and *consumer protection* against defects: *Henderson,* as seen, applies when the provider of advice can be taken to have *assumed responsibility* towards third parties who are likely to *rely* upon it; and it will be seen below that liability decided upon by a majority of the House of Lords in *White v. Jones (infra)* applies where the provider can be taken to have assumed a responsibility towards a third party who would foreseeably suffer financial loss through the adviser's failure to exercise due care. In whichever way the situation in *Aiken* is viewed, it seems quite clear that the defendant managing agents could be considered to have assumed responsibility towards future, not merely existing, members of the Names syndicate, and either it was the case that the latter would foreseeably rely upon this fact when they decided to join the syndicate (*Henderson*) or, even if not, it was wholly foreseeable that they would suffer economic loss if the defendants had failed to exercise sufficient care (*White v. Jones*). What Potter, J frankly should not have done therefore - although, it was understandable, given (*i*) the fact that he regarded the situation as falling outside the *Henderson* principle (p.1308), contrary to the present submission, and (*ii*) the House of Lords' decision in *White v. Jones,* restricting the more expansive approach of the Court of Appeal (see *infra*), had not yet been delivered - was to go on to find a general duty of care towards third parties for economic loss from negligent advice, under the *Caparo* principles. The danger from this is that unless such recovery is confined to the controls and principles in *Hedley Byrne* and to the progressions therefrom in *Henderson* and *White v. Jones,* instability and confusion may then arise through the *generalization* of the economic loss recovery process beyond those judicially constructed restrictions, contrary to the incremental approach hitherto adopted, of limiting economic loss to particular categories and circumstances.

2. *Third party is intended beneficiary of assumption of responsibility towards another irrespective of reliance, where the third party would otherwise suffer loss: White v. Jones [1995] 1 All ER 691, HL*

Courts have also shown themselves willing to allow a third party to recover his financial loss resulting from a *Hedley Byrne* misstatement or negligent advice between two other persons, *even though the third party himself was not within the special relationship nor relied upon the advice.*

One example of this is that of *job references:* X seeks

employment with firm Y, and Z is asked to provide a reference to Y, which he does, negligently. Obviously, Z, the referee may be liable towards Y, the employer, on normal *Hedley Byrne* principles if Y employs X in reliance on the reference and consequently suffers economic loss because X is incapable of performing his duties. But if Y decides not to employ X as a result of Z's negligence in writing the reference, does Z owe a duty of care towards X? In *Spring v. Guardian Assurance plc* [1994] 3 All ER 129, the House of Lords (by a majority of four to one) answered "yes", thereby reversing the Court of Appeal which had considered X's remedy to be solely in the tort of defamation of character, to which there would be a defence of "qualified privilege" in certain circumstances ([1993] 2 All ER 273, see *infra*, ch.26). The Lords, asking whether it would be fair, just and reasonable to impose such liability, considered that ex-employers would nonetheless remain willing to provide references, because these were so vital to industry, and even if the overall number decreased, it was in the public interest that they should be of a higher standard and properly drawn up, especially in view of the serious effects which a bad reference could have on a person's career prospects (pp.151, 153, 161-2, 168, 172, 177). Furthermore, it was not right that in this situation the recipient employer should have a remedy, as seen, under *Hedley Byrne* - but that there should be no duty of care in negligence towards the employee himself (p.161); and Lord Goff (pp.146-7) actually took the view, different from the other Lords, that the employee too was covered by *Hedley Byrne* itself, because the employer providing the reference had special knowledge, derived from his experience of the employee's character, skill and diligence in performing his duties, and the employee relied upon him to exercise due care and skill in preparing the reference before sending it. (Presumably, therefore, a personal reference, other than from an employer, would not give rise to such a duty: see pp.162-3, 179?)

Finally, the House of Lords considered that existence of a cause of action in the separate tort of defamation, together with its special defence of qualified privilege, would not have the effect of negativing what would otherwise be a duty of care in negligence, because the two torts protected different interests - the former, damage to reputation, irrespective of negligence, and the latter, economic loss (pp.151, 153, 160-1, 172-6). The result will doubtless be a decline in the use of defamation in such cases (if only because legal aid is there unavailable).

A further example of third party claims was *Ross v. Caunters* [1979] 3 All ER 580, in which the defendant solicitors had advised a subsequently deceased testator in making a will and had negligently failed to warn the testator that if the spouse of a beneficiary under the will were to witness the will, the beneficiary could not take thereunder. Pure economic loss to the disappointed beneficiary. Although the plaintiff beneficiary, whose husband had witnessed the will, had not herself been advised by nor had she relied upon the defendants' advice, nevertheless, the Vice-Chancellor held that the defendants owed a duty of care towards her. What possible basis could there have been for such finding? Was it, for example, that the plaintiff had somehow been *attracted* within the primary *Hedley Byrne* duty owed towards the testator, the idea being that because the economic loss to the plaintiff third party beneficiary was suffered *against a background* of *Hedley Byrne*-type relationship between the other two people - the testator and the defendant solicitor - this was sufficient to create a duty of care in negligent economic loss towards the plaintiff herself, outside the *Hedley Byrne* relationship sphere? The answer is "no". Quite simply Megarry, V-C preferred to base his decision entirely on the existence of reasonable foreseeability within *Donoghue v. Stevenson* that the plaintiff, as an individual or, at most, member of a limited class, would suffer damage - in view of the obvious absence of *Hedley Byrne* reliance by the plaintiff upon the defendant (pp.588, 591-2). The case was clearly vulnerable to criticism, as seeming to extend liability for negligent advice in the absence of any doctrinal justification and as threatening the principle of privity of contract whereby a third party upon whom a benefit is conferred by parties to a contract is nonetheless himself unable to enforce that contract; yet, it was not unique. Earlier, in *Ministry of Housing & Local Government v. Sharp* [1970] 2 QB 223, the defendant issued a search of the local land charge register to the purchaser of land, which negligently omitted to refer to a charge over the land in favour of the plaintiff, with the result that the purchaser took the land free of the plaintiff's charge. The defendant was held liable towards the plaintiff for the economic loss, notwithstanding that it had been the purchaser who was directly advised of the land search and who relied upon the report.

Furthermore however, *Ross v. Caunters,* though regularly applied as a first instance decision of the Chancery Division of the High Court, nevertheless became exposed to even more potential objections because, as will later be seen, more recent cases established the general inability to recover for pure economic loss resulting from negligent *acts* (see *Junior Books Ltd v. The Veitchi Co. Ltd* [1983] 1 AC 520, *Candlewood Navigation Corporation Ltd v. Mitsui OSK Lines Ltd, The Mineral Transporter* [1986] AC 1, and *Leigh and Sillavan v. The Aliakmon Shipping Co.* [1985] 1 QB 350 for criticism). In the light of these, it became questionable whether the *Ross v. Caunters* principle was still, if ever, correct, because whereas the negligent advice or statement in *Hedley Byrne* cases is a *statement* in relation to the person to whom it is made, nonetheless, from the point of view of third parties who may suffer as a result, arguably it has more of the character of a negligent *act*.

However, in the Court of Appeal in *White v. Jones* [1993] 3 All ER 481, in which defendant solicitors, who had negligently failed to alter a person's will as requested before the person died, were found to be liable towards the plaintiffs who had consequently lost the gifts they were intended to receive under the amended will - economic loss - it was expressly held that *Ross v. Caunters* remained good law (pp.492, 498, 504).

Notwithstanding the Court of Appeal's unanimous approval of *Ross v. Caunters* in *White v. Jones* however, the House of Lords subsequently reversed the latter decision on appeal in *White v. Jones* [1995] 1 All ER 691, HL, with the result that:

(i) *Ross v. Caunters* appeared to be rejected as a basis of liability towards third parties by Lord Goff in the majority in *White v. Jones,* on the ground that it failed to satisfy conceptual difficulties over privity of contract under English law whereby third parties to a contract could not enforce it, and in the light of inapplicability of *Hedley Byrne* itself (p.711), and by Lord Mustill in the dissenting minority who thought that *Ross v. Caunters* was decided in the old *liberal* times of *Anns v. Merton London Borough Council* two years earlier and that Meggary, V-C might have reached another conclusion "in the very different legal climate of 1994" (pp.724-5); and yet

(ii) at the same time *Ross v. Caunters* liability was replaced by a new, independent duty of care in negligence *sui generis,* not based upon *Hedley Byrne* nor on *Ross v. Caunters* itself, on the part of solicitors negligently preparing wills, towards disappointed beneficiaries - economic loss - supported by a majority of three Lords and vigorously objected to by the dissenting minority of two. Therefore, negligence existed, but not as a *Hedley Byrne* extension, nor on the *Ross v. Caunters* basis of ordinary *Donoghue v. Stevenson* reasonable foreseeability.

Lord Nolan in the majority in the House of Lords in *White v. Jones* actually supported *Ross v. Caunters,* as forming part of a more general principle of liability based on assumption of responsibility previously endorsed by the House of Lords in *Henderson v. Merrett Syndicates Ltd (supra,* p.117) (p.735), whereas Lord Browne-Wilkinson in the majority and Lord Keith in the minority did not refer to *Ross v. Caunters* at all.

So what exactly was the reasoning of the House of Lords

in *White v. Jones* [1995] 1 All ER 691, in greater detail?

The decision in the case, as seen, by a majority of three to two, was that solicitors acting for a testator, who had failed to carry out his instructions in the timely preparation of a new will, *were* liable *in damages for negligence* towards the intended beneficiaries, thereby upholding the result - though not the reasoning - in the Court of Appeal in 1993. The majority (pp.711, 716, 735) were heavily influenced by the earlier recent House of Lords decision in *Henderson v. Merrett Syndicates Ltd* [1994] 3 All ER 506, in which the *assumption of responsibility* by a defendant was found to be the general rationale underlying *Hedley Byrne* liability (*supra,* p.117) - distinguished from the situation in *White v. Jones,* however, by the minority Judges (pp.694-5, 730-1).

The first case which had to be confronted, however, was *Ross v. Caunters.* There, it will be recalled, the will had failed because the defendant solicitors had negligently omitted to have it properly attested - witnessed - whereas in *White v. Jones* it had failed because defendant solicitors negligently delayed to prepare a fresh will revoking the existing one and the testator died before the new will was completed. *Ross v. Caunters,* it was seen, was a first instance decision of Megarry, V-C (not binding on the higher courts), in which the beneficiary under the ineffective will was held entitled to recover damages for ordinary negligence liability against the solicitors.

It *might* have been possible to justify this as a kind of "attracted" *Hedley Byrne* liability - that is, ordinary negligence liability, based on reasonable foreseeability, towards an individual or member of a limited class, *against the background* of *Hedley Byrne* liability allowing economic loss, but not on the latter basis itself in view of absence of reliance by plaintiff upon defendant or intention by the defendant that the plaintiff should place such reliance. In this way, it might have been said that for recovery for economic loss to have taken place, the plaintiff was somehow allowed to benefit from the *Hedley Byrne* relationship between the solicitor and testator, in the absence of such a relationship between solicitor and plaintiff themselves. Thus, in *White v. Jones* the plaintiffs were the testator's daughters, who took nothing under the existing will, but would have benefited in the amount of £9,000 each under the new will, following a reconciliation with their father with whom they had previously quarrelled. So, the plaintiffs would argue, they too were owed a duty of care, as was the plaintiff in *Ross v. Caunters.*

However, the defendant solicitors in *White v. Jones* sought to challenge *Ross v. Caunters,* on the basis that the essentially contractual nature of the defendants' obligations precluded their liability in negligence towards the plaintiff *third parties to the contract* between the defendants and testator. Supposing, they said, there was a liability-exclusion clause in that contract: the defendant solicitor should be able to - but certainly could not - raise that against any such negligence claim (p.699). The plaintiffs' loss, furthermore, the defendants said, was merely one of expectation of a benefit - properly the concern of contract not tort - and not of a benefit itself (pp.699-700); and to allow the *Ross v. Caunters* basis for recovery could lead to liability towards indeterminate classes of person (p.700). In addition, Lord Goff considered a further possible objection that not only would the claim in tort be one for pure economic loss, but it would also be in respect of an *omission,* not normally applicable to negligence claims other than in special circumstances (see *infra,* p.195).

Lord Goff in the course of a comparative survey of different legal systems' solutions to the problem, conceded (p.701, *et seq.*) the strength of these arguments against negligence liability towards the third parties (p.698 *et seq.*) (albeit noting, at pp.699 and 704, that a solicitor *could* owe both contractual and *Hedley Byrne negligence* duties towards *his client,* in accordance with *Henderson v. Merrett Syndicates Ltd, supra,* p.117) and that there was great difficulty in holding the defendant solicitors liable in negligence towards intended beneficiaries in these circumstances: there was not necessarily any actual reliance by the plaintiffs on the exercise of skill by the defendants at the relevant time - they might not even have known of the solicitors' activities (p.704); furthermore, the English doctrines of contractual consideration and privity of contract preventing third parties to contracts from enforcing benefits thereunder were obstacles to contractual solutions to be found in foreign systems (pp.709-710). Therefore, for Lord Goff, both *Ross v. Caunters* and *Hedley Byrne* would not provide answers: the first was said to be inappropriate because the solution there of permitting an ordinary action in negligence - albeit in a *Hedley Byrne*-type context - between the main parties would not solve any of the conceptual difficulties over the tortious or contractual nature of the claim which had been raised (p.710); and the second because *Hedley Byrne* itself, as said, would not extend to the beneficiaries in the absence of special circumstances of assumed responsibility and corresponding reliance, here absent (*ibid.*) - from which it appears that *Ross v. Caunters* has, therefore, not survived *White v. Jones* in the House of Lords as the preferred basis of this type of liability towards third parties.

Consequently, the House of Lords was entitled to try to fill the gap in the law in order to *prevent an injustice,* because the essence of the situation here was that if the solicitors were negligent and this was not discovered until after the testator had died, there was no remedy if the beneficiaries who had lost out could not claim. There would be little point in damages in negligence going to the testator's estate, because this would solely benefit those entitled under the existing will, not the plaintiffs - for Lord Goff, a matter of "cardinal importance" in the case (p.702, and p.708).

In these circumstances, it was decided, *Hedley Byrne* was to be *developed* in the following way: *assumption of responsibility* by the defendant solicitor *towards his client* should be held to *extend* to the intended beneficiary whom the solicitor could *reasonably foresee* would otherwise suffer loss through the solicitor's negligence (p.710). This would, according to Lord Goff, produce practical justice for all parties and also had a number of additional beneficial consequences (*ibid.*):

1. no unacceptable circumvention of established principles of contract (that is, privity);
2. the purely economic nature of the beneficiary's loss was not a problem (having been rendered peripheral);
3. liability would be subject to any liability-exclusion term in the contract between testator and solicitor which would exclude the latter's liability towards the

former, though unlikely in practice;
4. since *Hedley Byrne* was founded upon an assumption of responsibility, the defendant might be liable for an omission, not merely negligent acts;
5. damages for loss of an expectation, recoverable in principle in contract, should not be excluded under *Hedley Byrne* as so developed, simply because the action was classified as tortious (pp.710-711).

Thus, according to Lord Goff, would all conceptual problems *fade innocuously away* (p.711). Limits to recovery were admitted to be necessary and could cause difficulties, but boundaries would be worked out in the future as practical problems came to light before the courts (pp.711-712). "... I can see no injustice in imposing liability upon a negligent solicitor in a case such as the present where, in the absence of a remedy in this form, neither the testator's estate nor the disappointed beneficiary will have a claim for the loss caused by his negligence. This is the injustice which, in my opinion, the Judges of this country should address by recognizing that cases such as these call for an appropriate remedy, and that the common law is not so sterile as to be incapable of supplying that remedy when it is required" (p.711) "... If by any chance a more complicated case should arise to test the precise boundaries of the principle in cases of this kind, that problem can await solution when such a case comes forward for decision" (p.712).

To which it is tempting to add: *and it was all done with mirrors.* If it is said often enough that things will all work out in the end, people will start to believe it.

How is Lord Goff's decision to be justified in principle? Was it perhaps due to the fact that a *contractual* relationship existed between the testator and the defendant solicitors: and that thereafter, by some sleight of hand, not only was the disappointed beneficiary *attracted* within this relationship, but additionally, the relations between solicitors and beneficiary miraculously *changed* from one in contract to tort at some point during the process, thereby affording a remedy in negligence to the plaintiff beneficiaries - all because *Hedley Byrne* liability depends upon actual reliance upon skills and advice, absent in the case of the plaintiff beneficiaries, and recovery for pure economic loss from negligent *acts* outside *Hedley Byrne* is of course heavily controlled?

Could, therefore, its justification be, not as suggested above in relation to *Ross v. Caunters,* namely:

(a) existence of a *Hedley Byrne* reliance relationship between testator and solicitor, X and Y,

(b) where the third party Z is allowed to benefit through bringing a negligence action, as having been attracted within the *X-Y Hedley Byrne* relationship, at least as a background to his own relations,

but instead:

1. "attraction" of third party Z into the *contractual* relationship between testator and solicitor, X and Y,
2. but then "conversion" of Z into a main party to

> a new, non-*Hedley Byrne* relationship with Y, as one of general *negligence,* on the basis of which he can bring a primary, "non-attracted" claim?

There is nothing to suggest that Lord Goff had any such thoughts in mind. He simply wished to do justice as he saw it, leaving the future - including scope and rationalization - to others?

Few people would be devoid of sympathy for the plaintiffs in the situation under discussion. Yet, it is hardly credible for Lord Goff to claim that his solution makes conceptual problems "innocuously fade away". On the contrary, it seems rather to ignore them completely and defiantly, which is hardly a prescription for future success.

A better approach, perhaps, recognizing the need to provide a remedy for beneficiaries, together with the absence of contractual relations between them and the defendants or necessarily of *Hedley Byrne* reliance on the solicitor's skills on their part, and yet the fact that solicitors will after all be insured against tortious liability, might have been to try to found an action in tort upon breach of - albeit delegated - statutory duty, that is, the duty of a solicitor under the Solicitors' Practice Rules 1990, rule 1, to do nothing to compromise or to impair *inter alia* the good repute of the solicitor or of the solicitors' profession or the solicitor's proper standard of work. (In *White v. Jones,* p.698, Lord Goff himself noted that a French *notaire* would be responsible even towards third parties for all fault causing damage, committed by him in the exercise of his functions.)

The effect of this would be to provide a remedy in tort in the one situation - negligent wills - in which most will agree that it should exist, without unnecessarily having to become involved with principles of assumption of responsibility said to underlie *Hedley Byrne,* using all the skills of an alchemist and potentially causing great uncertainty for the future development of the law in the course of doing so.

In truth, however, it is believed that the preceding suggestion would be *most* unlikely to gain acceptance in any quarter!

In *White v. Jones* Lord Browne-Wilkinson agreed with Lord Goff that the plaintiffs fell between the two stools of contract and *Hedley Byrne* reliance. Yet, for all that, a solicitor accepting instructions to draw up a will knew that the economic welfare of the intended beneficiary was dependent upon his careful execution of the task and assumed the responsibility to do so (pp.717-8) - an *assumption of responsibility* featuring in the two categories of *special relationship* (fiduciary, as in trusts, pp.713-4, and *Hedley Byrne,* pp.714-5) so far identified as giving rise to liability (see *Henderson v. Merrett Syndicates Ltd, supra,* p.117) - and it was immaterial that the task was only undertaken by the defendants by virtue of a contract with the testator. Not only was the relationship between the defendant solicitors and the plaintiffs therefore *analogous* to those permitting recovery (p.717), there were more general factors making it fair, just and reasonable to impose liability on the solicitors: the passing of property from one generation to another was dependent upon due discharge of their duties by solicitors (p.718 - see too Lord Goff, p.702, to like effect). Consequently, *society as a whole relied on solicitors to carry out their will-making functions carefully (ibid.).* It was unjust for beneficiaries not to receive what was rightfully theirs through the negligence of solicitors. The will-making function had unique features: there was no conflict of interest, since all wished the beneficiary to take, and in contrast to *inter vivos* transactions, the errors would not be discovered until after the death of a party, when they were irremediable (*ibid.*). (In this connexion, the case may be distinguished from the lifetime situation of *Hemmens v. Wilson Browne* [1993] 4 All ER 826, where a client instructed solicitors to draw up a document entitling the plaintiff to request a payment of £110,000. When the plaintiff did so, payment was refused. The court declined to impose a duty of care upon the solicitor for failing to draft an enforceable document, because the client was still alive and capable of remedying the position.) Thus, Lord Browne-Wilkinson concluded that "by accepting instructions to draw a will, a solicitor does come into a special relationship with those intended to benefit under it in consequence of which the law imposes a duty to the intended beneficiary to act with due expedition and care in relation to the task on which he has entered" (p.718).

The difficulties with Lord Browne-Wilkinson's treatment hardly need to be drawn attention to: *analogies* (with *Hedley Byrne*) do not take the place of principled doctrine - cats and dogs share many common physical features, and yet differ fundamentally in the final analysis; as for extending *Hedley Byrne* by analogy so that it is sufficient if *society relies* upon the defendant to exercise proper care, for social and economic reasons ...!

Lord Nolan agreed with the others, but wondered whether such a development in the law would be justified given that the testator's family as a whole - plaintiffs *and original beneficiaries* - would end up better off as a result of the defendants' negligence (p.734). Nevertheless, the testator's final wishes were firm, clear and attainable; the defendants were the family solicitors with whom the plaintiffs had had discussions about the preparation of the new will, so that the degree of proximity and reliance between them could hardly have been closer, and it would be absurd to suggest otherwise (pp.735-6). Contrary considerations "should not stand in the way of the simple justice of the respondents' claim --- entitled to --- the only remedy which the law can offer, notwithstanding the fortuitous aspects of the case and its unusual consequences" (p.735). True it was that not *all* potential beneficiaries who would lose out under an existing will could establish a sufficient relationship of proximity with defendants - but this was not inconsistent with the pragmatic case-by-case approach which the law now adopted towards negligence claims (p.736). (In other words, even if the limits were not known, work it out later.)

So there it was. The plaintiffs had *relied* on the defendants because they had been *involved in discussions* with the defendants over the revised will. Simple justice required that they should have a remedy. The problem with this use of the reliance concept however is that it fails to distinguish between *legal* reliance - based upon acceptance of a legal obligation by the person relied upon in the specific circumstances of *Hedley Byrne* or *Henderson v. Merrett Syndicates Ltd* - and everyday reliance, which is open-ended and not entirely stable as a criterion of tortious liability. We all rely on other people on a number of occasions throughout each day of our lives - yet, not all such situations can give rise to legal liability. Should a man gambling money on a horse to win a race be held to have a remedy against the person who trained the horse so negligently that it did not win, on the basis that the former relied upon the latter? With *Hedley Byrne,* we more or less know where we are. But with *White v. Jones,* there is no such certainty: Lord Nolan based his finding *as to actionable reliance* on the justice of the case and on the fact that the plaintiffs had some connexion with the defendants (*supra*). This provides little assistance to future litigants in quite different situations, who wish to work out potential liability. The "incremental" approach to development of duty of care in negligence assumes a *line of connexion of principle between existing and developed legal authorities,* not simply a series of random fact situations in which courts either will or will not find actionable reliance, which is hardly a prescription for stable and certain progress in the law.

In the latter connexion, it should at once be noted that Lord Keith, in the dissenting minority with Lord Mustill in the House of Lords in *White v. Jones,* dissented because he said that he could not reconcile allowing the plaintiffs' claim "with principle" nor accept that to do so "would represent an appropriate advance on the incremental basis from decided cases" (p.694). English contract law would not admit the *ius quaesitum tertio* (rights of third parties) and to allow a claim in tort would in substance be to circumvent this rule (*ibid.*). *Henderson v. Merrett Syndicates Ltd* (*supra,* p.117) had been different, because, in contrast to that case, the defendant solicitor in *White v. Jones* "was not engaged in managing any aspect of the plaintiffs' affairs" (p.695). In addition, unlike *Hedley Byrne* itself of course, in *White v. Jones* there was no direct relationship between plaintiffs and defendant, nor did the defendant solicitors do or say anything upon which the plaintiffs *acted* to their prejudice (p.694). Accordingly, conceptual difficulties involved in the claim were "too formidable to be resolved by any process of reasoning compatible with existing principles of law" (p.695).

Again, in the matter of reliance, Lord Mustill pointed out that *mutuality* was central to the *Hedley Byrne* decision (pp.729-730) - this was the only *solid basis* for permitting the accretive process of tortious recovery in favour of plaintiffs (p.731), and yet it was absent in the case of disappointed beneficiaries, all the more so where the latter, a charity for example, were not even to be taken to have been aware that they were intended to be favoured under a negligently prepared will (*ibid.*).

Lord Mustill could not accept the proposition that it was but a short step from *Hedley Byrne* to the situation in *White v. Jones,* attractive though this might appear, because this was not an "application of *Hedley Byrne* by enlargement ... but the enunciation of something quite different" (p.732). In *Hedley Byrne,* the fundamental point was that the defendants acted *for* the plaintiffs - in *White v. Jones* they did so *for the testator,* not for the plaintiff beneficiaries even though they knew that the latter were to benefit. This was why *Hedley Byrne* could not be used as a stepping stone to the newly developed liability and was that which distinguished *White v. Jones* from the recent House of Lords developments in *Henderson v. Merrett Syndicates Ltd* (see *supra,* p.117) which latter case "fell squarely within the concept of the undertaking of legal responsibility for careful and diligent performance in the context of a mutual relationship which in my opinion was the essence of the decision in *Hedley Byrne*" (p.731).

Lord Mustill went on to state that whilst a broad new type of claim might properly be met by a broad new type of rationalization as happened in *Hedley Byrne, rationalization* was the key word (pp.732-3) and it did not lead to the *orderly* development of the law or the *certainty* which practical convenience demanded "if duties are simply conjured up as a matter of positive law, to answer the apparent justice of an individual case" (p.733).

Exactly!

Lord Mustill saw nothing *unique* in the situation involved in *White v. Jones* which could have justified a special new rule, limited to those facts, without harming the general structure of the law, and consequently, if the principle propounded by the majority was to be considered sound, it would have to be so in every instance of the general situation where A promised B for reward to perform a service for B in circumstances where it was foreseeable that performance of the service with care would cause C to receive a benefit and that failure to perform it might cause C not to receive that benefit (p.733). "To hold that a duty exists, even *prima facie*, in such a situation would be to go far beyond anything so far contemplated by the law of negligence" (*ibid.*). This was not a case of *opening floodgates* as such - merely that it was not possible to discern a principled reasoning which could lead to the recognition of such an extensive new area of potential liability. An intermediate duty based upon the *precise facts* of the case, in which solicitor defendants, testator and plaintiffs had all been involved in discussions about the new will, had at first seemed possible, but on reflection was inappropriate because nothing had been proven to support this (*ibid.*).

Needless to say, this writer is in total agreement with Lord Mustill's dissenting judgment. Imagination in giving judgment is one thing, and is to be applauded. Fantasy is quite another.

It is a pity, therefore, that the possibility voiced by Lord Mustill in the closing words of his judgment, of *somehow* providing a remedy to the deserving beneficiaries, whilst at the same time limiting effects to the facts of the case, thereby preserving legal certainty, could not, seemingly, be achieved by framing the action against the solicitors as one for breach of (delegated) statutory duty (see above, p.148).

So that is *White v. Jones:* duty of care in negligence towards a third party, based on the existence of a contract between two other people for - or, at least, calculated to result in - the benefit of the third party.

Where does this leave the principle of privity of contract? What is the point of the latter control, if you can nevertheless obtain a remedy in tort?

The suspicion must be that *White v. Jones* will be limited to its facts - testator/solicitor/beneficiary - and only extended to specific situations, without also being generalized.

As Lord Mustill indicated, this is hardly the best method for development of legal doctrine, and it may well be that in order to take account of his concerns regarding lack of legal justification and threat to the fundamental privity of contract principle, there will have to be specific *legislation* awarding disappointed beneficiaries a remedy against a solicitor negligently preparing a will for another and that the House of Lords will overrule *White v. Jones* itself, as a dangerous piece of judicial legislation.

This will have to be seen.

In the meantime, *White v. Jones* was subsequently followed and applied by the Chancery Division of the High Court in *Penn v. Bristol and West Building Society* (1995) *The Times,* June 19, where defendant solicitors were held to be liable in negligence towards the plaintiff joint-owner of a house with her former husband, for failing to check whether she had truly consented to the sale of the house by the husband for whom they acted, which she had not. The husband had forged the plaintiff's signature on a contract of sale and transfer and he and the proposed purchaser were accomplices in an intended mortgage fraud. Thus, although the plaintiff had never been a client of the defendant solicitors, the court nevertheless considered that she ought reasonably to have been within their contemplation when they received the title deeds to the house, and her interest as co-owner was sufficiently proximate to the transaction in which they were engaged for the defendants to owe her a duty of care according to the principles pronounced upon by the House of Lords in *White v. Jones*.

On the other hand, in *X (Minors) v. Bedfordshire County Council etc* [1995] 3 All ER 353, HL (see *infra,* p.212), Lord Browne-Wilkinson, in assessing whether social workers and psychologists employed by the defendant local authorities to examine and provide for the plaintiff children alleging child abuse and failure to cater for special educational needs, were personally under a duty of care towards the children and their parents, for which the defendants themselves might then be "vicariously liable" (see ch.11), distinguished *Smith v. Eric Bush, Henderson* and *White* so far as the child abuse claims were concerned, on the ground that unlike the surveyor, managing agents and solicitor, the social workers and psychologists assumed no responsibility towards the children and parents themselves who were *not expected to regulate their conduct in reliance* on the reports (*a fortiori* if it had been a parent who was suspected of abuse), whereas the defendants were (p.383). This was to be contrasted with the educational needs claims, where parents would wish to rely on the advice and to follow it, for example, in the case of dyslexic reading difficulties of their children, so that personal duty of care of the social workers and psychologists and consequently also vicarious liability of the defendants would there be possible (p.393).

At the end of it all, it should be said that *Hedley Byrne* itself still comes in for continuing criticism on the ground that prudent recipients of advice should insure against or enter contracts establishing liability for negligent information, and that they are the first to profit if the advice is good; and some suggest that the courts are strongly influenced according to whether the plaintiff is acting in a private capacity, for example, as house purchaser (*Eric Bush*) or commercial (*Caparo*). Judicial discretion and justice again, sought to be presented as principled doctrine.

Before leaving this section of the discussion, it is pertinent to consider, by way of summary, how the elements of legal recovery for pure economic loss in *Hedley Byrne, Henderson* and *White* respectively now stand *in relation to each other*?

A particularly useful case to examine for this purpose is that of *Spring v. Guardian Assurance plc* [1994] 3 All ER 129, HL, concerning liability towards the subjects of negligent job references (see *supra*). This was a judgment delivered shortly before *Henderson* and of course before *White*. It is of interest because of the variety of grounds given in the four to one majority ruling for allowing the plaintiff to recover in negligence.

The facts of the dispute were that the plaintiff was dismissed as sales director and office manager by the defendant life assurance company when it took over the plaintiff's former employer. The plaintiff found it impossible to obtain a job elsewhere in the area and discovered that the defendant had provided a very poor reference to potential new employers who were required to obtain a reference under the insurance industry's code for the protection of the public. The plaintiff had been described in the reference as having no integrity, dishonest and keeping best business opportunities for himself in order to derive maximum commission. He sued in negligence and for implied breach of contract to provide a careful and accurate reference. At first instance he was found to have been incompetent, but not dishonest at his job. Yet, the defendants were not malicious in their reference and consequently enjoyed the defence of qualified privilege to a defamation or malicious falsehood claim (see *infra,* chs.26 and 27). It was also considered that the plaintiff had no contract with the defendant, or, if he did, there was no implied term as to reasonable care in preparing references. However, the defendants were nonetheless held liable towards the plaintiff in *negligence.*

The House of Lords upheld the defendants' negligence liability by a majority of four to one, Lord Keith dissenting.

Lord Keith's dissent was for the following reasons:

(a) a finding in favour of an ordinary duty of care in negligence would amount to an extension of the latter, unjustifiably, to pure economic loss (p.135);
(b) *Hedley Byrne* was inapplicable because *reliance* there required was by the addressee of the reference, not on the part of the subject thereof (pp.135-6); and
(c) in any event, public policy would be against allowing any such duty of care even if it could otherwise exist, because the effect would be to enable a plaintiff to circumvent the qualified privilege defence to defamation proceedings where there was failure to use reasonable care but no malice on the part of the defendant (qualified privilege is unavailable if there is malice - see *infra,* ch.26): "Those asked to give a reference would be inhibited from speaking frankly lest it should be found that they were liable in damages through not taking sufficient care in its preparation. They might well prefer, if under no legal duty to give a reference, to refrain from doing so at all. Any

> reference given might be bland and unhelpful and information which it would be in the interest of those seeking the reference to receive might be withheld (p.137) ... In general, precisely the same grounds of public policy which make the defence of qualified privilege available in an action for defamation strongly favour the exclusion of an action of damages for negligence in similar situations (p.142)."

As far as the majority were concerned, however, there was a variety of reasons for holding the defendants liable for negligence.

Lord Goff, with whom Lord Lowry agreed (p.152), made two significant findings:

First, the defendants' liability for economic loss towards the plaintiff fell within *Hedley Byrne,* on the ground of assumption of responsibility towards the plaintiff by the defendant referee and corresponding reliance by the former upon the latter (although, he admitted that this could be of limited authority, because counsel had not argued the point - pp.143 and 144): *Hedley Byrne* itself had concerned liability towards the recipient of the negligent statement, but its wider importance should not be lost sight of - being assumption of responsibility and reliance - and that was not the only way in which it could operate; liability here was satisfied towards the plaintiff through responsibility and reliance (pp.144-7).

Secondly, public policy arguments against such negligence duty of care as undermining the defence of qualified privilege in defamation were dismissed:

defamation principles were of no relevance to negligence and employers would not be any more reluctant to write references - they were usually careful anyway and would continue to be so (pp.149 and 151). Lord Lowry too thought that the idea of employers in future being deterred from providing references was a "spectre conjured up by the defendants to frighten your Lordships into submission" (p.153).

Lord Slynn followed a different approach. He considered that *Hedley Byrne,* applicable where a negligent misstatement was made to a person who then relied on it, did not therefore apply to the different circumstances of the present case, but nevertheless was a *pointer* towards liability (p.159). The question was not whether a referee was always, or never, liable toward the subject of his reference, but whether in the particular circumstances of the case, he satisfied the incremental approach of Lord Bridge (pp.573-4) in the *Caparo* progression (see [1990] 1 All ER 568) from *Donoghue v. Stevenson* (pp.159-160). As far as Lord Slynn was concerned, the *Caparo* three-stage test was satisfied on the facts, since it would be unacceptable if the addressee of the reference could sue the referee, but the subject could not (p.161). Defamation and duty of care in negligence were different and the former did not bar the latter, nor would employers be too frightened to give references (pp.162-3) - indeed, the development of liability in negligence had not even been contemplated at the much earlier date when defamation law was formulated (p.158). It would not be in *every* case that the duty of care would be owed, but incrementally from specific cases like the present - for example, it might be different if the referee was not a former employer but a mere social acquaintance (*ibid.*).

Lord Woolf, agreeing with the first instance Judge that the defendant's reference in the case had been "the kiss of death" to the plaintiff's career in insurance (p.168), agreed that the defendants were liable - that much is certain (p.171). What is less clear, however, is the precise ground for his finding. He referred both to the incremental approach in *Caparo* (pp.169 and 170) and to the basis of responsibility and reliance underlying *Hedley Byrne* - so that an *employer's* reference or reference *requested* of a social acquaintance by its subject would be likely to satisfy liability, whereas an unrequested social reference would be viewed in a different light (pp.170-1). Thus, there are in this elements of Lord Goff's and Lowry's *Hedley Byrne* and of Lord Slynn's *Caparo* - and like the latter, Lord Woolf further referred to the fact that the decision might not be the same in all cases, being subject to different facts on an incremental basis (p.179 - he admitted that this could produce uncertainty, but this would be better than a fixed rule of anticipation of other situations, *ibid.*). As with the others in the majority, however, Lord Woolf did not accept that public policy required the duty of care in negligence to be denied lest defamation defences be circumvented by the plaintiff (pp.172, 175, 176, 177-8).

So there was the line-up on liability (leaving aside public policy):

Keith	-	no *Hedley Byrne* and no *Caparo*
Goff and Lowry	-	*Hedley Byrne*

Slynn - *Caparo* but no *Hedley Byrne*
Woolf - either *Hedley Byrne* or *Caparo*

Stalemate on *Hedley Byrne*, if Lord Keith's dissenting judgment is included, possibly then leaving the field open to *Caparo*; two to one in favour of *Hedley Byrne* if it is not.

The problems with a simple application of *Caparo* to the case are (i) first, as Lord Keith pointed out (p.135), this would be to extend the ordinary duty of care in negligence to economic loss, contrary to general principles; and (ii) secondly, the so-called incremental approach, cited by Lords Slynn and Woolf as amounting to a control upon the floodgates of economic loss liability, should surely rather be applied to developments of doctrine and principle by the courts in relation to various fact categories, not merely willy-nilly to this or that fact situation which happens to come before the courts on one day, but not to a different set of factual circumstances on another. The former must be what is intended.

As for treating the case as falling within *Hedley Byrne* itself, as proposed by Lords Goff and Lowry (and possibly also by Lord Woolf), it is submitted with the greatest respect that this is incorrect. It can certainly be accepted, as Lord Goff explained, that the principle underlying *Hedley Byrne* is one of assumption of responsibility, coupled with reliance. Yet, the crucial question is: responsibility for *what*, and reliance upon *what*? The fact is that *Hedley Byrne* was a case concerning responsibility for and reliance upon a statement of advice. However much it is sought to generalize the underlying rationale or to extend the rule itself, the outer boundaries of the *Hedley Byrne* principle are thereby fixed at that point: assumption of responsibility for and reliance upon *the content of advice or statement.* There is an essential difference, therefore, between such reliance upon:

1. on the one hand, the *content* of the statement, and
2. on the other hand, the statement being *properly made.*

The plaintiff in *Spring* was reliant upon the latter alone - not the former. *He* certainly did not require the defendants to advise him about himself! It was potential employers who wanted that and the defendants would assume responsibility towards them for the content of their advice and reference, in accordance with *Hedley Byrne.* That is what the rule in *Hedley Byrne* is about - the quality of advice and its consequential usefulness, and, therefore, the care which must be shown towards the recipient addressee who will reasonably and foreseeably rely upon it. Legal responsibility towards somebody else - here, the plaintiff - who is not intended to use and to rely upon the *content* of the statement in this way, however, whatever the basis of such responsibility, if any, does not derive from *Hedley Byrne.* If it exists, its source is somewhere else (though, as pure economic loss, not *Caparo,* as explained). Thus, the same piece of advice or statement will have different legal effects - or at least sources thereof - according to the status of the plaintiff; and, in the case of a "third party" in the position of the plaintiff in *Spring,* the reference statement almost has more of the character of an *act* than a misstatement within *Hedley Byrne,* a point previously made above.

Essentially therefore, *Hedley Byrne* is properly to be regarded as being limited to those who rely upon the content of advice, rather than on its provision.

With regard to the latter class of persons who simply rely upon provision of advice or some other service, there are two situations which need to be distinguished.

(a) Where the plaintiff did not request (neither expressly nor impliedly) the defendant referee to provide the reference. In this situation, it is possible that the principle in *White* could apply - assumption of responsibility by defendant (referee) towards a third party (subject of reference) who could be harmed by lack of sufficient care in the defendant's transaction with the plaintiff's potential employer who sought the reference. However, this is not at all certain and the opposing argument would be to ask why should the referee so be taken to have assumed such a responsibility towards the plaintiff? The former's relations are with the addressee of the reference, not with the plaintiff. If the reference is inaccurate, the law of defamation - together with its defences - is available. The position is quite different from that in *White* where - for all the criticisms made of it above - at least the clear intention of the testator requesting the service was that the defendant solicitors should secure a benefit for the plaintiff beneficiaries, whereas, in *Spring* the addressee of the reference would have been quite neutral in relation to the interests of the plaintiff himself. However, notwithstanding such possible objections, the present writer's view is that, on balance, it rather depends upon the circumstances as to whether the referee should be taken to have assumed a responsibility

towards the subject of the reference, within *White.* If the potential employer's practice is only to take up references when it is seriously considering appointing the plaintiff, then, effectively, the potential employer *is* expecting the referee to perform so as to afford the plaintiff the opportunity to obtain employment where this is deserved; whereas if the potential employer takes references on all applicants for the job as a matter of course before making substantial further assessments of the plaintiff's suitability and qualification, expectation of assumption of responsibility by the referee is to that extent the less likely.

(b) Where the plaintiff who is the subject of the reference requested it (expressly or impliedly). Here, it is relatively easy to infer responsibility and reliance. Yet, the loss is purely economic, so that general tortious duty of care is inapplicable. *Henderson* itself too is not entirely apposite, since, notwithstanding responsibility and reliance, the latter relations are directly undertaken between defendants and plaintiff rather than arising indirectly from relations between the defendants (managing agents) and another (members' agents) as in *Henderson* - although, again, in particular circumstances, it might be possible to bring the case within *Henderson,* for example, by showing that plaintiff X specifically requested potential employer Z to "obtain" an assumption of responsibility towards X by defendant Y in the form of the reference, essentially a matter of perception of these arrangements by the court hearing the case. Nor is *White* exactly suitable, since, again, reliance and direct relations are present here.

Spring, accordingly, appears to represent a *new* situation, different from each of *Hedley Byrne, Henderson* and *White*: the plaintiff is not intended to rely upon the *content* of the statement (unlike *Hedley Byrne*); he is in *direct* relations with the defendants (unlike *Henderson*); and he does *rely* upon the accuracy of the statement (unlike *White*). Furthermore, if a remedy is to be given - *incrementally*, drawing upon principles of assumption of responsibility and reliance underlying the others - this must be accomplished in such a way as not to compromise the overall principle against recovery for pure economic loss in negligence through its capacity for generalization beyond the facts of *Spring*.

Which brings us to Lord Woolf . . .

It will be recalled that Lord Woolf appeared to have a foot in both *Hedley Byrne* and *Caparo* camps - or neither. Yet, whichever it might have been, Lord Woolf was unequivocal on one thing: the plaintiff in *Spring* should have a remedy in negligence. "If the law provides a remedy for references which are inaccurate due to carelessness this would be beneficial. It would encourage the adoption of appropriate standards when preparing references. This would be an important advantage as frequently an employee will be ignorant that it is because of the terms of an inaccurate reference, of the contents of which he is unaware, that he is not offered fresh employment ... The availability of a remedy without having to prove malice will not open the floodgates. In cases where the employee discovers the existence of the inaccurate reference, he will have a remedy if, but only if, he can establish, instead of malice, that the reason for the inaccuracy is the default of the employer, in the sense that he has been careless. To make an employer liable for an inaccurate reference, but only if he is careless, is, I would suggest, wholly fair. It would balance the respective interests of the employer and employee. It would amount to a development of the law of negligence which accords with the principles which should control its development. It would, in addition, avoid a rather unattractive situation continuing of a recipient of a reference, but not the subject of a reference, being able to bring an action for negligence" (p.172).

It is submitted that the approach of Lord Woolf, with which Lord Slynn's judgment itself is not wholly inconsistent, should be that which is adopted as the basis of *Spring,* rather than Lord Goff's (and Lowry's) *Hedley Byrne* application. Thus, it is logical and right that if X requests Y to provide a reference for X so that X can obtain employment with the addressee Z, Y should be taken to have assumed a responsibility towards X (not just Z) upon which X relies and that Y should consequently be liable for negligence towards X. The *logic* of this is that Y is liable towards Z, under *Hedley Byrne;* Y *could* be liable towards X, under *Henderson* in certain circumstances, if, say, X were to request Z to obtain a crucial reference from a suitable person, Y, upon whom X then relies; and Y *could* be liable towards X, under *White,* again, in certain circumstances, say, if Z, not requested by X, took it upon himself to obtain a reference for X from Y, making it clear to Y that his reference could be instrumental in the appointment or not of X.

Incrementally, therefore, *Spring* is a *new* variation of the principle of recovery of economic loss from negligent statements on the basis of assumption of responsibility and reliance, and the position reached, therefore, when generalized from the specific situation of references, now seems to be as follows:

1. If X requests advice from Y: *Hedley Byrne* liability of Y to X (Y responsibility; X reliance).

2. If X requests Z to obtain advice from Y for X's benefit: *Henderson* liability of Y towards X (Y responsibility; X reliance).

3. If Z requests Y for advice which is clearly calculated to confer a benefit upon X: *White* liability of Y towards X (Y responsibility).

4. If X requests Y to advise Z to the benefit of X: *Spring* liability of Y towards X (Y responsibility; X reliance).

5. If X requests Y to drive a package from London to Manchester or to build a wall for him, for which Y takes responsibility and upon which X relies ...? It will shortly be seen below that in these types of cases, concerning negligent acts rather than statements or advice, the English courts have now drawn the line, against recovery for pure economic loss (see *infra, Murphy v. Brentwood DC*). As will be concluded, there is no great logic in this, since responsibility for and reliance upon *acts* are essentially no different from the same in respect of statements or advice. The reason for the differential treatment, therefore, is not logic - but *policy,* in the control of potential claims. The floodgates argument - negligent statements made to a particular person or persons are easier for the law to provide for, in fairness to the defendant, than negligent acts which may have widespread and indiscriminate effects.

Nevertheless, it must therefore also be appreciated that if a negligent *act* would *not* have the feared uncontrolled effects in relation to a multitude of potential plaintiffs, there should be no reason in principle why responsibility and reliance should not then lead to recovery for pure economic loss in this case too, where a particular plaintiff has requested a service or materials upon which he relied and for which the defendant provider assumed responsibility - *a fortiori* in view of the fact that in *Spring, Henderson* and *White* themselves, as seen, the "statements" could in fact be looked upon as being rather more in the nature of *acts*, from the standpoint of the third party plaintiffs. As it happens, however, it will be seen below that where courts consider that the plaintiff and defendant were in such a *relationship* that the defendant could be taken to have assumed responsibility towards the plaintiff for the careful performance of an act, to the extent that the plaintiff relied upon this, the plaintiff *can* recover; and although the courts have narrowed economic loss from acts to this strictly confined area - so that, for example, where pure economic loss is caused to a number of strangers by the defendant's activities which were neither requested nor relied upon by them, recovery is not possible - the *Junior Books Ltd v. Veitchi Co. Ltd* case (see *infra*) which established the relationship principle has never in fact been overruled, and, confined though it may be, therefore still subsists.

(5) Exclusion of Hedley Byrne Liability

Under s.2(2) of the Unfair Contract Terms Act 1977, general liability for negligence can be excluded if *reasonable.* In *Harris v. Wyre Forest District Council* [1989] 2 WLR 790, the House of Lords rejected the argument that the "reasonableness" restriction in s.2(2) was inapplicable to

Hedley Byrne exclusion on the basis that the effect of an exemption clause upon *Hedley Byrne* liability would be to prevent duty of care and liability from arising in the first place rather than to exclude that which had arisen, because to accept that view would have been to destroy the whole point of s.2(2) to that extent and could not have been intended.

So, exclusion has to be "reasonable" to be effective. In *Harris* and in *Smith v. Bush,* a surveyor's exclusion of negligence liability towards the purchaser of a house (even if engaged for a valuation by the company lending the purchase price of the property to the purchaser), was held not to be fair and reasonable, as will exclusion no doubt frequently be held not to be reasonable in relation to most professional advice, except perhaps where the adviser is working on the borders of his field of expertise and large sums of money are at stake, or where the advice is given gratuitously at a party (or where the advisee can be expected to take independent advice, at least upon the legal effects of the disclaimer: *McCullagh v. Lane Fox* (1995) *The Times,* December 22, CA) - although the gap between such cases of effective exclusion and those where, in the circumstances, no liability would reasonably arise in the first place, may not be great.

(6) The Misrepresentation Act 1967

Liability for negligent misstatement under the Misrepresentation Act 1967 cuts across common law negligence in *Hedley Byrne.* In some respects, the Act is an easier mechanism to use in order to establish liability; but, importantly, in other ways, the scope of liability under the

Act is much narrower than that of *Hedley Byrne.*

The big limitation of the Act is that it only applies to negligent misstatements *which persuade people to enter into a contract.* That is its purpose. It does not deal with liability for loss generally from negligent misstatement. The only *effect* it deals with is where, as a result of the misstatement, the plaintiff *entered a contract* when he would not otherwise have done so.

Prior to the 1967 Act, where a person was persuaded to enter into a contract with another through the making of a false statement, he had no remedy in damages if he was outside a special *Hedley Byrne* relationship: he could not sue for the tort of *deceit* - *fraudulent* misrepresentation inducing contract - if the maker of the statement was merely negligent rather than intentional or reckless as to the truth of the statement.

However, under s.2(1) of the Act, a person who enters a contract as a result of a negligent misrepresentation can now sue for his losses: the principles of damages are those of tort rather than contract - although, unforeseeable losses are still recoverable, because they are treated as though based on deceit rather than negligence (*Royscot Trust Ltd v. Rogerson* [1991] 3 All ER 294). In addition, or alternatively, the plaintiff can terminate the contract - *rescission* - for misrepresentation.

It is, however, possible to bring the claim in the alternative under *Hedley Byrne* in this as in other cases. Proceedings under the Act may nevertheless be preferred to a common law *Hedley Byrne* action, because:

- reversal of the burden of proof: under s.2(1), where

the representation has been shown to be false, there is a heavy burden upon *the defendant* to prove that he was *not negligent* in making the false representation (*Howard Marine & Dredging Co. Ltd v. Ogden & Sons (Excavations) Ltd* [1978] QB 574), whereas at common law, the burden of proving negligence rests on the plaintiff; and

- proximity and reliance: there is no need specifically to satisfy the conditions of relationship and reliance elaborated in *Caparo v. Dickman.*

However, against this, it is reminded that the common law *Hedley Byrne* action is far broader, since s.2(1) only applies where a person *has entered a contract with the maker of the statement* as a result of the misrepresentation, and is also inapplicable where a contract was concluded, but not with the person who made the misrepresentation, or where no contract was concluded at all but resources were expended - a considerable restriction.

b. Negligent Acts

The development of this part of the law has been bound up with changes of governments of different political persuasions in the United Kingdom - and with losses suffered by the purchasers of defective buildings in the long, hot English summers of the mid-1970s!

There are three main periods of development to be drawn attention to.

(1) The pre-1970s position: no principle of recovery for pure economic loss from negligent acts

In *Spartan Steel & Alloys Ltd v. Martin & Co. (Contractors) Ltd* [1973] 1 QB 27, the defendants negligently cut into an electricity power cable, which brought the manufacturing process in the plaintiff's factory to a halt. Products in the course of being processed were damaged when the machinery stopped, and expected profits were lost; other products were unable to be processed at all. The Court of Appeal held that the plaintiff could only recover the financial profits lost on the products which were being processed, because this loss was accompanied by physical damage to those products; recovery of lost profits on the products yet to be processed, but not physically damaged, was not possible, as amounting to pure economic loss. Edmund Davies, LJ, who dissented, criticized this distinction and said that the whole loss should have been awarded; but Lord Denning, MR for the majority spoke of the policy nature of the decision and the need to avoid an unending list of claims. Much earlier than this, in *Cattle v. Stockton Waterworks Co.* (1875) LR 10 QB 453, the plaintiff was engaged to build a tunnel under a road, but the defendants negligently burst a water pipe which made the plaintiff's task more expensive. It was held that the plaintiff could not recover the additional costs, because these were purely economic losses and to allow recovery might open the floodgates of liability. Again, in *Weller v. Foot & Mouth Disease Research Institute* [1966] 2 All ER 560, the defendants negligently caused an outbreak of foot and mouth disease and farmers had to slaughter their cattle. The plaintiff cattle auctioneers were held to be unable to recover for their loss of business, which was purely economic damage. A further example of inability to recover was *Candlewood Navigation Corporation Ltd v. Mitsui OSK Lines Ltd* [1985] 2 All ER 935, where it was held that a time charterer (hirer) of a ship could not sue for lost profits while the ship was undergoing repairs following a collision caused by the defendant's negligence - the plaintiff had no proprietary interest in the damaged vessel and his loss was purely economic.

Moreover, a person who subsequently becomes owner of property damaged before he did so, cannot claim for the economic loss (*Leigh & Sillavan Ltd v. Aliakmon Shipping Co. Ltd* [1986] 2 All ER 145 - subject to an exception under the Latent Damage Act 1986, s.3, creating a statutory right of action from the date of acquisition of the interest where the damage could not have been discovered by the original owner).

(2) The 1970s: substantial increase of liability for pure economic loss

This was the decade of socialist government in Great Britain - what some people of the opposite political persuasion derogatively refer to as "the nanny state", meaning that agencies of the state, including the courts, would be expected to support and to favour those individuals in society who appeared to be too weak to help themselves, including plaintiffs who were victims of negligence.

Much of the development concerned claims brought by owners of buildings which were somehow defective, a not infrequent subject of litigation in the mid-1970s, when a sequence of dry, hot summers caused cracks to appear in the concrete foundations and walls of many houses.

Subsequent purchasers could not otherwise claim in contract against the original builders of those houses, with whom they were not in a contractual relationship; and their own contractual relations with the seller, as well as those of the original buyer with the builder-vendor, were covered by the rule of contract in respect of sale of land and buildings: *caveat emptor*.

What happened in response to this problem in the course of the following few years was that the courts opened up the scope of recovery for economic loss in tort from negligent acts:

- first, where the building was said to be *dangerous* to persons or to property
- thereafter, merely *defective*, and
- finally, generally to where persons other than merely the builders were held liable for causing economic loss, through *failure to warn* against a defect in a building.

Ultimately the point was reached at which it was possible to extrapolate a *general* principle of liability for pure economic loss - a presumption, in the absence of policy reasons against - beyond the specific sphere of defective buildings.

The stages along this route in the 1970s were as follows:

(a) Recovery on ground that building "defect" amounted to "physical damage" to the building itself: continued adherence to the principle of actual physical damage. In *Dutton v. Bognor Regis Urban District Council* [1972] 1 QB 373, the Court of Appeal held a local authority liable to compensate the

owner of a building for the cost of repairing defective foundations, on the ground that the local authority had carried out a defective inspection of the building work, with the result that the defect had *damaged the building itself.* Owners would have to spend money on repairs and prevention of the risk of further damage or injury.

Aside from the potential general effects of this decision upon recovery for economic loss from negligent acts, in the specific area of building defects it is worth pointing out that as the case was decided, the Defective Premises Act 1972 was passing through Parliament, making house builders strictly liable for defects, without needing to show negligence, for a six-year limitation period. The irony was that *Dutton* appeared to have opened the way for builders to be sued in any event for economic loss at common law. True it was that according to *Dutton,* plaintiffs, unlike those under the Act, would have to prove negligence, but, on the other hand, under the Act the limitation of actions period would begin when the building was completed, as opposed to when the damage *subsequently* manifested itself.

(b) Recovery where "mere threat" of damage to health or property, and even if not imminent. In *Anns v. Merton London Borough Council* [1978] AC 728, the House of Lords confirmed *Dutton* and added the further - in reality, quite fictional - justification that the defect might not only damage the building itself but also threaten the health and physical well-being of the occupants, moving away, therefore, from the idea that material damage had actually occurred through existence of the defect, yet still quaintly refraining from embracing pure economic loss in its totality and

attempting to link recovery to actual or threatened property or physical damage - although an important new advance was the sufficiency of mere *threatened* injury or damage for recovery for economic loss. In *Anns* the local authority had negligently failed to inspect the foundations of a block of flats in the course of construction. Years later defects appeared owing to faults in the foundations and, as indicated, the court held the defendants liable for the economic loss, linked to the fiction that the defective building could fall on people.

The fact that potential damage to the property itself or to health of occupiers and visitors and their property was merely being used as a convenient means to justify recovery for what was essentially pure economic loss, could be seen from the subsequent case of *Batty v. Metropolitan Property Realisations Ltd* [1978] QB 554 which took the law even further than *Anns.* In *Batty*, owners of what was now an unsaleable house, negligently built on land near an embankment and subject to slippage, and of which part of the garden had already fallen away, were able to claim successfully against the builders, on the ground that although neither house nor occupants were in danger at the present time, they probably would be in the future. So, not actual damage to property or health and safety; not even threatened imminent damage to the same; merely a *potential* threat. In truth, nothing more in essence than pure economic loss: the cost of making the premises safe.

(c) The highpoint of economic loss: "mere defect" in the building, where close proximity and reliance between the parties. This was *Junior Books Ltd v. Veitchi Co. Ltd* [1983] 1 AC 520. The

plaintiffs engaged main builders, and nominated the defendant subcontractors to be employed by the main builders to lay the floors, which they did, defectively. There was no contract between the plaintiffs and the defendants, so the claim against the latter was in negligence for the cost of repairs and further financial loss [see diagram]:

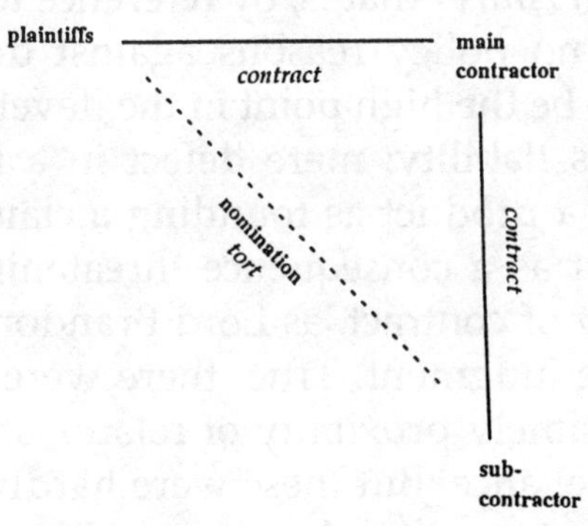

Although the defective floors were not going to cause further damage to the building and were not a danger to anyone's health or safety, the House of Lords held that the defendants owed a duty of care to the plaintiffs in economic loss, because of:

- the close *relationship of proximity* between the parties, and
- *reliance* by the plaintiffs upon the defendants, and
- the fact that the economic loss liability would *not be*

unlimited (policy), since it was quite obvious that it would be solely the plaintiffs who would raise any claim.

This case, in which the majority of the Lords actually affected to found recovery for pure economic loss upon the standard two-stage test of ordinary liability in tort in *Donoghue v. Stevenson* as pronounced upon by Lord Wilberforce in *Anns* - that is, by reference to proximity and reliance and no policy reasons against duty of care - is considered to be the high point in the development of pure economic loss liability: mere defect in a building or - if generalized - a product as founding a claim for economic loss, with tort as a consequence threatening to break the rule of privity of contract, as Lord Brandon pointed out in his dissenting judgment. True, there were certain alleged limitations: namely proximity of relationship between the parties, and reliance. But these were hardly strict controls: the first was extraordinarily vague, raising the question of when there would *not* be found to be such closeness - three parties between consumer victim and manufacturer of a product, perhaps two, but surely not merely one, the retailer? While, as for reliance, this must surely invariably be present - when you buy a product, you expect it to work and you accordingly rely upon the manufacturer and the seller that it does so.

After *Junior Books,* therefore, it seemed as though economic loss - at least from defective quality of goods and buildings, if not generally - had come of age.

(3) The 1980s and beyond: the retreat from Junior Books and away from recovery for pure economic loss

There was much adverse comment on *Junior Books*, which was viewed by critics as practically sanctioning a general liability for pure economic loss. The incoming Conservative government in 1979 heralded a change in the social and political environment. This was to be the age of the individual - self-sufficient and resourceful. He could not expect the state and its organs, including the courts, to come to his aid whenever he got into difficulties, and the Judges of the House of Lords were likely to reflect this difference in attitude.

Again, there were a number of steps on the road to the decline of the economic loss doctrine, just as there were when it was in its ascendency. Their fascination lies in the determined manner in which the House of Lords proceeded to retrace its footsteps backwards through *Junior Books,* past *Anns,* so as to arrive back at the position at which it had all started - a most restrictive regime for recovery of pure economic loss.

There were three main steps on this route backwards:

(a) No adequate reliance and proximity of relationship

The simplest method of getting round *Junior Books* was to distinguish other cases from it on its facts by holding that the very bases given for the decision in that case - proximity of relations between the plaintiff and defendant sub-contractor and reliance upon the latter - meaningless though these were, were not satisfied on the facts. The case usually cited to show this is *Muirhead v. Industrial Tank Specialities*

Ltd [1985] 3 All ER 705. The plaintiffs' business was to purchase lobsters at a low price, store them, and sell them later when the price had gone up. They purchased tanks for storage from one firm, but the lobsters could not be stored because the pumps for the tanks were defective (they were French and unsuitable for UK electricity mains). The plaintiffs sued the tank firm for breach of contract, but when that firm went into liquidation, the plaintiffs sued the defendant, from which the tank firm had bought the pumps, in negligence in respect of their losses. The Court of Appeal held that the action must fail, as one for pure economic loss (although recovery was awarded in respect of the dead fish - damage to property). *Junior Books* had to be limited to its special facts: *reliance* and *closeness/proximity* of relationship existed there, because the plaintiffs had actually *nominated* the defendant sub-contractor; not so in *Muirhead,* where they just relied on the *tank* firm and had nothing to do with the defendant *pump* firm.

In truth, of course, in *Muirhead,* even if the "sub-contractor" - the pump firm - was not nominated, proximity and reliance were not *that* different from *Junior Books.* When else would there also be held to be sufficient reliance? Was it the case that plaintiff and defendant now had to have some *personal contact* for pure economic loss to be recoverable on the ground of reliance and proximity - such as that which proceeds from a nomination of the latter by the former? The Court of Appeal doubtless had not worked out the full implications of its decision. One thing was clear. General recovery for pure economic loss was no longer on the agenda.

Two further cases made it even clearer that courts were

unhappy with *Junior Books*, and these went even further in almost strictly confining that judgment, never actually overruled, to the exact facts of the case, being *nomination of a sub-contractor to do building work* - although, it has to be said that even that decision might not have survived the two cases in question. Thus, whereas *Muirhead* in effect had held that where there was some kind of a relationship *gap* between plaintiff and defendant and no personal relations, recovery was not possible, the other two cases seemed to approach from the opposite direction, that is, if parties had *too much* of a relationship, and it was contractual, they should not be allowed to use economic loss in *tort*. If there was such a relationship between them, and it was *contractual,* it should be those contractual obligations which the plaintiff should be taken to have relied upon, and not on any tortious rights of economic loss, according to the first case; and in the second, even if there was no contract *between plaintiff and defendant,* nevertheless, if their roles and function formed part of an *overall structure or chain of contractual relationships* between various parties involved, again there could be no reliance and proximity between plaintiff and defendant *in tort,* such as would satisfy the principle in *Junior Books* - all glorious legal posturing, and outrageously begging the question of whether contractual relations *were* so intended to be exclusive in such transactions or at least in relation to a plaintiff.

But the effect would be devastating for economic loss, which was now apparently lodged somewhere between there being a sufficiently close relationship of *reliance and contact* between plaintiff and defendant (*Muirhead*), yet *no contract* between them and *no overall framework* of contractual relations.

The two cases in question were the following:

First, *Greater Nottingham Co-operative Society v. Cementation Piling & Foundations Ltd* [1988] 2 All ER 971, which established that there must be no contract between the parties. The plaintiff building owner made a contract with the defendant sub-contractor for the latter to exercise reasonable care to design certain equipment and in the use of materials. The plaintiffs lost money from the failure of the equipment to operate properly. The Court of Appeal held that the contractual regulation of the parties' relationship was exclusive of any further duties in tort. Since the contract made no mention of the manner of operating the equipment, this contractual omission should not be able to be avoided through resort to the law of tort.

The other case was *Simaan General Contracting Co. v. Pilkington Glass Ltd (No.2)* [1988] 1 All ER 791. A building owner withheld payment from the plaintiff main contractor under their contract, because glass panels supplied by the defendants were defective. The plaintiff had subcontracted the supply of panels to another firm under a contract which required the latter further to subcontract the manufacture of the panels to the defendants. Instead of suing the other firm in contract, the plaintiffs went straight to the defendants in tort. The Court of Appeal rejected the plaintiffs' claim for the economic loss caused. The *contractual structure and chain* of the building operation had been organized without bringing into being a direct contractual relationship between plaintiff main contractor and defendant, so that it would be quite wrong to impose obligations in tort where no obligations of any sort were meant to exist. The plaintiffs should have sued their subcontractor in contract and the latter could then have proceeded against the defendants under their own contract, thereby preserving the chain of contractual relations. Here, therefore, can be seen the other inhibiting factor upon the development of economic loss in England aside from the floodgates argument: unwanted interference of tort with privity of contract. For economic loss in tort, there would have to be a close relationship of proximity and reliance (*Muirhead*) - but not too close, directly (*Nottingham*) or indirectly (*Simaan*) *contractually* close.

Truly, these were cases providing a most impressive testimony to the resourcefulness and inventive ability of the English Judges! The result nevertheless appeared inescapable: goodbye to *Junior Books* as a general principle of recovery for economic loss from defects.

As to whether the two cases are still defensible in the light of the House of Lords' decision in *Henderson v. Merrett Syndicates Ltd* [1994] 3 All ER 506, actually concerning economic loss from negligent advice or statements (see *supra,* p.117), this remains to be seen. It will be recalled that in that case Lord Goff (pp.533 and 534) considered that contractual relations between parties, or forming part of a contractual structure, were not necessarily inconsistent with concurrent rights in tort enabling a plaintiff to choose, unless either the intention was to avoid a contractual exclusion clause or where the remedy in tort would clearly be inconsistent with contractual status and liability (see too *Holt v. Payne Skillington (a Firm)* (1995) *The Times,* December 22, CA, *supra, ibid.,* where the Court of Appeal reiterated that wider tort liability could be pleaded in the alternative, where not excluded by the contract). Those proceedings themselves, of course, were concerned with *Hedley Byrne* principles, and Lord Goff himself did accept that *Simaan* had been correctly decided and that in many cases tort claims *would* be so inconsistent (*ibid.*), so that perhaps in practice the effects will be minimal. At least it can be said, however, that following *Henderson,* any inference from *Greater Nottingham* or *Simaan* that contractual co-existence or chain is inconsistent with tort duties *as a matter of law* must now be rejected. The question is purely one of contractual construction - are tort duties thereby excluded, exceeded or co-extensive according to express or implied contract terms?

(b)(i) "Mere threat" of prospective or imminent damage to health or property insufficient for recovery - goodbye to Anns, and (ii) even actual damage to "same" property not enough - (almost) goodbye to Dutton: D & F Estates

Anns was the next stage effectively to be undone. It will be recalled that the justification given there for recovery for foreseeable economic loss was the fiction of a threat of imminent, and in *Batty* even merely prospective, damage to the defective building or to health and safety of its occupants. In *D & F Estates Ltd v. Church Commissioners for England* [1988] 2 All ER 992, some years after the construction of some flats, the occupiers sued the builders for the cost of repairs when plaster began dropping off the walls. The House of Lords held that there would be no recovery for the economic loss. The judgments of Lords Bridge and Oliver reveal the following lines of thought (pp.1006-7, 1012):

First, *actual* damage to the property or health of users or occupants from a product or building would be sufficient, on normal principles in *Donoghue v. Stevenson,* for the loss to be recovered; *but the fiction of threatened or prospective such loss was insufficient* and amounted to no more than a defect in quality, in respect of which the various parties would have to proceed against each other in contract if they could, all the way down the line to the initial person responsible ("if the defect is discovered before any damage is done, the loss sustained by the owner of the structure, who has to repair or demolish it to avoid a potential source of danger to third parties, would seem to be purely economic": p.1006, *per* Lord Bridge). Lord Brandon's dissenting opinion in *Junior Books,* based upon the essentially contractual, rather than tortious, nature of the plaintiff's claim and consequently subject to normal principles of privity of contract, was viewed with favour.

Secondly, doubts were expressed as to whether even actual damage to property would suffice for recovery for economic loss, *where the damage was to the defective product or building itself* (the idea first mentioned in *Dutton* and taken up in *Anns*), as constituting the cause rather than the effect of the problem - except that possibly, in the case of buildings (usually) rather than products, the property might be *complex* rather than *simple,* in which case it might be able to be said that parts of the property were sufficiently independent from each other for a defect in one part realistically to have been able to cause actual damage to a part different from itself: for example, a defect in the foundations of a building causes walls and ceilings to crack - *one* "part" causing damage to *another* "part". Lord Bridge elaborated (pp.1006-7) that in respect of such complex buildings, and possibly even products, it could be argued that one element of the structure was to be regarded as "distinct from another element, so that damage to one part of the structure caused by a hidden defect in another part may qualify to be treated as damage to other property" - that is, not purely economic, but physical damage.

So, following *D & F Estates,* damage to health or to property had to be *actual;* and in the case of property, actual damage would arguably not merely be to the defective property itself, unless defective and damaged parts were separable (in *Aswan Engineering Establishment Co. v. Lupdine Ltd* [1987] 1 All ER 135, at p.152, Lloyd, LJ seemed to think that a defective tyre could damage the car, or a defective cork, wine in the bottle - in the case itself, defendants, who had supplied the plaintiffs with containers for storing a chemical compound, which had burst causing the compound to be lost, were held not liable, because the damage was not reasonably foreseeable, but Lloyd, LJ did indicate, *ibid.,* that he regarded the containers and the compound as separate property of the plaintiffs). Effectively, therefore, this was the death of economic loss from acts: goodbye to *Anns* and almost goodbye to *Dutton.*

(c)(i) The final stage: present or imminent threat of danger to health or property confirmed as insufficient in the absence of actual damage - goodbye again to Anns; and (ii) damage to another part of the same structure is "not" enough and is not actual damage (defect in a part is defect in the whole) - goodbye to Dutton: Murphy

This was the effect of the House of Lords' decision in

Murphy v. Brentwood District Council [1990] 2 All ER 908, HL, which was to:

- confirm the finding in *D & F Estates* that imminent or prospective damage to health or property - that is, pure economic loss - was insufficient for recovery, and to
- reject the suggestion made in *D & F Estates* that certain property was sufficiently complex for one defective part to be held to be capable of causing damage to another part, different from itself, and
- expressly to overrule the cases of *Anns* and *Dutton.*

In *Murphy* itself, the plaintiff bought a house in 1970. The defendant local authority approved the foundations as complying with building regulations. In 1981 the plaintiff discovered that the foundations were defective and sold the house for £35,000 less than it should have been worth had its foundations not been defective. The plaintiff sued the local authority, claiming that gas and oil pipes had been broken by the settlement of the foundations and were an imminent threat to the health and safety of himself and of his family. The House of Lords held the defendants not liable.

Threatened damage to health or property,
even imminent, not enough

Where a latent defect had become apparent as a threat *before* it had *actually* caused physical damage or injury, it was purely economic loss, consisting in the cost to the owner of having it repaired so as to prevent such injury, and this was irrecoverable (nor could the owner have sued the previous owner in contract - as seen, the rule of *caveat emptor* applies to sales of land). The defect at that stage was merely economic and one of quality, and a non-contractual, tortious obligation in respect of defects in quality of goods or buildings was not to be introduced. In respect of defects discovered prior to injury, even if injury is threatened, Lord Keith remarked (at p.918): "The purchaser may incur expense in putting right the defect, or, more probably, discard the article. In either case the loss is purely economic." Lord Bridge said (at p.927): "If I buy a second-hand car and find it to be faulty, it can make no difference to the manufacturer's liability in tort whether the fault is in the brakes or in the engine, ie, whether the car will not stop or will not start. In either case the car is useless until repaired. The manufacturer is no more liable in tort for the cost of the repairs in the one case than in the other." Lord Oliver, too, explained that mere potential injury to body or property was not sufficient once the defect was no longer latent (p.935): the plaintiff then has the choice - repair the product or building or abandon it, both options amounting to pure economic loss.

Murphy was followed in *Department of the Environment v. Thomas Bates & Son Ltd* [1990] 2 All ER 943, where the House of Lords held plaintiffs unable to recover in tort from defendant builders the costs of strengthening a building. Low-strength concrete had incorrectly been used. The loss was purely economic, and as it happened, the structure, though incapable of supporting intended loads, was not dangerous.

Defect in one part of a building or product is defect in the whole, so no actual damage to property is caused. Goodbye to Dutton for good!

The distinction made in *D & F Estates* between complex and simple structures - recovery for damages being possible in the former, but not the latter case - was rejected, so that damage to walls and ceilings from defective foundations would not amount to the required actual damage to property separate from the foundations - it was all the same property. Lord Bridge stated (at p.928): "The reality is that the structural elements in any building form a single indivisible unit of which the different parts are essentially interdependent. To the extent that there is any defect in one part of the structure it must to a greater or lesser degree necessarily affect all other parts of the structure. Therefore any defect in the structure is a defect in the quality of the whole."

However, the Lords did seem prepared to contemplate that separate damage to a part of a building *could* be sustained:

(a) where the damage was caused to the building by a *defective installation,* such as a central heating boiler or electric wiring, or
(b) where an integral component of the structure was built by a *separate contractor,* for example, when a steel frame, erected by a specialist contractor, failed to give adequate support to floors and walls

(*per* Lord Bridge, at p.928 and Lord Jauncey at p.942 - there was also some discussion of whether a property owner might be able to recover for economic loss in preventing defects from leading to legal liability towards persons on neighbouring land or on the highway who might be injured, pp.475 and 489, but this remains largely unclear).

The problem with these possible exceptions is, first, where to draw the line, and secondly, the level of importance to be given to the factor of separate supplier of the defective part. Thus, when is an item an *installation* or an *integral component,* yet not also part of the structure? Why should it matter in the case of integral components that the supplier was not a separate specialist?

The truth, it is suspected, is that the Lords only included these qualifications because they did not want to shut the door completely on such economic damage liability. Yet, conceivably, if the "exceptions" are to be taken seriously, which still remains to be seen, there must surely be a strong presumption against sufficient separateness of a defective part, as an installation or integral component, for these purposes, which is then even harder - incrementally - to rebut where the supplier was not a separate specialist contractor.

Dutton and Anns overruled

These cases were expressly overruled, as amounting to judicial legislation (see pp.912 and 923) (only one of very few occasions on which the House of Lords had overruled itself since 1966 when the power was declared), and because consumer protection was best left to Parliament (p.943 - see too pp.930 and 938).

In the case of buildings, *Parliamentary* protection is in the form of the Defective Premises Act 1972 (see *supra,* p.177

and *infra*, pp.351) by which builders and architects have a strict duty to carry out their work in a workmanlike and professional manner. But the duty is broken only if, as a result of the defect, the building is *unfit for habitation* (requiring the owner to move out); and commercial properties are excluded.

The Latent Damage Act 1986 deals with periods of limitation of actions in the case of defective construction (*supra*, pp.175).

Lord Mackay, LC commented in *Murphy* (at p.912): "In these circumstances I have reached the clear conclusion that the proper exercise of the judicial function requires this House now to depart from *Anns* in so far as it affirmed a private law duty of care to avoid damage to property which causes present or imminent danger to the health and safety of owners, or occupiers, resting on local authorities in relation to their function of supervising compliance with building byelaws or regulations, that *Dutton* should be overruled and that all decisions subsequent to *Anns* which purported to follow it should be overruled."

So, there it was. The law had come full circle, in a mere 20 years.

Effectively, as a matter of policy, no further liability for pure economic loss caused by negligent acts, where defects in buildings or products had not *actually* caused damage to health or *other* property.

Damage could only be considered actually to have been caused by one part to a *different* part of the structure (or product) if it was somehow possible to regard it as a separate installation or integral component - unlikely, especially if not supplied by a different contractor.

Lacking in any real logic the position might be where economic loss not arising from breach of contract *is* foreseeable, since money spent in order to prevent or to repair prospective or actual injury or damage, either way, is all the same - an economic commodity.

Yet, if policy requires economic loss so to be restricted as a basis of negligence liability, there is little alternative other than to work backwards from that position and to distinguish it on the ground of lack of actual physical injury or damage to ascertainably different property.

Policy, not clarity of analysis, dictates the process, and as a result, recovery for pure economic loss from negligent acts once again is little more than a dead letter, both generally, as in the case of the broken electricity cable preventing profits, and specifically where the mere threat of danger exists to persons or to property from defective parts of a building or product.

One notable exception to this, which may be recalled from the treatment of negligent misstatement and the *Hedley Byrne* principle, was where a third party is the financial victim of a negligent misstatement or advice given between two other people and relied on by one of them. Although rather questionable in the light of *Murphy* - since, in relation to third parties suffering economic loss, the negligent advice may seem more like an *act* than a statement - nevertheless, in *Ross v. Caunters* [1980] Ch 297 it was held that a duty of care was owed to the third party in respect of the economic loss suffered, as, for example, where the third party would have benefited under a will but for the negligence of the solicitor who advised the person making the will; and, as seen, even following *Murphy*, this was subsequently held by the Court of Appeal still to be correct in *White v. Jones* [1993] 3 All ER 481 (see *supra*, p.140).

However, inclusion of third parties within ordinary negligence duty of care as in *Ross v. Caunters* was in fact moved away from by the House of Lords in its decision in *White v. Jones* [1995] 1 All ER 691, where the Court of Appeal's earlier support for *Ross v. Caunters* was replaced by a duty of care *sui generis* owed by solicitors to those disappointed under a will as a result of the solicitors' negligence, an approach, along with that in *Ross v. Caunters* itself, objected to by the dissenting minority of two Law Lords in *White v. Jones,* as lacking in legal principle and capable of being generalized to the destruction of the privity of contract rule (*supra*, p.152, *et seq.*).

Still, therefore, the subject of economic loss continues to excite controversy.

4. Omissions to act

You see someone drowning, but you do not dive into the water and save them even though you are a strong swimmer.

You hear a lorry driving out of control towards a deaf pedestrian, but you do not wave your arms to warn him.

You notice someone about to fall out of a train door, and you make no attempt to pull him back.

The situations are unlimited in which one person who has nothing at all to do with the danger in which another person finds himself, may choose to do absolutely nothing to help.

Will such an *omission* to act give rise to a duty of care in negligence, where it was reasonably foreseeable that injury would result? Certainly, in most cases, negligence is associated with a defendant's positive behaviour rather than his inaction. Are we expected to involve ourselves in the lives of complete strangers, or to pass by on the other side? Are we our brothers' keepers?

a. The general rule: no duty of care for omissions

Historically, the general principle has been clear: no liability in negligence for omissions, notwithstanding that damage was reasonably, even unequivocally, foreseeable.

So, if you happen to see somebody whom you do not like about to dive into a swimming pool, which you know has not yet been filled with water ... In *Yuen Kun Yeu v. Attorney-General of Hong Kong* [1988] AC 175 Lord Bridge said that there was no liability in negligence upon a person who saw another about to walk over a cliff with his head in the air and failed to shout a warning.

The reasons for the rule are fairly obvious: there might otherwise be intolerable pressure on people to go to the aid of others, whereas hopefully, voluntary help can frequently be relied upon in any event; there would be great uncertainty over who precisely could be regarded as being in a position to help, and over whom to sue if a whole crowd of people did nothing to assist.

The leading case is *Smith v. Littlewoods Organization Ltd* [1987] 1 All ER 710. The defendants had bought a cinema, which they intended to demolish and to replace with a supermarket. The building was left empty for a month and on a number of occasions, unknown to the defendants and to the police, intruders entered and tried to start a fire. Finally they succeeded and the fire damaged the plaintiff's property next door. Were the defendants negligent for not taking steps to prevent this possibility? The House of Lords held that the defendants were not liable towards the plaintiff. Lord Goff pointed out that there was no general duty of care to prevent a third party from wrongfully causing damage to a plaintiff, even if it was foreseeable that this could happen (pp.728-9 and 735). *Policy.* Following Lord Goff's approach, therefore, leaving your car unlocked in an area known to be frequented by "joyriders" does not give rise to a duty of care on your part towards persons knocked down and injured by the car thieves.

Finally, "omission" to act in this context means a pure omission. Omission to correct a negligent *act* already commenced - for example, failure to turn the steering wheel when driving negligently at excessive speed towards a pedestrian - would not of course be covered by the general principle against duty of care in the case of omissions. The absence of the necessary steering movement is just part of the overall positive act of negligence: the careless driving.

b. Exceptions to the general rule of no duty of care

The general principle of immunity is perfectly understandable.

But so, too, is the thought that exceptions may be necessary. It would be a rather pessimistic world if people were always expected as a matter of policy to walk past in total disregard of another person's difficulties, and the need for exceptions in special circumstances was recognized by all of the Lords in *Smith v. Littlewoods Organization Ltd.*

It is difficult to determine a generalized theory justifying the various exceptions.

One possibility mooted is that the source of the duty of care in these exceptional cases is not the omission to act - but an earlier *positive* act, or a status, or state of affairs, for which the defendant is responsible, so that a later omission to act is not in itself the sole cause of the damage. The *train of events* was set in motion by the earlier circumstance. (An analogy may be found in the law on contractual misrepresentation: normally, absence of a statement does not give rise to liability; not so, however, where a statement is made which is a half-truth, or which becomes untrue by the time of performance of the contract - it is the original statement, rather than absence of subsequent correction, which gives rise to liability, see *Dimmock v. Hallett* (1866) LR 2 Ch App 21.) In truth, however, it is questionable whether such an explanation would suffice to explain all those cases in which courts have held a duty of care to exist in the event of an omission to act.

It may be, therefore, that the law should simply be described in terms of those situations in which the courts have held as a matter of judicial policy that a duty of care should be considered to exist - and in all such cases, liability is not of course imposed unless the damage to the plaintiff was also reasonably foreseeable in accordance with the normal principle.

Categories of situations in which omission to act may lead to a duty of care are as follows:

(i) Defendant is in a relationship of control over another person who causes the damage

Types of relationship in which, as a matter of law, one party is obliged - not merely empowered as a fact - to exercise general control over another include:

- parent/teacher and child
- employer and employee
- hospital and patient, and
- police/prison and a person in custody.

Canadian authorities are even broader: for example, bar owner and drunken driver; competition organizer and drunken competitor; ice cream vendor and child.

In all such circumstances, the person with control has been held to be under a duty of care to prevent the other person from injuring himself or a third party, where the person with control knew of the danger and could have avoided it, that is, where there was foreseeability.

Consequently, for example, in *Carmarthenshire County Council v. Lewis* [1955] AC 549, the defendant local authority in charge of a school was held to be under a duty of care towards the plaintiff motorist who crashed in order to avoid a child rushing out of a school playground onto the road. The defendant had not taken steps to secure the playground.

Again, in *Home Office v. Dorset Yacht Co.* [1970] 2 All ER 294, the defendant was liable for allowing incarcerated young offenders to escape and to do damage on an outside trip. They should have been prevented from doing so through proper supervision.

In *Kirkham v. Chief Constable of Greater Manchester Police* [1990] 2 QB 283, the police were held liable for failure to prevent a man with a known mental disorder from committing suicide while he was in custody.

In *Newell v. Goldenberg* [1995] 6 Medical Law Review 371 a doctor was held liable for omitting to warn the plaintiff patient and his wife of the risk that an operation might fail.

However, failure to prevent a naval serviceman from becoming unconscious through drink was held not to be actionable in negligence in *Barrett v. Ministry of Defence* [1995] 1 WLR 1217 (CA).

(ii) Defendant has represented himself as someone who will take positive action to assist

Doctors, police, firemen, lifeguards, when on duty, and anyone else who takes the positive step of representing to the world, or at least to the plaintiff, that they will help people who are in danger, may be liable in negligence if they omit to do so, or do so negligently. For example, in *Mercer v. South Eastern & Chatham Railway Companies' Managing Committee* [1922] 2 KB 549, the defendants were held to owe a duty of care towards the public for failing to close a gate preventing people from crossing a railway line when it was unsafe to do so. The defendants were not in fact originally obliged to close and lock the gate. They merely did so as a matter of practice, so that when they omitted to lock the gate on one occasion, leading to injury to the plaintiff who had relied upon them, they were liable for negligence. Their action in total could be said to have led to the damage, where it was foreseeable that the plaintiff victim, in reliance on them, would take no further precautions. However, it does seem from the Canadian case of *Horsley v. MacLaren* [1970] 1 Lloyd's Rep 257, that the defendant - say, as a person who commenced an attempt to rescue the plaintiff - will not be liable in such cases, unless as a result of his partial efforts, the plaintiff was left in a *worse* condition (for example, because the defendant did not ask anyone else to help and lost valuable time). For, otherwise, there would be no incentive to help people - legally, it would be safer to pass by (see too *Barrett v. Ministry of Defence* [1995] 1 WLR 1217 (CA), *supra*, where the defendant was held not to be under a duty to prevent an airman from drinking himself unconscious, but fell under a duty of care to make him reasonably safe from choking *after* having assumed the responsibility to return him to his cabin).

The same has been held to apply when the defendant is relied upon, expressly or impliedly, to look after the plaintiff's property and omits to carry out the task properly. Looking at the defendant's actions as a whole - the positive step of taking custody of the property, as well as the omission to do what was necessary to secure it - the defendant's conduct has caused the loss. Thus, in *Stansbie v. Troman* [1948] 2 KB 48, a decorator was left alone in a house and told to lock up, which he failed to do, when he left. Thieves entered and stole property and the decorator was held liable for negligence. It seems unlikely that the duty in such cases depends upon the existence of any contract imposing obligations upon the defendant (see *Smith*, pp.724 and 730).

(iii) Statutory powers or duties

In the Australian case of *Sutherlandshire County Council v. Heyman* (1985) 60 ALR 1, at p.59, Deane, J stated that cases of liability for omissions included those involving "reliance by one party upon care being taken by the other in the discharge or performance of statutory powers, duties or functions, or of powers, duties or functions arising from or involved in the holding of an office or the possession or occupation of property."

In spite of this pronouncement of willingness to find a duty of care in respect of omission to perform a statutory function, courts have adopted a rather restrictive attitude towards recovery in cases of omission to exercise statutory powers, while, in the case of duties, the strict liability tort of breach of statutory duty may be more appropriate than negligence. Thus, in *East Suffolk Rivers Catchment Board v. Kent* [1941] AC 74, the House of Lords held that a public body would not be liable for *exercising a power negligently*, on the basis that no greater damage had been caused than if it had *failed altogether* to exercise the power; and that such failure would *not* have attracted liability: although, on the other hand, in *Anns v. Merton London Borough Council* [1978] AC 728, it was held that a local authority could be liable if its omission was *ultra vires* - beyond its powers so to fail to act in the particular situation. In *Curran v. Northern Ireland Co-Ownership Housing Association* [1987] AC 718, the defendant was not liable for failing to exercise its statutory power to inspect a property with sufficient care before making an award of a home improvement grant, because the purpose of the regulation was to ensure that public funds were spent properly, not to protect householders against building defects; and in *Yuen Kun Yeu v. Attorney-General of Hong Kong* [1988] AC 175, the defendant was held not liable for failing to take sufficient care to exercise a statutory function to remove a deposit-taking company from a register on suspicion of trading fraudulently.

The reason for this restrictive approach is the courts' reluctance to *interfere* with the exercise of discretion by statutory bodies. Thus, in *Sheppard v. Glossop Corporation* [1921] 3 KB 132, the defendants exercised a statutory discretion to turn off street lighting at 9.00 pm and were sued in negligence by the plaintiff who fell in the dark. The defendants were held under no duty of care. In *Rowling v. Takaro Properties Ltd* [1988] AC 473, the court pointed out that in many cases the plaintiff will have a public, administrative law remedy of judicial review of the public body's decision in any event.

However, recovery for negligent exercise of a statutory power is not *impossible.* In *Lonrho plc v. Tebbit* [1992] 4 All ER 280, the plaintiffs had given an undertaking to the United Kingdom's Minister of Trade that they would not acquire more than 30 per cent of the shares of the House of Fraser corporate group which owned Harrods store in London while the Monopolies Commission were assessing the validity of the takeover. Subsequently, the plaintiff, Lonrho, sold most of its shares to another company and, following the Monopoly Commission's report that the takeover would not be against the public interest, the other company acquired over 50 per cent of the shares. Thereafter, the Minister of Trade, the defendant, released the plaintiffs from their undertaking, but it was, of course, by then too late to proceed with the takeover and the plaintiffs sued the defendant for negligent delay in exercising his statutory discretion to release the plaintiffs. The Court of Appeal held that a duty of care was owed in the matter of discretion to release the plaintiffs from their undertaking, precisely because it was no longer in the public interest to keep the plaintiffs under the restriction - so the precondition for the latter was no longer satisfied and any discretion in the matter of release did not now exist.

Furthermore, Scottish courts in *Duff v. Highland and Islands Fire Board* (1995) *The Times,* November 3, disapproved of the restrictive nature of the majority judgments in *East Suffolk Rivers Catchment Board* and shared Lord Salmon's criticism of the case in *Anns,* yet noting that even in *East Suffolk* it was recognized that an authority which chose to exercise a statutory power came under a common law duty to take reasonable care not to inflict additional damage by doing so. However, the *Duff* judgment was in fact *obiter,* first, because the court took the view that it was a statutory duty which was involved in the case, not a mere power, and secondly, because the court did not accept on the facts that the defendant fire service had failed to check whether they had fully extinguished the fire in a house to which they had been called, which subsequently re-ignited and burnt down the property of the plaintiff who lived next door.

The preceding principles may now be viewed in the light of the judgment of Lord Browne-Wilkinson in the House of Lords in *X (Minors) v. Bedfordshire County Council* [1995] 3 All ER 353, HL, which involved claims for breach of duty of care in negligence and the tort of breach of statutory duty (see *infra,* ch.10) brought by children in care against local authorities.

One of the issues involved was whether an ordinary common law negligence duty of care could and would exist where the defendant local authority was acting in the exercise of a statutory discretion and power?

Lord Browne-Wilkinson made certain findings in the preceding respects, which ought to be drawn attention to in the context of the present account of duty of care as to statutory powers and discretion *generally* - although, these are dealt with in greater detail below (p.220, *et seq.*) in relation to public policy bars on negligence recovery against *public bodies*. Clearly, invariably, those exercising a statutory power will be a *public body*, so that the principles concerning duty of care in exercising a statutory discretion generally will, in any event, be subject to the encompassing - and to a large extent superimposed - principles concerning duty of care *of public bodies*. Nevertheless, it is not inevitable that a defendant exercising a statutory power must be a public body and, accordingly, it is considered justifiable to devote a separate section here to an examination of principles for exercise of a statutory power generally - *whoever* is responsible for its exercise.

It is recalled that previous cases tended to find against duty of care in the exercise of the power - unless perhaps the power was exceeded (*Anns*), or similarly the facts and conditions for exercise of the discretion no longer existed (*Lonrho*) (*supra*, p.203). All of which seems a fairly reasonable compromise. Not surprisingly then that Lord Browne-Wilkinson seemed to endorse this approach. He reemphasized that if decisions complained of fell within the ambit of the statutory discretion, they could not be actionable for negligence; but if they were "so unreasonable that it falls outside the ambit of the discretion conferred upon the local authority, there is no *a priori* reason for excluding all common law liability" (p.368), reciting dicta from *Anns* and *Dorset Yacht* (pp.368-369). However, quite correctly, he was careful to reject any idea that in order to be actionable at common law, it was sufficient to show that the exercise of the power was *ultra vires*, which would have been inaccurate (p.369). The requirement for negligence duty of care was, as seen, that the exercise was so unreasonable that it was no longer within the ambit of the discretion conferred (pp.369-370). Inevitably, therefore, this *would* make the exercise *ultra vires*: but there were other grounds upon which an exercise of a statutory power could be attacked for being *ultra vires* - for example, breach of rules of natural justice requiring those affected to be given a proper opportunity to object and to be heard (p.369) - and there could be no suggestion that *ultra vires* character of the exercise of the power on this ground could form the basis of a negligence action for breach of duty of care.

This was a useful regroupment of the principles previously developed:

- negligence duty of care can exist in respect of exercise of statutory powers,
- but only if the power is so poorly exercised that it no longer properly qualifies as an exercise of the power.

As to when this will be held to be the case, this is obviously a matter of degree for incremental development on the facts of each case. In *X (Minors)* itself, Lord Browne-Wilkinson did not dismiss the possibility that, if the case went to trial from the preliminary proceedings to establish whether a cause of action existed, it could be found that the defendant local authority, in failing to take proper steps to protect a child, had behaved so unreasonably that no reasonable local authority could have exercised its power in this way, so that its actions fell outside the ambit of its statutory discretion and consequently were able to found a negligence claim (p.380).

A possible exception to the general restrictive principle enunciated by Lord Browne-Wilkinson was floated by Lord Jauncey, the only other Law Lord to comment more than in the briefest terms. He took the view that if the statutory authority was to perform an act which would otherwise be a breach of duty through damage to another's person or rights, effectively the statute is then to be regarded as only a statutory defence to what would otherwise be a valid claim. Accordingly, since the statute would not have permitted careless performance of the act, if there is insufficient care, the defence no longer applies and ordinary negligence duty operates at common law and not as in any way created or permitted *under the statute,* nor, consequently, subject to the special restraints (p.362 - and *infra,* p.364).

It remains to be seen whether this elaborate argument will be taken up in the future by the courts. There must be some doubt, since most statutory powers conceivably otherwise involve tortious conduct, and such an exception could seriously weaken the general principle of unreasonable behaviour exceeding discretion propounded by Lord Browne-Wilkinson.

Finally, even if the general requirement laid down were to be satisfied by a plaintiff, there are two further sets of requirements which must also be fulfilled if recovery for negligence is to be possible:

(1) if the defendant is a *public body,* there are superimposed public policy considerations to be taken into account, namely, that the actions complained of must fall within the *operational* sphere of the power conferred, and not within the area of *policy* (see *infra,* p.218, *et seq.*); and

(2) even if the complaint is about operations rather than policy, and generally in any event whether the defendant is a public body or not, the fair, just and reasonable juridical policy stage of the *Caparo* three-stage test (as well as the others, of course) for duty of care in negligence must also be satisfied (see *infra*, p.212).

(iv) Control of dangerous things or land

In *Smith* (at p.30), Lord Goff envisaged as a special circumstance in which an omission could give rise to liability, a case "where the defendant negligently causes or permits to be created a source of danger, and it is reasonably foreseeable that third parties may interfere with it and, sparking off the danger, thereby cause damage to persons in the position of the plaintiff."

Presumably again, this can be justified if the positive act of possession of the object of danger and its subsequent use by third parties to cause damage, are viewed as a *continuum* rather than as separate stages, act and omission. Yet, the lack of any real logic is hard to miss. Virtually any object - even a baby's rattle, or toy gun - can be used in such a way as to inflict injury as a "source of danger", so that limitation of the exception to the more obviously dangerous objects - a box of fireworks - is difficult to justify. Perhaps it need not be. Maybe the "exception" applies to control of *all* land and property in principle, and the only other determinant of duty of care is then that of *reasonable foreseeability* of damage - also referred to by Lord Goff above - requiring positive steps to safeguard against this, in which event, the more dangerous the object, the more likely it is that possibilities of misappropriation and damage would have been foreseeable.

Lord Goff provided some examples of the duty, in *Smith* (at pp.730-1): *Haynes v. Harwood* [1935] 1 KB 146, where the owner of the horse-drawn van left in the street, which bolted when a boy threw a stone at the horses, was in *control* and should have foreseen the possibility of an accident, whether caused by wrongful behaviour or not; storage of fireworks in an unlocked garden shed, which the owner should foresee might be set off by mischievous boys, causing damage to neighbouring property. Again, however, it must be said that the empty building in *Smith* could be regarded as just as tempting to boys of a certain age as fireworks in a shed, so that the real distinction probably turns on a policy decision as to when damage from the omission is reasonably foreseeable or not, rather than upon absence of the *danger* or *control* element in the empty building case.

The courts have adopted a similar response to defendants who maintain their *land* in a dangerous state, which can be said to invite a third party to cause damage to another. For example, in *Cunningham v. Reading Football Club Ltd* (1991) *The Times,* March 22, the defendant football club was held liable to policemen who were injured when hooligans tore out loose pieces of concrete from the terraces and threw them at the police.

Would the principle also apply - just as in the case of control of dangerous things and land - where the defendant has brought about and is in control of a dangerous *situation?* For example, you park your car at the side of the road just before a bend. The driver behind quite wrongly pulls out to overtake you and hits a car driven by the plaintiff travelling in the opposite direction on the other side of the road. You must surely have known that this could happen when you parked the car and yet did nothing to warn oncoming traffic that there was danger ahead. Logically, there seems no reason why liability should not attach in this circumstance if it does so in the other cases mentioned. But, as said, the exceptions appear to be based more on policy as to foreseeability than on any inherent logic, and it is considered questionable whether the courts would impose a duty of care in respect of the omission in this type of case. Thus, for example, in *Topp v. London Country Bus Ltd* [1993] 3 All ER 464 (CA), the Court of Appeal held that the defendant bus company owed no duty of care towards the plaintiff's wife who was knocked down and killed by one of the defendants' buses which their driver had left on a road, unlocked and with its ignition key in it, for collection by the next driver in accordance with the usual practice, but which was then stolen and driven by an unknown person. This confirmed the first instance decision that, though foreseeable, it would not be fair, just and reasonable to impose the duty, incrementally, for this omission (p.460). How different it might have been had the thief been a naughty child and the defendant its responsible parent.

(v) Statutory body decides to act but delays

In *Stovin v. Wise (Norfolk County Council, third party)* [1994] 3 All ER 467, the highway authority knew that there was a danger to visibility on the road from an obstruction on neighbouring land belonging to the railway, and, having decided that action should be taken to remedy this, failed to do so. Three years later an accident occurred and the plaintiff was injured. The Court of Appeal, applying the incremental approach of Lord Bridge in *Caparo,* held that a common law duty of care was owed: this was not a case of omission, because the highway authority had taken a decision positively to proceed and having done so, its failure to carry through the proposed action would instead be regarded as *negligently performing* the activity and thereby amounting to breach of duty. The case is all the stronger for the fact that the court had previously concluded that the highway authority had not been in breach of its statutory duty under the Highways Act 1980 to maintain the highway, because the obstruction was on neighbouring land and not on the highway itself (but see now *infra,* Appendix Case 10).

5. Other Cases

(a) In *Marc Rich & Co. AG v. Bishop Rock Marine Co. Ltd (The Nicholas H)* [1995] 3 All ER 307, HL, the House of Lords (Lord Lloyd dissenting) held that it would not be fair, just and reasonable to impose a duty of care in negligence upon the defendant "classification society" responsible for a careless survey of a ship leading to its sinking and loss of the plaintiffs' cargo, because such societies were non-profit-making and set up for the collective welfare and safety and security of life and property at sea and lesser injustice would be done through not recognizing a duty of care (p.332, *per* Lord Steyn). The existing system affording cargo owners recourse against ship owners under the Hague Rules and insurance cover where necessary would otherwise be undermined (*ibid.*). Lord Lloyd dissented, but only on the ground - rejected by the rest - that the so-called "retreat from *Anns*", which case had emphasized foreseeability, at the expense of considerations of policy, had mostly concerned cases of pure economic loss, not also physical damage as here (pp.321-322 - the argument was also rejected by the House of Lords in *X (Minors) v. Bedfordshire CC*, at p.380, see *infra*).

This decision does serve to indicate, therefore, that the category of juridical policy against duty of care is by no means closed and confined to specific classes of case. Furthermore, as Lord Steyn made expressly clear, imposition of a duty of care in a particular action, even if the three-stage test *was* satisfied, would ultimately depend upon the facts of the case (p.327) - although a *further, independent* condition of this nature, it has to be said, is perhaps somewhat difficult to accept.

(b) *X (Minors) v. Bedfordshire County Council etc* [1995] 3 All ER 353, HL, it will be recalled, involved a number of cases brought by plaintiff children against various local authorities for common law negligence or breach of statutory duty in failing to protect against abuse or to provide for educational needs (see *supra*, p.204). On the assumption that the particular exercise of the power complained of by the defendants was justiciable in negligence (*supra*, p.204) and that there were no public policy objections against imposing a duty of care in ordinary negligence upon the defendant as a public body (see *infra*, p.218), Lord Browne-Wilkinson then had to assess whether the fair, just and reasonable condition of juridical policy for negligence duty of care was satisfied (p.380). Lord Browne-Wilkinson stated that it would not be just and reasonable to superimpose a common law duty of care on the defendant local authority in relation to performance of its statutory duties to protect or to educate the children, because this would *cut across the whole statutory system,* set up as an interdisciplinary structure for the protection of children at risk, based upon *extraordinarily delicate* provisions requiring the local authority to have regard not only to the physical well being of the child but also to the advantages of not disrupting its family environment (pp.380-381 - although, in principle it was perfectly possible for a common law duty of care in negligence to arise out of performance of a statutory duty, at p.368, see *infra,* p.364, *et seq.*, subject to the usual conditions for a cause of action in negligence, see *supra* p.204 and *infra*, p.220). In addition, a common law duty could not be imposed where it was inconsistent with, or had a tendency to discourage, the due performance by the authority of its statutory duties (pp.381, 391-392; and if there were any deficiencies in the operation of the statutory machinery in the Education Acts for special needs schooling, these should be dealt with administratively rather than through the courts in this case - p.392). On the other hand, had the local authorities specifically held themselves out as offering psychological services to the public, they would then have been under an ordinary common law duty of care (notwithstanding deriving their powers from statute), because they would have opened their doors to the public generally for a service which they were only required to provide for a certain section thereof (p.392), and a school headmaster himself (though not psychiatrists and social workers advising a local authority) would be under a separate duty of care in negligence towards his pupils, unaffected by the parallel statutory duty upon the local authority (p.395). "If such a head teacher gives advice to the parents ... he must exercise the skills and care of a reasonable teacher in giving such advice" (*ibid.*).

(c) As seen earlier, (*supra,* p.137), in *Spring v. Guardian Assurance plc* [1994] 3 All ER 129, the House of Lords considered whether it would be unjust on juridical policy grounds to impose a duty of care in negligence upon providers of references towards the person who was the subject of the reference and held that it would not: it was in the public interest and that of individual employees for whom references were provided by existing employers that these should be properly and accurately drawn up.

(d) Again, as seen earlier (*supra,* p.211) in *Stovin v. Wise (Norfolk County Council, third party)* [1994]3 All ER 467, the Court of Appeal thought it quite appropriate to impose a duty of care upon a highway authority to remove a danger to road users when it had decided to take such action but had failed to carry it out - and in most cases, this would not be too onerous, because the authority would possess a wide discretion upon whether to decide to take any action in the first place (but see now *infra,* Appendix Case 10).

(e) In *Bennett v. Commissioner of Police of the Metropolis* [1995] 1 WLR 488, the High Court held that even if it were to be held that a government minister was under a public duty to balance benefits of non-disclosure of documents against benefits of disclosure in the interests of the administration of justice, before objecting to such disclosure on the ground of public interest immunity, nonetheless it would not be fair, just or reasonable to impose a private law duty of care in respect of exercise of that public duty, in favour of a private litigant who wished to see the documents for the purposes of his litigation. The proper remedy was in public law for review of the government's actions.

(f) Again, in *West Wiltshire District Council v. Garland* [1995] 2 WLR 439, the Court of Appeal, while expressly confirming (p.448) that an ordinary duty of care in negligence *could* coexist with an action for the tort of breach of statutory duty (see *infra,* p.372), nevertheless held that it would not be fair, just or reasonable to impose a duty upon an auditor of a local authority's accounts towards any officer of that authority whose conduct he had occasion to criticize (p.449).

(g) In *Barrett v. Ministry of Defence* [1995] 1 WLR 1217 (CA), a 30-year-old naval airman drank himself into a state of unconsciousness during celebrations at a naval base, and was carried back to his bunk in his cabin where he suffocated to death from his own vomit. His widow brought proceedings for negligence. She argued that the navy owed the same duty of care towards the deceased to prevent him from harming himself as a school towards its pupils, employer towards employees and occupier to visitors. The

Court of Appeal held that there was no such duty towards the deceased and the position was quite distinct from those referred to: "I can see no reason why it should not be fair, just and reasonable for the law to leave a responsible adult to assume responsibility for his own actions in consuming alcoholic drink. No one is better placed to judge the amount that he can safely consume or to exercise control in his own interest as well as in the interest of others. To dilute self-responsibility and to blame one adult for another's lack of self-control is neither just nor reasonable and in the development of the law of negligence an increment too far" (p.1224, *per* Beldam, LJ). However, the defendants in fact accepted that they had not taken sufficient care of the deceased *after* he had fallen unconscious and when they had assumed responsibility for him, so that damages would be awarded in respect of their actions to this extent (although, these were reduced by two-thirds to take account of the deceased's contributory negligence, see *infra*, ch.29).

(h) In *Church of Jesus Christ of Latter-Day Saints (Great Britain) v. Yorkshire Fire and Civil Defence Authority* (1996) *The Times,* May 9, deputy High Court Judge William Crawford, QC, held that it would not be fair, just and reasonable to impose a common law duty of care in negligence upon the defendant fire brigade, which had allegedly negligently failed to ensure proper provision of water at the scene of a fire, which meant that the plaintiffs' premises were destroyed. However, the case was mainly decided on the grounds of *public policy* immunity of the fire service from duty of care, corresponding to that of the police (see *infra*), and against the background of *statutory* duties placed on the defendants, which themselves were held not to give rise to any private statutory duties towards individuals for breach of which they might claim (see ch.10). Furthermore, in *Capital and Counties plc v. Hampshire County Council* (1996) *The Times,* April 26, Judge Richard Havery, QC, held a few weeks later that the fire service did not enjoy public policy immunity from negligence liability in fighting a fire (see *infra* and Appendix)!

(i) In *Smolden v. Whitworth* (1996) *The Times,* April 23, Mr Justice Curtis in the High Court held that the referee of a "colts" (junior) rugby match was under a duty of care to ensure that "scrummages" (general linking of limbs and pushing of opposing team members in order to gain territory and possession of the ball) did not collapse dangerously, given the high risk of serious injury. This was fair, just and reasonable in a colts match - although, the Judge emphasized that this was not necessarily also so in relation to senior and international games.

That completes the cases in which judicial policy has played a large part in the operation of the duty of care in negligence - stage two of the three-stage process of duty of care, as here presented (*stage 3,* to stage 2 proximity, under the orthodox three-stage test): miscellaneous, nervous shock, economic loss, omission to act and exceptions, other situations. The third element of the three-stage process of duty of care according to the formulation above was *public policy* protecting state or society, as a negative influence upon the existence of the duty.

(iii) Public Policy Objections Against Duty of Care

1. *Public Bodies*

Under public - administrative - law, it is possible to attack the validity of an act or decision of a public body in the courts (called "judicial review") if it is *ultra vires* - in excess of their powers (for example, because the decision was made in bad faith or incorrect factors were taken into account).

The reasons for the restrictive position on suing public bodies in public law include the fact that so wide-ranging are their duties that they might otherwise never be out of the courts and that courts are not the most appropriate organs to review the discretion and expertise of what are sometimes elected bodies.

Consequently, for the same reasons and in order to prevent such public law limitations on liability from being circumvented by private law actions in negligence, courts have been reluctant to admit the existence of a duty of care in negligence on the part of public bodies, as a matter of public policy.

It would seem, therefore, that for tort liability to exist, a number of features have been held to be required to be present:

i. The body's actions must be *ultra vires* at public law (*Home Office v. Dorset Yacht Co. Ltd* [1970] AC 1004) - which, presumably, however, will automatically be so if the body has been negligent:

ii. The body's actions should be "operational" rather than

"policy", according to Lord Wilberforce in *Anns* (at p.755). For example, in *Home Office v. Dorset Yacht Co. Ltd,* a group of boys from a home for young offenders was taken on an outside trip to a boating harbour by three officers in accordance with Home Office policy for the rehabilitation of offenders. The three officers went off to bed and some of the boys were able to get out and caused damage to the plaintiff's boats. The House of Lords held that although the government department responsible could not be attacked for its policy of allowing offenders to be taken out in this way, even though the policy might be said to have been indirectly responsible for what had happened, nevertheless the *operational* execution of this policy in the particular case had been careless and the Home Office owed a duty of care in negligence towards the plaintiff. The same public policy reasons for not interfering with government decision-making or policy did not apply at the operational level.

Accordingly, if it were a local authority's policy to spend so little money that pavements were left in a dangerous condition and streets unlit, this decision could not be attacked for negligence if someone were to be hurt. But if the injury were caused by failing properly to carry out such street lighting and repairs to pavements as were decided on, an operational duty of care would exist. Clearly, however, the dividing line between *policy* and *operational* will not always be easy to draw and the matter remains one of degree (*Rowling v. Takaro Properties Ltd* [1988] 1 All ER 163, at p.172, *per* Lord Keith): nevertheless, if the issue is held to be one of policy, negligence will not be possible; while, if operational, the facts must still satisfy the usual requirements for a duty of care, such as reasonable foreseeability of damage to the plaintiff. Furthermore, even if a body's act is *ultra vires* at public law - for example, an irrelevant factor was taken into account - it still may not have been negligent in fulfilling its private law duty of care (*Takaro*).

These principles were the subject of confirmation and elaboration by the House of Lords in the case of *X (Minors) v. Bedfordshire County Council etc* [1995] 3 All ER 353, HL, previously referred to above (pp.204 and 212, concerning juridical policy restrictions upon claims in respect of statutory discretion and generally on fair, just and reasonable grounds). It will be recalled that the proceedings involved actions against several defendant local authorities brought by children claiming damages for negligence or breach of statutory duty in respect of failure to protect against abuse or to provide for special educational needs for children with learning difficulties.

In the case of actions against public bodies, there were a number of requirements to be satisfied, superimposed upon the rest (even duplicatory, in respect of those concerning statutory discretion itself generally: see *supra*, p.204). Lord Browne-Wilkinson considered that statutory duties now existed over such a broad range of activities that it was not possible to formulate one principle to cover all cases - nevertheless the following significant points could be identified (p.368):

(a) There would be no common law duty of care in negligence as to exercise of the discretion itself by the public body, as already seen (*supra*, p.204) in relation to exercise of statutory discretion generally:

with this the courts would not interfere. An example would be a decision on whether or not to close a school (p.368).

(b) But where it is implementation of a statutory function which is in issue, a distinction would be drawn between

- policy issues, as to which there would be no common law duty of care in negligence, and
- operational questions, which could be held to fall outside the discretion category and consequently to be actionable in common law negligence (pp.368 and 370).

(c) As to how to distinguish between policy and operational, beyond reciting expressions of the difficulties from *Anns* and *Rowling* (p.370), and providing, as examples of policy, decisions concerning allocation of scarce resources or distribution of risks (*ibid.*), and of operational, as the day-to-day running of a school which it has been decided as a matter of policy to keep open (p.368), Lord Browne-Wilkinson really had little more to offer in general terms. However, he did subsequently throw further light on the distinction in his application of the principles to the facts of the case. He thought that the defendant local authority's failure to take reasonable practical steps to remove children at risk from their parents, or to allocate a suitable social worker or to make proper investigations would not involve policy nor allocation of resources, whereas allegations that the defendant had failed to provide a level of service appropriate to the plaintiffs' needs would nevertheless do so (p.380).

Naturally, if common law negligence liability was *possible* against the public body in accordance with the preceding principles, it could only be established in fact if the harm was reasonably foreseeable (p.380) and liability fair, just and reasonable to be imposed (p.371) - the general requirements of duty of care.

Finally, three further points of general interest emerged from the proceedings.

(1) The psychiatrists and social workers engaged by the defendant local authorities to examine the plaintiff children for abuse and to advise the defendants were not themselves under a duty of care towards the plaintiffs, because of their immediate link with the defendants' statutory duties, and nor therefore were the defendants 'vicariously liable' (see *infra*, ch.11) for the actions of those persons (pp.383-384). Lord Browne-Wilkinson distinguished *Smith v.Eric S. Bush, Henderson v. Merrett Syndicates Ltd* and *White v. Jones (supra*, p.117, *et seq.*), on the ground that in *X (Minors)* the social workers and psychiatrists - unlike surveyor, managing agents and solicitors - simply undertook no responsibilities towards the "third party" plaintiffs and neither the latter nor their parents would be expected to regulate *their* conduct in reliance on the report (*a fortiori* if it had been a parent who was suspected

of abuse). It was solely for the defendant local authority to take action (p.383). Thus, it was for the latter reason that there could, conversely, be such a duty of care upon the social workers and psychologists involved in the special educational needs, rather than child abuse, claims, because in the former the parents themselves could be expected to rely upon the reports and to take the necessary steps to cooperate (pp.393-4). Lord Nolan, otherwise with the majority, differed from them on this aspect, on the ground that social workers and psychiatrists could fall under a general professional duty of care towards the children - although, he nonetheless agreed with Lord Browne-Wilkinson and the rest that the psychiatrist was exempt from the duty of care, on the ground of "witness immunity" protecting those conducting examinations likely to lead to legal proceedings (as in the case of child abuse) in which they might have to give evidence (p.400).

(2) A head of school in fact owed a duty of care in negligence at common law towards his pupils, and the fact that a local authority also had duties under statute would not affect the former (pp.395-6).

(3) The authority would have been under a common law duty of care if it had instead held itself out as offering a general psychological advisory service to the public, as well as for the children for whom it was bound to provide, even if it derived its powers from statute (pp.392-3).

As a final comment, it should be said that notwithstanding the preceding principles of control over negligence actions being brought against public bodies, there is nevertheless a growing feeling amongst commentators that notwithstanding the natural reluctance of courts to interfere with policy and discretion in the allocation of scarce resources, courts are, nonetheless, increasingly becoming dissatisfied at having to categorize certain acts and decisions as falling within the policy, rather than operational, category when individuals are hurt (see *Re HIV Haemophiliac Litigation* [1990] NLJ Law Rep 1349).

2. The Police

In carrying out their activities, policemen are under the same type of duty of care in negligence as other members of society - even if the standard expected of them may differ in order to take into account their special position and duties (*Marshall v. Osmond* [1983] QB 1034): for example, a police motor car driver in pursuit of a vehicle suspected of being involved in a crime and travelling at high speed could only sensibly be held liable for failing to meet such standards of care as could reasonably be expected of a public servant performing his duties in this way.

However, it is more in what the police *fail* to do than in their acts that the great potential for complaints and negligence claims against them exists. People expect a lot from their police force, and if crime increases and criminals are not apprehended, it is the police whom citizens tend to blame. The courts have shown themselves to be alive to this fact and are aware that if actions were frequently allowed to succeed, the police could spend a great deal of their time and resources defending actions in court, or following up every possibility in order to protect themselves against a future claim of negligence (see *Hill v. Chief Constable of West Yorkshire* [1988] 2 All ER 238). Thus, in *Calveley v. Chief Constable of the Merseyside Police* [1989] AC 1228, the defendant police authority was held not to be under a duty of care in negligence to notify the plaintiff police officers of complaints made against them by the public and to proceed swiftly to investigate the charges, because as a matter of public policy such a duty could hinder the investigation. Again, in *Hughes v. National Union of Mineworkers* [1991] 4 All ER 278, the plaintiff police officer, who was injured while trying to maintain public order during a strike, was held unable to sue his Chief Constable for negligently positioning the police force under his control, because it would be against public policy to hinder the conduct of policing public disorder by finding senior officers to be liable in negligence (see Appendix, *infra*).

Consequently, on public policy, there seem to be the following two basic controls on police duty of care, so as to avoid interference with the conduct of their investigation of crime:

First, there is the same distinction between policy and operational activities as with public bodies. In *Rigby v. Chief Constable of Northamptonshire* [1985] 2 All ER 985, police used tear-gas to drive a gunman out of property in which he was hiding, and unfortunately the gas set fire to the building. The court held that the police were not liable in negligence for the *policy* decision to make inflammable tear-gas available for such situations, but, nevertheless, they did owe a duty of care towards the owner of the building to bring with them fire-fighting equipment when the gas was used, as part of their *operational* sphere. It may be noted that in *Duff v. Highland and Islands Fire Board* (1995) *The Times,* November 3, Scottish courts held that the fire service did not have the same public policy immunity from liability in negligence as was enjoyed by the police - although, the standard of care to be expected by them was to be decided according to the usual principles applicable to those exercising professional judgment.

Secondly, in a number of situations, the courts simply find against police duty of care as a matter of policy, in order to protect the police from excessive liability, for example:

- failing to catch a multiple murderer (the "Yorkshire Ripper") before he killed another victim (*Hill v. Chief Constable of West Yorkshire* [1988] 2 All ER 238), although, it would be a different matter if the police had had him in custody and had negligently allowed him to escape;
- for failing to warn motorists of a danger caused by a third party and the malfunctioning of traffic lights (*Clough v. Bussan (West Yorkshire Police Authority)* [1990] 1 All ER 431);
- for failing to arrest a suspect out of a desire to obtain further evidence against him (*Jane Doe v. Metropolitan Toronto (Municipality) Commissioners of Police* (1990) 72 DLR (4th) 580);
- attending a shop at which the burglar alarm was ringing, but only checking the front of the property, whereas the burglars were at the back (*Alexandrou v.*

Oxford [1993] 4 All ER 328);
- failure for one year to interview or charge a person who was accused of seriously harassing a victim whom he eventually shot (*Osman v. Ferguson* [1993] 4 All ER 344).

Given this desire by courts to protect the police on the one hand and their growing unwillingness, referred to above, to find activities of public bodies to fall within the policy rather than operational sphere on the other, it is perhaps therefore highly appropriate that police and public bodies should be so categorized separately for present purposes, in case there should develop a more notable divergence in the application of such principles in the future. This said, however, it may be that the pendulum is beginning to swing against the police too, in the light of certain highly publicized instances of harassment of individuals, usually women - popularly known as "stalking" - in which the "stalker" commits no criminal offence and is therefore unable to be arrested by the police and yet goes on to harm his victim. It would appear that the European Commission of Human Rights has declared to be admissible an application that dismissal of one such negligence action against the British police was in contravention of the European Convention for the Protection of Human Rights and Fundamental Freedoms (see *The Times* (1996) May 18, p.2). If taken up by the English courts in future proceedings, the difficulty will then revolve around standard of care - what precisely are the police reasonably to be expected to do (see *infra,* ch.6)?

In *Elguzouli-Daf v. Commissioner of Police of the Metropolis* and *McBrearty v. Ministry of Defence* [1995] 2 WLR 173, the plaintiffs claimed negligence on the part of the Crown Prosecution Service (CPS) responsible for bringing criminal prosecutions in England and Wales (see [1995] 2 WLR, p.185), for alleged delays in deciding not to proceed against them, during which periods the plaintiffs remained in custody. The Court of Appeal held, following *Hill v. Chief Constable of West Yorkshire, supra* in relation to the police themselves, that as a matter of public policy and in the interests of the community as a whole, it would be wrong to inhibit the functions of the CPS by imposing such negligence liability upon it (pp.181-3, 186) - indeed, it was said that in some ways the arguments against a duty of care were even stronger than in the case of the police, because whereas much police work was operational in practice, the function of the CPS involved, to a large extent, matters of judgment and discretion (p.182). However, the previous first instance decision in *Welsh v. Chief Constable of the Merseyside Police* [1993] 1 All ER 692, in which the CPS had been held capable of being under a duty of care, was said not to have been incorrect, because in that case the CPS had specifically undertaken a particular responsibility towards the accused to inform a court about certain other criminal offences which had already been taken into account by another court (pp.183 and 186-7).

In *Swinney v. Chief Constable of Northumbria Police* (1996) *The Times,* March 28, CA, the Court of Appeal qualified the principle of public policy immunity in the case of the police themselves. The plaintiffs had supplied the police with confidential information which could help to identify the driver of a vehicle which had hit and killed a police officer when he had tried to stop it. The information was contained in a document including the plaintiffs' names. Although the police were aware that the persons allegedly involved in the accident might be of a violent disposition, the papers were left in a police vehicle and stolen when the vehicle was broken into. The persons alleged to have been concerned with the previous incident learnt of the information including the role of the plaintiffs and the latter were subsequently threatened with violence and arson (setting fire to property), being forced to give up their business running a public house. They sued the police for negligence. The Court of Appeal held that the police *were* capable of owing a duty of care in negligence in this situation. The normal public policy immunity of the police had to be weighed against the counterbalancing public policy that people giving information to the police had to be protected and encouraged to come forward without fear of risk of their identity becoming known to suspects or associates - following *Elguzouli-Daf (supra)* where the CPS was said to be able to be under a duty of care when voluntarily assuming responsibility towards an accused. All aspects of public policy should therefore be viewed in the round and consequently it was at least arguable that the general immunity did not apply.

3. The Fire Service

There are two cases, decided within a few weeks of each other, which seem to provide diametrically opposed authority.

In *Church of Jesus Christ of Latter-Day Saints (Great Britain) v. Yorkshire Fire and Civil Defence Authority* (1996) *The Times,*

May 9, a fire started on the plaintiff's premises one night and the defendant fire brigade was called. The defendants were unable to locate all of the water hydrants to be used in fighting the fire and those which were found failed to work, so that water had to be obtained from over half a mile away involving considerable delay. The building was destroyed. The plaintiffs alleged that the defendants had negligently failed to carry out regular inspections and repairs to the fire hydrants, one of which had become hidden by vegetation. The defendants claimed public policy immunity akin to that of the police.

Deputy High Court Judge William Crawford, QC, held that it would be contrary to public policy and interest for the fire service generally to be open to claims in negligence in respect of its fire fighting activities, including the provision of water and rescue operations. As with the police, the fire brigade was a true emergency service and to allow such claims would lead to distractions detrimental to its proper functioning and to potentially massive financial burdens unreasonably to be discharged by the taxpayer, whereas it was for the individual to insure his property against fire rather than for the community to bear the cost (nor was there a private action for breach of statutory duty under the Fire Services Act 1947: see *infra,* ch.10).

However, in *Capital and Counties plc v. Hampshire County Council* (1996) *The Times,* April 26, Judge Richard Havery, QC, sitting on official referee's business, appeared to reach the opposite conclusion. The plaintiff's premises were destroyed by fire when the defendant's fire officer at the scene ordered the water sprinkler system in the building to be shut off, having negligently concluded that it was no longer required or desirable. The Judge held the defendant liable for breach of the duty of care in negligence. He declined to accept that the fire service was in the same position as the police and that they enjoyed the same public policy immunity from negligence as the police:

- decisions made on site in fighting fires were entirely operational and did not require assessment of priorities of allocation of resources between one fire and another;
- the fire brigade's exclusive operational control was a factor against public policy immunity; and
- considerations similar to those specifically involved in the investigation and suppression of crime did not apply with anything like the same force to the fire-fighting activities of a fire-brigade, and potential liability was unlikely to lead to fire-fighting being carried on with a defensive frame of mind.

The reasoning in *neither* of the preceding cases is entirely satisfactory. With regard to the first, it is agreed that police and fire service ought to be equated so far as public policy immunity is concerned - yet the deputy Judge seemed to take insufficient account of the fact that the alleged negligence appeared to be purely operational as to proper inspections and repairs (unless this was part of fire brigade policy and use of resources). In the second case, where the breach of duty was even more clearly operational and the Judge's decision on the facts therefore quite correct, he nevertheless denied any public policy similarity between the fire service and the police and, consequently, presumably also that the former would even be immune with regard to policy decisions.

It is submitted accordingly that *Church of Jesus Christ* was correct on principle, but possibly not on application to the operational facts, and that *Capital and Counties* was the right decision on the facts, but somewhat adrift on principles.

The present writer's view is that on public policy the fire service ought to be equated with the police and other public bodies so far as protection against liability for policy discretion is concerned. Operationally however they should be subject to the ordinary duty of care in negligence - although clearly, the standard of care expected of them should be assessed in the light of the particular nature and circumstances of the complaint against them (for example, whether the alleged negligence took place in the course of battling against a dangerous and difficult fire emergency or in the preparations and training and provision made beforehand). At all events it is believed, the defendants in *Church of Jesus Christ* may consider themselves to have been rather fortunate in the court's decision (see further, Appendix).

4. Lawyers involved in litigation

Members of the legal profession, advising generally, owe a duty of care in negligence (*Al-Kandari v. J.R. Brown & Co.* [1988] QB 665). But where they are engaged in, or preparing for, litigation, lawyers - whether barristers or solicitors (see Courts and Legal Services Act 1990, s.62) - are under no duty of care towards their client as to the proper presentation of the case (*Rondel v. Worsley* [1969] 1 AC 191). They cannot be sued in negligence. The reasons are practical: lawyers might otherwise only take on the less complex cases; proceedings in which lawyers were found to be negligent would themselves have to be relitigated; and lawyers are under various duties towards the court to provide information or to present arguments in a particular form in the interests of the efficient administration of justice, in which case, a client who considered that this would not benefit his case would otherwise be able to sue his lawyer (*Rondel v. Worsley*). In *Rondel v. Worsley*, a person convicted of causing grievous bodily harm was unable to sue his barrister, who had failed to point out to the jury that the accused had carried out the attack with his teeth and hands, rather than - presumably, more seriously - with a knife.

The immunity from suit even extends to pre-trial work where this is closely connected with the litigation (*Saif Ali v. Sydney Mitchell & Co.* [1980] AC 198) - although, obviously, the line will not always be easy to draw.

At least, however, in these cases of no duty of care it is possible for courts to make an order that a lawyer should pay his client's wasted costs (Supreme Court Act 1981, s.51; *Antonelli v. Wade Gery Farr* (1993) *The Times*, December 29).

Judges, too, and arbitrators, enjoy immunity from negligence claims in the course of their office. The remedy is to appeal against their judgment (*Hunter v. Chief Constable of West Midlands* [1982] AC 529).

As a matter of public policy, court witnesses are also under no duty of care. *Expert* witnesses are in the same position in respect of work done and opinions given for use in the proceedings, whereas, their advice or report on the strength of a case prior to the litigation stage falls outside this immunity (*Palmer v. Durnford Ford* [1992] 2 All ER 122).

5. Partners in Crime

It would seem that people engaged in committing a common criminal offence may not owe each other a duty of care in negligence (*Ashton v. Turner* [1981] QB 137 - defendant driving away a getaway car from a burglary which the plaintiff and defendant had committed).

6. Miscellaneous Cases

There are a number of specific situations in which defendants have been held to owe no duty of care as a matter of policy, including:

- duty of examiners towards students, for negligent marking of university examination papers (*Thorne v. University of London* [1966] 2 QB 237);
- duty of schools to insure children against injury other than by negligence (*Van Oppen v. Clerk to the Bedford Charity Trustees* [1989] 2 All ER 389);
- duty of doctors towards a child born disabled, to have advised a mother with German measles to undergo an abortion (wrongful life action) (*McKay v. Essex Area Health Authority* [1982] QB 1166, and now Congenital Disabilities (Civil Liability) Act 1976, s.1(2)(b)), although, there is a duty of care towards the mother herself (wrongful birth);
- duty of an employer to ensure that employees' property is not stolen from the workplace (*Deyong v. Shenburn* [1946] KB 227);
- duty of a doctor performing an unsuccessful

vasectomy operation on a man, towards a future sexual partner of the man, not known of by the doctor at the time of the operation and who became pregnant (*Goodwill v. British Pregnancy Advisory Service* (1996) *The Times,* January 29, CA - compare *Thake v. Maurice* [1986] QB 644, where the doctor was liable to the man's wife, because he had advised both the man and his wife);

- duty of the Ministry of Defence towards the plaintiff soldier in a British army heavy artillery regiment whose hearing was damaged as a result of his commander's alleged negligence when firing a shell from a howitzer gun at the Iraqis during the Gulf War (*Mulcahy v. Ministry of Defence* (1996) *The Times,* February 27, CA).

However, in *Walpole v. Partridge and Wilson* [1994] 1 All ER 385, the Court of Appeal held that an action against solicitors for negligently failing to file an appeal in sufficient time against the plaintiff pig farmer's criminal conviction under the animal health legislation, would not be contrary to public policy as an abuse of the court's process through being a disguised attack upon a final court judgment - if only because the judgment in question, having been open to an appeal within the proper time, had to that extent *not* been a final judgment.

Such, then, is the first element of the tort of negligence: duty of care, according to the three-stage process in *Caparo v. Dickman* as here chosen to be presented, developed from the original two-stage test in *Anns* (foreseeability and public policy):

- reasonable foreseeability;
- no judicial policy reasons against and no absence of relationship of proximity;
- no public policy reasons against.

(Recall that under the *orthodox formula*, the three-stage test provides for (i) reasonable foreseeability, (ii) relationship of proximity, (iii) fair, just and reasonable on juridical policy.)

Once duty of care is held to exist on this basis, the second element of the tort of negligence has to be satisfied: the *breach* of that duty.

1. Duty of care.
2. Breach of the duty of care.
3. Causing damage.

Further reading:

Barker, "Unreliable Assumptions in the Modern Law of Negligence" (1993) 109 *Law Quarterly Review* 461.

Beale, "Valuer's Negligence and Falls in the Property Market" (1995) 111 *Law Quarterly Review* 571.

Brazier, *Street on Torts*, 9th ed, 1993 (Butterworth & Co., London): chs.11 and 12.

Cane, "Economic Loss in Tort: Is the Pendulum Out of Control?" (1989) 52 *Modern Law Review* 200.

Fleming, "Requiem for *Anns*" (1990) 106 *Law Quarterly Review* 525.

Fleming, J.G., *The Law of Torts*, 8th ed, 1992 (The Law Book Company, Sydney): ch.8.

Hepple, B.A. and Matthews, M.H., *Tort: Cases and Materials*, 4th ed, 1991 (Butterworth & Co., London): chs.2, 3, 4, 5 and 10.

Heuston, R.F.V. and Buckley, R.A., *Salmond and Heuston on The Law of Torts*, 20th ed, 1992 (Sweet & Maxwell, London).

Howarth, "Negligence after *Murphy*: Time to Re-Think" (1991) *Cambridge Law Journal* 58.

Howarth, D., *Textbook on Tort*, 1995 (Butterworth & Co., London): chs. 2, 3, 5 and 6.

Jones, M.A., *Textbook on Torts*, 4th ed, 1993 (Blackstone, London): ch.2.

Markesinis and Deakin, "The Random Element of their Lordships' Infallible Judgment: An Economic and Comparative Analysis of the Tort of Negligence from *Anns* to *Murphy* (1992) 55 *Modern Law Review* 619.

O'Dair, "*Murphy v. Brentwood District Council*: A House with Firm Foundations?" (1991) 54 *Modern Law Review* 561.

Rodger, "Lord Macmillan's Speech in *Donoghue v. Stevenson*" (1992) 108 *Law Quarterly Review* 236.

Rogers, W.V.H., *Winfield and Jolowicz on Tort*, 14th ed, 1994 (Sweet & Maxwell, London), chs.5 and 11.

Smith and Burns, "*Donoghue v. Stevenson*: The Not So Golden Anniversary" (1983) 46 *Modern Law Review* 147.

Stanton, K.M., *The Modern Law of Tort*, 1994 (The Law Book Company, Sydney): chs.10 and 16.

Stapleton, "Duty of Care and Economic Loss: A Wider Agenda" (1991) 107 *Law Quarterly Review* 249.

Stapleton, "Duty of Care: Peripheral Parties and Alternative Opportunities for Deterrence" (1995) 111 *Law Quarterly Review* 301.

Stevens, "*Hedley Byrne v. Heller*: Judicial Creativity and Doctrinal Possibility" (1964) 27 *Modern Law Review* 121.

Tan, "Nervous Shock: Bystander Witnessing a Catastrophe" (1995) 111 *Law Quarterly Review* 48.

Trindade, "Nervous Shock and Negligent Conduct" (1996) 112 *Law*

Quarterly Review 22.
Wallace, Duncan, "Beyond Repair" (1991) 107 *Law Quarterly Review* 228.
Wallace, Duncan, "No Somersault after *Murphy*: New Zealand follows Canada" (1995) 111 *Law Quarterly Review* 285.
Weir, T., *A Casebook on Tort*, 7th ed, 1992 (Sweet & Maxwell, London): chs.11 and 12.

Chapter 6

Breach of the Duty of Care. The Standard of Care Required in Negligence

Once it has been established that the defendant *owed* a duty of care towards the plaintiff as someone likely to be injured or to suffer damage *if the defendant did not act with reasonable care* (recall Lord Atkin in *Donoghue v. Stevenson, supra*, p.27), the obvious next question is: *did the defendant act with reasonable care?* Because, if he did not, he will be held to have been in breach of his duty of care towards the plaintiff.

The problem is: how is it to be decided whether the defendant acted with "reasonable"care? What is "reasonable"? What is the standard of care required of people in the position of the defendant? How far are they expected to go in order to safeguard against foreseeable possible harm to others?

Should those who know that a particular road is difficult for pedestrians to cross, drive at 10 miles an hour, or 15, or 25? Should they attach loudspeakers to the outside of their vehicles warning people to get out of the way? Should doctors carrying out difficult operations employ large teams of assistants to take over from them when they become tired? Should a baker pay special staff to check and to re-check that each loaf of bread has nothing harmful in it?

How far are we expected to go in order to ensure that nobody is harmed by our activities?

Again, what is the *standard of care*?

The truth of course is that the standard of care - reasonable care - is merely what the courts decide it to be on the facts of a particular case, in the light of certain established principles held to apply; and that those decisions will be carried out by the courts mindful of the serious economic effects of requiring various measures to be adopted as part of the standard of care and of the need to balance safety in the community with the flexible and tolerable conduct of ordinary life (see Mustill, J in *Thompson v. Smith Ship Repairers Ltd* [1984] QB 405). As always in the law of tort, policy - social, judicial and economic - has played a large part in shaping the courts' decisions in the area of standard of care in negligence. If duty of care were to be described as the *engine* of the negligence mechanism, starting off the entire process of liability and recovery, standard of care would have to be regarded as the *steering*, determining the extent and direction of the proceedings.

How, then, do the courts decide upon standard of care in a particular case?

1. The General Rule: Objective Standard of the Reasonable Man

In *Blyth v. Birmingham Waterworks Co.* (1856) 11 Exch. 781 at p.784, the Judge, Alderson, B, described negligence in the following manner: "Negligence is the omission to do something which a reasonable man, guided upon those considerations which ordinarily regulate the conduct of human affairs, would do, or doing something which a prudent and reasonable man would not do." Subsequently too, of course, in *Donoghue v. Stevenson* itself, Lord Atkin was to return to the theme in his famous statement (*supra*, ch.5, p.27): "... You must take reasonable care to avoid acts or omissions ..." - in the course of pronouncing upon the existence of a general duty of care in negligence.

That is the standard of care: the reasonable man. What would a reasonable person have done in all the circumstances?

It will immediately be understood of course that the concept of the reasonable man is simply a mechanism for Judges to be able to reach a decision, consistent with certain established principles, as to the standard of care which *they* believe the defendant ought to have exercised, and thereupon to justify their findings on the ground that the standard was *reasonable*.

Whether you call him the reasonable man, or the man on the Clapham omnibus, or the ordinary Joe, the reasonable man is really the invisible man: he does not exist other than in the mind of the Judge hearing the case, and in those of Judges who decided earlier cases - subject to altered social or legal perceptions of justice.

Accordingly, all that can be done in order to try to put some flesh on the bones of the reasonable man, is to examine the factors which courts have traditionally taken into account in arriving at their decisions on reasonableness, and the principles developed, with a view to calculating what their findings are likely to be in future situations.

2. Principles and Factors Determining Reasonableness

a. Standard objective, not subjective

This principle is fundamental. The standard is not *reduced* in order to take into account the particular disability of the defendant (although, it may be *increased* if the defendant is expected to possess certain extra skills, as will later be seen) (*Glasgow Corporation v. Muir* [1943] 2 AC 448). In *The Lady Gwendolen* [1965] P.294, the defendants were brewers using a ship to carry beer from Ireland to Liverpool who negligently collided with the plaintiffs' ship in foggy weather. They were held liable according to the standard of reasonable shipowners and not merely of reasonable (less knowledgeable) brewers hiring such a ship.

Thus, if a blind man drives a car, he will be expected to show the same degree of care as a man with full sight - and not merely the standard which could reasonably be expected of a blind man! Consequently, in *Nettleship v. Weston* [1971] 2 QB 691, the defendant, who was a mere learner driver, was nevertheless held liable for injuries to her instructor caused by her negligent driving. The Court of Appeal - no doubt mindful of the fact that the defendant was covered by compulsory liability insurance - held that the standard of care expected of a learner was the same as that required of an experienced driver, even if the defendant had acted to the best of her abilities; a variable standard of care would have led to great uncertainty. In that case, Salmon, LJ dissented on the ground that the *relationship* of learner-*instructor* or learner-*passenger* reduced the standard of care to that which could reasonably be expected of a learner. Yet, such relationship and knowledge of the defendant's inexperience on the part of the plaintiff probably goes more to the possible defence of consent than to absence of liability in the first place.

Similarly, an inexperienced doctor must reach the standard of an ordinary, competent doctor - no allowance is made for his inexperience (unless of course he is engaged in a less responsible capacity, specifically because of and taking into account his inexperience) (*Wilsher v. Essex Area Health Authority* [1986] 3 All ER 801). If he does not know what to do, he should request assistance. In *Roberts v. Ramsbottom* [1980] 1 All ER 7, even a defendant driver suffering a stroke which caused him to knock down the plaintiff was held liable according to the standard of the reasonable ordinary driver not affected by illness.

On the other hand, plaintiffs themselves are evidently expected to endure a certain degree of inconvenience, even damage, depending upon the circumstances of life. In *Hunter v. London Docklands Development Corporation* (joined with *Hunter v. Canary Wharf Ltd*) (1995) *The Times,* October 13, CA), the plaintiff householder sought damages for negligence through dust caused by the construction of a road by the defendants. The court held that although such a claim in respect of dust was possible provided that it had resulted in physical injury or damage to property, for example, to the plaintiff's carpets (see below, p.265), nevertheless, *some* dust was an inevitable incident of urban life, so that what was required for a successful action was damage from *excessive* dust and even after a reasonable amount of *household cleaning* by the plaintiffs.

b. Higher standard where defendants are expected to possess special skills

Where the defendant is carrying out an activity requiring a specialist skill, his required standard of care is above that which could be expected of a reasonable non-specialist called upon to perform the same task.

The main judgment in this field is that of McNair, J in *Bolam v. Friern Hospital Management Committee* [1957] 2 All ER 118 at pp.121 and 122, of which the following two elements should be noted in particular:

- the standard of an ordinary, reasonably competent specialist is enough - you do not have to be as good as the best in the field (nor keep up with *all* the latest developments - for example, in *Crawford v. Charing Cross Hospital* (1953) *The Times,* December 8, the defendant anaesthetist was held not liable for injuries he could have avoided had he read an article on the subject in the leading medical journal published six month earlier); and
- if there are different bodies of opinion in the field, the specialist is not liable if he acts in accordance with one and not the others, provided that the one he adopts is accepted by a responsible body of practitioners in the area.

This is known as "the *Bolam* test" and is frequently applied in medical negligence cases. In *Bolam* itself, there were two bodies of medical opinion concerning the use of relevant drugs when administering electric shock therapy to patients: one was in favour, but the other was against on the ground that the effect of the drugs could be to cause injuries to patients who were not restrained during the treatment. The patient's action failed, because in spite of the case against the use of such drugs, there was equally a responsible body of opinion which upheld their usefulness. Thus, in *Maynard v. West Midlands Regional Health Authority* [1984] 1 WLR 634, at p.638, Lord Scarman commented: "Differences of opinion and practice exist, and will always exist, in the medical as in other professions. There is seldom any one answer exclusive of all others to problems of professional judgment. A court may prefer one body of opinion to the other; but that is no basis for a conclusion of negligence."

Similarly, in *X (Minors) v. Bedfordshire County Council etc* [1995] 3 All ER 353, HL, (*supra,* p.223) Lord Browne-Wilkinson commented: "Psychologists hold themselves out as having special skills and they are, in my judgment, like any other professional bound both to possess such skills and to exercise them carefully. Of course, the test in *Bolam* ... will apply to them, ie, they are only bound to exercise the ordinary skill of a competent psychologist and if they can show that they acted in accordance with the accepted views of some reputable psychologist at the relevant time they will have discharged the duty of care, even if other psychologists would have adopted a different view. In the context of advice on the treatment of dyslexia, a subject on which views have changed over the years, this may be an important factor (p.393)."

In practice, what this means is that if the defendant doctor can find a colleague as an expert witness to back him, he will have met the standard of care, given that the requirement of a *responsible body* of supporting opinion is extremely vague and presumably only excludes that which is not a "body" (just one supporter?) and bodies which are not responsible (a group of inexperienced supporters?). So, in *Whitehouse v. Jordan* [1981] 1 All ER 267, a doctor specializing in childbirth, who delivered a baby with forceps rather than by carrying out a caesarian operation when the mother experienced difficulties with the birth owing to the smallness of her pelvis, was held not liable for brain damage caused to the baby, because expert evidence was provided in support of the doctor's decision. *Bolam* was applied. Furthermore, it would seem that *Bolam* does not just operate in relation to medical treatment itself, but also as to common practice on disclosure of risk or not to plaintiffs (*Sidaway v. Bethlem Royal Hospital Governors* [1985] AC 871, followed in *Gold v. Haringey Health Authority* [1987] 2 All ER 888 - although, see below, *Newell v. Goldenberg* [1995] 6 Medical Law Review 371).

Not surprisingly, *Bolam* has met with some criticism for encouraging professionals to "stick together" and to replace the courts as the arbiters of standards. In addition, attention has already been drawn to the difficulty over the meaning of "responsible body" of opinion. Would the test even include a practice favoured by a clear *minority* of experts, against the *majority?* In *Newell v. Goldenberg* (at p.374), Mantell, J considered that any medical body of opinion against warning that a vasectomy operation could reverse itself was not reasonable nor responsible. The reason? Because if "a couple believe that the operation is foolproof and pregnancy does occur, then it is bound to excite suspicion in the mind of the male partner or husband ... with consequent marital disharmony or tension"! - although, in any event, even if the opinion had been held to be responsible, the Judge would not regard this as sufficient if the defendant doctor himself did not usually follow it (see *infra*).

The courts do not allow defendants to have things all their own way, however. It remains in the courts' power to hold the practice of an entire profession or what is thought to be a responsible body thereof to be insufficient (*Lloyd's Bank Ltd v. E.B. Savory & Co.* [1933] AC 201). For example, in *Re Herald of Free Enterprise* (1987) *The Independent,* December 18, the court held that the practice of failing to check whether ferry doors were shut after setting sail represented a general failure of the industry to meet the required standard of care. Furthermore, although, as seen, professionals are not expected always to be totally up-to-date, they will be liable if they have fallen completely behind the times in their practices (*Bolam,* at p.122): there is no equality between two opinions when one is current and the other completely outdated and discredited (unless of course still supported by a "responsible body").

Finally, too, in relation to the connected duty to *warn* patients of risks, in the case of *Newell v. Goldenberg* [1995] 6 Med. LR 371, Mantell, J placed a restriction (see *supra*) upon the *Bolam* principle, to the effect that it was unable to be relied upon where a defendant admitted that his failure to warn, even if consistent with a responsible body of medical opinion, was contrary *to his own* usual practice. In that case itself, the defendant doctor was held to be negligent, not in the manner of carrying out a vasectomy operation, but for failing to warn the patient and his wife that there existed a one in 2,300 risk that the operation would reverse itself over the years, which it did, resulting in the birth of a third child to the plaintiffs. The defendant admitted that he normally warned people of this, but that he had omitted to do so in this case by an oversight. The Judge held that in these circumstances, the defendant could not rely on *Bolam* in any event, regardless of whether there was a responsible body of medical opinion in his favour (although, damages were not large, and were limited to distress, because the plaintiffs would have gone ahead with the operation in any event even if they had been warned). "The *Bolam* principle provides a defence for those who lag behind the times. It cannot serve those who know better" (p.374).

c. Learners

As previously seen from *Nettleship v. Weston* and *Wilsher v. Essex Area Health Authority*, where learners and trainees and generally the inexperienced engage in an activity (eg, driving) or fill a post (eg, as a doctor) which raises a certain level of expectation associated with their function, in assessing the standard of care, no allowance is made for their lack of knowledge and status. It would be a different matter if their activities or duties were limited to those regarded as suitable to their restricted knowledge, or if they specifically held themselves out as possessing a limited set of skills (for example, as an *amateur*) and no more. Thus, in *Phillips v. Whiteley* [1938] 1 All ER 566, the defendant jeweller was held not liable, when a person whose ears had been pierced fell ill with blood poisoning. He had done all that could reasonably be expected of a jeweller - washed his instruments in disinfectant and held them over a flame - and could not be expected to display the skills of a surgeon.

d. Age

Children are not frequently sued, so that there is very little authority as to the effects of childhood on the standard of care.

There seems to be a widespread view that children - whatever age that precisely denotes - should be judged according to the standards of a reasonable child of that age (*McEllistrum v. Etches* (1956) 6 DLR (2d) 1). Thus, in *McHale v. Watson* [1966] ALR 513, the defendant 12-year old boy struck the plaintiff nine-year old girl in the eye when he aimed a steel rod at a post from which it bounced onto the girl standing nearby. The boy was held not to have breached the standards of the ordinary 12-year old.

This statement of the rule may be too simplistic however. It seems acceptable where the child is doing something which children *normally do,* whether confined exclusively to childhood or not, for example, throwing stones at bottles on a wall, playing football, running about. But were a child to be involved in an activity normally reserved for adults, such as driving a car or flying an aeroplane, the child who steals the car and takes it for a drive must surely be judged according to the standard of the ordinary, competent adult driver. (Parents are not automatically or "vicariously" (*infra,* ch.11) liable for their childrens' negligence - only for failing to meet the standard of careful supervision and control which can reasonably be expected of a parent, taking into account the need to strike a balance between freedom and protection for the child: *Porter v. Barking & Dagenham London Borough Council* (1990) *The Times,* April 9).

e. Health

The position of sick defendants should arguably be analogous with that of childhood: no reduction in the standard of care if they are engaging in activities carried on by the rest of the population and not limited to the sick and disabled.

f. Situations requiring quick thinking

Where a person has to act in an emergency, or is involved in a fast-moving activity requiring quickness of thought and response, such as, for example, sportsmen or the police in a car chase, it would seem that the standard required is only that which can reasonably be expected of them in those circumstances. How could motor racing drivers in the Monaco grand prix possibly be asked to exercise the same degree of care and to travel at the same speed as a driver on an ordinary city street? They might never finish the race - and if they did, it would not be much of a spectacle. Thus, in *Wooldridge v. Sumner* [1963] 2 QB 43, in which a photographer attending a horse show was injured by one of the horses being ridden in the competition, and the defendant's failure to control his horse was held not to be negligent but a mere error of judgment, the Court of Appeal indicated that a lower standard of care than usual could be expected of participants in the heat of contest - even if the court did perhaps appear to overdo the point by intimating that recklessness would be necessary for the standard to be breached. On the other hand, in *Smolden v. Whitworth* (1996) *The Times,* April 23, the referee of a junior rugby match was held to have breached his duty of care to exercise a tight control over the game so as to prevent unnecessary injury to the plaintiff who was playing in one of the teams.

g. Practice

Common practice is strong evidence against negligence (all the more so in the case of specialist skills, according to the "*Bolam* principle", see *supra*), yet not conclusive, if itself shown to be negligent, as seen earlier (*Bank of Montreal v. Dominion Gresham Guarantee & Casualty Co.* [1930] AC 659). Conversely, non-compliance with common practice is evidence of negligence, although again, not conclusive: for example, in *Brown v. Rolls Royce Ltd* [1960] 1 WLR 210, the defendants provided washing facilities for employees, but not also creams usually supplied by other employers in the industry - however, although the plaintiff contracted dermatitis, the defendants were held not liable, because it was not proved that the plaintiff would not have suffered in the same way had the cream been provided.

In assessing common practice, courts have to decide what is the appropriate comparison to be made. In *Knight v. Home Office* [1990] 3 All ER 237, the court held that the common practice for supervising a violent prisoner with suicidal tendencies in a remand prison was that of such prison establishment (observation at not less than 15 minute intervals) and not of a psychiatric hospital (continuous observation), so that the prison service was not liable for breach of negligence duty of care when the prisoner committed suicide in his prison cell.

h. Miscellaneous matters relating to the activity, to be balanced together: extent of the risk, likely seriousness of the injury, usefulness of the activity and practicability and expense of precautions

How far must a person go in order to reduce the risk when he should foresee that a plaintiff *might* be injured were a certain sequence of events to occur and he is consequently under a duty of care towards the latter?

What is the level of that duty? What is the standard of care?

The courts *balance* a number of miscellaneous factors:

i. Extent of risk. If the risk is relatively low, the measures required to be taken to safeguard against damage are correspondingly reduced. In *Bolton v. Stone* [1951] AC 850, the plaintiff was injured by a cricket ball when he was standing in a quiet road about 18 metres from the cricket ground. The batsman was positioned about 70 metres from the boundary and there was an eight metre high fence. Cricket balls had only left the ground on six occasions in 30 years. The House of Lords held that the standard of care was not breached: the risk was not so substantial as to require the defendant to have taken greater precautions, and what was done was enough. Lord Radcliffe (at p.868) stated that the law of negligence was concerned "less with what is fair than with what is culpable."

This may be contrasted with cases where the risk was known to be higher, requiring further measures to prevent damage, and in which the defendant has consequently been held liable, such as:

(a) *Hilder v. Associated Portland Cement Manufacturers Ltd* [1961] 1 WLR 1434 - owners of land were held liable for allowing children to play football on it, when a ball was kicked onto an adjoining road 13 metres away and killed a motor cyclist, because the danger was there for all to see;

(b) *Haley v. London Electricity Board* [1965] AC 778 - defendants were liable when a blind man fell down a hole in the pavement which they had dug, because warnings were suitable for full-sighted pedestrians but not for the blind and there were sufficient numbers of blind people in London as to require special measures to be taken in order to protect them from this greater risk of serious accident;

(c) *Miller v. Jackson* [1977] QB 966 - defendants were held liable for hitting cricket balls out of the ground over the high fence eight or nine times a season.

So, the greater the risk, the higher the standard of care.

It is interesting to see how risk assessment operates together with the *Bolam* principle. In *Sidaway v. Governors of Bethlem Royal and Maudsley Hospitals* [1985] 2 WLR 480, the alleged negligence consisted in not informing a patient of a one per cent risk of paralysis from an operation. The House of Lords held that such a risk was too small to require the patient to be informed, according to a responsible body of medical opinion. A 10 per cent risk would have been quite a different matter, however -

and even a responsible body of medical opinion saying it was too small for a warning might not have been accepted by the court as justifying so big a risk. English courts have in fact shown themselves to be relatively lacking in support of patients' rights to be warned in this respect, whereas, in the Australian case of *Rogers v. Whittaker* (1992) Aust. Torts Rep. 81 on the other hand, a one in 14,000 risk of blindness from an operation was held to justify a warning. Nevertheless, in the recent English case of *Newell v. Goldenberg (supra,* p.246) a one in 2,300 risk of a vasectomy operation reversing itself was considered to be worthy of a warning.

ii. *Likely seriousness of damage.* Greater precautions are necessary to prevent potential loss of a limb than a scratch on the hand; and the standard is assessed in relation to the plaintiff individually. In *Paris v. Stepney Borough Council* [1951] AC 367, employers were held liable for failing to provide the plaintiff employee with protective goggles; although this was not done for employees in general, the defendants knew that he only had one eye, so that if an accident occurred he would be left totally blind, which is what happened. The seriousness of the injury for that particular employee was greater than for the rest: for Lord Simonds (at p.375) the risk of a greater injury was as significant as a greater risk of injury.

iii. *Social utility of the act causing damage.* "If all the trains in this country were restricted to a speed of five miles an hour, there would be fewer accidents, but our national life would be intolerably slowed down. The purpose to be served, if sufficiently important, justifies the assumption of abnormal risk" (*Daborn v. Bath Tramways* [1946] 2 All ER 333, *per* Asquith, LJ). Risk must be balanced against the social usefulness of the activity in question, such as, for example, where police cars have to chase criminals, and ambulances and fire engines have to reach accidents and fires - although, seemingly, not where a fire engine is driven through a red traffic light (*Ward v. London County Council* [1938] 2 All ER 341), presumably because the potential risk from this is greater than the damage from failing to fight the fire a minute or two earlier. In *Watt v. Hertfordshire County Council* [1954] 1 WLR 835, the plaintiff fireman was injured when heavy lifting equipment fell on him as he was helping to rescue a woman trapped under a vehicle - the equipment had been loaded onto an ordinary lorry because the special lorry was unavailable. The Court of Appeal held the defendant fire service not liable, because the danger to the woman justified the risk - it would have been otherwise had the objective been merely commercial and the motive to earn profits.

iv. *Practicality and expense of precautions.* Courts will try to take a common sense view: small reductions in risk at enormous expense, and large reductions at little cost, lead to the obvious conclusions - no liability and liability respectively - if not carried out. For the rest, it is a matter of degree. In *Latimer v. AEC Ltd* [1953] AC 643, the House of Lords held that a factory was not liable towards an employee who slipped on the factory floor which had become wet and slippery through heavy rainfall - the defendants had done all that could reasonably be expected of them in trying to cover the floor with sawdust, and the only alternative would have been to shut down the factory and risk losing business. The courts therefore balance cost and effectiveness of preventative measures against each other. If the damage is caused by a faulty design, courts are all the more aware of how serious it would be if the manufacturer were forced to withdraw a product or to incorporate new safety features (*Wyngrove v. Scottish Omnibuses Ltd*, 1966 SC (HL) 47). But if expensive steps are adjudged to be necessary, the *personal* shortage of resources of the defendant will not provide an excuse for failing to take such precautions. All such factors, accordingly - risk, cost, social utility, practicality - must be weighed together in order to achieve justice on the facts. In *Withers v. Perry Chain Co.* [1961] 1 WLR 1314, the defendant employers did all they could to put the plaintiff employee to work on activities not involving contact with grease to which she was allergic, but nevertheless she still caught dermatitis. The defendants were held not to have breached the standard of care, because the only other action left to them would have been to dismiss the plaintiff, which would have been unwelcome to all concerned.

v. Knowledge of the risk. This is, of course, required. A defendant cannot reasonably be expected to safeguard against risks which are not known of *at the time.* In *Roe v. Minister of Health* [1954] 2 QB 66, the plaintiff was paralysed while undergoing an operation, because the anaesthetic became contaminated by disinfectant. At the time, in 1947, it was not known that anaesthetics in glass containers stored in disinfectant could be affected in this way, because tiny cracks in the glass were unable to be detected. The defendants were held not liable. Denning, LJ (at p.84) said that the court should not look at the 1947 accident through 1954 spectacles, at which later time the danger was known.

So it is, therefore, that all such principles and factors are to be taken into account and *balanced together* in determining the standard of care and whether the duty of care has been breached.

An example of the process in practice was *Walker v. Northumberland County Council* (1994) NLJ 1659, [1995] IRLR 35, where the plaintiff, in his fifties, was employed by the defendant council as a child-care officer from 1974 to 1987. During that period the number of child abuse cases in his area rose from 15 to 88 and he suffered a nervous breakdown of his health owing to stress at work, crying uncontrollably. He had repeatedly had his requests for extra staff turned down by his employers. Six months after returning to work, the plaintiff fell ill again, because the defendants failed to reduce his workload significantly and he had to leave his employment. He claimed breach of a duty of care to provide reasonable assistance so as not to affect the plaintiff's health in a very stressful and sensitive job. The High Court held the employers liable: the plaintiff, following his first nervous breakdown, was a man distinctly more vulnerable to psychiatric damage than might otherwise have been the case; the risk in the case of the plaintiff that if he suffered a further crisis, it would create serious and lasting damage which would be likely to put an end to his career, was substantial; and the defendants knew of all these circumstances and yet did nothing to provide appropriate assistance in his tasks. The risk to his health, therefore, was quite foreseeable. Thus, it was all there: additional risk, serious consequences and knowledge. (Subsequently, the plaintiff accepted a payment of £175,000 in settlement of the claim: see *The Times* newspaper (1996) April 27, p.6.)

3. Method of Proving Breach of Duty

Problems of proof of negligence arise both in the case of *causation (infra,* ch.7) - that is, whether the defendant's actions actually caused the damage - and *breach of duty of care* - that is, whether the defendant behaved in such a manner or not as to satisfy the required standards.

In either case, the *burden* of proof is on the plaintiff, and the civil *standard* of proof is a balance of probabilities - although, the balance is likely to be harder to *tip* in the case of defendants who are professionals with complex procedures and high levels of skill (*Dwyer v. Rodrick* (1983) *The Times,* November 12).

There is an exception to this under the Civil Evidence Act 1968, s.11(1), whereby a person who is convicted of a crime - for example, dangerous driving (*Wauchope v. Mordecai* [1970] 1 WLR 317) - then has the burden of disproving his guilt in any civil proceedings - for example, for negligent driving - difficult, given previous satisfaction of the criminal standard of proof against him *beyond all reasonable doubt.*

In the case of both causation and circumstances of breach of duty, the courts are able to assist plaintiffs who may not know the precise details of the defendant's activities, through operation of the doctrine of *res ipsa loquitur* (meaning the thing speaks for itself).

a. Conditions for res ipsa loquitur

The basic meaning of *res ipsa loquitur* is that by its very nature, the occurrence could not have taken place other than through the defendant's negligence and failure to meet the required standard of care.

Conditions for operation of *res ipsa loquitur* were set out by Erle, CJ in *Scott v. London & St Katherine Docks Co.* (1865) 3 H & C 596, at p.601:

- the cause or circumstances are unknown;
- the defendant was in control of the situation;
- the accident was such as in the ordinary course of things would not have happened had the defendant used proper care and;
- the defendant has no other explanation.

Circumstances unknown

Res ipsa loquitur is only available when the *actual* cause or circumstances of the damage are not known (*Barkway v. South Wales Transport Co. Ltd* [1950] 1 All ER 392).

Defendant in control

It is essential that the defendant or his servants are shown to have been in control of the situation if *res ipsa loquitur* is to apply. Possible intervention by a third party, authorized or unauthorized, will destroy its operation. In *Easson v. London & North Eastern Railway Co.* [1944] KB 421, a passenger fell out of a train door in the course of a journey from Edinburgh to London. *Res ipsa loquitur* did not apply. At the time of the accident, the train was seven miles from its last stopping place and it was impossible to say whether an employee of the defendant railway company had left the door open or whether it was another passenger who had done this - the situation was not continuously under the sole control of the defendant railway company and its servants. On the other hand, in *Gee v. Metropolitan Railway* (1873) LR 8 QB 161 the plaintiff fell out of an underground train only a short time after it had left the station and the defendant was held liable.

Accident would not normally have happened without defendant's negligence and defendant cannot explain

There must be no innocent explanation other than the defendant's negligence.

In *Scott v. London & St Katherine Docks Co.* itself, the criteria of *res ipsa loquitur* were, as seen, set out, when bags of flour fell out of a warehouse window onto the plaintiff's head. Could it have been a puff of wind which blew over those heavy bags? It does not take much effort for it to be concluded that in the absence of a hurricane or divine intervention, the bags most probably were being handled without sufficient care. Similarly, in *Chapronière v. Mason*

(1905) 21 TLR 633, there was a stone in a bun delivered from the manufacturer - how could it have got there? Again, in *Mahon v. Osborne* [1939] 2 KB 14, a hospital patient died when a swab was left in his body after an operation - could there possibly have been an innocent explanation?

In the case of *products*, it should be noted that under the Consumer Protection Act 1987, a consumer can now sue for a defect in a *product* in certain circumstances without having to show negligence at all, so that *res ipsa loquitur* is then not necessary. Furthermore, courts are less willing to apply the doctrine in medical cases (because of diverse possible explanations and effects on medical insurance: *Hucks v. Cole* (1968) 112 SJ 483), although, in blatant cases - such as *Cassidy v. Ministry of Health* [1951] 2 KB 343, in which the plaintiff went into hospital with two stiff fingers and came out with four - the position would be the same as in non-medical complaints: someone, namely the defendant, must have been negligent.

b. Effects of res ipsa loquitur

The cases reveal two possibilities:

i. *Res ipsa loquitur* reverses the burden of proof. If this is so, the defendant has to prove absence of negligence on the facts, on a balance of probabilities - somewhat difficult in view of the circumstances of application of *res ipsa loquitur*. This derives support from a number of cases. In *Henderson v. Henry E. Jenkins & Sons* [1970] AC 282, in which the plaintiff's husband was killed by an unseen defect in his lorry's braking system, the House of Lords held that since it was not known whether the defendants were responsible, so that *res ipsa loquitur* applied, the defendants had to prove that they had always taken reasonable care to safeguard the lorry against hazards. Yet, they had provided no evidence to this effect. Furthermore, it was held not to be enough that unavoidable latent defect, not due to carelessness of the defendant, was a *possible* explanation. This was not *proof* on a balance of possibilities. Again, in *Ward v. Tesco Stores Ltd* [1976] 1 WLR 810, where the plaintiff slipped on yoghurt spilled on the defendant supermarket's floor, the yoghurt *might* only just have been spilled, so that there was a possible innocent explanation showing absence of negligence - but the defendants were unable to *prove* this and consequently were liable. Proof, therefore, might have been evidence that they had a fast and continuous safety checking system.

ii. *Res ipsa loquitur* raises merely a *prima facie* case of negligence. If this is correct, all that the defendant need do is to provide a *possible* alternative explanation for the occurrence, other than negligence, in which event the plaintiff must prove negligence without the aid of *res ipsa loquitur* - unlikely to be achieved in the circumstances. Support for this comes from *Colvilles Ltd v. Devine* [1969] 1 WLR 475, in which the House of Lords indicated that in order to neutralize *res ipsa loquitur,* the defendant need only produce an explanation of *equal* force to that of *res ipsa loquitur,* without having to exceed the latter: thus, if the balances are equal, the plaintiff loses. So, too, in *Ng Chun Pui v. Lee Chuen Tat* [1988] RTR 298, the Judicial Committee of the Privy Council (of which the decisions have persuasive authority in the United Kingdom), in a case where the defendant's coach skidded across a dual carriageway into a bus on the opposite side of the road, considered that *res ipsa loquitur* did not shift the burden of proof from plaintiff to defendant and only required the latter to answer the *prima facie* inference of negligence, even if unable to prove absence of negligence on a balance of probabilities - succeeded in here by showing that a car had cut in front of the defendant's coach, forcing the driver to swerve in order to avoid it, thereby rebutting the *res ipsa loquitur* inference.

The first approach preceding - reversal of the burden of proof - has been criticized as placing a *res ipsa loquitur* plaintiff in a better position than an unaided plaintiff who must discharge the burden of proof on the evidence; and as seen, in *Ng Chun Pui v. Lee Chuen Tat* [1988] RTR 298, at p.300, the Judicial Committee of the Privy Council expressly stated that the burden remained with the plaintiff (thereby favouring the second approach).

This seems quite acceptable. *Res ipsa loquitur* is a plaintiff's weapon to the extent that the plaintiff is spared from the *initial* burden of producing evidence to show negligence. But where the defendant is then able to provide a plausible alternative explanation, he should not also have to disprove negligence and substantiate the alternative possibility. It should remain with the plaintiff to prove his case. In *Scott v. London & St Katherine Docks Co.* itself, Erle, CJ's statement seemed to contemplate that mere explanation by defendants would be required in order to neutralize *res ipsa loquitur*, but not also actual discharge of the burden of proof by defendants.

Such, then, is the standard of care in negligence and methods of proof of its breach.

There have over the years been certain measures introducing strict (no-fault) liability, not requiring negligence to be shown: the best known example is the regulation of defective products, under the Consumer Protection Act 1987, implementing the EC Directive on Product Liability (see *infra*, ch.13 - and note too the Vaccine Damage Payments Act 1979). The important failures, however, have been the Pearson Commission's 1978 recommendation of no-fault liability for motor accidents, to be paid for by a special tax on petrol, not given effect to; and medical accident no-fault liability, unable to pass into legislation. Plaintiffs are therefore left with difficulties of proof and unco-operative defendants, and the difference between moral and legal responsibility - financial compensation for victims following solely upon the latter - remains.

Further reading:

Brazier, *Street on Torts*, 9th ed, 1993 (Butterworth & Co., London): ch.13.

Fleming, J.G., *The Law of Torts*, 8th ed, 1992 (The Law Book Company, Sydney): ch.7.

Hepple, B.A. and Matthews, M.H., *Tort: Cases and Materials*, 4th ed, 1991 (Butterworth & Co., London): ch.5.

Heuston, R.F.V. and Buckley, R.A., *Salmond and Heuston on The Law of Torts*, 20th ed, 1992 (Sweet & Maxwell, London): ch.8.

Jones, M.A., *Textbook on Torts*, 4th ed, 1993 (Blackstone, London): ch.3.

Markesinis, B.S. and Deakin, S.F., *Tort Law*, 3rd ed, 1994 (Clarendon Press, Oxford): chs.2 and 3.

Stanton, K.M., *The Modern Law of Tort*, 1994 (The Law Book Company, Sydney): ch.3.

Weir, T., *A Casebook on Tort*, 7th ed, 1992 (Sweet & Maxwell, London): ch.2.

Chapter 7

Damage in Negligence

This is the third major element which is required in the tort of negligence. There must be damage to the person, property, or, in the case of negligent misstatement, financial position, of the plaintiff. Negligence without a victim is not actionable. It may be morally - even criminally - wrong for a person to drive too fast, or to make a cake with contaminated ingredients. But this in itself will not give rise to liability in the tort of negligence.

In *Hunter v. London Docklands Development Corporation* (1995) *The Times,* October 13, CA (joined with a nuisance claim in *Hunter v. Canary Wharf Ltd,* see *infra,* p.539, *et seq.*), the plaintiff householders claimed damages in negligence for the annoyance and discomfort caused by dust resulting from the construction by the defendants of the Limehouse Link Road in East London.

The Court of Appeal confirmed that in order for dust to be able to found an action in negligence, it would have to be proved that physical damage, beyond mere discomfort and loss of utility, had been caused by the dust (and by unreasonably excessive dust, in accordance with the usual rule for breach of the standard of care: see above, p.243, *et seq.*). For example, it might be shown that the excess had been trodden into carpets by householders so as to bring about physical changes lessening the value or usefulness of the fabric. This was the damage. Again, in *Parrott v. Jackson* (1996) *The Times,* February 14, CA, the Court of Appeal held that a defendant in a personal injury action, who admitted negligence but not the resultant damage, was not thereby to be taken to have admitted to *liability* in the proceedings, because damage was the gist of a claim in negligence.

With regard to this fundamental requirement of damage in negligence, there are two important matters which have to be looked into: *causation* and *remoteness of damage.*

Each of these issues concentrates upon the *extent* of the damage suffered by the plaintiff, and the legal principles applicable may have the effect of preventing liability in negligence from arising.

Causation deals with the question of whether the defendant should be liable *at all* for the damage suffered: if it is considered that the damage claimed for was not in fact *caused* by the defendant's conduct, there will be no liability.

Remoteness is concerned with the issue of whether, if damage *was* caused to the plaintiff by the defendant's acts, the defendant should then be held liable for *all* the loss and damage suffered by the plaintiff, or whether some of the damage should be excluded on the ground that it is too distant, too *remote* from the original causation act.

Each of the issues will now be considered.

(i) Causation

Causation constitutes a problem in the law of negligence, because life is complex.

If a defendant drives his car too fast and consequently

loses control, so that the vehicle leaves the road and hits the plaintiff, who is just coming out of a restaurant and who subsequently dies of his injuries the following day, this seems simple enough. There can be no real doubt: the defendant *caused* the plaintiff's injuries and his subsequent death.

However, suppose that the situation is made somewhat more complex by additional factors. For example, the car would have gone out of control in any event, because the garage which serviced the defendant's car had left the steering mechanism in a defective condition; or the plaintiff would have died anyway, because the meal which he had just eaten in the restaurant was poisoned; or the plaintiff would not have died of his injuries had he not received incorrect medical treatment at the hospital to which he was taken following the accident; or, by chance, he was not only hit by the defendant's car, but also by another vehicle at exactly the same time; or another car had crashed into him 10 minutes before the defendant's and the impact of the defendant's car did not add to the plaintiff's injuries.

In all these cases, it is not so easy to conclude that the *defendant* caused the injury - other people were involved, whether before, at the same time, or after the defendant. The plaintiff himself may not have been entirely blameless - he may have left the restaurant in a drunken state and was about to walk straight into the middle of the road and into the path of a juggernaut lorry when the defendant's car hit him.

Who can be said to have "caused" the injuries in such cases when so many people, apart from the defendant himself, were part of the overall sequence of events leading to the plaintiff's injuries?

In order to do justice in these circumstances, the law has to establish principles of liability; and because the issue is closely connected with the link between *act* and *damage*, it is referred to as "causation". It is expressed that the defendant is liable if he is held to have "caused" the damage. But in truth, of course, "caused" is a quite meaningless expression in the legal context - except to the extent of indicating, *as a fact*, that the defendant's acts played *a* part in the chain of events leading to damage, or that they had no such effect at all. For the rest, causation is entirely a legal conception, governed by principles which, as Lord Denning, MR said in *Lamb v. Camden LBC* [1981] QB 625, at p.636, are shaped by policy considerations and Judges' desire to achieve what they view as the just outcome to a case.

It is necessary, therefore, to consider the principles which have been developed by the courts, as to when a defendant will or will not be held, legally, to have caused the plaintiff's damage, so as to become liable for negligence.

1. Elimination of Defendants from Causation: the "but for" Test

The "but for" method is used in order to establish that the defendant was at least part of the cause of the damage, even if, ultimately, he is held, legally, not to be *the* cause.

The formula is: if the damage would not have occurred *but for* - without - the defendant's acts, the latter, potentially, are the cause. However, if the defendant's behaviour made no difference whatsoever to the course of events leading to damage, the defendant cannot then be held to have caused it (see *Cork v. Kirby MacLean Ltd* [1952]

2 All ER 402 *per* Lord Denning).

Cases usually cited in this connexion are the following:

First, there was *Barnett v. Chelsea & Kensington Hospital Management Committee* [1969] 1 QB 428, where a man went into hospital complaining of severe stomach pains and the hospital doctor sent him home, telling him to see his local doctor. He died - someone at his place of work had put arsenic in his tea. A good hospital doctor might have examined the man, but this was not done. Nevertheless, it still had to be asked whether the death would not have occurred *but for* the hospital doctor's behaviour? The answer to this question would be no - the man would have died anyway, because there was no known treatment for arsenic poisoning. The hospital's negligence therefore was not *a* cause of the death. It was not *the* cause. The hospital was not liable.

The other case is *Robinson v. Post Office* [1974] 2 All ER 737, in which a patient needed an immediate anti-tetanus injection. The doctor negligently failed to carry out a test in order to discover whether the man was allergic to the injection, which he was. The court held, however, that the doctor's negligence was not a cause of the allergic reaction, because the man would still have had to have undergone the injection whatever the test would have said, and furthermore the injection would have had to have been given before the results of the test were known. The absence of a test had therefore altered nothing.

A case in which the courts were prepared to apply the *but for* test very generously in favour of the defendants was *McWilliams v. Sir William Arrol & Co. Ltd* [1962] 1 WLR 295. Defendant employers had been negligent in failing to supply a steel erector with a safety belt, and he died in a fall. Evidence was given that he had never worn a belt before and would most likely have ignored it if it had been provided. The House of Lords concluded that the accident would have happened anyway. The defendants' behaviour was not a cause. They were not liable. Similarly, in *Newell v. Goldenberg*, *supra*, p.246, the plaintiffs, whom the defendant doctor had negligently failed to warn of the risk of reversal of a vasectomy operation, merely received damages of £500 for distress and anxiety caused by the failure, and not in respect of the costs of upbringing of the child born as a result of the operation's lack of effect, because the evidence was that they would have gone ahead with the operation in any event even if they had been told of the risk.

Accordingly, the "but for" test tells us whether a defendant "could" or "could not" be liable.

2. Causation When the "but for" Test is Satisfied

It is one thing to say that the defendant's acts were *a* cause of the damage, because the damage would not have occurred but for his actions. Yet, it is quite another to go on from there to conclude that the defendant legally caused the loss.

So, what is the next step?

How is it to be decided whether the defendant's behaviour is legally *the* cause - *causa causans* rather than merely *causa sine qua non* - when it was merely one of a number of elements in the overall sequence of events?

In *Liesbosch Dredger v. SS Edison* [1933] AC 449, at p.460, Lord Wright commented: "In the varied web of affairs, the law must abstract some consequences as relevant, not perhaps on grounds of pure logic but simply for practical reasons."

This seems to sum up the position. Courts have tried to steer a pragmatic course through the complex combinations of factual circumstances which may arise, and have decided upon "cause" in order to give effect to a policy of doing justice in the individual case.

An example of the distinction between where, on the one hand, a defendant's acts are merely the *occasion* of the loss, but legally not the cause, and where, on the other hand, they are held to be the effective cause, was *Young v. Purdy* (1995) *The Times,* November 7, CA. There, the defendant solicitor broke his contract with the plaintiff to proceed against the plaintiff's former husband for financial maintenance. The plaintiff made the claim herself and was unsuccessful, in the first place because her application was defective and secondly because she remarried before remedying the defect, which barred her from claiming the financial relief. The plaintiff alleged that the defendant's breach of contract had negligently caused the loss of her claim against her former husband. The Court of Appeal held, first, on the facts, that the plaintiff's action in making the claim herself against her former husband without further legal representation could not have been reasonably foreseen by the defendant solicitor, so that a duty of care did not exist. Secondly, as for causation, the test was whether the defendant's breach of contract was the *effective* cause of the plaintiff's making the claim herself and not merely the *occasion* for the latter and an occurrence without which the latter would not have taken place (criticizing the "common sense" approach in *Galoo Ltd v. Bright Grahame Murray, infra,* p.291, as an unsure guide). The unanimous view of the Court of Appeal was that - had a duty of care been held to exist - causation would still not have been satisfied on the facts, because the defendant's acts were merely the occasion of the damage and not the cause.

The following are some of the factors which have been taken into account, and the solutions applied, in determining effective cause:

i. Material contribution to damage. As a general guide, it would seem that if the defendant's act was a *material contribution* - that is to say, not relatively insignificant in relation to the remainder - he will be held to have "caused" the damage (see *Bonnington Castings Ltd v. Wardlaw* [1956] AC 613, dealt with below in connexion with *proof* of causation). In *Hotson v. East Berkshire Area Health Authority* [1987] 2 All ER 909, the plaintiff had an injury to his hip from a fall for which no one was to blame, and there was a 75 per cent chance that his disability would be permanent. The defendant medical authorities failed to treat the hip for five days because of an incorrect diagnosis and the result was a 100 per cent certainty of disability. The House of Lords held that the defendants had not "caused" the disability. Even if the defendants had applied the correct treatment, there was still a 75 per cent possibility of permanent disability. Therefore the fall, not the faulty diagnosis, had caused the disability and the defendants were not liable. Perhaps, then, it is the case that where there are only two causative factors, including the defendant's act, "materiality" of contribution actually means a simple majority - 51 per cent? In *Hotson,* the defendants were only 25 per cent to blame, against 75 per cent causation from the blameless event. Furthermore, it may be important in this type of case that the defendant's 25 per cent contribution was *subsequent* to the blameless event or to the plaintiff's own, and not contemporaneous. However, it would surely be excessive to require a 51 per cent contribution from a defendant as a condition of liability, where there were multiple causative acts and not merely two.

ii. Material increase in the risk. In *McGhee v. National Coal Board* [1972] 3 All ER 1008, the plaintiff became ill from contact with brick dust at his place of work. The employers were not negligent in this respect, because it was a normal hazard of the job. However, they were negligent in failing to provide washing facilities, so that workers had to go home covered in dust. It was impossible to say for certain whether the plaintiff would not have become ill if he had been able to wash. But what was clear was that the lack of washing facilities must have *materially increased the risk.* For the House of Lords, this was enough. Innocent exposure and culpable lack of washing facilities had *together* led to illness - and the culpable part had created a material increase in risk, which *material* increase would not have taken place *but for* the lack of washing facilities. The defendants had therefore caused the damage. Here, it will be noted, in contrast to the position in *Hotson,* the defendants' actions were more or less contemporaneous with the innocent exposure to the dust.

iii. Prior event must not have caused the same damage. If a prior event did so, the defendant's actions are not the "cause". In *Performance Cars Ltd v. Abraham* [1962] 1 QB 33, the defendant crashed into the plaintiff's Rolls Royce, necessitating a re-spray. However, someone else had also crashed into the vehicle about a week earlier, with the consequence that a re-spray was already needed! The defendant had not *caused* the damage therefore. This was common sense. A not altogether satisfactory application of this principle was adopted in *Cutler v. Vauxhall Motors Ltd* [1971] 1 QB 418, where the defendant negligently grazed the plaintiff's leg, but the plaintiff was only able to establish liability in respect of the graze and not also for pain and suffering from an operation due to a pre-existing condition of the veins in his leg, aggravated by the graze, but which would have had to have received medical treatment eventually in any event. The decision seems acceptable if the grazing injury and veins condition are treated as having a separate existence - the one new and the other already present. If they were not to be so dealt with, and the decision were instead to be regarded as being based upon unforeseeable remoteness of damage, then according to the "eggshell skull" principle (see below, p.311) this would be incorrect, because a special vulnerability or condition of the victim will not lead to damage being held to be too remote.

iv. Subsequent event increases the damage. It would seem that courts draw a distinction between subsequent *innocent* acts and those which are torts.

(a) If the subsequent event is an innocent occurrence, a natural misfortune, the defendant is released and is no longer treated as the cause. This seems illogical, but is arguably fair from a defendant's point of view. If, for example, the defendant scratches the plaintiff's car door negligently and subsequently a roof slate crashes into it in a storm through nobody's fault and destroys the door, it does not seem wholly unfair that the greater natural disaster should so eliminate the earlier tort. Thus, in *Carslogie Steamship Co. Ltd v. Royal Norwegian Government* [1952] AC 292, a ship was damaged in a collision, through the defendant's negligence, and required repairs for about 10 days. Before the repairs were carried out, the ship suffered further damage through an innocent event, so that it would take 51 days in all to be repaired. The House of Lords held that the defendants were not liable for the 10 days' loss of use of the ship - they were no longer the "cause" of this, which had been taken over by the subsequent innocent event.

(b) However, if the subsequent event is itself a tort, committed by somebody else, the first defendant remains liable, because, as a principle of tortious remedies, a tortfeasor is said to take his victim as he finds him and consequently the subsequent tortfeasor is only liable for causing the *additional* damage (*Beaco Ltd v. Alfa Laval Co. Ltd* [1994] 3 WLR 1179, CA). This means that the victim would be undercompensated if the prior defendant were to be released from causation in such circumstances. Thus, in *Baker v. Willoughby* [1970] AC 467, the plaintiff suffered a stiff leg in a road accident with the defendant.

Subsequently, the plaintiff was shot in the same leg during a robbery at work and the leg was amputated. The House of Lords held that had the robbers been sued in tort, they would only have been held to have caused the additional loss of amenities from the use of the leg, not also those of which the plaintiff had already been deprived as a result of the defendant's negligence; the defendant therefore remained the cause of the latter.

A case which seemed to fall between the preceding two situations in its outcome was *Jobling v. Associated Dairies Ltd* [1982] AC 794, in which the subsequent event was innocent, but the defendants were not completely released - they remained liable for the damage "caused" until the time of the subsequent event. Thus, the plaintiff's back had been injured at work through the negligence of the defendant employers, resulting in a 50 per cent reduction in his earning capacity. Three years later he contracted a disease which meant that he could not work at all. The House of Lords held the defendants to be liable for the plaintiff's loss of earnings for three years, after which their liability ceased. Were it not to have been so terminated, victims of tort might be in a better position than others who became affected by disease.

It is submitted that the difference between this case and *Carslogie,* in which, as seen, the defendants were completely released, is that there, the original damage - the 10 days' loss of use of the ship - did not begin to *bite* before the subsequent innocent damage took over; in *Jobling,* however, the damage began up to three years before the subsequent innocent event took place.

These cases demonstrate how meaningless is the concept

of legal *causation* in reality. The truth is that courts attempt to reach what appear to them to be just decisions on the facts - if two tortfeasors are responsible, they should share the blame, whereas, if natural causes intervene, the defendant should be wholly or partially released - and then try to express their findings in terms of causation, which inevitably leads to criticism.

Of all three cases, it may be said that *Baker* seems the most *logical* and ought to be extended to the innocent-subsequent-event situation. If a subsequent tort injures the plaintiff more seriously than the first, the plaintiff remains a more-seriously-*injured*-plaintiff - that does not cease to be the case; yet, similarly, if a subsequent innocent event had the same effect, again, the plaintiff continues to be an *injured*-plaintiff affected by the subsequent innocent event - the fact of his prior injuries and damage may indeed now be submerged by the new and greater innocent injuries, but the former do not cease to exist conceptually, and should not do so legally. Better too, surely, that the defendants' insurers should pay the plaintiff, rather than his being forced to resort to provision made by the social welfare authorities. Doubtless, there will be those who disagree.

v. Novus actus interveniens. In certain cases, the courts have held that an event subsequent to the defendant's acts has *broken the chain of causation* between defendant and damage, so that the defendant cannot be said to have caused it. These differ from preceding situations in that there the damage was already caused by the defendant, whereas here not so. It is a new act which brings it about, even though the "but for" test is satisfied in relation to the defendant's own actions. Furthermore, in one sense *novus actus* is the mirror image of causation through material increase of risk above (p.273): in the former case, the defendant is released, in the latter he becomes liable.

In summary, for a subsequent event to amount to a *novus actus interveniens* breaking the chain of causation, it must fall into either one of two main categories, as follows:

(1) Where a third party or the plaintiff himself does something unreasonable (and, at least in the former case, unforeseeable) which directly brings about the damage, or materially adds to the damage, or materially increases the risk of its occurrence. For example, a negligent cyclist knocks over the plaintiff who is taken to hospital for examination; the hospital then provides a painkiller, which negligently contains arsenic and kills the plaintiff: *novus actus interveniens.*

(2) Where an uncontrollable natural event intervenes, for example, a flash of lightning strikes the hospital building and kills the plaintiff who is undergoing treatment.

A number of different types of *intervening acts* have been held *not* to break the chain of causation, however.

(a) *Reasonable reaction of a third party.* Provided that the actions of the third party in response to the situation created by the defendant are held to be reasonable - in the sense of being understandable in the circumstances - the third party's intervention will not be held to have broken the chain of causation. Thus, in *The Oropesa* [1943] P.32, two ships, one of them *Oropesa,* collided in bad weather owing to the negligence of *Oropesa's* captain. The other ship began to sink and its captain decided to row his crew across to *Oropesa* in a boat, but the boat turned over in the water and a member of the crew drowned. Did the action of the other ship's captain break the chain of causation between the original negligence of *Oropesa* and the eventual damage, being death of the seaman? The Court of Appeal held that it did not, because the reactions of the captain of the other ship were perfectly reasonable in the circumstances. Lord Wright commented (at p.39): "To break the chain of causation it must be shown that there is something which I will call ultroneous, something unwarrantable, a new cause which disturbs the sequence of events, something which can be described as either unreasonable or extraneous or extrinsic." Presumably, the justification for the principle is that the reasonable acts of third parties should have been reasonably foreseen by the defendant - although the two are by no means automatically equivalent.

(b) *Acts of third party reasonably foreseeable.* Even if the actions of a third party are wholly unreasonable - even illegal - they will not amount to *novus actus* breaking the chain of causation if they should reasonably have been foreseen by the defendant (*Knightley v. Johns* [1982] 1 All ER 851). For example, in *Scott v. Shepherd* (1773) 2 Wm Bl 892, the defendant threw a firework into a crowded market and it landed on a stall. The stallholder picked it up and threw it onto another stall whose owner did the same, and it exploded on the next stall, blinding the plaintiff. The defendant was held liable and the chain of causation unbroken. It may not have been entirely reasonable for the intervening stallholders to have tossed the firework at each other - but it was perfectly foreseeable that people would react in this way. A case on the borderline was *Philco Radio & Television Corporation of Great Britain Ltd v. J. Spurling Ltd* [1949] 2 All ER 882, in which the defendant negligently sent inflammable paper to the plaintiff's address; one of the plaintiff's employees began to play around with it, and it exploded and damaged the plaintiff's property. Was the employee's behaviour *reasonable*? Probably not - harsh though it may sound, employees are not supposed to *fool about*. Yet, was it nonetheless foreseeable that someone might try to light the paper? This seems rather unlikely. However, the Court of Appeal must have thought so, because they held the defendant to be liable and evidently the chain of causation not to have been broken (seemingly, the result could have been different had the defendant been able to prove that the employee had *intentionally* started the fire, see pp.886, 887-8, 889).

The *Philco* case reveals how imprecise and open to judicial policy and discretion the tests of reasonable conduct and foreseeability are.

It would seem too from *Knightley v. Johns* [1982] 1 All ER 851 that courts will be more or, as the case may be, less willing to find a third party intervention to have broken the chain of causation on preceding bases of lack of reasonable conduct or lack of foreseeability, according to the circumstances. The following factors may provide a guide:

- Positive acts are (as less reasonable and less foreseeable) more likely than omissions to break the chain, as are intentional acts rather than those which are innocent.

- Negligent acts (as being less reasonable and less foreseeable) are more likely than innocent to cause a break: for example, in *Knightley v. Johns* [1982] 1 All ER 851, the defendant caused a traffic accident at the end of a tunnel, and the plaintiff policeman was injured when his colleague negligently forgot to shut the tunnel and directed him to ride his motorcycle in the wrong direction through the tunnel in order to close it; the defendant was held not to have caused the plaintiff's injuries, because there was a *novus actus*. However, if the nature of the third party negligence is more closely linked to the original act of negligence than it was in *Knightly*, so as to make the former a reasonably foreseeable occurrence, it may be that it will not break the chain of negligence and that contributions will be ordered from both the defendant and third party. For example, in *Rouse v. Squires* [1973] QB 889 the first defendant's negligent driving made his lorry jack-knife across the road and the second defendant then negligently crashed into the vehicles involved in the first accident a few minutes later, killing the plaintiff. The first defendant was held to be 25 per cent liable for causing the death - the chain of causation was not broken.
- Reckless acts are more likely than negligent to break the chain (because the former are less reasonable and less foreseeable): in *Wright v. Lodge* (1993) 142 NLJ 1269, the defendant negligently stopped her car on a motorway in fog and a lorry driver, driving recklessly, crashed into it and crossed the carriageway, smashing

into a number of other vehicles. This would not have happened if the lorry driver had merely been driving negligently. The court held the lorry driver's actions to be *novus actus interveniens* and the defendant had not caused the damage to the other cars.

- Criminal acts most of all and those which are otherwise intentional are likely to constitute *novus actus interveniens* (as the least reasonable and least foreseeable): in *Lamb v. Camden London Borough Council* [1981] QB 625, the defendant negligently damaged a water main leading to the plaintiff's house, forcing the plaintiff to move out because of consequent subsidence. While the house was empty, squatters moved in illegally and caused a lot of damage. The Court of Appeal held that the presence of the squatters and their criminal acts were not foreseeable, so that the defendant had not caused the damage - there was a *novus actus interveniens*. However, even in the case of criminal intervention, breach of the chain of causation is not inevitable. For example, in *Ward v. Cannock Chase District Council* [1985] 3 All ER 537, the defendants left their property in a derelict and disused state, so that it damaged the plaintiff's adjoining property. Vandals entered and caused further, criminal damage to the plaintiff's property. The court held that this eventuality, though criminal, was quite foreseeable and that the defendants had caused the damage. This seems more realistic than the outcome in *Lamb* above.

(c) *Acts of a third party who is not responsible for his own conduct.* Intervening acts, for example, of a child or mentally disordered person, where they are not responsible for their own actions, will apparently not break the chain of causation. This may seem illogical, but it is probably not so, on the basis that one is expected generally to *foresee* all such acts of children or others. For example, in *Haynes v. Harwood* [1935] 1 KB 146, the defendant was held liable for negligently leaving a horse-drawn van unattended in the street - the horse bolted when a boy threw a stone at it and the plaintiff was injured in attempting to prevent the horse from harming other people in the area. The defendant was held to have caused the injuries to the plaintiff and the boy's intervention did not affect this. In fact, it may be felt that this was not really a pure case of *novus actus interveniens* at all, because the boy's "intervention" was not truly an intervention - on the contrary, it was the very substance of the complaint against the defendant, in that until the boy threw the stone, the horse had not yet bolted, and the defendant should have foreseen that an unattended horse might have been disturbed by children. However, the attitude of the court was clear: a defendant may not hide behind the acts of youths.

(d) *Acts of the plaintiff himself which are reasonable.* If the plaintiff himself reacts to the defendant's actions in such a manner as leads to damage or further loss, this will not amount to *novus actus* if the plaintiff's reactions were reasonable; *aliter* if the plaintiff's actions were unreasonable. Courts seem to focus upon reasonableness rather than also upon foreseeability in the case of plaintiff's own intervening actions, which can obviously be advantageous to plaintiffs in certain circumstances. Thus, in *Wieland v.Cyril Lord Carpets* [1969] 3 All ER 1006, the court held that it was reasonable for the plaintiff to have attempted to walk down a flight of steps, even though as a result of the defendant's negligence, the plaintiff had to wear a surgical collar which made it impossible for her to look down through her bifocal glasses - the defendants were therefore held to have caused the further damage which the plaintiff suffered when she fell down the stairs. It was quite reasonable and sensible for people to try to carry on as normal as far as possible following injury, even if the further accident may not have been exactly foreseeable.

Again, in *Sayers v. Harlow Borough Council* [1958] 1 WLR 623, the plaintiff was faced with the ultimate nightmare - the lock on the door of the public toilet which she had just used jammed and she was unable to get out. She decided to try to climb out by standing on the revolving toilet roll holder, but it moved and she fell, suffering injuries. It was held that the chain of causation had not been broken: even though the plaintiff may well have panicked unnecessarily, her reaction in this respect could not be said to be wholly unreasonable. Who would not feel just a little *determined* when faced with the prospect of spending a night in a toilet? Seemingly, too, plaintiffs involved in rescue attempts will not be held to have acted unreasonably (*Cutler v. United Dairies (London) Ltd* [1933] 2 KB 297); nor will a woman who refuses to have an abortion when a sterilization operation is performed negligently be so held (*Emeh v. Kensington & Chelsea & Westminster Area Health Authority* [1984] 3 All ER 1044).

However, in *McKew v. Holland & Hannen & Cubitts (Scotland) Ltd* [1969] 2 All ER 1621, on similar facts to *Wieland*, the defendants were held not to be liable, where the plaintiff, whose leg they had previously negligently injured, fell down a flight of stairs with no handrail - the plaintiff knew perfectly well that his leg could give way at any time and it was most unreasonable for him to have attempted to use the stairs in this way. It mattered not that it was not wholly unforeseeable that a person in the position of the plaintiff might try something like this. In this case, therefore, the focus upon plaintiff-reasonableness rather than defendant-foreseeability actually worked to the disadvantage of the plaintiff. Foreseeability may be felt to be a more reliable criterion to adopt than reasonableness from this perspective, even though in a majority of cases it may reliably be supposed that reasonable and unreasonable intervening behaviour of plaintiffs will be found to be respectively foreseeable or unforeseeable as the case may be, or at least presumed to be so until the contrary is proven.

It should be added that even where the plaintiff's actions are held overall not to amount to *novus actus* - a complete break in the chain of the defendant's negligence - nevertheless, the court may decide to reduce his damages in order to take into account his own contributory negligence. This occurred in *Sayers v. Harlow UDC*. Again, in *March v. E & M H Stramore Pty Ltd* [1991] 99 ALR 423, the defendant parked his lorry negligently across a highway and the plaintiff, who was drunk, hit it with his vehicle. The Australian High Court held that the defendant caused the plaintiff's injuries, and the action of a drunk would not affect this - however, damages would be reduced by 70 per cent for the plaintiff's contributory negligence.

(e) *Acts of a plaintiff who is not responsible for his actions.* As with third party intervention, it seems that a defendant will not be released from causation where the plaintiff intervened but is held not to be a fully independent person. An example is the preceding case of *March v. E & M H Stramore Pty Ltd,* where the plaintiff was drunk. In the cases of *Pigney v. Pointers Transport Services Ltd* [1957] 1 WLR 1121 and *Kirkham v. Chief Constable of the Greater Manchester Police* [1989] 3 All ER 882, the plaintiffs committed suicide following injury while their minds were irrational and unhinged - this was held not to be *novus actus interveniens,* because they were not responsible for their actions. Perhaps a more extreme example, however, was *Meah v. McCreamer* [1985] 1 All ER 367, in which the plaintiff, who had suffered a personality change following an accident caused by the defendant's negligence, was imprisoned for life for carrying out sex attacks, and obtained damages from the defendant in respect of his imprisonment. His criminal activities evidently did not amount to *novus actus interveniens* given his state of mind (although, the Judge held that the defendant was not liable for the plaintiff's loss to the extent of damages he had had to pay to two of his victims in respect of their injuries - justifiable on the ground of excessive "remoteness" of the further damage, rather than as a matter of causation it may be considered, *infra,* p.299, *et seq.*). (Note too Appendix, Case 4, *infra.*)

It will have been noted that the law in this area of *novus actus interveniens,* and in causation generally, unfortunately is not as clear as might have been hoped. Some of the *novus actus interveniens* cases may easily be felt to be more a matter of remoteness of damage than causation, in that the question was not truly whether the defendant had caused loss to the plaintiff notwithstanding that a *novus actus* was the new event which had directly brought it about and but for which there would have been *no* damage, but instead whether the defendant was liable for having "caused" the *additional* loss to the plaintiff which arose as a result of the *novus actus,* and where the original damage would have occurred even without the *novus actus* (see, for example, *Meah v. McCreamer, supra*). This can be seen quite clearly in the case of *Banque Bruxelles Lambert S.A. v. Eagle Star Insurance Co. Ltd* [1995] 2 WLR 607 (CA) (see *infra,* p.298), where the plaintiff lender of £800,000 on a property worth £500,000 and negligently valued by the defendants at £1 million, claimed damages on default in repayment by the borrower, including the additional loss suffered on sale of the secured property by the plaintiff at the fallen market value of £300,000. The defendants claimed that the latter fall in market value was *novus actus interveniens* and that therefore they had not caused the additional loss of £200,000 (from £500,000 down to £300,000). The Court of Appeal held that it was quite foreseeable by the defendants that if the borrower from the plaintiffs were to fail to repay the loan, as occurred, the plaintiffs would have to sell the secured property and that the market value might have decreased, so that the fall was not to be treated as having "broken the link between the valuer's negligence and the damage which the lender has suffered" (p.636, *per* Sir Thomas Bingham, MR). Yet - how could it have "broken the link"? There was no *link*. All that there was was the damage claimed, as the fall in value (together with the existing £300,000 shortfall). This was *solus actus,* not *novus actus.*

Nevertheless, in spite of this regrettable lack of precision in the cases, the principles are still able to be used as a guide to further development and clarification of the law and to answer some of the many questions outstanding.

3. Separate Concurrent Acts as an Exception to the "but for" Test

In certain cases, the courts have been prepared to abandon the "but for" test, on the grounds of policy - or, as the Court of Appeal put it in *Galoo v. Bright Grahame Murray* [1994] 1 WLR 1360, according to common sense (or "the man in the street", *per* Lord Wright in *Yorkshire Dale Steamship Co. Ltd v. Minister of War Transport* [1942] AC 691) - although, *Galoo* itself was criticized by Leggatt, LJ in the Court of Appeal in *Young v. Purdy* (1995) *The Times,* November 7, as an unsure guide to whether a breach of duty of care resulting in loss was to be judged in law as having caused it. To put it simply, in these proceedings, the Judges believed that a defendant should bear some of the responsibility for his acts, and were not prepared to see this objective defeated by the legal technicalities of causation. The trouble has been that in order to overcome the logical objections, the courts have used some rather questionable reasoning. It might have been simpler if the courts had openly stated that *legally,* for liability to exist it was sufficient to be a separate *concurrent* cause, even if not exclusive. Thus, in *Bonnington Castings Ltd v. Wardlaw* [1956] AC 613, an employee sued his employers for allowing silica dust to escape into the air which caused him to become ill:

the dust came from two sources, one which the employers were not responsible for, and one for which they were. It was not known in what proportion the dust came from the two sources, but probably most was from the first source for which the defendants were not culpable. Clearly, the plaintiff would not be expected to satisfy the "but for" test: he would have fallen sick anyway even if the employers had not been negligent. However, the House of Lords held that since the dust escaping from the second source had made a *material contribution* to the illness, the employers were liable for the full extent of the injury.

The message seemed to be that if the acts - one negligent and the other not, or both negligent but by different defendants - were somehow *mixed together at the same time,* the defendant should be held to have caused the damage, provided that his acts were "material", that is, at the very least, not completely insignificant in comparison to the others, and probably a good deal more. Otherwise, an extraordinary situation might arise in which two different defendants were negligent towards the plaintiff - they drove their cars in opposite directions straight into the victim - but *neither* could be held to have caused the injuries and to satisfy the "but for" test, because the other defendant would have caused the damage on his own in any event.

Furthermore, the suspicion must also be that the court in *Bonnington* was by no means reluctant to find a *material* contribution to the sickness on the part of the defendants, even though there was very little evidence to show what part their actions had really played.

The case of *McGhee v. National Coal Board* was also noted earlier, in which defendant employers were held liable for causing injury through failing to provide washing facilities in a factory, even though the plaintiff would probably have suffered injury in any event - yet, the defendants' omission was held to have materially increased the risk of this. It all happened at the same time.

Indeed, for a period following *McGhee* it was thought that so long as the defendant could be shown to have increased the risk of damage, then if the damage occurred it would be for the defendant to disprove causation - reversal of the burden of proof.

However, in *Wilsher v. Essex Area Health Authority* [1988] 1 All ER 871, the plaintiff was a premature baby who was born blind. The plaintiff had received excessive oxygen through the defendants' negligence and this was known to be a cause of blindness. However, there were five other possible causes of blindness apart from excess oxygen, and the House of Lords held that just because the defendants had increased the chances and risk of blindness by adding a further possible cause, this did not remove the burden from the plaintiff to prove on a balance of probabilities that the defendants had caused the damage - simply to show that it could have been so caused was insufficient, and any suggestion by Lord Wilberforce in *McGhee* that where the damage might have been caused by the defendant or other factors, the burden should shift to the defendant was said to be incorrect. Thus, in accordance with *Bonnington,* it had to be established that the lack of oxygen was a material contribution to the damage - which a majority of the Court of Appeal had held to have been achieved. Furthermore, the case of *Hotson* was also previously seen - this was an attempt to get round the rules of proof by arguing that it was enough for the plaintiff to show that there was a *chance* that the defendants had caused the plaintiff's injuries, rejected by the House of Lords. To complete the trilogy of restrictive decisions subsequent to *McGhee*, in *Kay v. Ayrshire and Arran Health Board* [1987] 2 All ER 417, the court held that the plaintiff's deafness was caused by his meningitis rather than by the defendants' administration of an overdose of penicillin to treat it, but that had there been evidence to show that such an overdose would materially increase the risk of deafness, *McGhee* would have been applicable and the defendants liable for causation. Thus, for *McGhee* to operate there must at least be separate evidence to support the harmfulness of the defendant's behaviour as a separate source of the damage; it is not enough that it simply occurred in conjunction with the other competing cause and that damage resulted.

At the end of it all, it will now be understood that causation is an art, not a science. Judges have had to construct a body of rules to govern an infinite variety of factual situations, with one eye to the overall systematic consistency of the doctrine, but with the other to ensuring a just outcome in the individual cases before them. Unfortunately, the two objectives are not always reconcilable and the result may be viewed as a somewhat unclear and at times an analytically rather questionable tapestry of different rules and decisions on causation for the poor observer to contend with. In the Court of Appeal in *Galoo Ltd v. Bright Grahame Murray* [1994] 1 WLR 1360, Glidewell, LJ came to the decision that in both contract and tort, causation was without doubt one of the most difficult areas of the law. In his estimation, it was insufficient to show that the defendant's breach of duty was merely the occasion for the loss; instead it had to be the effective or dominant cause. As to how this test would be applied, Glidewell, LJ considered that the answer in the end would depend upon *the application of the court's common sense.* In that case itself, the plaintiffs alleged that negligently audited accounts had caused their losses through continued trading and payment of dividends. However, the Court of Appeal held that whilst the defendants' breach of duty gave the opportunity to the plaintiffs to continue to incur trading losses, it had not caused those losses in the sense described. Again, in *Banque Bruxelles Lambert S.A. v. Eagle Star Insurance Co. Ltd* [1995] 2 WLR 607 (CA), Sir Thomas Bingham, MR, stated (at p.621) that the approach of courts to issues of causation was in principle simple, pragmatic and commonsensical, and that the event which a plaintiff alleged to be causative "need not be the only or even the main cause of the result complained of; it is enough if it is *an* effective cause" (*ibid.*). Furthermore, an event would not be causative in law, if it did no more than provide the occasion for the result complained of: "If X assaults a fellow guest Y at a party given by Z, it is plain that Z's invitation of X provides the occasion for the assault. But for his invitation the assault would not have occurred. But it could not possibly be said, without more, that Z caused the assault" (*ibid.*)

Nowhere have the difficulties over defining and solving problems of causation been more marked than in cases involving claims for what is referred to as "the loss of a chance" of a financial or other gain. There are two reasons for the problems in this area: first, by its very nature, a *chance* of a gain is not a certainty and consequently may never have taken place, even in the absence of the defendant's negligence - so how can the defendant be said to have *caused* the loss of a gain which might not have come into existence in the first place?; and, secondly, it may be that what is at issue in these cases is not really causation at all, but quantification of damages - that is to say, if the defendant has caused some damage to the plaintiff, then in assessing the overall amount, the court will try to estimate the value of any lost chance as part of the award.

The matter arose in *Allied Maples Group Ltd v. Simmons & Simmons* [1995] 1 WLR 1602, CA, where the plaintiffs entered a transaction to take over another business, which included the transfer of some tenancies to the plaintiffs. It subsequently emerged that the plaintiffs would be subject to substantial liabilities under the tenancies and they claimed damages from the defendants, their solicitors, for allegedly negligent advice in the takeover. At first instance, the defendants were held liable for breach of duty and causation: had the defendants given the correct advice, the plaintiffs would have requested an indemnity against liability under the tenancies from the transferor and the court considered they would have been granted this. The defendants appealed to the Court of Appeal. They were unsuccessful. The Court of Appeal considered that causation and quantification of damages were very closely linked and that it was hard to say where the one ended and the other began (p.1609). In deciding these matters, the court distinguished three types of case: (1) Negligence as a *positive act*. Here, causation was said to be a historical fact, to be determined on a balance of probabilities, after which the plaintiff would then be entitled to a remedy in damages, with no discount at this stage for the fact that he had only just managed to discharge the burden. As to quantification of his loss, the court simply had to make an assessment and, if this consisted of loss of a chance, for example, winning the national lottery had the defendant not negligently driven into the plaintiff preventing him from buying a ticket, the court would decide the percentage of risk that the plaintiff would have won the lottery. (2) Negligence consisting of an *omission*. An example might be omission to give proper advice, or to register a lottery ticket for the owner. Again, the plaintiff must satisfy the court on a balance of probability that he would have taken the required action to avoid risks or to capitalize on chances if the defendant had not been negligent. Thus, in the present case, they had to show that had the defendants correctly advised them, they would have used that advice in order to obtain proper protection in their transaction, and the court considered that they had succeeded in this. The prospects that they would have sought such protection are then quantified for amount of damages. (3) Plaintiff's loss depends wholly or partly upon how a *third party would have acted*. In the present case, for example, would the other side in the transaction have agreed to the plaintiffs' request for protection? The rule here was not that the plaintiff should prove on a balance of probability that the third party would have provided the benefit; it was that the plaintiff must show that he had a "substantial chance rather than a speculative one". If, for purposes of subsequent quantification of damages, the chance lost were then assessed as less than 50 per cent likely to have occurred, say, 30 per cent (clearly "substantial"), the plaintiff would not of course lose the claim on causation - he would simply receive 30 per cent of the loss as a matter of quantum of damages. Thus, the words of Stuart-Smith, LJ should be noted (p.1614): "... the plaintiff must prove as a matter of causation that he has a real or substantial chance as opposed to a speculative one. If he succeeds in doing so, the evaluation of the chance is part of the assessment of the quantum of damage, the range lying somewhere between something that just qualifies as real or substantial on the one hand and near certainty on the other. I do not think that it is helpful to seek to lay down in percentage terms what the lower and upper ends of the bracket should be." On the evidence, the plaintiffs succeeded in proving to a majority of the three Judges in the Court of Appeal that there was a sufficiently substantial chance that they would have successfully negotiated protection with the other side, had the defendants properly advised them to do so (the dissenting Judge, on the other hand, considered the chance to be merely speculative on the available evidence). After this, it would then be necessary to make a financial assessment of the *value* of the chance lost (including the degree of likelihood, as part of the calculation) in order to carry out *quantification* of damages (p.1621, Hobhouse, LJ).

In other words, a summary of the principles governing this type of loss of chance claim would be: (a) existence and loss of a substantial chance on a balance of probability from the evidence opens the door of *causation* - "substantial" appearing to mean a real or realistic chance, rather than a particular minimum percentage; and (b) once this is satisfied, the court then makes a more precise assessment of the likelihood as part of the value of the lost chance, for the purpose of *quantifying* the damages and providing a compensation remedy.

A subsequent illustration of the process was *Stovold v. Barlows* (1995) *The Times,* October 30, CA. In this case the plaintiff had received an offer to buy his house and the prospective purchaser had requested that the title documents should be sent to his own solicitor by a particular date so that the transaction could be concluded. In the meantime, the prospective purchaser was viewing another property for which the title documents had arrived. The plaintiff's solicitors failed to send the documents to arrive in time and the prospective purchaser bought the other property. The plaintiff claimed damages of about £90,000 from the defendant solicitor amounting to the difference between the price offered and the sum eventually obtained from another purchaser. The Court of Appeal held that the first instance court had been incorrect in finding that if on a balance of probabilities, it was considered that the prospective purchaser would have bought the plaintiff's house had the documents arrived, the plaintiff should receive the *full* loss, otherwise nothing. The proper procedure was as follows:

1) *Causation.* As a matter of causation, the plaintiff had to prove that he had a real or substantial chance, as opposed to a merely speculative one.

2) *Quantum of damages.* If he was successful, the evaluation of the extent of the chance lost was part of the assessment of quantum of damage, the range lying somewhere between something that only just qualified as real or substantial on the one hand and near certainty on

the other (from *Allied Maples Group Ltd v. Simmons & Simmons*).

Thus, *existence* of the chance could be said to go to causation; *extent and nature* of the chance, to damages.

On the facts of the case, therefore, the Court of Appeal sought to determine existence and extent of the chance that the sale to the prospective purchaser would have gone ahead in the absence of the defendant solicitor's negligence. In this respect, two things could have gone wrong so as to reduce the chances that the sale would have taken place: first, that even if the documents had been sent, they might not have arrived in time; and secondly, that even if they had arrived on time, the prospective purchaser might have decided that he preferred to buy the other house in any event.

Accordingly, on this basis the Court of Appeal held that there had been a *50 per cent chance* that the prospective purchaser would have proceeded with the purchase of the plaintiff's house: this was the existence (causation) and extent (quantum) of the chance. This was what the plaintiff was considered to have lost as a result of the defendant's negligence. Full damages claimed would thus be reduced by 50 per cent.

A further recent decision upholding these principles was *First Interstate Bank of California v. Cohen Arnold & Co.* (1995) *The Times*, December 11, CA. Here the plaintiff bank lent nearly £5 million pounds to a customer to finance a property transaction. In June 1990 the plaintiffs asked the defendant accountants to advise them as to their client's worth, which the defendants assessed as over £45 million. However, in August 1990 the defendants admitted that their client had assets worth no more than £57,000! Thereafter, in September the plaintiffs had the property sold for £1.4 million. They sued the defendant accountants for damages for loss of a chance: their argument was that if they had received the correct advice in June, they could have sold the property for £3 million. The defendants contended, however, that even if the plaintiffs had known the true position in June, they would still have waited until September to sell the property. The Court of Appeal applied *Allied Maples Group Ltd v. Simmons & Simmons:* (a) *causation* was satisfied since it could be proven on a balance of probabilities that the plaintiffs would have put the property on the market in June and the evidence was that there was a real and substantial, as opposed to a merely speculative, chance that the property would then have been sold for a higher price; and (b) as to *quantification* of damages for loss of the chance, it was here that the value of the chance, including precise likelihood, would be assessed. The court thereupon valued the chance at 66⅔ per cent likelihood of occurring. Difference between June and lower September selling price was therefore reduced by 33⅓ per cent for calculation of damages.

Banque Bruxelles Lambert S.A. v. Eagle Star Insurance Co. Ltd [1995] 2 WLR 607 (CA) involved similar facts. The plaintiff lender lent £800,000 on the security of property negligently valued by the defendants at £1 million. In fact the value was £500,000 and when eventually the property was sold on the borrower's default, it fetched £300,000 owing to a fall in market values. However, the case was not argued out over the issue of loss of a chance, because the plaintiffs did not appear to claim that the loss on the market fall could have been avoided had the defendants notified them of the over-valuation. The matter of the sum representing the market fall (£200,000) was dealt with on the basis of foreseeability and causation: the plaintiffs would not have entered the transaction had they known of the over-valuation; accordingly, the latter was the effective cause of that part of the loss as well as the rest and was recoverable (p.634). Indeed, such a loss through market falls was quite foreseeable and for this reason it was not even argued by the defendants that the damage was too "remote" (p.620). (But see now *infra,* Appendix Case 4.)

(ii) Remoteness of Damage

This is the second issue which requires to be dealt with in respect of the damage requirement in the tort of negligence.

Some might take the view that when one person negligently causes damage to another, it is only fair that the former should pay for *all* of the consequent losses, even if some of them were unusual and not at all foreseeable in the normal course of events.

Others would argue - and the law would support them - that there has to be a limit upon such liability and a fair division of risk in society. The line must be drawn somewhere. Consider the following example. A dog taken for a walk by its owner is known to become excited whenever it sees a cat. The owner negligently fails to fasten the dog's lead and the dog chases across the road when it spots its feline adversary. A car is forced to swerve in order to avoid hitting the dog, and narrowly misses a man carrying a parrot in a cage. The cage is dropped and the parrot escapes and flies through the open door of a café where it knocks over a boiling cup of coffee onto a man's hand. The man, who is a mechanic at a nuclear power station, is unable to use his hand properly in order to screw a cover onto a pipe at the plant. As a result, the cover falls off without anyone knowing, nuclear fuel escapes and there is a huge nuclear explosion. The Russians believe that they have been attacked by the Americans and release their entire stock of nuclear weapons upon the United States. The Americans retaliate. All life on earth is destroyed. Legally speaking, was a dog to blame for all of this?

The courts say no; and they have developed various rules as to which elements of loss and damage from a negligent act are, and which are not, recoverable for. Those which are not recoverable for are said to be too *remote* from the negligent event at the origin of the damage; and the rules of limitation of damage in question are those for the *remoteness of damage.* Loss which is held not to be too remote, however, is recoverable.

Thus, once the plaintiff has established existence of a duty of care towards the plaintiff on the part of the defendant (through reasonable foreseeability that the plaintiff would suffer some damage, subject, as seen, to judicial and public policy), and then breach of that duty, and sufficient causation, he must thereupon establish the extent of his recoverable loss. Like the rest, the eventual decision of the court upon this issue of remoteness will include a large policy dimension, as follows.

1. *The Foreseeability Rule*

(a) General

The previous law was that defendants were liable for all direct consequences of their negligent acts, whether these were foreseeable or not.

The leading case was *Re Polemis and Furness, Withy & Co. Ltd* [1921] 3 KB 560, in which a shipworker negligently dropped a plank of wood into the ship's hold. It might have been foreseen that someone in the hold could have been injured, or that the ship would have been damaged by the impact; but what actually occurred could not reasonably have been foreseen - benzine had been leaking into the hold, the plank ignited it and the resulting fire destroyed the ship. The defendant was held liable. Scrutton, LJ in the Court of Appeal said "once the act is negligent, the fact that its exact operation was not foreseen is immaterial."

However, then came the case of *The Wagon Mound (No.1)* [1961] AC 388. Although decisions of the Judicial Committee of the Privy Council - equivalent in judicial personnel to the House of Lords - on final appeal from courts in British Commonwealth countries are merely persuasive not binding, it is generally accepted that the Judicial Committee's judgment in *The Wagon Mound* now accurately represents the law on remoteness and spells the end for the Court of Appeal's judgment in *Re Polemis.* In *The Wagon Mound,* oil was carelessly being loaded onto the defendant's ship, *The Wagon Mound,* in Sydney Harbour in Australia, and some of the oil flowed into the water. Normally, the oil would merely have fouled the plaintiff's wharf and would not have been dangerous. But on this occasion it was picked up by floating rubbish in the water which was subsequently ignited by sparks from welding work on the other side of the harbour. The fire caused serious damage to the plaintiff's wharf. If *Re Polemis* had applied, all direct consequences would have been recoverable for. However, the Judicial Committee considered *Polemis* to be wrong, and wished to see it replaced by a rule of reasonable foreseeability, not satisfied on the facts: *some* damage to the plaintiff's wharf was reasonably foreseeable, but the type of fire which actually occurred and the way in which it did so were not. Viscount Simonds (at p.422) said that *Polemis* could lead to injustice and that it did not "seem consonant with current ideas of justice or morality that, for an act of negligence, however slight or venial, which results in some trivial foreseeable damage, the actor should be liable for all consequences, however unforeseeable and however grave, so long as they can be said to be 'direct'."

The Privy Council's favoured approach has been taken up by courts in later cases; and the rule of foreseeability of damage applies too in other torts, such as nuisance (see *The Wagon Mound (No.2)* [1967] 1 AC 617, below, ch.23). However, where "intentional" torts, such as deceit and the economic torts (below, chs.19 and 20), are concerned, and torts of strict liability, including breach of statutory duty (below, chs.9 and 10), the *Polemis* principle governs (*Quinn v. Leatham* [1901] AC 495, 537).

(b) Foreseeability of likelihood of occurrence, or of possibility of occurrence

It is submitted that arguments to the effect that for damage to be recoverable as being not too remote, the damage must be reasonably foreseeable as being *likely* to occur and not merely as being a *possible* occurrence however unlikely, are over-elaborate.

Concepts of foreseeability, likelihood and possibility merge into the single test of reasonable foreseeability of occurrence. Otherwise, *how* likely or possible would the occurrence have to be for its reasonable foreseeability to be capable of leading to recovery? The reasonable foreseeability criterion itself is essentially a policy tool for the Judges to reach the just decision in a case where any doubt at all exists as to foreseeability on the facts, and if they believe recovery to be correct, they will hold the damage's occurrence - irrespective of its designation as likely or possible or not - to have been reasonably foreseeable (see Lord Upjohn in *The Heron II* [1969] 1 AC 350, at p.422).

(c) The type and circumstances of damage to be foreseen

If a man is driving a car too fast, it is reasonably foreseeable that he will knock someone over and cause physical injuries. It is not reasonably foreseeable that a bridge towards which he is travelling will collapse before he has time to stop and that his car will damage a ship passing underneath.

Thus, the courts have sought to place limits upon foreseeability by reference to *type* of damage and *nature* of events leading to it - or else it would almost be possible for all damage to be regarded as having been reasonably foreseeable, if damage were sufficiently broadly defined as, say, *injury* from *wrongful acts*.

However, this said, it should further be pointed out that

courts have been careful not to go too far in the opposite direction, so as not to restrict plaintiffs' opportunities of recovery to an excessive degree - they have, therefore, only required the type of damage suffered and, in particular, the manner and circumstances of its occurrence, to be *generally* consistent with what they consider to have been reasonably foreseeable.

Type of Damage

Thus, in *Bradford v. Robinson Rentals Ltd* [1967] 1 All ER 267, the plaintiff was sent by his employers on a long journey in a van lacking a heater, in bitterly cold weather. He suffered frostbite. He was held entitled to recover for this foreseeable *type* of injury, even if an effect as serious as frostbite might not have been the precise and exact injury contemplated from the unheated car. Similarly, in *Margereson and Hancock v. J.W. Roberts Ltd* (1996) *The Times*, April 17, CA, the plaintiffs recovered damages against the defendant owners of an asbestos factory, having developed a serious disease of the lung called mesothelioma, through playing in the factory's loading bay as children round about 1933 when the defendants had deposited a large amount of asbestos dust outside their premises. The Court of Appeal held that it was sufficient for recovery if *some* injury to the lungs had been reasonably foreseeable, even if mesothelioma itself had not been.

However, in *Tremain v. Pike* [1969] 3 All ER 1303, the plaintiff worked on the defendant's farm which was home to a large population of rats. He contracted *lepto spirosis*, which is a rare disease caused through contact with rats' urine. He was held to be unable to recover, because although bites or food poisoning from the rats might have been foreseen, this particular rare condition was not a *type* of damage which was reasonably foreseeable (compare the remoteness rule in contract in *H. Parsons (Livestock) Ltd v. Uttley Ingham & Co. Ltd* [1978] QB 791, where defendants were held liable in full for breach of contract in supplying mouldy nuts to pigs which contracted a rare disease as a consequence, because some damage was foreseeable). The decision has been criticized as being too restrictive - foreseeable injury should have been categorized more broadly as *that caused by rats.* After all, with such a description, there is very little direct injury which a rat could perpetrate which would not be foreseeable (otherwise of course, in the case of indirect injuries, as, for example, where a rat were to chew through an electric cable, causing fire).

These cases demonstrate the unscientific and policy nature of courts' classification of "type" of damage foreseeable, and the consequent difficulties of prediction. Certainly, from *The Wagon Mound* itself, it would seem that fouling or impact damage may be regarded as of a different type from fire damage; and *Hughes v. Lord Advocate* [1963] AC 837 (see below, p.309) indicates that fire damage will not be considered to be different from an accompanying explosion, where the former might have been foreseen, yet the latter not so. *Tremain v. Pike* suggests that courts may be more reluctant to find foreseeable type in personal injuries cases than in those concerned with damage to property. However, *Hughes v. Lord Advocate* is a contrary indication, and, in any event, the "eggshell skull" exception to foreseeability, which will probably more frequently apply to injuries than to damage, helps to remove any inequality in this respect (see below, p.311).

The imprecision of the whole foreseeability process may be seen from the fact that in the different proceedings in *The Wagon Mound (No.2)* [1967] 1 AC 617, a different Judge held on the evidence that fire damage from the escaping oil *was* foreseeable, so that the plaintiffs here, owners of two ships damaged in the fire, were able to recover for the not too remote loss.

Finally, three further points need to be made:

(1) First, if the type of loss was foreseeable, this is recoverable even if the damage turned out to be more serious and expensive than might have been expected. In *Vacwell Engineering Co. Ltd v. BDH Chemicals Ltd* [1971] 1 QB 88, the foreseeable explosion caused by the mixture of the defendants' chemicals was even more violent than might have been contemplated, yet recovery for the full damage was held not to be too remote; and in *Hughes v. Lord Advocate* [1963] AC 837, at p.845, Lord Reid said: "No doubt it was not to be expected that the injuries would be as serious as those which the appellant in fact sustained. But a defender is liable, although the damage may be a good deal greater in extent than was foreseeable. He can only escape liability if the damage can be regarded as differing in kind from what was foreseeable."

(2) Secondly, once the type of damage is held to be foreseeable in the matter of remoteness of damage, the defendant has to pay the full extent of the plaintiff's loss, large or small, as a matter of measure and quantification

of damages: the tortfeasor takes his victim as he finds him (see *The Arpad* [1934] P.189, at p.202). From a defendant's point of view, therefore, or his insurer's, it is preferable to run down a pauper than a millionaire.

(3) Thirdly, it now seems to be the position, following the decision of the House of Lords in *Page v. Smith* [1995] 2 All ER 736, HL, that in the case of nervous shock as damage, courts should no longer regard physical and mental injury as constituting different *types* of damage for purposes of foreseeability in remoteness of damage. *Page v. Smith* was previously dealt with above in the discussion of nervous shock (p.72, *et seq.*). It will be recalled that the case involved a car accident in which the plaintiff was not physically injured but claimed damages for nervous shock. A majority of the House of Lords led by Lord Lloyd held that where the plaintiff suffering nervous shock was himself the "primary" victim of the defendant's negligence, in the sense that his fears were for his own safety, rather than those of a mere "secondary" victim experiencing concern for another, it was sufficient for liability that he was able to satisfy the court that physical injuries were foreseeable (other usual conditions of liability for nervous shock also quite logically being held to be inapplicable), and it was not then required to prove reasonable foreseeability of nervous shock itself (*supra,* ch.5). (Previously, it had been possible to claim for nervous shock through fear for one's own safety - see *Dulieu v. White & Sons* [1901] 2 KB 669 - but, it is submitted, the assumption would have been that the defendant ought reasonably to have foreseen that such nervous shock would be suffered.) The minority, Lords

Keith and Jauncey, dissented on the ground that nervous shock itself had to be reasonably foreseeable, seemingly on the basis that whereas foreseeability of "any" damage to health was sufficient to establish a *duty of care* in negligence, nevertheless the principle remained for purposes of *remoteness of damage* that damage suffered had to be of the same type as that which would have been reasonably foreseeable (see pp.740 and 748 "Taking your victim as you find him however is relevant, not to the existence of a duty owed to him but rather to the question of damages payable in respect of breach of a duty otherwise established"). Against the latter view, however, it has to be said that the majority did succeed in providing justification, at least in principle, for their finding: this was that there was no longer considered to be any essential difference in type between physical and mental injuries - medical knowledge had developed so much that any such distinction sought to be drawn would be quite artificial (p.754 "... recent developments suggest a much closer relationship between physical and mental processes than had previously been thought"; p.759, *supra*, p.72; 761 "There is no justification for regarding physical and psychiatric injury as different 'kinds' of injury)." Thus, the decision in *Page v. Smith* which now represents the law is to a greater or lesser extent acceptable according to whether the latter thesis is agreed with or not. The present writer's view may here be recalled that it is not. The ultimate test of equivalence or similitude of type must surely be that of foreseeability - the foreseeability of one form of injury necessarily importing the same in relation to the other - not the other way round. Consequently, since it is not true to say that (foreseeable) physical injuries in a car accident will *always* - even invariably - be accompanied by nervous shock on the part of the victim, the two sorts of effects ought not to be considered to amount to the same type for such purposes (see Lord Jauncey, p.743).

At least, however, where physical injuries themselves were not reasonably foreseeable by the defendant, yet nervous shock - perhaps through mistaken apprehension of the former by the "primary" victim - was so, the principle of *Dulieu v. White* remains, upholding recovery for nervous shock by the victim.

Finally, it will further be recalled from the earlier discussion of *Page v. Smith (supra*, ch.5, p.72) that Lords Browne-Wilkinson and Lloyd in the majority (pp.753-4, 760, 768) indicated that nervous shock, on the facts of the case arising from the plaintiff's particular susceptibility to the condition known as ME, would fall within the eggshell skull - here eggshell *personality* - exception to remoteness of damage requirements in any event (see *infra*, p.311, *et seq.*), whether physical and mental illnesses were treated as the same or not. However, the view put earlier was that this approach was hardly justifiable, since the eggshell exception ought properly to be confined to damage and injuries *of the same type* which are more severe than ordinarily foreseeable, owing to the plaintiff's special condition and should not therefore cover a case in which a different kind of damage was sustained as a consequence thereof (see *infra*, p.313).

Circumstances of Occurrence

In *Hughes v. Lord Advocate* [1963] AC 837, the House of Lords seemed to go to great lengths in order to find that the general nature of the events leading to the damage were foreseeable, even if the precise circumstances were not. The defendants had negligently left a hole in the road uncovered and surrounded by a striped tent and paraffin lamps. Two boys entered the tent, taking one of the lamps with them. The lamp fell down the hole and exploded causing one of the boys to be badly burnt. Although an explosion was held not to have been foreseeable, nevertheless, the House of Lords found that the *general nature of the occurrence* - fire from the lamps leading to burns - was so, and this was enough for the defendants to be held liable. Lord Guest said (at p.856): "I cannot see that these are two different types of accident. They are both burning accidents and in both cases the injuries would be burning injuries." Again, in *Wieland v. Cyril Lord Carpets Ltd* [1969] 3 All ER 1006, at p.1009, Eveleigh, J commented that "the precise mechanics of the way in which the negligent act results in the original injury do not have to be foreseen."

However, plaintiffs in other cases have not been so fortunate in their claims.

In *Doughty v. Turner Manufacturing Co. Ltd* [1964] 1 QB 518, the plaintiff employee suffered burns when an asbestos lid fell into a tank of sulphuric acid at his place of work and exploded. The Court of Appeal held that this damage from a chemical reaction was too remote. It was foreseeable that there might have been some splashing from the lid falling into the boiling liquid - but the consequent explosion was an unforeseeable circumstance leading to injury.

Thinking of *Hughes* - general nature of fire and burns -

both that case and *Doughty* perhaps only go to prove that if you ask the correct questions, you can come up with the right answers.

Again, in *Crossley v. Rawlinson* [1981] 3 All ER 674, the plaintiff failed to satisfy the remoteness test. The defendants' vehicle was negligently on fire. The plaintiff was rushing towards it with a fire extinguisher when he tripped in a hole in the road and was injured. The defendants were not liable and the damage was too remote: injury through the fire was foreseeable, but the actual circumstances - running towards the fire to put it out, rather than engaging in that activity in close contact - were not.

Thus, reasonable foreseeability is the general test of remoteness and recoverability - as it is in respect of existence of the duty of care towards the plaintiff in the first place:

- duty of care: foreseeability that the *plaintiff* would be injured;
- remoteness: foreseeability that the *type* and *circumstances* of damage suffered by the plaintiff would occur.

In either case, the Judge has a lot of discretion to reach the correct decision on juridical policy: and the only controls would seem to be academic scrutiny and public disapproval or ridicule.

2. *Exception to the Foreseeability Rule: Eggshell (Thin) Skulls*

As previously indicated, if *some* damage to the plaintiff is foreseeable, there is a general principle that a tortfeasor takes his victim as he finds him and must pay for *all* damage of the same type. The principle is no less applicable and the defendant cannot escape liability if the reason why injuries turn out to be more serious than could possibly have been foreseen *is that of the plaintiff's special weakness or vulnerability* (such as an eggshell thin skull, or a weak heart, or a nervous disposition!): "... if a man is negligently run over or injured in his body, it is no answer to the sufferer's claim for damages that he would have suffered less injury, or no injury at all, if he had not had an unusually thin skull or an unusually weak heart" (*Dulieu v. White & Sons* [1901] 2 KB 669, at p.679 *per* Kennedy, J). This was so held in *Smith v. Leech Brain & Co. Ltd* [1962] 2 QB 405, where the plaintiff's husband was splashed on the lip with molten metal at work. The burn itself was healed, but since the husband had a pre-cancerous condition of the lip, the burn acted as an agent to activate the cancer of which the plaintiff's husband died. The defendants could not have foreseen the husband's special vulnerability, but they were held liable for his death: the burn was foreseeable even if the cancer was not, and that was enough. Again, in *Robinson v. Post Office* [1974] 2 All ER 737, defendants were held liable towards a plaintiff who had to have an anti-tetanus injection after slipping on the step of a ladder in the course of his employment as a result of their negligence and who suffered an allergic reaction to it. Recoverable damage extended to the full effects of the particular allergy to which the plaintiff was subject and was not confined to his cut shin.

The eggshell skull principle probably applies to damage to property as well as to physical injuries, and to mental disorders (*Malcolm v. Broadhurst* [1970] 3 All ER 508): although, in the case of damage to property, it has been argued that the eggshell skull rule should be limited to where the unforeseeable damage was of the same *type* as the foreseeable, or else the *Wagon Mound* principle would seriously be threatened, since objects can easily be viewed as having a special propensity to suffer whatever damage happens to occur to them, foreseeable or not. Thus, if a car negligently crashes into a house so that some damage is foreseeable, the driver will be liable if unknown to him, the house has suffered subsidence, and is completely demolished when it collapses - eggshell foundations. But should he also be liable if the house was being used to store inflammable material and blows up - eggshell contents? Probably not.

It is submitted that in principle - if not all that likely in practice - the same restriction should apply to personal injuries: so that if it were to be held that a particular type of personal injury suffered were of a completely different nature to that which was reasonably foreseeable and that the former was due to the victim's special susceptibility thereto, the defendant should not then be held to be liable according to the eggshell skull rule. Thus, in *Tremain v. Pike* the plaintiff failed to recover for rat disease. Why should it make any difference that he only contracted this by reason of his special vulnerability? There is a fundamental difference between degree and type: there is no recovery at all for the latter without foreseeability and it is illogical that this should be able to be affected by eggshell skull considerations. If this writer's previous criticism of *Page v. Smith (supra,* p.79) for abolishing the distinction between physical and mental injury were ever to be taken up, the submission here made would be all the more significant. Susceptibility to mental illness - not reasonably foreseeable - would be of a different type to physical injuries, reasonably foreseeable. In practice, however, as observed, the views here put may make little difference in the area of physical injuries, since it is expected that courts will continue to treat all physical conditions - for example, heart disease - other than the most unusual - such as lepto spirosis from rat's urine - as essentially no different a *type* of damage than a minor (foreseeable) personal injury. The fact that the greater *degree* of damage through heart attack was not reasonably foreseeable because the victim had latent heart disease should not then prevent recovery: eggshell heart.

What does at least seem to be clear furthermore, is that the eggshell skull principle will not be applied to *financial* weakness, that is, where a plaintiff suffers special damage because of lack of funds. The plaintiff will be expected to react to the negligent conduct as a person of ordinary means would do. Thus, in *Liesbosch Dredger v. SS Edison* [1933] AC 449, the defendants negligently sank the plaintiffs' boat. The plaintiffs did not have enough money to buy a replacement in order to fulfil their contracts, so that they had to hire one instead at a very high cost. The House of Lords held that the plaintiffs could only recover for the lower cost of purchasing a new boat. The defendants could not have foreseen the reasons for the extra loss to the plaintiffs, and the eggshell skull principle would not be applied to the plaintiffs' difficult financial position. Nevertheless, the *Liesbosch* restriction has been weakened in recent years, where courts have allowed recovery arising from shortage of funds if the plaintiffs were exercising good commercial sense or practice in not incurring replacement costs, presumably on the basis that the possibility of such a reaction should be reasonably foreseen in any event. For example, in *Dodds Properties (Kent) Ltd v. Canterbury City Council* [1980] 1 WLR 433, the plaintiffs were held by the Court of Appeal to have acted sensibly in waiting until after judgment had been reached against the defendants - eight years - before carrying out repairs even though costs were then much higher; money was scarce and would be better used for other purposes should the case against the defendants ultimately have proved to be unsuccessful and the plaintiffs unable to recover expenses from the defendants. Again, this was presumably generally foreseeable good sense and not limited specially to the plaintiffs. Similarly, in *Mattocks v. Mann* (1992) *The Times*, June 19, the plaintiff was held quite reasonably to have waited until her insurers paid out and to have hired in the meantime, rather than paying money herself, which she did not in fact possess, to have her own vehicle repaired.

3. *Summary of foreseeability for nervous shock*

(a) Where the plaintiff is the secondary victim: foreseeability of *nervous shock* (ex post facto) is required for the defendant to be liable. How could it be of *physical* damage to the plaintiff, when it is not *the plaintiff* who is physically injured nor in danger?

(b) Where the plaintiff is the primary victim: it is here that the majority in the House of Lords in *Page v. Smith* said that foreseeability of *physical* injury was enough for recovery in nervous shock because physical and mental were the same type of damage.

Thus, although this makes no difference to foreseeability for *duty of care*, because foreseeability of *any* admissible harm to the plaintiff is enough for such purpose, it does affect *remoteness*, because the plaintiff has to establish that the *type* of damage which occurred and which was claimed for (namely, nervous shock) was reasonably foreseeable - so that it would not otherwise have been sufficient to show that a different type of loss (that is, physical) was reasonably foreseeable if it were sought to claim for nervous shock.

Further reading:

Atiyah, "*Res Ipsa Loquitur* in England and Australia" (1972) 35 *Modern Law Review* 337.

Brazier, *Street on Torts*, 9th ed, 1993 (Butterworth & Co., London): ch.14.

Fleming, J.G., *The Law of Torts*, 8th ed, 1992 (The Law Book Company, Sydney): chs.9 and 14.

Hepple, B.A. and Matthews, M.H., *Tort: Cases and Materials*, 4th ed, 1991 (Butterworth & Co., London): ch.6.

Howarth, D., *Textbook on Tort*, 1995 (Butterworth & Co., London): ch.4.

Jones, M.A., *Textbook on Torts*, 4th ed, 1993 (Blackstone, London): ch.4.

Markesinis, B.S. and Deakin, S.F., *Tort Law*, 3rd ed, 1994 (Clarendon Press, Oxford): ch.2.

Reece, "Losses of Chances in the Law" (1996) 59 *Modern Law Review* 188.

Rogers, W.V.H., *Winfield and Jolowicz on Tort*, 14th ed, 1994 (Sweet & Maxwell, London): ch.6.

Scott, "Causation in Medico-Legal Practice: A Doctor's Approach to the 'Last Opportunity' Cases" (1992) 55 *Modern Law Review* 521.

Stanton, K.M., *The Modern Law of Tort*, 1994 (The Law Book Company, Sydney): ch.4.

Weir, T., *A Casebook on Tort*, 7th ed, 1992 (Sweet & Maxwell, London): ch.4.

PART V

Chapter 8

Liability of Occupiers of Property Towards Persons Who Enter

Introduction

Liability of occupiers of property for injuries caused to visitors has had a separate, though related, development to that of negligence generally.

This field is now governed largely by statute, as supplemented by the common law. Prior to the 1957 legislation, an occupier's liability towards his visitors would depend upon the circumstances of the visit, and, in particular, on whether the visitor entered under a contract (a "contractual licensee"), or had a common interest with the occupier (an "invitee"), or was granted permission to enter (a "licensee"), or entered without permission (a "trespasser"). The lowest standard of care was owed towards the last category - trespassers.

Following the 1957 and later legislation, the only two categories for distinction now are "lawful" and "unlawful" visitors. Lawful visitors are the concern of the Occupiers' Liability Act 1957; liability towards unlawful visitors is dealt with by the Occupiers' Liability Act 1984.

There is also a body of common law concerning the liability of *non-occupiers*, supplemented by the Defective

Premises Act 1972, s.4 specifically in relation to duties of landlords.

The main questions to arise in this area relate to physical injuries caused to visitors, or damage to their property, resulting from the condition of the premises or possibly also from activities carried out there - although, damage to adjoining premises is excluded and is instead covered by the torts of nuisance and by *Rylands v. Fletcher.*

It should be said that legal rules in this area have to take account of special sensitivities due to the fact that they may affect what people do in their own homes - the *Englishman's castle.* Many injuries which occur in private dwellings are not claimed for in any event, because house contents insurance, covering occupiers' liability, is not compulsory and few people would wish to sue their relatives.

The following account will be divided into a number of sections:

(i) liability of occupiers towards lawful visitors;
(ii) liability of occupiers towards persons other than lawful visitors;
(iii) liability of non-occupiers.

(i) Liability of Occupiers Towards Lawful Visitors

1. Scope of the legislation

Liability is governed by the Occupiers' Liability Act 1957.

It will be seen below that s.2(1) places an occupier of premises under a common duty of care towards his visitors in so far as this is not lawfully excluded. This raises the question of the precise scope of this provision. What are *premises?* Who is an *occupier?* Who are *visitors*?

a. Premises

These are defined by s.1(3)(a) so as to cover any fixed or movable structure, including any vessel, vehicle or aircraft. Courts have construed these widely so as to extend, for example, to chairs, ladders, scaffolding and lifts, as well as to the obvious, such as land, houses, shops and factories (*Wheeler v. Copas* [1981] 3 All ER 405). Seemingly, therefore, any object accommodating physical presence of a person is liable to be found to amount to premises.

It should in addition be mentioned that under s.1(3)(b), the duty of care includes damage to property brought onto the premises by the visitor, even if it does not also belong to the visitor.

b. Occupier

Section 1(2) says that common law meanings should apply.

The test at common law is one of *control.* Courts developed a number of principles as to the degree of control less than exclusive possession and ownership which may be considered to be sufficient for the purposes.

First, it would seem that an occupier need only have an immediate right to enter and to use the premises, even if he is not in actual physical occupation at the time of the injury. In *Harris v. Birkenhead Corporation* [1976] 1 All ER 341, a local authority compulsorily acquired a house and then served notice to quit on the tenant who left. The local authority left the property empty and made no attempt to display its ownership. Nonetheless, it was held to be an occupier.

The leading case in this area is *Wheat v. E. Lacon & Co. Ltd* [1966] AC 552. The defendants owned a public house, which was run by a manager - an employee - who lived in a flat above the public house and who was allowed to take in paying guests. The manager had no proprietary interest in the premises and was a mere contractual licensee to use these, with the defendants retaining the right to enter and repair. A guest fell down an unlit staircase and died. The House of Lords held the defendant owners to be an occupier (but not in fact liable for the act of a stranger in removing the light bulb from its fitting): although they were not in actual occupation, they nevertheless had sufficient control. It would have been different had the defendants instead granted exclusive occupation to the manager under a tenancy, with no retained right to enter and repair.

Secondly, it is further evident from *Wheat v. E. Lacon & Co. Ltd* that control is not dependent upon the existence of property rights in the premises -the manager himself was also considered to be an occupier in the alternative; and in addition, it follows that there may be more than one occupier, and of different parts of premises. Occupation may even be limited to specific purposes, for example, structural maintenance rather than general safety and repairs (*Collier v. Anglian Water Authority* (1983) *The Times*, March 26).

At bottom, therefore, the courts' decisions on existence of sufficient control will not be taken in total disregard of policy considerations concerning whether particular interests in premises should be considered to import corresponding responsibility for the safety of visitors thereto.

c. Lawful visitor

The first point to be made is that s.2(6) provides that persons entering premises *in the exercise of a right conferred by law* are to be treated as visitors, whether or not the occupier has granted permission. This will include policemen and firemen - but *not* those exercising a public or private right of way (*Greenhalgh v. British Railways Board* [1969] 2 QB 286). Section 1(1)(a) of the Occupiers' Liability Act 1984 now imposes the Act's duty of care towards persons exercising a *private* right of way (although, where the plaintiff is a third party, who is liable: the owner of the right of way, or of the land through which it runs?). *Public* rights of way are excluded from both the 1957 and 1984 Acts (*Greenhalgh v. British Railways Board* [1969] 2 QB 286), so that the common law applies (except in the case of negligence on the highway, governed by the Highways Act 1980, see *infra*), whereby it may be that the duty owed towards the user of such right is the same as that towards a trespasser at common law (see *Thomas v. British Railways Board* [1976] 3 All ER 15, *infra*). This has lately been confirmed by the House of Lords in *McGeown v. Northern Ireland Housing Executive* [1994] 3 All ER 53.

Secondly, s.5(1) says that where people enter in pursuance of a contract - for example, hotel guests, or plumbers - there is an implied term imposing the common duty of care, subject to any express provision increasing or reducing the duty.

Beyond this, however, s.1(2) merely says that a visitor is someone who would have been an *invitee* or *licensee* at common law: that is to say, a person sharing a common interest with the occupier, or someone expressly or impliedly permitted to enter.

The main distinction, therefore, is between lawful visitors and those entering without express or implied permission - *trespassers.* It is even possible for a person who enters with permission to have this withdrawn by the occupier, upon which, after a reasonable time in which to leave, he becomes a trespasser.

As to these categories of lawful visitor, there cannot be much difficulty in determining when a person has expressly been invited to visit. The problems usually involve deciding whether a person has implied authorization to enter or is a mere trespasser who is there without permission. Implied permission is a question of fact which courts will not readily treat as having been given.

The following are some of the principles applied.

People entering upon property in order to knock at the door of a house, perhaps in order to sell something or to ask for their ball back if it was kicked into the garden, have implied permission (*Robson v. Hallet* [1967] 2 QB 939).

However, mere knowledge of entry cannot be presumed also to be implied consent, yet may be taken to be such where a perfectly simple and reasonable means of indicating disapproval were available but not exercised. Thus, in *Edwards v. Railway Executive* [1952] AC 737, the court held that repeated trespass did not confer implied permission: and in fact the occupier had tried to prevent it by mending a fence. On the other hand, in *Lowery v. Walker* [1911] AC 10, the defendant occupier took no steps at all to prevent people using his field as a short route to the railway station and the plaintiff was injured by a dangerous horse which the defendant had placed in the field without notice. The plaintiff was held to be a lawful visitor.

Courts have been more willing to imply permission in the case of children who are tempted - "allured" - onto premises by an attractive object. In *Glasgow Corporation v. Taylor* [1922] 1 AC 44, the defendant occupiers were held liable towards a seven-year-old child attracted to poisonous berries which the child ate and died. However, if the child had been told to leave by the occupier, he would have remained a trespasser (*Liddle v. Yorkshire (North Riding) County Council* [1944] 2 KB 101), and since, following the Occupiers' Liability Act 1984, trespassers are not treated as harshly as before, courts may be less prepared to imply permission to enter in the case of children, although, allurements will still be relevant to foreseeability and causation under the common duty of care.

Even where permission to enter is granted, this may be limited in time and space so that the visitor becomes a trespasser if he exceeds either of these by, for example, going to another part of the premises, even accidentally, or by staying too long. In *The Calgarth* [1927] P.93, Scrutton, LJ made his famous remark that "when you invite a person into your house to use the stairs, you do not invite him to slide down the bannisters." Thus, in *Gould v. McAuliffe* [1941] 2 All ER 527, the plaintiff was bitten by a dog when searching for a toilet in a drinking bar - the court held that had the defendant clearly indicated that there was no permission to enter that part of the building, the plaintiff would have been a trespasser. Similarly, the plaintiff's husband in *Stone v. Taffe* [1974] 1 WLR 1575 was not a trespasser when he died falling down steps outside a drinking bar after licensing hours, because the defendants' manager had not indicated to the plaintiff's husband that he had to leave at that time. Again, in *R. v. Smith and Jones* [1976] 1 WLR 672, the accused was held to be a trespasser, because his reason for entry to his father's house - to steal a television set - was not one for which he had general permission to enter.

Finally, it would seem that an employer occupier will be liable towards a visitor brought onto the premises by an employee against the employer's express instructions, if the visitor honestly and reasonably believed that he had permission and was unaware of the arrangements between employer and employee (*Ferguson v. Welsh* [1987] 2 All ER 777).

2. *The common duty of care under the Act*

Section 2(1) provides that an occupier of premises owes the same duty, the common duty of care, to all his visitors except in so far as he is free to and does extend, restrict, modify or exclude his duty to any visitor or visitors by agreement or otherwise.

Common duty of care means that it applies to all lawful visitors and that there is no longer any distinction between invitees and licensees.

The duty, it will be noted, is to make the visitor safe, not the premises.

There is a view that under the Act, the duty exists solely as to the state of the premises, rather than also as to activities carried out there (see *Ogwo v. Taylor* [1987] 2 WLR 988). However, the majority of the House of Lords in

Ferguson v. Welsh [1987] 3 All ER 777 appeared to take the opposite approach.

As for the standard of care, s.2(2) defines this as a duty to take such care as in all the circumstances is reasonable to see that the visitor will be reasonably safe in using the premises for the purposes for which he is invited or permitted by the occupier to be there: *reasonable* care in all the circumstances to see that the visitor is *reasonably* safe. In other words, the same as in the case of negligence (*Roles v. Nathan* [1963] 2 All ER 908). Circumstances will include *inter alia* balancing risk against expense, and anticipating reasonably foreseeable unlawful actions by other visitors, such as ripping pieces of concrete out of a football stand and throwing them around (*Cunningham v. Reading Football Club Ltd* (1991) *The Independent*, March 20).

If the visitor uses the premises for an unauthorized purpose, he becomes a trespasser to that extent and subject to the 1984 Act. You do not expect your milkman to practice his golf swings in your back garden.

3. *Specific provisions on the common duty of care*

Some guidance is included in the Act as to operation of the common duty of care in particular cases.

a. Children

Section 2(3)(a) specifically provides that an occupier must be prepared for children to be less careful than adults. It will be recalled that prior to the 1984 Act which improved the position of trespassers, courts seemed prepared to find an implied licence to enter in favour of children who were said to have been "allured" into a "trap" by some tempting object which would have had no appeal for an adult so as no longer to be trespassers: for example, the poisonous berries which were not fenced off or warned against in the botanical garden in *Glasgow Corporation v. Taylor* (but not a mere heap of stones in *Latham v. R. Johnson & Nephew Ltd* [1913] 1 KB 398).

However, notwithstanding the improved position of trespassers, which may lead courts to be less willing to find implied consent in favour of children, s.2(3)(a) still requires a potentially higher standard of care towards children: occupiers should reasonably anticipate that child visitors may act less carefully than adults and reasonably guard against this. For example, in *Moloney v. Lambeth London Borough Council* (1966) 64 LGR 440, the occupier was held liable when a boy aged four fell through a gap in railings on a staircase, when an adult could not have done so. Presumably, too, a sensible adult would not also have eaten the poisonous berries in *Glasgow Corporation v. Taylor*.

Ultimately, reasonable care is a question of fact and the younger the child, the higher the standard of care that is likely to be required. The problem with this is that it is not entirely practical for all businesses, homes and public places to be made 100 per cent *child-proof*. To accommodate this, courts developed the principle that children of a very young age, or in certain circumstances whatever their age, could not reasonably be expected to be unaccompanied by an adult to look after them. The result is that courts will either hold the child entering without a parent to be a trespasser, in breach of the conditional licence to enter only if in the company of a parent, or even if not, find that the occupier's reasonable standard of care towards a child being looked after by its parent had not been broken. Thus, in *Phipps v. Rochester Corporation* [1955] 1 QB 450, a five-year-old boy was injured when he fell into a hole dug on a housing estate under construction while crossing to pick berries. The occupiers were not liable: the boy was not a trespasser because the occupiers knew that children often played there and had done nothing to warn them off, and the occupiers should also reasonably have foreseen that children may go where they should not. However, the court felt that no reasonable parent would have permitted a child to play on a building site and the occupiers could therefore reasonably assume that a child would not be unaccompanied. The Judge said that responsibility for the safety of little children rested primarily on the parents and that it would be socially undesirable for that burden to be shifted as a matter of course to occupiers of bits of land.

This is a disturbing doctrine, unless applied highly restrictively. The world is full of unreasonable parents, or parents who through financial exigencies may feel that they have no option but to allow their child to go unaccompanied, and of children who disobey their most reasonable and caring parents to go looking for their stray dog. Should not occupiers reasonably recognize this and take safety precautions - especially since it has already been seen that occupiers are generally expected to anticipate unreasonable behaviour of third parties (*Cunningham v. Reading Football Club Ltd, supra*)? Nevertheless, the same approach as in *Phipps* was applied in *Simkiss v. Rhondda Borough Council* (1983) 81 LGR 460, in which occupiers were held not to be liable towards a seven-year-old girl who was injured sliding down a grass bank where her father had allowed her to picnic, because the defendants could assume that a parent would not allow a child to play where it was dangerous.

The father himself admitted that he did not consider the slope to be dangerous, which is why he did not accompany his daughter.

As said, this is worrying. By all means take account of the father's views in assessing how reasonable and unreasonable parents might be expected to affect the behaviour of children. But occupiers should not simply be allowed to place conclusive reliance upon the parents' views or actions.

b. Workmen

Section 2(3)(b) states that a person in the exercise of his trade will appreciate and guard against any special risks ordinarily incidental to it, so far as the occupier leaves him free to do so. This is the opposite of the preceding category relating to children: less care rather than more. People who repair rooves may slip; window cleaners can fall. They know they can and may be expected to guard against these ordinary, special risks of their trade, so that the occupier is not in breach of the common duty of care if he has taken no special steps over and above the normal to make them safe. In *Roles v. Nathan* [1963] 2 All ER 908, two chimney sweeps were killed by poisonous fumes from a central heating boiler while cleaning a chimney. The occupier was held not to be liable, because fumes were a special risk ordinarily incidental to the activity of a chimney sweep and the sweeps should have known this - in addition to which, the occupier was also not liable since the sweeps had been warned by the occupier not to carry out the cleaning while the boiler was lit.

However, the standard of care is only affected by risks *ordinarily incidental* to the trade. So, for example, if the occupier had knocked a saucepan of boiling water over the chimney sweep, or the stairs had given way as workmen made their way to repair a roof, s.2(3)(b) would be inapplicable (*Bird v. King Line Ltd* [1970] 1 Lloyd's Rep 349 - shipworker falling over empty bottle on ship's deck not ordinarily incidental). Furthermore, it would seem that "special" means risk special to the trade and not special beyond those ordinarily encountered in that trade.

Nevertheless, the fact remains that even within the sphere of the workman's special risks, it is not impossible for the occupier to be held to be in breach of the common duty of care. He must still make conditions as safe as is reasonable for a person exercising the trade and cannot absolve himself completely from taking care. One should not invite someone to repair the roof and fail to inform him that all the slates are loose if one is aware of this. Thus, in *Salmon v. Seafarer Restaurants Ltd* [1983] 3 All ER 729, firemen were injured trying to put out a fire at a fish and chip shop. The court rejected the occupiers' argument that they could not be liable other than for risks which were beyond those ordinarily incidental to a fireman's activities.

c. Warnings

Section 2(4)(a) says that where damage is caused to a visitor by danger of which he has been warned by the occupier, the warning is not to be treated *without more* as releasing the occupier from liability, unless in all the circumstances it was enough to enable the visitor to be reasonably safe.

Furthermore, the warning is ineffective to reduce the occupier's standard of care if:

(a) it would not be *understood* by a reasonable person, for example, a child, blind person or foreigner, depending on all the circumstances, and

(b) even if it is capable of being understood, it may not be *sufficient* if the visitor cannot do anything to avoid the danger. Thus, it is for the occupier to make the visitor safe. It is no good warning the postman to be careful of a savage dog, without also tethering the canine aggressor (*Rae v. Mars (UK) Ltd* [1990] 3 EG 80 - unlit pit should be fenced off). So, in *Roles v. Nathan* [1963] 2 All ER 908 it was said that there was no point in warning a visitor that a footbridge was rotten if this was the only access to the house, whereas, if there was another perfectly good bridge, the notice would be sufficient to make the visitor reasonably safe.

Finally, certain distinctions must be kept in mind in respect of the following notices:

1. "Be careful of the steps - they might be slippery."
2. "Use these steps at your own risk."
3. "No liability accepted for injuries to people using these steps."

Number 1 is a s.2(4)(a) *warning* which may affect the occupier's standard of care. Number 2 may found the *defence* of consent (*volenti non fit injuria,* see *infra,* ch.29). Number 3 is an *exclusion* of the occupier's liability (*ibid.*). Which of them it is is a matter of construction and may have differing legal consequences. Naturally, a notice could contain more than one of these formulae.

d. Work done by independent contractors

Section 2(4)(b) provides that where damage is caused to a visitor by a danger due to faulty construction, maintenance or repair by an independent contractor employed by the occupier, the occupier is not to be treated without more as answerable for the danger if in all the circumstances he acted reasonably in entrusting the work to an independent contractor and had taken such steps, if any, as he reasonably ought in order to satisfy himself that the contractor was competent and that the work had been properly done.

Occupiers have to employ others to carry out skilled work to premises. They can only reasonably be expected to do so much to ensure that the work has been properly executed. Section 2(4)(b) seeks to lay down some ground rules in this respect.

Faulty Construction, Maintenance or Repair

Other types of work are excluded from the reduced standard, although maintenance and repair do seem quite wide. In *Ferguson v. Welsh* [1987] 3 All ER 777, the House of Lords supported a broad and purposive construction of the words, and held that construction included demolition (including minor such work *AMF International Ltd v. Magnet Bowling Ltd* [1968] 1 WLR 1028).

Acted Reasonably in Employing Independent Contractor

This will depend *inter alia* on the complexity of the task. Compare *Haseldine v. CA Daw & Son Ltd* [1941] 2 KB 343 and *Woodward v. Mayor of Hastings* [1945] KB 174. In the former the occupier was held to have acted reasonably in employing a contractor to maintain a lift in a block of flats; in the latter, a local authority was held not to have been reasonable in leaving it entirely to cleaners to make safe an icy step at a school on which a child slipped. In the latter, the Judge commented that whilst the "craft of the charwoman may have its mysteries ... there is no esoteric quality in the nature of the work which the cleaning of a snow-covered step demands."

Reasonable Steps to Check Competence

Most householders have limited ability to assess competence of workmen and must accept whatever service is provided, trying to avoid obvious risks and using Chambers of Commerce and trade associations for advice where possible. In *Ferguson v. Welsh* the plaintiffs failed to prove that the defendant ought reasonably to have had doubts about the contractor.

Reasonable Steps to Check Work Was Properly Carried Out

The same arguments apply - although the occupier should ask surveyors and architects to validate major or important work if possible. In *AMF International Ltd v. Magnet Bowling Ltd* [1968] 1 WLR 1028, the occupiers were held liable towards the plaintiff supplier of bowling equipment which was damaged when water flooded the defendant's bowling alley in the course of being built by the defendant's contractor. The occupiers had done nothing to check the state of the contractor's work for themselves after receiving the latter's assurance. On the other hand, in *Haseldine v. Daw,* it was not reasonably possible for the occupiers to check the contractors' lift maintenance work, so that the occupiers were not liable when the lift fell to the bottom of the shaft killing its occupants.

Similarly, in *Ferguson v. Welsh* the plaintiff employee was injured through the contractor's unsafe system of work and sued the local authority occupier. The House of Lords held that the occupier escaped liability under s.2(4)(b): unless there were grounds to suspect the contractor's competence, it was not reasonable to expect the occupier to supervise everything the contractor did.

4. *Defences*

As previously indicated, the occupier can rely upon a number of defences.

a. Consent of the visitor

Section 2(5) preserves *volenti non fit injuria:* occupiers do not owe a duty to visitors in respect of risks willingly accepted by the visitor: "Enter at your own risk". Thus, a professional rugby player accepts the risks of playing on rugby grounds complying with standards set by the Rugby League, the game's governing body (*Simms v. Leigh Rugby Football Club Ltd* [1969] 2 All ER 923).

However, s.2(5) has to be read together with s.2(4)(a) on effects of warnings when the latter are said to be the basis of the alleged consent (see *supra*, p.329). Thus, in such cases the occupier is not excused, unless the effect of the "consent" is to make it reasonable for the occupier to take no further steps to make the premises safe (*Bunker v. Charles Brand & Sons Ltd* [1969] 2 QB 480). Furthermore, if the plaintiff had no true choice other than to enter and to accept the state of premises - for example, an employee - this will not amount to consent (*Burnett v. British Waterways Board* [1973] 2 All ER 631).

b. Contributory negligence

If the visitor's own negligence contributed to the harm suffered, damages are apportioned under the Law Reform (Contributory Negligence) Act 1945, as in an ordinary negligence action (see *infra*, ch.29).

c. Exclusion of liability

It will be recalled that the common duty of care is imposed under s.2(1) of the 1957 Act except in so far as the occupier is free to and does extend, restrict, modify or exclude his duty to any visitor or visitors by agreement or otherwise.

With regard to methods of exclusion, s.2(1) says that this may be by agreement *or otherwise*. This, therefore, includes a notice. In *Ashdown v. Samuel Williams & Sons Ltd* [1957] 1 QB 409, there were notices on the defendant's land excluding liability for negligence. The plaintiff visitor was injured by some railway trucks. The court held the exclusion to be effective, because the plaintiff had only been allowed entry on such conditions, and could have chosen to keep out altogether. Again, in *White v. Blackmore* [1972] 2 QB 651, there was a notice at the entrance of a car race track and elsewhere on the course excluding organizers' liability for injuries. A man was killed when a competitor's car crashed. The court held that the notice was effective to exclude the defendants' liability. Those were the terms of entry.

However, it will be apparent from the *Ashdown* case that there are limits to the ability to exclude liability by notice:

(a) the notice must be reasonably capable of being understood by plaintiffs, including children, or blind or illiterate persons, if entry by these people could reasonably have been anticipated (*Geier v. Kujawa* [1970] 1 Lloyd's Rep 364), and

(b) again, as in the case of consent, liability cannot be excluded in this way where the visitor has no choice but to enter (*Burnett v. British Waterways Board*).

There are in fact further statutory restrictions on exclusion which must be mentioned here.

i. *Section 3(1) of the 1957 Act*. This provides that where an occupier is bound by a contract to permit persons who are strangers to the contract to enter or use the premises, the common duty of care owed to the strangers as visitors by the occupier cannot be excluded or restricted by the contract. This means that a landlord occupying the common parts of a block of flats cannot exclude his common duty of care towards his tenants' visitors by the terms of his contracts with the tenants.

ii. *Unfair Contract Terms Act 1977.* The restrictions upon liability exclusion in this Act apply only to business liability and to breach of duty arising from the occupation of business premises (s.1(3)). "Business" includes professions, local or central government departments, schools and hospitals (s.14). However, entry for recreational or educational purposes is expressly excluded from the Act's restrictions on exclusion (for example, people permitted to enjoy a walk across a farmer's land), unless these are the very purposes of the business (for example, a swimming pool or leisure centre) (s.1(3)). Private occupiers are of course outside these provisions.

The restriction in the Act is as follows:

(a) exclusion of liability for death or personal injury through negligence arising from the state of the premises, by contract or notice, is void (s.2(1)); and

(b) exclusion of liability for loss or damage to property is only valid to the extent that the contract term or notice is reasonable in all the circumstances (s.2(2)). (Occupiers cannot escape the reasonableness requirement by pleading consent instead of exclusion as a defence, because s.2(3) expressly says that agreement or awareness of an exclusionary term or notice does not of itself amount to voluntary acceptance of any risk.)

(ii) Liability of Occupiers Towards Persons Other Than Lawful Visitors. Trespassers

1. The earlier law

Traditionally, the law of tort was very harsh towards persons who were injured on the occupier's premises when they were there against his knowledge or will, that is to say, towards *trespassers.* The occupier would only be liable if he had intentionally injured (deliberately set a man-trap for or otherwise intended to harm) trespassers, or recklessly injured them (did not care whether trespasser was injured or not). Mere failure to exercise reasonable care for a trespasser's safety - that is, negligence - would not lead to liability. In *Robert Addie & Sons (Collieries) v. Dumbreck* [1929] AC 358, occupiers of a mining colliery were held not liable towards a child seriously injured when playing on machinery, because children were frequently chased off by employees of the colliery so that the child was a trespasser and the injuries were neither intentional nor reckless. No one invites a trespasser to come onto his land.

2. Later developments

A number of methods were used in order to improve the harsh treatment of trespassers. In the case of children, it was seen earlier that courts developed a practice of often finding implied consent where there was a tempting allurement on the premises, so that they were not then held to be trespassers and the ordinary duty of care in negligence was owed to them.

In addition, following the Lord Chancellor's Practice

Statement of 1966, in which for the first time the House of Lords was permitted to depart from its previous judgments where it was right to do so, the House of Lords was able to establish a duty of "common humanity" towards trespassers in the case of *British Railways Board v. Herrington* [1972] AC 877, where occupiers were held liable towards a six-year-old child trespasser who was injured by an electric rail on the track, having crawled through a hole in the fence which the defendants knew the public regularly used for a short cut and yet had done nothing to repair. The Lords held that although the defendants were not liable for negligence (*quaere* whether their action did not amount to reckless disregard for the safety of trespassers in any event in the circumstances?), they did owe a duty of common humanity towards trespassers, which they had broken on the facts, since it would have been very easy for them to repair the broken fence in order to prevent people, including children, from entering and crossing the track.

The precise nature of this duty of common humanity was as follows:

i. Humanity

The duty would be broken where a reasonable man, possessed of the defendant's knowledge of the existence of the danger, would have regarded it as *inhumane* not to give a warning or to take reasonable steps to protect the trespasser, and the defendant took no such action: a combined subjective-(based on defendant's actual knowledge)-objective-(reasonable man would consider protective action humane whatever the defendant himself might think) test.

ii. Danger

A similar subjective-objective approach applied to whether the premises were to be regarded as dangerous or not.

iii. Reasonable steps to protect

Again, both subjective and objective considerations would come into play. What steps was it reasonable to expect the occupier to take (objective) having regard to his actual resources, skills and abilities (subjective) - a balance of expense and risk (analogy with private nuisance is impossible to avoid). The defendants held liable in *Herrington* would have had no difficulty in repairing the fence.

In most reported cases, the occupier was held liable, all the more so if he had actually created the danger on the premises rather than failing to repair natural dilapidation. Thus, in *Southern Portland Cement Ltd v. Cooper* [1974] AC 623, PC, defendants were liable where a pile of waste sand in a quarry had been placed near a 33,000 volt electric cable overhead, enabling a 13-year-old boy to climb up to play which led to an accident. Again, in *Pannett v. McGuiness* [1972] 2 QB 599, an occupier of a building site was held liable towards a five-year-old child trespasser, because safety measures could reasonably have been taken; and in *Harris v. Birkenhead Corporation* [1975] 1 All ER 1001, the occupier of empty properties was held liable even though the child trespasser who had fallen out of a top floor window had smashed the front door down, because the occupier knew that children habitually went in and ought reasonably to have provided a warning as well as attempting to board up the properties.

On the other hand, the duty of common humanity was held not to have been broken in *Penny v. Northampton Borough Council* (1974) 72 LGR 733 where a child threw an aerosol can onto a burning fire on a 50-acre council rubbish tip. It would have been extremely costly to local ratepayers for the council to have built a fence around so large a site.

3. The Occupiers' Liability Act 1984

In 1972 the Lord Chancellor asked the Law Commission to consider the law relating to liability towards trespassers, in the light of the *Herrington* case. The Commission reported that the *Herrington* principles should be extended to all trespassers, not just children in practice (Law Com No. 75, Cmnd 6428 (1976)), and as a consequence the 1984 Act was passed, which replaces, but substantially repeats, the principles of common humanity of the common law.

a. Scope

The 1984 Act only applies to personal injuries, not also to damage to the property of trespassers (s.1(8)).

"Premises" and "occupier" are defined as in the 1957 Act (s.1(2)) and liability arises from dangers due to the state of the premises, or from things done or omitted to be done on them, provided that what is done in some way concerns the state of the premises and is not completely unrelated thereto (s.1(1)).

b. Persons other than the occupier's visitors

Section 1(1)(a) provides that the duty is owed to such

persons. The main category is that of trespassers.

However, it also includes people exercising a statutory right of way under s.60 of the National Parks and Access to the Countryside Act 1949, and people exercising a private right of way. The latter were plainly intended by the Law Commission to be covered by the 1984 Act - yet it is evident from previous case law that an owner of land over which a right of way passes will not always be an "occupier" of the right of way (*Holden v. White* [1982] QB 679). If he is not, the 1984 Act is inapplicable and common law principles will have to govern, according to which there is no liability for failure to act (non-feasance) as opposed to positive negligence (misfeasance).

It will be recalled that persons using a public right of way were excluded from the 1957 Act (*Greenhalgh v. British Railways Board* [1969] 2 QB 286). This is continued by the 1984 Act - s.1(7) says that the Act does not apply to people using the highway. In fact, s.58 of the Highways Act 1980 now imposes liability for negligent acts or omissions of highway authorities leading to physical injuries or damage to property. Other public rights of way are subject to the common law on this matter, which holds the defendant liable for acts but not omissions (although, in *Thomas v. British Railways Board* [1976] 3 All ER 15, involving a two-year-old child, the court seemed to apply *Herrington* principles of common humanity).

c. Existence of the duty of care

Section 1(3) specifies when the duty is owed. This will be where:

(a) the occupier is aware of the danger or has reasonable grounds to believe it exists;
(b) knows or has reasonable grounds to believe the other person is in or may come into the vicinity of the danger (whether that person has lawful authority or not); and
(c) the risk is one against which in all the circumstances the occupier may reasonably be expected to offer the person some protection.

This is a mainly objective test:

- the occupier knows of the danger, or ought reasonably to;
- he knows that the other person will be near the danger, or ought reasonably to; and
- he ought reasonably to think about providing some protection.

However, it seems likely that the *Herrington* subjective-objective combination is nonetheless preserved, because courts are likely to consider whether the occupier should reasonably (objective) have known of danger, presence of the person and possible need for protection, on the basis of facts *actually known* (subjective) to the occupier. Again, therefore, it would seem that the occupier is not required to go looking for conditions amounting to dangers on his premises of which he is unaware, and it is not sufficient to establish liability that a reasonable occupier would have known of the danger and possible presence of the trespasser.

Thus, in *White v. St Albans City & District Council* (1990) *The Times,* March 12, the Court of Appeal declined to conclude from the fact that an occupier had taken steps to prevent unauthorized entry by blocking a short cut to a car park, that it was necessarily reasonably foreseeable or known to the occupier that people might try to enter and come within the vicinity of danger for purposes of s.1(3)(b). The defendants were not aware that the short cut was used in this way, nor of any facts to suggest that it might be being so used, and it mattered not whether a reasonable man would have guessed that people were using the short cut.

With regard to s.1(3)(c), existence of the duty further depends upon the subjective-objective test of whether *this* occupier, in all the circumstances - including those taken into account under s.1(4) concerning *standard* of care, such as extent of risk and steps required - ought reasonably to have done anything at all to protect the entrant. One difference from *Herrington* is that it seems doubtful whether *personal resources* of the occupier will be taken into account in the assessment under s.1(3)(c) of whether some action is reasonably to be taken to protect the plaintiff (similarly under s.1(4) on standard) - the subjective element will consist in drawing conclusions on reasonableness of taking any protective steps in the light of facts known to the occupier.

d. Standard of care

Section 1(4) sets the standard of care under the duty - such care as is reasonable in all the circumstances of the case to see that the trespasser does not suffer injury on the premises by reason of the danger.

As commented earlier in relation to existence of the duty under s.1(3)(c), all circumstances will include *inter alia* balancing reasonable cost against extent of risk, as well as the character of trespasser as a child or otherwise, seriousness or likely injury and public or private nature of premises. Thus, s.1(3)(c) says (together with (a) and (b)) whether appropriate and reasonable care should be taken at all to protect the plaintiff, and s.1(4) states what that reasonable care is - if anything - if it is to be so taken. The test under s.1(4), as with s.1(3)(c), will not take account of the defendant's resources and abilities, but will nonetheless subjectively assess the occupier's state of knowledge of the facts in order to determine objective reasonableness of any protective steps to be taken.

Accordingly, one may assume that the reasonable standard of care towards a child will be higher than towards a thief who climbs over a garden fence and crashes into a glass greenhouse, if only because thieves can be expected to be aware of dangers of their activities, not to mention the greater level of unreasonableness of a thief's behaviour compared to that of a mischievous child.

In *Revill v. Newbery* [1996] 1 All ER 291, CA, the defendant was a 76-year-old man asleep in a shed on his garden allotment when he was awoken by the plaintiff attempting to break in. The defendant poked his shotgun through a hole in the door and blasted it, hitting the plaintiff at about five feet. The plaintiff claimed damages for personal injuries, as a trespasser. The Court of Appeal held the defendant liable (subject to the plaintiff's own *substantial* contributory negligence, pp.300, 301-2): he had used greater violence than was justified in self-defence and was negligent by reference to the standard of care to be expected from a reasonable man. The shot fired was not merely a warning, but was aimed at body height, horizontally (p.300). Millett, LJ explained: "For centuries the common law has permitted reasonable force to be used in defence of the person or property. Violence may be returned with necessary violence. But the force used must not exceed the limits of what is reasonable in the circumstances. Changes in society and in social perceptions have meant that what might have been considered reasonable at one time would no longer be so regarded; but the principle remains the same. The assailant or intruder may be met with reasonable force but no more; the use of excessive violence against him is an actionable wrong ... Mr Newbery's conduct was not reasonable. It was clearly dangerous and bordered on reckless" (pp.301-2).

Section 1(5) supplements the general provision in s.1(4), in providing that a duty may be discharged by taking reasonable steps to *give a warning* of the danger or to discourage persons from incurring risk.

Occupiers may therefore be taken to have done all that is required to discharge their duty if they put up warning notices, even if they do nothing else to make the premises safe and to remove the danger. As to what is a reasonable warning, this will depend on the circumstances: very small children can reasonably be expected not to be unaccompanied by their parents; young children cannot necessarily read - even if they can, some will disregard what they read (*Pannett*); non-English-speaking foreigners might frequently be amongst those trespassing; in some cases, consequently, a mere notice will not be enough and another deterrent may be necessary to discourage trespassers if the duty is to be discharged, for example, alarms and flashing lights (even these might not be sufficient in the case of a trespassing foreigner, or deaf-blind child). In *Westwood v. Post Office* [1973] 1 QB 591, a notice on a lift engine room door said "Only Authorized Attendant is Permitted to Enter." In the circumstances, the court considered that a normal intelligent person would not simply understand this to relate to privacy, but as indicating danger from which they should keep away.

Conceivably, a warning notice may be so clear - for example, "Keep Out. There are dangerous live wires which can trip you up and kill you" - as actually to lead to the conclusion that any unauthorized entrant is in fact *consenting* to the risk under s.1(6) (see below).

e. Defences

i. *Consent.* Section 1(6) retains *volenti non fit injuria.* Courts are not particularly reluctant to apply the defence of consent in the case of trespassers if it is clear that the trespasser understood that there was a sufficiently serious risk of danger (*Westwood v. Post Office, supra*).

ii. *Exclusion.* Unlike the 1957 Act, the 1984 Act does not say whether liability towards trespassers thereunder can be excluded. Furthermore, in the case of business occupiers, the Unfair Contract Terms Act 1977 is thought not to have applied to restrict exclusion of the common law duty of common humanity towards trespassers, and s.1(1)(b) and (c) of the 1977 Act only mention the common law duty of care and that under the 1957 Act.

Does this mean that since the 1957 Act allows exclusion but the 1984 does not, it is better to be a trespasser (or other person who is not a visitor, for example, user of a private right of way) rather than a lawful visitor to a household, where the occupier has excluded his liability? This is precisely the argument in favour of permitting exclusion under the 1984 Act. The argument against such exclusion is that the law has set a minimum standard towards trespassers in the 1984 Act which should not be able to be reduced any further.

The courts will eventually have to decide.

One suspects that most people would support exclusion where this is properly brought to the trespasser's attention so as to be effective. *"I do not authorize you to enter. But even if you do, I shall exclude such liability as the law imposes upon me not to put you in danger."*

iii. Illegality not a Defence

In *Revill v. Newbery* (*supra*, p.344), the defendant argued that no duty of care could be owed towards a trespasser who was engaged upon a criminal activity, such as theft: *ex turpi causa non oritur actio*. The Court of Appeal held there to be no such principle of law under the 1984 Act which had intended to regulate liability towards trespassers whether they were criminals or otherwise and not to turn the plaintiff into an "outlaw" (p.299). The plaintiff's behaviour rather involved the defence of contributory negligence, as satisfying fault and responsibility (pp.300-301).

iii. Liability of Persons Other than Occupiers

1. Independent contractors

If they have sufficient control of the premises on which they are carrying out works, they are "occupiers" under the 1957 and 1984 Acts.

If not, they are subject to the ordinary law of negligence, whether the plaintiff is lawful visitor or trespasser (*AC Billings & Sons Ltd v. Riden* [1958] AC 240). This hardly differs from that under the 1957 Act. Thus, in *Buckland v. Guildford Gas Light & Coke Co.* [1944] 1 KB 410, contractors stretching an electricity cable through a tree's branches on a farmer's land ought reasonably to have foreseen that the plaintiff trespasser might have climbed the tree and been electrocuted.

2. *Landlords*

It will be recalled that a landlord may himself remain an occupier where:

(a) he has a right to enter, inspect and maintain (*Wheat v. E. Lacon & Co. Ltd*), or
(b) as to the common parts of the premises, such as stairways and entrance hall, over which he retains control (*Jacobs v. London County Council* [1950] AC 361).

What is the position where a landlord is not an occupier for the purposes of the Acts?

At common law, if the landlord (of unfurnished property) did not create the danger himself - for example, the premises were already dangerous when he bought the property - he would not be liable for omitting to make them safe. Thus, in *Cavalier v. Pope* [1906] AC 428 the tenant's wife fell through the kitchen floor which had not been repaired by the landlord. The latter was held not liable for the omission.

As a result of what was perceived to be a failure of the law sufficiently to control landlords, the Defective Premises Act 1972 was passed.

Section 4(1) says that where a landlord has an obligation towards a tenant under a tenancy to maintain or repair the premises, the landlord owes to *all* persons who might reasonably be expected to be affected by the defective state of the premises a duty to take such care as is reasonable in all the circumstances to see that they are reasonably safe from personal injury or damage to their property caused by a relevant defect.

Section 4(2) says that the duty is only owed if the landlord knows or ought in all the circumstances to have known of the relevant defect.

Section 4(3) defines relevant defects very broadly as:

- existing *at* or after the material time, and
- arising from or *continuing*
- because of an act *or omission* of the landlord

constituting a failure of his obligation towards the tenant to repair or maintain.

Section 4(4) extends the duty to where the landlord has a mere *power* to enter and repair.

Under s.4(5), an obligation of a landlord to repair may

be expressed, implied or laid down by statute. An example of the latter would be the Landlord and Tenant Act 1985 requiring a lessor of a dwellinghouse for a term under seven years to keep the structure, exterior and water, gas and electricity installations in good repair.

Section 6(3) provides that s.4 duties cannot be excluded or restricted by any term of the agreement.

It will be noted that under s.4(1) the duties are owed to *all* persons who might reasonably be expected to be affected: the tenant, his family, their visitors, trespassers, and even people using the adjoining highway or on neighbouring land.

3. Builders

The position at common law regarding liability of builders for defective premises was noteworthy:

(a) if the builder also owned the premises and then sold or let them, he was treated as seller or lessor rather than builder - this meant the rule of sales and leasing contracts, *caveat emptor*, applied, and there was no liability in negligence (*Bottomley v. Banister* [1932] 1 KB 458); but

(b) if the builder did not own the property, he was liable in negligence to people injured by defects.

Furthermore, it used to be thought that rights in tort could not exist alongside a seller's or lessor's contractual duties.

Then, in 1972, two things happened to change this:

i. The Defective Premises Act 1972. Section 3 provided that any duty of care otherwise owed to persons who might reasonably be expected to be affected by building defects would not be prevented by subsequent disposal of the premises by the person owing the duty.

ii. Case Law. As it happened, while the 1972 Act was proceeding through Parliament, the courts were, in any event, undoing the old law.

In *Dutton v. Bognor Regis Urban District Council* [1972] 1 QB 373, the Court of Appeal held that a builder who sold property *did* owe a duty of care in negligence - approved in *Anns v. Merton London Borough Council* [1978] AC 728. Thus, in *Rimmer v. Liverpool City Council* [1984] 1 All ER 930, the defendant lessor owed a duty in negligence towards the tenant for injuries through faulty construction or design as builders and designers, notwithstanding their additional status as landlords.

Dutton and *Anns* were in fact subsequently overruled by the House of Lords in *Murphy v. Brentwood District Council* [1990] 2 All ER 908, in the matter of the type of loss which can be recovered for: that is, to the extent that they upheld a principle of claiming (against a local authority) in negligence for defects in the building itself (purely economic loss) through failure to check a builder's work and his compliance with building regulations, thereby threatening imminent danger to the health and safety of occupants (see *supra*, p.192, *et seq.*).

However, it is generally accepted that the principle of a builder's ordinary liability in negligence for injuries caused to any person or to property other than the building itself by latent defects in the building, survived *Murphy* - and the same duty was in fact conceded by the defendant there to be placed on a local authority negligently inspecting and certifying the work.

What is a plaintiff to do, however, in respect of damage to the building itself, excluded from an ordinary negligence claim as pure economic loss in accordance with *Murphy*?

There are three possibilities:

(1) *Murphy* would allow an ordinary negligence action where the defect was caused by a separate contractor's installation or integral component part distinct from the damaged part (*supra*, p.191).

(2) It is possible that an action could be brought for breach of the statutory duty to comply with building regulations, under s.38 of the Building Act 1984, but this is uncertain.

(3) An action could be brought under s.1 of the Defective Premises Act 1972, applicable to building, conversion and enlargement of *dwellings,* not business premises. Thus, s.1

- imposes a duty upon the builder, engineer, architect, surveyor or other person taking on the work to see that the work is done in a "workmanlike" or "professional" manner and with proper materials, so that the dwelling will be fit for habitation when completed,
- towards the person ordering the work and towards anyone subsequently acquiring an interest in the dwelling.

These duties are therefore more extensive than those in negligence. They apply even to cases where defects subsequently appear because of the poor workmanship - for example, through rising damp - and not merely to those arising at the actual date of the work (*Andrews v. Schooling* [1991] 1 WLR 783).

There are limitations upon the operation of s.1, however. In the first place, the builder has a defence if he worked according to the plaintiff's instructions, unless he should have warned the plaintiff that the instructions were defective. Secondly, s.2 excludes dwellings which are subject to "approved schemes", for example, the National Housebuilders Protection Scheme covering almost all new houses for 10 years from completion of building (under which builders agree to obtain insurance against any unsatisfied judgment against them and at the same time guarantee that the house is properly constructed). This means that, effectively, s.1 is only applicable to extensions and conversions, not to main construction. Thirdly, the limitation period is six years from the date of completion of the building, whereas in common law negligence time runs from the date of damage, extendable under the Latent Damage Act 1986. Fourthly, to bring the claim under s.1(1), the plaintiff must show that the premises are unfit for habitation (*Thompson v. Clive Alexander & Partners* (1992) 28 Con LR 49).

Further reading:

Brazier, *Street on Torts*, 9th ed, 1993 (Butterworth & Co., London): ch.16.
Fleming, J.G., *The Law of Torts*, 8th ed, 1992 (The Law Book Company, Sydney): ch.22.
Hepple, B.A. and Matthews, M.H., *Tort: Cases and Materials*, 4th ed, 1991 (Butterworth & Co., London): ch.9.
Heuston, R.F.V. and Buckley, R.A., *Salmond and Heuston on The Law of Torts*, 20th ed, 1992 (Sweet & Maxwell, London): ch.11.
Howarth, D., *Textbook on Tort*, 1995 (Butterworth & Co., London): ch.8.
Jones, M.A., *Textbook on Torts*, 4th ed, 1993 (Blackstone, London): ch.6.
Rogers, W.V.H., *Winfield and Jolowicz on Tort*, 14th ed, 1994 (Sweet & Maxwell, London): ch.9.

PART VI

Chapter 9

Strict Liability

One of the oft-cited advantages of proceeding against a defendant in an action for breach of contract rather than in tort where this is possible is that liability in contract is strict, in the sense that if a person has contractually undertaken to perform an obligation, and yet fails to do so properly, or at all, he will be legally liable for the breach of the agreement whether or not he could have done anything to prevent it, and whether or not the breach was foreseeable. The solemn and binding promise was sacred and the law will protect the integrity of the bargain in this way, subject to whatever defences might exist including permitted liability exclusion and failure of the basis of the contract, known as "frustration".

As previously seen, however, the law of tort does not always see things in quite the same way. The whole of the common law tort of negligence is based upon the idea of "fault", according to *Donoghue v. Stevenson:* liability dependent upon whether harm to the plaintiff was foreseeable and if so, whether the defendant's conduct which caused it was unreasonable. Even in the major litigation area of motor vehicle accidents, no-fault liability, alongside the provision made for compulsory insurance, has not been able to be introduced (*supra,* Ch.4). This reflects the greater burden of justification to be discharged where the imposition of obligations derived from state or social policy rather than from the communal wills of the disputant parties is the subject of discussion.

In certain instances, however, even in the law of tort, liability may exist, irrespective of whether (a) the defendant ought reasonably to have foreseen that harm would occur or of (b) whether his behaviour was reasonable or not, or (c) even of whether his own actions were the direct cause of any damage which has arisen.

It is this species of tortious obligation which is referred to as that of *strict* liability.

Examples may include the breach of a statutory duty, vicarious liability for the activities of employees, liability for animals and for fire (see *infra,* Ch.10 *et seq.*).

Even so, as will become clear, strict liability will rarely be totally *unrestricted.* There will invariably be conditions attached which, in many ways, indirectly resemble factors otherwise taken into consideration for normal purposes of negligence: for example, did the statutory duty in question merely require the defendant to do all that might be regarded as reasonable, or was it more absolute; or did the employee commit the tort when carrying out the range of duties which had been laid down for him to perform by his employer as would be needed to be shown for the employer to be vicariously, strictly liable?

Some torts may incorporate one of the main elements of strict liability (say, disregard of defendant's reasonable care), but not the other (irrelevance of foreseeability). To this extent they could be said to be strict - yet not *wholly* so (see *infra,* chs.23 and 24).

The imposition of liability which, to a greater or lesser

extent, is not dependent upon a defendant's own blameworthiness and reasonableness of behaviour, is clearly a socio-legal policy matter. As to the scope and limitations of such liability in tort, this may now be understood from reading the chapters following in Part VI.

Further reading:

Fleming, J.G., *The Law of Torts*, 8th ed, 1992 (The Law Book Company, Sydney): ch.15.

Jones, M.A., *Textbook on Torts*, 4th ed, 1993 (Blackstone, London): ch.8.

Stanton, K.M., *The Modern Law of Tort*, 1994 (The Law Book Company, Sydney): ch.11.

Chapter 10

Breach of Statutory Duty

Introduction

Many statutes passed each year by the United Kingdom's Parliament impose duties to act upon persons, companies and authorities, or prohibit them from acting in a particular manner.

Some of these statutes will expressly provide for civil liability in the event of their breach, for example, the Consumer Protection Act 1987, s.41. Others may specify a criminal penalty for breach. Most, however, will say nothing at all about the effects of failure to comply - no doubt because Parliament could not conceive that so law-abiding a populace would ever contravene the duties laid down. It is with the latter type of statute, together also with those containing solely criminal sanctions, that the tort of breach of statutory duty is concerned - and very often, the cases will involve statutes dealing with industrial safety legislation.

As to which of the preceding effects such statutes are to be taken to have, this is a matter of statutory construction in order to determine the legislature's intention (*Cutler v. Wandsworth Stadium Ltd* [1949] AC 398; *X (Minors) v. Bedfordshire County Council etc.* [1995] 3 All ER 353, HL; *Church of Jesus Christ of Latter-Day Saints (Great Britain) v.*

Yorkshire Fire and Civil Defence Authority (1996) *The Times,* May 9; *John Munroe (Acrylics) Ltd v. London Fire and Civil Defence Authority* (1996) *The Times,* May 22): and in some cases, the liability in tort of those in contravention, for such breach of statutory duty, held to have been intended by the legislature, will be treated as providing for *strict* liability, whereas, in others, merely for liability in *negligence.* Some people doubt whether such decisions are in truth based upon any sound legal principles and the suspicion is that they are in fact merely policy judgments which are then sought to be justified subsequently. In *Ex parte Islands Records Ltd* [1978] Ch. 122, Lord Denning, MR thought that courts might just as well "toss a coin to decide it" (p.135).

Many of the most important principles in this area were restated by the House of Lords in recent times in X *(Minors) v. Bedfordshire County Council, supra,* where two further important points were made clear:

1. even if an action for breach of statutory duty is held not to be available on the facts of the case, nonetheless, it is perfectly possible for a defendant to become subject to an ordinary common law negligence duty of care in carrying out its duties and activities under a statute (p.368), if the usual conditions therefor are satisfied (see *supra*, pp.204, 212 and 220); and
2. in the absence of an available claim for breach of statutory duty or for common law negligence, there is no alternative possibility of an action for careless exercise of a statutory power or duty (p.367).

The following are the elements which have to be satisfied

for a successful action for breach of statutory duty to be brought.

(i) Construction of Statute as Imposing Civil Liability for Breach

In *Ex parte Island Records Ltd, supra,* Lord Denning, MR considered that statutes should be construed in the light of the language used and the earlier law, without resorting to presumptions.

However, it seems from the House of Lords' decision in *Lonrho Ltd v. Shell Petroleum Co. Ltd* [1981] 2 All ER 456, approving the earlier statement of Lord Tenterden, CJ in *Doe dem. Murray, Lord Bishop of Rochester v. Bridges* (1831) 1B & AD 847, that presumptions *do* exist in the matter of statutory construction of a civil remedy for breach of statutory duty, as follows:

(1) if the statute imposes an obligation, but provides *no remedy* for its breach, the presumption will be that there is a right of action for breach of statutory duty;
(2) if the statute does *specify a remedy,* this is presumed to be exclusive, subject to two exceptions referred to by Lord Diplock in *Lonrho.*

These two presumptions are now examined.

1. *Presumption of liability for breach of statutory duty when statute prescribes no remedy*

The presumption here is that an action lies for breach of statutory duty.

In *Dawson v. Bingley Urban District Council* [1911] 2 KB 149, s.66 of the Public Health Act 1875 required local authorities clearly to identify the position of fire plugs for use in extinguishing fires, and yet the statute specified no penalty or remedy for their failure to do so. The plaintiff's property suffered greater fire damage because the fire brigade were unable to locate the fire plugs for some time. The defendant local authority was held liable for breach of its statutory duty: where a statute was silent as to consequences of breach, the proper remedy was in damages. Again, in *West Wiltshire District Council v. Garland* [1995] 2 WLR 439, auditors who were under an express statutory duty towards local electors and taxpayers were held by the Court of Appeal also to owe a duty towards the local council, as the body or class whose accounts were to be audited, and since the statute provided no remedy for its contravention, Parliament was to be taken to have intended the local councils to be able to claim for breach of statutory duty.

It should immediately be added, however, that there are certain qualifications which have to be made to this statement of principle, which is therefore only applicable if certain conditions are satisfied, as follows:

a. No existing common law remedy

Even if the statute itself provides no remedy for breach, if a means of obtaining compensation already exists at common law, an action for breach of statutory duty should not be permitted, since Parliament must be taken to have legislated with such common law remedy in mind (*Phillips v. Britannia Hygienic Laundry Co. Ltd* [1923] 2 KB 832). Thus, in *McCall v. Abelesz* [1976] QB 585 there was no remedy of breach of statutory duty in s.1 of the Protection from Eviction Act 1977 prohibiting unlawful harassment of an occupier, either because the occupier could sue for breach of covenants of quiet enjoyment under the tenancy agreement or, if the latter were terminated, for the tort of private nuisance. Some, however, have argued that even if there is a remedy at common law, breach of statutory duty should still be allowed if it *adds* to the latter. So, in *Monk v. Warbey* [1935] 1 KB 75, s.35 of the Road Traffic Act 1930 prohibited a vehicle owner from permitting his car to be driven by an uninsured driver. The plaintiff was injured by the latter's negligence, but he could not obtain payment of damages from the driver. The court held that he could therefore sue the owner for breach of statutory duty.

The question arises of whether a public law action for judicial review of an administrative decision is to be regarded as an existing *common law remedy* in the present context? In *Hague v. Deputy Governor of Parkhurst Prison* [1991] 3 All ER 733, the House of Lords treated such remedy for breach of the Prison Rules as excluding an action for breach of statutory duty, although not conclusively. Support for this conclusion may also be drawn from Lord Browne-Wilkinson's judgment in *X (Minors) v. Bedfordshire County Council etc* [1995] 3 All ER 353, at p.397.

b. Statutes passed for the general benefit of the public or community at large

It would seem that if a statute is passed for the benefit of a particular class of people (for example, the homeless: *Thornton v. Kirklees Borough Council* [1979] QB 626), there is a further presumption that an action for breach of statutory duty exists (*Solomons v. Gertzenstein Ltd* [1954] 2 QB 243). This in fact was expressly stated by Lord Diplock in *Lonrho* as one of the two exceptions to the presumption *against* a breach action where a statute does provide a specific remedy, and the difficulty of course is to discern when exactly a statute has been passed for the benefit of a class (see below).

However, for purposes of the present discussion, the opposite presumption applies if a statute has been passed for the general benefit of the public or community: no action for breach of statutory duty at the suit of an individual, notwithstanding absence of remedy in the statute. This is especially so where the statute has very general wording or gives a wide discretion (for example, "so far as is reasonably practicable") to the relevant authorities, such as that to provide safe conditions of work under ss.1-9 of the Health and Safety at Work Act 1974. Thus, in *Phillips v. Britannia Hygienic Laundry Co. Ltd* [1923] 2 KB 832, the Court of Appeal held that the duty to maintain a motor vehicle in a roadworthy condition under statutory regulations of 1904 was owed to the public at large, and consequently, the plaintiff, whose own van was damaged in an accident with the defendants' unroadworthy vehicle, was unable to claim damages for breach of statutory duty. Nevertheless, once again, it has to be said that in *Lonrho,* the second of Lord Diplock's exceptions to the presumption *against* liability for breach of statutory duty when a statute does provide a specific remedy was where the statute was passed for the benefit of the public in general, *but a particular member of the public suffered additional damage different from the rest*, which, in principle, therefore, should also apply in the present situation of absence of remedy in the statute.

Preceding principles came to be applied in *X (Minors) v. Bedfordshire County Council etc.* [1995] 3 All ER 353, HL, involving a number of cases brought by children against local authorities for failing to perform duties under various statutes to protect them against abuse and to provide for special educational needs. In the House of Lords, Lord Browne-Wilkinson confirmed that in the ordinary case a breach of statutory duty would not give rise to a private law cause of action, but that the latter could be held to exist if, as a matter of statutory construction, a statutory duty were found to have been imposed:

- for the protection of a limited class of the public such as children at risk, and
- Parliament intended to confer upon that class a private right of action for breach of the duty, especially if there were only limited machinery for enforcing the statutory duties imposed (p.378).

As to when a statute would be considered to have such effect, there was said to be no general rule, but certain indicators, as follows: (a) if the statute provided no other or insufficient remedy for its breach to secure the statutory protection (see *supra*); (b) if there was a statutory means of enforcement, normally, in accordance with *Cutler* and *Lonrho (infra),* there would be no private cause of action, except that it would still be possible to show a statutory intention to protect the class through private remedy, for example, duties of employers in respect of factory premises (*Groves v. Lord Wimborne* [1898] QB 402) (pp.364-5).

Thus, Lord Browne-Wilkinson explained (at p.378) that the child care statutes in question were all concerned to establish an administrative system designed to promote the social welfare of the community: "The welfare sector involved is one of peculiar sensitivity, involving very difficult decisions how to strike the balance between protecting the child from immediate feared harm and disrupting the relationship between the child and its parents. Decisions often have to be taken on the basis of inadequate and disputed facts. In my judgment in such a context it would require exceptionally clear statutory language to show a parliamentary intention that those responsible for carrying out these difficult functions should be liable in damages if, on subsequent investigation with the benefit of hindsight, it was shown that they had reached an erroneous conclusion and therefore failed to discharge their statutory duties ... When one turns to the actual words used in the primary legislation to create the statutory duties relied upon ... they are inconsistent with any intention to create a private law cause of action."

He thereupon proceeded to construe the child care legislation and concluded that since the duty of the defendant to take child care proceedings thereunder was conditional upon its *subjective* judgment and *discretion* to take such steps as were *reasonable,* it was not possible to deduce a private right of action of the child based thereon (pp.378-9). Corresponding conclusions were reached in respect of the education statutes (p.398). Breach of statutory duty was not available (*ibid.*).

However, as previously noted, even if an action for breach of the statutory duty was not possible, the House of Lords nonetheless confirmed that it remained possible for an ordinary *common law duty of care in negligence* to be given rise to, subject to various restraints (see *supra*, pp.204, 212 and 220), in respect of the defendant's actions in the course of carrying out the statutory duties (p.368). The restrictions referred to were, first, no common law negligence liability as to exercise of discretion and policy matters, as opposed to the purely operational, by statutory bodies, on public policy grounds, and secondly, satisfaction of the three-stage test for common law negligence liability if this is sought to be established (see ch.5, pp.204, 212 and 220, *supra*). In the case itself, the court's view was that it would not in fact be fair just and reasonable for a common law duty of care to be imposed upon the local authority defendants, because this would cut across the statutory system set up to deal with very delicate and sensitive issues (*supra*); nor would mere careless performance as such of a statutory duty give rise to an action for breach, in the absence of either an action for breach of statutory duty or for common law negligence -there was no such third alternative of a claim for careless performance of a statutory power or duty (pp.367 and 399: although, note the dissenting view of Lord Jauncey - otherwise with the majority - on this, p.362, to the effect that a statutory power only extends to its careful performance and that otherwise it ceases to constitute a defence to the common law tort against which the statutory authority protects).

2. *Presumption against liability for breach of statutory duty where the statute provides a specific remedy*

This presumption was confirmed, as seen, by the House of Lords, subject to two exceptions, in the *Lonrho* case and thereafter in *X (Minors) v. Bedfordshire County Council etc.*

Such remedies specifically provided by statutes may be in tort, or by way of criminal penalty, or administrative remedy, or procedure.

Accordingly, in *Atkinson v. The Newcastle and Gateshead Waterworks Co.* (1877) LR 2 Ex. D. 441, under s.42 of the Waterworks Clauses Act 1847 there was a duty to keep water in pipes under a certain pressure and a penalty of £10 for failure to do so. The defendants contravened this duty and, as a result, the plaintiff's house could not be saved from fire. The Court of Appeal held that the statutory £10 penalty on the defendants was exclusive and that no further action could be brought for breach of statutory duty. Again, in *Wentworth v. Wiltshire County Council* [1993] 2 WLR 175, s.1 of the Highways (Miscellaneous Provisions) Act 1961 imposed a duty to keep roads in repair and s.59 of the Highways Act 1959 provided a method to enforce this. It was held that no action was possible for breach of statutory duty. In the *Atkinson* case, the court seemed to be influenced by the fact that it was dealing with a public utility supplier - water - which meant that the water company could otherwise have been subject to very extensive liability for breach of statutory duty at the hands of individual members of the public, whose houses could generally be expected to be insured against fire in any event. On the other hand of course, in *Monk v. Warbey*, in allowing an action for breach of statutory duty, the court obviously took into account the fact that the *defendant* owner of the motor car was covered by insurance - although, it has to be said that courts have not always been prepared to allow such actions where contravention of the road traffic legislation has been of a comparatively trivial nature, as otherwise being too hard on defendants. Policy considerations intervene here.

In *CBS Songs Ltd v. Amstrad Consumer Electronics plc* [1988] Ch. 61, the Court of Appeal even refused to grant an injunction to the plaintiff record companies against the defendant tape recorder manufacturers for allegedly encouraging their purchasers to record the plaintiffs' songs and thereby to commit a criminal offence in breach of the Copyright Act 1956. The remedy was to bring a criminal prosecution. In *McCullagh v. Lane Fox and Partners Ltd* (1995) *The Times*, December 22, CA, Sir Christopher Slade reasoned in the Court of Appeal that since the Property Misdescriptions Act 1991 protected the public by making estate agents criminally liable for certain false statements, without also providing a civil remedy, it was to be inferred that the latter was already available under ordinary common law negligence in respect of misstatements - an interesting way of indirectly avoiding the controversies of breach of statutory duty!

There are, however, three exceptions to the presumption against breach of statutory duty liability in such situations, two of which come from the *Lonrho* case.

a. Statutory remedy inadequate

It will be recalled from the previous section (*supra*, p.361) that even if the statute does provide a remedy, courts may nonetheless allow an action for breach of statutory duty if they regard that particular remedy as incapable of providing sufficient protection - all the more so if it is merely discretionary - in view of which it may be taken only to have been intended to be in addition to the damages claim. In *Reffell v. Surrey County Council* [1964] 1 All ER 743, the specific provision for judicial order to compel local authorities to perform their duties under the Education Act 1944 was held not an adequate penalty to protect a school pupil who was cut by glass. Again, in *Groves v. Lord Wimborne* [1898] 2 QB 402, s.5(3) of the Factory and Workshop Act 1891 imposed an obligation on employers to fence dangerous machinery, with a fine of up to £100 which could be applied in whole or in part for the benefit of the injured employee at the discretion of the government minister. The discretionary nature of the remedy and the fact that there was a maximum amount, assessed on penal rather than compensatory principles, were taken to indicate that breach of statutory duty was not excluded.

b. Statute passed for the benefit or protection of a particular class of persons

This was Lord Diplock's first exception to the presumption against breach of statutory duty in *Lonrho Ltd v. Shell Petroleum Ltd* [1981] 2 All ER 456.

The alternative ground for the Court of Appeal's upholding of breach of statutory duty in *Groves v. Lord Wimborne* was that the statute there was passed for the benefit of a particular class.

The principle deviating from the normal position simply because a class is involved is a little difficult to comprehend, yet nevertheless is established. In *Ex parte*

Island Records Ltd [1978] Ch. 122, s.1 of the Dramatic and Musical Performers' Protection Act 1958 imposed a criminal penalty where a musical or dramatic performance was recorded without the written consent of the performer. The Court of Appeal held that there was also an action for breach of statutory duty, because the Act was passed to protect a particular class of individuals - musicians and actors. Compare it with *Atkinson v. The Newcastle and Gateshead Waterworks Co.* (above) where the statutory duty to keep water in pipes at a certain pressure was for the benefit of the public in general.

As to whether a particular class of persons is so intended to be benefited, this is a matter of construction of the specific legislation. Employees are usually accepted as a class under works safety statutes, as are members of the public using pedestrian crossings under traffic laws.

However, in accordance with the principle applicable generally to claimants in breach of statutory duty cases (see below), there must be an intention to benefit *that particular* class under the legislation. Thus, in *Ex parte Island Records Ltd,* it was held that actors and musicians were the class intended to be protected against unauthorized recordings, but not also record companies. Similarly, in *Cutler v. Wandsworth Stadium Ltd* [1949] AC 398, s.11(2)(b) of the Betting and Lotteries Act 1934 required owners of race tracks to provide space for bookmakers on the track. The plaintiff bookmaker claimed breach of statutory duty through being excluded from the track. The House of Lords held that the action was inadmissible, because it was the public who were intended to benefit from these provisions, not the bookmakers, who were only incidental beneficiaries.

Again, in *R. v. Deputy Governor of Parkhurst Prison, ex parte Hague* [1992] 1 AC 58, breach of the Prison Act 1952 by the prison authorities was held not to give rise to a claim for breach of statutory duty on the part of a prisoner, because the purpose was to ensure proper administration of prisons in the public interest, not to benefit a particular class, namely, prisoners themselves. Similarly, in *T v. Surrey County Council* [1994] 4 All ER 577, the object of certain child care legislation placing duties upon local authorities to register child-minders was held not to be specifically to benefit children as a particular class, but to ensure a proper management of the system.

A rather curious decision in this context was *Richardson v. Pitt-Stanley* [1995] 2 WLR 26. There the plaintiff employee was seriously injured in the course of employment but his employer had not insured under s.1 of the Employers' Liability (Compulsory Insurance) Act 1969 and subsequently became insolvent so that it was unable to satisfy the plaintiff's judgment. Consequently, the plaintiff sued the employer company's directors on the ground that since failure to insure was an offence under s.5 of the Act, they were able to be claimed against in tort for breach of statutory duty. A majority of the three Court of Appeal Judges held that the defendants were not liable, because, on a construction of s.5, there was no express or implied provision for such civil liability. The dissenting Judge, however, considered that the *Lonrho* exception of statutory protection of a particular class of individuals ought to have applied. Clearly, policy is alive and well in the decisions of Judges in this area as to the principal purpose of statutory provisions.

Finally, even if it is considered that a particular class is intended to be benefited by a statute, availability of the private tortious remedy is still subject to the overall construction of the Act. Thus, in *X (Minors) v. Bedfordshire County Council etc (supra)*, the House of Lords was prepared to assume that child care and education statutes were for the benefit of children as a particular class, but nevertheless concluded that there was nothing in the legislation which demonstrated a parliamentary intention to give that class a right of action for damages (p.398). Lord Browne-Wilkinson stated (at pp.398-9): "I have never previously come across a statutory procedure which provided for such close involvement of those who would be affected by a decision in the making of that decision or which conferred more generous rights of appeal. To suggest that Parliament intended, in addition, to confer a right to sue for damages is impossible."

c. *Statute creates a public right but an individual member of the public suffers special damage*

Lord Diplock's second exception in *Lonrho*. There is much uncertainty over what "public rights" are. The immediate assumption would be that it includes any statute imposing duties which are not specifically restricted to protection of a particular class or individuals: in other words, the statute was not passed in order to protect a class or individuals (*supra*), yet such person or persons in fact suffered special damage. However, *Lonrho* suggests a more literal meaning - that there may be statutes which confer no such *rights* upon the *public,* either because all they do is to impose obligations on the public with no corresponding rights, or because it is not the public which is intended to benefit from any rights or protection but the state itself or the international community. The statute in question in *Lonrho* was the Southern Rhodesia Act 1965 which made it a crime to supply oil to what was then Southern Rhodesia (now Zimbabwe). The plaintiffs claimed that the Act was for the public benefit and that they had suffered special commercial damage as a result of the defendant's breach: thus, the plaintiffs, *Lonrho,* had duly shut down their pipeline to the defendant Shell's oil refinery in Rhodesia, but Shell had allegedly contravened the statute by continuing to supply oil to the illegal government by other means, and had thereby helped to keep it in power longer than would otherwise have been the case - and the plaintiffs' pipeline out of use. The House of Lords held that no public right was created by the Act; on the contrary, its purpose was to *remove* a previous right to supply oil to Southern Rhodesia - the objectives were political rather than for the public or any section thereof.

(ii) Further Conditions of Liability

In the preceding section, it was shown that courts will make a general assessment of existence of statutory duty according to whether the statute does or does not already provide a specific remedy.

In addition, it was noted that a number of policy considerations intervene in the course of deciding upon the construction of statutes and availability of the civil remedy for breach: is the plaintiff or defendant insured (*Atkinson, Monk*); extent of potential liability (*Atkinson*); whether the protection is physical and concerned with employment

(*Groves*) or merely commercial (*Cutler*); whether statutory remedies are penal and non-compensatory and merely discretionary (*Groves*).

However, beyond this there are a number of further conditions for existence or satisfaction of liability which must always be taken into account.

1. Duty owed towards the plaintiff

The plaintiff must fall within the protection of the statutory provision - a matter of construction.

In *Knapp v. Railway Executive* [1949] 2 All ER 508, the statute requiring the defendants to maintain railway level-crossing gates was intended to protect members of the public, not the plaintiff train driver. Again, in *Hartley v. Mayoh & Co.* [1954] 1 QB 383 statutory regulations were held to be intended to protect employees, not firemen visiting the premises. Similarly, in *Hewett v. Alf Brown's Transport Ltd* [1992] ICR 530, Control of Lead at Work Regulations placed duties on employers in order to protect employees against lead, not also the wife of an employee, who suffered lead poisoning when she cleaned her husband's work clothes.

2. Circumstances covered by the statute

If the duty is imposed in respect of certain premises but not others, its breach on the latter is not covered (*Chipchase v. British Titan Products Co. Ltd* [1956] 1 QB 545).

3. Damage is of the type covered by the statute

In *Gorris v. Scott* (1874) 9 Exch. 125, an Order was made

requiring animals transported by ship to be kept in pens. The defendant shipowner failed to comply and the plaintiff's sheep were washed overboard into the sea. The plaintiff's breach of statutory duty claim failed because the purpose of the pens was to prevent the spread of contagious disease amongst the sheep, not to stop them from drowning - the wrong type of damage.

4. Defendant's breach of statutory duty caused the damage

It would seem that this will not be satisfied if it can be proved that the plaintiff would not have made use of statutory safety measures even if they had been provided (*McWilliams v. Sir William Arrol & Co. Ltd* [1962] 1 All ER 623).

(iii) Nature of Liability for Breach of Statutory Duty

Even if the courts hold that an action exists for breach of statutory duty in respect of a particular statute, the question still arises as to whether the statutory duty which it is claimed has been breached is one of strict liability or based on negligence and fault. The answer to this is that it can be either, depending upon the usual textual - and doubtless also policy - construction of the legislation. If the court finds that the duty is intended to be strict, no amount of care taken by the defendant to comply will be sufficient to prevent liability.

It may be that use of words like "shall" or "must" in statutes will be taken to indicate strict liability. In *Galashiels Gas Co. Ltd v. Millar* [1949] AC 275, s.22(1) of the Factories Act 1937 stated "every ... lift shall be properly maintained."

This was held to impose liability even if failure to the lift mechanism had been impossible to foresee. Again, in *John Summers & Sons v. Frost* [1955] 1 All ER 870, s.14(1) of the Factories Act 1961 provided that every dangerous part of machinery shall be securely fenced. This was held to impose strict liability.

On the other hand, in *Brown v. National Coal Board* [1962] 1 All ER 81, "such steps as were necessary" was held not to indicate strict liability.

"In so far as reasonably practicable" probably means having to do *everything* possible in order to avoid liability, but not being strictly liable beyond that. As to what is *reasonable,* the courts will try to balance the sacrifice and expense necessary to avoid the risk against the level of risk involved (*Edwards v. National Coal Board* [1949] 1 All ER 743). In *McCarthy v. Coldair Ltd* [1951] 2 TLR 1226, the factories legislation required safe access for workers, so far as reasonably practicable. The plaintiff fell when a ladder he was climbing slipped. The employers were held liable for breach of statutory duty. The court thought that it would not usually be required to have another man holding a ladder steady, balancing the cost of this against the minor degree of risk. However, in this case the floor in question was known to be wet and slippery, greatly increasing the risk, and it would therefore have been reasonable to have the ladder held by another employee.

(iv) Defences Against Liability for Breach of Statutory Duty

1. *Volenti non fit injuria (consent)*

There is some doubt over whether, as a matter of public

policy, consent can be a defence to breach of statutory duty - especially where plaintiff and defendant are employee and employer respectively (*Baddeley v. Earl Granville* (1887) 19 QBD 423) - except where an employee himself was responsible for the employer's breach (*ICI v. Shatwell* [1965] AC 656). In *Ginty v. Belmont Building Supplies Ltd* [1959] 1 All ER 414, statutory regulations required special crawling boards to be used for work carried out on a roof. The plaintiff employee failed to use them. The court held that the employer was not liable (otherwise if the employer's breach had been committed through a *different* employee from the plaintiff).

2. *Contributory negligence*

This is available to the defendant, subject to special leniency between employer and employee in favour of the latter (*Caswell v. Powell Duffryn Associated Collieries Ltd* [1940] AC 152). Thus, in *Westwood v. Post Office* [1974] AC 1, the defendants claimed that the plaintiff post office employee had been contributorily negligent in entering a lift room at a telephone exchange, to which entry was forbidden and where the plaintiff fell through a trap door to his death. The court held the defendant employers to be in breach of their statutory duty under the Offices, Shops and Railway Premises Act 1963, and the plaintiff not to have been contributorily negligent.

This chapter should fittingly end with the following quotation from the judgment of Lord Browne-Wilkinson in *X (Minors) v. Bedfordshire County Council etc* [1995] 3 All ER 353, at pp.364-5, HL, which admirably summarizes many of the preceding principles:

> "The principles applicable in determining whether such statutory cause of action exists are now well established, although the application of those principles in any particular case remains difficult. The basic proposition is that in the ordinary case a breach of statutory duty does not, by itself, give rise to any private law cause of action. However, a private law cause of action will arise if it can be shown, as a matter of construction of the statute, that the statutory duty was imposed for the protection of a limited class of the public and that Parliament intended to confer on members of that class a private right of action for breach of the duty. There is no general rule by reference to which it can be decided whether a statute does create such a right of action but there are a number of indicators. If the statute provides no other remedy for its breach and the Parliamentary intention to protect a limited class is shown, that indicates that there may be a private right of action since otherwise there is no method of securing the protection the statute was intended to confer. If the statute does provide some other means of enforcing the duty that will normally indicate that the statutory right was intended to be enforceable by those means and not by private right of action: see *Cutler v. Wandsworth Stadium Ltd* [1949] 1 All ER 544, [1949] AC 398 and

Lonrho Ltd v. Shell Petroleum Co. Ltd [1981] 2 All ER 456, [1982] AC 173. However, the mere existence of some other statutory remedy is not necessarily decisive. It is still possible to show that on the true construction of the statute the protected class was intended by Parliament to have a private remedy. Thus the specific duties imposed on employers in relation to factory premises are enforceable by an action for damages, notwithstanding the imposition by the statutes of criminal penalties for any breach: see *Groves v. Lord Wimborne* [1898] 2 QB 402, [1895-9] All ER Rep 147.

Although the question is one of statutory construction and therefore each case turns on the provisions in the relevant statute, it is significant that your Lordships were not referred to any case where it had been held that statutory provisions establishing a regulatory system or a scheme of social welfare for the benefit of the public at large had been held to give rise to a private right of action for damages for breach of statutory duty. Although regulatory or welfare legislation affecting a particular area of activity does in fact provide protection to those individuals particularly affected by that activity, the legislation is not to be treated as being passed for the benefit of those individuals but for the benefit of society in general. Thus legislation regulating the conduct of betting or prisons did not give rise to a statutory right of action vested in those adversely affected by the breach of the statutory provisions, ie, bookmakers and prisoners: see *Cutler v. Wandsworth Stadium Ltd* and *Hague v. Deputy Governor of Parkhurst Prison* [1991] 3 All ER 733, [1992] 1 AC 58. The cases where a private right of action for breach of statutory duty have been held to arise are all cases in which the statutory duty has been very limited and specific as opposed to general administrative functions imposed on public bodies and involving the exercise of administrative discretions."

Further reading:

Brazier, *Street on Torts*, 9th ed, 1993 (Butterworth & Co., London): ch.22.

Fleming, J.G., *The Law of Torts*, 8th ed, 1992 (The Law Book Company, Syndey): ch.8, s.8.

Hepple, B.A. and Matthews, M.H., *Tort: Cases and Materials*, 4th ed, 1991 (Butterworth & Co., London): ch.12.

Heuston, R.F.V. and Buckley, R.A., *Salmond and Heuston on The Law of Torts*, 20th ed, 1992 (Sweet & Maxwell, London).

Howarth, D., *Textbook on Tort*, 1995 (Butterworth & Co., London): ch.7.

Jones, M.A., *Textbook on Torts*, 4th ed, 1993 (Blackstone, London): ch.9.

Rogers, W.V.H., *Winfield and Jolowicz on Tort*, 14th ed, 1994 (Sweet & Maxwell, London): ch.7.

Stanton, K.M., *The Modern Law of Tort*, 1994 (The Law Book Company, Sydney): ch.25.

Chapter 11

Vicarious Liability

Introduction

Where the law imposes liability in tort upon one person, X, the defendant, towards another, Y, the plaintiff, in respect of the tort committed by a third person, Z, against Y, the defendant X is said to be "vicariously liable" for the tort of Z. It is a form of strict liability, because it does not depend upon the defendant's having been at fault in any way. The liability is imposed solely by virtue of the defendant's relationship with the third party, Z. The most common example is an employer's vicarious liability for acts of his employees carried out in the course of their employment. This type of liability developed as a matter of legal policy at a time when a *master* had overwhelming control over the conduct of his *servants,* but nowadays it has more to do with the greater economic resources of employers to satisfy judgments in tort, especially when they are insured against such risks.

Vicarious liability does not depend upon existence of any duty of the defendant towards the plaintiff (*Staveley Iron & Chemical Co. Ltd v. Jones* [1956] AC 627), and the third party's personal liability to the plaintiff continues to exist at the plaintiff's option, as will any contractual liability of the third party towards the defendant himself.

Yet, the third party's liability must be established, in the absence of any primary liability of the defendant arising out of the facts, if vicarious liability is to exist. In *X (Minors) v. Bedfordshire County Council etc* [1995] 3 All ER 353, HL, the plaintiffs sought, *inter alia,* to hold the defendant local authorities vicariously liable for the personal negligence of social workers and psychiatrists in carrying out their duties, but failed, since they were unable to prove existence of a duty of care on those persons (p.384 - see too pp.399 and 400, and *supra,* p.222, *et seq.*). Not so, however, in the case of the defendant local authority's staff of educational psychologists, who were capable of coming under a duty of care towards the plaintiffs and for whose activities the defendant accordingly might be vicariously liable (pp.393-4).

In certain cases, a defendant may also be subject to a primary duty towards the plaintiff, co-extensive with the vicarious liability: for example, an employer's duty towards employees to select competent fellow employees, broken where an unqualified employee injures the plaintiff who is another employee. This could be important where the defendant employer would not be subject to the vicarious type of liability, because, for example, the unqualified employee injured the plaintiff otherwise than in the ordinary course of his duties (*Hudson v. Ridge Manufacturing Co. Ltd* [1957] 2 QB 348).

Accordingly, such departures, in the case of vicarious liability, from the principle of fault in tort are usually sought to be justified on the grounds of:

(a) fairness - the employer makes the profits and consequently should bear the losses, and he is usually able to insure against such liability, whereas it is not worth suing an employee with few financial resources;

(b) efficient loss distribution - this means that employers' insurance premiums can be met through higher prices to consumers; and

(c) safety - employers are encouraged to provide safe systems of work and recruitment.

The truth is, essentially, therefore, that the system only works if those who can pay are made to do so within reasonable bounds.

(i) Elements of Vicarious Liability of Employers

There are two:

1. the tort must have been committed by an *employee*
2. who was *acting in the course of his employment.*

1. Employees (servants)

A person who carries out work for another may be legally classified as one of two things:

(a) an employee ("servant" is the older term, meaning the same, just as "master" preceded "employer"), or

(b) an independent contractor.

The significance of the difference in tort is that employers are vicariously liable without fault for the torts of employees, but not for those of independent contractors.

Another form of description is to say that employees have contracts *of service,* whereas independent contractors are under contracts *for services.*

Unfortunately, no one has yet succeeded in formulating a comprehensive formula to define the distinction between the two, which is not only important for vicarious liability but also in tax, EU laws on free movement and the law relating to unfair dismissal. Some cases present no difficulties: if you employ a person to carry out maintenance and decoration work on your property indefinitely, in return for an agreed weekly payment, he is your employee; if you agree to pay a man £1,000 to paint your factory once, he is an independent contractor. As always though, it will be the situations falling between these two clear cases which cause the problems: the man in the latter example is told to work according to your directions, at times of the day set by you, with materials supplied by yourself; or the man in the former example is given the freedom to choose his own working hours provided that he gets the jobs done, and he can use his own tools.

In practice, the courts will try to balance a number of factors together and attempt to achieve some degree of doctrinal clarity and consistency, at the same time as reaching the decision as to vicarious liability or not which they consider to be just and appropriate.

The following are relevant factors to be considered:

Control

This is the traditional test. In *Yewens v. Noakes* (1880) 6 QBD 530, Bramwell B indicated that a person was an employee when he could be told not only *what* to do but also *how* he was to go about doing it.

Clearly the control test has its limitations in modern times when employees - doctors, academics, computer operators - may possess high degrees of skill and would be indignant if told by managers and administrators how to do their jobs. Accordingly, control is only of particular help to the extent that it is consistent with the nature of the duties. Beyond that, it has been said to become a "when and where" test, rather than merely "how"; and an *employee* will be expected at least to be subject to his employer's overall direction as to general working practices and conditions, including provision of tools and method of payment of tax and agreed terms of remuneration and dismissal. If all else fails, courts may have to fall back on simply looking for "lawful authority to command so far as there is scope for it" as an indicator of employee status (*Zuijs v. Wirth Brothers Pty Ltd* (1955) 93 CLR 561).

In *Stevenson Jordan and Harrison Ltd v. McDonald and Evans* [1952] 1 TLR 101, Denning, LJ stated: "One feature which seems to run though the instances is that, under a contract of service, a man is employed as part of the business, and his work is done as an integral part of the business; whereas, under a contract for services, his work, although done for the business, is not integrated into it but is only accessory to it." However, this at first sight attractive-looking test is nevertheless too vague and subjective to be of much use. Presumably, casual or part-time workers will be considered to be employees, and yet they are difficult to view as an integral part of the business (*Lee Ting San v. Chung Chi-Keung* [1990] IRLR 236, PC).

As a result of the inadequacies of control and integration

criteria, courts often have to look at a whole variety of factors in addition, including:

a. expressed intentions and descriptions in the contract - but these are by no means conclusive when inconsistent with the facts (*Mersey Docks and Harbour Board v. Coggins and Griffiths (Liverpool) Ltd* [1947] AC 1), especially since both workers and the firms engaging them may have certain ulterior motives in their description of the relationship as being other than one of employment, the former in order to obtain various tax advantages and the latter to escape the burdens of employment protection legislation (see *Young and Woods v. West* [1980] IRLR 201);
b. method of payment - a lump sum indicates independent contractor (even if payable in instalments), weekly or monthly payments an employee;
c. use of employer's tools suggests employee.

One rather more useful modern approach has been to ask whether the worker can reasonably be said to be in business *on his own account*, which would then be inconsistent with the status of mere employee (*Market Investigations Ltd v. Minister of Social Security* [1969] 2 QB 173). This may be the case where he pays his own tax, hires his own assistants and bears costs of exceeding time periods - or otherwise is very skilled and has a wide discretion to decide upon how the work should be carried out (see *Lane v. Shire Roofing Co. (Oxford)* (1995) *The Times*, February 25, CA - here the Court of Appeal showed an awareness of the extrinsic factors, such as those relating to taxation, which could lead both employer and employee to wish to attach a label other than that of employment to their relationship, but when it came to the question of liability, the court would look at realities and here the plaintiff injured roofworker was closer to being an employee of the defendant than not, even though the former was normally self-employed and only started working for others when his own building jobs became scarce in the economic recession).

Thus, in *Ready Mixed Concrete (South East) Ltd v. Minister of Pensions and National Insurance* [1968] 1 All ER 433, lorry drivers responsible for delivering concrete to the company's customers were required to purchase their own vehicle painted in the company's colours, through a finance company, with an option to the company to purchase it, and the lorry was not to be sold without the company's permission, nor to be used for private purposes. Drivers agreed to obey company rules and orders as if employed, and were paid for haulage at a rate *per* mile. In spite of the extensive control of the company over the drivers, the court held that they were not employees for purposes of national insurance contributions, because drivers had to make their vehicles available at their own expense for the relevant period and risked their own profits if unable to do so. "A man does not cease to run a business on his own account because he agrees to run it efficiently or to accept another's superintendence."

In general, therefore, treatment as an employee or not will be a mixture of legal principle, where this is able to apply, together with an active element of judicial policy to reach a decision consistent with justice and proper social policy.

Finally, there are certain situations which require particular mention.

First, since the setting up of the state national health service, health authorities are considered to be vicariously liable for the torts of their staff (*Cassidy v. Ministry of Health* [1951] 2 KB 343). Hospitals are actually funded for this purpose.

Secondly, by statute, chief constables are vicariously liable for torts of the police in their area, although damages are not paid by them personally.

Thirdly, what happens when one employer lends an employee to another on a temporary basis and the employee commits a tort in the course of his work? Which employer is vicariously liable?

The question is one for the court to decide upon in all the circumstances so as to determine who was the employer at the relevant time. The court will take into account the usual factors for assessment of whether a person is an employee as opposed to independent contractor, but in this context it will be carried out on a comparative basis as between the two employers: who pays the wages and can terminate employment; how long is the employee to work for the other employer; whose tools are used; who has control over *how* as opposed to *what* work to do. In other words, it is only to be expected that the employee will carry out whatever tasks the alternative employer asks of him - that is after all why he is there. However, does he do so in accordance with the general practices, methods, training and overall work instructions of the original or alternative employer? Only if the latter, is the alternative employer vicariously liable.

These principles derive from the leading case of *Mersey Docks & Harbour Board v. Coggins & Griffith (Liverpool) Ltd* [1947] AC 1, from which it is equally clear that the burden is on the original employer to satisfy the court that the employee on loan became the employee of the borrowing employer for the purposes of vicarious liability - a burden which will be most difficult to discharge and only exceptionally so. In that case, a crane operator was hired out by his employer, the Mersey Docks & Harbour Board, to a firm of stevedores, in the course of which arrangement the operator injured a third party through negligence. The docks board continued to pay the operator's wages and retained the power of dismissal during the hiring period. The stevedores could tell the operator which ships to load but not how he was to operate the crane in doing so. The contract between the docks board and the firm of stevedores actually provided that the operator was to be the servant of the stevedores. The House of Lords held on the facts that the operator remained the employee of the original employer during the period of loan. Insufficient control and authority had passed to the stevedore firm to displace the heavy burden on the dock board to show change of employment.

It will further be noted from the case that an express term in the contract between the two employers will not be conclusive as to the employee's status for the purposes, although it may impose an obligation upon the borrowing employer to indemnify the lending employer against vicarious liability for the employee's torts.

Fourthly, the courts have held that where the owner of moveable property - usually a motor vehicle - permits another person to use it, in the course of which a tort is committed by the user, the owner is vicariously liable for the tort, *provided the owner had an interest in the use.* A loan out of generosity will not be sufficient for liability. The justification appears to be that liability arises out of some sort of agency relation between owner and user. In *Ormrod v. Crossville Motor Services Ltd* [1953] 1 WLR 1120, the owner of a motor car asked another person to drive it to Monte Carlo for him where he would later join him for a holiday. The driver had an accident en route and the owner was held vicariously liable. Compare *Britt v. Galmoye* (1928) LR 8, where the owner was held not to be vicariously liable for a car accident, because the driver had borrowed it for his own use. In *Morgans v. Launchbury* [1973] AC 127, a wife lent her car to her husband to go for a drink with his friends, and he promised that he would ask someone else to drive it home if he himself was too drunk, which occurred. As it happened, the friend was also drunk and crashed the car. The plaintiff claimed that the wife was vicariously liable for the friend's negligent driving. The friend himself was uninsured. The House of Lords held that a mere permission to the friend to drive the car, without a personal interest of the wife, was not sufficient to establish vicarious liability of the wife - rather curious, since one might have thought that most wives would have had some interest in seeing that their husband arrived home safely.

This seems a strange extension of vicarious liability - and indeed, if the agency justification is sought to be relied upon for the outcome, it has to be said that agents have far more of the appearance of independent contractors, for whom employers are not held vicariously liable, than of employees, for whom they are so. One can appreciate the desire to protect the public against uninsured drivers (there is always, however, the possibility of a claim to the Motor Insurers' Bureau in such cases, or against the owner for breach of statutory duty in allowing an uninsured person to drive the vehicle). Yet in these situations it should surely be assessed whether the owner has *primary* liability in tort for setting in train the events leading to the accident, whereas vicarious liability hardly seems appropriate.

2. *Employee acting in the ordinary course of employment*

This is the second condition of employers' vicarious liability. It would not be fair if employers were held to be liable for *everything* an employee did during working hours.

The issue is one of fact, yet there is general agreement amongst commentators that there is an absence of complete consistency in the various decisions of courts, because judgments are frequently based on a policy of achieving justice in the particular circumstances of the case.

The limited success of the "in the course of employment" formula is therefore merely to set a minimal standard for vicarious liability - that the employee's activities must in some way be related to his contractual employment activities. Thus, for example, if he is entertaining guests socially at home whom he negligently poisons, the guests can hardly expect to enjoy a remedy against the man's employer simply because they happen to be fellow employees.

If any test for assessment of acts as being in the course

of employment can be said to derive from the cases, it appears essentially to depend upon whether at the time of the tort the employee *was still acting generally within the express or implied duties of his employment* (other than in respect of the tortious manner of performance itself, of course, since, clearly, it would be unusual for an employer actually to have authorized an employee to commit a tort as part of his duties, and if the employer did so - as, for example, where a delivery firm or coach service were to instruct its drivers to meet their schedules at all costs - the employer would himself be subject to *primary* tort liability not merely vicarious).

The issue for the court to decide, therefore, as a matter of fact and degree, is whether the employee could be said to have gone outside the express and implied duties and authority of his job at the time the tort occurred? If so, the employer would not be vicariously liable. In *Joel v. Morison* (1934) 6 C&P 501, Parke, B famously asked whether the servant was engaged on his master's business at the time of the tort, and not on some sort of a detour or "frolic of his own".

An illustration of implied or incidental authority would be *Poland v. John Parr & Sons* [1926] All ER Rep 177, where an off-duty employee negligently injured a boy whom he was trying to prevent from stealing sugar from his employer's wagon. The boy fell under a wheel of the wagon. The employer was vicariously liable: it was an implied part of the employee's duty to protect his employer's property when he could and he was therefore acting in the course of his employment on a broad view. It is even arguable that an employer is vicariously liable when he *holds out* - that is to say, represents - the employee as having authority, even though the employee has no express or implied actual authority to carry out such activities, so that the employer is *estopped* (prevented) from denying that the tort was committed in the course of the employee's employment (*Armagas Ltd v. Mundogas SA* [1986] 2 All ER 385).

Examples of a number of standard situations appear from the following cases:

Limpus v. London General Omnibus Company (1862) 1 H&C 526

An accident occurred when bus drivers tried to drive faster than each other, and the defendant's driver then blocked the other's way in order to pick up two passengers, thereby causing an accident. Their employer was vicariously liable: driving was their job.

Whatman v. Pearson (1868) LR 3 CP 422

The employee's duty was to safeguard his horse and cart during use. The horse bolted when the employee made a short detour to have lunch at his home and left it unattended. The employer was vicariously liable: it was the employee's task to look after the horse and cart at all times during working hours. Clearly, had the employee travelled 50 miles away with horse and cart to have lunch, he would have taken himself outside his employee duties and authority, as would also have been so had he completed the duties assigned to him by his employer at the time of the detour (*Storey v. Ashton* (1869) LR 4 QB 476 - visit to brother-in-law when deliveries finished).

Bayley v. Manchester, Sheffield & Lincolnshire Railway Co. (1873) LR 8 CP 148

The defendant railway company was vicariously liable towards the plaintiff, who was dragged off one train by a porter and put on the wrong train: it was part of the porter's job to "help" passengers to catch the right train.

Beard v. London General Omnibus Company [1900] 2 QB 530

A bus conductor responsible for collecting fares from passengers tried to turn a bus around while the driver was not there. The bus company was not vicariously liable: it was no part of the conductor's duties to drive the bus. However, compare this with the following three cases. In *Ricketts v. Thos. Tilling Ltd* [1915] 1 KB 644, the bus company was held vicariously liable for the negligence of the driver in permitting the conductor to turn the bus round, as part of the driver's duties. Similarly, in *Ilkiw v. Samuels* [1963] 1 WLR 991, a lorry driver asked a third party to move his lorry and an accident occurred. This was within the scope of his duties, although unauthorized, and the employers were vicariously liable. Again, in *Kay v. ITW Ltd* [1968] 1 QB 140, the driver of a fork-lift truck and small vans drove a lorry out of his way. The employers were held vicariously liable: the driver was attempting to continue his duties by clearing his route.

Century Insurance Co. Ltd v. Northern Ireland Road Transport Board [1942] AC 509

A petrol tanker driver discharged his load at a petrol filling station and caused an explosion when he lit a cigarette and threw the match to the ground. The employers were held liable, because although his smoking, which led to the tort, was not authorized, it occurred in the course of performing his duties.

Recreational activities, such as smoking and having lunch, have consistently challenged the courts. In *Crook v. Derbyshire Stone Ltd* [1956] 1 WLR 432, employers were held not vicariously liable for tort of a lorry driver permitted to stop for a lunch break; whereas, in *Harvey v. R.G. O'Dell Ltd* [1958] 2 AB 78, the employer was found to be liable. Presumably, in the latter case, the nature of the employment agreement was that the driver was treated as burdened with his duties even during the luncheon period. Again, in *Hilton v. Thomas Burton (Rhodes) Ltd* [1961] 1 All ER 74, workmen drove off for an unauthorized tea break. The employers were not vicariously liable and the workers were on a frolic of their own: going off in this way could not be said to have any connexion with their duties.

Journeys to and from work have similarly exercised the courts. The House of Lords provided some guidance in *Smith v. Stages* [1989] 1 All ER 833: (1) an employee travelling to and from work is not ordinarily acting in the course of employment, unless perhaps where required to use his employer's vehicle; (2) an employee travelling from home to a workplace as part of his duties to act on behalf of his employer or from workplace to workplace for this purpose, should be taken to be acting in the course of his employment. In that case itself, employees who were sent to another town for a day's work and paid eight hours travelling time for the return journey were held to be acting in the course of their employment when an accident occurred during the journey home.

A rather curious case held to be the employees' frolic of their own was *General Engineering Services Ltd v. Kingston and Saint Andrew Corp.* [1988] 3 All ER 867, in which employers were held not to be vicariously liable for negligence of firemen taking industrial action by "going slow". The fire engine took 17 minutes to arrive instead of what should have been three-and-one-half minutes and the property was destroyed. One would have thought that travelling to a fire to put it out was precisely what the firemen were employed to do - albeit that they were carrying it out in an unauthorized manner. Perhaps the explanation for the Judicial Committee's decision therefore is that the action of the firemen was so outrageous and unacceptable where lives and property were at risk as to take their behaviour completely outside the normal parameters of their duty (the "very negation" of carrying out their duties, in the words of Lord Ackner, at p.870).

The effects of two particular factors upon the preceding principles should also be discussed.

Contractual Prohibition of Conduct

There is not always a very helpful distinction between:

(a) where the prohibition restricts the *scope* of the employee's duties, in which case negligence in the course of a breach of such condition will take the activity outside the ordinary course of employment; and

(b) where the prohibition merely affects the *mode* of performing the duties, in view of which the tort will remain in the ordinary course of employment.

The difficulty of course is to decide when a prohibition is as to scope or mere mode (sometimes referred to as the difference between doing an unauthorized act on the one hand, and doing an authorized act in an unauthorized manner on the other). If a driver is told not to go off for refreshments in working hours outside lunchtimes, is this scope or mode? Or suppose that he is told not to include alcohol in his refreshment?

Cases where courts have held prohibitions merely to relate to mode are as follows:

Limpus v. London General Omnibus Co. (1862) 1 H&C 526

Bus driver told not to race other drivers; employers vicariously liable when he did so.

Canadian Pacific Railway Co. v. Lockhart [1942] AC 591

Driver told not to drive uninsured; employers vicariously liable when he did so.

London County Council v. Cattermoles (Garages) Ltd [1953] 1 WLR 997

Employee told to shift vehicles manually and not to drive them; employers vicariously liable when he drove one.

Rose v. Plenty [1976] 1 All ER 97

A milkman's job was to drive his milk float, deliver bottles of milk to houses, and collect money. He was told not to use young boys to help him. He did so and a 13-year-old boy was injured. A majority of the Court of Appeal held the employers vicariously liable.

A judgment inconsistent with the preceding was that in *Twine v. Bean's Express Ltd* [1946] 1 All ER 202, where the employer was held not to be vicariously liable towards a hitch-hiker to whom the employee had given a ride against his employer's instructions. However, it would seem that this decision was based upon an old-fashioned idea that trespassers - which appears to have been the view taken of the hitch-hiker - were not owed a duty of care, and should not therefore be regarded as surviving *Rose v. Plenty*. (In the latter, Lord Denning, MR indicated that the outcome would depend upon whether the employee's act in contravention of instructions was done for the employer's benefit or not - but this would be a very uncertain test). Nevertheless, seemingly contrary to both *Rose v. Plenty* and *Limpus v. London General Omnibus Co.*, was the case of *Conway v. George Wimpey & Co. Ltd* [1951] 2 KB 266, where drivers who were employed by the defendants to take workers to a building site were instructed not to give lifts to employees of other firms. There the defendants were held not to be vicariously liable to the plaintiff who was one such worker from another company injured through the negligence of one of the defendants' drivers when being given an unauthorized lift, because the driver's breach of his orders was held to have gone beyond mere mode of performing his duties. This outcome seems to demonstrate the suspected policy nature of courts' determination of the in-the-course-of-employment requirement and the precise designation of the employee's job in relation to the act causing damage in some of these cases.

This conclusion would appear to be supported by Lord Jauncey's finding in *Racz v. Home Office* [1994] 2 WLR 23, HL - in which a plaintiff prisoner sought to hold the defendant government department vicariously liable *inter alia* for assault allegedly carried out upon him by prison officers - that it was "likely to be a question of fact and degree whether the prison officers were engaged in a misguided and unauthorized method of performing their authorized duties or were engaged in what was tantamount to an unlawful frolic of their own" (p.28).

Criminal Acts of Employee

Certain criminal activities - for example, fraud and assault - are also torts.

Can an employer be vicariously liable for an employee's tort in these circumstances? Can criminal behaviour ever be regarded as being in the ordinary course of employment?

The answer is that, applying the usual principles (see above), the criminal nature of the act will normally take this outside the normal scope of the employee's duties, so that the employer will not be vicariously liable in tort nor for the crime itself (unless, of course, the employer authorized the employee, say, to drive dangerously and to commit the criminal office of dangerous driving, or was negligent in employing an untrustworthy employee, in which cases the employer will be subject to primary - not mere vicarious - liability for negligence: *Nahhas v. Pier House (Cheyne Walk) Management Ltd* (1984) 270 EG 328). Thus, in *Warren v. Henley's Ltd* [1948] 2 All ER 935, employers of a petrol pump attendant who assaulted a customer when the latter said that he was going to report him for rudeness, were held not to be vicariously liable, because the attendant had gone outside the course of his duties.

However, where the criminal offence and tort are committed against property passing through the employee's hands as part of his actual or ostensible duties, the employer may be vicariously liable (*Morris v. C.W. Martin & Sons Ltd* [1966] 1 QB 716 - fur coat stolen by employee of cleaning firm). Thus, in *Lloyd v. Grace, Smith & Co.* [1912] AC 716, a solicitor's clerk fraudulently persuaded a client of the firm to transfer funds into his name, which the firm had held him out as authorized to do. The firm was vicariously liable. On the other hand, employers are not vicariously liable for crimes committed on the occasion of and facilitated by the employment opportunity (*Heasman's v. Clarity Cleaning Co. Ltd* [1987] IRLR 286: unauthorized use of customer's telephone by cleaner; *Irving v. Post Office* [1987] IRLR 289: defacing letters posted to the addressee by writing racist remarks on the envelope; *Armagas v. Mundogas SA, The Ocean Frost* [1986] AC 717: unauthorized hire of a ship).

Not surprisingly, in the case of *assault* as a crime and tort, vicarious liability is less likely, being more difficult to relate to performance content. Thus, *Warren v. Henley's Ltd, (supra)*, will be recalled, and similarly in *Keppel Bus Co. Ltd v. Ahmad* [1974] 1 WLR 1082, the employer was not vicariously liable when the employee bus conductor hit a passenger with his ticket machine. On the other hand, in *Petterson v. Royal Oak Hotel Ltd* [1948] NZLR 136 a nightclub "bouncer" (responsible for ensuring the good behaviour of those attending) went too far in keeping order and committed an assault for which the employer was held vicariously liable.

(ii) Indemnity of Employers Against Vicarious Liability

At common law, there is an implied term of a contract of employment that the employee will exercise all reasonable care and skill in carrying out his duties.

Consequently, if the employee is negligent towards a third party, for which the employer is held vicariously liable, the employer, or his insurer, can claim to be indemnified by the employee for its losses towards the third party, in an action for breach of contract (*Lister v. Romford Ice & Cold Storage Co. Ltd* [1957] AC 555).

Some people feared that such actions could adversely affect industrial relations, so insurance companies entered a "gentleman's agreement" (non-binding) not to bring such claims against employees in the absence of wilful misconduct by them or collusion between employee and employer to procure a successful claim.

(iii) Employers' Liability for Independent Contractors

The difference between an employee and an independent contractor has previously been drawn attention to, generally speaking, on the basis of a number of rather imprecise factors, including employer's control of methods of work, degree of integration of employee in the business, and whether workers can more or less be considered to be in business on their own account, in which case they are likely to be considered to be independent contractors. It has previously been pointed out that the major significance of the distinction between employees and independent contractors for present purposes is that employers are vicariously liable for the torts of the former but not for those of the latter. It will further be seen in the following ch.12 that in certain circumstances, employers' liability for actions of independent contractors will nonetheless be primary, and *strict.*

(iv) Agents and Partners

Partners are expressly made vicariously liable for torts committed by other partners when acting in the ordinary course of their firm's business or with the other partners' authority, under s.10 of the Partnership Act 1890.

As seen earlier, so too would it seem that principals are also so liable for torts of their agents carried out in the course of their agency duties (*Ormrod v. Crossville Motor Services* [1953] 1 WLR 1120).

Further reading:

Fleming, J.G., *The Law of Torts*, 8th ed, 1992 (The Law Book Company, Sydney): ch.19.

Hepple, B.A. and Matthews. M.H., *Tort: Cases and Materials*, 4th ed, 1991 (Butterworth & Co., London): ch.17.

Heuston, R.F.V. and Buckley, R.A., *Salmond and Heuston on The Law of Torts*, 20th ed, 1992 (Sweet & Maxwell, London): ch.21.

Howarth, D., *Textbook on Tort*, 1995 (Butterworth & Co., London): ch.14.

Jones, M.A., *Textbook on Torts*, 4th ed, 1993 (Blackstone, London): ch.8.

Rogers, W.V.H., *Winfield and Jolowicz on Tort*, 14th ed, 1994 (Sweet & Maxwell, London): ch.21.

Stanton, K.M., *The Modern Law of Tort*, 1994 (The Law Book Company, Sydney): ch.6.

Weir, T., *A Casebook on Tort*, 7th ed, 1992 (Sweet & Maxwell, London): ch.6.

Chapter 12

Independent Contractors

Introduction

In the preceding section, employers were shown to be vicariously liable for torts committed by their *employees* in the course of their employment; and employees were distinguished from *independent contractors,* carrying out works for an employer, on the basis of factors such as lack of sufficient control of the employer and of sufficient integration of the independent contractors in the employer's business.

The significance of the distinction: employers are not vicariously liable for the torts of independent contractors. The rationale is that being, by definition, in business on their own account, independent contractors have the responsibility and possibly also the financial means to satisfy or to insure against liability for torts committed in the course of their work. In *Morgan v. Incorporated Central Council of the Girls Friendly Society* [1936] 1 All ER 404, the plaintiff was injured in the defendants' lift which had been negligently repaired by independent contractors. The defendants were held not liable.

Nevertheless, the law does not absolve itself entirely from imposing liability upon employers for the activities of their independent contractors.

There are in fact two situations in which an employer can find himself liable as a result of the activities of his independent contractor.

(i) Primary Liability of the Employer in Negligence

This liability is not strict at all. The employer was contracted to perform a task; he engages an independent contractor to carry out the work, which the independent contractor performs negligently, so that a third party is injured. If it can be established that the employer did not take reasonable care to select competent and qualified independent contractors, or allowed them to continue after discovering their incompetence, or did not provide a safe system of checking that their work was correct, the plaintiff has a primary claim for negligence against the employer whose responsibility it was after all to accomplish the work (*Pinn v. Rew* (1916) 32 TLR 451). There is nothing strict about this liability, therefore. The employer was negligent.

(ii) Primary Strict Liability of the Employer for Non-Delegable Duties

However, even where the employer himself has fulfilled the preceding primary liability in negligence to take reasonable care as to selection of contractors and system of work, the employer may still find himself to be liable for the contractor's torts in certain situations where the duties carried out by the independent contractor, in the course of which a tort was committed by the latter, are said to be *non-delegable* on the part of the employer - that is to say, duties for which an employer remains liable and cannot escape by asking an independent contractor to perform them. To this extent, therefore, the continuing, primary liability of the employer is *strict:* he cannot get out of it by showing that he did everything which could reasonably be expected of him to ensure that no torts were committed by the independent contractor. In such cases, the employer's duty is said to be *to provide that care is taken* rather than *to take reasonable care* (*The Pass of Ballater* [1952] P.112). Thus, in *Cassidy v. Ministry of Health* [1951] 2 KB 343, Denning, LJ stated that where an employer is himself under a duty of care, he cannot get rid of his responsibility by delegating the performance of it to someone else, no matter whether the delegation is to a servant under a contract of service (vicarious liability) or to an independent contractor under a contract for services (strict liability).

In these circumstances the employer remains strictly liable for the torts committed by the independent contractor in the course of performance: and the torts themselves may be in negligence, as where the contractor fails to use reasonable care, or strict, as, say, in the case of breach of statutory duty.

Consequently, the nature of this species of *strict* liability of an employer should be understood as the following:

1. the employer is subject to a duty, which itself need only be in negligence and not necessarily strict if the employer were to perform it himself;
2. however, by delegating the performance to an independent contractor and to that extent losing control over it, the employer's duty can be *converted* into a form of strict liability, so that the employer does

not profit unjustifiably nor the other party so suffer through the delegation;

3. thus, if the duty is designated as *non-delegable,* the employer will be strictly liable if the independent contractor is negligent, whether the employer himself was negligent or not in selecting the independent contractor to perform the job - the independent contractor's negligence is treated as the employer's negligence and the employer cannot escape performing properly himself by such delegation; the other party is entitled to the employer's - to be assumed - non-negligent *performance* and does not have to make do with the independent contractor's negligent performance nor with the employer's performance by way of non-negligent selection of the independent contractor; the other party should get what he contracted for *from the* employer, and because of this, a form of strict liability enters into existence upon the employer in relation to the delegation arrangement, perfectly fairly;
4. yet, if the employer's duty to the other party is held to be *delegable,* the position is exactly the opposite, namely, that the employer's duty is limited to that of delegation to this extent and will be correctly discharged if he is not negligent in his choice and supervision of independent contractor, even if the latter himself then performs negligently.

The important question, therefore, after all this is when are employers' duties in tort delegable and non-delegable?

1. Delegable duty to take reasonable care

If the law merely imposes a duty upon a person to take reasonable care - for example, to ensure that a vehicle is roadworthy - reasonable care in selection of and delegation to a contractor to carry out this duty may be able to satisfy the person's duty in the event of a tort by the independent contractor, provided that the duty is construed as merely being a duty to take reasonable care, rather than as a strict duty to ensure that reasonable care is taken, which is quite different (see above) (*Stennett v. Hancock* [1939] 2 All ER 578).

2. *Non-delegable duties*

In some cases as seen, the law states that a duty on the employer cannot be so discharged by his reasonable care and is strict upon the employer (liable in the alternative to liability of the independent contractor himself, and with a right of indemnity against the latter if chosen to be proceeded against by the plaintiff). Such duties can arise by statute or at common law. There seems to be no general principle for the designation of duties as falling within such categories of non-delegable. However, case law is able to reveal which duties have been so classified.

Non-delegable statutory duties or powers

This is a matter of statutory construction.

Nor are these limited to strict duties or powers under a statute such as the many under the Factories Act 1961. They can also be construed as duties to ensure that reasonable care is taken in carrying out an activity (that is to say, even though liability would not arise in the absence of such negligence by the performer), so that the employer is liable if the independent contractor is negligent in so doing (*Darling v. Attorney-General* [1950] 2 All ER 793). Thus, in *Riverstone Meat Co. Pty Ltd v. Lancashire Shipping Co. Ltd* [1961] AC 807, the statutory duty was to apply "due diligence" to ensure that a ship was seaworthy. The firm was held strictly liable for the repairer's negligence and in breach of the duty, even though they had made sure that the independent contractor employed to repair the ship was competent and had had the repairs inspected by a Lloyd's shipping surveyor. On the other hand if the duty is merely construed as being one to take reasonable care, delegation is possible and discharges the employer's duty if reasonably so delegated.

Common Law Duties

There are a number of common law duties in tort which have been treated as non-delegable on the part of employers.

a. Ultra hazardous activities inherently dangerous

You cannot escape legal liability for these by employing an independent contractor to carry them out. Such cases may involve liability through escape of fire.

In *Balfour v. Barty-King* [1957] 1 QB 496, the defendant was held liable when he called in a contractor to thaw out his frozen pipes in the loft and the contractor started a fire by using a blow-lamp, which spread to the plaintiff's property. Again, in *Honeywell and Stein Ltd v. Larkin Bros.*

Ltd [1934] 1 KB 91, a company was asked to carry out work to improve the sound effects in a theatre and employed an independent contractor to take photographs of the work when it was finished. The photographer used magnesium powder to create the flash, but did so too close to the curtains which caught fire. The company was held liable, because the photography work was inherently dangerous and the company could not avoid liability by asking another to carry it out.

Similarly, the duty to prevent the escape of dangerous things kept on land in *Rylands v. Fletcher* is held to be non-delegable.

b. Private nuisance

Generally, an occupier's duties in private nuisance are *not* non-delegable. An exception is the duty not to withdraw support from neighbouring land (*Bower v. Peate* (1876) 1 QBD 321). However, in *Matania v. National Provincial Bank Ltd* [1936] 2 All ER 633, defendants were held liable for damage caused by their independent contractors in carrying out alterations to premises - but this may have been because the activities were considered to be ultra-hazardous.

c. Public nuisance and activities on or adjoining the highway (public roads and footpaths)

The employer is liable: the duty in public nuisance is non-delegable. In *Tarry v. Ashton* (1876) 1 QBD 314, the defendant was an occupier of land adjoining the highway and asked a contractor to repair a lamp overhanging the highway. The lamp fell on a passer-by. The defendant was liable.

The principle extends to any public place, not just the highway, for example, railway stations (*Pickard v. Smith* (1861) 10 CB (NS) 470), but the employer is not liable if the work is not on but merely near the highway. For example, in *Salsbury v. Woodland* [1970] 1 QB 324, the defendant was not liable when the contractor cut down a tree which fell across the highway from 28 feet away. Furthermore, the employer is also not subject to non-delegable duties in relation to activities involving use of vehicles on the highway: for example, as seen previously, the duty to ensure that a vehicle is in roadworthy condition is regarded as delegable through reasonable care to a competent repairing contractor (*Stennett v. Hancock, supra*) - except that it would seem that a minicab firm which employs independent contractors to drive taxis will be prevented from denying liability towards passengers who do not know that the firm itself does not own the taxis (*Rogers v. Night Riders* [1983] RTR 324).

d. Bailees

A bailee is someone to whom a person entrusts property - a bailee for reward (as opposed to gratuitous bailment) when the bailment is undertaken in return for money, for example, by clothes cleaners or a furniture storage firm or warehouse. Duties of a bailee for reward are non-delegable, unless the bailment contract specifies that they are delegable (*Morris v. C.W. Martin & Sons Ltd* [1966] 1 QB 716).

e. Employer's common law duties towards employees

The employer has certain duties towards his employees at common law, including due regard to health and safety and provision of a safe system and operation of work (*McDermid v. Nash Dredging and Reclamation Company Ltd* [1987] 2 All ER 878, HL; *Morris v. Breaveglen Ltd* [1993] ICR 766; *Nelhams v. Sandells Maintenance Ltd* (1995) *The Times*, June 15 - see below, Ch.16, *Liability of Employers*). These duties are non-delegable and the employer remains liable for the independent contractor's work (*Wilsons & Clyde Coal Co. Ltd v. English* [1938] AC 57). Similar non-delegable duties are placed upon hospitals and schools to look after patients and children respectively.

Understandably perhaps, in *Davie v. New Merton Board Mills Ltd* [1959] AC 604, the House of Lords held that an employer was not thus liable for the supply of a defective tool to an employee, which the employer had purchased, since the manufacturer was not to be equated with an independent contractor employed by the employer and for whose torts towards employees the employer would be non-delegably liable. Employers did not have a primary duty to manufacture their tools and equipment. (The effect of the decision was in fact subsequently reversed by the Employers' Liability (Defective Equipment) Act 1969 under which employers became liable for personal injuries to employees from defective equipment in circumstances there specified.)

So too, it will be recalled from *Aiken v. Stewart Wrightson Members Agency Ltd* [1995] 1 WLR 1281 (see *supra*, ch.5), the plaintiff Lloyd's Names sued *inter alia* their members' agents in negligence for failing properly to insure against their losses. The plaintiffs failed to persuade Potter, J that the defendants' duty of care in negligence was co-extensive with the higher contractual duty according to its terms (and unfortunately for the plaintiffs the action in contract itself was time-barred, see *ibid.*). Consequently, the plaintiffs tried a second line of approach: the defendants had delegated the conduct of the underwriting business on the plaintiffs' behalf to managing agents, in accordance with the contract between plaintiffs and defendants. Thus, the plaintiffs argued that although the defendants had quite properly delegated their duties to the managing agents as independent contractors, the defendants' duties in tort towards the plaintiffs were *non-delegable*, which meant that whereas the defendants may have exercised all reasonable care in delegating to the managing agents, nonetheless, the defendants remained liable for the managing agents' lack of care in conducting the business (p.1295): although this was not a case of employer's duty to provide a safe system of work or of hazardous operations, the plaintiffs asserted that the categories of non-delegable duties were never closed (p.1302).

Potter, J concluded, however, that there were no policy reasons for him to hold that members' agents' tortious duties towards Lloyd's Names were non-delegable by nature (p.1305) and accordingly, the defendants' duty was merely to exercise care in the plaintiffs' general interests and in respect of delegation of activities to managing agents. It was not also to ensure that care was taken by the managing agents to whom the functions of underwriting and day-to-day business management had been delegated (pp.1301-2).

In the Course of Duties

Just as employers are only vicariously liable for torts committed by employees in the course of their employment, so too they are only liable for non-delegable duties in respect of torts committed by independent contractors in the course of carrying out the delegated work and not for what is referred to as collateral or casual tort.

As usual, it is not always easy to decide whether acts of tort were committed in the course of the delegated activities or not. The test here appears to be more restrictive of employers' liability than in the case of vicarious liability for employees. Thus, in *Padbury v. Holliday & Greenwood Ltd* (1912) 28 TLR 492, the Court of Appeal indicated that the employer should only be held to be strictly liable where the independent contractor committed the tort whilst carrying out that part of the work -for example, the ultra-hazardous aspect - which had justified the non-delegable nature of the duty in the first place.

Accordingly, in *Padbury* itself, installation of a window by an independent contractor carrying out building work on a house, in the course of which a tool, which had been put to one side, was dropped onto the plaintiff walking along the highway, was considered merely to be collateral to the main building activities, and the employer was held not liable; whereas, in *Holliday v. National Telephone Co.* [1899] 2 QB 392, the explosion on the highway was caused by dropping a blowlamp during performance of the very act of laying telephone wires which the independent contractor was engaged to perform. Clearly too, therefore, torts committed in the course of work which is merely preparatory to the non-delegable activity are particularly likely to fall outside the non-delegable category.

Further reading:

Brazier, *Street on Torts*, 9th ed, 1993 (Butterworth & Co., London): ch.27.

Fleming, J.G., *The Law of Torts*, 8th ed, 1992 (The Law Book Company, Sydney): ch.19, s.5.

Howarth, D., *Textbook on Tort*, 1995 (Butterworth & Co., London): ch.8.

Jones, M.A., *Textbook on Torts*, 4th ed, 1993 (Blackstone, London): ch.8.

Weir, T., *A Casebook on Tort*, 7th ed, 1992 (Sweet & Maxwell, London): ch.7.

Chapter 13

Product Liability

Introduction

Product liability law is partly strict liability. There are *two* possible routes to recovery of compensation in tort which are open to a plaintiff injured by a defective product:

- an action under the common law of negligence: not strict liability; or
- a claim under the Consumer Protection Act 1987, giving effect in the United Kingdom to the European Union's Product Liability Directive: strict liability.

Things were not always so. The nineteenth century was the age of contract law, not tort, and remedies for defective products had to be sought under the former.

Even today there are marked advantages to be gained from bringing such actions in contract rather than in tort: (a) liability for breach of contract is strict, not based on fault, subject to the doctrine of frustration of contracts - whereas actual proof of fault is a major problem in tort where manufacturers may naturally be reluctant to co-operate and *res ipsa loquitur* has to be relied upon; (b) terms are implied by law into contracts as to the quality of goods or services and their fitness for purpose, even if these are not dangerous and have caused no injuries - while in tort, whereas *Junior Books v. Veitchi* [1983] 1 AC 520 represented an attempt to enable tortious recovery for defects in quality, this was eventually condemned in *Murphy v. Brentwood District Council* [1990] 2 All ER 908 as a prohibited claim for pure economic loss, except where the defectively manufactured part was separate from the rest of the property which it had damaged (*supra*, ch.5); and (c) contractual damages may include loss of an expected profit, whereas compensation in tort is restorative.

The major problem with contract law, however, as those first seeds of the later consumer society were sown at the end of the nineteenth century, was the doctrine of "privity of contract" whereby a stranger to a contract was unable to enforce it, which meant that plaintiffs injured by defects in products which they had not purchased directly from the manufacturer had no contractual claim against the latter. All that they could do was to sue their immediate seller for breach of contract, who might do the same to his seller, and so on, all the way up to the manufacturer. But supposing the injured plaintiff did not have a contract with anyone - for example, he received the defective product as a present from a friend - or he did conclude a contract, but the seller did not have sufficient resources to meet his claim? Could the plaintiff then sue the manufacturer in tort as an alternative? The answer was no: unless a product was inherently dangerous, courts said that injured parties should not be allowed to escape the privity of contract rule by suing in tort instead (*Winterbottom v. Wright* (1842) 10 M&W 109).

The change came in 1932 with the House of Lords'

decision in *Donoghue v. Stevenson* [1932] AC 562 that a duty of care could exist in negligence, irrespective of the absence of contractual remedies of the plaintiff against a manufacturer (*supra,* ch.5) - from which the common law of product liability against manufacturers was subsequently to be developed. This will now be examined, followed by a consideration of the more recent statutory remedy under the Consumer Protection Act 1987.

(i) Common Law of Product Liability. Manufacturers' Duty of Care in Negligence

1. Liability

In *Donoghue v. Stevenson,* the plaintiff, who claimed illness from drinking a bottle of ginger beer alleged to contain the remains of a decomposed snail, had no contract with the defendant manufacturer, nor with the café owner because her friend had purchased the drink. Mindful precisely of this fact, the House of Lords held that a manufacturer who put products onto the market which could injure a consumer's life or property if reasonable care was not taken in their manufacture or preparation, owed a duty towards the ultimate consumer to take such reasonable care.

There it was: the origin of product liability at common law, based upon fault, negligence.

In subsequent years, the scope of application of the principle was to be broadened beyond the facts of *Donoghue v. Stevenson,* itself involving a food product and a manufacturer defendant. Many different types of product have been brought within it - including cars, tombstones, and even defectively manufactured woollen underpants

(*Grant v. Australian Knitting Mills* [1936] AC 85); and defendants have gone beyond manufacturers to include others in the sales chain, such as repairers or suppliers who knew of or ought reasonably to have inspected for a defect in the product (*Watson v. Buckley, Osborne Garrett & Co. Ltd* [1940] 1 All ER 174). In addition, the duty is a continuing one. Manufacturers are not liable for defects undetectable through scientific tests or unknown design defects at the date of manufacture. But if these defects become known after the products have been put onto the market and are in circulation, the manufacturer has a duty in negligence either to recall the products or at least to issue an appropriate warning (*Hobbs (Farms) Ltd v. Baxenden Chemical Co. Ltd* [1992] 1 Lloyd's Rep 54). They will frequently insure against this possibility and ought to have an efficient system of warning or product recall.

One possible limitation on the principle of liability arose from Lord Atkin's statement in *Donoghue v. Stevenson* that the duty of care arose where the manufacturer put the product on the market "with no reasonable possibility of intermediate examination", as for example would be the case with a sealed bottle of ginger beer. Would this mean that if products could be examined in the hands of an intermediate supplier, but were not, or if the woollen underpants containing the chemicals in *Grant v. Australian Knitting Mills Ltd* had been expected to be washed before being worn, but were not, the manufacturer would escape liability for defects which might have been revealed by such an intermediate examination or treatment?

The answer given by one writer (see Jones, *Textbook on Torts*, 1993, pp.305-6) is that the courts have interpreted

Lord Atkins' no reasonable *possibility* condition in favour of plaintiffs and rather as meaning no reasonable *probability* of examination, so that even if an inspection would be perfectly possible, the manufacturer would remain liable if consumers were not usually in the habit of using such opportunities (*Haseldine v. CA Daw & Son Ltd* [1941] 2 KB 343). Certainly, if the manufacturer gives a warning to the consumer or intermediate seller to test the product or follow instructions before use, this will be capable of satisfying the manufacturer's duty. In *Holmes v. Ashford* [1950] 2 All ER 76, manufacturers of a hair dye were not liable to the plaintiff, because the hairdresser had failed to test it as required before use; and in *Kubach v. Hollands* [1937] 3 All ER 907, manufacturers of a chemical were held not liable towards an injured schoolgirl, because neither the seller nor the school had tested it before use as instructed by the manufacturer. Whether the warning does release the manufacturer, whether it should be given to the consumer rather than intermediate supplier or seller, and whether it is foreseeable that the warning is likely to be ignored in any event, are all questions to be decided on the facts of the case (*Good-Wear Treaders Ltd v. D & B Holdings Ltd* (1979) 98 DLR (3rd) 59) - as is the issue of the precise standard of reasonable care to be exercised, in the light of balance of risks against costs or benefits of products such as medicines (Jones, p.308).

It should be added, however, that although a manufacturer may remain liable where a consumer simply does not utilize a perfectly good opportunity to inspect goods before use, the consumer himself can be held to have been contributorily negligent to this extent so that the damages will be apportioned - but this will not be the case if the consumer had no real choice other than to use the product, albeit as carefully as he could (*Targett v. Torfaen Borough Council* [1992] 3 All ER 27). Thus, for example, if you climb a ladder to the roof of your house and then notice that one of the steps is weak, presumably it would not be held to be totally unreasonable for you nevertheless to try to make your way down the ladder by avoiding that step.

2. *Proof*

As usual with negligence claims, the plaintiff must prove that it was a defect in the product or in its design which actually caused the damage, not always easy in product liability cases, where scientific evidence may therefore prove vital to the success of a claim (*Evans v. Triplex Safety Glass Co. Ltd* [1936] 1 All ER 283 - windscreen manufactured by defendants shattered causing injuries one year after car purchased, but plaintiff unable to prove defendants at fault). In practice, however, courts will frequently assume that a defect originated with the manufacturer in the absence of evidence that this might have taken place at an intermediate stage (*Mason v. Williams & Williams Ltd* [1955] 1 All ER 283).

3. *Damages*

With regard to recovery of loss from product defects, it will be recalled that physical injuries and damage to property distinct from the defective product, together with any consequent economic loss (for example, cost of hiring a replacement) can be recovered for in negligence (*Spartan*

Steel & Alloys Ltd v. Martin & Co. (Contractors) Ltd [1973] 1 QB 27). But pure economic loss and damage to the product itself cannot be recovered, as amounting to mere defect in quality, requiring repair or abandonment (*D&F Estates Ltd v. Church Commissioners for England* [1988] 2 All ER 992 and *Murphy v. Brentwood District Council* [1990] 2 All ER 908 - *supra*, ch.5). The remedies in such cases remain those in contract where available. In *Murphy* the House of Lords declined to accept the complex-structure possibility mentioned in *D&F Estates,* whereby constituent parts of complex buildings or products could be regarded as separate and consequently as legally capable of causing *physical* damage to each other - except in the case of separate defective installations or integral components of the whole structure built or made by a different contractor. Thus, it would seem from *Aswan Engineering Establishment Co. v. Lupdine Ltd* [1987] 1 All ER 135 that defective containers may be separate products from their contents for these purposes, tyres from cars and corks from wine in bottles.

Such was the position at common law prior to the Consumer Protection Act 1987: fault-based liability for defects in products, subject to the usual conditions of negligence and difficulties of proof. (In addition to which, under s.75 of the Consumer Credit Act 1974, a consumer using a credit card to purchase products on credit is able to sue the credit card company if the goods or services are defective.)

(ii) Statutory Strict Liability for Defective Products The Consumer Protection Act 1987 Part I

1. General

Notwithstanding preceding judicial developments in the law of negligence, there remained a perceived need for more radical reforms involving strict liability, especially in view of certain highly publicized cases of medical product defects causing severe injuries.

The EU then produced the European Community Directive on Liability for Defective Products 1985 (85/374/EEC), introducing strict liability and implemented in the United Kingdom by Part I of the Consumer Protection Act 1987, entering into force on March 1, 1988 and applicable to damage from products put into circulation by the producer following that date (s.50(7) and SI 1987/1680). In its recital, the Directive considered that producer's liability without fault was the only way of solving the problem of the fair apportionment of risk inherent in modern technological production, in addition to which it may be said that manufacturers will traditionally insure against breach of contract and negligence claims and spread the costs amongst consumers through the pricing mechanism.

This new statutory strict liability exists alongside established common law remedies in negligence and contract for defective products which will have to be relied upon where the statutory conditions or scope remain unfulfilled. In addition, Part II of the 1987 Act imposes criminal liability for breach of certain consumer safety regulations, and s.41 specifically provides that an action for breach of statutory duty may be brought by an injured party on this basis.

Part I has had its critics. One view is that by reason of the United Kingdom's use of "development risks" defence, excluding liability for unforeseeable defects to that extent (see *infra*), as well as of the very meaning of "defective" in relation to products, results may not differ greatly from those under the common law of negligence, where, in certain circumstances, fault is all but presumed from existence of a defect, in the absence of contrary proof. Secondly, s.1(1) provides that Part I is to be construed as is necessary in order to comply with the product liability Directive. This is intended to avoid any possible proceedings being brought before the European Court of Justice against the United Kingdom for its failure fully to implement the Directive - also capable of leading to a judgment for damages in favour of an aggrieved person (see *Francovitch v. Italian Republic,* Cases C-6/90 and C-9/90 [1991] ECR I-5403) - in view of differences in wording between Act and Directive. The problem is that this creates uncertainty: will courts apply the Act or the Directive where these differ?

2. *Strict Liability*

Section 2(1) provides that where any damage is caused wholly or partly by a defect in a product, every person to whom s.2(2) applies *shall be liable* for the damage.

The plaintiff therefore proves that it was a defect in the product which caused the damage. Liability is then strict and unreliant upon fault and foreseeability.

Section 7 prohibits exclusion or limitation of this liability by contractual term or otherwise.

3. *Claimants*

It is implicit in the expression "any damage" in s.2(1) that any person who sustains damage through the defect can claim. This may be the consumer himself, or a third party injured by the defect.

4. *Persons liable*

Section 2(2) and (3) specify who can be sued.

(a) Producer. Under s.1(2), this includes:

- the manufacturer of the product or component part (both are liable if the component was defective, but not vice versa, *a fortiori* in circumstances specifically covered by s.4(1)(f));
- extractor of non-manufactured products, say oil;
- processor, if product's essential characteristics are attributable to industrial or other process.

(b) Own-branders, that is, people who hold themselves out as the producer by putting their own name on the product made by others, as many supermarkets and clothing outlets may do.

(c) Importer in the course of a business from outside the EU into a member state, in order to supply others.

(d) Supplier who fails, within a reasonable time from being requested by the person suffering damage, to identify the producer, own-brander, importer or his own supplier of the finished product (if the supplier does supply the information, the plaintiff could still proceed against him for common law negligence or in contract). Shops are therefore well-advised to keep records of their suppliers if they are to avoid this secondary liability.

Liability of all such persons is joint and several. The plaintiff can sue all or just one.

Difficult questions arise as to the meaning of "industrial", "processes" and "essential characteristics" of a product.

5. Product

Section 1(2) defines product as:

- any goods, which s.45 says include substances, growing crops and things comprised in land by virtue of being attached to it and any ship, aircraft or vehicle;
- electricity (defects, not power cut);
- subject to s.2(3), products comprised in other products as component part, raw material or otherwise (from the Directive and s.46(3), it appears that buildings are excluded, whereas building materials may be included even though buildings themselves are not - information in books is also widely thought to be covered).

Section 2(4) specifically excludes agricultural produce and game, except if they have undergone an industrial process so as to give them their essential characteristics. What is an "industrial process" - freezing, canning, slicing, cleaning? Is the "essential characteristic" of sliced beetroot or chunky grapefruit the slicing and chunking?

6. Defect

Section 3(1) provides that there is a defect in a product if the safety of the product is not such as persons generally are entitled to expect. Although this approaches from the direction of the plaintiff rather than from that of reasonable conduct of defendants, it is this aspect of the whole process which is said to bring the liability closest to negligence: products may be *deficient* as to safety, but if they do not fall below whatever is held to be the standard which persons generally - that is, not the plaintiff in particular - are entitled (no doubt meaning reasonably) to expect, they are not *defective* so as to give rise to strict liability under the Act.

As to that which persons are so entitled to expect in so far as safety of products is concerned, s.3(2) requires all the circumstances to be taken into account, including:

- the manner and purposes of marketing, marks, instructions and warnings;
- reasonably expected use;
- the date of supply.

Defendants can therefore protect themselves with warnings and instructions. Misuse of products will stop these from being held to be unsafe, unless such misuse was itself reasonably to be expected. As to timing, it may be that people should reasonably expect safety of certain products to have deteriorated after a period, whilst subsequent improvements to the safety of products do not necessarily mean that older models now fall below the standards of safety which people are entitled to expect.

It is partly these preceding considerations, appearing to offer producers a way out of liability almost through demonstrating absence of fault, so as to prevent products from being held to be *defective,* which some critics feel to compromise the strictness of the liability and to reduce the differences from common law negligence duties.

7. Excluded damage

Section 5(1) defines allowable damage as death or personal injury or any loss of or damage to property, including land.

Certain types of loss are excluded, however, in accordance with s.5(2) to (4):

(a) loss of or damage to the product itself (pure economic loss), or to a product caused by a defective component supplied with it - so if a car's battery blows up, personal injuries and damage to other vehicles can be claimed for, but not also damage to the car itself, nor to the battery, although it is otherwise if the battery were supplied subsequent to the previous purchase of the car as a substitute for the original worn-out battery;

(b) damage to business property, not ordinarily intended for private use, occupation or consumption and intended by the person suffering the loss or damage mainly for his own private use, occupation or consumption - so a manufacturer supplying a faulty electric fire to an office, which catches fire and burns down the office, is safe from strict liability, but not so if it is a dwelling home which is destroyed;

(c) property damage valued under £275.

8. Caused wholly or partly by a defect

Section 2(1) clearly means that the defect need not be the *sole* cause of the damage for strict liability to be imposed. Some commentators draw attention in this respect to the fact that at common law, a manufacturer may escape negligence liability by showing that an intermediate inspection was probable (see *supra*, p.419), whereas under s.2(1) the defendant will remain strictly liable - unless it were to be held that the reasonable expectation of such inspection, in accordance with s.3(2), would prevent the product from being held to be defective in the first place (*supra*, p.426).

9. Defences

What is *not* a defence, by virtue of s.7, is the limitation or exclusion of liability under the Act by any contract term, notice or other provision. Such attempted exclusion is ineffective thereunder.

However, s.4(1)(a) to (f) does permit a defendant to establish a number of defences.

(a) Defect due to compliance with statute or EU obligation. This seems quite unlikely. It would arise where the defendant was required to use some ingredient which proved to make the overall product harmful. It does not apply to mere statutory permission, but presumably it does to *omission*: for example, if EC law prevented certain vehicles from being sold with seat belts. The reason why this defence does not seem very likely to be widely relied upon in practice is that existence of such statutory regulations could well materially affect the finding as to defectiveness and reasonable expectations as elements in the establishment of liability in the first place.

(b) The defendant did not supply the product to another. This excludes things stolen from him, remnants and waste products thrown away - fake products too if this can be proved.

(c) The defendant did not supply the product in the course of a business: for example, where he baked cakes for the village fair or brought back presents to the EU from a holiday in the United States.

(d) The product was not defective when the defendant supplied it. This means that the product was affected after it left the defendant's control. Difficult questions of proof can arise and producers are well advised to have efficient checking systems. Of course, a product which was *certain* subsequently to deteriorate or was *easily* able to be interfered with is likely to be held to have been defective at the date of supply by the defendant in any event.

(e) "Development risks" are a defence against liability: the state of scientific and technical knowledge at the time at which the defendant supplied the product was not such that a producer of products of the same description as the product in question might be expected to have discovered the defect if it had existed in his products while they were under his control.

This is the equivalent of the "state of the art" defence in common law negligence (*Roe v. Minister of Health* [1954] 2 QB 66, *supra*, p.256): no one could have known of the defect at the relevant time on the basis of scientific knowledge then available - a defence unavailable in contract. The defence was included after great pressure from manufacturers, particularly of drugs, who said that otherwise there would be reluctance to advance medical science and technology. It was not compulsory, but the United Kingdom decided to include it in the 1987 legislation.

The criticism of the defence is that within its - potentially very wide - sphere, it reintroduces negligence via the back door by a reversal of the burden of proof, and further that product insurance is the proper loss-bearing solution. Some critics assert that in referring to scientific knowledge of *producers of the product in question* rather than to *general* scientific skills, the Act makes it too easy for producers to escape liability and that to this extent the Act does not properly implement Article 7 of the EC Directive omitting the narrower formula ("... the state of scientific and technical knowledge at the time when he put the product into circulation was not such as to enable the existence of the defect to be discovered"), which may consequently have to be considered by the European Court of Justice in the event of an action for infringement of EC law being brought by the European Commission. They further query what exactly is "knowledge" and when mere theory becomes such?

(f) In the case of a defendant sued in respect of a component part of another product, where the defect is wholly due to the design of the other product or to compliance with the instructions given by the producer of the other product. This protects defendants in a situation over which they may have little control - although it should be said that just because they can rely upon the statutory defence, this does not also mean that they are immune from an ordinary common law action in negligence if the events affecting the plaintiff were reasonably foreseeable.

In addition to these preceding, the plaintiff will be subject to apportionment of damages for contributory negligence. *Volenti non fit injuria* (consent) is the subject of some doubt, especially in view of the prohibition of liability *exclusion* under s.7. However, it could be that in circumstances of *volenti,* products would not be regarded as being defective in the first place, given consenting plaintiffs' level of reasonable expectations.

With regard to time limitation of actions, under Schedule 1 to the Act:

(a) the plaintiff cannot commence his action more than 10 years after the defendant supplied the product, even if the defect was deliberately concealed; and

(b) the plaintiff must commence the action not more than three years after

i. the date on which the damage occurred, or
ii. if later, the date of his knowledge of it, although, in personal injuries cases, the court has a discretion to override the three-year limit (but not the overall 10-year period).

Development risks, the primary role of causation (though partial is enough), exclusion of agricultural products through farmers' pressure, application of *res ipsa loquitur* and almost presumed causation from defects in any event at common law, have all led commentators to question the merits of the 1987 legislation, which may nevertheless at least be said to have prompted industrialists and suppliers to examine their safety and records systems so as to protect consumers - and their own positions in the event of litigation.

Further reading:

Brazier, *Street on Torts*, 9th ed, 1993 (Butterworth & Co., London): ch.18.
Clark, "The Conceptual Basis of Product Liability" (1985) 48 *Modern Law Review* 325.
Fleming, J.G., *The Law of Torts*, 8th ed, 1992 (The Law Book Company, Sydney): ch.23.
Heuston, R.F.V. and Buckley, R.A., *Salmond and Heuston on The Law of Torts*, 20th ed, 1992 (Sweet & Maxwell, London): ch.12.
Howarth, D., *Textbook on Tort*, 1995 (Butterworth & Co., London): ch.8.
Jones, M.A., *Textbook on Torts*, 4th ed, 1993 (Blackstone, London): ch.10.
Markesinis, B.S. and Deakin, S.F., *Tort Law*, 3rd ed, 1994 (Clarendon Press, Oxford): ch.6.

Newdick, "The Development Risk Defence of the Consumer Protection Act 1987" (1988) 47 *Cambridge Law Journal* 455.

Rogers, W.V.H., *Winfield and Jolowicz on Tort*, 14th ed, 1994 (Sweet & Maxwell, London): ch.10.

Stanton, K.M., *The Modern Law of Tort*, 1994 (The Law Book Company, Sydney): ch.11.

Whitaker, "European Product Liability and Intellectual Products" (1989) 105 *Law Quarterly Review* 125.

Chapter 14

Liability for Animals

Strict liability already existed at common law on the basis of knowledge of an animal's dangerous character. This was abolished and replaced by strict liability under the Animals Act 1971. However, the general provisions of common law torts such as negligence also remain applicable to wrongs committed through animals, as by any other actionable means.

(i) Common Law

Any reasonably foreseeable harm resulting from the keeping of an animal, for example, failing to control it on a busy road, will be actionable in negligence.

Allowing dogs to bark or pigs to stink can amount to nuisance (ch.23) - even *Rylands v. Fletcher* (ch.24) if the pet alligator escapes from the bath.

Teaching a pet parrot to say rude things about the neighbours may be defamatory. Training a dog to attack them may be battery.

These standard principles will still have to be resorted to where the 1971 Act is inapplicable, as, for example, in the case of a *non-dangerous* species where the keeper did not know of the particular animal's character but ought reasonably to have foreseen that the animal could have caused injuries (many normally docile animals may react violently if subjected to provocation, as may humans) (*Draper v. Hodder* [1972] 2 QB 556) - and as part of a duty of care in negligence, keepers should take reasonable steps to control any animal until they have had a proper chance to assess whether it has a dangerous character or not (*Smith v. Prendergast* (1984) *The Times,* October 18).

(ii) Animals Act 1971

There is a distinction between inherently *dangerous species* and *non-dangerous* - meaning not normally dangerous - species.

1. Dangerous species

Section 2(1) makes the keeper of an animal belonging to a dangerous species *strictly liable* for damage caused by it (expressly including death and personal injuries, but probably also property damage), except where otherwise provided by the Act.

"Keeper" is:

- the owner, if in possession;
- head of household, if keeper is under 16;
- an existing keeper who loses ownership or possession, until there is a new keeper.

"Dangerous species" is a species:

i. not commonly domesticated in the British Isles; *and*
ii. which, when fully grown, unless restrained, is *either* likely to cause severe damage *or* is such that any damage which it does cause is likely to be severe.

Dangerous, accordingly, is a question of law, and if the species is dangerous it is not a defence to prove that the particular animal is not so (*Behrens v. Bertram Mills Circus Ltd* [1957] 2 QB 1). Beware, therefore, of keeping a pet rhinoceros in the garden.

"Damage" which is recoverable for under s.2(1) is not confined to that normally associated with the dangerous nature of the non-domesticated species, such as crushing or goring. An animal being transported by road in a trailer might move suddenly and cause the vehicle to swerve off the carriageway.

The Dangerous Wild Animals Act 1976 requires keepers of dangerous wild animals to take out compulsory insurance against liability for damage caused to third parties and to be licensed by the local authority.

2. *Non-dangerous species*

Section 2(2) provides that, subject to the Act, the keeper is strictly liable for damage caused by the animal if:

(a) the damage is of a kind which the particular animal, unless restrained, *either* is likely to cause *or* if caused is likely to be severe; *and*

(b) such likelihood is due to characteristics of the particular animal not normally found in animals of the same species or not so except at certain times or in certain circumstances; *and*

(c) those characteristics were known to:

  (i) the keeper; or

  (ii) at any time to the keeper's servant having charge of the animal; or

(iii) known to another keeper under 16 being a member of a household of which the keeper is head.

Damage

Courts have interpreted "likely" to cause or to be severe, widely, in the plaintiff's favour, as a *material risk* rather than merely as *probable (Smith v. Ainger* (1990) *The Times,* June 5). Furthermore, they have not been reluctant to give a broad classification to the type of damage an animal is likely to cause. An animal which has already bitten may be held just as likely to jump on and scratch as to bite. However, the damage caused must fall within that type, as so construed, which the particular animal's characteristics thus make likely or likely to be severe (*Curtis v. Betts* [1990] 1 All ER 769) - it is not sufficient, for example, if a dog known to jump on people sets up an allergic reaction to its fur in the plaintiff. In *Curtis v. Betts* the plaintiff was bitten on the face by his neighbours' dog whom he had known since it was a puppy. It was held that the damage was not likely, because of the normally gentle and inactive nature of the dog, but the severity of such an injury was likely and was seemingly due to the dog's unusual characteristic of reacting violently when disturbed while taking up its position in the family car.

Abnormal Characteristics

With regard to abnormal characteristics, or those not normal *except at certain times or in certain circumstances* - for example, during the mating season or when protecting the young -

it is expressly made clear that the latter does not convert the animal into a temporarily dangerous species: it is merely that the particular animal's behaviour is treated as an abnormal characteristic of the otherwise non-dangerous species. Thus, in *Cummings v. Grainger* [1977] 1 All ER 104, an Alsatian guard dog injured the friend of an employee of the firm using the dog. The court held that Alsatians were not a dangerous species, and although in fact it was not at all abnormal for Alsatians to be aggressive in the circumstances of being used as a guard dog, the particular dog in question was held to have characteristics falling within the non-dangerous category of liability.

For liability, it is not necessary for the particular animal's abnormal characteristics in relation to the species actually to consist of violent behaviour towards other animals or people. In contrast to the pre-Act law, it is sufficient if the animal's characteristics are those of unreliability or nervousness which lead to the plaintiff's injures (*Wallace v. Newton* [1982] 2 All ER 106 - horse's reaction to being loaded into a trailer is not normal characteristic of horses; *Kite v. Napp* (1982) *The Times,* June 1 - dog attacking people carrying bags not usual for such dogs).

Finally, "species" is not limited to different types of animal - dogs, cats, snakes and crocodiles. It also descends into different breeds of each of the types (*Hunt v. Wallis* (1991) *The Times,* May 10). If an entire breed of dogs has a particular characteristic, the latter consequently is not abnormal, even though the majority of dogs do not share it.

Knowledge of the keeper

Other than in the case of servants and keeper members of the household under 16, the keeper's knowledge must be actual - the mere fact that he ought reasonably to have known of the abnormality is not enough and will therefore have to form the basis of a common law action for negligence instead (*Draper v. Hodder* [1972] 2 All ER 210). The characteristics of which the keeper is required to have knowledge need not correspond with the actual behaviour complained of, merely with the features which led to it, for example, a violent and aggressive nature.

3. *Defences*

Section 2 provides a number of defences.

a. Contributory Negligence

No liability for damage due *wholly* to the fault of the person suffering it (s.5(1)) - entering a lion's den, pushing fingers through the bars of a cage. If the plaintiff's negligence merely *contributed* to the loss, damages will be apportioned (s.10).

b. Volenti

Voluntary assumption of risks is a defence (s.5(2)), but not if this is a risk ordinarily incidental to employment (s.6(5)) - for example, as in the case of a lion tamer's assistant.

c. Trespassers

No liability exists if the keeper proves *either* that the animal was not deliberately kept in order to protect persons or property *or* if it was, that this was not unreasonable (s.5(3)). In *Cummings v. Grainger, supra,* p.438, guard dogs in a scrap yard were held not unreasonable by the Court of Appeal, whereas the first instance court had held this to be excessive. But what else could the defendants do, asked Lord Denning, MR in the Court of Appeal? - the dog in question might indeed have been very fierce, yet "a gentle dog would be no good". ... the yard was "in the East End of London where persons of the roughest type come and go"! The Guard Dogs Act 1975 now makes it a criminal offence, however, for a guard dog to be allowed to roam free on premises without a handler. This could also be held to make the dog's presence unreasonable for purposes of s.5(3). Occupiers are therefore advised to provide a clear warning of the dog so that the defence of *volenti* is independently available both under the 1971 Act and the Occupiers' Liability Act 1984 where the latter applies.

Under the 1971 Act, however, there are no defences of Act of God and act of a stranger, applicable elsewhere in strict liability (see *infra,* ch.29).

(iii) Straying Animals

The 1971 Act also has a number of distinct heads of strict liability for damage caused by *straying* animals - those which escape free from human control and wander off.

1. Straying of livestock onto land

Section 7 establishes strict liability on owners for damage caused to a person's land or property on it (but not personal injury) from livestock straying onto his land, and the person can sell the livestock in order to obtain compensation for damages and expenses of keeping the livestock. "Livestock" means farming animals such as cattle, horses, pigs, poultry and sheep - not dogs and cats (s.11). This derives from the ancient common law action of cattle trespass.

Usual defences of *volenti* and contributory negligence are available - but s.5(6) specifically provides that failure to fence is not a defence, unless the owner or occupier was under a duty (say, by contract or custom) to fence. In addition, s.5(5) makes it a defence if the animal was lawfully on the highway when it strayed (in former times, animals had to be marched along highways to market), although the keeper can still be liable for common law negligence in the circumstances (*Gayler & Pope Ltd v. Davies & Son Ltd* [1924] 2 KB 75). In *Matthews v. Wicks* (1987) *The Times,* May 25, it was held that sheep which had been left to graze overnight on common land and which had then strayed onto the highway and subsequently from there into the plaintiff's garden were not *lawfully on the highway* for these purposes, and that the defendants could not use the defence.

2. Animals straying onto the highway

Section 8(1) applies the ordinary duty of care in negligence to require persons to act reasonably in order to prevent animals - any, not just livestock - from straying onto the highway. Birds should be caged, dogs kept on a lead and fenced in, yet cats ... who could possibly be expected to have the slightest influence in controlling the activities of a cat?

Section 8(2) provides that the duty of care is not breached merely through placing animals on common land or a village green, which then wander onto the highway.

At common law, owners had no duty at all to keep their animals from straying onto the highway.

3. Damage to livestock by dogs

Section 3 makes the keeper liable if a dog kills or injures livestock. This is regardless of knowledge or of abnormal characteristics.

Defences exist: where the livestock strayed onto land of the dog's owner and the dog was kept there; *volenti*; contributory negligence.

There is also a defence to killing or injuring a dog in order to protect livestock on land belonging to the defendant or his employer, provided that the police are informed within 48 hours (s.9). Protection of livestock for the purposes means a reasonable belief that:

(a) the dog was worrying or about to worry the livestock and that there were no other reasonable means to stop it, or

(b) that the dog had been worrying livestock, had not left the area, was not under any person's control and no practicable means existed to find out who owned it.

The defence is inapplicable if under s.5(4) the owner of the dog would not have been liable because the livestock had strayed.

(iv) Remoteness of Damage

Foreseeability is inapplicable - keepers are liable for all direct damage in the absence of express treatment in the 1971 Act. It will be recalled, however, that damage from non-dangerous species is limited to that resulting from the abnormal characteristics - although the precise damage within that category need not have been reasonably foreseeable.

Further reading:

Brazier, *Street on Torts*, 9th ed, 1993 (Butterworth & Co., London): ch.21.

Fleming, J.G., *The Law of Torts*, 8th ed, 1992 (The Law Book Company, Sydney): ch.18.

Hepple, B.A. and Matthews, M.H., *Tort: Cases and Materials*, 4th ed, 1991 (Butterworth & Co., London): ch.11.

Heuston, R.F.V. and Buckley, R.A., *Salmond and Heuston on The Law of Torts*, 20th ed, 1992 (Sweet & Maxwell, London): ch.14.

Howarth, D., *Textbook on Tort*, 1995 (Butterworth & Co., London): ch.8.

Jones, M.A., *Textbook on Torts*, 4th ed, 1993 (Blackstone, London): ch.8.

Markesinis, B.S. and Deakin, S.F., *Tort Law*, 3rd ed, 1994 (Clarendon Press, Oxford): ch.6.

Rogers, W.V.H., *Winfield and Jolowicz on Tort*, 14th ed, 1994 (Sweet & Maxwell, London): ch.16.

Stanton, K.M., *The Modern Law of Tort*, 1994 (The Law Book Company, Sydney): chs.11 and 19.

Weir, T., *A Casebook on Tort*, 7th ed, 1992 (Sweet & Maxwell, London): ch.12.

Chapter 15
Escape of Fire

This is nowadays usually a matter for insurance rather than litigation. Nevertheless, actions exist at common law and by statute, which may be of use where a victim has not paid his insurance premiums or the insurance company decides to sue.

(i) Common Law

Liability for escape of fire is an ancient common law form of action.

There are doubts over whether it was strict or fault-based.

Today, fire damage may be brought within several different types of action.

1. Rylands v. Fletcher-type liability

This is possible (*infra,* ch.24) if the defendant brought things onto the land which were likely to catch fire, kept them there for some non-natural use, in circumstances making it likely that any fire would spread to neighbouring property, and this occurred (*Mason v. Levy Autoparts of England* [1967] 2 QB 530). Thus, in *E. Hobbs (Farms) Ltd v. The Baxenden Chemical Company Ltd* [1992] 1 Lloyd's Rep 54, the defendants were held liable under *Rylands v. Fletcher* when fire spread from underneath a workbench to the property next door.

It should be noted that required likelihood of escape relates to the fire itself not to the thing which might catch fire: this is why this form of liability is referred to as *Rylands v. Fletcher*-"type" liability, rather than as *Rylands v. Fletcher* itself.

In *H & N Emanuel Ltd v. GLC* [1972] 2 All ER 835, Lord Denning, MR suggested that in view of the need to assess *likelihood* of things catching fire, there was not much difference between this and ordinary liability in negligence, where the fire spread to adjoining land. Indeed, it is likely that defendants undertaking hazardous operations involving creating fire will also be under a non-delegable duty and liable in negligence for independent contractors, even if not personally at fault, regardless of conditions of escape or non-natural user of land applicable to *Rylands v. Fletcher* (see *Honeywell and Stein Ltd v. Larkin Bros (London's Commercial Photographers) Ltd* [1934] 1 KB 191).

The *Rylands v. Fletcher*-type liability will also exist for acts of persons under the occupier's control, such as employees and even independent contractors (*Balfour v. Barty-King* [1957] 1 QB 496) - but not for those acting without the authority of the occupier ("acts of a stranger") or Acts of God.

2. *Nuisance*

An occupier may be liable for failing to take reasonable steps to stop the spread of a fire which began naturally, for example, through lightning or through the act of a stranger (*Goldman v. Hargrave* [1967] 1 AC 645), and which then interferes with a neighbour's use or enjoyment of his property or causes physical damage.

3. Negligence

A normal claim in negligence may be brought (*Musgrove v. Pandelis* [1919] 2 KB 43), or proceedings under the Occupiers' Liability legislation.

(ii) Statute

The Fires Prevention (Metropolis) Act 1774, s.86 provides that no one is liable for fires which start accidentally. *Accidentally* has been restrictively interpreted, so that it does not provide a defence to *Rylands v. Fletcher* or negligence liability (nor to fires started intentionally, even if the spread was accidental). In *Filliter v. Phippard* (1847) 11 QB 347, in which the defendant lit a fire on his property in order to burn some weeds, which he then negligently left so that it spread to the plaintiff's neighbouring land and burnt a hedge, it was held that the immunity only applied to fires started by mere chance or of which the exact cause was unknown. This was said to exclude fires started accidentally, but which spread through negligence, in *Musgrove v. Pandelis* [1919] 2 KB 43, where the defendant's motor car engine accidentally caught fire when he started it up in his garage, yet the fire then spread to the plaintiff's premises above through negligence of the defendant's employee. However, in *Collingwood v. Home & Colonial Stores* [1936] 2 All ER 200 the defendants were held not liable for fire from faulty wiring, because negligence could not be proved; a similar result was achieved in *Sochaki v. Sas* [1947]

1 All ER 344 when a spark jumped out of a domestic fire grate.

The Act, therefore, does not reduce the standard of liability for common law negligence or *Rylands v. Fletcher* - but merely clarifies the legal position at the lower level of accidental cause outside the preceding circumstances.

Since at common law railways were held to have a defence of statutory authority, in the absence of negligence, when sparks from trains set fire to properties alongside the track (*Vaughan v. Taff Vale Railway Co.* (1860) 5 H & N 679), the Railway Fires Acts 1905 and 1923 were passed, creating liability, yet limiting damages to £200 for losses to land and crops.

Further reading:

Fleming, J.G., *The Law of Torts*, 8th ed, 1992 (The Law Book Company, Sydney): ch.17.

Hepple, B.A. and Matthews, M.H., *Tort: Cases and Materials*, 4th ed, 1991 (Butterworth & Co., London): ch.14.

Heuston, R.F.V. and Buckley, R.A., *Salmond and Heuston on The Law of Torts*, 20th ed, 1992 (Sweet & Maxwell, London): ch.13.

Howarth, D., *Textbook on Tort*, 1995 (Butterworth & Co., London): ch.11.

Jones, M.A., *Textbook on Torts*, 4th ed, 1993 (Blackstone, London): ch.8.

Stanton, K.M., *The Modern Law of Tort*, 1994 (The Law Book Company, Sydney): ch.21.

PART VII

Chapter 16

Liability of Employers

Introduction

Employers' liability towards their employees is not only of great social importance, but also provides a useful study of how different forms of liability in negligence, vicarious liability, non-delegable strict liability and breach of statutory duty, may all co-exist and complement each other in respect of the single employment relationship. There may of course be some overlap, for example, where an employer is both vicariously liable for the actions of one of his employees towards another and primarily liable for the same injury under his non-delegable duty of safety. This is not particularly surprising when it is understood that the latter doctrine was created at a time when employers were not in fact held vicariously liable for the actions of employees towards each other - the so-called rule of "common employment", eventually abolished under s.1 of the Law Reform (Personal Injuries) Act 1948. The primary non-delegable duty nonetheless remains of importance where the employer has no vicarious liability because the employee causing the injury was not acting in the course of his employment or was not an employee but an independent contractor, and employers are therefore obliged to insure against liability for personal injuries of employees

(Employers' Liability (Compulsory Insurance) Act 1969). A range of special social security benefits is also available to employees in respect of injuries suffered at work.

(i) Non-Delegable Strict Liability of Employers

Employers' duties of safety towards their employees are strict, to the extent of being personal and non-delegable to others.

That is to say, the employer is liable for breach of the duty delegated to others, even though he himself may not be personally at fault: he thought that the other person was competent and took reasonable steps to confirm this. Yet nevertheless, the non-delegable duties were broken.

The actual standard of care to be exercised by the employer himself or by his delegate in the performance of the safety duties, however, is not strict as such - reasonable efforts not to breach these in all the circumstances of the case is all that will be expected and will vary with the nature of and dangers involved in the work (*Davie v. New Merton Board Mills Ltd* [1959] AC 604), although courts will naturally try to set a standard sufficient to give proper protection to employees (*Winter v. Cardiff Rural District Council* [1950] 1 All ER 819), balanced against practicality of precautions to be expected from employers (*Withers v. Perry Chain Co. Ltd* [1961] 1 WLR 1314) and against employees' own duties under their employment contract (*Johnstone v. Bloomsbury Health Authority* [1991] 2 All ER 293).

This (non-delegable) duty of employers to ensure that reasonable care is taken for the physical safety of employees can be sub-divided into a number of categories as follows.

1. Duty to employ competent staff

Part of the employer's duty towards an employee to create a safe working environment is to select fellow-employees with care and to ensure that they are properly trained to use equipment (*General Cleaning Contractors Ltd v. Christmas* [1953] AC 180). This may involve refusing to employ, or disciplining, other employees who have a reputation for playing practical jokes or causing trouble (*Hudson v. Ridge Manufacturing Co. Ltd* [1957] 2 QB 348). The employer's primary non-delegable duty is all the more important in this respect where the other employee is held not to have been acting in the course of his employment in causing injury to the plaintiff employee so that the employer is not also vicariously liable for the former's actions towards the plaintiff.

2. Duty to provide safe place and system of work

The employer is expected to do what is reasonable in the circumstances, having regard to the nature of the employee's work and level of control exercised. If, for example, the employee spends a lot of his time away from his employer's premises, for example, in the case of social workers or auditors of company accounts, the employer cannot reasonably be expected to make a thorough check of the outside premises visited (*Wilson v. Tyneside Window Cleaning Company* [1958] 2 QB 110). Nor was it held reasonable to expect the Ministry of Defence to maintain *a safe system of work* for the plaintiff British soldier serving in a heavy artillery regiment which was firing shells at the Iraqis during the Gulf War and whose hearing was affected by the blasts (*Mulcahy v. Ministry of Defence* (1996) *The Times*, February 27, CA).

Safe systems may involve proper training in the use of tools and equipment as well as provision of supervisors where reasonable (*Nolan v. Dental Manufacturing Co. Ltd* [1958] 1 WLR 936), together with the warnings of dangers where appropriate (*Pape v. Cumbria County Council* [1992] 3 All ER 211: employers should have warned a cleaner about the risk of catching dermatitis from the cleaning materials used should the employee decide not to use the gloves provided; and should provide a proper level of assistance to prevent severe stress where the workload is extremely heavy: *Walker v. Northumberland County Council* (1994) NLJ 1659. In *General Cleaning Contractors v. Christmas* [1953] AC 180, it was held that a window cleaner ought to have been provided with wedges to prevent windows from falling shut and should have been advised to test the window first before standing on the window sill, in which case this would have been sufficient to discharge the employer's duty, since there was nowhere to attach safety ropes as a further safety measure.

However, it would seem that the employer's duty to warn is generally restricted to the employee's physical well-being and does not also extend, for example, to advice on economic benefits of insurance (*Reid v. Rush & Tomkins Group plc* [1990] 1 WLR 212).

Where the duty does apply, this is not merely to introduce a safe system, but also to ensure that it is operated safely (*McDermid v. Nash Dredging and Reclamation Co. Ltd* [1987] AC 906).

Employers should also anticipate that safety instructions

may from time to time be ignored by employees and have procedures to enforce these (*Clifford v. Charles H. Challen & Son Ltd* [1951] 1 KB 495). Where an employee works off site, the employer may have to go and inspect the outside premises himself in order to establish their safety - in other cases it may be enough to ensure that the firm for which the employee will be temporarily working is generally trustworthy (*Cook v. Square D Ltd* [1992] ICR 262). The employer must have regard to the general health of the employee, not merely the avoidance of specific injuries (*Johnstone v. Bloomsbury Health Authority* [1991] 2 All ER 293 - hospital doctor becoming ill through working more than 100 hours a week).

If an employer can show that he has followed the general practice of his particular trade, the employee's claim will be very difficult to establish (*Thompson v. Smiths Ship Repairers (North Shields) Ltd* [1984] 1 All ER 881) - but by no means impossible where the practice is shown to be defective.

Whether an employer should create an elaborate overall system, or leave safety matters largely to each individual employee, or not only have a general system but actually ensure safety in respect of separate individual activities of employees will depend upon the nature of the job and its safety requirements (*Speed v. Thomas Swift & Co. Ltd* [1943] KB 557). Clearly, if work is repetitive and presents common features without great variations, an overall system is likely to be both sufficient and required (*General Cleaning Contractors Ltd v. Christmas* [1953] AC 180).

3. *Proper plant and equipment*

The employer has a duty to take reasonable care to provide, maintain, instruct in the use of and regularly inspect proper tools and equipment for his employees (*Smith v. Baker* [1891] AC 325). There is a defence of lack of causation if the employer can prove that the employee would not have used safety equipment (properly or even at all) even if it had been provided (*Parkinson v. Lyle Shipping Co.* [1964] 2 Lloyd's Rep 79), or if the latent defect could not be ascertained (*McWilliams v. Sir William Arrol & Co. Ltd* [1962] 1 WLR 295). However, under s.1(1) of the Employers' Liability (Defective Equipment) Act 1969, an employer is made strictly liable for supplying an injured employee with equipment which was negligently manufactured (reversing *Davie v. New Merton Board Mills Ltd* [1959] AC 604, where the House of Lords had held that an employer was not liable for manufacturers' negligently-made equipment, if a reasonable inspection would not reveal this) - and the employer can then claim an indemnity from the manufacturer. The courts will adopt a broad construction of "equipment" covered by the Act (*Knowles v. Liverpool City Council* [1993] 4 All ER 321). In *Coltman v. Bibby Tankers Ltd* [1988] AC 276, the expression was actually held to include a ship which had sunk, and it was said not to be restricted to equipment merely ancillary to the employee's main workplace.

Finally, these duties are only applicable where the plaintiff is an employee of the defendant, which may not be the case where the plaintiff was hired out to another firm by his main "employer" at the time of his injury. In *Morris v. Breaveglen Ltd* (1992) *The Times,* December 29, the plaintiff was injured when he was sent by the defendant firm to work for contractors at Dartmoor Prison: the arrangement between the defendants and contractors was that the former would continue to maintain employers' liability insurance, but that the contractors would have control over the plaintiff's activities. The defendants were held liable for injuries caused to the plaintiff by an unsafe system of work at the prison. However, the Court of Appeal also stated that had the injured person been a third party and not the employee himself, it would then have been the contractors and not the defendants who would have been liable, because the contractors were in control. Similarly, in *Johnson v. Coventry Churchill International Ltd* [1992] 3 All ER 14, the defendant English employment agency was held liable towards the plaintiff employee for injuries suffered by him from an unsafe system of work on a building site in Germany to which he had been sent by the defendant agency: the plaintiff was paid by the defendants and there would have to have been very strong evidence before the court would conclude that he had become the employee of the German contractors. Again, in *Nelhams v. Sandells Maintenance Ltd* (1995) *The Times*, June 15, defendant employers were held liable towards the plaintiff employee who had been sent to work for another firm where he was injured because a ladder which he had been asked to climb was unsafe (although, the defendants were also found to be entitled to a complete indemnity from the other firm which was directly responsible for the accident).

(ii) Breach of Statutory Duty

The Health and Safety at Work Act 1974 imposes duties of

safety and penalties upon employers, together with other legislation to similar effect such as the Factories Act 1961, and further regulations are able to be made thereunder.

In the case of some of these duties, a civil action for breach will be available (see *supra*, ch.10). The precise nature of the statutory duties of employers is a matter of interpretation as to scope and as to whether these are strict (*John Summers & Sons Ltd v. Frost* [1955] AC 740) or merely to do what is reasonably practicable, which latter involves balancing risk against costs and extent of measures required (*Edwards v. National Coal Board* [1949] 1 All ER 743). In *Latimer v. AEC Ltd* [1953] AC 643, a floor was required to be kept in an "efficient state", which was held to be necessary to determine on the basis of which injuries were reasonably foreseeable.

Clearly, there are many obstacles of uncertainty and interpretation to overcome before such actions may be brought for breach of statutory duties in industrial safety legislation. Yet, if this is possible there may be substantial advantages of proof for employees over an ordinary negligence action.

(iii) Defences

These used to be considerable, in employers' favour, and included the doctrine of "common employment" whereby an employee injured by another could not sue their common employer. This obstacle was abolished in 1948 (*supra,* p.448), and in addition contributory negligence ceased to be a complete bar and employees' own negligence was treated less harshly in the light of the changed perceptions of the twentieth century. *Volenti* (consent) too was required to be freely given by employees before it would be applied.

1. Volenti non fit injuria (consent)

In *Smith v. Baker & Sons* [1891] AC 325 the House of Lords accepted that mere continuation in work knowing of the risks was not sufficient without more to amount to *volenti,* because people generally had no choice other than to work.

Public policy probably bars the defence where the employee's action is for breach of statutory duty by the employer - except where the employee himself took part in the breach with the other employee who injured him (*ICI Ltd v. Shatwell* [1965] AC 656), or where the plaintiff put the employer in breach of his statutory duty through vicarious liability (*Ginty v. Belmont Building Supplies Ltd* [1959] 1 All ER 414).

2. Contributory negligence

Courts are quite generous to employees in applying this defence to negligence and breach of statutory duty actions (*Bux v. Slough Metals Ltd* [1974] 1 All ER 262) - and may even hold that employers had a duty precisely to take reasonable steps to safeguard employees from injuries due to their own negligence (*Flower v. Ebbw Vale Steel Iron & Coal Ltd* [1934] 2 KB 132).

Actions for breach of statutory duty, alongside negligence, development of non-delegable duties of employers, reduction in effectiveness of employers' defences, and employers' compulsory liability insurance, have all combined to bring about a relative improvement in employees' legal position in modern times. In addition, there are social security payments by the state to injured employees, financed by employer and employee contributions, and in fact most employees will bring their claim under the no-fault industrial injuries scheme administered by the social security authorities, rather than institute proceedings in tort through the courts.

Further reading:

Fleming, J.G., *The Law of Torts*, 8th ed, 1992 (The Law Book Company, Sydney): ch.24.

Hepple, B.A. and Matthews, M.H., *Tort: Cases and Materials*, 4th ed, 1991 (Butterworth & Co., London): ch.12.

Howarth, D., *Textbook on Tort*, 1995 (Butterworth & Co., London): ch.8.

Jones, M.A., *Textbook on Torts*, 4th ed, 1993 (Blackstone, London): ch.5.

Markesinis, B.S. and Deakin, S.F., *Tort Law*, 3rd ed, 1994 (Clarendon Press, Oxford): ch.6.

Rogers, W.V.H., *Winfield and Jolowicz on Tort*, 14th ed, 1994 (Sweet & Maxwell, London): ch.8.

PART VIII

Chapter 17

The Tort of Trespass to the Person

Introduction

The law has provided a civil remedy for physical interference with a person - trespass to the person - from the earliest times.

As will be seen, for historical reasons connected with development of different forms of action under the procedural writ system, trespass came to be distinguished from the tort of negligence in the following manner:

(1) trespass is *intentional* harm, negligence can be unintentional;
(2) trespass is *direct* interference, negligence direct or indirect: hit the plaintiff with a stick and it is trespass; leave the stick in his path without a warning so that he falls over it, and it is negligence.

Thus, it was confirmed by Diplock, J in the High Court in *Fowler v. Lanning* [1959] 2 WLR 241 that for trespass to the person to succeed, it was not sufficient for the act complained of to have *directly* caused harm to the plaintiff: it also had to be *intentional*. If the interference was unintentional, whether purely accidental or negligent, the action would have to be brought in negligence, not trespass, so that if the plaintiff merely alleged that the defendant had shot him without also revealing whether this was intentional or unintentional, this would found a claim neither in trespass nor in negligence. This was subsequently approved by a majority of the Court of Appeal in *Letang v. Cooper* [1965] 1 QB 232, where the defendant negligently and unintentionally ran over the plaintiff's legs with his car while she was sunbathing, and the court held that the action was in negligence, not trespass in the form of battery (see *infra*) and consequently was time-barred after only three years (and again in *Wilson v. Pringle* [1986] 2 All ER 440, CA). If this approach is followed, it means that unintentionally, including negligently, inflicted harm to the person must be claimed for under the tort of negligence and cannot form the basis of an action in trespass. This is significant because trespass, unlike negligence, is actionable *per se* - that is, without proof of actual damage - rules of "remoteness" of damage are more favourable to the plaintiff in trespass (see *infra*), and an action in negligence could be barred by limitation rules after a shorter period of time (see *supra, Letang v. Cooper*).

There are different forms of trespass to the person, as follows:

(i) Assault and Battery

These may take place, the latter consequent upon the former, or either without the other. Their meaning?

Assault is where the defendant does something (or possibly even merely says something, for example, "Give me your money now or I shall kill you" see *R. v. Wilson* [1955] 1 WLR 493) which reasonably causes the plaintiff to expect immediate unlawful physical force to be applied to him. *Battery* is such an application of unlawful force (*Collins v. Wilcock* [1984] 3 All ER 374).

Assault

Examples from the cases include raising a clenched fist or pointing a gun at someone. So long as the plaintiff's expectation of force was reasonable ("reasonable apprehension"), it is no defence that the assault could not have been carried out because, for example, the gun was unloaded (*R v. St George* [1840] 9 Car & P 483); nor need it be proved that the plaintiff was frightened (*Stephens v. Myers* [1830] 4 C & P 349).

Expectation of an immediate attack is necessary, so that if the defendant workers on strike are making threatening gestures towards those continuing to work but are being held back by the police for the time being, the expectation cannot sensibly exist as to immediate force.

Both immediacy and reasonableness of apprehension from a defendant's actions may be removed by virtue of his accompanying words (and *vice versa*, of course, as where a seemingly verbal threat is countered by friendly gestures demonstrating that the defendant is not being serious). Thus, in *Tuberville v. Savage* (1669) 1 Mod 3, the defendant placed his hand on his sword and declared "If it were not assize-time, I would not take such language from you." There was no assault because the words showed there would be no swordplay that day.

Naturally, if the violence does not, in fact, take place, there is assault without battery. Conversely, there will be battery without prior assault if the defendant creeps up on the plaintiff without prior warning or threat of the attack and then hits him.

Battery

This is where the physical attack is actually carried out. Being a trespass, it must be direct, as where the defendant punches the plaintiff on the nose, or hits him with a stick or shoots a bullet at him, or throws a stone, or kicks a chair from underneath him, poisons his food, infects him with a disease or dyes his hair without permission. However, in practice, the courts are reluctant to classify intentionally inflicted harm as *indirect:* for example, damage was held to be direct in *Scott v. Shepherd* (1773) 2 W BL 892 - tossing a firework into a market place, which was automatically thrown onwards by a number of people, eventually injuring the plaintiff; *Wilkinson v. Downton* [1897] 2 QB 57 - causing nervous shock by playing a trick on the plaintiff that her husband had been involved in a serious accident (at the time, liability for nervous shock had not yet been developed in negligence); *Janvier v. Sweeney* [1919] 2 KB 316 - threat to make embarrassing public disclosures unless documents were produced, causing nervous shock; *DPP v. K* [1990] 1 WLR 1067 - leaving acid in a hot air dryer, which shot out when pressed on. Some commentators have argued that battery should break loose from its origins in trespass prohibiting recovery for indirect loss and that, on the basis of *Wilkinson v. Downton,* any intentional physical harm, whether direct or indirect, should be entitled to be compensated for. This would amount to a broader new tort and consequently must await future developments before its existence may be confirmed.

There is an old principle that "the least touching of another in anger is a battery" (*Cole v. Turner* (1704) 6 Mod 149, Holt, CJ). However, there are three qualifications to be made in relation to this principle. The first is that "social touching" - say, congratulating with a shake of the hand or slap on the back, or pushing in a queue or busy shop - is not to be regarded as battery in spite of the reference to the *least* touching (*Wilson v. Pringle* [1986] 2 All ER 440 -playing around by pulling a schoolboy's bag hanging from his shoulder so that he fell and was injured); otherwise, the common conduct of social relations might become intolerable. The second qualification though, conversely, is that, depending upon the circumstances, the touching need not be *hostile* for it to amount to battery. Gross rudeness and roughness may not be uncommon socially, yet it is nonetheless unacceptable to the victim and will be held to constitute a battery, for example, an unwanted kiss, holding someone back so that they can hear what you have to say, or excessive fun-making by pushing someone into a swimming pool, or carrying out a medical operation without permission (*Collins v. Wilcock* [1984] 3 All ER 374; *F v. West Berkshire Health Authority* [1989] 2 All ER 545). Thirdly, some have argued that a person should be able to be held liable for battery, or at least as a new tort being an extension of battery, where harm is intentionally inflicted, notwithstanding the complete absence of touching, as where mental anguish less than nervous shock is intentionally caused by harassment and breach of privacy, say, through annoying telephone calls (*Khorasandjian v. Bush* [1993] 3 WLR 476; see Townshend-Smith, Harassment as a Tort in English and American Law: the Boundaries of *Wilkinson v.*

Downton (1995) 24 Anglo-American Law Review 299).

Intention

Connected with the preceding point is the fact that whereas *intention to apply force* is necessary for battery to be committed - thereby, incidentally, distinguishing the tort from that of negligence - intention *to injure* is not also required.

Relationship with the Criminal Law

(a) Criminal injuries compensation

Usually assaults and batteries are crimes as well as torts. People injured by certain crimes of violence may receive *ex-gratia* compensation payments from an administrative body funded by the state - the Criminal Injuries Compensation Board - placed on a statutory basis by the Criminal Justice Act 1988, ss.108-117 when brought into force. This can be of great value where criminals would not possess the resources necessary to satisfy damages awards. The Board (not the courts or the police) assesses compensation on similar principles to those relating to damages in tort, yet on a less generous basis (a *fortiori* where exemplary damages are available against the police); and if tort damages are subsequently recovered, the award must be repaid. There are a number of other restrictions upon claims, relating, for example, to the claimant's own behaviour and to the type of criminal offence involved, and traffic offences are not included, being subject to compulsory insurance and to their own compensation scheme for the uninsured. In addition, a civil claim will have to be relied upon where there are no personal injuries to the victim. Awards are not dependent upon a person being charged with or convicted of an offence against the claimant. Such commission and injuries are for the Board to determine.

(b) Compensation by a convicted criminal to the victim of personal injury, or for loss or damage from a crime

Courts have the power to make such orders under the Powers of Criminal Courts Act 1973, ss.35-8. There are a number of limitations, including those in relation to dependants and road traffic offences, where insurance or remedies in tort must be used. Amounts of awards will depend upon the convicted person's financial means and there may be ceilings on sums awarded.

If a criminal prosecution for assault and battery is brought in the lower courts (magistrates' courts), a civil action in tort cannot then be brought. Thus, victims should either bring their civil case first, or wait for the criminal prosecution to proceed and after that apply to the Criminal Injuries Compensation Board for criminal compensation.

(ii) False Imprisonment

The plaintiff need not show that he has actually been put into prison. All that is necessary is that:

- intentionally; and
- without lawful justification,

his freedom of movement from a particular place has been

completely prevented (*Collins v. Wilcock* [1984] 3 All ER 374). Examples are locking someone in a room, or putting a guard outside the door in order to prevent their exit; holding the plaintiff down or by the arm; standing in front or either side of the plaintiff so that he cannot walk out of the way; threatening him with violence if he moves; restraining a person in a shop without reasonable grounds for suspicion until the police can question him about theft of products; and the police as well as anyone else are capable of committing this tort, for example, where they continue to detain the plaintiff for questioning when there are no longer reasonable grounds for suspecting that he committed a crime, or even putting sufficient pressure on a person as to compel him to go to a police station against his will without lawful justification. Quite large sums are paid out by the police in total, as damages (including exemplary) and out-of-court settlements, to victims of police assault and battery, false imprisonment or defamation (*Taylor v. Metropolitan Police Commissioner* (1989) *The Times*, December 6). People have the right to move where they wish in the street or to leave premises when they choose. Restraint, for however short a period, is false imprisonment. Nor would it seem that the plaintiff need be aware of his imprisonment for the tort to be committed - he may be unconscious or mentally disordered (*Murray v. Ministry of Defence* [1988] 2 All ER 521, HL) (although, in these circumstances, damages may be reduced to purely nominal).

There are limits. In the first place, the restraint upon the plaintiff's freedom to move away must be total. It is not false imprisonment to obstruct a person from passing in one direction, if he can, nevertheless, escape in another which is reasonably available for use and not excessively dangerous. Thus, in *Bird v. Jones* (1845) 7 QB 742 there was no false imprisonment when the plaintiff was prevented from crossing a bridge: he was free to go back in the direction from which he had come.

Secondly, where an occupier of property admits a person, subject to conditions for leaving, restraint from departure until the conditions are fulfilled *may* not amount to false imprisonment. In *Robinson v. Balmain Ferry Co. Ltd* [1910] AC 295, the plaintiff was required to pay one penny to board a ferry between Sydney and Balmain and a penny to get off at the other end. Once he had boarded, he changed his mind before the ferry set sail and wanted to get off without paying another penny, but he was prevented by the defendant ferry company. The Judicial Committee of the Privy Council held that this was not false imprisonment, because the plaintiff had agreed to pay a penny in order to leave the ferry. Similarly, in *Herd v. Weardale Steel Coal and Coke Co. Ltd* [1915] AC 67 it was not false imprisonment where employers refused to transport a miner to the surface before the end of his shift after he had complained that conditions underground were dangerous. The difficulty with these decisions, however, is that *remedies for breach of contract* lie in damages, not physical compulsion of performance by the contracting party seeking enforcement. It may be that a distinction should be drawn according to whether the plaintiff was prevented from leaving when he could otherwise have done so unaided - false imprisonment - or where he would require the defendant to take action which he was not otherwise bound to do, such as to stop a train or aeroplane at an unscheduled stop - not false imprisonment: although, even in the former case, it might be argued that a certain level of restraint is nonetheless justified if this can be construed either as an objection against breach of contract, or as part of the process of lawful ejection of the plaintiff who has become a trespasser through breach of his conditions of entry.

Thirdly, where a person is already lawfully imprisoned so that he has previously lost his liberty, the prison authorities will not be liable for false imprisonment if, within the prison, he is then locked in a cell or placed in solitary confinement (*Weldon v. Home Office* [1992] 1 AC 58 - nor even if a prisoner on remand remains in prison after expiry of the time limit notwithstanding that the Crown Prosecution Service failed to apply for an extension, because a remand prisoner in such circumstances is entitled to bail but not to unconditional release, as so held by deputy High Court Judge Barbara Dohmann, QC in *Olotu v. Secretary of State for the Home Department* (1996) *The Times,* May 8); if prison regulations are broken, his remedy lies in administrative law or in the tort of negligence (*Hague v. Deputy Governor of Parkhurst Prison* [1991] 3 All ER 733 HL - similarly in the case of serving members of the armed forces: *Pritchard v. Ministry of Defence* (1995) *The Times,* January 27). It is a different matter, however, where the prisoner is the victim of prison officers acting outside the scope of their authority, or of fellow prisoners - here, actions for false imprisonment and other torts are possible.

Fourthly, false imprisonment must be *without lawful justification*. This is not the case, therefore, if there is "lawful arrest" (nor is there a battery). "Arrest" is where a policeman or other person detains a person by use of force or by words indicating that force will be used if necessary in connexion with the commission of crime. The police also have powers to stop and search people in the street if they suspect a crime and can enter property to seize and search (Police and Criminal Evidence Act 1984 - "PACE"). They also have power to take body samples and fingerprints at police stations, subject to prescribed procedures involving written consent of the suspect and the permission of senior officers. If the procedures are followed, there is no false imprisonment and there is also a defence to battery.

Arrests may be carried out by the police with a magistrates' warrant, or by the police or ordinary citizens without a warrant. Citizens have this power at common law where they honestly and reasonably believe that it is necessary to prevent a breach of the peace (meaning an assault on someone or general public alarm and excitement involving danger: *Albert v. Lavin* [1982] AC 546), whether the person arrested started the breach or not. Additionally, under s.24 of PACE, there is power to arrest without warrant a person who is reasonably suspected to be committing or to have committed certain crimes - but the power of ordinary citizens to do so is considerably reduced by the requirement thereunder that if the arrested person is acquitted, someone else must actually be found to have been guilty for the arrest to remain lawful (*R. v. Self* [1992] 3 All ER 476). There are Codes of Practice assisting with the meaning of *reasonable grounds for suspicion*, including that these must not be founded upon personal factors alone, such as age, height, dress, colour or stereotype, and reasonableness must be based on objective factors and not upon the arresting citizen's or policeman's own mental state. Merely to provide the police with incorrect information leading to the arrest of a person by the police at their own discretion will not normally amount to false imprisonment on the part of the provider, even if the latter is a professional, for example, a store detective (see *Davidson v. Chief Constable of North Wales Police* [1994] 2 All ER 597, CA) - although it is noteworthy that in the related area of malicious prosecution, the House of Lords has held that the defendant, though technically not the prosecutor, can nonetheless be liable if in substance responsible for the prosecution having been brought (see *Martin v. Watson* (1995) *The Times*, July 14, HL - *infra*, ch.28).

The police themselves, of course, are given much wider powers to arrest without warrant on reasonable suspicion that a crime has been, is being or is about to be committed, under ss.24 and 25. Section 28 PACE further requires the arrested person to be informed of the grounds for his arrest, even if these are obvious, at the time of arrest or as soon as reasonably practicable thereafter, otherwise the arrest is unlawful as from the time at which the information should have been given (so damages run from that point up to when he is eventually informed); and a person helping police with their inquiries, but who is not arrested, has to be informed of his right to leave the police station at any time, under s.29. Section 117 confers the power upon the police to use reasonable force to exercise their powers under PACE, this being a question of fact in the individual case (*Farrell v. Secretary of State for Defence* [1980] 1 All ER 166). In addition, there are time limits for reviews of arrest and for release in the absence of sufficient evidence to charge the arrested suspect, and for bringing him before a court.

Breach of these rules will constitute false imprisonment or battery, and even ultimate conviction of the person who was originally falsely imprisoned will not release the defendants from liability for such false imprisonment (*Hill v. Chief Constable of South Yorkshire Police* [1990] 1 All ER 1046).

(iii) Defences against Trespass to the Person

1. Consent

Some commentators consider that it is for the plaintiff to prove absence of his consent to the trespass for liability in trespass to be established in the first place, rather than for the defendant to raise the matter as a defence to liability (*Freeman v. Home Office [No.2]* [1984] QB 524).

Frequently, however, consent is dealt with as a defence.

Consent to assault and battery may be expressed or implied.

In sports, there may be implied consent to inevitable and reasonable physical contact and to minor breaches of the rules ("fouls") which are commonplace, but this is not also the case where there is a serious assault and battery quite outside the rules, like a punch in the face by a footballer in the opposing (or plaintiff's own!) team, or a deliberate bone-breaking tackle (*McNamara v. Duncan* [1979] 26 ALR 584).

Where there is a general "punch-up" between two or more people and it cannot be said who started it, consent will be a defence and *ex turpi causa* - meaning plaintiffs who are guilty of wrongdoing are unable to bring their claims - will also be available; if the plaintiff is shown to have begun the fight, the defendant will have the defence of consent (as well as that of self-defence), provided that the force of his response did not unreasonably exceed that of the plaintiff's attack (*Barnes v. Nayer* (1986) *The Times,* December 19); but if it is the person attacked who is the plaintiff, the plaintiff's efforts to defend himself should not give rise to the defence of consent.

Medical cases raise many issues concerning consent. Treatment without the patient's consent will amount to a battery and an adult patient has the right to refuse treatment notwithstanding that this leads to his death (*Airedale NHS Trust v. Bland* [1993] 1 All ER 821).

Normally, when a patient visits his doctor's or dentist's surgery, his consent to treatment there will be implied (*O'Brien v. Cunard* (1891) 28 NE 266 - standing in line and holding out arm, as consent to vaccination); and usually a person about to have surgery at a hospital is asked to sign a standard form of consent. Consent is not a defence, however, if a different treatment from that agreed to is applied (*Schweizer v. Central Hospital* (1975) 53 DLR [3d] 494).

The overriding requirement is that consent should be genuinely and freely given. This may involve explaining risks to the patient, but in trespass it is sufficient for the defence that the doctor has given a broad description of risks and effects of the operation (*Chatterton v. Gerson* [1981] 1 All ER 257), and as to whether and how far specific risks and details should have been explained, this is a matter of reasonable standard of care for the avoidance of liability in the tort of negligence and not trespass, even if the patient requires such specific details (*Sidaway v. Governors of Bethlem*

Royal Hospital [1985] 1 All ER 643), and to which the *Bolam* test of responsible body of medical practice will apply (see *supra*, ch.6).

Where the patient is unconscious, in an emergency it is thought that doctors have the defence of implied consent to operate; and in *F v. West Berkshire Health Authority* [1989] 2 All ER 545, the House of Lords held that the defence of "necessity in the best interests of the patient" also applied, subject itself to the *Bolam* test. The latter is also the position with patients suffering a mental disorder (court's permission should still be sought if desirable or there is doubt) - although, treatment should not go further than is necessary to deal with the condition during the absence of consciousness and rational thought (*Murray v. McMurchy* (1949) 2 DLR 442). Treatment for patients in a persistent vegetative state is said not to be in their best interests and need not be continued, notwithstanding the fatal consequences (*Airedale NHS Trust v. Bland* [1993] 1 All ER 821, HL).

So far as treatment of children is concerned, s.8 of the Family Law Reform Act 1969 has the effect that children between 16 and 18 years are treated like adults for medical consent; under 16, a child with sufficient understanding and intelligence can give an effective consent to medical treatment (*Gillick v. West Norfolk and Wisbech Area Health Authority* [1985] 3 All ER, HL 402); beneath that, parental or court consent is required for the defence - and in each of the latter cases, doctors also have the defence if the parents or court consent, notwithstanding the child's own refusal.

The usual obstacles to freedom of consent apply to the

defence to battery. Thus, threats of violence destroy consent to sex, as may undue influence, fraud and misrepresentation where the victim is ignorant as to the nature and purpose of the battery - though not merely as to its effects or surrounding circumstances. So, women tricked into having sex on being told that this was a medical operation (*R. v. Flattery* (1877) QBD 410), or voice therapy (*R. v. Williams* [1923] 1 KB 340), were held not to have genuinely consented, but to have done so where agreeing to sex without knowing of the other person's venereal disease (*R. v. Clarence* (1888) 22 QBD 23) - a distinction taken from the criminal law and subject to some academic and other criticism in favour of there being found to be a lack of consent in the latter case as well (*Re T [Adult: refusal of medical treatment]* [1992] 4 All ER 649). In *Re T,* consent to *refusal* of medical treatment was negatived where a car accident victim's mother, a Jehovah's Witness, persuaded her daughter, who was in a poor state, to refuse a blood transfusion, so that doctors administering the blood had not committed a battery.

2. *Self defence*

This defence against battery exists where the defendant:

- used reasonable and proportionate force,
- in order to defend himself against an actual or threatened attack against his person or property, or to eject a trespasser from property in his possession.

He need not, therefore, wait until he himself is struck if the threat is immediate (*Chaplain of Gray's Inn Case* (1400) YB

2 Hen 4, fol. 8, pl. 40).

The common law has been extended by s.3(1) of the Criminal Law Act 1967 so as to cover use of reasonable force to prevent a crime, including that against a third party, and common law itself probably allows the defence in order to prevent an attack upon another, even if there were a defence to the latter crime.

Reasonableness and proportionality of force are questions of fact dependent upon the circumstances of the threat. In *Cook v. Beal* (1697) 1 Ld Raym, it was not self defence for the defendant to draw a sword and cut off the hand of the plaintiff who had struck him; similarly, in *Collins v. Renison* (1754) Say. 138, tipping up a ladder on which a trespasser was standing in order to eject him from the defendant's property was held to have amounted to excessive force. Similarly, in *Revill v. Newbery* [1996] 1 All ER 291, 301-2, CA (see *supra*, p.344) the defendant, who injured a trespasser who was attempting to break into his garden shed in the middle of the night while the defendant was asleep inside the shed, was held to have used excessive force. The defendant, a 76-year-old man, had poked his shotgun through a hole in the door and fired it.

3. Necessity

Lord Goff listed three categories of necessity as a possible defence in *F v. West Berkshire Health Authority*:

- protection of damage to the public;
- prevention of damage to one's own property or person;
- helping another person without his consent.

Whether these are a defence in a particular case will depend upon its facts. Sacrifice of one life in order to save many members of the public can clearly be expected to qualify, but there is much uncertainty over whether it would be justified to sacrifice another person simply to protect oneself - pushing someone else in front of an escaped tiger, for example. As for assistance to the plaintiff himself, it has already been seen that necessity, alongside implied consent in some cases, can be a defence to unauthorized medical treatment of an unconscious or mentally defective person if this was reasonably considered to be in the best interests of the patient (*F v. West Berkshire Health Authority* - sterilization of a mentally deficient woman held to be of necessity) - always in accordance with the *Bolam* test of reasonableness, of course, in medical cases. However, it was also shown that doctors have no right of necessity to operate in order to save a conscious adult who refuses treatment (*Re S* [1992] 4 All ER 671; *Sidaway v. Governors of Bethlem Royal Hospital* [1985] 1 All ER 643, *supra*), and, consequently, the decision in *Leigh v. Gladstone* (1909) 26 TLR 139, in which the forced feeding of a suffragette prisoner on hunger-strike was held to be justified by necessity, seems unlikely to stand at the present day.

4. *Lawful arrest*

This was examined in connexion with false imprisonment. If the arrest is lawful and procedures involving bodily contact connected with it are properly followed, there is a defence to battery.

5. Other defences

Parents have a statutory right to restrain and punish children where this is reasonable and for the child's welfare, and mental health legislation enables certain mentally disordered people to be detained in hospital. In some cases too, contributory negligence, statutory authority, or illegality can also be used as a defence against trespass to the person (*Barnes v. Nayer* (1986) *The Times,* December 19, CA; *Revill v. Newbery, supra*).

(iv) Remedies

A person falsely imprisoned or unlawfully arrested can use *self help* to obtain his release through reasonable force, either to resist or to escape.

It is also possible to apply to a court for a prerogative order of *habeas corpus* in an emergency in order to obtain release.

The main remedy, however, is damages, and these can include exemplary damages where the defendant authorities have behaved in an arbitrary manner, even though, unlike negligence, trespass is actionable *per se,* that is, without proof of actual damage. Thus, for example, in *Taylor v. Metropolitan Police Commissioner* (1989) *The Times,* December 6, an award of £70,000 was made against the police as damages for false imprisonment and malicious prosecution.

In addition, the victim of unlawful arrest and false imprisonment may also be able to bring proceedings for defamation of character.

Further reading:

Brazier, *Street on Torts*, 9th ed, 1993 (Butterworth & Co., London): ch.3.
Fleming, J.G., *The Law of Torts*, 8th ed, 1992 (The Law Book Company, Sydney): chs.2 and 5.
Hepple, B.A. and Matthews, M.H., *Tort: Cases and Materials*, 4th ed, 1991 (Butterworth & Co., London): ch.13.
Heuston, R.F.V. and Buckley, R.A., *Salmond and Heuston on The Law of Torts*, 20th ed, 1992 (Sweet & Maxwell, London): ch.7.
Howarth, D., *Textbook on Tort*, 1995 (Butterworth & Co., London): ch.9.
Jones, M.A., *Textbook on Torts*, 4th ed, 1993 (Blackstone, London): ch.12.
Makesinis, B.S. and Deakin, S.F., *Tort Law*, 3rd ed, 1994 (Clarendon Press, Oxford): ch.4.
Rogers, W.V.H., *Winfield and Jolowicz on Tort*, 14th ed, 1994 (Sweet & Maxwell, London): ch.4.
Stanton, K.M., *The Modern Law of Tort*, 1994 (The Law Book Company, Sydney): chs.9 and 23.
Weir, T., *A Casebook on Tort*, 7th ed, 1992 (Sweet & Maxwell, London): chs.8 and 9.

PART IX

Chapter 18

Torts Over Goods

Introduction

The general tort of negligence applies as much to damage to goods ("chattels") as to any other form of property or to the physical or mental state of a person.

However, there are certain - in some cases rather old - torts which developed specifically to safeguard the integrity of goods and dominion over them.

(i) Trespass

Immediate and direct unauthorized interference with another person's goods.

This will include using, removing, touching or destroying: for example, scratching a car door with a key (*Fouldes v. Willougby* (1841) 8 M & W 540), or ripping the car's tyres with a knife - not, however, leaving a piece of jagged glass on the road for the car tyres to drive over, which would be *indirect* interference.

The unauthorized interference must be deliberate and intentional - although it is not a defence that the trespasser believed by mistake that the goods were his. Traditionally, it is assumed that the trespass is actionable *per se* and that actual damage need not be shown to exist.

It is the person in possession of the goods at the time of the trespass or who has an immediate right to possession, who is entitled to sue, even if his own possession is illegal. The owner out of possession with no immediate right to possess cannot sue.

(ii) Conversion

Dealing with goods in a manner inconsistent with the rights of the true owner, provided that the defendant thereby intends to deny the owner's rights or to assert a right inconsistent with the owner's (*Lancashire and Yorkshire Ry v. MacNicoll* (1919) 88 LJKB 601, Atkin, J).

Examples are purchasing goods from a thief, selling another's goods, destroying them, or intentionally exposing them to such dangers by, for example, lending them to an irresponsible person (*Willis v. British Car Auctions* [1978] 1 WLR 438) - but not merely verbally denying ownership without accompanying acts (Torts (Interference with Goods) Act 1977, s.11(3)).

Conversion is committed even if the defendant honestly believed that he was the owner of the goods; and contributory negligence is not a defence (s.11(1), 1977 Act).

As in trespass, an owner who wishes to sue for conversion must show either actual possession or an immediate (probably proprietary, including equitable, as opposed to mere contractual) right to it. Thus, in *Gordon v. Harper* (1796) 7 Term Rep 9, a landlord could not sue in conversion a person who wrongfully took furniture from the let property while the property was in the tenant's possession during the lease. On the other hand, under s.8(1) of the 1977 Act, a defendant in wrongful interference proceedings, whether for trespass or conversion, is entitled to claim that a third party has a superior right to the goods to that of the plaintiff and to have the third party joined in the proceedings.

In the case of finders of lost goods, subject to exceptions, the finder has a right to the goods superior to that of all except the real owner, and can sue for wrongful interference any third parties who take the goods from him (*Armory v. Delamirie* (1721) 1 Stra 505) - chimney sweep's boy who found a jewel could recover from the jeweller to whom he gave it for valuation). The first exception to this is in the case of employees who find goods in the course of their employment - the employer, not the employee, is treated as the finder (*Parker v. British Airways Board* [1982] 1 QB 1004). Secondly, if the finder discovers the goods on land occupied by a third party, the latter is treated as having earlier possession, even if unaware of the goods, if the goods are buried there or positioned so as to indicate exclusive possession of the occupier (*South Staffordshire Water Co. v. Sharman* [1896] 2 QB 44 - workmen finding gold rings when cleaning out a company's pool). However, if the public have access to the land and the circumstances are such that the occupier cannot be said to have exercised exclusive control over goods left there by third parties, the finder (provided that he is not a trespasser) may gain a superior right to that of the occupier (*Parker v. British Airways Board* - gold bracelet found on floor of lounge at Heathrow Airport could be kept, against British Airways).

(iii) Detinue

Section 2(1) of the 1977 Act abolished the tort. It consisted in the wrongful refusal to deliver goods to the person entitled or in having custody of a person's goods and then losing them.

(iv) Reversioner's Action

A reversioner is a person with a future right to possession of goods, for example, the owner who has hired out his goods to another person or who has lent them to someone for a definite period. During such time when the reversioner is not in actual possession and has no immediate right to repossession, he is unable to bring actions for trespass or conversion against third parties. He can, nevertheless, bring a special "reversioner's action" if he can prove that the third party's acts have had a lasting effect upon his reversionary interest, because, for example, the goods are permanently damaged or will never be found (*Mears v. LSW Ry* (1862) 11 CB (NS) 850).

(v) The Torts (Interference with Goods) Act 1977

As seen, s.2(1) abolished detinue. However, s.2(2) states that the old detinue situation in which a person who has custody of another's goods - a "bailee" - loses or destroys them should now fall within the action for *conversion;* and some people argue that even the other detinue category mentioned above, that of wrongful detention of goods, also amounts to conversion in any event, although opponents object that such detention is merely evidence of conversion.

The Act refers to trespass, conversion and all torts involving damage to goods as "wrongful interference with goods" (s.1) and then lays down various general rules concerning such interference, including remedies and extinction of the plaintiff's title to goods on the payment of damages, together with the exclusion of the contributory negligence defence to conversion and intentional trespass and awards of compensation to people who improve goods and on disposal of uncollected goods.

(a) Section 7 prevents double liability of a defendant by requiring apportionment of any damages when he is sued by two claimants with possessory rights, and requires a single claimant to account to another person who would be entitled to claim, according to their respective interests.

(b) In *Munro v. Willmott* [1949] 1 KB 295 the plaintiff *temporarily* left her car in the defendant's yard and then went away. Years later, the defendant spent £85 renovating the car, worth £20 before that, and sold it for £100. The plaintiff reappeared and the defendant was held liable for conversion. The car was worth £120, but the plaintiff was given £35 damages because the defendant had spent £85.

It seems that this common law rule in favour of improvers continues to apply even after the 1977 Act, but s.6(1) replaces it where improvements were made to another's goods in the mistaken but honest belief that they belonged to the improver - damages are reduced to the extent that the value of the goods at the time of valuation for damages is attributable to the improvement.

(c) Remedies are set out under s.3(2) - orders for delivery and payment of any damages, or for optional payment of the value of the goods and any damages, or damages alone. The claimant's title to the goods is extinguished under s.5 where payment of the value or of damages satisfies the plaintiff's claim.

(vi) Defences to Torts Against Goods

1. Consent

In *Smith v. Baker and Sons* [1891] AC 325, at p.360, Lord Herschell said: "One who has invited or assented to an act being done towards him cannot, when he suffers from it, complain of it as a wrong."

Thus, in *Arthur v. Anker* (1995) *The Times,* December 1, CA, the plaintiff was a motorist who trespassed on private land, where the defendant then fixed a wheel clamp to the plaintiff's motor car which he had parked there. The plaintiff sued the defendant for damages for tortious interference with the vehicle, but was unsuccessful. The Court of Appeal held that the plaintiff had consented to the risk that his car would be clamped and detained until he had paid the release fee of £40: the plaintiff had seen the warning notice on the land to the effect that vehicles parked there without authority would be wheelclamped and only released on payment of a fee. Consent was a defence.

However, Sir Thomas Bingham, MR did go on to lay down certain conditions for a plaintiff to be treated as having given consent: a) the release fee should be reasonable; b) the plaintiff would be most unlikely to be taken to have consented to any damage being done to the car, whatever the warning; c) there should be no delay by the defendant in the release of the car after the plaintiff has offered to pay; and d) there has to be effective means for the plaintiff to communicate his offer of payment of the fee to the defendant.

2. Distress damage feasant

This is not only a defence against the torts of interference with goods, but also a *remedy* available to an occupier of land against someone who trespasses upon the occupier's land (see *infra,* p.520).

In short, the occupier is permitted to seize and detain - not to sell or use - property brought onto the land by the trespasser until the trespasser pays for any damage caused and then leaves: distress (*seizure for*) damage feasant (*caused*).

However, in *Arthur v. Anker, supra,* the Master of the Rolls did not believe that wheelclamping of motor cars in private car parks in urban city centres was likely to have been in the contemplation of those who developed this ancient remedy (nor was he inclined to undertake "heroic surgery" to adapt it to twentieth century conditions!) and he doubted whether the remedy should apply to such facts for the following reasons:

(a) the purpose of the self-help remedy was to bring to an end the trespass as quickly as possible and to obtain security for any damage caused;

(b) whereas, the object of wheelclamping was not to prevent or to compensate for damage, nor even to eject the trespassing object, but to deter future trespassers. Damage compensation, not deterrence, was at the root of the original remedy;

(c) it followed too that actual damage or obstruction from the trespass should be shown, for example, that the plaintiff's motor car had obstructed the entrance or exit of the car park; and

(d) the flat charge of £40 for release of the car in all circumstances demonstrated that the payment was not compensatory at all.

Thus, neither the defendant wheelclamping firm, nor the occupiers of the property for whom they acted as agents, had suffered any actual damage. There was no defence of distress damage feasant on these facts.

Further reading:

Brazier, *Street on Torts*, 9th ed, 1993 (Butterworth & Co., London): ch.4.

Fleming, J.G., *The Law of Torts*, 8th ed, 1992 (The Law Book Company, Sydney): chs.4 and 5.

Heuston, R.F.V. and Buckley, R.A., *Salmond and Heuston on The Law of Torts*, 20th ed, 1992 (Sweet & Maxwell, London): ch.6.

Howarth, D., *Textbook on Tort*, 1995 (Butterworth & Co., London): ch.10.

Rogers, W.V.H., *Winfield and Jolowicz on Tort*, 14th ed, 1994 (Sweet & Maxwell, London): ch.17.

Stanton, K.M., *The Modern Law of Tort*, 1994 (The Law Book Company, Sydney): ch.23.

Weir, T., *A Casebook on Tort*, 7th ed, 1992 (Sweet & Maxwell, London): ch.13.

PART X

Chapter 19

Economic Torts

Introduction

So-called "economic torts" concern intentional harm to a person's or firm's business interests, frequently in the context of industrial disputes or unfair competition.

At the turn of the last century, the House of Lords laid down the fundamental principles of this area of law, in an age of free trade and economic liberalism, as follows:

1. Intentional economic harm from unfair or aggressive trading is not actionable in tort. For a remedy to be available, the activity must be *unlawful.*

   In *Mogul Steamship Co. Ltd v. McGregor, Gow and Co.* [1892] AC 25, the defendants cut the price of tea in order to drive the plaintiff shipowners out of business and thereby to obtain a monopoly in the tea trade, which is precisely what happened. The plaintiffs were held to have no cause of action; the defendants had done nothing unlawful. Businesses may try to gain advantage by undercutting each other.

2. A threat to strike unless other workers were dismissed was not unlawful.

   In *Allen v. Flood* [1898] AC 1, the defendant official of

the ironworkers' union informed employers that if they did not dismiss the plaintiff woodworkers from doing certain work, he would bring his members out on strike, which the employers therefore complied with. The woodworkers were held to possess no cause of action: calling a strike was not unlawful and the employers had lawfully terminated the woodworkers' contracts, so that the defendant had not unlawfully interfered with these either. Whether the defendant had a spiteful or malicious motive or not was irrelevant.

3. Where persons conspire together to inflict unjustified financial harm with an improper motive, there is a cause of action in tort.

This was the case of *Quinn v. Leatham* [1901] AC 495. The defendant trade union officials were unable to persuade the plaintiff meat supplier not to employ non-unionmen, so they told their members employed by the butcher who was the plaintiff's main customer not to handle the plaintiff's meat. It appeared that the defendants would not be liable, in accordance with *Mogul* and *Allen,* because they had not acted unlawfully - the members were not asked to break their contracts. The House of Lords held them nonetheless to be liable because they had *conspired together* to harm the plaintiff maliciously and without justification. Illogically, according to some, what was quite lawful for one, was nevertheless tortious for more.

Outside these general principles forming the overall background to the law, a number of individual economic torts can be isolated, each requiring intention to harm for liability to exist, as follows.

(i) Tort of Conspiracy

In *Mulcahy v. R* (1868) LR 3 HL 306, Willes, J defined the tort of conspiracy as "the agreement of two or more to do an unlawful act, or to do a lawful act by unlawful means."

The following elements are therefore required.

1. Two or more persons

A company is a separate legal person and consequently can conspire with its directors (*Belmont Finance Corp v. Williams Furniture Ltd (No. 2)* [1980] 1 All ER 393), as can husband and wife (*Midland Bank Trust Co. Ltd v. Green (No. 3)* [1982] Ch. 529).

2. *Agreement*

This need not be a legally binding contract - more a "combination" for a common purpose (*Belmont*).

3. *Causing damage to the plaintiff*

This is required. Conspiracy is not actionable *per se*.

4. *Alternatively, unlawful act or lawful act by unlawful means*

(a) *Unlawful act*

Unlawful acts will include crimes, tort and, as most believe, breach of contract (left open in *Rookes v. Barnard* [1964] AC 1129).

The essential prerequisite to this type of conspiracy action is that the defendants must have had an intent to injure the plaintiff.

In *Lonrho Ltd v. Shell Petroleum Co. Ltd (No. 2)* [1982] AC 173, the plaintiffs built a pipeline from a port in Mozambique to the defendants' oil refinery in what was then Southern Rhodesia. Subsequently, in 1965, the UK government made it illegal to supply oil to Southern Rhodesia. The pipeline ceased to be used, but the plaintiffs sued the defendants for allegedly conspiring with others to continue to supply oil to the illegal Rhodesian regime in breach of sanctions, causing additional loss to the plaintiffs through prolongation of the illegal government and the consequent continued compulsory closure of the plaintiffs' pipeline. It was held that the defendants were not liable for conspiracy, because their predominant purpose was not to injure the plaintiffs but to serve their own interests. This was followed in *Metall und Rohstoff AG v. Donaldson Lufkin and Jenrette Inc.* [1990] 1 QB 391 - but subsequently overruled by the House of Lords in *Lonrho Plc v. Fayed* [1992] 1 AC 448, to the effect that it need only be shown that the defendants intended to injure the plaintiff, whether or not this was the predominant purpose in the case of unlawful act conspiracy. (In *Lonrho Plc v. Fayed (No.5)* [1993] 1 WLR 1489, it was held that whereas financial loss could be claimed from conspiracy, harm to reputation and feelings was solely for the tort of defamation.)

(b) *Lawful act by unlawful means*

As previously seen, this was established in *Quinn v. Leatham*.

Here, however, for liability to exist, there is the

prerequisite that the defendants' *predominant* motive must have been to injure the plaintiff's interests rather than to serve their own. In *Crofter Hand Woven Harris Tweed Co. Ltd v. Veitch* [1942] AC 435, trade union officials in the hand-spun yarn industry ordered docker members on the Isle of Lewis not to handle cheaper imported machine-spun yarn because this was driving down wages paid to hand-spun yarn workers on the island. The dockers obeyed the instruction without breaching their contracts of employment. The plaintiffs suffered a loss through the action taken against the machine-spun yarn, but were held unable to claim against the defendants for conspiracy because their predominant purpose was to protect their members' interests, not to harm the plaintiffs.

It would seem that defendants will not be held to have acted out of self-interest, if they were motivated by spite and ill-will. Thus, in *Huntley v. Thornton* [1957] 1 WLR 321, the defendant trade union officials were held liable for damages for conspiracy when they prevented the plaintiff from obtaining employment anywhere in their area, because they were not protecting their interests but behaving maliciously.

(ii) Tort of Intimidation

In 1964, in the case of *Rookes v. Barnard* [1964] AC 1129, the House of Lords laid down the four elements required for the tort of intimidation to be committed. In *Rookes v. Barnard* itself, the defendant union officials had an informal agreement with an airline that all its employees would be members of the union. When the plaintiff employee resigned from the union, the defendants threatened to call a strike unless the airline dismissed the plaintiff from his job, which the airline did, lawfully. The defendants were held to have committed the tort of intimidation against the plaintiff. The four elements required for intimidation are:

1. a threat to the third party, not a mere warning - obviously a matter of construction of the strength of words used;
2. the threat must be to do something unlawful - a crime, tort or breach of contract;
3. the third party must have complied with the threat and have done what was asked;
4. the plaintiff must prove that he suffered damage.

There seems to be some doubt over whether there is a defence of justification to the tort of intimidation, based on legitimate industrial reasons. If there were, it would surely smash the tort wide open, and in effect confine it to the narrow area of personal grudge and enmity.

It may be, too, that intimidation could apply in a two-party situation, where, say, the defendant threatens the plaintiff in order to force the plaintiff to allow the former to breach their contract (*Godwin v. Uzoigwe* (1992) *The Times*, June 18), although remedies in contract itself may seem the more obvious route to recovery.

(iii) Tort of Inducing Breach of Contract

1. Types of inducement

There are three ways in which the tort can be committed (*D.C. Thomson and Co. Ltd v. Deakin* [1952] Ch. 646). They are:

(a) *The defendant persuades a third party to break a contract with the plaintiff.* In *Lumley v. Gye* (1853) 2 El and Bl 216, the defendant theatre owner was held to have committed the tort when he offered more money to persuade a famous opera singer to break her contract to sing only for the plaintiff rival theatre owner. The plaintiff (though not the singer herself) was entitled to damages. It is for the court to construe whether, on the facts, the defendant's words had the effect of inducement.

(b) *By unlawful means, the defendant prevents performance.* A common example is if the defendant were to hide a contracting party's tools.

(c) *Defendant's inducement of a fourth party to break his contract with a third party, who, as a consequence, is unable to perform his contract with the plaintiff.* This is, therefore, a combination of the preceding two cases: the persuasion is there, but not directed at the party whose contract is with the plaintiff; and prevention of contractual performance by that party also consequently takes place. The defendant must know of the contract between plaintiff and third party, have intended to procure its breach by inducing a fourth party to break his contract with the third party, and breach of the former must have been a necessary consequence of breach of the latter. In *Thomson v. Deakin* itself, the defendant union officials, in an effort to force the plaintiff newspaper publishers to employ union workers, which they had refused to do, instructed their members (fourth parties) not to deal with supplies of paper to the plaintiff. The members' employer (third party) then broke its contract to supply paper to the plaintiff for fear that this would cause an industrial dispute with its workers. On the facts, the plaintiffs failed to establish the tort, because there was no evidence that the members had actually broken their contract with the employer, which was essential for liability. An injunction to restrain the defendants was accordingly refused. However, in *J.T. Stratford and Sons Ltd v. Lindley* [1965] AC 269, the plaintiffs had a contract to hire barges to a third party, and the defendant union officials, in order to place industrial pressure on the plaintiff, instructed members who were employees (fourth parties) of the third party not to handle the plaintiffs' barges. The plaintiffs sought an injunction, which was granted by the House of Lords, because the employees had been persuaded to break their contracts of employment with the third party employer.

A variation on this theme is where a defendant *enables or facilitates the inducement by* a third party of a second party to break the second party's contract with the plaintiff.

In this situation, it would seem that the defendant will not be liable towards the plaintiff, unless the former's transaction with the third party is itself unlawful, for example, because it is in contravention of an injunction or other court order.

Thus, in *Law Debenture Trust Corporation v. Ural Caspian Oil Corporation Ltd* [1994] 3 WLR 1221 company X acquired the shares in four other companies. The plaintiff company agreed with X and the four others that if the latter received compensation from the Russian government in respect of assets which had been confiscated in 1917, this would be paid to the plaintiff to be held on trust for shareholders in the four companies. X agreed not to transfer its shares unless the transferee were to agree that the plaintiff would so receive any compensation as trustee. However, in breach of the latter agreement, X transferred the shares to Y, which then transferred them to defendant Z.

The plaintiff sued Z on the ground that Z, by taking, procuring or causing the transfer of the shares, had prejudiced any claim in tort which the plaintiff might have had against Y which could have led to an order to re-transfer the shares to X: Z had procured and facilitated Y's tortious inducement of X's breach of contract with the plaintiff.

The plaintiff's claim against Z before the Court of Appeal was unsuccessful: although Y had tortiously induced X's breach of contract with the plaintiff, so that the plaintiff would have been able to obtain an injunction against Y's transfer to Z and an order to Y to re-transfer the shares to X, no such injunction had been granted, and accordingly, the actual transfer by Y to Z was not tortious and unlawful and there was no cause of action against Z for acceptance of the transfer.

2. *Defendant's intentions*

The defendant must have intended the contract to be broken.

However, courts are seemingly very willing to infer this (*Merkur Island Shipping Corp. v. Laughton* [1983] 2 AC 570); and recklessness as to whether the contract is broken or not should be sufficient (*Emerald Construction Co. Ltd v. Lowthian* [1966] 1 WLR 691).

3. *Breach*

Torquay Hotels Co. Ltd v. Cousins [1969] 2 Ch. 106 suggests that it may be sufficient for the contract in question to have been *interfered with* even if it is not actually broken. In the course of an industrial dispute, the defendants persuaded oil companies not to deliver to the plaintiffs. Esso complied because its drivers were union members. There was, however, a clause in Esso's contract with the plaintiffs excluding Esso's contractual liability for failure to perform through industrial action, so that Esso were not, in fact, in breach of contract. Nevertheless, the defendants were held liable for the tort. This could be explained on the basis that there *was* a breach of the contract between Esso and the plaintiffs even though Esso's own liability for that breach was excluded - although Lord Denning preferred the more direct approach of saying that the tort was still committed if contractual performance was prevented or interfered with even without breach. In *Merkur Island Shipping Corp. v.*

Laughton, Lord Diplock thought that this might be the case in the *Thomson v. Deakin* category of inducement, whereas, in the other types of inducement, breach would appear to be the necessary effect. So, for example, inducing a third party to negotiate a variation of the original contract with the plaintiff, unfavourable to the plaintiff, would not amount to the tort.

4. Damage to the plaintiff

This must be shown to have arisen from the breach.

5. Defence of justification

This applies in either of two cases: (1) where the contract interfered with is inconsistent with a previous contract with the interferer, or (2) where there was a moral duty to intervene (*Edwin Hill and Partners v. First National Finance Corporation* [1989] 1 WLR 225). Thus, in *Brimelow v. Casson* [1924] 1 Ch. 302, it was held that the defendant union official was justified in inducing actresses to break their contracts with the plaintiff theatre, because their pay was so low that they had been forced to take to prostitution in order to make ends meet. However, commercial interests of the defendant or revenge against the plaintiff, who had previously broken a separate contract with the defendant, would not be a defence.

(iv) Passing Off

1. Meaning

The defendant gives the impression that the plaintiff's

products are the defendant's. He passes off the plaintiff's goods and any reputation they enjoy as his own, leading to a loss to the plaintiff. The plaintiff makes his claim in a passing off action, not in the tort of deceit, because *he* has not been deceived as to the source of the product - *that* fate falls upon the general public.

In *Erven Warnink Besloten Vennootschap v. J. Townend & Sons (Hull) Ltd* [1979] AC 731, Lord Diplock noted the five things which a plaintiff has to prove in a passing off action:

> (1) misrepresentation (2) made by a trader in the course of trade (3) to prospective customers of his or ultimate consumers of goods or services supplied by him (4) which is calculated to injure the business or good will of another trader (in the sense that this is a reasonably foreseeable consequence) and (5) which causes actual damage to a business or good will of the trader by whom the action is brought or (in a *quia timet* action) will probably do so.

2. *Types of passing off*

(a) *Using a similar name to that of the plaintiff's product*

This is the most obvious type of case. In effect, the defendant is appropriating the reputation attached to the plaintiff's products by confusing the public into believing that they are buying the plaintiff's. Thus, there are many examples from the cases: *Reddaway v. Banham* [1896] AC 199 - use of the words "Camel Hair Belting" to describe the defendants' camel hair belting when the plaintiff used the same words together with a camel design; *J. Bollinger v.*

Costa Brava Wine Co. Ltd [1960] Ch. 262 - description of their wine as "Spanish Champagne" by the defendant Spanish wine producers when it was not from the plaintiff's Champagne district in France; *Erven Warnick BV v. J. Townend & Sons (Hull) Ltd* [1979] AC 731 - use by the defendants of the name "Old English Advocaat" to describe their drink when the plaintiffs had sold their drink called "advocaat" for many years; *Taittinger v. Allbery Ltd* [1994] 4 All ER 75, CA - again, description of a sparkling fruit drink as "Elderflower Champagne" was a passing off offence against champagne.

(b) *Using the plaintiff's name*

In *Maxim's Ltd v. Dye* [1977] 1 WLR 1155, it was held to be passing off to open a French restaurant called "Maxim's" in Norwich, England, when there was already a world-famous restaurant of that name in Paris. Similarly, the "British Diabetic Association" was able to restrain the "Diabetic Society" from continuing to use that name ((1995) *The Times*, October 23).

However, suppose that the defendant in such cases is using his own name - does this make a difference? Not even here, if the public is likely to be deceived (*Parker-Knoll Ltd v. Knoll International Ltd* [1962] RPC 265).

(c) *Similar appearance of product*

This can be as deceptive as use of a similar name. In *White Hudson & Co. Ltd v. Asian Organization Ltd* [1964] 1 WLR 1466, the plaintiffs sold cough sweets in Singapore in red wrappers, and customers, most of whom did not read

English, would ask for "red paper cough sweets". It was passing off when the defendants began selling their own cough sweets in Singapore under a different name - in red wrapping paper. The restriction extends also to distinct advertising slogans for products (*Cadbury-Schweppes Pty Ltd v. Pub Squash Co. Pty Ltd* [1981] 1 WLR 193).

(d) *Sale of product as that of the plaintiff*

This is the most extreme form of passing off. There is no attempt to confuse or to lead the public to reach their own conclusions, but an actual claim to be the goods of the plaintiff. In *Lord Byron v. Johnson* (1816) 2 Mer 29, the defendant publishers advertised poems as having been written by Lord Byron when they were not: passing off.

3. *Conditions*

In all such cases, the court has to assess whether the public is *likely* to be confused into believing that it is the plaintiff's product which they are purchasing, or the plaintiff with whom they are dealing. *Intention* to deceive is not a requirement (although, it is not *wholly* irrelevant to assessment of likely confusion: *Harrods Ltd v. Harrodian School* (1996) *The Times,* April 3, CA) and the defendant's innocence is not a defence (*Gillette UK Ltd v. Edenwest Ltd* (1994) *The Times,* March 9). If the only purchasers of goods are professionals, who will know the difference between those and the plaintiff's, there is no deception (*Hodgkinson & Corby Ltd v. Wards Mobility Services Ltd* [1994] 1 WLR 1564).

To succeed in the passing off action, the plaintiff should

usually establish that plaintiff and defendant are in the same trade and in the same geographical marketing region. Thus, in *McCullough v. May* [1947] 2 All ER 845, the plaintiff children's broadcaster called "Uncle Mac" failed to prove that the public would be confused by the defendants' breakfast cereal called "Uncle Mac's Puffed Wheat"; and in *Granada Group Ltd v. Ford Motor Co. Ltd* [1972] FSR 103, the plaintiff entertainments group were unable to prevent the defendants from calling their car models "Granada". In *Harrods Ltd v. Harrodian School* (1996) *The Times*, April 3, CA, the plaintiffs, Harrods department store, failed to establish passing off against the defendants, a private school, also in South-West London. A majority of the Court of Appeal held that what was required for passing off was appropriation by the defendant of the plaintiff's goodwill through deception of the public - clearly not satisfied here where the two activities were wholly different. It was not sufficient for passing off that use of the similar name, although not causing actionable deception, nonetheless contributed to the general *erosion of the distinctiveness* of the plaintiff's name which might degenerate into common use. Millett, LJ expressed an "intellectual difficulty" in accepting the idea that the law insisted upon both confusion and damage, and yet were to recognize as sufficient a head of damage (erosion) which did not depend on confusion (not that there was considered to be any real danger of "Harrods" becoming a generic term for retail shops for luxury goods)!

4. Remedies

The plaintiff may claim damages for his losses and an account of the defendant's profits from passing off, but his main remedy is likely to be an injunction to restrain the defendant from continuing to pass off the plaintiff's goods as his own. An injunction is discretionary and may be granted subject to the condition that the defendant should be allowed to continue his products provided that he takes proper steps to demarcate these from the plaintiff's - or refused if the plaintiff delayed in taking action, leading to substantial extra costs for the defendant (*Dalgety Spillers Foods Ltd v. Food Brokers Ltd* (1993) *The Times,* December 2).

(v) Possible General Economic Torts

The law does not stand still. People and courts are for ever alert to the development of more extensive areas of liability than those traditionally acknowledged to exist. In the area of economic torts, one such possible extension is that of economic duress, making a contract voidable if "economic" pressure was exerted on a person to enter the transaction and entitling the victim to damages in tort, claimed to exist by Lord Scarman in *Universe Tankships Inc. of Monrovia v. International Transport Workers Federation* [1983] 1 AC 366. It remains to be seen whether this invitation to develop what is clearly a far broader concept than existing established economic torts will be taken up. In addition, Lord Denning has suggested that any unlawful conduct which has the effect of interfering with trade should be actionable as a tort (*Torquay Hotels Co. Ltd v. Cousins, supra,* p.495). There have been decisions indicating some support. For example, in *Department of Transport v. Williams* (1993) *The Times,* December 7, the crime of obstructing the highway under the highways legislation was held also to give rise to tortious liability for interference with trade by unlawful means. The difficulty at present is that there is much uncertainty as to the conditions of operation of such tort: must the defendant have intended to harm the plaintiff's trade specifically; when are means unlawful?

(vi) Statutory Immunities

As a concession to political realities and industrial relations, certain statutes provide defendants with immunity from liability for certain economic torts where these are committed in the course of industrial action - *in contemplation or furtherance of a trade dispute.* Thus, s.13 of the Trade Union and Labour Relations Act 1974 grants such immunity for the torts of:

- conspiracy to injure by lawful means, and, partly, by unlawful (no immunity if the latter would be actionable in tort if carried out by one person); and
- intimidation and inducing breach of contract subject to the prescribed conditions.

Some commentators perceive as a major omission from such immunity the emerging tort of interference with trade by unlawful means, which may therefore figure as an increasingly important component of plaintiffs' armoury of legal weapons in economic torts.

Further reading:

Brazier, *Steet on Torts*, 9th ed, 1993 (Butterworth & Co., London): chs.8, 9 and 10.

Fleming, J.G., *The Law of Torts*, 8th ed, 1992 (The Law Book Company, Sydney): ch.30.

Hepple, B.A. and Matthews, M.H., *Tort: Cases and Materials*, 4th ed, 1991 (Butterworth & Co., London): ch.15.

Heuston, R.F.W. and Buckley, R.A., *Salmond and Heuston on The Law of Torts*, 20th ed, 1992 (Sweet & Maxwell, London): ch.16.

Howarth, D., *Textbook on Tort*, 1995 (Butterworth & Co., London): ch.10.

Markesinis, B.S. and Deakin, S.F., *Tort Law*, 3rd ed, 1994 (Clarendon Press, Oxford): ch.7.

Rogers, W.V.H., *Winfield and Jolowicz on Tort*, 14th ed, 1994 (Sweet & Maxwell, London): ch.18.

Sales, "The Tort of Conspiracy and Civil Secondary Liability" (1990) *Cambridge Law Journal* 491.

Stanton, K.M., *The Modern Law of Tort*, 1994 (The Law Book Company, Sydney): ch.15.

PART XI

Chapter 20

Tort of Deceit

Introduction

Deceit, or fraud, or fraudulent misstatement/misrepresentation, as it is known, is where a false statement is made to a person upon which the latter relies and as a consequence suffers damage. It is a tort.

It is closely connected to negligent misstatement (whether leading to conclusion of a contract or otherwise generally relied upon to a person's detriment) - except that mere negligence of the defendant is not enough in fraudulent deceit, where something more is required, namely, knowledge or recklessness as to the false nature of the statement.

Many of the elements of the tort, nevertheless, will be those also found in negligent misstatement.

The following conditions apply to establish liability for deceit.

1. False representation

There must be a statement or conduct amounting to a representation which is false. For example, walking into a shop in Oxford wearing academic dress, thereby falsely representing oneself as a member of the university in order to obtain credit (*R. v. Barnard* (1837) 7 C & P 784).

Generally, mere silence is not a representation. There are certain exceptions, however, where a party has a duty of disclosure: (a) a half-truth ("this car runs well over a speed of 50 miles per hour", omitting to say that whilst this may be true between 50 and 55 miles per hour, nevertheless, over 55 miles per hour it breaks down); for example, in *Notts Patent Brick and Tile Co. v. Butler* (1886) 16 QBD 778, a solicitor acting for the seller of land informed the purchaser that he did not know of any restrictive covenants affecting the property, which was only true because he had not even searched; or (b) statements initially true but which have become inaccurate to the maker's knowledge during the relevant period, as in *With v. O'Flanagan* [1936] Ch 575 where a medical practice was valued at £2,000 when negotiations for sale began, but which was worthless when contracts were signed five months later through the defendant seller's illness, undisclosed to the plaintiff buyer; or (c) contracts *uberrimae fidei,* such as insurance, which rely upon good faith and where consequently there is a duty to disclose all material facts *in utmost good faith,* and fiduciary relationships between parties not of equal status with regard to each other.

Whatever representation is made, this must, as a matter of fact, be false.

2. *Of Fact*

A number of other types of statement will not suffice for liability:

(a) puffs - advertisers talking up products with acceptable commercial exaggeration, not intended to lead to legal liability - "The best brush in the world"; or
(b) of opinion - unless there were no reasonable grounds for the defendant to have held such an opinion, in which case he misrepresented the fact of truly holding it (*Smith v. Land and House Property Corporation* (1884) 28 Ch D 7);
(c) of intention - again subject to an exception where, as a fact, the defendant did not really have his expressed intention (*Edgington v. Fitzmaurice* (1885) 29 Ch D 459 - intention was to use debenture issue to pay off corporate debts, not to expand business as stated in company prospectus); or
(d) of law.

3. Knowing or reckless as to whether statement is false

Mere negligence - lack of reasonable grounds to believe that the representation is true - is not enough for deceit. The defendant must know that his statement is untrue, or not care whether it is true or not - recklessness. Anything less than such knowledge or indifference as to the truth can only found an action for negligent misrepresentation either at common law under *Hedley Byrne* or under s.2 of the Misrepresentation Act 1967 (see *supra,* ch.5). The problem for the plaintiff in *Derry v. Peek* (1889) 14 App Cas 337, was that at that time there was not yet such liability for mere negligent misstatement so that the plaintiff, who had bought shares in a company having read the statement by the directors in the company's prospectus that the company intended to run trams, brought an action for deceit when it turned out that the company required the government's approval to do this, which it did not however receive, consequently having to be wound up. Unfortunately for the plaintiff, the directors had honestly believed that the company would receive approval for its plans, so that whether or not this belief was reasonable, they were not guilty of deceit.

The test for deceit is subjective, relating to the defendant's actual knowledge and state of mind - although, obviously, unreasonableness of his belief could be used as evidence of such actual mental state (*Angus v. Clifford* [1981] 2 Ch 449).

4. Plaintiff is the person or one of a class of persons to whom the representation was addressed

Thus, in *Peek v. Gurney* (1873) LR 6 HL 377 a false statement was made in a company's prospectus on the issue of shares. However, the plaintiff bought his shares subsequently on the stock exchange, and the court held that the prospectus was only addressed to initial purchasers of the shares from the company itself, and the defendants were consequently not liable towards the plaintiff for what was said in the prospectus. The result would be different if the statement was more widely circulated in the press and advertising instead of being confined to the prospectus (*Andrews v. Mockford* [1896] 1 QB 372).

5. The plaintiff relied upon the defendant's representation

The representation need not have been the sole reason for

the plaintiff's subsequent actions leading to loss; it need only have been material, in the sense of being one of the factors which together led to this course of action (*Edgington v. Fitzmaurice*).

It is a question of fact whether the plaintiff did so rely upon the defendant's statement, or whether he was unaware of it, ignored it or took independent advice. It is not sufficient to destroy reliance that the plaintiff could - even should - reasonably have made checks and inquiries which would have revealed the truth (*Redgrave v. Hurd* (1881) 20 CH D 1).

6. Damage

The plaintiff must have suffered damage from the defendant's deceit.

It would seem from *Doyle v. Olby* [1969] 2 QB 158 that the test of remoteness of damage in deceit is the *Polemis* principle of liability for all direct losses, rather than the reasonable foreseeability test of *The Wagon Mound* (see *supra*, ch.7), since the fraudulent defendant should not gain the benefit of the latter. The damages remedy is calculated on the tortious basis of difference between actual value of the product acquired by the plaintiff and the higher price paid by him as a result of the fraudulent misrepresentation ("out-of-pocket" rule) - although, in *Smith New Court Securities Ltd v. Scrimgeour Vickers (Asset Management) Ltd* [1994] 1 WLR 1271, the Court of Appeal considered that damages should represent the difference between the sum paid and the value which the assets held according to the state of knowledge in the market at the date the cause of action arose and not their lower value on a subsequent date at which further damaging information had been revealed. The House of Lords gave leave to appeal this judgment (see [1995] 1 WLR 30).

7. *Contributory negligence*

It would seem that this defence may be unavailable against deceit. *Alliance and Leicester Building Society v. Edgestop Ltd* [1994] 2 All ER 38 was a claim brought by the plaintiff building society against the defendant estate agents for deceit by fraudulently over-valuing properties as part of a mortgage fraud so that the plaintiffs would make excessive loans. The defence was that the plaintiffs had been contributorily negligent in not making sufficient inquiries. Mummery, J held that this defence was unable to be pleaded in the case of deceit under ss.1(1) and 4 of the Law Reform (Contributory Negligence) Act 1945, since it was an intentional tort.

Further reading:

Fleming, J.G., *The Law of Torts*, 8th ed, 1992 (The Law Book Company, Sydney): ch.28.

Heuston, R.F.V. and Buckley, R.A., *Salmond and Heuston on The Law of Torts*, 20th ed, 1992 (Sweet & Maxwell, London): ch.18.

Markesinis, B.S. and Deakin, S.F., *Tort Law*, 3rd ed, 1994 (Clarendon Press, Oxford): ch.4.

Stanton, K.M., *The Modern Law of Tort*, 1994 (The Law Book Company, Sydney): ch.15.

PART XII

Chapter 21

Torts Against or From Immovable Property

Land, as, historically, amongst the oldest of assets to receive legal protection under the English legal system in its earliest stages of development, still excites peculiar responses from lawyers, courts, litigants and the citizenry in general. Little surprise really, in view of its value, normally exceeding that of most movable objects except for jewels, machinery, ships, Rolls Royces and shareholdings, and in the light of its particular status as a place of relaxation and personal development, a sanctuary from an often cruel and hostile world. Protection of use and enjoyment of interests in land was therefore the subject of the earliest *writs of trespass* at the very birth of the common law and retains its special appeal, therefore, to those concerned to administrate justice in torts within a stable and continuing legal system.

Yet, times change - the social and economic environment, out of all recognition. The legal context itself is no longer the exclusive province of landowner and state. Instead, it now accommodates the sprawling amorphous "infant", the tort of negligence, with few obvious boundaries and even appearing to possess the capacity to extend itself into those areas traditionally the province of the "senior" tort of trespass to property. The latter, nevertheless, it will be seen in the succeeding chapter, still has a few *tricks up its sleeve* with which to fight off the impudent youngster, alongside the sister tort of continuing nuisance.

But interests have to be balanced properly in a complex society. The advantage cannot always lie with the landowner. The tort of nuisance has needed to adjust itself to this reality, as seen in Ch.23; while, landowners themselves cannot simply be given a free hand to terrorize and to oppress the rest of the community standing outside their borders, and the law has therefore had to afford suitable protection against escape of danger from inside a person's landed property, the subject of ch.24.

Further reading:

Stanton, K.M., *The Modern Law of Tort*, 1994 (The Law Book Company, Sydney): ch.18.

Chapter 22

Trespass to Land

(i) General Characteristics of the Tort of Trespass

Trespass to land is one of the oldest actions at common law. It is about the interference with a person's land - the main subject of private litigation in early times.

In former years trespass was also a crime, but this is no longer so other than under certain public order statutes (hence the misguided use of signs outside houses stating "Trespassers will be Prosecuted").

The usual description of trespass is: *unauthorized interference with a person's possession of land.*

Clearly, other tort actions may also be possible in such cases, for example, the later and ever-increasing tort of negligence, as well as those of nuisance and *Rylands v. Fletcher*. However, trespass has certain distinct features which may mean that only that tort can be used on the facts. What are these special characteristics of trespass?

1. Intention to commit the tort is not required

A person is liable for trespass if he intentionally (or possibly even negligently: *League Against Cruel Sports Ltd v. Scott* [1985] 2 All ER 489) carries out an interference with the plaintiff's land, even if he does not intend to commit trespass - for example, he believes that he himself owns the land which he enters (*Basely v. Clarkson* (1681) 3 Lev 37), or that the owner has authorized his entry (*Conway v. George Wimpey & Co. Ltd* [1951] 2 KB 266).

However, if the act itself, otherwise amounting to trespass, is involuntary and unintentional, this will be a defence ("inevitable accident") - for example, a person is thrown or pushed onto the plaintiff's land (*Smith v. Stone* (1647) Style 65); although, if the act in question derived from negligence, the interference is then actionable (*River Wear Commissioners v. Adamson* (1877) 2 App Cas 743).

Therefore, for trespass, intentional (or negligent) entry is required, but not also intent to commit the trespass.

2. *Damage need not be proved*

Unlike nuisance and negligence, trespass is actionable *per se*: that is to say, it is not necessary to prove damage to the property entered upon, because one of the original purposes of the action was to prevent a breach of the peace - people tend to become quite angry if they find a stranger on their property.

However, if there is no actual damage, the plaintiff will only receive nominal damages of a trivial amount - and may also be penalized in costs for bringing the action in the first place. An injunction can also be obtained in order to prevent repetition or continuation.

3. *Direct interference*

Trespass is restricted to direct interference with the plaintiff's land, whereas in nuisance the action complained of may be an indirect invasion. This means that in the former case, the defendant's act itself must be the interference, rather than merely the cause thereof: for example, throwing a stone onto the land, or planting a tree on it is trespass; whereas, it would be nuisance but not trespass if the defendant had piled stones next to the plaintiff's land and they fell onto it, or if the tree was planted next to the land and its branches or roots intruded, or if smoke blew over onto the land (*Davey v. Harrow Corporation* [1958] QB 60).

(ii) Nature of Interference

As seen, any direct invasion of possession of land will amount to trespass:

- entry, or staying, without permission, or using the land in an unauthorized manner (but not staying on after expiry of a lease, because the defendant himself originally entered as a possessor - contrast a mere licensee);
- placing an object on or against part of the land, including its boundary, or a wall or fence (*Westrip v. Baldock* [1938] 2 All ER 799), even leaning against it (*Gregory v. Piper* (1829) 9 B & C 591), or parking a car, or leaving rubbish on it.

Furthermore, the trespass is entry onto land. What is *land*?

Land includes buildings and fixtures on it, as well as the airspace above it and the soil beneath (for example, driving a stake into the subsoil owned by another: *Cox v. Moulsey* (1848) 5 CB 533), and this also includes improper use of public roads ("the highway"), such as picketing in a strike

(*Hubbard v. Pitt* [1976] QB 142), stopping longer than is reasonable (*Randall v. Tarrant* [1955] 1 WLR 255), walking up and down a short space of road in order to keep watch on a racehorse in training (*Hickman v. Maisey* [1900] 1 QB 752), or standing in the road, opening and shutting an umbrella in order to scare pheasants away from a pheasant shoot (*Harrison v. Duke of Rutland* [1893] 1 QB 142). This may overlap with public nuisance.

Thus, it will have been noted, trespass can be "vertical" as well as "horizontal" - for example, unauthorized digging, tunnelling, mining or building structures intruding into the air space over land, or throwing objects across it, stretching overhead telephone wires, the arm of a crane or shooting bullets (*Bulli Coal Mining Co. v. Osborne* [1899] AC 351). In *Kelson v. Imperial Tobacco Co. Ltd* [1957] 2 QB 334 there was held to be trespass when an advertising board stretched eight inches onto the plaintiff's land.

With regard to height, there has to be some limit on trespass liability. Consequently, this is set at the level at which the plaintiff's use and enjoyment of the land and structures on it are interfered with. In *Bernstein v. Skyviews & General Ltd* [1978] QB 479, it was held not to be a trespass for an aeroplane to fly over land taking aerial photographs at several hundred feet - the Judge feared that otherwise owners of satellites in space would continually be committing trespass on a multiple scale! Lower flying, interfering with peace and quiet, would, of course, be another matter, as well as extending into the area of nuisance - although, in this connexion it should be noted that the Civil Aviation Act 1982, s.76 removes any right of action for trespass or nuisance from flying at a height which is reasonable in the circumstances, including weather conditions; but to balance this, the section makes the aircraft owner strictly liable for any damage caused by the aircraft to persons or property on land or water.

(iii) Persons Who Can Sue For Trespass

Trespass is committed against persons who have an immediate right to exclusive possession of land, not against owners as such. Consequently, only the former can sue and owners without possession cannot. This ability to sue covers tenants and landlords respectively - and indeed the former may sue the latter (*Jones v. Llanrwst UDC* [1911] 1 Ch. 393). However, mere lodgers and licensees (for example, hotel guests) do not have such rights to exclusive possession (*Allan v. Liverpool Overseers* (1874) LR 9 QB 180) - although a person in *de facto* exclusive possession, yet without right or authority, can sue anyone else in trespass who has no immediate right to recover possession of the property (*Graham v. Peat* (1861) 1 East 244).

(iv) Defences

1. Licensee

A person who enters land having express or implied permission and who stays within the scope of the invitation to do so is a licensee: he is not a trespasser. If the permission ends, he becomes a trespasser after a reasonable period of time in which to leave (*Robson v. Hallett* [1967] 2 QB 939). Examples are traders calling at home (implied permission), people attending theatres (express permission) and lodgers or hotel guests (express permission).

Gratuitous licences for no payment may be revoked at any time and the former licensee becomes a trespasser if he does not leave within a reasonable time: you can invite someone to your home, but you are entitled to change your mind and ask them to leave.

In the case of licences granted under a contract not providing for revocation, it would seem that if the courts would grant specific performance of, or an injunction to prevent breach of, contract, the licence is irrevocable, so that an action for the tort of assault is available to the licensee if the licensor attempts to eject him as a trespasser (*Winter Garden Theatre (London) Ltd v. Millenium Productions Ltd* [1948] AC 173); in other cases, the licence terminates and the licensee becomes a trespasser, but can sue for damages for breach of contract (*Wood v. Leadbitter* (1845) 13 M & W 838).

In addition, what is referred to as a "licence coupled with an interest" is irrevocable (*Thomas v. Sorrell* (1674) Vaugh 330): for example, a flat is sold with permission to use a parking space - the buyer would not have bought the flat if the parking space had not been available, so that the permission to use the parking space cannot be revoked, because it is attached to the buyer's interest in the flat.

2. *Necessity*

This is a defence. For example, in *Rigby v. Chief Constable of Northamptonshire* [1985] 2 All ER 985 the defendant police authority could rely on this defence where they fired CS gas into the plaintiff's shop in order to remove a psychopath (although, as seen earlier, in ch.5, they were liable in negligence for failing to bring fire-extinguishing equipment), as was also the case in *Esso Petroleum Co. Ltd v. Southport Corporation* [1956] AC 218, where oil was discharged in order to save a ship.

Thus, necessity means in order to avoid greater loss - not to fulfil moral or other general needs (*Southwark LBC v. Williams* [1971] Ch 734).

At common law, there was no right to enter a neighbour's land as a matter of necessity in order to repair a dangerous structure (*John Trenberth Ltd v. National Westminster Bank Ltd* (1979) 253 EG 151). Consequently, the Access to Neighbouring Land Act 1992 enables courts to make an order permitting such entry, subject to any conditions of insurance against damage and payment of consideration to the neighbouring landowner as the court considers reasonable.

3. Rights of entry

These may exist at common law - for example, a public or private right of way or easement (other right over another person's land), or to abate (terminate) a nuisance - or under statutes permitting the police or other officials to enter for specific purposes. If the latter are abused or exceeded, the entrant is treated as a trespasser *ab initio* from the point in time when he entered, contrary to the normal rule of limiting trespass to the date of abuse (*The Six Carpenters' Case* (1610) 9 Co. Rep. 146a).

(v) Remedies

There are a number of these.

1. Injunction

This can and normally will be granted in order to prevent a repetition or to terminate continuing trespass. It may be in addition to damages, or instead of these where the actual damage is small (*Anchor Brewhouse Developments Ltd v. Berkley House (Docklands Developments) Ltd, supra*).

2. Damages

These will be nominal if actual damage is small or non-existent, unless the plaintiff is able to argue that he could have charged the defendant money for permission to enter (*Anchor Brewhouse*). If damage is suffered, damages are paid to the extent of the reduction in the value of the land, not for repair costs (*Lodge Holes Colliery Co. Ltd v. Wednesbury Corporation* [1908] AC 323).

3. Action for recovery of land (previously called ejectment)

The plaintiff must show a better title to the property than the defendant (*Martin d Tregonwell v. Strachan* (1742) 5 D & E 107 n).

4. Re-entry

At common law, a person can re-enter his property and use reasonable force to evict a trespasser (*Hemmings v. Stoke Poges Golf Club* [1920] 1 KB 720) - although, in *Burton v. Winters* [1993] 1 WLR 1077, it was held that the remedy should only be used in the clearest and simplest cases, and any excessive force amounts to trespass to the person. Holding a trespasser down and restraining him from waving and shouting may qualify as no more than reasonable force (*Harrison v. Duke of Rutland* [1893] 1 QB 142).

However, use of force in order to enter may be a criminal offence under s.6 of the Criminal Law Act 1977.

5. Abatement and distress damage feasant

As in nuisance, the occupier can himself remove any object extending onto his land, unless this would damage the defendant's property to a disproportionate degree.

Similarly, the occupier can keep (though not sell or use) property left on his land until any actual damage is paid for - *distress damage feasant*. In these circumstances, the occupier will have a defence against the tort of interference with goods and the "remedy" thereby becomes a "defence". However, the Court of Appeal declined to apply the doctrine to the modern practice of *wheelclamping* motor cars which are parked without authority on private land, in *Arthur v. Anker* (1995) *The Times,* December 1, CA (see *supra,* p.484). The court considered that the object of distress damage feasant was to obtain compensation for any damage caused by the trespass, whereas wheelclamping was intended as a deterrent - even to make a profit for the wheelclamping firm. Nevertheless, it was further held that if the motorist sees the warning sign, subject to certain conditions the defendant wheelclamper will still have the defence of plaintiff's *consent* (*supra*, p.484).

6. Action for mesne profits

This is an action for loss of money which could have been

earned from use and occupation of the land, including costs of any deterioration in its condition and costs of recovery of possession.

Further reading:

Brazier, *Street on Torts*, 9th ed, 1993 (Butterworth & Co., London): ch.5.

Cooke, "Trespass, Mesne Profits and Restitution" (1994) 110 *Law Quarterly Review* 420.

Fleming, J.G., *The Law of Torts*, 8th ed, 1992 (The Law Book Company, Sydney): chs.3 and 5.

Hepple, B.A. and Matthews, M.H., *Tort: Cases and Materials*, 4th ed, 1991 (Butterworth & Co., London): ch.14.

Heuston, R.F.V. and Buckley, R.A., *Salmond and Heuston on The Law of Torts*, 20th ed, 1992 (Sweet & Maxwell, London): ch.4.

Howarth, D., *Textbook on Tort*, 1995 (Butterworth & Co., London): ch.5.

Jones, M.A., *Textbook on Torts*, 4th ed, 1993 (Blackstone, London): ch.11.

Markesinis, B.S. and Deakin, S.F., *Tort Law*, 3rd ed, 1994 (Clarendon Press, Oxford): ch.5.

Rogers, W.V.H., *Winfield and Jolowicz on Tort*, 14th ed, 1994 (Sweet & Maxwell, London): ch.13.

Stanton, K.M., *The Modern Law of Tort*, 1994 (The Law Book Company, Sydney): ch.19.

Weir, T., *A Casebook on Tort*, 7th ed, 1992 (Sweet & Maxwell, London): chs.8 and 9.

Chapter 23

Nuisance

1. General

There are two types of tortious nuisance: private and public.

Private nuisance is where the defendant's activity interferes with the enjoyment and use of *a particular person's* - the plaintiff's - land. The offender will usually be the person who lives next door, but not always: it might be someone visiting the neighbour; it could even be somebody standing in the road outside the victim's house.

Public nuisance is interference with rights of the public generally. Usually, the right offended against is to have unobstructed use of public roads - the *highway*.

Use of land is and always has been one of the most delicate and sensitive issues confronting the law of tort. The balance between allowing people unrestricted enjoyment of their home, and yet preventing them from spoiling the enjoyment of the people who live next door, is extremely hard to achieve. Loud stereo music at midnight may be all that Mr Smith lives for. But it may also be the means to destroy the peacefulness of his neighbour, Mr Brown's, life.

Whom is the law to favour? Part of the problem lies in the fact that there is nothing inherently wrong and immoral in Mr Smith's act itself. It is purely the *effects* of his activities which may require the law to decide upon the appropriate regulation of mutual co-existence of persons within society. All that one can do is to consider the principles developed and the cases decided, in order to try to calculate what will and will not be actionable as nuisance.

2. Private Nuisance

(i) The General Nature

Since the law of nuisance is made up of individual cases and categories in which courts have held liability to exist, attempts at definition are of limited use. The general nature of such legal nuisance is usually said to be that it involves "unlawful interference with a person's use or enjoyment of land and rights over it". Yet, what is "unlawful" to be taken to mean?

Smells, slime, sleaze and sex could be an alternative explanation.

Vitally, it involves *land,* including buildings, crops, fixtures, rights of way *et alia* within the definition of land in s.205 of the Law of Property Act 1925, and not other property. If a colleague consistently spills coffee over one's jacket as he walks past one in the canteen at work, this may well be considered to be a thorough nuisance, but it is not a legal nuisance.

In *Crown River Cruises Ltd v. Kimbolton Fireworks Ltd* (1996) *The Times*, March 6, Potter, J held in the High Court that nuisance could be caused to a barge and a passenger vessel permanently moored on the River Thames in London. They had been set on fire as a result of a 20-minute firework display on the Thames in 1990, organized to commemorate the Battle of Britain. The vessels were permanently attached to a mooring on the bed of the river, of which the plaintiffs had exclusive use and occupation pursuant to a licence.

The types of nuisance that may interfere with a person's use and enjoyment of land are as broad as the imagination can conjure up, and case law examples include: physical collapse of a building, such as may occur from tree roots sucking moisture; shaking; noise; pollution of rivers; blasting in quarries, smells from candle-making or manure; dust; fumes; telephone calls; sex shops and brothels.

Is nuisance a tort of "strict liability" (see *supra,* ch.9)?

Whatever past perceptions may have been, it is now clear that nuisance is not fully so. It will be recalled (see ch.9) that there are two elements which must be present for *full* strict liability without fault to exist:

1. the defendant is liable even if it was not reasonably foreseeable that his actions would cause damage to the plaintiff; and
2. even if he took all reasonable care to avoid harming the plaintiff.

The position in nuisance is that whereas the latter is true, the former is not: reasonable foreseeability of damage is required for an action in damages for nuisance (and, in practice, in any event, the nuisance will be known to the defendant where an injunction is sought - see [1994] 1 All ER 53, at p.71). This was confirmed in the judgment of Lord Goff in the House of Lords in *Cambridge Water Co. Ltd v. Eastern Counties Leather plc* [1994] 1 All ER 53, HL. The plaintiffs sued the defendants in negligence, nuisance and the tort of *Rylands v. Fletcher* dealing with the escape of dangerous things on land (see *infra,* ch.24), in respect of chemicals used by the defendants which had contaminated the plaintiff's water source one mile away. In the House of Lords the case was mainly fought out on the *Rylands v. Fletcher* liability, which was thought - incorrectly - to be fully strict, because the finding of the courts below that damage had not been reasonably foreseeable for the purposes of negligence and nuisance was not appealed against (p.67). Nevertheless, Lord Goff, delivering the leading judgment, decided to consider the question of whether reasonable foreseeability was in fact required in nuisance, as a preliminary to its examination for purposes of *Rylands v. Fletcher* itself, because of the close relationship between the two (p.69) and notwithstanding that nuisance was no longer, strictly speaking, a live issue in the case (p.71).

Lord Goff began with "reasonable care": it was still the law "that the fact that the defendant has taken all reasonable care will not of itself exonerate him from liability" (pp.71-2). However, Lord Goff nevertheless did point out that there was a form of *control mechanism* on defendants' liability when they had acted reasonably, which was that this would be taken into account in determining, as a matter of balance, whether the defendants' acts amounted, in their *effects,* to legal nuisance (p.72). Thus, it will be seen below that general reasonableness or otherwise of the defendant's behaviour will be a material factor in deciding upon nuisance, and will carry greater or less weight according to the circumstances: for example, if physical damage or damage to a proprietary right over land is caused, reasonableness of the defendant's behaviour would seem to carry very little weight at all in preventing nuisance liability (*infra*, p.532, *et seq.*), whereas if the interference complained of is merely with the use and enjoyment of land, reasonableness of the defendant's conduct can matter a great deal (*infra*, p.535, *et seq.*).

With regard to the issue of reasonable foreseeability of harm from (private or public) nuisance, referring to the speech of Lord Reid in the Judicial Committee of the Privy Council in *The Wagon Mound (No.2)* [1966] 2 All ER 709, at 717 (although, actually considering that Lord Reid had been discussing *remoteness* of damage, rather than establishment of liability itself, not necessary to decide which in *Cambridge Water*: p.72), Lord Goff concluded that reasonable foreseeability of damage to the plaintiff *was* required to establish nuisance liability: "... it by no means follows that the defendant should be held liable for damage of a type which he could not reasonably foresee; and the development of the law of negligence in the past 60 years points strongly towards a requirement that such foreseeability should be a prerequisite of liability in damages for nuisance, as it is of liability in negligence. For if a plaintiff is in ordinary circumstances only able to claim damages in respect of personal injuries where he can prove such foreseeability on the part of the defendant, it is difficult to see why, in common justice, he should be in a stronger position to claim damages for interference with the enjoyment of his land where the defendant was unable to foresee such damage. Moreover, this appear to have been the conclusion of the Privy Council in *The Wagon Mound*

(No.2) ... It is widely accepted that this conclusion, although not essential to the decision of the particular case, has nevertheless settled the law to the effect that foreseeability of harm is indeed a prerequisite of the recovery of damages in private nuisance, as in the case of public nuisance" (p.72).

This message of Lord Goff is therefore unequivocal: reasonable foreseeability is required for nuisance liability.

Unfortunately, however, perhaps even inevitably with a Judge as brave and innovative as Lord Goff, the reasoning is not always quite as clear as might have been hoped. Some of his statements in the case betrayed a lack of certitude over whether the test of reasonable foreseeability which he was propounding was as to *liability* in nuisance in the first place or merely as to remoteness of damage ("... foreseeability of harm of the relevant type ...", p.71; "... liable for damage of a type which he could not reasonably foresee ...", p.72). In spite of this ambiguity, however, there can be little doubt that Lord Goff intended to refer to reasonable foreseeability as a prerequisite to nuisance *liability* ("... foreseeability of harm of the relevant type is an essential element of liability ...", p.71; "... such foreseeability should be a prerequisite of liability in damages for nuisance ...", p.72).

As it happens, it probably does not matter whether the authority drawn upon by Lord Goff concerned liability or merely remoteness of damage, for the simple reason that even if reasonable foreseeability were considered to be limited to the remoteness question, effectively this would necessarily entail its applicability to liability as well. What would be the point of establishing - unforeseeable - liability if damages were not recoverable at all in the absence of foreseeability? Lest it be responded that at least an injunction might still be available in such circumstances, Lord Goff himself intimated that for an injunction to be sought, the defendant would in practice actually have to be aware of the continuing harm being caused to the plaintiff against which an injunction is sought and have refused or failed to terminate it (p.71).

The real question, therefore, is not whether the reasonable foreseeability requirement governs not just remoteness of damage but also liability - one way or another, it plainly does - but whether this is in fact justified as a precondition of nuisance?

The present writer believes that it is not. Very simply, the function of negligence is to allocate compensation to a plaintiff where the defendant has transgressed. The emphasis is equally upon the defendant's behaviour and the plaintiff's claims to recompense for injury. Whereas, the object of nuisance is to protect the *plaintiff*, regardless of whether the *defendant* is at fault or not. Nuisance is primarily plaintiff-orientated, even though, as Lord Goff pointed out, reasonableness of the defendant's behaviour will not be discounted as a control mechanism for liability in assessment of the plaintiff's protective requirements (p.72). (Indeed, it will be seen that in *public* nuisance, the plaintiff must be able to demonstrate that he has suffered extra damage beyond that sustained by others, as a condition of being permitted to claim, *infra*, p.562.) It does seem illogical, therefore, for this point of no-fault nuisance liability, on the one hand effectively to be conceded in permitting nuisance liability notwithstanding exercise of all reasonable care by the defendant, and yet, on the other hand, to draw back from this position in the matter of reasonable foreseeability. This is a half-way house: in one direction - no requirement of reasonable care - lies real strict liability; in the other, if reasonable foreseeability were to be required also for nuisance, lies negligence and probably the end of nuisance as a distinct tort. The latter would be regrettable. Nuisance *is* necessary for societal protection. If the decision were reached that nuisance existed in all the circumstances, irrespective of the fact that the defendant's behaviour and demeanour had not been unreasonable and that harm to the plaintiff had been (subject to defences of act of God or act of a stranger, *infra*) completely unforeseeable, then it is believed that the plaintiff should be entitled to recover for all direct damage flowing from that nuisance. That is only logical and consistent with the plaintiff-protective policy essentially underlying the doctrine of nuisance - to be contrasted with the plaintiff-defendant equality basis of negligence.

However, to adopt a perhaps rather appropriate expression ... seemingly this is now all *water under the bridge.*

(ii) The Elements of Nuisance

These are:

1. Interference with use or enjoyment of land

Unlike trespass, nuisance is not actionable *per se* from an act of land encroachment alone. There must be an effect, an interference with the normal processes of life - damage, for want of a better term - in relation to a person himself, his land, rights over the land, or to the person's enjoyment of it (*Cambridge Water Co. Ltd v. Eastern Counties Leather plc*

[1994] 1 All ER 53, 67, HL). Such "interference" can be of different types.

a. Physical damage

Liability may be expected to be easier to establish where there is some physical damage resulting from the defendant's activities; and the amount of physical damage need not be great (*St Helen's Smelting Co. v. Tipping* (1865) 11 HL Cas 642).

b. Interference with "servitudes"

"Servitudes" mean proprietary rights granted over someone else's land, for instance, rights of light, air, water or of way, *et alia* - known as easements - and natural rights not deriving from any grant, such as support and flow of water in a defined stream. (There is a difference between a defined stream of water and water flowing in an undefined way - "percolating" - under the ground. In the case of the stream, the natural right is to have the flow uninterrupted, *infra,* p.533; with percolating water, the (*natural*) right is to block, divert or extract it, *infra,* p.533.)

Here too, as in the case of physical damage, a substantial interference will make it easier to establish legal nuisance (*Cambridge Water Company Ltd v. Eastern Counties Leather plc* [1994] 1 All ER 53, HL). For example, the defendant removes a bank of earth on his land, so that the plaintiff's house on neighbouring land collapses from interference with the right of support: this constitutes nuisance irrespective of whether the defendant's actions were considered reasonable or not (*Dalton v. Angus* (1881) 6 App

Cas 740). In the case of water running in a stream over the plaintiff's land, it will be a nuisance if the defendant affects its flow (*Miner v. Gilmour* (1858) 12 Moo PC 131). But it is not nuisance where the water flows in an undefined way ("percolates") underneath the plaintiff's property and the defendant interferes with this, even deliberately in order to force the plaintiff to sell his land to the defendant at a low price (*Chasemore v. Richards* (1859) 7 HL Cas 349; *Bradford Corporation v. Pickles* [1895] AC 587, HL). Thus, in *Home Brewery plc v. William Davis and Co. (Loughborough) Ltd* [1987] 1 All ER 637, the defendants filled in two clay pits on their land, which meant that water was unable to drain away from the plaintiffs' neighbouring property and the latter had to install pumps, the costs of which were claimed in the nuisance action. The court held there to be no legal nuisance.

c. Interference with comfort and enjoyment

This is a more difficult type of nuisance to deal with, and the operation of other factors will be critical. Interference with someone's enjoyment of their property cannot *per se* be held to give rise to a claim for nuisance. The interference has to be *balanced* against the restrictions which would be placed upon the freedom of the defendant to continue his own activities: "give and take, live and let live" is the guiding principle (*Bamford v. Turnley* (1862) 3 B & S 66, at pp.79 and 84), as will now be discussed.

2. *Reasonableness of interference*

a. *Physical damage, servitudes and certain miscellaneous cases: liability regardless of whether or not activity reasonable*

Physical Damage and Servitudes

Where there is physical damage from the defendant's activities, or interference with servitudes, the courts will not spend as long assessing the "reasonableness" or otherwise of the effects of the defendant's conduct against his own claims to an unobstructed existence and activities. Live and let live becomes ... *let live:* legal nuisance. Smoke and smells from factories in an industrial area may be unpleasant, but are an inevitable part of the landscape in these localities and may have to be suffered without recourse to the law of nuisance (see below); but if the smoke is so hot that it melts the window frames of the plaintiff's house, or makes him violently sick, such physical damage to property or health affecting his use of land alters the situation and makes justification of the defendant's activities through other factors and reasonableness most unlikely (*St Helen's Smelting Co. v. Tipping*). Certain commentators conclude that in the case of physical damage and servitudes, the defendant is liable in nuisance wholly regardless of whether this is reasonable or not (see Veale, J in *Halsey v. Esso Petroleum Co. Ltd* [1961] 1 WLR 683). This seems quite correct in practice, although rather doubtful in principle, and in theory, at any rate, reasonableness may remain a remote possibility.

This virtual *immunity* of physical - and servitudes' - nuisance from the requirement of reasonableness has been criticized, and some have even argued that they should be transferred from the tort of nuisance to negligence. For the time being, however, the distinction between physical and servitude interference on the one hand, and other types of interference on the other, should probably be taken to exist, at least as one of substantial degree.

Miscellaneous Cases Where Reasonableness is not a Major Factor

(a) **Defendant exercising a servitude.** There is also the converse of the previous case of interference with the plaintiff's natural right or servitude: if it is the defendant neighbour whose interference consists in the exercise of a natural right or easement - for example, he extracts water percolating underneath his land, so that the water is denied to the adjacent property, or he digs for fuel so that support is lost - reasonableness or unreasonableness of his conduct is also not here the issue. It is not nuisance (*Langbrook Properties Ltd v. Surrey County Council* [1970] 1 WLR 161). (Note that in *Cambridge Water Co. Ltd v. Eastern Counties Leather plc* [1994] 1 All ER 53, at p.68, HL, Lord Goff distinguished the natural right not to have the flow of water in a defined stream onto one's land interrupted, from the "*natural*" right to abstract water percolating beneath one's land in an undefined way and thereby to interrupt its flow to one's neighbour: the latter was merely a *right* to take water without this being unlawful as a tort; it certainly was not a natural right not to have the flow of the percolating water underneath one's land interrupted.)

Thus, neither the exercise nor the breach of a natural right or easement requires a substantial inquiry into reasonableness in practice: the one is not, and the other is, a legal nuisance. Liability, therefore, is respectively non-existent and strict.

(b) **Nuisance from natural condition of land.** However, in the case of interference through the *natural condition* of land - for example, from thistles blowing and taking root, rocks falling - although this used to be thought to be incapable, like exercise of a natural right or servitude, of amounting to a nuisance (provided that the plaintiff was permitted to enter the defendant's land in order to remove the nuisance: *Giles v. Walker* (1890) 24 QBD 656), this is no longer the position today (*Leakey v. National Trust* [1980] QB 485), and reasonableness is now also a consideration in this type of case (see *Cambridge Water Co. Ltd v. Eastern Counties Leather plc* [1994] 1 All ER 53, 71 HL; and *infra*, p.544).

(c) **Views.** Conversely, the natural right to enjoy a *beautiful view* is the province of nature, not the law of nuisance, even if obstruction could be considered to be wholly unreasonable (*Hunter v. Canary Wharf Ltd* (1995) *The Times*, October 13, CA). Some writers deduce too that recreation generally is not protected, especially since in *Bridlington Relay Ltd v. Yorkshire Electricity Board* [1965] Ch 436, the court held the defendant not liable for interfering with enjoyment of the land when it erected electricity pylons which interfered with the plaintiff's television broadcasts. This, however, would seem to be a somewhat excessive conclusion to draw, both for its generality and because times change, even in 30 years (in *Nor-Video Services Ltd v. Ontario Hydro* (1978) 84 DLR (3d) 221, Canadian courts held that interference with television reception on a wide scale amounted to a nuisance towards the plaintiff television company).

b. *Non-physical/non-servitudes/non-miscellaneous cases: reasonableness*

Smells, vibration, smoke, fumes, dust and sex shops

The infinite number of ways in which neighbours are able to succeed in annoying each other if they try hard enough!

Here, the test of private nuisance is *whether the defendant's interference with the plaintiff's enjoyment of his land is unreasonable* taking into account a number of factors and principles.

> "The question ... entirely depends on the surrounding circumstances - the place where, the time when, the alleged nuisance, what, the mode of committing it, how, and the duration of it, whether temporary or permanent, occasional or continual ..." (*Bamford v. Turnkey* (1862) 3 B & S 66 at p.79, per Pollock, CB).

This *control mechanism* of reasonableness was confirmed by Lord Goff in *Cambridge Water Co. Ltd v. Eastern Counties Leather plc* [1994] 1 All ER 53, 72, HL.

Unlike instances of physical and servitude damage in which those physical effects substantially serve to remove any doubts over lack of justifiability of the defendant's activities, in the non-physical cases the courts have the task of reaching a decision as to which party's interests should be protected in society - plaintiff's or defendant's - on the facts of a particular case. *Reasonableness* here is not the same as in the law of negligence, where it largely centres upon the nature of the defendant's conduct, foreseeability of harm and appropriate standards of behaviour ([1994] 1 All ER 53, 71-2). In nuisance, it has a far broader meaning: regardless of whether or not the defendant's conduct on its own can be regarded as reasonable, moral or immoral, ultimately it is the *effects* upon the plaintiff's enjoyment of his land which is the issue. Consequently, however unreasonable in a general sense the defendant's behaviour on its own may be considered to be, and however reasonably foreseeable the disturbance to the plaintiff, the resultant interference might nonetheless not be held to be "unreasonable" so as to amount to nuisance in all the circumstances. The court must balance interests of plaintiff and defendant in society. Imitating the sound of a hyaena at three o'clock in the morning might seem rather strange and unreasonable behaviour: but the interference itself would not be unreasonable, if carried out on a farm in the middle of the countryside; whereas a private all-night bus service would seem a perfectly reasonable and acceptable objective, yet the interference would be highly unreasonable if the bus depot were placed in a residential street.

Reasonableness, then, in these non-physical cases in nuisance, is for assessment in the overall circumstances.

"Ought this inconvenience to be considered in fact as more than fanciful, more than one of delicacy or fastidiousness, as an inconvenience materially interfering with the ordinary physical comfort of human existence, but according to plain and sober and simple notions among the English people?" (*Walter v. Selfe* (1851) 4 De G & Sm 315, per Knight Bruce, VC).

"Of course, although liability for nuisance has generally been regarded as strict, at least in the case of a defendant who has been responsible for the creation of a nuisance, even so that liability has been kept under control by the principle of reasonable user - the principle of give and take as between neighbouring occupiers of land, under which 'those acts necessary for the common and ordinary use and occupation of land and houses may be done, if conveniently done, without subjecting those who do them to an action'" (*Cambridge Water Co. Ltd v. Eastern Counties Leather plc* [1994] 1 All ER 63, at pp.70-71, *per* Lord Goff).

Factors taken into account in determining *reasonableness* of interference and in the balancing of interests for these purposes include the following.

i. Duration. The more temporary the interference, the more unlikely it is to be held to be an unreasonable nuisance, especially if the remedy sought is an injunction rather than damages (*Harrison v. Southwark & Vauxhall Water Co.* [1891] 2 Ch 409). Yet, if it is serious, even a temporary inconvenience will constitute nuisance: an example would be using noisy and dusty pile-driving machinery at night (*De Keyser's Royal Hotel Ltd v. Spicer Bros Ltd* (1914) 30 TLR 257). Similarly, in *Crown River Cruises Ltd v. Kimbolton Fireworks Ltd* (1996) *The Times,* March 6, the plaintiffs' vessels permanently moored on the River Thames in London were damaged when they caught fire during a fireworks display in 1990 organized to commemorate the Battle of Britain. The defendants argued that a 20-minute firework display was too short to be capable of amounting to a nuisance. However, Potter, J, in the High Court rejected this, on the ground that the holding of a firework display in a situation where it was inevitable that for 15 or 20 minutes debris would fall upon nearby property of a potentially flammable nature, created a nuisance actionable at the suit of property owners like the plaintiffs who suffered as a result.

A single act is most unlikely to be held to amount to a nuisance: except that it can do:

- if the court considers that the act is the first of a potential series (for example, *British Celanese Ltd v. A.H. Hunt (Capacitors) Ltd* [1969] 2 All ER 1252, where metal strips blew off the defendant's land onto the plaintiff's electricity station and caused a power failure); or
- if the court regards the nuisance as consisting of a continuous state of affairs relating to the defendant's land which threatened to, and eventually did, give rise to the final act, rather than of the latter itself (*Miller v. Jackson* [1977] QB 966, where safeguards to stop cricket balls being knocked out of the ground were ineffective).

Short length of time, therefore, must be balanced against seriousness of the effects, while longer duration lends much weight to the nuisance claim.

ii. Locality. "What would be a nuisance in Belgrave Square would not necessarily be so in Bermondsey." Thus did Thesiger, LJ successfully secure for himself a place in the history books with this statement in *Sturges v. Bridgman* (1878) 11 Ch D 852, at p.865. (Note to readers: It may reasonably be assumed that Judges from time to time have shown a preference to live in Belgravia rather than in Bermondsey.)

The nature of the environment has to be taken into account in assessing whether interference is unreasonable: smoke is a part of the landscape in an industrial area; not so in a select residential neighbourhood. Accordingly, in *Laws v. Florinplace Ltd* [1992] 3 WLR 449 and *Thompson-Schwab v. Costaki* [1956] 1 All ER 652, prostitution and sex centres were regarded as incompatible with a good-class residential street. However, in *Hunter v. Canary Wharf Ltd* (1995) *The Times,* October 13, CA, the plaintiffs claimed damages *inter alia* for private nuisance through interference with their television reception at their homes in East London, caused by the construction of Canary Wharf Tower, which was a very tall building and with metal windows. The Court of Appeal, whilst accepting the importance of television to its viewers, nevertheless noted that tall buildings were a quite common feature of the landscape in urban areas, and consequently, interference to television was no more of a nuisance than loss of a pleasant view would have been. The plaintiffs therefore were unsuccessful (although leave to appeal to the House of Lords would be granted). Thus, whilst the authorities which established the limits of the tort of nuisance were old, the reasoning behind them was not only sound but was applicable to modern conditions (*ibid.*).

This does not mean that people in industrial areas are unprotected (*Roshmer v. Polsue and Alfieri Ltd* [1906] 1 Ch 234 - noise at night from a new printing machine in an area with many printing firms held nuisance): the test is what is customary in the area and whether the interference exceeds this ... "what is reasonable according to the ordinary usages of mankind living in society, or more correctly, in a particular society" (*Sedleigh-Denfield v. O'Callaghan* [1940] AC 880, at p.903). Interference beyond this constitutes nuisance (*Halsey v. Esso Petroleum Co. Ltd* [1961] 2 All ER 145).

However, as seen earlier, in *St Helen's Smelting Co. v. Tipping* (1865) 11 HLC 642, where smoke damaged the plaintiff's trees in an area wholly given over to the copper smelting industry, the House of Lords held that locality was only relevant when there had been no physical damage to the plaintiff's land. Consequently, the defendant was liable for nuisance.

iii. Plaintiff's abnormal sensitivity. "A man cannot increase the liabilities of his neighbour by applying his own property to special uses, whether for business or pleasure" (*Eastern and South Africa Telegraph Co. v. Cape Town Tramways* [1902] AC 381, at p.393, per Lord Robertson).

What is normal? This is for Judges to decide on the facts.

If a normal activity and use of the plaintiff's land would *not* also have been affected, the interference is not unreasonable. In *Robinson v. Kilvert* (1889) 41 Ch D 88, the plaintiff stored brown paper for sale above the defendant's premises where boxes were manufactured at hot temperatures. The plaintiff could not continue because the paper would dry out and its value would be reduced. However, ordinary paper would not have dried in this way and the Court of Appeal held the defendant not liable: the plaintiff's paper was exceptionally sensitive. Similarly, the television broadcasting relay station interfered with by electric pylons in *Bridlington Relay Ltd v. Yorkshire Electricity Board* [1965] Ch 436 was abnormally sensitive, and to be distinguished from interference with ordinary television sets (subject to reasonableness or otherwise of the cause - see *Hunter v. Canary Wharf Ltd, supra,* p.539): no nuisance. Thus, in *Gaunt v. Fynney* (1872) 8 Ch App 8, at p.13, Lord Selborne, LC commented: "... a nervous, or anxious, or prepossessed listener hears sounds which would otherwise have passed unnoticed, and magnifies and exaggerates into some new significance, originating within himself, sounds which at other times would have been passively heard and not regarded."

However, if "normal" activities would also have been affected, abnormality of the plaintiff's use will not prevent the nuisance from being held to be unreasonable. In *McKinnon Industries Ltd v. Walker* (1951) 3 DLR 577, fumes from the defendant's neighbouring premises affected the growth of the plaintiff's crop of exceptionally delicate orchids. This was held to be a nuisance, because ordinary flowers would also have been affected.

iv. Public usefulness of defendant's conduct. Public utility is certainly not a *defence* to nuisance (*Adams v. Ursell* [1913] 1 Ch 269 - service to the less affluent members of the community held not a defence against smells from fish and chip shop opened in up-market residential area). But it will undoubtedly be taken into account in balancing reasonableness against interference to the plaintiff, on the ground that public benefit *per se* is, without more, wholly desirable and reasonable.

Thus, in *Miller v. Jackson* [1977] AB 966, although the

majority of the Court of Appeal held that despite the fact that the defendant cricket ground was of benefit to the local community, the frequency with which balls were hit out of the ground made it unreasonable. Nevertheless, Lord Denning, dissenting, came down in favour of cricket.

Furthermore, even if public utility does not prevent nuisance liability, it should be remembered that the remedy of an injunction for nuisance is purely *discretionary* (see *infra*, p.555).

v. Motive. Maliciousness, recklessness, even sheer bloody-mindedness are not, in ordinary parlance, reasonable. Consequently, a defendant's motives can affect the outcome of nuisance: the defendant's activities carried out with motives such as these will reduce the overall claims for his conduct to be regarded as reasonable as a balance to interference with the plaintiff's enjoyment of his land.

Perhaps no better example can be provided as to the operation of this principle in practice than *Christie v. Davey* [1893] Ch 316. The plaintiff family was highly musical: mother and daughter were music teachers, and the son played the cello - although father was deaf. The defendant, who lived next door, complained unsuccessfully to the plaintiffs about the noise of music and singing, which, he claimed, sounded like a dog howling. After that he took stronger measures: when the music began, he would blow a whistle, bash trays and bang on the wall. The Judge held the defendant's behaviour to amount to nuisance, because it was malicious and intended to annoy the plaintiffs - that was its sole purpose. How could this compete with the plaintiffs' contrasting claims to enjoyment and to the freedom, reasonably, to indulge their love of music?

Again, in *Hollywood Silver Fox Farm Ltd v. Emmett* [1936] 2 KB 468, the defendant unsuccessfully requested the plaintiffs to stop advertising fox-breeding activities on their land, because he feared it might stop people from purchasing his own land. The foxes bred by the plaintiffs were very nervous and would eat their young if frightened. This occurred when the defendant deliberately began firing a gun on his own land near to the breeding pens. The defendant was held liable in nuisance (a strong case, because the silver foxes were unusually sensitive - see *supra*, p.540).

Clearly, too, if the defendant, though not malicious, has been careless, this will likewise affect the reasonableness equation in nuisance and certainly will not assist the defendant. However, carefulness by the defendant will not necessarily lead to a finding against unreasonableness of his interference: *Rapier v. London Tramways Co.* [1893] 2 Ch 588).

An exception to the effects of malice upon what might otherwise not be considered to be a nuisance is where the defendant maliciously extracts or diverts water flowing generally and in an undistinguishable form - *percolating* - under his land, so that neighbouring properties are deprived. It will be recalled that this is a "natural right" (it is otherwise, if it flows in defined channels: *Chasemore v. Richards* (1859) 7 HL Cas 349) and accordingly will not constitute a nuisance, malicious or otherwise (*supra*, pp.530 and 533): reasonableness is simply not a major factor, and even to the extent that it is, malice will be incapable of outweighing the importance of uninterrupted freedom over such natural rights. The defendant did this in *Bradford*

Corporation v. Pickles [1895] AC 587, in order to "encourage" the plaintiffs to purchase his land from him at a good price (see too *Langbrook Properties Ltd v. Surrey County Council* [1969] 3 All ER 1424, where the pumping of water on the defendant's land caused the plaintiff's neighbouring buildings to settle).

vi. Interference from the natural state of the land. Formerly, the defendant would not be liable for nuisance if, for example, weeds spread or thistles blew (see *supra,* p.534). This was changed by the Privy Council in *Goldman v. Hargrave* [1967] 1 AC 645. The defendant cut down a burning tree struck by lightning in Australia, but the wind blew the fire up again and it spread to the plaintiff's land. The defendant was held liable, apparently on the basis that he had not taken reasonable steps to prevent the foreseeable damage to the plaintiff's property - actually the language of *negligence* (see *Cambridge Water Co. Ltd v. Eastern Counties Leather plc* [1994] 1 All ER 53, 71, HL, *per* Lord Goff).

This principle applied in *Leakey v. National Trust for Places of Historic Interest or Natural Beauty* [1980] QB 485, where a steep hill suffered erosion causing landslips of rocks, soil and tree roots to threaten buildings at the bottom of the hill. The Court of Appeal held this to amount to a nuisance, where the defendant occupier had failed to do all that was reasonable in the circumstances to prevent or minimize dangers to neighbouring buildings from the forces of nature. Megaw, LJ was not impressed with the alternative of plaintiffs having to wait for land to fall on them or hoping that it would not, with no legal remedy in the meanwhile to put a stop to the risk. In *Bradburn v. Lindsay* [1983] 2 All

ER 408, dry rot, a natural fungus, spread from one joined house to another. This was a nuisance which the defendants ought to have taken reasonable steps to prevent by treatment.

However, it would seem from *Leakey* that the personal position of the defendant will be taken into account in determining what it would have been reasonable to expect of him: could he afford to take the measures to reduce the danger; was he too old or sick to do it himself; should the plaintiff himself have lent assistance?

Some commentators appear startled by the latter departure from normal *objective* standard and principles of negligence. Yet, why should they be? The inquiry remains one in nuisance, not negligence. Old, sick and poor people form part of society, just as do the young, rich and healthy. What is reasonable for an old defendant is a perfectly proper factor to be *balanced* against interference to the plaintiff, in accordance with the usual process for determining private nuisance. In principle too, the approach surely need not be limited to cases concerning disturbance caused by the natural condition of land.

(iii) Those Who Can Sue for Nuisance

Anyone with an interest in the affected land can sue.

What is an *interest*? The following:

- ownership;
- possession;
- any other proprietary interest.

There has been some doubt over whether those who are

merely in occupation, but who lack a proprietary interest, such as a licensee (say, a hotel guest), or spouse or child of the owner, have a right of action (*Street v. Mountford* [1985] 2 All ER 289). Thus, in *Malone v. Lasky* [1907] 2 KB 141, the plaintiff, who was the wife of the tenant, was sitting on the toilet one day when the toilet cistern fell on her as a result of being loosened by vibrations from the defendant's electricity generator next door. The Court of Appeal held that she could not sue for nuisance, because she had no proprietary interest in the premises.

In recent years, however, there have been indications that courts will permit mere occupiers to sue: spouses now have a statutory right of occupation of the home under the Matrimonial Homes Act 1967; and Canadian courts have refused to follow *Malone v. Lasky,* while, in *Khorasandjian v. Bush* [1993] 3 WLR 476, a majority of the Court of Appeal held that a series of unwanted telephone calls were a nuisance towards the plaintiff having no proprietary interest in the property, and noted that sometimes earlier decisions had to be reconsidered in the light of changed social conditions. This change now appears to have been confirmed by the Court of Appeal (although leave to appeal to the House of Lords on the issue was granted) in *Hunter v. Canary Wharf Ltd* (1995) *The Times,* October 13, CA. The court, in fact, held in any event in the circumstances that there was no nuisance to the plaintiffs through interference with their television reception by a tall building (see above, p.539). However, if this were wrong, what was the position on interest in the property affected: were the plaintiffs required to have such to sue for private nuisance? The court's finding was that although a substantial link between the person enjoying the use of the affected property and the latter was essential, nevertheless, the trend had been to give mere occupants protection in some circumstances, so that it was no longer tenable to limit the sufficiency of the link to the requirement of proprietary or possessory interests in the property. Occupation of property as a home, therefore, was sufficient to enable the occupier to sue in private nuisance. Clearly too, if the licence to use and occupy is exclusive, arguments in favour of the right to sue are even stronger (see *Crown River Cruises Ltd v. Kimbolton Fireworks Ltd* (1996) *The Times*, March 6 - *supra*, p.523).

Finally, a plaintiff can sue for damage already caused, even if he acquired his interest in land subsequent to the nuisance, and knew of it at the time of acquisition (*Masters v. Brent LBC* [1978] QB 841).

(iv) Those Who can be Sued for Nuisance

1. The person who created the nuisance

He remains liable even after leaving the land on which the nuisance was created (*Thompson v. Gibson* (1841) 7 M & W 456).

Furthermore, it is not necessary for the creator to be in occupation of the land from which the nuisance derives: he can be a visitor. It is even possible to create a private nuisance when on a public road: for example, striking miners demonstrating in the road outside a factory (*Thomas v. NUM (South Wales Area)* [1986] Ch 20), or lorries going in and out of a depot on a road outside the plaintiff's house (*Halsey v. Esso Petroleum* [1961] 1 WLR 683).

One interesting point which emerged in *Cambridge Water*

Co. Ltd v. Eastern Counties Leather plc [1994] 1 All ER 53, HL, was that the dangerous substance which had escaped and caused damage to the water source, was continuing to do so. It was argued for the plaintiffs that although the nuisance had not been reasonably foreseeable on the facts when it was created, thereby negating liability in nuisance, nevertheless, clearly the defendants *were* now aware of its damaging effects on a continuing basis and consequently would satisfy the reasonable foreseeability requirement of liability in nuisance. Not surprisingly, Lord Goff rejected this: foreseeability was to be judged as at the date of creation of the nuisance (p.77 - and at most, if the case *were* one of nuisance, contrary to Lord Goff's view, then he considered that it would have to be treated as having become one of interference from the natural state of the land within *Leakey, supra,* p.544, so that the defendant's personal circumstances and difficulties could be taken into account, *ibid.*).

2. *The person in occupation of land*

He is liable not just for his own acts of nuisance but also for those of the following other persons on his land:

a. Visitors, servants and those under his control

Normal principles of vicarious liability apply.

b. Independent contractors

This is an exception to the normal rule according to which parties are vicariously liable for the acts of their employees, but not for those of independent contractors whom they engage to carry out work for them. Thus, an occupier is liable for any nuisances considered to be the inevitable consequences of activities of the independent contractor. In *Matania v. National Provincial Bank Ltd* [1936] 2 All ER 633, dust and noise from building work above the plaintiff's flat were held to be a nuisance, as the unavoidable consequences of the builders' activities; by its very nature, the work being carried out involved a special danger of nuisance, against which the defendant had failed to safeguard. However, if the nuisance was not inevitable, the occupier is not liable for nuisance created by the independent contractor's negligent work (*Angus v. Dalton* (1881) 6 App Cas 740).

c. Previously created

A person is liable for nuisance created on his property before he acquired his interest, if he knows or ought reasonably to know about it - he is then said to have *adopted* it (*St Anne's Well Brewery Co. v. Roberts* (1929) 140 LT 1).

d. Trespassers

The occupier is liable for nuisance caused by trespassers if he:

- adopts, or
- continues the nuisance.

To *adopt* the nuisance is to make use of it; *continuing* it is where the occupier knows or ought to know of its existence, but does nothing to end it. In *Sedleigh-Denfield v. O'Callaghan* [1940] AC 880, the local authority trespassed on the defendant's land to lay a drainage pipe in the defendant's ditch running alongside the plaintiff's land. Over the years, the end of the pipe became blocked with leaves and debris, because the local authority workers failed to fix a cover on it. After a heavy rain storm, the ditch overflowed and flooded the plaintiff's land. The House of Lords held the defendant liable for nuisance. On the facts:

- the defendant knew of the absence of a cover on the pipe and of the consequent risk of flooding: *continuation* of the nuisance; and
- the defendant also made use of the pipe in order to drain water from his own land: *adoption* of the nuisance.

All that is required in order to prevent nuisance in such cases is that the occupier took such reasonable steps as he could - if any were possible - to discontinue the nuisance (*King v. Liverpool City Council* [1986] 1 WLR 890; *Cambridge Water Co. Ltd v. Eastern Counties Leather plc* [1994] 1 All ER 53, 71, HL).

3. One of several creators

If a person combines with others to create a nuisance which would not have been caused by his act alone, the person is nonetheless liable. Thus, in *Pride of Derby & Derbyshire Angling Association v. British Celanese Ltd* [1953] Ch 149, the defendant factory was held liable for nuisance in polluting a fishing river, although they were not the only factory to have done so.

4. *Landlords*

Even though landlords may be neither occupiers nor creators of a nuisance on property let to a tenant, they will be liable, in addition to the tenant occupier himself, in the following circumstances (see Jones, Textbook on Torts, 1993, p.227 *et seq.*):

(a) where the nuisance was part of the normal use for which the premises were let (*Harris v. James* (1876) 45 LJQB 545 - land let for blasting operations and lime-burning; *Tetley v. Chitty* [1986] 1 All ER 663 - land let for go-karting); or

(b) where the nuisance existed before the tenancy and the landlord knew or ought reasonably to have known of it - even if he obtained the tenant's agreement to remove it (*Brew Brothers Ltd v. Snax (Ross) Ltd* [1970] 1 QB 612); or

(c) where the landlord has reserved the right to enter and repair (*Mint v. Good* [1951] 1 KB 517) because this amounts to retention of control by the landlord, even if he neither knew nor ought to have known of the nuisance (*Wringe v. Cohen* [1940] 1 KB 229) - although the landlord actually has a duty of care towards *anyone* reasonably expected to be affected by defects in the state of the premises - not just to adjoining landowners - under s.4 of the Defective Premises Act 1972, which is therefore wider than common law nuisance (see *supra,* ch.8).

(v) Defences

1. Prescription

Continuation *as a nuisance* for an uninterrupted period of 20 years gives rise to a prescriptive right to commit it.

It is not the activity, but the nuisance, which must be at least 20 years old. In *Sturges v. Bridgman* (1879) 11 Ch D 852, the noise and shaking from the defendant's sweet-making business had gone on for more than 20 years - but this was not sufficient as a defence, because it only became a nuisance when the plaintiff built a set of medical consulting rooms in his garden near the defendant's sweet-making building and this was less than 20 years previously.

2. Statutory authority

It is a defence if the defendant had the express or implied right under a statute to carry on the activity causing the nuisance, provided that the defendant can prove that the nuisance was inevitable and could not have been avoided by the exercise of reasonable care (*Manchester Corporation v. Farnworth* [1930] AC 171).

An example of implied statutory power was *London, Brighton & South Coast Railway v. Truman* (1886) 11 AC 45, where the statute authorized the railway to acquire yards to keep cattle to be transported by rail. The House of Lords held that, since, of necessity, the yards had to be near the stations and people living close to them, the interference with those inhabitants through the noise of the cattle must have been impliedly authorized by the statute and could not amount to nuisance. Again, in *Allen v. Gulf Oil Refining Ltd* [1981] AC 1001, a statute authorized the defendants to acquire land compulsorily for construction of an oil refinery at Milford Haven in South Wales, but did not expressly permit *operation* of the refinery. Local inhabitants complained of smells, traffic and fumes when the refinery was built. The House of Lords held that the operation of the refinery was impliedly authorized by the legislation and consequently the defendants had a defence - provided that the interference caused by the refinery did not go beyond what was the inevitable consequence of operating such a refinery. Lord Diplock said (at p.1014): "Parliament can hardly be supposed to have intended the refinery to be nothing more than a visual adornment to the landscape in an area of natural beauty. Clearly the intention of Parliament was that the refinery was to be operated as such ...". Lord Roskill (at p.1023) too, considered that in these cases, ".. the lesser private rights had to yield to the greater public interest." The latter, however - public benefit - it will be recalled (see *supra*, p.541) although a relevant factor in considering reasonableness in the first place, is not a general defence to nuisance (*Adams v. Ursell* [1913] 1 Ch 269 - fish and chip shop in residential street a nuisance, even though of public benefit).

It would appear too that the grant of *planning permission* to construct a tall building will not be regarded as statutory authority for purposes of providing a defence to nuisance (*Hunter v. Canary Wharf Ltd* (1995) *The Times*, October 13, CA - leave given to appeal to the House of Lords). Thus, in *Wheeler v. J.J. Saunders Ltd* [1995] 3 WLR 466 (CA), the Court of Appeal held that the grant of planning permission to facilitate intensification of pig farming on a farm already used for that purpose did not provide the farmer with a defence to a nuisance action by neighbours complaining about the smell - it was not for an administrative authority to decide on legal nuisance (pp.474, 479 and 481, distinguishing the defence of statutory authority from mere planning authorization). It would have been different had the planning permission authorized a complete change of use, *altering the character of the neighbourhood* as in the public nuisance case of *Gillingham Borough Council v. Medway (Chatham) Dock Co. Ltd* [1993] QB 343: here, if the new use was consistent and reasonable in accordance with the changed character of the locality, the effect would be the absence of nuisance liability (pp.473, 478-9, 481) - and the planning authority no doubt would have balanced competing interests in the neighbourhood in deciding to grant the permission for change of use (p.480).

3. Contribution and consent

The Law Reform (Contributory Negligence) Act 1945 applies as a defence to nuisance, so as to reduce damages if the plaintiff contributed to the loss. So does *volenti non fit injuria* (consent), to the extent that the court will take into account the plaintiff's apparent acceptance of the interference, in its initial assessment of whether the interference should be held to be unreasonable or not. Act of God and act of a stranger can provide a defence, in the absence of adoption or continuation of the nuisance by the defendant. Ignorance of the nuisance on the part of the defendant has previously been considered to negate liability (*Noble v. Harrison* [1926] 2 KB 332). Since *Cambridge Water* confirmed foreseeability of damage as a prerequisite of nuisance, this seems inevitable. How can the defendant reasonably be expected to foresee a nuisance from a state of affairs of which he is unaware? It could be a different matter of course if he were aware of the state of affairs, but unaware of its effects upon the plaintiff; or probably also where the defendant ought to have known of the activities creating the interference, but had wilfully shut his eyes to the situation.

As seen earlier, nuisance resulting from several persons will not be a defence to an action brought against just one (*Thorpe v. Brumfitt* (1873) LR 8 Ch App 650; *Pride of Derby & Derbyshire Angling Association Ltd v. British Celanese Ltd* [1953] Ch 149).

(vi) Coming to the Nuisance is not a Defence

It would be natural to assume that this was a defence: the plaintiff knew what he was letting himself in for. But it is not a defence (*Bliss v. Hall* (1838) 4 Bing NC 183).
The reason?

This seems to be that buyers would otherwise be reluctant to purchase land if there was a nuisance next door and a purchaser would have no remedy; and people would otherwise acquire a permanent "right" of nuisance over neighbouring land once it had been sold to a new owner or if there was a new occupier. The plaintiff doctor in *Sturges v. Bridgman* knew that there was a sweet-manufacturing business next door when he built his new consulting rooms in the garden near to it, yet the sweet business thereby became a nuisance. However, even if coming to a nuisance is no defence, the court may still take the factor into account in connexion with remedies, by refusing to grant an injunction to the plaintiff (*Miller v. Jackson* [1977] QB 966 - the plaintiffs knew of the risk when they bought a house near a cricket ground, which had been there for 70 years before the houses were even built, so damages would have to suffice in lieu of an injunction); furthermore, the locality factor in assessment of reasonable interference will be a further control upon actions for nuisance - people moving into an area with existing interference conforming to the general character of the neighbourhood do not have things all their own way (*supra*, p.538, *et seq.*).

(vii) Remedies

1. Damages

Physical damage and damage to land are not hard to calculate on normal principles. But what of smells and discomfort? In *Bone v. Seal* [1975] 1 All ER 787, rules on loss of amenity - loss of life's enjoyment - in personal injuries cases were used on analogy in the absence of damage to health or property of the plaintiff: £1,000 was awarded to the plaintiff for having had to suffer the smell of a pig farm for more than 12 years.

Damages may be awarded on their own or combined with an injunction. The test for remoteness is reasonable foreseeability (*The Wagon Mound (No.2)* [1967] 1 AC 617; and *Cambridge Water Co. Ltd v. Eastern Counties Leather plc* [1994] 1 All ER 53, at p.72, HL, *per* Lord Goff, see *supra*, p.524, *et seq.*).

2. Injunction

These are discretionary, but very common so as to restrain the continuation of the nuisance (*Redland Bricks Ltd v. Morris*

[1970] AC 652).

The court has the power to award damages in lieu of an injunction under s.50 of the Supreme Court Act 1981 where:

- the interference with the plaintiff is small; and
- can be calculated in money; and
- will be satisfied by a small money payment; and
- it would be oppressive to the defendant to grant an injunction (*Shelfer v. City of London Electric Lighting Co.* [1895] 1 Ch 287, at p.372, per A.L. Smith, LJ).

Normal principles for exercise of the equitable discretion apply (for example, the plaintiff should not have delayed unreasonably in seeking a remedy).

Normally courts are not particularly impressed with claims as to the disastrous and oppressive effects of injunctions for defendants (*Attorney-General v. Birmingham Corporation* (1858) 4 K & J 528). Furthermore, interference with a plaintiff from the nuisance has to be *very* small for damages to be awarded in lieu of an injunction, so that richer defendants cannot effectively purchase plaintiffs' claims to an injunction with damages (*Elliott v. London Borough of Islington* [1991] 10 EG 145 - tree roots encroaching into the plaintiff's garden held not a trivial matter). Refusal of injunctive relief in *Miller v. Jackson* (cricket balls landing on the plaintiff's house), on the ground that the public's interests in sport and recreation should prevail over those of individuals in maintaining their uninterrupted and unspoilt private enjoyment of land, seems out-of-step with this approach - although, the fact that the plaintiffs "came to the nuisance" in that case was clearly a material factor, as was the fundamental social utility and importance of the game of cricket to the English way of life! Thus, in *Kennaway v. Thompson* [1981] QB 88, the Court of Appeal re-affirmed that private interests would prevail over the public's, so that damages in place of injunction were exceptional and not appropriate where the plaintiff occupier's peace and quiet was disturbed by the defendant's power boat racing on a nearby lake.

3. *Abatement*

This is a form of self-help - an old remedy not greatly beloved of the courts in modern times. The victim takes steps himself to remove the nuisance, if necessary by entering upon the wrongdoer's land to do so, and will have a good defence to trespass in the absence of unnecessary damage.

The victim must notify the perpetrator of the nuisance before carrying out the abatement, except where:

(a) there is an emergency threatening life or property; or
(b) he can remove the nuisance without entering upon the land.

Abatement and legal proceedings are alternative remedies - plaintiffs cannot try both, except in respect of past damage.

The usual examples are encroachment by tree branches and roots. When they are cut, they must be returned.

(viii) Legal Nature of Nuisance Liability

It is often debated whether liability in nuisance is strict or fault-based.

Most commentators deny that it is strict, except in the case of physical damage or interference with natural rights or servitudes, where, it was previously seen (*supra*, p.532, *et seq.*), the defendant tends to be held to be liable regardless of whether his conduct was reasonable or not. Lord Wright in *Sedleigh-Denfield v. O'Callaghan* [1940] AC 880, at p.904) said that liability for nuisance was not, at least in modern law, a strict or absolute liability; and in *The Wagon Mound (No.2)* [1967] 1 AC 617, Lord Reid commented that although negligence in the narrow sense was not required, nevertheless, fault of some kind was almost always necessary for liability in nuisance (from which decision it is further clear that the test for remoteness of damage in nuisance is reasonable foreseeability, as in the case of negligence, *supra*, p.556). This of course has now been confirmed by Lord Goff in *Cambridge Water Co. v. Eastern Counties Leather* [1994] 1 All ER 53, HL: no liability without reasonable foreseeability; but liability even if the defendant behaved reasonably. The truth therefore lies somewhere between the two extremes of fault and strict liability. Nuisance still has a distinct role. Certainly, if plaintiffs are unable to establish a breach of a duty of care by the defendant in negligence through lack of reasonable care, they would then be well advised to try nuisance. Taking into account elements including differences in remedy-structures, levels of fault, potential plaintiffs and defendants and other factors previously considered, torts of nuisance and negligence should continue to be regarded as doctrinally, if not also conceptually, independent and, in practice, in many cases will be pleaded in the alternative.

3. Public Nuisance

(i) Meaning

In *Attorney-General v. PYA Quarries Ltd* [1957] 2 QB 169, at p.184, Romer, LJ described public nuisance as an act "which materially affects the reasonable comfort and convenience of life of a class of Her Majesty's subjects." Examples include queuing or picketing on the public highway; holding a noisy pop concert; blocking or interfering with a waterway; making obscene telephone calls to women in a particular area.

1. Crime

Public nuisance is also a crime, which will be prosecuted by the Attorney General on behalf of the public (*R. v. Shorrock* [1993] 3 WLR 698; and see *R. v. Johnson, infra* Appendix).

2. Relationship with private nuisance

Some of the elements are very different.

Public nuisance is caused *to the public.* Members of the public can sue even if they have no interest in land and no land is affected, although, if it is, public and private nuisance can then overlap. There is no defence of 20-year prescription in public nuisance; nor is there in practice a need for repetition over a period. As will be seen, there are other important differences concerning the ways in which the two torts are constituted.

(ii) Materially Affects Reasonable Comfort and Convenience of a Class

1. Material

Whether the effect is *material* is a question of fact.

2. Reasonable

As in private nuisance, the plaintiff must first persuade the court that the interference caused to the comfort and convenience of life is not reasonable (see *Hunter v. Canary Wharf Ltd* (1995) *The Times*, October 13, CA, *supra*, p.539 - conclusion that interference with television reception by a tall building in an urban area was not a private nuisance said also to apply to public nuisance).

The essence of public nuisance is that it must affect the *public*: not the entire population, but a class, a number of people. Nor need it affect all members of the class potentially involved (*AG v. PYA Quarries Ltd*).

In *AG v. PYA Quarries Ltd*, the defendants were held liable for creating a public nuisance through dust and vibrations caused by their quarrying operations, even though they had contended that not enough people were affected for it to be a public nuisance.

The real question therefore is whether a sufficient section of the locality has been so affected as to deserve the protection of the law? Infrequent stock-car racing in *AG v. Hastings Corporation* (1950) Sol J 225 was held not to be a public nuisance, because not enough people were inconvenienced by the occasional meetings (but see *infra* Appendix).

(iii) Extra Damage

The plaintiff who sues for the tort of public nuisance must show that he has suffered particular damage, more than others affected by the nuisance.

The additional damage and inconvenience must be substantial. This will not be difficult to prove, where it consists of physical damage. In other cases, the court must simply assess the facts. In *Boyd v. Great Northern Railway Co.* [1895] 2 IR 555, 20 minutes delay for a doctor at a railway crossing was considered sufficiently substantial, even though delay will not usually be so (*Winterbottom v. Lord Derby* (1867) LR 2 Ex 316). Where obstruction of the highway also prevented customers gaining access to the plaintiff's shop, this was sufficient in *Benjamin v. Storr* (1874) LR 9 CP 400; and in *Rose v. Miles* (1815) 4 M & S 101, it was sufficient for the plaintiff to recover that the defendant had blocked a canal with his boat, so that the plaintiff had had to unload his barge and transport the cargo by land at great expense.

All members of the public can complain of the *crime* of public nuisance; but only those particularly affected can bring proceedings in tort.

(iv) Public Nuisance on the Highway

Many of the modern cases of public nuisance concern *obstruction of* or *danger on* or *from* the "highway" - public roads and pavements (and probably also navigable rivers: see *Crown River Cruises Ltd v. Kimbolton Fireworks Ltd* (1996) *The Times,* March 6, QBD, Potter, J).

1. Obstruction

This consists of acts preventing the public from being able to pass and re-pass.

In *Jacobs v. London County Council* [1950] AC 361, at p.375, Lord Simmonds adopted the description of "any wrongful act or omission upon or near a highway, whereby the public are prevented from freely, safely and conveniently passing along the highway."

This has long been a crime as well. The obstruction may take many forms: a ditch, rocks, theatre queues, crowds, strike pickets, funeral procession, lorries at night, a pipe laid across a pavement causing the plaintiff to trip, a barge on a public river, a person standing in the way, a vehicle blocking the road - and the court must assess whether inconvenience to the plaintiff, over and above that to the public in general, is unreasonable. If, for example, the obstruction is merely temporary, it may not be considered an unreasonable inconvenience (*Harper v. Haden & Sons Ltd* [1933] Ch 298 - temporary scaffolding obstructing access not a nuisance). It is all a question of reasonableness of interference, whether or not the defendant actually intended to create the nuisance (*Lyons v. Gulliver* [1914] 1 Ch 631). Benefit to the public is no defence to the nuisance (*R. v. Train* (1862) 2 B & S 640), but will be a material factor in assessing reasonableness of interference with the plaintiff's comfort and convenience.

Naturally, a state of affairs may be both an obstruction of the highway and within the next category - a danger on or to the highway.

2. *Dangers*

On the highway. These can be from an obstruction (*Burgess v. Gray* (1845) 1 CB 578 - pile of rubble; *Ware v. Garston Haulage Co.* [1944] KB 30 - unlit vehicle parked on road); slippery piece of fat from a butcher's shop (*Dollman v. Hillman* [1941] 1 All ER 355); or smoke, affecting drivers' visibility (*Holling v. Yorkshire Traction Co.* [1948] 2 All ER 662).

The criterion remains one of reasonableness, taking into account the existence of the danger. In *Trevett v. Lee* [1955] 1 All ER 406, the plaintiff fell over a hosepipe stretching across a country lane *in daylight* and this was held not to amount to a public nuisance in all the circumstances (compare *Dymond v. Pearce* [1972] 1 QB 496 - lorry parked overnight under street lamps held public nuisance).

The action can be more useful than one in negligence, because the plaintiff can claim for pure economic loss (*Rose v. Miles* (1815) 4 M & S 101 - cost of extra transport).

Danger from premises adjoining highway. Occupiers of premises adjoining the highway are liable for public nuisance for dangers to passersby: a falling lamp, a loose slate, a collapsing wall, a dilapidated fence - all can cause damage and injury. In *Castle v. St Augustine's Links* (1922) 38 TLR 615, golf balls were continually being hit onto the road and eventually went through the windscreen of the plaintiff's car: public nuisance.

It would seem that:

(a) when the danger is man-made, public nuisance can exist whether or not the defendant knew or ought to have known of it; but

(b) where it was through natural causes, for example, a tree root, or caused by a hidden defect such as defective foundations causing subsidence, or by a trespasser, the person responsible for repair is only liable if he knew or ought to have known of the danger (*Wringe v. Cohen* [1940] 1 KB 229).

Thus, in *British Road Services v. Slater* [1964] 1 All ER 816 it was not foreseeable that an overhanging tree branch would knock a packing case off a passing lorry into the path of the vehicle behind; nor in *Caminer v. Northern and London Investment Trust Ltd* [1951] AC 88 that a tree with rotten roots would fall across a road: no public nuisance.

In the case of liability for man-made dangers, the person with responsibility for maintaining the premises in a state of repair is even liable for an independent contractor engaged to carry out maintenance (*Tarry v. Ashton* (1876) 1 QBD 314 - falling lamp).

Clearly, however, if *Cambridge Water* were now to be extended to public nuisance, even in the case of man-made danger reasonable foreseeability by the defendant would be required for liability to exist (see Lord Goff, at p.72, equating public and private nuisance for recovery of damages).

Liability of the highway authorities. At common law, the public highway authorities were liable if they carried out repairs or maintenance negligently ("misfeasance"), but not if they failed to repair the roads at all ("non-feasance").

Their liability is now specifically regulated by the

Highways Act 1980 which removes the distinction between misfeasance and non-feasance and makes the authority liable for breach of statutory duty, unless they took reasonable care to ensure that the highway was not dangerous. It seems that the burden of proving such reasonable steps may rest upon the defendant authority (*Griffiths v. Liverpool Corporation* [1967] 1 QB 374).

However, according to the Court of Appeal, the authority is only liable for physical, not purely economic, damage (*Wentworth v. Wiltshire County Council* [1993] 2 WLR 175).

(v) Defences

These are as in tort generally - although, in *Hunter v. Canary Wharf Ltd* (1995) *The Times,* October 13, CA, the Court of Appeal indicated, first, that grant of planning permission to build would not amount to statutory authority for the purposes, and secondly, statutory authority would not amount to a defence to public nuisance in any event (leave to appeal to the House of Lords was granted to the parties, see *supra,* p.553) (possibly though, planning permission *might* be a defence to public nuisance alleged to arise out of the *activities* carried on subsequently to construction of the structure for which consent was granted - as opposed to that caused by the building work itself - on the ground that the construction had thereby changed the character of the neighbourhood: see the High Court decision in *Gillingham Borough Council v. Medway (Chatham) Dock Co. Ltd* [1993] QB 343, and that of the Court of Appeal in *Wheeler v. J.J. Saunders Ltd* [1995] 3 WLR 466, CA, relating to private nuisance, *supra*).

(vi) Remedies

1. Damages

These are available for physical or financial loss suffered by the plaintiff. Exemplary damages will not be awarded for public nuisance (*Gibbons v. South West Water Services Ltd* (1992) *The Times,* November 26). It would seem from *dicta* of Lord Goff in *Cambridge Water Co. Ltd v. Eastern Counties Leather plc* [1994] 1 All ER 53, at p.72, HL, that the test of remoteness of damage in (private or) public nuisance is one of reasonable foreseeability.

2. *Injunctions*

These may be awarded - but are discretionary as usual.

Further reading:

Brazier, *Street on Torts,* 9th ed, 1993 (Butterworth & Co., Ltd): ch.19.

Fleming, J.G., *The Law of Torts,* 8th ed, 1992 (The Law Book Company, Sydney): ch.21.

Gearty, "The Place of Private Nuisance in the Modern Law of Torts" (1989) 48 *Cambridge Law Journal* 214.

Hepple, B.A. and Matthews, M.H., *Tort: Cases and Materials,* 4th ed, 1991 (Butterworth & Co., London): ch.14.

Heuston, R.F.V. and Buckley, R.A., *Salmond and Heuston on The Law of Torts,* 20th ed, 1992 (Sweet & Maxwell, London): ch.5.

Howarth, D., *Textbook on Tort,* 1995 (Butterworth & Co., London): ch.11.

Jones, M.A., *Textbook on Torts,* 4th ed, 1993 (Blackstone, London): ch.7.

Kodilinye, "Public Nuisance and Particular Damage in Modern Law" (1986) 6 *Legal Studies* 182.

Kodilinye, "Standing to Sue in Private Nuisance" (1989) 9 *Legal Studies* 284.

Markesinis, B.S. and Deakin, S.F., *Tort Law,* 3rd ed, 1994 (Clarendon Press, Oxford): ch.5.

Newark, "The Boundaries of Nuisance" (1949) 65 *Quarterly Law Review* 480.

Rogers, W.V.H., *Winfield and Jolowicz on Tort*, 14th ed, 1994 (Sweet & Maxwell, London): ch.14.

Spencer, "Public Nuisance: A Critical Examination" (1989) 48 *Cambridge Law Journal* 55.

Stanton, K.M., *The Modern Law of Tort*, 1994 (The Law Book Company, Sydney): ch.20.

Weir, T., *A Casebook on Tort*, 7th ed, 1992 (Sweet & Maxwell, London): ch.10.

Chapter 24

The Rule in Rylands v. Fletcher

(i) No Longer Wholly Strict Liability

This was traditionally considered to be a true tort of strict liability, not requiring *fault* on the part of the defendant in respect of damage caused by dangerous things kept on land, in the following dual sense:

- foreseeability of harm to the plaintiff would not be required as a condition of liability (see Mann, LJ in the Court of Appeal proceedings in *Cambridge Water Co. Ltd v. Eastern Counties Leather plc* [1994] 1 All ER 53, at p.61, CA), and
- nor would the defendant be able to escape liability by showing that he had exercised all reasonable care to avoid causing damage to the plaintiff.

The preceding two classic features correspond to the equivalent former perception of the tort of nuisance, to which *Rylands v. Fletcher* is closely related (see *supra*, ch.23).

Thus, in *Rylands v. Fletcher* (1866) LR 1 Exch 265, (1868) LR 3 HL 330, Blackburn, J in the Exchequer Chamber, spoke the words which formed the basis of the rule:

"We think that the true rule of law is, that the person

who for his own purposes brings on his lands and collects and keeps there anything likely to do mischief if it escapes, must keep it in at his peril, and, if he does not do so, is *prima facie* answerable for all the damage which is the natural consequence of its escape. He can excuse himself by showing that the escape was owing to the plaintiff's default; or perhaps that the escape was the consequence of vis major, or the act of God; but as nothing of this sort exists here, it is unnecessary to inquire what excuse would be sufficient. The general rule, as above stated, seems on principle just. The person whose grass or corn is eaten down by the escaping cattle of his neighbour, or whose mine is flooded by the water from his neighbour's reservoir, or whose cellar is invaded by the filth of his neighbour's privy, or whose habitation is made unhealthy by the fumes and noisome vapours of his neighbour's alkali works, is damnified without any fault of his own; and it seems but reasonable and just that the neighbour, who has brought something on his own property which was not naturally there, harmless to others so long as it is confined to his own property, but which he knows to be mischievous if it gets on his neighbour's, should be obliged to make good the damage which ensues if he does not succeed in confining it to his own property. But for his act in bringing it there no mischief could have accrued, and it seems but just that he should at his peril keep it there so that no mischief may accrue, or answer for the natural and anticipated consequences. And upon authority, this we think is established to be the law whether the things so brought be beasts, or water, or filth, or stenches."

The dictum was subsequently approved in the case by the House of Lords, which added, however, that the defendant's use of the land was required to be *non-natural,* and the latter condition was subsequently used by courts as a way of imposing policy restrictions upon the operation of the rule.

So this principle, borne of an age of industrialization, thenceforth came to be known as "the rule in *Rylands v. Fletcher*".

Recently, however, in the case of *Cambridge Water Co. v. Eastern Counties Leather* [1994] 1 All ER 53, HL, Lord Goff in the House of Lords, agreed with by the other Lords, reviewed the rule of liability for escape of dangerous things in *Rylands v. Fletcher,* as a result of which it is now clear that *Rylands v. Fletcher* is not a general rule of wholly strict liability for escape of dangerous substances: it is simply a specific branch of the law of nuisance, applicable to *isolated* incidents (consequently, not otherwise capable of constituting a nuisance) of *escape.* Accordingly, as in the case of nuisance, no longer actually in issue in the proceedings in the House of Lords (see *supra,* ch.23 - because the plaintiff had recognized that reasonable foreseeability was a requirement, held not to be satisfied on the facts, for negligence and nuisance liability, but wished to fight its application to *Rylands v. Fletcher*), the position held to exist in respect of *Rylands v. Fletcher* liability was:

1. it was strict to the extent that a defendant would be found to be liable notwithstanding that he had exercised all reasonable care to avoid causing damage to the plaintiff, but

2. not also in the matter of reasonable foreseeability of damage - this would be required as a precondition of liability.

The facts of *Cambridge Water* were that the defendant leather manufacturer used a certain chemical in its tanning process, which spilled on the concrete floor of its premises, until its practices were changed in 1971. All that was foreseeable from the spillage at the time was that workers could have been affected by fumes. What in fact occurred was that the chemical seeped through the floor into an underground water hole a mile away and contaminated the water which the plaintiff water company began to draw in 1979. The plaintiffs had to spend £1 million developing a new water source, because an EU Directive had entered into force in the United Kingdom in 1985 prohibiting use of water containing the particular chemical. These consequences were not foreseeable by the defendants.

The House of Lords through Lord Goff held that neither in nuisance (or negligence, dropped in the appeal) nor in *Rylands v. Fletcher* were the defendants liable for the unforeseen consequences of their activities: liability in nuisance was strict to the extent that the creator would not have a defence that he had taken all reasonable care to prevent interference; yet, just as *The Wagon Mould (No.2)* was relied on previously in support of the finding of a rule of reasonable foreseeability of loss for nuisance liability, so should it be in respect of *Rylands v. Fletcher*, essentially an extension of the law of nuisance to cases of isolated escape (p.75).

In coming to this conclusion, Lord Goff first noted that

in *Rylands v. Fletcher*, Blackburn, J spoke of "anything *likely* to do mischief if it escapes" and "which he *knows* to be mischievous" and liability to "answer for the natural *and anticipated* consequences" - all of which suggested reasonable foreseeability; yet he also indicated that the defendant had to keep the thing in *at his peril* whether the escape was *by negligence or not* (p.73). Accordingly, Lord Goff concluded: "The general tenor of his statement of principle is therefore that knowledge, or at least foreseeability of the risk, is a prerequisite of the recovery of damages under the principle; but that the principle is one of strict liability in the sense that the defendant may be held liable notwithstanding that he has exercised all due care to prevent the escape from occurring (p.73)."

Lord Goff went on to consider the case authorities on the matter of reasonable foreseeability in *Rylands v. Fletcher.* He found these to be inconclusive and academic opinion divided (pp.73-5), in view of which he felt that he was entitled to approach the question *as a matter of principle* open for consideration by the House of Lords (p.75). Thus, for a number of reasons, the rule should be that reasonable foreseeability of damage *was* required in order to establish liability in *Rylands v. Fletcher*: a) because of its historical connexion with nuisance; and b) one leading commentator had convincingly demonstrated that in his judgment in *Rylands v. Fletcher,* Blackburn, J did not regard his statement as breaking new ground but merely as extending the law of nuisance to cases of isolated escape - and consequently, it was logical to apply the same rule of reasonable foreseeability from *The Wagon Mound (No.2)* as governed nuisance to *Rylands v. Fletcher* (p.75). Lord Goff thought that there were serious difficulties with the opposite approach which was to regard *Rylands v. Fletcher* not as an extension of nuisance but as a separate tort of strict liability for damage resulting from ultra-hazardous operations as in the United States, so that costs would be part of business overheads instead of for victims, insurers or the community at large to discharge (p.75): a) in the first place, if accepted, such a principle should apply without restrictions, and the rule in *Read v. J. Lyons & Co. Ltd* (*infra*, p.584) that the defendant is only liable if there is an *escape* of the dangerous object, seemed inconsistent with this (pp.75-6); and b) the Law Commission in its Report on *Civil Liability for Dangerous Things and Activities* (Law Com No.32) 1970 had doubts about applying a rule of strict liability to ultra-hazardous activities (p.76).

Thus, Lord Goff concluded:

> "If the Law Commission is unwilling to consider statutory reform on this basis, it must follow that Judges should if anything be even more reluctant to proceed down that path.
>
> "Like the Judge in the present case, I incline to the opinion that, as a general rule, it is more appropriate for strict liability in respect of operations of high risk to be imposed by Parliament, than by the courts. If such liability is imposed by statute, the relevant activities can be identified, and those concerned can know where they stand. Furthermore, statute can where appropriate lay down precise criteria establishing the incidence and scope of such liability.
>
> "It is of particular relevance that the present case is

concerned with environmental pollution. The protection and preservation of the environment is now perceived as being of crucial importance to the future of mankind; and public bodies, both national and international, are taking significant steps towards the establishment of legislation which will promote the protection of the environment, and make the polluter pay for damage to the environment for which he is responsible - as can be seen from the WHO, EEC and national regulations to which I have previously referred. But it does not follow from these developments that a common law principle, such as the rule in *Rylands v. Fletcher,* should be developed or rendered more strict to provide for liability in respect of such pollution. On the contrary, given that so much well-informed and carefully structured legislation is now being put in place for this purpose, there is less need for the courts to develop a common law principle to achieve the same end, and indeed it may well be undesirable that they should do so.

"Having regard to these considerations, and in particular to the step which this House has already taken in *Read v. Lyons* to contain the scope of liability under the rule in *Rylands v. Fletcher,* it appears to me to be appropriate now to take the view that foreseeability of damage of the relevant type should be regarded as a prerequisite of liability in damages under the rule. Such a conclusion can, as I have already stated, be derived from Blackburn, J's original statement of the law; and I can see no good reason why this prerequisite should not be recognized under the rule, as it has been in the case of private nuisance. In particular, I do not regard the two authorities cited to your Lordships, *West v. Bristol Tramways Co.* [1908] 2 KB 14, [1908-10] All ER Rep 215 and *Rainham Chemical Works Ltd v. Belvedere Fish Guano Co. Ltd* [1921] 2 AC 465, [1921] All ER Rep 48, as providing any strong pointer towards a contrary conclusion. It would moreover lead to a more coherent body of common law principles if the rule were to be regarded essentially as an extension of the law of nuisance to cases of isolated escapes from land, even though the rule as established is not limited to escapes which are in fact isolated. I wish to point out, however, that in truth the escape of the PCE from ECL's land, in the form of trace elements carried in percolating water, has not been an isolated escape, but a continuing escape resulting from a state of affairs which has come into existence at the base of the chalk aquifer underneath ECL's premises. Classically, this would have been regarded as a case of nuisance; and it would seem strange if, by characterizing the case as one falling under the rule in *Rylands v. Fletcher*, the liability should thereby be rendered more strict in the circumstances of the present case" (pp.76-7).

Finally, and, in view of the foregoing, to no great surprise, Lord Goff reached the decision on the facts that the damage could not reasonably have been foreseen at the time when the dangerous substance was brought onto the defendant's land, nor even later when it was being used.

The claim for damages under the rule in *Rylands v. Fletcher* would fail (pp.77 and 78).

Criticisms of the Lords' judgment to equivalent effect in

relation to nuisance liability has previously been registered (see *supra*, p.528, *et seq.*). The comments are equally apposite to *Rylands v. Fletcher* liability, indeed more so in view of the additional seriousness of escapes. Nuisance and *Rylands v. Fletcher* have as their underlying objective the protection of vulnerable interests in society - and foreseeability could still have been permitted to act as a restriction on damages as a rule for remoteness of damage, in accordance with *The Wagon Mound (No.2)*, in all probability thereby fulfilling its proper role. In this writer's opinion, to apply reasonable foreseeability to initial liability in nuisance and *Rylands v. Fletcher* constitutes a major deviation from their true function and development. No more need be said.

In the future, therefore, it has to be accepted that *Rylands v. Fletcher* is no longer a tort of strict liability in the fullest sense:

(a) liability for isolated escape will continue to exist where the traditional elements are satisfied, even where the defendant used all reasonable care to prevent damage; but
(b) now the defendant can only be held to be liable if the danger which occurred was reasonably foreseeable.

(ii) Elements of the Rule in Rylands v. Fletcher

The facts of *Rylands v. Fletcher* were that the defendant mill owners employed independent contractors to build a water reservoir on their land. The contractors failed to ensure that old mineshafts on the property leading to the plaintiff's mines were blocked up, and when the reservoir was filled, the plaintiff's mines were flooded. There could be no nuisance liability because the event complained of was an isolated act; nor had the defendants themselves been negligent and they would not be vicariously liable for the actions of the independent contractor; and trespass would not exist because the interference was indirect. However, the court held the defendants liable for escape of a dangerous thing on their land: *water*.

The following, therefore, are the elements which have traditionally been required to be established for liability to be made out under the rule in *Rylands v. Fletcher*:

1. *Anything likely to do mischief if it escapes: dangerous things*

The "thing" should be capable of causing damage in the event of its escape from the land - for example, gas, water, electricity, chemicals - all foreseeably dangerous substances in the event of escape, although, in practice, anything which actually escapes and causes damage is likely to be held to be dangerous by virtue of that very fact.

2. *Brings on the land and collects and keeps there*

The rule does not apply to the escape of things naturally on the land, such as rocks which have not been dug up, weeds not planted and water naturally accumulated (*Giles v. Walker* (1890) 24 QBD 656). Instead, the plaintiff must try to succeed in nuisance (if repeated or continuing) or negligence (if duty of care broken).

3. *For his own purposes*

It is not enough if the potentially dangerous thing is brought onto the land by the defendant for the benefit of another person, say, by a landlord for his tenant (*Rainham Chemical Works v. Belvedere Fish Guano Co. Ltd* [1921] 2 AC 465).

4. *Non-natural user*

This was the condition added by Lord Cairns, LC in the House of Lords in *Rylands v. Fletcher* (1868) LR 3 HL 330: and was commented upon by the House of Lords in *Cambridge Water.*

What did it mean?

Prior to *Cambridge Water*, in *Rickards v. Lothian* [1913] AC 263, at p.280, Lord Moulton described it as "some special use bringing with it increased danger to others and must not merely be the ordinary use of the land or such a use as is proper for the general benefit of the community." Furthermore, it would appear that "special" and "ordinary" were to depend upon the customs of the time and place and judicial recognition of this: "... all the circumstances of the time and place must be taken into consideration, so that what might be regarded as dangerous or non-natural may vary according to those circumstances" (*Read v. J. Lyons & Co. Ltd* [1947] AC 156, at p.176, per Lord Porter). In *Rickards v. Lothian* itself, the plaintiffs were tenants of offices on the second floor of a building occupied by the defendants. The plaintiffs' offices were flooded because a sink on the fourth floor had been blocked with soap and string and the tap turned on by a malicious third party. The defendants were not liable. Installation of a sink and tap to provide water was an ordinary use of land.

Clearly, policy considerations by the courts would play a leading role in decisions upon whether usage is natural or not.

Is it natural to garage a car with a full tank of petrol? Seemingly in 1919, it was not so (*Musgrove v. Pandelis* [1919] 2 KB 43). What of munitions in wartime? Again, not so in 1921 (*Rainham Chemical Works Ltd v. Belvedere Fish Guano Co. Ltd*), but possibly in 1947 (*Read v. J. Lyons & Co. Ltd*). Domestic water and electricity on the other hand, were held to constitute natural user (*Collingwood v. Home & Colonial Stores Ltd* [1936] 3 All ER 200).

It seemed from Lord Moulton's statement in *Rickards v. Lothian (supra)* that in assessing non-natural quality of user, courts would balance:

- increased risk with
- general benefit to the community

and courts were thereby enabled to reach policy decisions as to when strict liability should properly be imposed.

Fire risks from storage of combustible materials, for example, could frequently expect to be held to be non-natural user (*Mason v. Levy Auto Parts of England Ltd* [1967] 2 QB 530).

The criterion of general benefit to the community gave courts the freedom to find natural user on policy grounds. The key word was "proper": many dangerous activities could be said to be for the benefit of the community, but not always even then was it *proper* in the restricted policy context of legal liability for escape. If not, user would be classified as non-natural.

Nevertheless, all of the preceding must now be regarded as highly suspect, following the *Cambridge Water* case.

There, Lord Goff made a number of pronouncements about the meaning of non-natural user, which were strictly speaking *obiter dicta* since he had already held the reasonable foreseeability requirement for recovery under *Rylands v. Fletcher* not to have been satisfied and the plaintiff consequently to be unable to recover (*supra*, pp.576, *et seq.*).

(a) *Factual as opposed to evaluative meaning.* Lord Goff pointed to the fact that the meaning of the expression had changed and developed over the years. There was no doubt that Blackburn, J had originally intended it in a factual sense, to describe things which the defendant had brought onto his land and which were not there - naturally - before; and in the House of Lords in *Rylands v. Fletcher,* Lord Cairns, who had coined the phrase "non-natural use", was also said to have been unlikely to have intended anything more than Blackburn, J in the court below (p.78).

(b) *Developed meaning as a policy restriction.* Nevertheless, the law had "long since departed from any such simple idea, redolent of a different age" and at least since *Rickards v. Lothian* natural use had been extended to embrace the concept of *ordinary* use of land, whether domestic or even recreational and certain industrial usage (p.78). The benefit of this development was thought to be its flexibility: strict liability under *Rylands v. Fletcher* could be controlled through policy decisions as to what was and what was not held to amount to non-natural user (pp.78-9); and earlier in his judgment, Lord Goff had contemplated that the natural use criterion, as it had developed in *Rylands v. Fletcher,* might be regarded as the equivalent of the "reasonableness of defendant's behaviour" control mechanism in the law of nuisance (p.71).

On the other hand, there were a number of objections to the vague concept of non-natural use as it had developed, in particular to the supposed 'general benefit to the community' alternative to ordinary use of land in *Rickards v. Lothian (supra)*: Lord Goff doubted whether this concept should be extended beyond provision of services to local industry, so as also to cover the wider interests of the local community or of the community at large, since otherwise it was "difficult to see how the exception can be kept within reasonable bounds" (p.79 - munitions in wartime, as discussed in *Read v. J. Lyons & Co. Ltd*?). Lord Goff himself did not feel able to accept that "the creation of employment as such, even in a small industrial complex, is sufficient of itself to establish a particular use as constituting a natural or ordinary use of land" (*ibid.*). As it happened, however, it was unnecessary for Lord Goff to attempt any redefinition of the concept of natural or ordinary use in *Cambridge Water,* because, on the facts, even according to the developments described, he considered the storage of substantial quantities of chemicals on industrial premises to be "an almost classic case of non-natural use" and that creation of employment as a benefit to the local community would not convert the case into one of natural user (p.79).

In the end, Lord Goff intimated that the natural use and benefit to the community criterion was likely to lose much of its influence in the light of his further finding in the case that reasonable foreseeability was a requirement of liability in *Rylands v. Fletcher*. The latter was now the main policy control on liability and non-natural user was likely to become less technical and could revert to its originally intended factual meaning of anything which was brought onto the land and which would be dangerous if it escaped:

> "It may well be that, now that it is recognized that foreseeability of harm of the relevant type is a prerequisite of liability in damages under the rule, the courts may feel less pressure to extend the concept of natural use to circumstances such as those in the present case; and in due course it may become easier to control this exception, and to ensure that it has a more recognizable basis of principle" (p.79).

Thus, after *Cambridge Water* it may be the case that dangerous things which were not already on the land but were brought onto it by the defendant may no longer be saved from giving rise to liability by a finding that their use is not out of the ordinary or is otherwise proper for the benefit of the community - even though on the facts of *Cambridge Water* itself, it was not necessary to go this far in redefining the rule in *Rylands v. Fletcher* so as expressly to incorporate such a development.

5. *Escape*

For the rule to apply, the dangerous thing or its effects must have escaped from the land in question: indeed, according to the terms of Blackburn, J's statement (*supra*, p.570) the thing need only be dangerous *if* (meaning in the event that) it escapes, and otherwise is harmless. In *Read v. J. Lyons & Co. Ltd* [1947] AC 156, the plaintiff was injured when an artillery shell exploded on the production line at the defendant munitions factory where she was employed as an inspector during the Second World War. The defendants were held not liable under *Rylands v. Fletcher* because the explosion was confined to the factory and had not escaped. In *Crown River Cruises Ltd v. Kimbolton Fireworks Ltd* (1996) *The Times,* March 6, Potter, J in the High Court considered *obiter* that escape in *Rylands v. Fletcher* would cover intentional release of the dangerous substance, not merely accidental escape - albeit that he expressed himself to be conscious of "current judicial and academic reserve" towards extension of *Rylands v. Fletcher* beyond its present limits.

6. *Defendants*

There is thought to be no requirement that the defendant should have ownership or possession of the land from which the dangerous thing escapes. He need only be the occupier.

7. *Plaintiffs*

Because of its similarity to nuisance (see *supra*, ch.23), suggestions have been made that a plaintiff in *Rylands v. Fletcher* (see *supra,* pp.450-1, and proceedings must be an occupier or have some other interest in the affected land (*Weller & Co. v. Foot & Mouth Disease Research Institute* [1966] 1 QB 569 - auctioneer's business affected by escape of foot and mouth disease, unable to recover).

Many commentators take the opposite view, however,

on the ground that this would be inconsistent with the objective of *Rylands v. Fletcher*, being the control of dangerous activity.

8. *Type of damage*

Damage to neighbouring land, or to things on it are covered (*Halsey v. Esso Petroleum Co. Ltd* [1961] 2 All ER 145 - paintwork of a car parked on a public road).

Doubts were expressed in *Read v. J. Lyons & Co. Ltd* over whether personal injuries were recoverable for under *Rylands v. Fletcher* (see too Newark (1949) 65 *Law Quarterly Review* 480, 488). It is thought that adjoining occupiers of land could claim for such (*Hale v. Jennings Bros* [1938] 1 All ER 579 - tenant of a fairground shooting stall struck by a chair flying off a chair-o-plane ride). It may be, however, that non-occupiers could not. The position is uncertain. Those who liken *Rylands v. Fletcher* to nuisance will no doubt argue against such claims.

Others would once more disown such a distraction on the ground that dangerous activities are a risk to all who may be unfortunate enough to fall within their range, whether occupiers or not (*Perry v. Kendricks Transport Ltd* [1956] 1 WLR 85: *Rylands* held applicable in a case where a boy was injured by a bus's exploding petrol-tank - although the action failed on the ground of the defence of act of a stranger, *infra*, p.587).

9. *Defences*

a. Consent

Plaintiff's consent to presence of danger is a defence and

may be implied. For example, in *Peters v. Prince of Wales Theatre (Birmingham) Ltd* [1943] KB 73, the plaintiff's consent to existence of a dangerous fire sprinkler system was implied from the fact that he took up occupation of the property. Similarly, in *Kiddle v. City Business Premises Ltd* [1942] 2 All ER 216, the plaintiff shopkeeper was held to have consented to a water drainage system shared with others, which became full of dust and consequently flooded the plaintiff's shop.

This is all the more so if the dangerous thing is for the plaintiff's own benefit: in *Kiddle* the plaintiff was stated to have taken the premises as they were and to have consented to the presence there of the installed water system with all its advantages and disadvantages (at p.79).

b. Act of God

In *Tennent v. Earl of Glasgow* (1864) 2 M (HL) 22, at p.26, Lord Westbury described this as an event "which no human foresight can provide against, and of which human prudence is not bound to recognize the possibility." Thus, in *Nichols v. Marsland* (1876) 2 Ex D 1, exceptional rainfall caused artificial lakes to break their banks and flood the plaintiff's land - Act of God; a natural occurrence - an earthquake or tornado in England perhaps - of a most exceptional and unexpected nature (although each has occurred in the area of Norwich, England in recent years!). Yet, heavy rain as an Act of God has subsequently been doubted, the suggestion being that the criterion for an Act of God is not reasonable foreseeability of the event, but whether or not human foresight and prudence could reasonably have contemplated the *possibility* and whether any practical measures could reasonably have been expected to be taken in order to safeguard against the possibility (*AG v. Cory Bros* [1921] 1 AC 521).

Thus, in *Greenock Corporation v. Caledonian Railway Co.* [1917] AC 556, a children's paddling pool overflowed in very heavy rainfall. The defendants were liable under *Rylands v. Fletcher* and the rainfall was not an Act of God: unlikely it may have been, but impossible to contemplate as capable of occurring it was not.

c. *Act of a stranger*

A "stranger" is a person who is not under the defendant's control and who causes the escape. He might be a trespasser; or someone performing an act on land other than the defendant's. The matter is a question of fact. Examples are available. In *Box v. Jubb* (1879) 4 Ex D 76, the defendant's reservoir overflowed because a third party emptied his own into the source of the first: no liability of defendant. Again, it will be recalled (see *supra*, p.579) that in *Rickards v. Lothian* [1913] AC 263, the defendants were not liable when a third party blocked their sink which then flooded the plaintiff's offices.

It would seem that the defence will only apply when the third party stranger's intervention was unforeseeable by the defendant. Thus, in *Perry v. Kendrick Transport Ltd* [1956] 1 WLR 85, a disused bus on the defendants' land blew up and injured the plaintiff, when two young trespassers threw a lighted match into its petrol tank. Someone had removed the petrol cap. The defendants were held not to be liable for the act of a stranger, because what had happened was unforeseeable. In the event that the stranger's act is held to have been foreseeable, however, so that the act-of-stranger defence is unavailable, arguably the cause could then be regarded, effectively, as having been transformed into one of negligence to this extent.

Not unexpectedly too, where the escape is caused by the plaintiff himself - not truly a "stranger" - the defendant will not be liable (*Dunn v. Birmingham Canal Co.* (1872) LR 7 QB 244: plaintiff dug mine beneath the defendant's canal, causing water to fall through and damage mine; *Ponting v. Noakes* [1894] 2 QB 281: plaintiff's horse reached over fence and ate defendant's poisonous berries). The same is true where the cause of damage is special sensitivity of the plaintiff's property (*Eastern & South African Telegraph Co. Ltd v. Cape Town Tramways Companies Ltd* [1902] AC 381, PC).

d. Statutory authority and necessity

A statute may authorize a dangerous activity, in which case this will provide a defence (*Green v. Chelsea Waterworks* (1894) 70 LT 547 - defendants had statutory authority to lay water mains). However, there may still be liability in tort for breach of statutory duty or negligence (see *supra*, chs.10 and 5). Necessity too may excuse a deliberate release of a dangerous substance.

10. Remoteness of damage

Traditionally, since *Rylands v. Fletcher* was regarded as a tort of strict liability, the defendant could be expected to be held liable for all direct consequences of escape, whether reasonably foreseeable or not: "the natural consequence of its escape" (Blackburn, J).

However, as a result of the House of Lords' judgment in *Cambridge Water*, referred to above (p.576, *et seq.*), it will be recalled that Lord Goff treated the tort as being subject to a requirement of reasonable foreseeability on the basis of the earlier nuisance case of *The Wagon Mound (No.2)*, in view of which - whatever criticism may be made of such application of the latter to the question of liability existence as opposed to mere remoteness of damage (*supra*, pp.528 and 576-7, *et seq.*) - it would certainly seem that remoteness itself must now be regarded as being subject to the foreseeability condition for recovery.

Further reading:

Brazier, *Street on Torts*, 9th ed, 1993 (Butterworth & Co., London): ch.20.

Fleming, J.G., *The Law of Torts*, 8th ed, 1992 (The Law Book Company, Sydney): ch.16.

Hepple, B.A. and Matthews, M.H., *Tort: Cases and Materials*, 4th ed, 1991 (Butterworth & Co., London): ch.14.

Heuston, R.F.W. and Buckley, R.A., *Salmond and Heuston on The Law of Torts*, 20th ed, 1992 (Sweet & Maxwell, London): ch.13.

Howarth, D., *Textbook on Tort*, 1995 (Butterworth & Co., London): ch.11.

Jones, M.A., *Textbook on Torts*, 4th ed, 1993 (Blackstone, London): ch.8.

Markesinis, B.S. and Deakin, S.F., *Tort Law*, 3rd ed, 1994 (Clarendon Press, Oxford): ch.6.

Rogers, W.V.H., *Winfield and Jolowicz on Tort*, 14th ed, 1994 (Sweet & Maxwell, London): ch.15.

Stanton, K.M., *The Modern Law of Tort*, 1994 (The Law Book Company, Sydney): ch.21.

Weir, T., *A Casebook on Tort*, 7th ed, 1992 (Sweet & Maxwell, London): ch.11.

PART XIII

Chapter 25

Torts of Damage to Reputation

English law provides for civil liability where one person makes a false statement about another to a third party, and *which harms the other person's reputation*. This is known as the law of defamation. If the defamation is written, it is called libel; if it is spoken, it is slander. The need to protect the legal interest of a person to maintain his good reputation has to be balanced, however, against society's interest in freedom of speech and the press. The law therefore provides a number of defences against defamation, for example, privilege of persons speaking in Parliamentary debate or of witnesses in judicial proceedings.

Special procedural features of defamation actions are: the presence of a jury to decide issues of fact and the amount of damages, now rare in civil trials; confinement of actions to the High Court and unavailability of legal aid; injunctions against mere threatened defamation; high legal costs; liability even where the person to whom the defamatory statement was published did not believe it to be true.

Defamation is an old tort, protecting peoples' reputations. Some of its traditional characteristics have been criticized and reform is in the air.

What the English law of defamation does not do, and about which there is some dissatisfaction, is to protect peoples' privacy and personality generally: not against publication of true and highly personal facts (unless information was provided to the defendant in confidence, in which case a breach of confidence action may be brought); not against taking a person's picture without their permission using a long lens camera; not against monitoring conversations with high powered listening devices. Consequently, there have been numerous proposals to legislate for privacy, particularly against the press, but none has come to pass. The existence of individual victims of excessive press zeal and intrusion has been regarded as not too high a price to pay for the fundamental freedom of the press, and it is considered that the balance may better be provided through education of the public to distinguish good from bad reporting. In the meantime, other methods have to be found to protect privacy: actions for breach of confidence; torts of malicious falsehood and malicious prosecution; the case of *Tolley v. Fry* [1931] AC 333 (see below) where a well-known amateur golfer's picture was used in order to advertise chocolate without his authority, held to be defamatory of his amateur reputation as *implying* that he had been paid for the use of his image - by no means comprehensive, however, in respect of personality.

Defamation remains the main weapon in the armoury against improper assault upon the reputation (and at the time of writing, there is a Defamation Bill of February 8, 1996 before Parliament, reforming rather than revolutionary, to which reference is hereinafter made - although, doubtless, changes will be effected to it in the course of its legislative progress).

The requirements for a successful action will now be examined.

Further reading:

Fleming, J.G., *The Law of Torts*, 8th ed, 1992 (The Law Book Company, Sydney): ch.26.

Wilson, "Privacy, Confidence and Press Freedom: A Study in Judicial Activism" (1990) 53 *Modern Law Review* 43.

Chapter 26

Defamation

1. Liability

(i) Defamatory Nature of a Statement

In this fast-moving, stress-ridden modern world with all its daily tensions, people are frequently heard to complain about one another. When do they cross the legal borderline so that what they say or write about each other is held to be "defamatory"?

1. Effects of the statement

The defamatory nature of a publication depends upon its *objective effects.* Subject to the defence of *unintentional defamation* in special circumstances dealt with under s.4 of the Defamation Act 1952 (see below, p.610), it is no less a defamation just because the defendant did not intend the effects to be defamatory or did not believe that they were so.

Whether the words used are *capable* of being defamatory or not is a matter of law for the Judge; and if so, whether they *are* in fact defamatory is a question left to the jury (*Gillick v. British Broadcasting Corporation* (1995) *The Times,* October 20, CA).

If the jury finds that the words did have the defamatory

meaning suggested, it is no defence that the person(s) to whom the statement was made did not actually believe it to be true (*Morgan v. Odhams Press Ltd* [1971] 1 WLR 1239). Thus, all that the plaintiff has to establish is that defamatory words were used, after which it is for the defendant to escape liability by raising a defence, for example, that the statement was true.

However, the all-important question is what do the "effects" of a statement have to be for the statement to be regarded as *defamatory* in nature?

These are stated by Lord Atkin in *Sim v. Stretch* [1936] 2 All ER 1237 who thought that the traditional test that words were used which exposed the plaintiff to "hatred, ridicule or contempt" should also be extended to any statement which "tends to lower the plaintiff in the estimation of right thinking members of society generally."

Thus, there are two possibilities:

- lowering of public esteem; and/or
- exposure to hatred, contempt or ridicule.

A case in the first category (and probably also the second) would be where it had been indicated in the course of a live television discussion that the plaintiff was morally responsible for the deaths of pregnant girls who had committed suicide following the successful stage of the plaintiff's campaign to prevent doctors from giving contraceptive advice to young girls without their parents' consent (*Gillick v. British Broadcasting Corporation* (1995) *The Times,* October 20, CA).

An example of the second category might be where the

plaintiff was said to have been severely disfigured in an accident. Hopefully, this would not lower peoples' respect for him, yet many might decide to avoid him out of fear or contempt. Another situation would be where the plaintiff was the subject of a comical or satirical portrayal subjecting him to ridicule or contempt (*Dunlop Rubber Co. Ltd v. Dunlop* [1921] 1 AC 367) - although this may attract the defence of fair comment in the public interest (see below, p.640).

Who are these "right thinking members of society generally" upon whose judgment the plaintiff's case and the defendant's fate depend?

One thing at least is clear, which is that the views of society *generally* must be assessed, not merely those of smaller circles in which the plaintiff moves. In *Byrne v. Deane* [1937] 1 KB 818, gambling machines illegally kept at a golf club were removed by the police after an informant had notified them. The defendant subsequently put a note on the club notice board which said that whoever had informed should "*byrnn* in hell". The plaintiff member, Mr Byrne, was not amused. The court held that the words were not defamatory: it might be that members of the golf club would be extremely contemptuous of the person who had informed upon them - but society as a whole would admire and applaud someone who had performed his public duty and assisted the police. Similarly, the test would operate in the reverse case in which society generally looked down upon a particular description - for example "villain" - but a smaller group approved of it.

As for the rest, it would seem that we are back into the territory of the ordinary, reasonable or sensible man -

neither naive nor unduly suspicious (*Hartt v. Newspaper Publishing plc* (1989) *The Times,* November 7) - the Judge deciding whether the effects upon the reasonable man in society generally could possibly have been defamatory and the jury whether they were so.

The problem, unfortunately, is that large sections of a particular society may not always be *reasonable*. The so-called ordinary man may harbour many fears and prejudices which would not automatically be regarded as reasonable - and yet, are plaintiffs not also to be protected against contempt felt by such people? Certainly, it is the case that if they were, the implicit recognition accorded to such bigoted views would not necessarily be permanent, since moral attitudes and behaviour are constantly changing. The effects of calling somebody a "homosexual" in 1935 may be somewhat different from the outcome in 1996 - in which connexion it should be added that reports of statements made in the past have to be assessed in the light of that past period for their defamatory effects (*Mitchell v. Book Sales Ltd* (1994) *The Independent*, March 25).

Further help is provided by the House of Lords' decision in *Charleston v. Newsgroup Newspapers Ltd* [1995] 2 All ER 313, HL, in which it was held that it was the reaction of the *single* category of ordinary, reasonable and fair-minded reader to the statement which was to be assessed for liability and damages, on the assumption that such was the sole meaning in which all readers would have understood the publication, and that the jury should not therefore consider that different groups of readers might have read different parts of the publication - for example, some of them only the headlines - and consequently understood different things. In the case itself, the plaintiffs were actors who played a respectable married couple in the Australian television programme *Neighbours*. The defendant publisher and editor of the *News of the World* newspaper showed, under a suggestive headline ("Strewth! What's Harold up to with our Madge?"), large pictures of the plaintiffs (with the words "Censored Down Under" superimposed) apparently having sex - but in much smaller writing underneath and alongside the pictures, there was an explanation that their faces had been put on these faked pictures without their knowledge by the makers of a pornographic computer game. The plaintiffs claimed that readers who saw the headline and pictures would have concluded either that the plaintiffs had consented to their faces being put on the pictures, or that they really were the people in the photographs: yet they also admitted that if readers had read the accompanying article, they would have understood that this was not the case. Accordingly, the plaintiffs asserted that they should be entitled to a remedy if it was possible to identify a particular group of readers who would not read beyond the pictures. The House of Lords, however, held that liability and damages must be based upon the assumed under-standing of the single category of the notional ordinary, reasonable and fair-minded reader - being that which was to be understood as the natural and ordinary meaning of the words used, the test applied in the absence of alleged legal innuendo from the circumstances known to some of the readers (see *infra*, p.606) - and it would be destructive of the principle that a publication had the one and only meaning which the readers as reasonable men should have collectively understood the words to bear, to allow the plaintiffs to assert that different groups of readers read different parts of the entire publication and for that reason understood it to mean different things, some defamatory, some not. The one principle (that is, of singular meaning) necessarily followed upon the former (that is, the test of understanding of the ordinary, reasonable and fair-minded reader). Thus, the ordinary, reasonable, and fair-minded reader, it was considered by the House of Lords, would have read on beyond the headlines and pictures to discover the full - *non-defamatory* - story (pp.318-9, 319-320).

Finally, where it is clear that the otherwise defamatory description of the plaintiff would not reasonably be taken to be *seriously meant* - it was a joke, or an abusive insult in the course of an argument, which right thinking members of society would recognize as such - the statement will not be held to be defamatory in its effects (*Parkins v. Scott* (1862) 1 H & C 153). To describe somebody as *a drunk and a rapist* - or a woman as a "tramp" (*Fields v. Davis* [1955] CLY 1543) - in the midst of a furious rage may have different effects from such a statement made in the course of providing a job reference. Conversely, it would seem that if the statement is written, it is not to be taken to have been written in anger - perhaps rather unrealistically, since people have been known to have written letters which, from tone and handwriting, were obviously affected by uncontrolled rage. Furthermore, in *Gillick v. BBC* (1995) *The Times,* October 20, CA, Neill, LJ in the Court of Appeal considered that the fact that a defamatory statement had been made in the course of a serious television discussion lessened the possibility that it had been merely flippant or ill-considered.

Examples from the cases of factors held to have lowered the estimation of the plaintiff in the mind of the reasonable man have been a BBC television holiday programme which accompanied a feature on a holiday camp in the Spanish resort of Majorca with the theme music from a popular television programme about a prison camp; description of an actress as having a "big bum" (meaning a large bottom) and "the kind of stage presence that blocks lavatories", and of a performer as "the summit of sex - the pinnacle of masculine, feminine and neuter. Everything that he, she or it can ever want ... a deadly, winking, sniggering, snuggling, chromium-plated, scent-impregnated, luminous, quivering, giggling, fruit-flavoured, ice-covered heap of mother love" (*Liberace v. Daily Mirror Newspapers* (1959) Current Law Yearbook, 1864). Others have included "kiss and tell bimbo" (indiscrete, unintelligent female), "tart" (promiscuous woman) and "boring".

In *Gillick v. British Broadcasting Corporation* (1995) *The Times,* October 20, CA, a majority of the Court of Appeal held that a statement made in the course of a television discussion, which suggested that a campaigner against giving contraceptive advice to young girls without their parents' consent bore moral responsibility for the suicides of pregnant girls, was capable of being defamatory and should be put to the jury, because the death of two or more young women was a most distressing event and reasonable viewers might well have taken an unfavourable view of anyone who was even remotely to blame, so that the plaintiff's reputation could certainly have been affected in the estimation of reasonable persons generally.

2. *Determination of whether a statement which has defamatory effects was made*

In the preceding section, the discussion dealt with the nature of a defamatory effect of an allegation or description (lowered public esteem or ridicule) and how it is adjudged that an allegation or description would have such an effect (standard of right thinking members of society generally).

However, there is an additional issue which really has to be decided upon in particular disputes before even the preceding is settled: this is whether what has been said and/or done actually bears that meaning which it is claimed - even accepted - would have the defamatory effects in the minds of right-thinking members of society? Nobody can seriously deny that to allege that someone is a *murderer* would be defamatory. But the question may arise as to whether the defendant can be taken to have made this allegation, according to whatever it was that he said or did?

There are two main types of case:

a. Statement defamatory on the face of it

Here, the defamation is clear from the natural and ordinary meaning of the words used: there is no ambiguity in calling someone an alcoholic, or a criminal, or a bigamist.

On the other hand, this is not to say that the natural and ordinary meaning of a statement will always be absolutely clear. It may be necessary for the court to construe the words used in order to determine whether they are capable of having a particular meaning which a jury may decide is defamatory. The test used by the courts in carrying out such a construction, it may already have been appreciated, is the same as that for determining whether a meaning decided upon is actually capable of being defamatory - that is to say, the understanding of the ordinary and reasonable reader or listener. Thus, in *Charleston v. News Group Newspapers Ltd* [1995] 2 All ER 313, at p.317, HL, Lord Bridge stated: "... where no legal innuendo is alleged to arise from extrinsic circumstances known to some readers, the 'natural and ordinary meaning' to be ascribed to the words of an allegedly defamatory publication is the meaning, including any inferential meaning, which the words would convey to the mind of the ordinary, reasonable, fair-minded reader."

This principle can be seen from the decision of the majority (2:1) of the Court of Appeal in *Gillick v. British Broadcasting Corporation* (1995) *The Times,* October 20, CA, where the plaintiff took part in a live television discussion with the defendants concerning advice on contraception to young girls. At the time, the plaintiff had succeeded in her campaign, before the Court of Appeal, to prevent doctors from providing such advice without the consent of the girls' parents - a decision which was subsequently overturned by a majority in the House of Lords. In the course of the television programme, one of the defendants, who favoured availability of contraceptive advice, stated that following the plaintiff's successful action in the Court of Appeal, there had been at least two reported cases of suicide by girls who were pregnant. The plaintiff's claim was that this statement *could be taken to mean* that she was morally responsible for the deaths - and further that such meaning was therefore defamatory as reducing her esteem in the eyes of right thinking members of society generally (as so held by the majority in the Court of Appeal: see *supra*, p.599).

As to the meaning alleged, Neill, LJ, in the majority, after confirming that it was a matter of law for the court to determine whether the words were capable of having the meaning alleged - whereas whether they then did so or not was an issue for the jury - adopted the formula set out by Sir Thomas Bingham, MR in the unreported case of *Skuse v. Granada Television Ltd* (1993) March 30, for the purposes of deciding upon the meaning of words used in this context, which was:

1. the sense should be the natural and ordinary meaning of the ordinary, reasonable viewer;
2. the hypothetical reasonable viewer was not naive, but not unduly suspicious and he could "read between the lines" implications which a lawyer might not - and might be guilty of some loose thinking, especially where a remark was derogatory - yet, he was not eager for scandal and would not automatically choose a bad meaning rather than good;
3. courts should avoid over-elaborate analysis of what was said;
4. a television audience would not give the analytical attention of a lawyer, auditor or academic;
5. courts were entitled, if not bound, to take account of the overall impression of the statement (the *bane and the antidote* in libel parlance), when considering the reaction of the hypothetical reasonable viewer;
6. courts should not take too literal an approach;
7. statements should be taken to be defamatory if they tended to lower the plaintiff in the estimation of right-

thinking members of society generally or were likely to affect a person adversely in the estimation of reasonable people generally.

Thus, the view of the majority of the Judges of the Court of Appeal in *Gillick* was that the words used were able to be construed as meaning that:

- there was a clear link between the plaintiff's successful campaign against contraceptive advice at that time and the suicides, and
- that within the reasonable spectrum of meanings of which the words were reasonably capable was the meaning that the plaintiff was in some sense to blame for the girls' deaths and morally responsible for this,

and accordingly the issue should go to a jury to determine whether the statement should in fact be so construed in this manner.

Furthermore, as seen, the majority Court of Appeal decision was also that, if the defendant's words were to be construed as having such meaning, this would in addition satisfy the test for defamatory effects, of tending to lower the plaintiff's esteem in the view of right thinking members of society in general (*supra,* p.599).

b. Statement defamatory by innuendo

Here the words used are seemingly quite innocent. Yet they are also capable, in the circumstances, of bearing a defamatory meaning. This is known as "innuendo":

There are two types of innuendo.

i. False/popular innuendo

In this case, the jury looks beyond the natural and ordinary meaning of the words used to a different, defamatory meaning, which may depend either upon another, popular sense, applicable in the particular context, or upon whatever other actions or words accompany the statement, thereby altering its meaning without the need for any further, extrinsic evidence of such popular meanings.

Thus, to take an obnoxious example, if a lady is referred to as "the town bicycle", the jury must determine whether the defendant for some reason intended to designate her as a useful two-wheeled conveyance, or alternatively meant to indicate the popular sense of the expression, being a sexually promiscuous person. Equally, if a male employer describes his female secretary as extremely willing and prepared to do anything to help, is he being genuinely complimentary, or is he casting aspersions on her morals - perhaps the latter if his words were accompanied by lascivious grimacing, winking eyelids and lustful gestures with throat and arm. Similarly, placing a waxwork model of somebody adjacent to a sign marked "chamber of horrors" could also amount to a statement defamatory of that person (*Monson v. Tussauds Ltd* [1894] 1 QB 671).

Further examples of false (popular) innuendo from the cases include where a traffic policeman was photographed saying that he wished he could bathe his feet in the defendants' products, which was held to be defamatory by innuendo - people would think that the plaintiff's feet smelt so badly that only the defendants' fluid would relieve the condition.

In *Lewis v. Daily Telegraph Ltd* [1963] 2 All ER 151, the defendant newspaper reported that the Fraud Squad was inquiring into the plaintiff's affairs. The House of Lords considered how the ordinary, reasonable man would react to this report and concluded that whilst he would not necessarily jump to the conclusion that the plaintiff was guilty of fraud, nevertheless, he might not merely believe that there was a simple investigation, but instead that the plaintiff was actually suspected of fraud, which amounted to defamation by false innuendo. In the House of Lords, Lord Reid said that the ordinary man "does not live in an ivory tower and he is not inhibited by a knowledge of the rules of construction ... so he can and does read between the lines in the light of his general knowledge and experience of world affairs" (p.154). A new trial was therefore ordered for a jury to decide whether the words were thus defamatory, as giving rise to a suspicion of fraud.

A somewhat less realistic conclusion was reached by a majority of the House of Lords in the earlier case of *Capital & Counties Bank Ltd v. Henty & Son* (1882) 7 App Cas 741. There the defendant firm was in dispute with the plaintiff bank and wrote to its own customers notifying them that it would not accept cheques drawn on the plaintiff, which caused a lot of the bank's account holders to withdraw their funds from the plaintiff bank fearing that it was insolvent. A majority of the Lords considered that the defendant's notice was not defamatory as false innuendo. Surely, however, it would not be wholly *unreasonable*, on receipt of such a message from the defendant without further explanation, for a customer to conclude that the plaintiff's finances might not be as healthy as one would wish?

ii. True/legal innuendo

This is where the defamatory allegation does not appear from the words used or actions carried out themselves, neither from the natural and ordinary meaning nor from popular innuendo - but nevertheless does so when these are taken together with some outside fact known to the recipient which has to be *pleaded and proved in evidence* (so-called "extrinsic evidence"). Witnesses must be found who are willing to testify that they knew of the facts which had led them to draw the defamatory conclusions (so that if a true/legal innuendo is incorrectly merely pleaded as a popular/false innuendo, the plaintiff will lose).

Thus, in *Tolley v. J.S. Fry & Sons Ltd* [1931] AC 333, the plaintiff, a famous *amateur* golfer, appeared on an advertising poster praising the defendants' chocolate, without the former's permission. The House of Lords held this to be defamatory by legal innuendo. Provided that the plaintiff pleaded evidence of his known amateur status, a reasonable member of society would infer from the picture that the plaintiff had betrayed his amateur status by accepting money from the defendants in return for his support for their product.

Another example is *Cassidy v. Daily Mirror Newspapers Ltd* [1929] 2 KB 331. A racehorse owner was photographed in the defendant newspaper in the company of a lady to whom, according to the man himself, he was said to be engaged to be married. The plaintiff was the man's existing wife from whom he was separated, but with whom he occasionally stayed. Her complaint was that the newspaper could be taken to suggest that she was not married to the man, so that anyone *who knew that he visited her* might think that she was co-habiting immorally with him. (This *was* in *1929*.) The Court of Appeal held the newspaper report to be defamatory by innuendo, where readers were aware of the additional fact that the man stayed with the plaintiff.

It should immediately be said, however, that in this situation - where the words were not defamatory on their face and the publisher did not know of the plaintiff nor of the circumstances amounting to the defamation - there is a type of defence under s.4 of the Defamation Act 1952, which will be dealt with below (p.610).

(ii) The Plaintiff must be Referred to

The plaintiff must be the subject of the defamatory statement.

This will be so where:

(a) he is expressly named; or
(b) even if not, he could nevertheless be identified by a "hypothetical sensible reader who knew of the special facts."

In *Morgan v. Odhams Press Ltd* [1971] 1 WLR 1239 the defendant reported that a certain girl had been kidnapped by a dog-doping gang. This was not so and she was in fact staying with the plaintiff. The House of Lords held that readers who knew of the latter situation could reasonably conclude that the plaintiff was a member of the dog-doping gang - ordinary readers would not be taken to scrutinize such reports with the accuracy of a lawyer, but quickly in order to form a general impression. Some satirical broadcasts or magazines, for example, will have comical names for politicians which are easy to identify with the latter.

Is it sufficient that the plaintiff is not personally identified but is a member of a whole class of persons referred to?

"All academics are lazy and idle." "All footballers are overpaid and under-talented." Can a particular lecturer or player sue?

It would seem not, generally, on the ground that the plaintiff member of the class is not himself referred to (even if known to be an academic or footballer) - although, perhaps a more principled basis would be that no reasonable and right thinking member of society could possibly hold such a sweeping statement to be true or seriously meant. Thus, in *Knupffer v. London Express Newspaper Ltd* [1944] AC 116, the plaintiff was the head of a pro-German British group of about 24 members during the last war. The House of Lords held that an article about the group could not be taken to refer to the plaintiff personally and that this was likely to be the case in most group situations.

However, there are two circumstances in which an individual member may be able to sue: (i) where he is personally identified in the overall statement, for example, by name or picture; and (ii) where the group is so small and limited that in effect each member is personally referred to and each is able to claim, for example, in the case of a small solicitors' firm or a particular sports team (*Browne v. D. C. Thomson & Co.* (1912) SC 359).

Finally, supposing that reference is made to the plaintiff,

but it is unintentional: for example, a name is used in the statement which - unknown to the defendant - is the same as that of the plaintiff: "Fred Brown was convicted of theft"; or the plaintiff's name is given to a fictitious character in a book or play, who does not inspire great respect in the reader? This will still amount to a defamation of the plaintiff as being referred to, and the defendant must try to protect himself by adding further description to the name in the report in order to distinguish the person from others (personal features, height, job and so forth), or by specifying that all characters in the book are fictitious. Thus, in *Hulton v. Jones* [1910] AC 20 a newspaper reported on immoral behaviour by a man called Artemus Jones from Peckham, South London, at a motor festival in Dieppe. Jones, who was a church official, was said to have been accompanied by his mistress. The House of Lords held that the plaintiff, a barrister called Artemus Jones, had been defamed, even though the defendants had not intended this nor were they even aware of his existence. Similarly, in *Newstead v. London Express Newspaper Ltd* [1940] 1 KB 377, the defendant newspaper stated that "Harold Newstead, 30 year-old Camberwell man" was convicted of the crime of bigamy (undergoing a marriage ceremony while already lawfully married to another). The plaintiff, a hairdresser from Camberwell, South London, called Harold Newstead was held to have been defamed, because reasonable right thinking members of society would believe that the article referred to him, whereas in fact it was a barman of that name who was the subject of the report. Plaintiffs in this position generally should produce witnesses to testify that they understood the statement to refer to those plaintiffs.

It should be said, however, that in such cases where a person is unintentionally defamed through not being properly distinguished, or in the earlier situation of true/legal innuendo, there is a special statutory defence, which will now be considered.

(iii) Statutory Defence to Unintentional Defamation and Legal Innuendo

Section 4 of the Defamation Act 1952 provides a special type of defence in respect of "innocent defamation", defined to cover two types of case dealt with previously, where, in addition to the fact that the publisher took all reasonable care in relation to the publication (that is, he was not negligent):

1. he did not intend to refer to the plaintiff and did not know of circumstances whereby it might be understood to refer to him (*Hulton, Newstead*); or
2. the words were not defamatory on their face and the publisher did not know of circumstances by virtue of which they might be understood to be defamatory of the plaintiff (*Cassidy*).

In either case, the publisher must make an "offer of amends", defined as an offer (a) to publish a suitable correction and apology and (b) to take reasonably practicable steps to notify persons to whom copies of the statement were distributed that the words were defamatory. If the offer is accepted and carried out, the publisher can no longer be sued for the defamation. But if the offer is rejected, the publisher still has a defence in court if he shows that (a) the publication was innocent, (b) the offer was made as soon as practicable after the defendant discovered that the words were or might be defamatory of the plaintiff, and was not withdrawn, and (c) if he was not the author of the statement, the author made it without malice.

Therefore, the defence is not particularly easy to use. In *Ross v. Hopkinson* (1956) 223 LT 97 an actress's name was used for an unsympathetic character in a novel with whom, nevertheless, she shared a number of similarities. The s.4 defence failed because although the plaintiff actress was not very well known (nonetheless, the daughter of a well-known playwright), the defendant had not used all reasonable care in checking whether a public person of that name existed and she was in fact acting in a play in the centre of London at that time and was entered in a professional directory.

Section 4 of the Defamation Act 1952 is to be repealed by Schedule 3 to the proposed Defamation Act 1996, on the ground that it is little used in practice.

However, in its place there will be statutory defences under: (a) clause 1 - for defendants other than author, editor or publisher (that is, for those who are mechanical publishers, see *infra,* pp.615-6); and (b) clauses 2-4 - for defendants generally, who, as under s.4 of the 1952 Act, may offer to make amends (see *infra,* p.647).

(iv) Publication of the Statement

The essence of defamation is that the plaintiff's reputation is lowered in the eyes of right thinking members of the public. It is not to protect plaintiffs against suffering personal feelings of hurt.

Accordingly, if the plaintiff alone is aware of the statement, the defamation has not been "published" and the defendant is not liable (*Powell v. Gelston* [1916] 2 KB 615). It is one thing to write to the plaintiff stating him to be a swine - it is another to declare this to a third party.

So, *publication* is essential.

When does it occur?

1. Publication intended or reasonably foreseeable

Writing evil thoughts in a diary and putting it in a locked drawer will not be publication if some unscrupulous person breaks the lock and reads the diary. However, leaving the diary in a place where the writer either intends or should reasonably have foreseen that somebody would be tempted to read it would be publication. This is essentially a question for the jury.

A number of situations of publication have arisen in the cases:

(a) Addressing letters to the wrong person through lack of care (*Hebditch v. MacIlwaine* [1894] 2 QB 54).

(b) Speaking in a loud voice so that people nearby will hear (*White v. J.F. Stone (Lighting and Radio) Ltd* [1939] 2 KB 827).

(c) Sending a letter to a person in circumstances in which it is reasonably foreseeable that someone else might open it, for example, a clerk or typist dealing with the post (*Pullman v. Walter Hill & Co. Ltd* [1891] 1 QB 524) - husbands too have been known to open their wives' letters intentionally or by mistake. In *Theaker v. Richardson* [1962] 1 All ER 229 the plaintiff recovered damages for defamation where her husband opened an envelope addressed to her believing it to be an election circular. The letter alleged that she was a whore and a brothel keeper. The Court of Appeal held that the question for the jury was whether the husband's action was so unusual and extraordinary that it could not reasonably have been anticipated by the defendant, or was it something which could quite easily and naturally happen in the ordinary course of events? On the other hand, sending letters to the plaintiff in an unsealed envelope will not be regarded as publication, nor was it held in *Huth v. Huth* [1914-15] All E Rep 242 that a letter from a separated husband to his wife, denying their marriage and declaring the children illegitimate, opened by a butler, had been published, since it was not part of a butler's duties to open letters addressed to his employers.

(d) Sending a postcard or telegram identifying the plaintiff, which will be presumed to have been read by post office officials and members of the addressee's household (*Sandgrove v. Hole* [1901] 2 KB 1).

(e) Failing to remove unauthorized defamatory material from premises over which the defendant has control (*Byrne v. Dean* [1937] 1 KB 818).

2. *Repetition*

The first point to make is that the maker of the statement himself is liable for every intended, or authorized or reasonably foreseeable repetition (*Parkes v. Prescott* (1869) LR 4 EX 169) - although also for an unauthorized repetition of the "sting" of the statement if this was the likely consequence. Thus, in *Slipper v. BBC* [1991] 1 All ER 165 the defendant was liable not only for the original television broadcast but for subsequent newspaper reports of it which were easily foreseeable.

Secondly, those who repeat or report a defamatory statement are also liable for publication (*Cutler v. McPhail* [1962] 2 QB 292: newspaper liable for publishing defamatory letter, as well as writer) - every fresh repetition is a new cause of action for which the plaintiff can claim, even if the intention was merely to report rather than to defame the plaintiff (see *Stern v. Piper* (1996) *The Times,* May 30, CA - *infra* Appendix). Consequently, in the case of a book or newspaper containing a defamatory article, persons liable will include the author, newspaper owner, editor, printer, distributor, bookshop, newsagent and librarian - although there is a defence in some of these cases (see below, p.615), and frequently only the defendants with sufficient resources will be sued in any event in practice.

3. *Circumstances where there is no publication*

The following examples fall within this category:

a. *Statements to the defendant's (but not to the plaintiff's) own spouse (Wennhak v. Morgan (1888) 20 QBD 635)*

If pillow talk between husband and wife were actionable,

what would this do to the state of married life?

b. Repetition by the plaintiff himself

A letter sent to the plaintiff, describing him as a cad, a liar and a swine who steals from less well-off members of society, which the plaintiff then shows to other people, is not published: although, were the envelope to be addressed to "The Swindler", for everyone to see, this would be a quite different matter.

c. Unintentional and unforeseeable publication

For example, if a letter is marked "private and confidential", it is reasonable to presume that the confidential nature of the communication will be respected.

d. Unauthorized and unforeseeable repetition

This will be regarded as breaking the chain of causation, so that the original maker of the statement will not be liable for the repetition (*Ward v. Weeks* (1830) 7 Bing 211).

e. "Mechanical publishers"

That is, booksellers and libraries, rather than author, publishers and printer ("producers") are relieved from liability for publication, on a policy of fairness (innocent dissemination) if they can prove that they did not know that the material contained a defamatory statement and that there were no circumstances which should reasonably have alerted them to it. Thus, in *Vizetelly v. Mudie's Select Library Ltd* [1900] 2 QB 170, the defendant library was liable because in spite of the publisher's warning to return certain books which could be libellous, they had no system of examining books for defamation. Printers are not protected (except when they hand back the printed work to the author) - but usually ask publishers to agree to indemnify them for damages. The safest measure of all for a bookseller, who is concerned about a particular book or journal, is not to stock it at all -not unheard of in the case of certain "dangerous" magazines.

Clause 1 of the Defamation Bill 1996 proposes to include this mechanical defence on a statutory basis (see *infra,* p.646).

f. Statement made in a foreign language which the recipient did not understand

A sensible defence.

(v) Libel and Slander as Different Forms of Publication

1. Difference between libel and slander

Following the preceding discussion as to the meaning of publication, it may be important to determine the form in which defamatory material has been published.

According to such form of publication, there are two possible types of defamation: *libel* and *slander,* which developed in different courts in the Middle Ages.

The general distinction is that libel is written and slander is spoken words or gestures, so that traditionally the former was regarded as the more serious through its permanence. In modern times, however, the distinction is blurred because broadcasting and recording techniques will mean that the "spoken" word can be as permanent as if it were written, and perhaps the real distinction now, as a result of legislative intervention, is between the *permanent* and the *transient*. It is certainly not entirely accurate to describe libel and slander as being perceived by eyes and ears respectively.

How are various methods of communication classified in this context?

Oral statements and books are no problem: slander and libel.

Letters: libel when published to a third party, but probably slander when dictated to a typist. If the letter is *read* to a third party, this is libel (*Forrester v. Tyrrell* (1893) 9 TLR 257).

Signs: in *Monson v. Tussauds Ltd* [1894] 1 QB 671, placing a wax model of the plaintiff near a sign saying "chamber of horrors" was held to be libellous. The Judge said that although libels were generally written or printed, they could be some other permanent form, such as a statue, a caricature, an effigy, chalk marks on a wall, signs or pictures.

Broadcasting: by radio or television, libel (Broadcasting Act 1990, ss.166, 201; Defamation Act 1952, s.16).

Theatre performances: libel (Theatres Act 1968, s.4).

Records and tape recordings: there is academic disagreement because whilst they are permanent (suggesting libel), they are not perceived until spoken and played (indicating slander). Surely the former is correct.

Films and videos: libel (*Youssoupoff v. MGM Pictures Ltd* (1934) 50 TLR 581 - plaintiff shown as seduced by Rasputin).

It should be noted that Clause 17(1) of the Defamation Bill 1996 defines "statement" *in the Bill* as meaning words, pictures, visual images, gestures or any other method of signifying meaning - clearly covering *both* libel and slander.

2. *Legal significance of distinction*

Libel is *actionable per se.* This means that the plaintiff does not have to prove damage.

Slander, on the other hand, subject to exceptions, requires "special damage" to be shown - that is, material or pecuniary loss to the plaintiff's trade or other financial opportunity beyond general damage to his reputation itself (and subject to the normal limitation of remoteness of damage) (*Chamberlain v. Boyd* [1883] 11 QBD 407).

The exceptions where slander is actionable *per se* are the following slanderous statements about the plaintiff:

(a) he is guilty of a crime punishable by imprisonment (*Hellwig v. Mitchell* [1910] 1 KB 609);
(b) he has a contagious disease - aids, leprosy, venereal disease (*Bloodworth v. Gray* (1844) 7 Man & G 334);
(c) a woman has been immoral, is a lesbian, or has been raped (Slander of Women Act 1891; *Kerr v. Kennedy* [1942] 1 KB 409; *Youssoupoff v. MGM*);
(d) he is unfit to carry on a trade, business or

> profession (and the allegation no longer needs to be based upon actions actually carried out in the course of the business or professional activities, provided that it generally demonstrates unfitness) (Defamation Act 1952, s.2).

The distinct treatment of libel and slander in this way has not surprisingly been criticized and its abolition recommended in favour of the former being applicable to both.

3. Libel as a crime

In practice, criminal libel is virtually obsolete. It used to be based upon the idea that a serious libel could cause so much offence as to threaten a breach of the peace. Similarly, for this reason, there was no requirement of publication to a third party beyond the plaintiff; and the defamed person did not even have to be alive.

(vi) Restrictions on Suit

If a defamed person is already dead when the defamatory statement is made, or dies before the termination of the proceedings, the defendant cannot be sued. The action does not survive and it is buried with the deceased. Equally, the estate of a deceased defendant cannot be sued in respect of defamatory statements made by the deceased in his lifetime.

Companies can sue to defend the corporate reputation (*South Hetton Coal Company v. North Eastern News Association Ltd* [1894] 1 QB 133; *Derbyshire County Council v. Times Newspapers Ltd* [1993] 2 WLR 449, but local or central government authorities cannot (*Derbyshire County Council v. Times Newspapers Ltd*), in view of the perceived need to safeguard fearless public criticism (although individual officers can bring proceedings on their own behalf). They must therefore defend themselves through public statements. Trade unions too are unable to sue through lack of separate personality for the purpose (*Electrical, Electronic, Telecommunication & Plumbing Union v. Times Newspapers Ltd* [1980] QB 585).

Employers may be vicariously liable for defamation by an employee committed in the course of performing his duties, subject to the defence of qualified privilege (*Riddick v. Thames Board Mills Ltd* [1977] QB 881) (see below, p.630, *et seq.*).

2. Defences to Liability

A plaintiff may succeed in establishing that a statement about him was defamatory. But that is not necessarily the end of the story.

The defendant may be able to use one or more of a number of defences in order to escape liability.

The major defences to defamation are the following:

(i) Consent

In *Chapman v. Lord Ellesmere* [1932] 2 KB 431, one of the conditions of the plaintiff's licence from the Jockey Club as a racehorse trainer was that the Jockey Club could withdraw the licence and publish this fact in the *Racing Calendar.* When one of his horses was found to have been doped, the Club published a warning in the *Racing Calendar* and in *The Times* newspaper. The plaintiff was held to have consented to the former but not to the latter.

(ii) Justification

1. General

If the defendant can prove that his words were *true*, this is a complete defence, and is called "justification". It is a defence, even if the defendant was malicious in making the statement and wanted to harm the plaintiff: *EXCEPT THAT* under s.8 of the Rehabilitation of Offenders Act 1974 (see Defamation Bill 1996 for consequential amendments), the defendant cannot raise the defence of justification, if the plaintiff is able to prove that the defendant was malicious when he stated that the plaintiff had committed a criminal offence covered by the Act. (Under the Act, certain offences of a less serious nature are to be treated as though they had never occurred after a period of time. They are then known as "spent" convictions, that is, lapsed.)

The burden is upon the defendant to prove the truth of his statement on a balance of probabilities (not for the plaintiff to show that a statement is untrue):

- a mere honest belief in the truth, however reasonable, is not enough for the defence; and
- even if the defendant is merely repeating what a third party has said, the defendant himself must still prove its truth, if the defence of justification is to succeed (*'Truth' (NZ) Ltd v. Holloway* [1960] 1 WLR 997).

2. *Extent of truth to be shown*

It is said that the defendant need only prove the "sting of the charge" (*Sutherland v. Stopes* [1925] AC 47, at p.79, per Lord Shaw).

This means that he must show that the main substance of the defamatory allegation is true - it is not also necessary that every aspect of the charge should be substantiated. As to what is the "substance", this is essentially a matter of fact and degree in each individual case. Thus, for example, allegations of *theft* or *imprisonment* will usually be regarded as the serious substance of a defamation, so that if these are proved, any inaccuracies concerning, say, the precise dates, or terms of imprisonment, are likely to be disregarded and the defence will be established (*Alexander v. North Eastern Railway Co.* (1865) 6 B & S 340).

Further, where the plaintiff proves to the jury an *innuendo* meaning, it is not sufficient for the defendant to establish that the literal meaning of the statement was true. If, for example, the defendant makes a statement that the plaintiff is "helping police with their inquiries" into a murder, then even if the defendant is able to establish the literal truth of this statement, he must also go on to prove the accuracy of any innuendo arising from it to the effect that the plaintiff is suspected by the police of being guilty of the murder - and must actually specify the particular respect in which he alleges that the statement is true (*Lucas-Box v. News Group Newspapers Ltd* [1986] 1 WLR 147). In addition, the defendant may argue that the sting of an alleged defamation was broader than the particular meaning claimed and then prove that in the wider sense it is true. Thus, in *Williams v. Reason* [1988] 1 All ER 262, an amateur rugby player was accused by the defendant publishers of accepting money during his career for writing a book. The court permitted the defendants to provide evidence that the plaintiff had generally accepted payments for matches, thereby compromising his amateur status, on the ground that the latter broader claim was the essence of the charge against him.

A remarkable principle of common law was that proof of conviction of a crime would *not* justify the statement that the convicted person had committed the offence - the defendant had to prove the latter himself. This was altered by s.13 of the Civil Evidence Act 1968 which makes proof of conviction of crime conclusive evidence of its commission in defamation proceedings - although, conversely, if a plaintiff proves acquittal, it is still possible for the defendant to try to show that the plaintiff really was guilty (*Loughans v. Odhams Press Ltd* [1963] CLY 2007). Section 13 only applies to criminal convictions. Accordingly, if the statement was that the plaintiff left university without obtaining a degree and the innuendo was that he had failed in his examinations or was in breach of discipline, proof that the plaintiff was asked to leave may not be sufficient for the defence. Clause 12 of the Defamation Bill will limit conclusiveness - though not evidential admissibility - of the conviction to where the convicted person himself is the plaintiff, and not another.

In *Aspro Travel Ltd v. Owners Abroad Group plc* (1995) *The Times*, July 11, CA, the plaintiff travel company alleged defamatory comments about them by the defendants, made to hoteliers and travel agents in various countries. The Court of Appeal held that it was not sufficient for defendants to point to the existence of hearsay and rumours as justification for the assertion of the fact of the truth of the rumours. Nevertheless, there could be circumstances where a person, the defendant, had repeated rumours before ascertaining that they were true, and then plead in justification that there were in fact such rumours. A subtle distinction indeed!

3. Justification in multiple defamation

The common law rule was favourable to plaintiffs. If several different charges were alleged in the defamatory statement, proof of the truth of one or more of them would not also amount to a defence against the rest.

Section 5 of the Defamation Act 1952 altered this. It provides that where a defamatory statement contains *two or more distinct* charges against the plaintiff, the justification defence does not fail only because the truth of *every* charge is not proved, if the words not proved to be true do *not materially injure the plaintiff's reputation, having regard to the truth of the remaining charges.*

For example, if the defendant alleged that the plaintiff was a thief, a wifebeater and incapable of playing chess, the defendant could plead justification if able to prove the thief and wifebeating charges, even if not also the chess allegation, if the latter did little damage in view of the truth of the former.

Plaintiffs can try to get round s.5 by confining their claims solely to the charge against them, the truth of which the defendant is unable to prove, if this tactic is in the plaintiff's interests in terms of any damages hoped for. The defendant will not then be permitted to introduce evidence of truth of his other charges as a means of proving substantial justification. In *Speidel v. Plato Films Ltd* [1961] AC 1090, the plaintiff, commander of Axis Forces in the Second World War, was charged with a number of offences in the defendant's film, including war crimes, but the plaintiff only sued in respect of the allegation that he had betrayed Rommel as well as murdering the King of Yugoslavia. The House of Lords held that the defendants were not permitted to introduce evidence of the truth of the war crimes and atrocity allegations as a defence to the actual claim, nor in mitigation of damages (although this would not stop the defendants from showing that the plaintiff generally had a poor reputation, as a means of reducing damages). This is thought to be unfair to defendants and the Faulks Committee on Defamation (*infra*, p.658) recommended its reversal, so that defendants could rely upon the truth of the excluded parts of their statement in defence of the claim. In the meantime, prior to any such reforms, defendants are at least assisted by the wording of s.5 requiring two or more *distinct* charges: if they can succeed in showing that excluded and non-excluded parts of the statement are not distinct and have the *common sting*, the defendant will be permitted to adduce evidence of truth of the excluded parts in overall justification of the non-excluded (*Polly Peck (Holdings) plc v. Trelford* [1986] 2 All ER 84). Thus, if the statement alleged that the plaintiff had committed adultery with a particular person and generally been sexually promiscuous, yet the claim was only in respect of the former, the defendant might successfully argue that the non-excluded and excluded charges were all part of a single theme and that consequently, proof of truth of the latter, but not the former, would nonetheless justify the common sting of the statement (*Khashoggi v. IPC Magazines Ltd* [1986] 1 WLR 1412). In addition, the defendant may in any event refer to excluded parts in order to argue for a particular meaning to be given to the non-excluded words in the context of the overall statement.

(iii) Absolute Privilege

In certain cases, the law permits a defence to defamation, regardless of malice on the part of the maker of the statement.

These situations fall into a number of well-known categories - although difficulties will always exist as to the exact limits of their scope. They tend to be resolved on the basis of past case law and of the underlying policy of the defence, which is that of public interest and policy in freedom of speech and communication, yet without unduly and unnecessarily facilitating its abuse.

The following are the categories of absolute privilege:

1. Parliamentary proceedings

Those who govern us should not be inhibited, through fear of legal proceedings, from communicating their true opinion on matters of state. This principle was first set down in the Bill of Rights in 1688.

The absolute privilege attaches:

(a) to statements made by Members of the House of Commons and of the House of Lords and by witnesses called to give evidence in debates, committees and documents laid before Parliament; and also

(b) to publication of reports of such proceedings by order or authority of Parliament, by virtue of the Parliamentary Papers Act 1840, s.1 (although publication of mere extracts only attract *qualified* privilege, under s.3, see below, as, in all likelihood, does the televising of Parliament).

However, Members of Parliament are not protected with regard to their statements made outside Parliamentary proceedings.

In *Prebble v. Television New Zealand Ltd* [1994] 3 All ER 407, the defendants asserted, on the basis of certain Australian decisions, that absolute Parliamentary privilege was unavailable where it was the Member of the Legislature himself who had brought proceedings for libel and the defendants wished to justify their allegations by demonstrating that his Parliamentary statements were untrue. The Judicial Committee of the Privy Council rejected this argument and upheld the defence of absolute privilege in these cases on the ground that its purpose was to protect Parliament, not its individual Members as such - although it might be, nevertheless, that proceedings would have to be stayed if the effects of Parliamentary privilege were such as to make it impossible to determine the issues between the parties in the light of whatever evidence was otherwise available.

2. *Court proceedings*

Judges, lawyers, parties to litigation, juries and witnesses are all protected as to their statements in court (*Dawkins v. Lord Rokeby* (1875) LR 8 QB 255).

There is a qualification, however: the statement must not be completely unconnected with the case (*More v. Weaver* [1928] 2 KB 520). Thus, a Judge cannot say to a convicted person: "I sentence you to five years in prison ... and by the way, did you know that my wife is a loose woman?"

Courts, for these purposes, will include other tribunals exercising judicial functions, such as professional disciplinary committees, but not also administrative and licensing offices and government departments, nor even the EC Commission when carrying out investigations into possible breach of EC Treaty Articles 85 and 86 prohibitions upon trade restrictions (*Hasselblad (GB) Ltd v. Orbinson* [1985] 1 All ER 173, CA).

Communications between lawyers and clients relating to litigation, actual or contemplated, are absolutely privileged - but those not involving judicial proceedings are probably only covered by qualified privilege (*Minter v. Priest* [1930] AC 558, HL).

Fair and accurate newspaper reports of judicial proceedings (Law of Libel Amendment Act 1888, s.3), subsequently extended to United Kingdom radio and television reporting (Defamation Act 1952, s.9(2); Broadcasting Act 1990, sch.20, para.2), are privileged - generally believed to be absolute although not expressly stipulated - provided that they are published at the same time as the proceedings are conducted (see below, p.637, for where they are not). Reporting must therefore be factually correct and put both parties' arguments.

Clause 14 of the Defamation Bill 1996, if enacted, will

clarify preceding uncertainties. It confirms that a fair and accurate report of proceedings in public before any United Kingdom court or the European Court of Justice is *absolutely privileged* if published contemporaneously with the proceedings; "court" includes any tribunal or body exercising the *judicial* power of the state; a report required by court order or statutory provision to be postponed is to be treated as published contemporaneously if published as soon as practicable after publication is permitted. Schedule 3 will repeal s.3 of the Law of Libel Amendment Act 1888.

3. Public officials

Statements in the course of official communications between government Ministers or high civil servants are covered by absolute privilege (*Chatterton v. Secretary of State for India* [1895] 2 QB 189 - statement by the Secretary of State for India to an Under-Secretary of State; *Fayed v. Al-Tajir* [1987] 2 All ER 396 - foreign ambassador).

A Prime Minister can only describe one or more of his Ministers as "bastards" if this is done in the course of official business.

The problem with this branch of the defence is where to draw the line: are the army and police force included, and if so, at what ranks? Army officers, it would seem, are covered (*Dawkins v. Lord Paulet* (1865) LR 5 QB 94: Major-General), in the public interest, but not a high ranking police officer (*Merricks v. Nott-Bower* [1965] 1 QB 57: Deputy Commissioner in the Metropolitan Police).

Certain officials, such as the Director General of Fair Trading and the Ombudsman, are specifically granted absolute privilege in the exercise of their functions by the

Courts and Legal Services Act 1990, s.69(2); otherwise they would be particularly vulnerable to legal action.

(iv) Qualified Privilege

1. Circumstances in which it applies

Where the defendant is covered by qualified privilege, this will be a defence, unless the plaintiff is able to prove that the defendant acted with *malice.*

The law grants this defence - and sets the limits at malice - in those of life's situations in which a defendant requires protection against unreasonable legal liability on a balance of plaintiff's and defendant's interests, "for the common convenience and welfare of society" (*Toogood v. Spyring* (1834) 1 CrM & R 181, p.193).

The circumstances in which a defendant may be held to be entitled to qualified privilege are extremely varied, but are commonly categorized as follows:

a. The defendant has a duty to make the statement and the recipient a duty or interest to receive it (Adam v. Ward [1917] AC 309, p.334 per Lord Atkinson): reciprocation of duties

In these circumstances, life could otherwise be very difficult.

Lord Atkinson made it clear that the duty to communicate could be *legal, social or moral.* Furthermore, it is for the court to determine existence or not of the duty - and the fact that a person wrongly but honestly believes that he is under a duty, will not satisfy the defence (*Davidson v. Barclays Bank Ltd* [1940] 1 All ER 316).

Examples of such duties include those of employees under contracts of employment to pass on information to their employer; of the public to inform the police about crimes; of a bank about an account-holder's credit rating; of a referee to supply details to a prospective employer - all the more significant since in *Spring v. Guardian Assurance plc* [1993] 2 All ER 273, the Court of Appeal (overruling the earlier decision in *Lawton v. BOC Transhield* [1987] 2 All ER 608) had held that a referee was not liable in negligence towards the subject of the reference, so that - subject to qualified privilege - the latter's only remedy against the referee was in defamation. The Court of Appeal's decision itself, however, was subsequently reversed by the House of Lords in *Spring v. Guardian Assurance plc* [1994] 3 All ER 129 by a majority of four to one, which held that an employer was liable towards the employee in negligence for failure to take sufficient care in preparing a reference, and a cause of action in defamation, with its defence of qualified privilege, was not inconsistent with this, because the two torts were to protect different interests, the one, reputation, the other, economic loss (pp.136, 151, 153, 158 and 172-6 - and see *supra,* ch.5). Clearly, as a result of this finding, the number of cases in which defamation is relied upon in the matter of references is likely to decline.

It is still difficult, however, to state with certainty all those situations in which a social or moral duty is likely to be held to exist. In *Stuart v. Bell* [1891] 2 QB 341, p.350, Lindley, LJ stated the test to be "would the great mass of right-thinking men in the position of the defendant have considered it their duty under the circumstances to make the communication?" Clearly not where the plaintiff made a justified criticism of the defendant's business and the defendant defamed him in response (*Fraser-Armstrong v.*

Haddow (1994) *The Times,* January 21).

Furthermore, even if a duty to communicate is held to exist, that is not the end of the story. Qualified privilege is only available as a defence, in the absence of malice, if:

- the statement does not exceed in its scope that which its maker has a duty to impart; and
- is made to the particular person who has a duty or interest to receive it.

It is no defence if the defamatory reference is shown to a third party by the referee and not to the prospective employer, or if the referee takes the opportunity to make a defamatory comment about an unconnected third party in the reference.

As to the recipient, he must have a duty or interest to receive the information, for example, a prospective employer, the police, a Member of Parliament receiving a complaint about harm allegedly done to one of his constituents whom he represents, a mother about danger to her child, or a host about the character of a guest.

A case demonstrating these principles was *Watt v. Longsdon* [1930] 1 KB 130. The plaintiff and defendant were respectively the overseas manager and director of a company. The defendant received a letter concerning the plaintiff's alleged sexual improprieties and showed it to the company chairman and to the plaintiff's wife, an old friend of the defendant, without first having established the truth of the allegations, with the result that the wife petitioned for divorce. As it happened, the charges against the plaintiff's behaviour were quite false. The court held (i) the communication to the chairman was subject to qualified privilege, because the defendant had a duty to pass on and the chairman an interest to receive the information, but that (ii) the disclosure to the wife was not covered, since there was no legal, social or moral duty upon a friend to inform the plaintiff's wife of her husband's alleged but unproven infidelities, even if she had an interest in learning of these.

What also emerges from Lindley, LJ's statement of principle in *Stuart v. Bell, (supra),* and from the case of *Watt v. Longsdon* previously considered, is that existence of duty can depend on particular circumstances, such as whether parties are in a relationship of confidence, or whether untrue allegations had at least first been investigated. The fact that the recipient had requested the information may be particularly influential in demonstrating an interest to receive it, if the details provided are limited to the scope of that interest, for example, to factors relevant to employment where a prospective employer seeks a reference, or to credit worthiness where a finance company makes inquiries about a prospective borrower's credit rating (*London Association for Protection of Trade v. Greenlands Ltd* [1916] 2 AC 5). Similarly, it will be more difficult for a defendant informant who is a stranger to the recipient to prove interest of the latter than if they were close friends or family (*Todd v. Hawkins* (1837) 8 C & P 88). In particular, it may not be easy for a defendant to show that the general public had an interest in - *a fortiori* a duty to act upon - the receipt of unsubstantiated information or suspicion. Perhaps this would be satisfied where a newspaper reported on a "food scare" or "security alert" where the maxim "better to be safe than sorry" might apply. In *Chapman v. Ellesmere*

[1932] 2 KB 431, it was reported in *Racing Calendar* and *The Times* newspaper that the plaintiff had been warned after an inquiry by the Jockey Club into the doping of race horses. The court held that qualified privilege (and consent, *supra*, p.620) applied to the first - but not to the second - publication: the racing public had an interest in recept of this publication and the implicit suspicion directed at the plaintiff, but not the public generally.

Finally, the scope of the defence fell for consideration by the Court of Appeal in *Watts v. Times Newspapers Ltd* (1995) *The Times*, September 22, CA, where a newspaper, in the course of publishing an apology for previously defaming *X*, included, at the request of *X*'s solicitors, a statement in the apology which allegedly defamed *Y*. The Court of Appeal held that the newspaper was not entitled to rely on qualified privilege, because their duty was only to publish so much of an apology as was necessary to correct their mistake and not to make further explanations at the request of *X*, including the alleged defamation.

b. Statements to protect an interest

The preceding section dealt with cases in which the defendant had a legal, social or moral *duty* to make a statement.

The present covers situations where the defendant can prove that he has an *interest* - recognized at law for the purpose - to communicate to another *who has a duty or interest to receive it*: the reverse of the former.

The types of interest protected by qualified privilege in this way are the defendant's *private* interest, *common* interest or, in certain circumstances, *public* interest.

Private interest. For example, where the defendant is accused of a crime and blames the plaintiff, whom he suspects of being guilty of fraud, for fear that his commercial reputation may suffer. People are entitled to a degree of flexibility in application of the law of defamation - although not going beyond what is reasonably necessary - to protect their own interests when these are threatened. In *Turner v. Metro-Goldwyn-Meyer Pictures Ltd* [1950] 1 All ER 449 this right was linked to that of self-defence in criminal law - although the analogy is not entirely apposite. In *Osborne v. Boulter* [1930] 2 KB 226, the defendant beer brewer was held entitled to the defence when he dictated a letter to his secretary, accusing the plaintiff of watering down the defendant's beer - the defendant had previously complained that the beer was of poor quality. All the defendant was doing was protecting his business.

Again, in *Watts v. Times Newspapers Ltd, supra*, p.634, the Court of Appeal considered that the defendant newspaper, which had published the allegedly defamatory apology for an earlier libel, being the guilty party rather than victim, could not be said to have an interest within the meaning of *Adam v. Ward* so as to be entitled to rely upon the defence of qualified privilege. Not so, however, in the case of the solicitors for their previously defamed client, who had requested inclusion of the allegedly defamatory words in the newspaper's published apology towards their client. The client was the victim and consequently had an interest in having his point of view put forward within reasonable bounds, so that both he and his solicitors as his representatives were protected by qualified privilege.

Common interest. Defendant's and recipient's interests in the information communicated are the same, for example, where members of a trade association are informed about the alleged conduct of one of their number, or employees are informed by the employer of the reason for dismissal of the plaintiff employee, or a landlord is complained to by a tenant about the behaviour of another tenant, the plaintiff - the common interest being protection of the trade association, employer's business and landlord's property together with their members, employees and other tenants respectively (*Knight v. Gibbs* (1834) A & E 43). In *Bryanston Finance Ltd v. De Vries* [1975] QB 703, the defendant was protected by qualified privilege when dictating a memorandum to a secretary, because of common business interest.

Public interest. The defence of the general public's interest is, as seen earlier, unlikely to succeed, unless a very strong case for protection of the public can be shown. In *Blackshaw v. Lord* [1983] 2 All ER 311, the Court of Appeal held publication by a national newspaper of an unproven claim that the plaintiff was implicated in the loss of large sums of public money was not covered by qualified privilege, being mere rumour and "tittle-tattle". However, Stephenson, LJ did indicate that dangers from suspected terrorists, drugs or poisoned food would justify reporting. One type of communication which will be justified in the public interest is that concerning conduct of public officials, including Judges, made to the appropriate authorities rather than to the public generally through the newspapers (*Harrison v. Bush* (1856) 5 E & B 344). It should usually be safe to complain to a Member of Parliament about matters suspected of occurring in his constituency (*Beach v. Freeson* [1972] 1 QB 14) - although statements published by candidates in national or local elections are not automatically covered by privilege just by reason of their Parliamentary connexion (Defamation Act 1952, s.10).

c. Reports of public proceedings

(1) *Parliamentary proceedings.* Fair and accurate reports, whole or partial, verbatim or not, written or broadcast, are protected by qualified privilege at common law and by statute (*Wason v. Walter* (1868) LR 4 QB 73; Parliamentary Papers Act 1840, s.3; Defamation Act 1952, s.9(1); Broadcasting Act 1990, sch.20, para.1).

(2) *Judicial proceedings.* Again, fair and accurate reporting is protected, provided that it is not blasphemous or obscene - even when not carried out at the same time as the proceedings, in which circumstances, it will be recalled, absolute privilege is unavailable.

(3) *Other proceedings.* Section 7 of the Defamation Act 1952 grants qualified privilege to fair and accurate newspaper accounts or broadcasts of certain proceedings specified in the Schedule to the Act which are of public concern and benefit. The Schedule contains two different categories of statement, which are treated differently: (i) statements privileged without explanation or contradiction (Schedule Part I) - these include those relating to foreign Commonwealth legislatures, courts and public inquiries,

international courts, and UK judicial notices; and (ii) statements privileged subject to explanation and contradiction (Schedule Part II) - here qualified privilege is lost if the plaintiff requested the defendant to publish in the same source as the original account a reasonable statement of explanation or contradiction and the defendant failed to do so; these include fair and accurate reports of decisions of trade, cultural or sporting associations; of public inquiries and local government meetings; meetings of public companies; and official notices, including media broadcasts by the police (*Boston v. W.S. Bagshaw & Sons* [1966] 2 All ER 906).

Clause 15 and Schedule 1 to the Defamation Bill 1996 will replace ss.7-9(2) and (3) of the 1952 Act, to be repealed by Schedule 3 to the 1996 proposed legislation along with Broadcasting Act 1990, Schedule 20, paras.2 and 3. In brief: a) Part I statements having qualified privilege without explanation or contradiction are to be extended to fair and accurate reports of *inter alia* legislatures, courts, public inquiries and international organizations or conferences *anywhere in the world*; and b) Part II statements privileged subject to explanation or contradiction are notably to be extended to fair and accurate reports of proceedings of European institutions, and of any other bodies which may be designated.

Clause 15 elaborates, in respect of Part II statements, that there is no defence thereunder if the plaintiff shows that the defendant was requested to publish in a suitable manner a reasonable letter of explanation or contradiction and refused or neglected to do so - suitable manner meaning in the same manner as the publication complained of or in a manner that is adequate and reasonable in the circumstances. The clause goes on to provide that it does not apply to publication to the public of a matter which is not of public concern and publication of which is not for the public benefit.

2. *Requirement of absence of malice on the part of the defendant*

If the plaintiff can prove malice, the defendant is unable to rely upon the defence of qualified privilege (*Telnikoff v. Matusevitch* [1991] 4 All ER 817).

The defendant will be guilty of malice if:

(a) he did not believe his statement to be true (*Horrocks v. Lowe* [1975] AC 135) - although an honest but negligent belief in its truth will not remove the privilege (*Clark v. Molyneux* (1877) 3 QBD 237); or
(b) he was motivated to make the statement by spite or ill-will towards the plaintiff or recklessness as to the truth.

Malice on the part of the defendant is a question to be decided by the jury (provided that the Judge decides that there is sufficient evidence for consideration by the jury) in the light of all facts and circumstances including the parties' relationship, language used, past conduct and behaviour in court (*Broadway Approvals Ltd v. Odhams Press Ltd* [1965] 1 WLR 805).

Suppose that there are several defendants - for example, newspaper editor, publishers and author - but only one of them was malicious: does this mean that all are deprived of the defence? The answer is no - the others are still protected (although a principal is liable for the malice of his agent, but seemingly not vice versa). Thus, in *Egger v. Viscount Chelmsford* [1965] 1 QB 248, the plaintiff sued the committee members and secretary of the Kennel Club in respect of a letter written by the secretary as instructed by the committee which was entitled to qualified privilege. The Court of Appeal held that only those amongst the defendants whom the jury had found to have been motivated by malice were *deprived of the defence.*

Clause 15 of the Defamation Bill 1996 preserves this restriction upon qualified privilege where it is shown that the publication was made with malice.

(v) Fair Comment

This defence is intended to protect reasonable freedom of speech.

There are a number of elements which must be satisfied for the defence of fair comment to apply:

- the comment is on a matter of public interest;
- it is opinion, not fact;
- it is fair;
- the plaintiff is unable to prove malice.

1. Matters of public interest

The decision on this issue is a question of law for the Judge; if the Judge holds against public interest, the defendant must then rely on privilege.

Broadly, comments on public personalities, activities and materials should be covered by the defence, because these are matters which are "such as to affect people at large, so that they may be legitimately interested in, or concerned at, what is going on; or what may happen to them or to others; then it is a matter of public interest on which everyone is entitled to make fair comment" (*London Artists Ltd v. Littler* [1969] 2 QB 375, p.391, *per* Lord Denning MR). This, therefore includes politicians, Judges, books, plays, concerts, television programmes, the Royal family and any other "public figures" - provided that the comment is referable to their public position (wide terms of reference indeed). In the *London Artists* case, the defendants successfully pleaded fair comment in having published a letter alleging that the plaintiffs had conspired to bring to an end a play by persuading four main performers to terminate their contracts - the court said that the public had a legitimate interest in things which happened in the world of the theatre and in particular in the closure of a successful play. The public also has an interest in learning that certain rented housing is in an insanitary condition (*South Hetton Coal Co. Ltd v. North-Eastern News Association Ltd* [1894] 1 QB 133).

2. *Comment confined to opinion not fact*

It is for the jury to decide whether the statement should be construed as one of opinion or fact (although the Judge determines as a matter of law whether it is capable of being so). If the statement is one of fact, the defendant must seek to prove truth or privilege. As to methods of distinguishing opinion from fact, one common suggestion of commentators is that the former should be limited to statements which are incapable of objective confirmation: for example, X says Y is a scoundrel - opinion; X says Y is a thief - fact (*Dakhyl v. Labouchère* [1908] 2 KB 325: plaintiff, who described himself as medical specialist, called "quack of the rankest species" by defendant - opinion). The problem, of course, is the grey area in the middle: can there be anyone who does not believe that a proven thief is a scoundrel? Perhaps so - Robin Hood, the kind-hearted thief may be a case in point - mere opinion to call him a scoundrel.

In *Telnikoff v. Matusevitch* [1991] 4 All ER 817, a majority of the House of Lords held that in deciding whether the defendant's letter to a newspaper implying that the plaintiff was a racist, was fact or opinion, the defendant could not cite the wording of the plaintiff's own earlier letter to the newspaper which led to the defendant's response, because it could not be assumed that readers of the defendant's letter would also have read the plaintiff's. Thus, the jury should reach a view on fact or opinion solely with regard to the words of the defendant's letter.

There is a further requirement.

If the facts upon which the opinion is based are included in the statement, they must be substantially correct or the opinion will not be protected. However, there are three qualifications to this requirement. First, s.6 of the Defamation Act 1952 expressly provides that the defence of fair comment does not fail just because some of the facts alleged are not proved, if the opinion is fair comment having regard to such of the allegations of fact which have been proved. For example, the defendant says of the plaintiff that he is not fit to be the club treasurer because he is a *thief, innumerate* and has *no financial qualifications.* It may be considered that proof of any one of these factual bases for the opinion as to lack of fitness would be sufficient. Secondly, although any facts upon which the comment was based, and which are included in the statement of opinion, must be accurate, they need only consist of sufficient facts in the circumstances to enable the recipient to judge the opinion's worth, and not all of them. The leading case is *Kemsley v. Foot* [1952] AC 345 where the defendant, Michael Foot, one time leader of the Labour Party in opposition, wrote an article accusing a newspaper of the "foulest piece of journalism ... for a long time" and headed "Lower than Kemsley". Kemsley, the plaintiff, was a different newspaper proprietor who had no connexion with the first newspaper, and he brought defamation proceedings against Foot for implying that Kemsley's standards were otherwise the lowest in journalism. The House of Lords held that the defence of fair comment applied, because there was sufficient indication of fact in the comment, as a matter of construction thereof, upon which the defendant's opinion of the plaintiff could be based: namely, the fact of whether or not the plaintiff's newspaper knowingly published falsehoods. Further facts need not be provided: the defendant need only get his "basic facts right" (*London Artists Ltd v. Littler, per* Lord Denning).

Thirdly, as will have been gathered from the preceding case, although sufficient facts must be included (you cannot just say "X is a fool", without providing facts in support of the opinion), the factual basis of the opinion need not always be expressly set out and can be inferred through construction of the words used.

3. Comment is fair

What is *fair* in this life? Is it the fact that the defendant, however unreasonably, honestly believed his comment to be correct, which makes the comment "fair" - the subjective test, or does the actual content of the opinion expressed in the comment itself have to be reasonable for it to be fair - the objective approach? In *Slim v. Daily Telegraph* [1968] 1 All ER 497, the subjective test appeared to be favoured - was the defendant an honest man expressing his genuine opinion? However, it is now clear from *Telnikoff v. Matusevitch* [1994] 4 All ER 817 that the objective approach applies and that if this is satisfied by the defendant, it is then for the plaintiff to try to prove malice as a lack of honest belief in the truth of the comment on the part of the defendant, so that what is otherwise the defence of fair comment will no longer operate. In that case, the House of Lords held that the defendant did not have to prove his honest belief in the statement to be protected by fair comment, and adopted the objective formulation of the test that the defendant merely had to establish that any fair-minded person could honestly have expressed the opinion on the proved facts. In other words the defendant need not prove that *all* reasonable men would have held the opinion he did - an absolute standard of fairness - he need only show that it was possible for a person to share the opinion and still be regarded as reasonable, even if other people - perhaps a majority - would reasonably have taken a different view. Respectable differences of opinion are quite capable of arising in such matters. The *Bolam* test in defamation. The burden is then on the plaintiff to prove malice. Thus, in *Lyon v. Daily Telegraph Ltd* [1943] KB 746, the defendant newspaper published a letter from a reader who gave false details of identity, without checking this. It was held that if it was possible for the opinion in the letter reasonably to be held, it did not also have to be shown that it was honestly held for fair comment to be available.

Clearly, the more *extreme* the view expressed, the harder it may be for the defendant to satisfy the objective requirement that *any* reasonable man could have held it - although this is not to say that the opinion itself must be reasonable, bearing in mind that many reasonable people can make mistakes and draw the wrong conclusions about others from the facts (*Campbell v. Spottiswoode* (1863) 3 B & S 769 - no reasonable basis for believing that the plaintiff's purpose in spreading Christianity in China was to sell more newspapers, even if the defendant himself honestly believed it).

4. Malice destroys fair comment

It is open to the plaintiff to prove malice as in the case of qualified prejudice.

The meaning is basically the same - the defendant did not genuinely believe what he said to be true and instead acted from spite or some other improper motive, for example, so as to bring about the failure of a rival play, book or business (*Thomas v. Bradbury Agnew & Co. Ltd* [1906] 2 KB 627 - book review held to have been inspired by malice from wording and defendant's behaviour as a witness in court).

In the case of several defendants pleading fair comment, *Egger v. Viscount Chelmsford* [1965] 1 QB 248, was a case on malice and qualified privilege, holding the latter to continue in relation to the non-malicious defendants (*supra,* p.640). Presumably, this is also the position in respect of fair comment, where malice can be proved on the part of one defendant - say, a cinema critic - but not also on that of another - a magazine's editor or publisher (*Lyon v. Daily Telegraph Ltd*).

(vi) Defamation Bill 1996

This contains two new statutory defences.

1. "Mechanical" publishers - Clause 1

This places on a statutory footing the defence already developed by the courts (see *supra,* pp.615-6).

The defendant will have a defence if he shows that

- he was not the author, editor or publisher;
- took reasonable care in relation to the publication complained of; and
- did not know, and had no reason to believe, that what he did caused or contributed to the publication of a defamatory statement.

Authors, editors and publishers are then defined - and do not include *inter alia* those only involved in printing, producing, distributing or selling printed material containing the statement, or in processing, copying, distributing, exhibiting or selling film or sound recordings or electronic media containing the statement, or in operating equipment; nor do they include the broadcaster of a live programme containing the statement where the broadcaster has no effective control over the maker of the statement; nor the operator of a communications system for such statements made by a person over whom he has no effective control. Employees of author, editor or publisher have the same liability as these latter to the extent that they are responsible for the content of the statement or the decision to publish it.

Finally, the clause assists in determination of whether a person took reasonable care or had reason to believe that what he did caused or contributed to the publication. It requires regard to be had to the extent of his responsibility for the content of the statement or the decision to publish it; nature or circumstances of publication; and previous conduct or character of author, editor or publisher.

2. *Offer to make amends - Clauses 2-4*

Subject to one qualification (see *infra*), this is intended to broaden the existing defence in Defamation Act 1952, s.4 - to be repealed by Schedule 3 - which at present only applies to "unintentional" defamation (*supra,* p.610). It will in future apply whenever a person has published an allegedly defamatory statement and may be used at any time prior to serving a defence in defamation proceedings. There are provisions as to the form of the offer to make amends, and content - being to publish correction or apology and to take practicable steps to notify readers and to pay any agreed or determined compensation (clause 2). Other rules (clause 3) relate to the acceptance of the offer, subject to the supervision of the court, and to determination of compensation and costs. If the offer is not accepted, it is available to the offeror to be used as a defence in defamation proceedings brought by the offeree, or in mitigation of damages (clause 4).

The qualification to the generality of the new statutory defence, mentioned above, is that:

(a) the defence is still unavailable if the person making the statement knew or had reason to believe that the statement referred to the complainant or would be likely to be understood to do so (that is, by innuendo) and was false and defamatory - so far closely following 1952 Act, s.4;

(b) but, in future, *it shall be presumed until the contrary is shown that he did not know and had no reason to believe* that that was the case: reversal of the burden of proof through rebuttable presumption of innocence (clause 4(3)).

3. Remedies

(i) Damages

In *John v. MGN Ltd* (1995) *The Times,* December 14, CA, Sir Thomas Bingham, MR described damages as the *primary remedy* in defamation claims.

Juries decide on the amount of damages for defamation (notwithstanding that Judges may hint at the amount as a rough guide to the jury, for example, "the cost of an ordinary family saloon car") and appeal courts are reluctant to interfere unless they consider the sum to be so inappropriate as not to have been decided upon according to rational and proper principles.

Previously, if the appeal court did hold the award to be too high or too low, the case had to be re-heard at first instance. Now, however, Rules of the Supreme Court Order 59, r.11(4) empowers the appeal court to substitute its own figure.

The following are types of damages awards:

1. Compensatory amount

The principle is one of compensation for loss of reputation and hurt feelings. Not surprisingly, amounts are hard to predict and most ordinary people do not bother to sue, for fear of the legal costs in the event that they lose. Furthermore, there has been some concern and indignation that defamation awards appear to be higher than those in "more deserving" spheres such as personal injuries. One judgment for libel in connexion with allegations about wartime activities was for £1.5 million (see, however, *infra,* p.654, *Tolstoy v. United Kingdom* (1995) *The Times,* July 19). Jason Donovan, the pop star, obtained £100,000 in 1992 and Jeffrey Archer, the novelist and former Member of Parliament, £500,000 in 1987. Graham Souness, the football manager, was awarded £750,000 in 1995.

2. Nominal damages

The jury can award "nominal damages" - a very small sum - if it considers that the plaintiff suffered little or no actual damage from a libel.

3. Contemptuous damages

These low awards may be made where the plaintiff wins

his defamation case even though his conduct was not of a very high standard. Thus, in *Dering v. Uris* [1964] 2 QB 669, the jury awarded damages of one halfpenny to a plaintiff who had proved that defamatory statements were made, but who, it was alleged, was nonetheless guilty of war crimes.

4. Exemplary damages

Defamation is one of the exceptional cases where English courts are permitted to award exemplary damages (*Cassell & Co. v. Broome* [1972] AC 1027). Their object is to penalize a defendant where the gains which were intended or expected to be derived from the defamation (for example, through additional sales) would exceed the damages which would normally be ordered to be paid.

5. Aggravated damages

These will not be awarded as a separate head of damages in defamation. Nevertheless, the jury can increase the amount of its award to take account of the fact that there is a need for greater compensation because of the defendant's particularly bad behaviour in, for example, refusing to admit that the statement was false or continuing to publish it (*Sutcliffe v. Pressdram* [1990] 1 All ER 269).

6. Payment into court

If a defendant offers to settle the action and pays a certain sum of money into court by way of settlement, a plaintiff who refused the offer must pay both sides' legal costs from the date of payment in if the eventual damages award does not exceed the amount paid in (*Roach v. Newsgroup Newspapers Ltd* (1992) *The Times,* November 23). If a plaintiff agrees to settle for such amount, the defendant cannot then claim that he only paid the sum for commercial reasons (*Charlton v. EMAP plc* (1993) *The Times,* June 11).

There are two provisions in the Defamation Bill 1996 which should be drawn attention to in connexion with damages.

First, it will be recalled (see *supra*, p.647, *et seq.*) that where an offer to make amends is not accepted by the offeree, the offeror can rely upon this fact in mitigation of damages, whether or not it was also relied on as a defence - encouragement indeed (clause 4(5)).

Secondly, clause 13 brings out any skeletons from the plaintiff's cupboard. He cannot recover damages for injury to his reputation beyond those to which he would be entitled if all relevant facts affecting his reputation were generally known - and the defendant is permitted to adduce evidence of such facts in mitigation of damages. However, it is further expressly provided that the court can exclude evidence of specific facts if it appears that it would be in the interests of justice to do so, having regard to the time which has elapsed since the matters in question occurred and their relative unimportance in the quantification of damages - clearly a provision inserted in order to preserve some of the fun in libel lawyers' lives!

(ii) Injunction

The plaintiff may also seek an injunction if there is a real fear of repetition. Even before publication, he can ask for an interim injunction to prevent a potentially defamatory broadcast or publication (*Gulf Oil (GB) Ltd v. Page* [1987] Ch 327) - but this will be very hard to obtain when the defendant pleads one of the defences (*Femis-Bank (Anguilla) Ltd v. Lazar* [1991] Ch 391).

(iii) New Approaches to Remedies

Common criticisms of the law of libel are that awards are too high and are as uncertain as a lottery.

In *Rantzen v. Mirror Group Newspapers* [1993] 3 WLR 953 the Court of Appeal indicated a possible new approach to the principles of compensation for defamation, based on the fact that s.8 of the Courts and Legal Services Act 1990 enabled the Court of Appeal to alter a jury's award of damages which it regarded as excessive or inadequate (previously, the award had to be "divorced from reality"): Article 10 of the European Convention on the Protection of Human Rights and Fundamental Freedoms (signed by the United Kingdom in 1951 but not yet incorporated into English law) provided that freedom of speech could only be limited by *necessary* restrictions, and so, according to the Court of Appeal, *excessive* in s.8 was to be interpreted in the light of the latter - whether a reasonable jury could have thought that the award was *necessary to compensate the plaintiff and to re-establish his reputation* was to be the test for the Court of Appeal in future cases. A new body of case law was to be built up by juries, aside from past awards, taking account of current purchasing power of awards and of how much was really necessary to restore the plaintiff's reputation, and without looking at previous non-s.8 awards or at those in personal injuries actions. At least this appeared to be a more scientific-*looking* test.

(iv) Restatement of Damages Practice: John v. MGN Ltd

In recent times, the Court of Appeal brought about a major restatement and reform of previous English practice in the grant of damages awards in defamation cases, in its judgment in the case of *John v. MGN Ltd* (1995) *The Times*, December 14, CA.

In summary, amounts were to be reduced, significantly in some cases, to the level of those in personal injury disputes, since it was considered to be offensive to public opinion that the former should exceed the latter, sometimes by a substantial amount. In addition, previous practice would be changed, so that Judges and parties' lawyers would in the future be permitted to make suggestions to the jury as to appropriate sums of damages. Furthermore, the limits on awards and amounts of exemplary damages were reasserted.

In the case itself, the popular performer, Elton John, sued the publishers of the defendant newspaper in respect of a defamatory article. The High Court jury awarded £75,000 compensatory damages and £275,000 exemplary damages. On appeal, the Court of Appeal reduced these sums to £25,000 and £50,000 respectively and delivered directions for the practice to be followed by juries in future cases, based upon justice to plaintiffs and defendants and such public interests as might be involved.

The Court of Appeal dealt with both compensatory and exemplary damages.

Compensatory

In contrast to personal injury cases, where Judges sat alone without juries and were able to develop broadly comparable systems of damages awards, Judges in defamation proceedings had avoided providing anything but the broadest guidelines on damages to juries, out of respect for the juries' role. Juries were simply told to make *reasonable* awards, yet not also what might be considered to be reasonable. As a consequence, sums of money awarded could be wholly disproportionate to the damage to the plaintiff's reputation. But, as the Master of the Rolls pointed out, this was not the fault of juries. They were like sheep let loose with no shepherd.

There had been some improvements: in *Sutcliffe v. Pressdram Ltd* [1991] 1 QB 153, the Court of Appeal recommended that juries' attention should be drawn to the purchasing power of awards; under RSC Ord.59, r.11(4) the Court of Appeal could substitute its own figure; and in *Rantzen,* it had directed that whereas reference should not be made to past awards preceding the new power of substitution, the Court of Appeal's own awards would eventually grow into a valuable source to be referred to. Yet it rejected the idea of comparative reference to (generally lower) personal injuries awards. Thus, in *John,* the defendants requested the Court of Appeal to reconsider the previous rejection, since the number of Court of Appeal decisions to refer to on defamation itself was not yet very large and awards still seemed too high. Elsewhere in courts in the British Commonwealth, personal injury damages had begun to be taken into account, Article 10 of the European Convention on Human Rights (*supra,* p.652) had been held to correspond with English common law, and in *Tolstoy v. United Kingdom* (1995) *The Times,* July 19, [1995] 20 EHRR

442, the European Court of Human Rights had held that the size of the defamation award by the English courts against the applicant (£1,500,000 - see *supra*, p.649) was a violation of his freedom of expression under Article 10 (at that time, the Court of Appeal did not yet have the power to substitute its own figure for the jury's - see *supra*, p.649).

Accordingly, the Court of Appeal agreed to look again at the position, believing it to be unhealthy for libel law to fail to command general respect and to be regarded by some as a road to untaxed riches.

The following is a summary of the Court of Appeal's findings:

(1) *Rantzen* was correct that juries should not look at old awards made in the absence of specific guidelines.

(2) It was also agreed that valuable reference could be made to the Court of Appeal's own confirmed or substituted awards under 1990 Act, s.8, although these would not develop very rapidly.

(3) However, in relation to personal injuries awards, it was not agreed with *Rantzen* that such sums could not serve as guidance for juries in defamation cases. Although it was not being suggested that exact *equivalence* was possible (confirming *Broome v. Cassell & Co. Ltd* [1972] AC 1027, 1071) - for how could effects of libel be compared with severe brain damage? - nevertheless, personal injuries levels might certainly act as a *control* upon defamation amounts. Therefore, even though no exact comparison and guide was possible, the jury in a

very serious libel case might still be made aware of the maximum award for serious brain damage (about £125,000) and be asked to consider whether sums for damage to a person's reputation ought to exceed this. The expressed view of the Court of Appeal itself was that it would be quite offensive to public opinion to reach such a conclusion and wholly proper that the Judge should be able to draw the jury's attention to comparative levels of awards.

(4) Finally, previous practice was that neither Judge nor parties' advocates could suggest amounts of damages to the jury. The Court of Appeal now considered that this was wrong. In personal injuries litigation, it had become common for both sides' lawyers to make such suggestions, which were helpful to, but not binding upon, the Judge. The court therefore saw no reason why Judges and lawyers should not indicate responsible amounts when addressing juries; and controls on sums so indicated would exist through plaintiffs' desire not to appear too greedy, and defendants' wish not to seem unrepentant. Consequently, figures put were likely to amount to the upper and lower brackets of awards: juries would not be bound by the Judge's or lawyers' suggestions and they would be directed to make up their own minds (conscious too that if they went outside the sums indicated, the Court of Appeal would be likely to prefer their judgment on the matter to that of Judge and advocates).

The Court of Appeal described the preceding as *modest but important* changes of practice, which, far from undermining the constitutional position of the English libel jury (of which, historically, in any event, the more significant role involved decisions on defamatory nature of statements, rather than the assessment of quantum of damages), would in fact improve it by making their awards more rational and consequently the more acceptable to public opinion.

Exemplary damages

The Court of Appeal dealt with limits on their award and amount.

Awards were exceptional, especially in the light of Article 10 of the European Convention on Human Rights limiting restrictions upon freedom of expression to those prescribed by law and necessary for protection of reputation in a democratic society.

(1) *Conditions for exemplary awards for defamation were the following:*

   (a) The defendant must have had no honest and genuine belief in the truth of the defamatory statement - or have been reckless, meaning that he suspected that it was untrue but failed to take the obvious steps to check. Mere carelessness as to the truth by the defendant would not be sufficient for grant of exemplary damages.

   (b) The defendant must have had the motive of financial or material gain (a precise calculation, however, is not necessary) and the civil standard to prove this would not be easy for plaintiffs to discharge.

(c) A compensatory amount of damages would not be enough to punish the defendant and to deter others.

(2) *Amount of exemplary damages.* Relevant factors included the defendant's resources, his degree of fault and the profit he made. Since such damages were not compensatory, their amount should never exceed the minimum necessary to satisfy their underlying public purpose of punishment, prevention of profit from tort and deterrence. This was said to be quite consistent with Article 10 of the European Convention. Although the latter was not in force as such in the United Kingdom, there was no conflict between it and the common law, so that the same result would have been reached independently of the Convention or even if it did not exist.

4. Legislative Reform

In 1975 the Faulks Committee on Defamation (Cmnd 5909) made various proposals for reform, some of which were:

- abolish the distinction between libel and slander, in favour of the former;
- live broadcasts from Parliament should enjoy the defence of qualified privilege;
- exemplary damages for defamation should be abolished;

- a dead plaintiff's personal representatives should be able to continue the defamation action on behalf of the estate, and relatives of the deceased should be able to sue for an injunction;
- there should be a three-year limitation period from the date of publication, in place of the current six, in defamation actions;
- legal aid should be available for defamation; and
- juries should be at the Judge's discretion and should only make recommendations on damages.

Mostly, the recommendations have not been implemented.

However, as previously seen, there is now a Defamation Bill 1996 before Parliament (February 8, 1996 version).

This promises to make some interesting reforms, although most of the preceding are not included.

Many of the provisions of the Bill have already been noted above in the relevant sections:

(a) Clause 1 on the defence for mechanical publishers (*supra*, p.646, *et seq.*);
(b) Clauses 2-4 on the defence by way of offer to make amends (*supra*, p.647, *et seq.*);
(c) Clause 12 on evidential value to the defendant of proof of criminal conviction of the plaintiff (*supra*, p.623);
(d) Clause 13 on evidence of a plaintiff's reputation in assessment of damages for defamation (*supra*, p.651, *et seq.*);
(e) Clause 14 confirming the defence of absolute privilege for fair and accurate contemporaneous

reporting of United Kingdom and European Court of Justice court proceedings (*supra*, pp.628-9); and

(f) Clause 15 (together with Schedule 1) extending qualified privilege to fair and accurate reports of proceedings of specified bodies anywhere in the world in some cases, and to European institutions and designated bodies in others (*supra*, p.638).

The following further provisions should also be noted.

i. Limitation of actions - Clause 5

The limitation period for libel, slander and malicious falsehood is reduced from three years to one year from the date on which the cause of action accrued (and the Limitation Act 1980 accordingly amended). However, the court is given a discretion to disregard the period and to allow the action to proceed if this is considered equitable in all the circumstances, including possible prejudice to plaintiff or defendant, length of and reasons for the plaintiff's delay in institution of proceedings, when relevant facts became known to the plaintiff, the extent to which he acted promptly and reasonably after that time, and availability and cogency or otherwise of the evidence in the light of the delay.

ii. Court rulings on meaning of a statement - Clause 7

This provision prevents parties from seeking preliminary rulings from courts on whether a statement is "arguably capable" of bearing a particular meaning. They will be allowed by rules of court (see Clause 10, *infra*) to seek rulings on what meanings the statement is actually capable of bearing.

iii. Summary disposal of claims - Clauses 8-10

This is a new power of Judges to dispose of a defamation claim summarily. The claim may be dismissed if it appears to the court that it has no realistic prospect of success and there is no reason why it should be tried. Conversely, the court can give judgment for the plaintiff and grant him summary relief if it appears that there is no defence to the claim which has a realistic prospect of success and that there is no other reason why the claim should be tried.

The court can act on application by the plaintiff or of its own accord to grant summary relief, but in the latter event, it must be satisfied that the summary relief will adequately compensate the plaintiff for the wrong he has suffered. The court is required to have regard to a number of factors in considering whether a claim should be tried, for example, whether all possible defendants are before the court, any conflict of evidence, seriousness of the alleged defamation, as to content and extent of publication, and justification for trial in all the circumstances. Furthermore, the summary relief proceedings *are heard and determined without a jury* (Clause 8).

Summary relief itself is then defined to include: declarations that the statement was false and defamatory of the plaintiff; orders to the defendant to publish a suitable correction and apology; damages not over £10,000; and orders restraining (further) publication. Content, time, manner, form and place of publication of any correction and apology will be for parties to agree, and for the court's direction in the absence of parties' agreement (Clause 9). Provision is made for rules of court to determine the procedures relating to applications for and conduct of summary disposal proceedings (Clause 10).

iv. Miscellaneous

Clause 17(1) defines "statement" in the 1996 Bill as meaning words, pictures, visual images, gestures or any other method of signifying meaning. Both libel *and slander* are therefore alive and well under the proposed legislation (and Clause 20 expressly states that nothing in the legislation is to affect the law of criminal libel).

Under Clause 19, Clauses 1, 5, 6, 12 and 13 *et al* will come into effect at the end of two months following Royal Assent; most of the rest will do so on an appointed day.

Further reading:

Brazier, *Street on Torts*, 9th ed, 1993 (Butterworth & Co., England): chs.23, 24 and 25.

Fleming, J.G., *The Law of Torts*, 8th ed, 1992 (The Law Book Company, Sydney): ch.25.

Hepple, B.A. and Matthews, M.H., *Tort: Cases and Materials*, 4th ed, 1991 (Butterworth & Co., London): ch.16.

Heuston, R.F.V. and Buckley, R.A., *Salmond and Heuston on The Law of Torts*, 20th ed, 1992 (Sweet & Maxwell, London): ch.8.

Howarth, D., *Textbook on Tort*, 1995 (Butterworth & Co., London): ch.12.

Jones, M.A., *Textbook on Torts*, 4th ed, 1993 (Blackstone, London): ch.13.

Markesinis, B.S. and Deakin, S.F., *Tort Law*, 3rd ed, 1994 (Clarendon Press, Oxford): ch.7.

Rogers, W.V.H., *Winfield and Jolowicz on Tort*, 14th ed, 1994 (Sweet & Maxwell, London): ch.12.

Stanton, K.M., *The Modern Law of Tort*, 1994 (The Law Book Company, Sydney): ch.24.
Weir, T., *A Casebook on Tort*, 7th ed, 1992 (Sweet & Maxwell, London): ch.14.

Chapter 27

Malicious (Injurious) Falsehood

This is a tort of publication of false statements about a person's goods or services, which damages him economically as opposed to his personal reputation (although damages for his injured feelings can also be granted). In *Ratcliffe v. Evans* [1892] 2 QB 524, the plaintiff succeeded against a newspaper which had maliciously and falsely reported that the plaintiff's firm had gone out of business, which caused the plaintiff to suffer serious business losses.

There are other differences from defamation:

(a) a deceased defendant's estate can be sued for malicious falsehood;
(b) legal aid is available - juries are not;
(c) the plaintiff must prove malice on the part of the defendant;
(d) unlike in libel, the plaintiff must prove actual loss;
(e) the plaintiff must prove that the statement was untrue - this is presumed in defamation in the absence of contrary proof, if the words are defamatory (see above, p.594, *et seq.*);
(f) damages are lower than for defamation.

The difference from the tort of deceit is that in the latter the false statement causing loss is made by the defendant *to* the plaintiff rather than to a third party *about* the plaintiff.

Particularly because of the availability of legal aid, a plaintiff might think of trying to use malicious falsehood in place of defamation, or in the alternative if jury trial is also desired, although this does not happen frequently. In *Joyce v. Sengupta* [1993] 1 All ER 897 the defendants published false statements accusing the plaintiff of stealing intimate letters from Princess Ann and sending them to the press. The plaintiff's action for malicious falsehood entitled her to legal aid, but was struck out as an abuse of process at first instance on the ground that the claim should have been for libel. The Court of Appeal disagreed however. Appropriateness of a grant of legal aid was a matter for the Legal Aid Board to decide upon, not the courts; and the plaintiff did seem to have an arguable case of malice on the part of the defendants and of financial loss through reduced employment opportunities.

In order to succeed, the plaintiff must show that the defendant made a statement of *fact* about the plaintiff's business, not mere opinion or a "trader's puff" (that is, acceptable advertising exaggeration about the merits of one's product). The authorities show that if the defendant simply says that his own produce is better than the plaintiff's, this is likely to be taken as a puff, non-actionable (*White v. Melin* [1895] AC 154). However, if he goes further and seriously and falsely suggests that the plaintiff's product is unsatisfactory, he will risk liability for malicious falsehood (*Lyne v. Nichols* (1906) 23 TRL 86). In *De Beers Products v. Electric Co. of New York* [1975] 1 WLR 972, the court noted there to be a difference between the defendant, on the one hand, saying that his goods were better than those of the plaintiff, and, on the other, adding that this was because the plaintiff's goods were rubbish, without any justification, which would found liability for malicious falsehood.

Malice in malicious falsehood is the same as in defamation, that is, the defendant knew that the statement was false or was reckless as to its truth and acted out of spite or ill will or in order to harm the plaintiff (even if he also intended to further his own business: *Joyce v. Motor Surveys Ltd* [1948] Ch 252). Thus, in *Greers Ltd v. Pearman & Corder Ltd* (1922) 39 RPC 406, the court held that it would presume malice from the fact that the defendant had knowingly made false allegations; but malice will not exist if the defendant had an honest belief in the truth of his statement, or was merely negligent and had no malicious intention (*Balden v. Shorter* [1933] Ch 247).

Particular *damage* must be proved by the plaintiff, which can be difficult, but s.3 of the Defamation Act 1952 enables the court to assume general loss of business where the defendant intended to harm the plaintiff's interests. In *Allason v. Campbell and Others* (1996) *The Times,* May 8, Drake, J held that although the plaintiff Member of Parliament and author had succeeded in establishing falsehood and malice on the part of one of the defendants, Mirror Group Newspapers, in respect of a Daily Mirror newspaper article about him (it had overstated the number of MPs who had invited him to contribute certain libel damages he had won to people who were "Maxwell pensioners" and had also failed to state that the MPs were all in the opposing political party), nevertheless, he was unable to prove that he had lost any book contract as a result of the article nor that he had suffered any other financial loss. The defendants were not liable for malicious falsehood in the absence of such damage.

Malicious falsehood, it will be noted (together with *slander of title* to land and *slander of goods* which are now in practice superseded by malicious falsehood) is expressly included in Clause 5 of the Defamation Bill 1996, alongside libel and slander. It will be recalled (see *supra*, p.660, *et seq.*) that Clause 5 seeks to reduce the current six-year limitation period for such claims to just one year from the date of accrual of the cause of action, subject to equitable extension.

Further reading:

Fleming, J.G., The Law of Torts, 8th ed, 1992 (The Law Book Company, Sydney): ch.30.

Heuston, R.F.V. and Buckley, R.A., Salmond and Heuston on The Law of Torts, 20th ed, 1992 (Sweet & Maxwell, London): ch.18.

Howarth, D., Textbook on Tort, 1995 (Butterworth & Co., London): ch.12.

Markesinis, B.S. and Deakin, S.F., Tort Law, 3rd ed, 1994 (Clarendon Press, Oxford): ch.7.

Chapter 28

Malicious Prosecution

This is a tort where a defendant has abused the facility of judicial process against the plaintiff.

It is an old tort which has its origin in a period when there was no public police authority to concern itself with the proper prosecution of offenders, and nowadays it is very hard to succeed, because of a policy that prosecution of offenders should not be undesirably obstructed.

Consequently, there are a number of hurdles for the plaintiff to jump if he is to prove successful.

(i) Defendant Initiated a Criminal Prosecution Against the Plaintiff

Usually it will be a policeman who is the defendant as being "actively instrumental" in putting the processes of law in force (*Danby v. Beardsley* (1840) 43 LT 603). A person who merely reported a suspected crime to the police, who then investigated the matter before charging the plaintiff, is not liable for initiating the prosecution of the plaintiff. He must have done more, such as signing a charge sheet and agreeing to appear as a witness, upon which the prosecution is substantially based, as may be the position in the case of department store detectives. Even in the latter case, however, it seems that the normal assumption will be that it was the police, not the provider of information, who were responsible for the effects (see *Davidson v. Chief Constable of North Wales* [1994] 2 All ER 597, on false imprisonment, *supra*, ch.17). However, in *Martin v. Watson* [1995] 3 WLR 318 the House of Lords adopted, unanimously, an even more extensive construction of malicious prosecution, where the defendant, who was in dispute with the plaintiff, her neighbour, falsely accused him of indecently exposing himself to her. The plaintiff was arrested, but subsequently discharged and he sued the defendant for malicious prosecution. The problem for the plaintiff was that it was the police who had initiated the prosecution on the complaint being made by the defendant. Nevertheless, the House of Lords held that the fact that a defendant was not technically the prosecutor should not enable her to escape liability where she was *in substance the person responsible for the prosecution having been brought* (p.326). Simply giving information to the police would not make a person the prosecutor, but where the circumstances were such, as here, that the police were reliant solely upon the defendant's evidence so that it was virtually impossible for the police to exercise any independent discretion, the defendant would be held to have procured the prosecution: criminal penalties for perjury or wasting police time would not adequately compensate the plaintiff, whereas, a *bona fide* defendant who had complained to the police without malice and with reasonable cause, had nothing to fear (p.328).

It is not certain whether the Crown Prosecution Service, which reviews cases sent to them by the police for possible prosecution, can be liable for malicious prosecution in view of the major role played by the police in the system. It may be that the administrative remedy of judicial review would be more appropriate. Certainly it was seen above (p.227) that in *Elguzouli-Daf v. Commissioner of Police of the Metropolis* [1995] 2 WLR 173, the Court of Appeal held that as a matter of public policy, the CPS was not under a common law duty of care in negligence towards an accused person in custody on the ground of delays in processing the case.

(ii) Without Reasonable and Probable Cause

The plaintiff must prove absence of reasonable and probable cause for the prosecution, which is not easy especially if the defendant acted on legal advice.

The test seems to be a mixture of objective and subjective factors: that is, in the light of facts known to the defendant at the time (whether true or not), were there reasonable grounds for believing that the plaintiff was probably guilty of the crime (objective) *and* did the defendant honestly believe that the plaintiff was probably guilty (subjective) - the former for the Judge and the latter for the jury (*Dallison v. Caffery* [1965] 1 QB 348).

(iii) Malice

The plaintiff must also satisfy the jury that the defendant was motivated by malice.

This means that the sole or dominant motive for the prosecution was something other than that of bringing the accused to justice (*Brown v. Hawkes* [1891] 2 QB 718).

Where reasonable and probable cause exists, there is no liability, irrespective of the defendant's malicious motives; but if there is no reasonable and probable cause, malice is not presumed.

The burden of proof on the plaintiff is very hard to discharge. The plaintiff succeeded in *Taylor v. Metropolitan Police Commissioner* (1989) *The Times,* December 6, where a police officer had planted cannabis on the plaintiff.

(iv) Prosecution of the Plaintiff Fails

This is required, otherwise the tort might be used in order to retry the criminal case.

The plaintiff need not actually have been found "not guilty" and acquitted on the merits of the case: acquittal on a technicality, or the quashing of conviction on appeal, or discontinuance, is enough (*Herniman v. Smith* [1938] AC 305).

(v) Damage

The plaintiff must prove that he has suffered damage to his reputation, body or liberty, such as detention, or financial loss, for example, defence costs not recovered - upon which he can also claim damages for his distress and hurt feelings (*Savile v. Roberts* (1698) 12 Mod 208).

Except for malicious bankruptcy proceedings, no action in tort for malicious process can be brought in respect of *civil* proceedings. In principle, the victim's remedy is in recovery of his costs, although, in practice, this will be most unlikely to be accomplished in full.

Further reading:

Fleming, J.G., The Law of Torts, 8th ed, 1992 (The Law Book Company, Sydney): ch.27.

Howarth, D., Textbook on Tort, 1995 (Butterworth & Co., London): ch.9.

Jones, M.A., Textbook on Torts, 4th ed, 1993 (Blackstone, London): ch.12.

Rogers, W.V.H., Winfield and Jolowicz on Tort, 14th ed, 1994 (Sweet & Maxwell, London): ch.19.

Part XIV

Chapter 29

Defences to Torts

Even if the plaintiff succeeds in establishing the elements of a particular tort, the defendant may still be able to raise a defence to liability, which releases him either wholly or partially.

The following are the main defences which are open to a defendant:

(i) Volenti Non Fit Injuria (Consent)

1. General

This is the defence of *voluntary assumption of risk:* the plaintiff cannot complain if he is held to have consented to the conduct otherwise amounting to a tort.

It is a complete bar to recovery - which is why courts may prefer the defence of contributory negligence, which, since 1945, has permitted them to reduce damages and to apportion loss between plaintiff and defendant according to relative responsibility, rather than barring the plaintiff completely from recovery as in *volenti.*

The great age of *volenti* was the latter part of the nineteenth century, the era of individualism and entrepreneurial spirit, when, for example, employees were to be taken to have consented to dangerous conditions of service as the price of obtaining work.

2. *Elements of volenti non fit injuria*

The following conditions must be satisfied for the *volenti* defence to be able to be pleaded successfully:

a. Agreement

There must be an agreement - voluntary as will be seen - to take the risk. Such agreements may be express or by conduct.

i. Express. It is conceivable that the plaintiff is expressly warned by the defendant that the defendant is not going to act with proper regard for the plaintiff's safety, which the plaintiff accepts: for example, the defendant offers the plaintiff a lift in his car and states that the brakes are faulty - "no problem", says the plaintiff. That is express agreement, *volenti* (although it could be argued in the alternative that liability would not arise in the first place in any event, because of the reduced standard of care upon the defendant - see *infra*).

The matter is one of evidence and construction of words used: did the parties agree upon a course of action, according to which the plaintiff was consenting to the very conduct otherwise amounting to an actionable tort? If so, there can be no claim: *volenti,* express agreement.

This circumstance, however, must be distinguished on the evidence from another situation which appears to be the same or very similar, and yet is fundamentally distinct: that is where the agreement between the parties is that the plaintiff will *excuse the defendant* for his negligent acts. If the latter is the proper construction of the agreement on the evidence, then s.2(1) of the Unfair Contract Terms Act 1977 must be taken into account, which prohibits such notices or agreements excluding business liability (s.1(3)) in the case of death or personal injuries, and s.2(2) otherwise prevents such agreements and notices in respect of other loss or damage where they are not reasonable (*Johnstone v.Bloomsbury Health Authority* [1991] 2 All ER 293) - and s.2(3) expressly states that mere knowledge or awareness of the exclusion term or notice is not of itself to be taken as indicating voluntary acceptance of any risk.

ii. By Conduct. Courts are very reluctant to find consent from conduct, not least because they prefer the defence of contributory negligence, under which blame can be apportioned between the parties more equitably.

Mere knowledge of a risk of negligence is not regarded as sufficient for agreement (*Lynch v. Ministry of Defence* (1983) NI 216; *Woodley v. Metropolitan District Railway Co.* (1877) 2 Ex D 384). Consequently, for *volenti* to operate as a defence it would seem that there has to be something about the plaintiff's conduct which demonstrates that:

- he is not merely agreeing to a mere *risk* that the defendant *might* act negligently or commit some other tort (*Nettleship v. Weston* [1971] 2 QB 691);
- the circumstances are such that the risk of likelihood of tort is so strong that he is not merely consenting to the *possibility* thereof, but virtually no less than to the negligent act itself (*Morris v. Murray* [1991] 2 QB 6).

Some commentators express this distinction in terms of the

reasonableness or otherwise of the plaintiff's behaviour: conduct amounting to consent to negligence must be foolhardy and unreasonable for *volenti* to operate. However, whilst this description is broadly acceptable as a general, non-technical explanation, it is not entirely suitable, because it runs the risk of colliding with the different defence of contributory negligence which does indeed focus upon the plaintiff's behaviour as well as on that of the defendant. This said however, it is possible that a court might prefer *volenti* to contributory negligence in a situation where the plaintiff has been extremely unreasonable in his behaviour, because, under contributory negligence, the plaintiff would have to receive some damages. Thus, in *ICI Ltd v. Shatwell* [1965] AC 656, the plaintiff's job was to detonate explosives in a quarry. One of the detonators was faulty and the plaintiff and a colleague tested them in order to determine which. They did this from close by, which was against company rules, and there was an explosion, which injured both of them. The plaintiff sued the defendant company in respect of the other worker's negligence, and the House of Lords, having openly recognized that contributory negligence was not a complete bar to recovery, preferred instead to find *volenti* to exist on the part of the plaintiff in view of his leading role in causing the accident with the other worker, so that the plaintiff was unable to receive any damages at all.

This distinction, referred to above, between implied agreement to mere risk of tort - not *volenti* - and to the tort itself - *volenti* - may further be seen from cases involving drunken drivers and sports.

Drunk drivers

At common law, in *Dann v. Hamilton* [1939] KB 509 Asquith, J held that where a passenger accepts a lift in a car from an obviously drunk driver, the defendant cannot plead *volenti* as a defence, unless the drunkenness had so blatantly incapacitated the driver that allowing him to drive the plaintiff was like "intermeddling with an unexploded bomb or walking on the edge of an unfenced cliff" (p.518).

In other words, courts make a distinction on policy between, on the one hand, acceptance of a mere risk - not implied agreement and *volenti*, on the assumption that the plaintiff will nevertheless expect the defendant to do his best not to be negligent in the circumstances - and, on the other hand, agreement to virtually inevitable negligence - *volenti*. The position is the same for plaintiff passengers of defendant *learner* drivers, who will not necessarily be defeated by *volenti*, although there will probably be a reduction in damages for contributory negligence (*Nettleship v. Weston* [1971] 2 QB 691). In any event, s.149 of the Road Traffic Act 1988 now excludes the *volenti* defence where a defendant driver has compulsory insurance (see *Pitts v. Hunt* [1991] 1 QB 24). However, common law principles previously described will continue to apply in other situations. Thus, in *Morris v. Murray* [1990] 2 All ER 801, the plaintiff knew that the defendant was completely drunk when he accepted a ride in a stolen light aircraft piloted by the defendant. The aeroplane crashed and the defendant was killed. The plaintiff sued his estate in respect of the personal injuries he himself had suffered. The Court of Appeal held that, in the circumstances, the plaintiff was *volenti*: following *Dann v. Hamilton*, accepting the ride was like meddling with an unexploded bomb; the pilot was so drunk as to make the crash almost inevitable. Certainly, too, drunkenness is even more likely to lead to disaster where aircraft are concerned than in the case of cars!

Sports

Sports involve injuries. They are sometimes unavoidable. Danger is one of the things which makes sport exciting to both participants and spectators. Football, rugby and cricket can, and frequently do, lead to injuries to one or more of the players in the course of a match.

With regard to *participants,* the response of the courts appears to be:

- if the injury is suffered inside the normal rules of the game (including "reasonable" fouling), the plaintiff is *volenti,* since, by playing, he is impliedly accepting the inevitability of occasional injury, but
- if it was suffered outside the rules, it is not *volenti*: he might have accepted the *possibility* that an opponent might break the rules, but not its *inevitability.*

In *Simms v. Leigh Rugby Football Club* [1969] 2 All ER 923, the defendants were able to plead consent where the plaintiff was both tackled and thrown against a wall in a game of rugby. The evidence showed that the injury had arisen from the tackle, within the rules. Had it occurred from being thrown against the wall, outside the rules, consent would then not have been available.

In *Smoldon v. Whitworth* (1996) *The Times,* April 23, the plaintiff was injured when a rugby scrum collapsed (see *supra*, chs.5 and 6). Curtis, J held that the defendant *referee* was in breach of his duty of care in negligence to exercise proper control over the dangerous aspects of the game. Certainly, therefore, it is highly unlikely that sportsmen will be taken to have consented to more than merely minor and understandable errors of judgment on the part of referees and umpires when these lead to injuries - a further burden to add to a thankless task (although, the Judge did emphasize that this was a junior match and that there would not necessarily also be a breach of duty in a senior or international contest, played according to different rules)! Significantly however, the plaintiff lost his negligence claim against the opposing player.

As for sporting *spectators,* once again, they are taken to have impliedly consented to the inevitable risks within the rules of the game (*Wooldridge v. Sumner* [1963] 2 QB 43). If one stands in the crowd at a grand prix, one knows that one may be hit by a flying wheel. In *Murray v. Harringay Arena Ltd* [1951] 2 KB 529, defendants were held not liable when a spectator was struck by the puck at an ice-hockey match. However, again, spectators do not impliedly consent to more than the usual circumstances of injury.

It should be said, nevertheless, that although these sporting cases usefully illustrate the boundaries of consent for purposes of *volenti,* in fact they are not themselves instances of *volenti*: they were either cases in which the tort of *battery* was unable to be established in the first place owing to the victim's *consent,* or where the standard of care itself in *negligence* was significantly reduced in the light of the plaintiff's consent to a certain level of risk. Thus, in *Wooldridge v. Sumner* [1963] 2 QB 43, the plaintiff, a professional photographer, was injured by a horse which was being ridden too quickly round a bend at a horse show and crashed into a seating area. The Court of Appeal dealt with the case on the basis of standard of care to be shown in a fast-moving sport, where not every lapse of skill or judgment could be held to fall below the required legal standard. The rider would have had to have shown an almost reckless disregard for the spectators' safety to breach the standard of care, and this was not so on the facts.

b. Voluntary

Whatever it is that the plaintiff says or does which is held to amount to an agreement to accept the risk, he must have said it or done it *voluntarily*. It is not sufficient if he was compelled to do so or if he did not understand and appreciate what he was doing.

i. Pressure negating volenti. In *Bowater v. Rowley Regis Corporation* [1944] KB 476, at p.479, Scott, LJ commented: "A man cannot be said to be truly 'willing' unless he is in a position to choose freely and freedom of choice predicates ... the absence from his mind of any feeling of constraint so that nothing shall interfere with the freedom of his will."

Employees are frequently under great economic pressure. Everyone needs to work in order to live. Courts now recognize this and are reluctant to permit the *volenti* defence to succeed in actions against employers where the employee plaintiff has continued to work in unsafe conditions after having protested about these to the employer (*Smith v. Charles Baker & Sons* [1891] AC 325). His "agreement" to do so would not be said to be voluntary.

On the other hand, if the job is inherently dangerous, employees may encounter a successful plea of *volenti* by the employer. In *Gledhill v. Liverpool Abattoir Co. Ltd* [1957] 1 WLR 1028, *volenti* was successfully pleaded in an action brought by the plaintiff employee of a slaughter house who was struck by a hanging pig - an obvious risk.

ii. Protest. Agreement cannot be voluntary if given under protest. In *Smith v. Charles Baker*, the plaintiff worked in a quarry underneath a crane used to lift rocks over his head without warning. He made regular complaints to the defendant employer about this, but to no avail. Eventually, he was struck by a rock. The court held against *volenti*: the plaintiff had done all that he could by way of protest, but, other than to resign, there was little more that he could have done in order to show his disapproval.

iii. Drunk or mentally disordered plaintiffs. Where a person in protective custody, for example, in hospital or a police station, is negligently allowed to injure himself or to commit suicide in a drunken or mentally disordered state, his act will not be regarded as voluntary, and consequently *volenti* is unavailable; the converse is so when he was *compos mentis* at the relevant time at which he started upon his inevitably destructive course of action (*Kirkham v. Chief Constable of the Greater Manchester Police* [1990] 3 All ER 246).

iv. Rescuers. As is frequently the case, the courts have been fairly generous towards rescuers. The defence of *volenti* is no longer available against rescuers - even those who are professional (see *Salmon v. Seafarer Restaurants Ltd* [1983] 3

All ER 729: defendants liable towards a fireman, the aptly named Mr. Salmon, who was injured trying to put out a fire in a fish and chip shop) - unless the rescue was not truly necessary (see *Cutler v. United Dairies (London) Ltd* [1933] 2 KB 297, where *volenti* was successfully pleaded, because the plaintiff went into a field to calm some horses when there was no risk to anyone; compare *Haynes v. Harwood* [1935] 1 KB 146, in which a defendant was liable towards a policeman who stopped a runaway horse from galloping down a street towards some children).

c. Knowledge of the plaintiff

For consent to be voluntary and meaningful, the plaintiff must have had full knowledge of the risk (*Osborne v. London & North Western Railway Co.* (1888) 21 QBD 220).

The test is *subjective* not objective - did *this* plaintiff understand the true nature and extent of the danger of negligence or other tort? If he was himself too drunk to do so, he could not be *volenti (Morris v. Murray)* - although, damages can be reduced for his own contributory negligence in getting drunk in the first place.

d. Medical cases

These throw up particular questions of consent and knowledge. Lack of consent may not merely mean the absence of a defence against the tort of negligence, *but can actually give rise to a cause of action* for unlawful medical treatment, the tort of battery.

i. Consent to treatment. If people refuse consent to medical treatment - for example, Jehovah's Witnesses who will not have blood transfusions on religious grounds - it is to commit the torts of assault and battery to treat them against their will ; similarly if a person were to be injected with a long-term contraceptive drug which had not been requested and which was not known about, at the same time as receiving a vaccination for rubella.

Where patients are under 16 years of age, in accordance with their jurisdiction under s.100 of the Children Act 1989 to decide what is in the best interests of the child, courts hold that doctors may treat the patient notwithstanding the parents' objection (*Re J* [1990] 3 All ER 930) - unless the treatment would cause the child greater suffering. As to consent by the child itself, the doctor must assess whether the child has sufficient maturity to comprehend what the treatment is (see *Gillick v. West Norfolk and Wisbech Health Authority* [1985] 3 All ER 402). Where the patient is over 16, consent of the patient is required (Family Law Reform Act 1969, s.8(1)). The court's consent should be obtained to treatment of a mentally disordered person (*F v. West Berkshire Health Authority* [1989] 2 All ER 545).

ii. Negligence. The amount of knowledge provided to the patient can affect negligence. In *Wells v. Surrey Area Health Authority* (1978) *The Times,* July 20, the plaintiff signed a consent form to a caesarian section operation and sterilization in the course of a long and difficult birth. She later said that as a Roman Catholic she would not have agreed to be sterilized had she not been in such pain, that it had not previously been mentioned, and that she had been given no advice on the implications. The court held that she had not consented to the sterilization operation and doctors were negligent in not advising her properly.

Thus, even if an operation or treatment is itself carried out with all reasonable care, the doctor may still be negligent in doing so without properly obtaining the plaintiff patient's consent or giving them suitable warning of risks.

This, however, is subject to the principle that doctors do not in any event breach the standard of care in negligence if, in failing to provide any or sufficient information, they are acting in accordance with a responsible body of medical opinion and practice (*Bolam v. Friern Hospital Management Committee* [1957] 2 All ER 118 - see *supra,* ch.6). Thus, doctors enjoy a lot of freedom to decide how much information it is necessary to give a patient, so far as the establishment of negligence in the first place is concerned. In *Sidaway v. Governors of Bethlem Royal Hospital* [1985] 2 WLR 480, a one per cent chance of serious damage to an arm from surgery was considered by the House of Lords to be too small for the plaintiff to be informed about it. On the other hand, in *Rogers v. Whitaker* (1992) Aust Torts Rep 81, Australian courts seemed to consider that *Bolam* should only apply to diagnosis and treatment, not also to the duty to inform of risk. Thus, in that case, a woman who was not informed of a one in 14,000 chance of blindness from an eye operation, was held to be able to recover for negligence. Furthermore, even in the English High Court it has been held that if a defendant doctor's *own* normal practice was to warn of a one in 2,300 risk that a vasectomy operation would reverse itself, *Bolam* would not then provide a defence on the ground that a responsible body of medical opinion would not consider a warning to be necessary, where the defendant failed to warn the plaintiffs of the risk (see *Newell v. Goldenberg* [1995] 6 Med LR 371, *supra*, p.247) - in fact, the plaintiffs were awarded greatly reduced damages, because evidence showed that they would have accepted the risk even if they had been warned).

Where a plaintiff *has* been warned of a risk and the risk materializes, clearly here in normal circumstances the defendant will have the defence of *volenti.*

However, when an operation is carried out negligently, the mere fact that the patient agreed to such treatment (otherwise a battery) does not of course also mean that he consented to negligence; consequently, *volenti* is not available.

3. Distinction between volenti and exclusion of liability

As seen earlier (*supra*, pp.674-5), there is a very thin line between the *volenti* defence and exclusion of tort liability.

Volenti is a consent to the acts of the defendant otherwise amounting to negligence or other tort.

Exclusion of liability is where the plaintiff did not consent to the defendant's tortious behaviour - it was merely agreed that *if* the defendant did commit the tort, he would not be legally liable for it towards the plaintiff.

The distinction is important. Section 149 of the Road Traffic Act 1988 now prohibits both exclusion *and volenti* in relation to death or injury to motor vehicle *passengers*. But s.2 of the Unfair Contract Terms Act 1977 appears to prohibit only *exclusion* of (business) liability for negligence, not also *volenti* (although, it is expressly stated in s.2(3) that a person's agreement or awareness of a negligence exclusion term or notice is not of itself to be taken as indicating his voluntary acceptance of any risk).

(ii) Illegality of the Plaintiff's Conduct

A burglar is making his getaway after robbing your house. He climbs down the drainpipe, which gives way because you failed to mend it properly. Should you be liable to pay him damages for negligence? Of course not. Public policy demands that people engaged in criminal conduct should be denied access to civil remedies in respect of damage suffered in the course of those criminal activities. *Ex turpi causa non oritur actio* (no action should be founded upon illegal activity).

Thus, burglars bitten by dogs have no complaint (*Cummings v. Grainger* [1977] 1 All ER 104). A woman giving birth to a malformed child could not sue the hospital for failing to detect the abnormality and to advise on an abortion, when, at the time, abortion would have been illegal (*Rance v. Mid-Downs Health Authority* [1991] 1 All ER 801). An injured plaintiff cannot include a claim in respect of lost earnings from his profession *as a burglar (Burns v. Edman* [1970] 2 QB 541).

As is often the case in such matters, however, the problem is where to draw the line? Just because a plaintiff was convicted of stealing apples from a shop 20 years ago, he should not be prevented from suing the same shop for negligence today if he cuts himself on a jagged piece of metal sticking out from one of the shelves in the shop or if he slips on the wet floor.

The basis of the defence is public policy against permitting recovery (*Ashton v. Turner* [1981] QB 137).

1. The basic requirement

It would seem that illegality will only act as a defence where the claim relates to tort committed *in the course of the criminal activity in question*. So this will not apply where, for example, a burglar on his way home with his illegal gains is struck by a negligent driver; otherwise, of course, if the burglar is being pursued by the police from whom he is attempting to escape, so that the crime is still actively being carried on.

It would seem too from *Kirkham v. Chief Constable of the Greater Manchester Police* [1990] 3 All ER 246, 251, that the principle also applies to *immoral*, as well as to criminal behaviour (and *Revill v. Newbery* [1996] 1 All ER 291, at p.298, CA).

Seemingly, however, even if the tort *is* committed in the course of the crime, illegality will still not be a defence where the minor scale of the criminal offence is out of all proportion to the greater seriousness of the tort (*Barnes v. Nayer* (1986) *The Times*, December 19). It would be wrong to deprive an injured plaintiff of half a million pounds damages for serious personal injuries because he was stealing a ball-point pen at the time.

Thus too, in *Revill v. Newbery* [1996] 1 All ER 291, CA, the Court of Appeal held a 76 year-old man to be liable in negligence for personal injuries inflicted upon the plaintiff who had tried to break into the defendant's garden shed in the middle of the night. The defendant was awoken inside the shed and poked his shotgun through a hole in the door and fired it, hitting the plaintiff. The court considered the appropriate defence to be one of contributory negligence (see *supra*, chs.6 and 8) - although, in fact, the decision is not of general application on *ex turpi causa*, because, as Neill, LJ explained at p.299 (see too Evans, LJ at p.301 and Millett, LJ at p.302), the latter doctrine was in fact superseded, in the case of criminals who were also *trespassers* to the plaintiff's land, by s.1 of the Occupiers' Liability Act 1984, which specifically regulated the occupier's duty of care: "It seems to me to be clear that, by enacting s.1 of the 1984 Act, Parliament has decided that an occupier cannot treat a burglar as an outlaw and has defined the scope of the duty owed to him ... There is in my view no room for a two-stage determination whereby the court considers first whether there has been a breach of duty and then considers whether notwithstanding a breach the plaintiff is barred from recovering by reason of the fact that he was engaged in crime (*ibid.*)." Millett, LJ further expounded, at p.302, "there is no place for the doctrine *ex turpi causa non oritur actio* in this context ... If the doctrine applied, any claim by the assailant or trespasser would be barred no matter how excessive or unreasonable the force used against him."

2. *The rationale of the defence*

It will not have escaped the reader's notice that the defence of illegality seems extremely imprecise. When is the tort sufficiently closely connected with the criminal conduct for the latter to be a defence? When is the criminality to be considered to be of a "minor" scale when compared with the tort? Such questions depend for an answer upon the decision of the courts on the facts of each case - and in truth also upon judicial attitudes towards the plaintiff and the merits of his claim.

Courts have at times sought to justify their decisions on either of two alternative bases (see *Revill v. Newbery, supra, per* Neill, LJ at pp.298-9).

i. The impossibility of adjudication approach. Under this method, Judges affect to throw their hands up in the air in resignation and to say that the upright nature of their own lives makes it impossible for them to assess the standard of care to be expected towards those who operate in a criminal manner, because they know so little of their *modus operandi* and expected reactions; and consequently, particularly where both plaintiff and defendant are engaged on a common criminal activity, it is not possible to set a standard of care in favour of the plaintiff. *A plague on both their houses.* In *Pitts v. Hunt* [1991] 1 QB 24, the plaintiff and defendant were drunk when they left a discothèque and the defendant drove off on a motorcycle with the plaintiff as a passenger. The plaintiff urged the defendant, who had no licence and was uninsured, to drive recklessly; they crashed and the defendant was killed and the plaintiff injured. The majority of the Court of Appeal held that the plaintiff was barred by illegality: the injuries arose directly from the joint illegal behaviour, so that a standard of care from the defendant towards the plaintiff could not be set. The impossibility approach was preferred to the public conscience test below, because public reaction was considered frequently to be irrational and emotive and it was difficult to compare degrees of immorality in public eyes.

ii. Affront to the public conscience. This is the alternative basis for non-recovery, and is preferred by those who say that the impossibility of adjudication test is unrealistic since it is difficult maybe, but not impossible, to assess the standard of care owed by one criminal to another and that it is of no use anyway where the defendant himself is not also engaged in a criminal act.

In *Ashton v. Turner* [1981] QB 137, which involved an injury to the plaintiff passenger in a getaway car, Ewbank, J (at p.146), said that courts might not recognize a duty of care by one criminal to another, when they were participants in the same crime, in relation to acts done in the commission of that crime, as a matter of public policy. Again, in *Euro-Diam Ltd v. Bathurst* [1988] 2 All ER 23, Kerr, LJ commented: "The *ex turpi causa* defence ultimately rests on a principle of public policy that the courts will not assist a plaintiff who has been guilty of illegal (or immoral) conduct of which the courts should take notice. It applies if, in all the circumstances, it would be an affront to the public conscience to grant the plaintiff the relief which he seeks because the court would thereby appear to assist or encourage the plaintiff in his illegal conduct or to encourage others in similar acts" (pp.28-9).

On the other hand, in *Tinsley v. Milligen* [1993] 3 WLR 126, a majority of the House of Lords expressed doubts about the public conscience test, as amounting to a "revolution" in the law.

The advantage of the public conscience test over the impossibility of adjudication method is that it gives the courts a free hand to off-load responsibility onto the public rather than claiming that they themselves are unable to proceed. *Don't blame us. It's the public's wish.* Thus it would seem that the public would not be too affronted at the thought of a claim arising from suicide (*Kirkham v. Chief Constable of the Greater Manchester Police*), or where the plaintiff had offended against a statute intended for her own protection (*Progress and Properties Ltd v. Craft* (1976) 135 CLR 651). In other cases, it will depend upon the relative seriousness of crime and tort, and how connected they are. People committing minor traffic offences are not quite in the same category as bank robbers communally engaged in blowing up a safe (*Gala v. Preston* [1991] 100 ALR 29). Similarly, a person intending to commit a robbery in Northern Ireland was mistakenly thought to be a terrorist and shot dead by a soldier - the defence of illegality was not accepted (*Farrell v. Secretary of State for Defence* [1980] 1 All ER 166). In *Saunders v. Edwards* [1987] 2 All ER 651, the defendant was liable for the tort of deceit arising out of fraudulent misrepresentation towards the plaintiffs on the sale of a flat to them, and was not permitted to raise the defence of illegality on the ground that the plaintiffs had used the incorrect value in order to evade paying stamp duty tax on the purchase to the Inland Revenue authorities, Kerr, LJ (at p.660) considering that the defendant's moral culpability greatly outweighed that of the plaintiffs, so that the former should not be allowed to "keep the fruits of his fraud".

So, courts which are requested to apply the illegality defence have the task of balancing the factors in order to determine whether a bar on the claim would be accepted as justifiable from the general public and judicial viewpoint.

Perhaps that is precisely how it should be. No neat rule of thumb should serve to replace the innate good sense of the courts exercising a discretion in such cases. Judges are, after all, ultimately entrusted with the efficacy and integrity of the administration of justice. The irony of it all of course is that if the defence of illegality is able to be raised against the claim of one joint criminal against another, the defendant, the latter escapes liability in tort as a consequence. Perhaps the Latin expression *ex turpi causa non oritur actio* should be replaced by the English: *people who lie down with dogs get up with ...*

(iii) Inevitable Accident

This is a very limited defence indeed, consisting of the defendant's plea that no amount of reasonable care would have prevented the occurrence.

It has no relevance as a defence to negligence, because it is simply taken over by the issues of whether the defendant owed a duty of care on the basis of reasonable foreseeability in the first place, or otherwise satisfied the test of reasonable standard of care.

Nor does it apply in torts of strict liability, where fault is not an issue in any event.

It used to be able to apply to trespass to the person, as in *Stanley v. Powell* [1891] 1 QB 86, where a shotgun pellet bounced off a tree at a peculiar angle and hit the plaintiff; but *intention* is now even required for trespass (see *supra*, pp.458-9), once again therefore substituting for inevitable accident the overall inquiry led by the plaintiff into whether the defendant has failed to act with reasonable care.

(iv) Necessity

This is where the defendant justifies his interference with the person or property of the plaintiff by claiming that not to have done so could have led to even greater harm.

The court has to assess whether the defendant was correct on the basis of facts known at the time - although the requirement is that the defendant must merely have acted reasonably, even if ultimately proved wrong. For example, in *Cope v. Sharpe* [1912] 1 KB 496, the defendant trespassed on the plaintiff's land in order to stop the spread of fire which he thought - as it turned out, incorrectly - would get out of control. He was held to have behaved reasonably and so was entitled to the defence of necessity, as appeared to him to be the position at the time.

The courts today are more reluctant than they were to allow the defence. In *Leigh v. Gladstone* (1909) 26 TLR 139, forced feeding of suffragette prisoners on hunger strike - otherwise a battery - was held justified by medical necessity. However, in *Malette v. Shulman* (1990) 67 DLR (4th) 321, in more modern times, a doctor was held liable for the tort of battery in giving a blood transfusion to save the life of an unconscious Jehovah's Witness carrying a transfusion refusal card, and this would also no doubt be the case on refusal of treatment by a conscious plaintiff in danger of his life. It would be otherwise if an unconscious patient in grave danger had no refusal card (*F v. West Berkshire Health Authority* [1989] 2 All ER 545); also in the case of young children (*Re J* [1990] 3 All ER 930) and mentally disordered people (*F v. West Berkshire Health Authority)* if it is in their best interests to be treated. In *Southwark LBC v. Williams* [1971] Ch 734, at p.744, Lord

Denning, MR refused to allow homeless squatters and trespassers to use the defence of necessity: "Necessity would open a door which no man could shut ... an excuse for all sorts of wrongdoing. So the courts must, for the sake of law and order, take a firm stand. They must refuse to admit the plea of necessity to the hungry and homeless: and trust that their distress will be relieved by the charitable and good." Similarly, in *Burmah Oil Co. v. Lord Advocate* [1965] AC 75, Lord Upjohn said at p.165: "No man now, without risking some action against him in the courts, could pull down his neighbour's house to prevent the fire spreading to his own; he would be told that he ought to have dialled 999 and summoned the local fire brigade."

Since necessity is *material* to whether or not the defendant acted reasonably, it has been argued by some observers that it will not operate as a defence to negligence. A duty of care would not be owed nor breached in the first place. However, this statement may be too simplistic, since events causing damage may be complex and made up of multiple actions, only some of which were dictated by necessity.

(v) Defendant's Mistake

This is not a defence to tort: not even in defamation.

It can be *material* to liability, however, where motive is relevant to the latter. For example, in an action for deceit, the plaintiff must prove lack of honest belief on the part of the defendant. Thus, if the defendant was mistaken as to the truth of his statement, he can nevertheless be said to have had an honest belief in it.

In other cases, mistake is not central to any defence. A person still commits trespass to another person's land even if he mistakenly believed that he owned the land (*supra*, ch.22); and in negligence, mistaken belief by the defendant that his misstatement was correct is simply submerged in the broader question of whether the defendant was reasonable or not in his belief for the purposes of liability.

(vi) Contributory Negligence

1. General

Before 1945, contributory negligence by the plaintiff was a complete defence to his action in negligence; and the slightest degree of culpability on his part would suffice to bar the remedy (*Butterfield v. Forrester* (1809) 11 East 60).

This unfair situation led to the difficult "last opportunity rule": even if the plaintiff did contribute to the damage, nevertheless if the defendant was the one who had the last opportunity to avoid it, he should be held wholly responsible. Thus, in *Davies v. Mann* (1842) 10 M & W 546, where the plaintiff left a donkey in the street as it became dark and the defendant, not looking where he was going, collided with it. The defendant was said to have had the last opportunity to prevent the accident from occurring.

The last opportunity rule was unsuitable for fast-moving motor accidents, and an international maritime convention at the beginning of the 20th century provided for apportionment (division) of damages in collisions between ships according to respective degrees of fault.

The law on contributory negligence generally was ready to be reformed. Reform came in the shape of the Law Reform (Contributory Negligence) Act 1945. Section 1(1) provides that where damage is due to the fault of both plaintiff and defendant, damages are to be reduced:

- to such extent as the court thinks just and equitable; and
- having regard to the plaintiff's share in the responsibility for the damage.

This is the principle of *equitable apportionment.* The defendant's liability is reduced - not wiped out completely (compare *volenti non fit injuria*).

2. *Actions to which the 1945 Act applies*

Section 4 specifically mentions negligence, breach of statutory duty and other acts or omissions giving rise to liability in tort.

Thus, negligence and nuisance are covered by this defence - probably battery too, although, clearly, the plaintiff's behaviour would have to be quite serious to be held to have contributed to the defendant's battery (*Barnes v. Nayer* (1986) *The Times,* December 19), say, for example, where a wife jokingly tells her husband that she has flushed his boyhood collection of stamps down the toilet because he refused to do the washing up.

Deceit, on the other hand, appears to be excluded from this defence because of the strong element of intentional harm required for the tort of deceit to be made out (*Alliance and Leicester Building Society v. Edgestop Ltd* [1994] 2 All ER 38). It has been questioned whether *Hedley Byrne* negligent misstatement could be subject to contributory negligence, because either the plaintiff reasonably relied on the defendant's statement or he did not: if the plaintiff should have taken independent advice and negligently did not do so, the defendant would not be liable for negligent misstatement in the first place (see Jones, Textbook on Torts, 1993, p.405). Nevertheless, courts do seem to treat it as applicable: in *Edwards v. Lee* (1991) *The Independent*, November 11, the plaintiff was held to be contributorily negligent for not exercising further safeguards when he took up a negligent reference; and in *Gran Gelato Ltd v. Richcliff (Group) Ltd* [1992] 2 WLR 867, the court held contributory negligence to apply to claims for negligent misrepresentation under the Misrepresentation Act 1967 - although the Judge rather reduced this finding to the level of pointlessness by his further pronouncement that failure by the plaintiff to make further inquiries would not lead to a just and equitable reduction of damages, because the plaintiff had done exactly what the defendant intended him to do, that is, relied solely on his statement (see Jones, *op. cit.*, p.406). Accordingly, unless there is some other way - that is, apart from omission to make further inquiries - in which the plaintiff might himself contribute to fault, without negativing reliance upon the defendant at the same time, there does not seem to be great scope in practice for the defence of contributory negligence to operate in relation to negligent misstatement: perhaps a possible case might be where the defendant's advice was negligent and incorrect in any event, yet the defendant was not assisted in this respect by inaccuracies in the instructions given to him by the plaintiff.

A further difficulty is whether the defence can apply to actions *in contract* (see Jones, *ibid.*)? Section 1 refers to damage suffered through "fault" and s.4 defines fault, as seen, *inter alia*, as including negligence and other acts giving rise to liability in tort. In *Forsikringsaktieselskapet Vesta v. Butcher* [1986] 2 All ER 488, the Court of Appeal held that where the plaintiff could have brought his claim in tort rather than in contract - for example, in cases of professional negligence or employer's liability - the contributory negligence defence should apply in order to prevent its avoidance.

It seems unlikely, however, that contributory negligence could apply to strict contract claims not also covered by tort, unless of course the plaintiff's negligence directly led to damage (*Lambert v. Lewis* [1981] 1 All ER 1185 - Jones, *op. cit.*, p.407). As to the other situation mentioned in *Forsikringsaktieselskapet Vesta v. Butcher*, that is, where the contract imposes an obligation of reasonable care, but not corresponding to a tortious standard, this too would appear to be excluded from the 1945 Act according to that decision. This does not seem too objectionable: if a contract requires a certain level of care, perhaps its terms should be considered to be exclusive as to liability, since it did not also express what was to happen in the event of the plaintiff's own negligence.

3. *Contribution*

The defendant must prove that the plaintiff "contributed" to the tort.

It does not matter whether the plaintiff is shown to have contributed:

- to the accident itself (for example, where the defendant is driving too fast and the plaintiff passenger tells him that traffic lights approaching are green when they are red, or even getting into a car knowing the driver to be drunk (*Owens v. Brimmell* [1977] QB 859); or

- to the damage, for example, by failure to wear a seatbelt (*Froom v. Butcher* [1976] QB 286) or a crash helmet (*O'Connell v. Jackson* [1972] 1 QB 270).

4. Causation

Closely linked to the meaning of *contribution* are questions of causation.

The rule is that the plaintiff's negligent behaviour must have been *causa causans* together with the defendant's, not merely *causa sine qua non*. It is not enough that the plaintiff's intervention enabled the defendant's negligent act to cause damage; it must have been partially responsible.

In *Jones v. Livox Quarries Ltd* [1952] 2 QB 608, against the rules of his employment, the plaintiff rode on the back of a traxcavator and was crushed when another employee negligently drove his vehicle into the back. The plaintiff was held to have been contributorily negligent: what had happened was within the foreseeable risk of riding on the back of the traxcavator, in addition to other dangers like falling off. Similarly, the plaintiff, who was killed in a collision caused by negligent driving, was held to be guilty of contributory negligence in riding on the offside steps of a dustcart, in *Davies v. Swan Motor Co.* [1949] 2 KB 291.

On the other hand in *Smithwick v. Hall & Upson Co.* (1890) 59 Conn 261, 21 A 924 (SC Conn), the plaintiff was told not to go to a part of a platform which was icy and where there were no railings. He ignored this and when he stood there a wall fell on him. It was held that he was not a contributory cause even though he would not have been injured had he not been there: what occurred was not within the foreseeable risk he had placed himself into - it would have been otherwise had he slipped on the ice or fallen off the platform without railings and then been injured by a defendant negligently colliding with him.

In *Jones v. Livox Quarries Ltd,* (p.616) Denning, LJ spoke of the plaintiff's negligence being "so much mixed up with his injury that it cannot be dismissed as mere history ... dangerous position on the vehicle was one of the causes of his damage ..."

On the other hand, of course, if the plaintiff's behaviour, though unreasonable, made no difference whatsoever to the accident or damage, or these were otherwise outside the range of injuries to which the plaintiff had exposed himself, clearly he will not be held to have been a contributory cause. Thus, for example, if a drunk is run over, but his sobriety would not have saved him, he will be held not to have contributed; and in *Froom v. Butcher* [1976] QB 286, Lord Denning (at p.296) said that failure to wear a seatbelt would not amount to contributory negligence if the injuries would have happened anyway - but there would be a 15 per cent reduction in damages if the belt would have led to less serious injuries and a 25 per cent reduction if the belt would have prevented any injuries from happening at all. In *O'Connell v. Jackson* [1972] 1 QB 270 the plaintiff's injuries were much worse for lack of a crash helmet when riding his motorcycle, so the damages were accordingly reduced.

The courts will therefore examine the evidence in order to determine what part the plaintiff's conduct played in the accident. In *Owens v. Brimmel* [1977] 2 WLR 943, the plaintiff and defendant were drunk and the defendant crashed the car, from which the plaintiff was thrown, suffering severe injuries. The court reduced the plaintiff's damages by 20 per cent because of his contributory negligence in *going out drinking with* the defendant and intending to drive home knowing the risks, even though at the time of getting into the car, the plaintiff was too drunk to realize the danger ("... a passenger may be guilty of contributory negligence if he rides with the driver of a car whom he knows has consumed alcohol in such quantity as is likely to impair to a dangerous degree that driver's capacity to drive properly and safely. So, also, may a passenger be guilty of contributory negligence if he, knowing that he is going to be driven in a car by his companion later, accompanies him upon a bout of drinking which has the effect, eventually, of robbing the passenger of clear thought and perception and diminishes the driver's capacity to drive properly and carefully", p.949) - *volenti* had the former actually consented to negligence rather than the mere risk (see *supra*, p.677). However, because the defendant could not explain precisely how the accident had taken place nor whether a seat belt would have prevented or reduced the plaintiff's injuries, the court in *Owens* held that there could be no contributory negligence with regard to the *failure to wear a seat belt.*

It should be noted that wearing of seat belts in front and back seats of cars is now compulsory in England under the Road Traffic Act 1988, s.14, which may therefore raise the possibility of introducing the illegality defence - unlikely, however, in the case of serious negligence by the driver leading to severe injuries to the plaintiff (see *supra*, p.687, *et seq.*; note too that *volenti* is excluded where a driver has compulsory insurance, *supra*, p.677, unable to be circumvented by claiming 100% contributory negligence, *infra*, p.707).

In *Revill v. Newbery* [1996] 1 All ER 291, before the Court of Appeal, it was considered that a plaintiff who was injured by a shotgun in the course of an attempt to carry out a burglary, would satisfy conditions of fault and responsibility for a defence of contributory negligence to be raised (p.300). The trial Judge had found the plaintiff to be two-thirds to blame for his injuries.

5. Standard of care

This is partly objective and partly subjective. It is necessary to start by asking what is reasonable? In *Tremayne v. Hill* [1987] RTR 131, the plaintiff pedestrian was held not to have acted unreasonably in failing to look out for negligently driven cars when traffic lights were at red for vehicles.

On the other hand, failure to wear a seatbelt (now compulsory) has been held to be objectively unreasonable, even if the plaintiff truly believed it to be safer without (*Froom v. Butcher*) (and even though at that time, the vast majority of drivers in England did not choose to wear the belt). Nevertheless:

- the courts have been willing to look at the plaintiff himself and to find the lack of a seat belt to be reasonable for him, for example, because he is extremely stout, or possibly, absolutely terrified of being trapped by the belt, or because she is pregnant;

and

- section 1(1) of the 1945 Act does require the courts to reduce damages where it is *just and equitable,* which clearly imports subjective considerations as to the degree of fault which the plaintiff is considered to be responsible for; and
- concessions, it will be seen, are made for, *inter alia,* the young, the old and the sick.

Furthermore, clearly what is expected of the plaintiff is not a duty of care towards the defendant but towards the plaintiff *himself* - to take such steps as are reasonable in order to prevent harm to himself through what is reasonably foreseeable, including the possibility of the defendant's negligence (see *Jones v. Livox*).

Courts may well be expected to require less of plaintiffs than of defendants in terms of standards of reasonableness, in view of the financial consequences for plaintiffs who are not covered by insurance, and as a throw-back to earlier times when contributory negligence was a complete bar to recovery.

Additional concessions appear to be made as to what may reasonably be expected of children, the old, the sick, those faced with a dilemma or an emergency, and of employees who may be reliant upon care taken, and compliance with, safety regulations by the employer.

Children

In *Gough v. Thorne* [1966] 3 All ER 398, at p.399, Lord Denning, MR commented: "A very young child cannot be guilty of contributory negligence. An older child may be;

but it depends on the circumstances. A Judge should only find a child guilty of contributory negligence if he or she is of such an age as reasonably to be expected to take precautions for his or her own safety."

Therefore, it is a matter of what can reasonably be expected, by way of sensible behaviour, of a child of the particular age of the plaintiff - not much, if anything, if he is very young - and taking into account any special characteristics of the plaintiff himself, such as his immaturity. Seemingly, from the cases, a five-year-old, but not a three-and-a-half-year-old may reasonably be expected not to run into the road; while, a nine-year-old boy is not expected to be aware of the dangers of purchasing petrol on the false pretences that his mother needed it for her car.

Drunks

It was seen from *Owens v. Brimmel* (*supra*, p.699) that drunks will not be contributorily negligent for what they did without comprehension in their drunken state (getting into the car with a driver who is also drunk); yet, they will be held to be so if they set off to get drunk, knowing that what would later occur was a distinct possibility. In *Barrett v. Ministry of Defence* [1995] 1 WLR 1217 (CA), the deceased naval airman had a heavy drinking session at the base and eventually fell unconscious. He was taken back to his cabin and put in his bunk. There he suffocated through choking on his own vomit. Although the defendant was under no duty of care to prevent the deceased from becoming drunk (see *supra*, ch.5), the defendant accepted that insufficient care had been taken for the deceased's safety thereafter. However, the Court of Appeal held that damages ought to be reduced by two-thirds to take account of the deceased's contributory negligence: "... his lack of self-control in his own interest caused the defendant to have to assume responsibility for him. But for his fault, it would not have had to do so" (p.1225).

Sick and old

Again, the yardstick is what is reasonable. It would normally be unreasonable for a blind or elderly person to stroll across a six-lane motorway when the traffic had temporarily cleared.

Employees

Courts are reluctant to find contributory negligence when employees sue employers for breach of regulations meant for employees' protection, since it is often intended that those very rules should act as a safeguard against employee carelessness induced by boredom and repetition (*Staveley Iron & Chemical Co. Ltd v. Jones* [1956] AC 627). To hold otherwise could undermine the purpose of the statute or regulations in question (*Caswell v. Powell Duffryn Associated Collieries Ltd* [1940] AC 152). However, as the case of *Jones v. Livox Quarries Ltd* has shown, the courts will have no hesitation at all in finding an employee to have been contributorily negligent where he clearly bears a measure of responsibility, of one degree or another, for what took place. For example, in *Jayes v. IMI (Kynoch) Ltd* [1985] ICR 155, the plaintiff, who was an experienced worker, was held to have been contributorily negligent when he cleaned a machine without its safety guard having been fixed to it and lost the tip of his finger; and in *Bux v. Slough Metals Ltd* [1974] 1 All ER 262, the plaintiff declined to wear goggles provided by the defendant employer because they misted up when used, and he had received no response when he requested a better pair. The defendants were liable in negligence for failing to ensure that the injured plaintiff wore goggles when dealing with molten metal, but the plaintiff himself was contributorily negligent in not making full and proper use of such equipment as was provided.

Dilemmas and Emergencies

Less care can reasonably be expected of plaintiffs who have to make up their mind what to do in order to avoid danger in a very short space of time.

In *Jones v. Boyce* (1816) 1 Stark 493, the plaintiff, fearing for his safety, jumped out of a negligently driven coach and broke a leg. This was held to be reasonable and the plaintiff was not contributorily negligent. The case, it should be noted, was decided long before the 1945 Act introduced apportionment of damages, and contributory negligence would have been a complete defence to recovery.

In contrast, in *Holomis v. Dubuc* (1975) 56 DLR 3d 351, a passenger jumped out of a sea plane which was letting in water, and drowned, whereas he would have survived if he had remained in the plane. Damages were reduced by 50 per cent for his contributory negligence in leaping out of the plane without wearing a life jacket. Similarly, if one finds oneself trapped in a toilet, certainly, it is reasonable to try to escape - but not to contribute to the negligence by stepping onto a revolving toilet roll holder (*Sayers v. Harlow UDC* [1958] 1 WLR 623).

6. Apportionment

Section 1(1) of the 1945 Act requires the court to reduce damages to such extent as the court:

- thinks just and equitable
- having regard to the claimant's share in the responsibility for the damage.

The court first calculates the sum which would have been awarded but for the contributory negligence - and then reduces it in order to take account of the latter. In making the assessment, the court will consider the extent to which the plaintiff departed from the objective standard of reasonableness (*Westwood v. Post Office* [1974] AC 1). Apportionment is treated as a matter of fact (although it is assumed that damages under the Act can never be reduced by a full 100 per cent).

However, in order to provide a degree of certainty, courts tend to adopt standard reductions in respect of particular actions. *Froom v. Butcher* will be recalled, in which Lord Denning mentioned standard percentage reductions for a plaintiff's failure to wear a seat-belt: no reduction if it made no difference; 15 per cent if it would have reduced the injuries; 25 per cent if it would have prevented them. Similarly, the reduction for a motorcylist's failure to strap his helmet would be less than for not wearing a helmet at all (*Capps v. Miller* [1989] 2 All ER 333).

In *Stapley v. Gypsum Mines Ltd* [1953] AC 663, a miner was killed when a roof fell on him. He and another miner had been told by the foreman to make the roof safe by knocking it down, but they were unable to do so and decided to work on. The other miner was held liable for "causing" the accident - but the damages were reduced by 80 per cent because of the plaintiff's own "contribution" to the cause of the collapse.

If there are two defendants, the plaintiff's contribution will be assessed in relation to their joint fault, rather than as against each of them separately. Thus, in *Fitzgerald and Lane v. Patel* [1989] AC 328, the plaintiff stepped into the road without looking and was struck by the first defendant's negligently driven vehicle, which knocked him further into the road, where he was hit by the second defendant's negligently driven car. At first instance, the Judge held all three equally to blame and reduced the plaintiff's damages by 33⅓ per cent. The House of Lords held this to be incorrect: the plaintiff's "equal" share of fault had to be assessed against that of a notional *single* defendant. Plaintiff- and defendant-blame was therefore equal - half and half. The plaintiff's damages were reduced by 50 per cent (his half share of the blame). Otherwise, it would be better for a contributorily negligent plaintiff to be hit by a whole car load of drunks rather than by one on his own.

(vii) Exclusion of Liability in Tort

Section 149 of the Road Traffic Act 1988 prohibits exclusion of liability, or the *volenti* defence, in the case of compulsory insurance of car drivers against death or personal injury of passengers.

Section 7 of the Consumer Protection Act 1987 prevents exclusion of liability for defective products under Part I of the 1987 Act.

But what of the general situation in which the defendant seeks to exclude or restrict his liability by notice ("No liability accepted/Enter at your own risk") or agreement ("It is hereby agreed that no liability will attach in respect of the carrier's negligence")?

Under s.2 of the Unfair Contract Terms Act 1977, a person cannot exclude or restrict his liability for negligence in the course of a business (s.1(3)):

- at all in the case of death or personal injuries; and
- unless reasonable in other cases.

"Reasonable" means in all the circumstances, including: parties' relative bargaining power; alternative sources of supply; difficulty of the activity in question; practical consequences of exclusion, including parties' ability to bear the loss and insure. In *Smith v. Bush* [1989] 2 WLR 790, the House of Lords rejected the argument that a disclaimer in the case of negligent misstatement prevented the duty of care from arising in the first place (as negativing proximity and reliance) so that there was no "exclusion" for the Act to prohibit.

Although exclusion of business liability for negligence is prohibited or restricted under the Act, nonetheless, since an amendment in 1984, there has been an exception for farmland entered for educational or recreational purposes, which is no longer to be treated as being for business liability purposes. So the farmer can put up a notice saying *enter at your own risk, no liability accepted* and he is protected in respect of the dangerous condition of the land.

In *Aiken v. Stewart Wrightson Members Agency Ltd* [1995]

1 WLR 1281, Potter, J confirmed that plaintiffs could sue in contract or tort in the alternative *except where* the purpose of bringing the action in tort was to circumvent a contractual liability-exclusion clause (p.1301, see *supra*, ch.5 - following the House of Lords in *Henderson v. Merrett Syndicates Ltd, supra*, ch.5).

(viii) Limitation of Actions

1. General

The Limitation Act 1980 provides "limitation periods" - periods after which actions generally in tort cannot be brought at law:

- six years from when the tort cause of action accrued;
- three years in defamation (to be reduced to one year, extendable, under the Defamation Bill 1996, Clause 5 - *supra*, ch.26).

Date of accrual of the cause of action is that of *damage* in negligence (contrast date of *breach* in the case of contract) - date of *act* in torts which are actionable *per se*.

2. Personal injuries

The special limitation period (s.11) is *three* years from the *later* of:

- the date of accrual of the cause of action, and
- the date on which the plaintiff first had knowledge (defined by s.14 as meaning knowledge that he had suffered a significant injury, caused by the defendant's

allegedly negligent act or omission).

The plaintiff is deemed to have knowledge of facts which he should reasonably discover either by himself or with expert advice (s.14).

Knowledge merely means that the plaintiff knew or ought reasonably to have realized that something was significantly wrong with him, for example, following surgery, even if the full details were not appreciated by him (*Broadley v. Guy Clapham & Co.* [1994] 4 All ER 439, CA). Furthermore, provided that the plaintiff is aware of his injury, this is sufficient for knowledge, notwithstanding that he only subsequently learnt that the wrong done to him was tortiously actionable. Thus, in *Dobbie v. Medway Health Authority* [1994] 4 All ER 450, the Court of Appeal ruled the plaintiff out-of-time, where her breast was removed in surgery but was then discovered to have been non-cancerous. Fifteen years later, the plaintiff heard of a similar case and issued proceedings. She was barred, because she knew at the earlier time following the operation that she had suffered a significant "injury" as a result of the defendant's act or omission even though she may not have realized that this was actionable.

The preceding may seem hard on a plaintiff, but, as Stuart-Smith, LJ explained in the Court of Appeal in *Forbes v. Wandsworth Health Authority* (1996) *The Times,* March 21, CA, any other construction of ss.11 and 14 might make them unworkable, since a plaintiff could delay indefinitely before seeking expert advice as to whether anything had gone wrong with his medical treatment and still then fall within the limitation period, which would be contrary to the whole purpose of the Act which was to "prevent defendants being vexed by stale claims which it was no longer possible to contest".

In that case, the plaintiff's deceased husband had had a heart by-pass operation at the defendant's hospital in 1982. Since it was not a success, a second operation was carried out the next day towards midday, which too was unsuccessful and as a result of which the plaintiff's husband's leg had to be amputated in order to prevent gangrene. It was only in 1991 that the husband sought legal and expert advice on the operation and was informed that had the hospital not negligently delayed to perform the second operation and to restore the blood supply, the amputation would not have been necessary.

The writ claiming damages for medical negligence was issued in December 1992, more than 10 years after the negligent amputation. The husband died in 1995.

The question was: when was the date of the husband's "knowledge" for purposes of s.11?

The Court of Appeal made a number of interesting findings, as follows:

(1) It was sufficient to start the limitation period running that the husband had knowledge of:

- the fact of the injury, being the amputation
- that it was significant, and
- that it was caused by the failure of the second operation.

Seemingly, the husband was considered to have had actual knowledge of the first two of the three preceding factors within a very short time of the amputation, but not the third. Accordingly, there was insufficient *actual* knowledge for the limitation period to have started in 1982.

(2) Nevertheless, did the husband have deemed knowledge of causation under s.14, on the ground that he ought reasonably to have sought expert advice at an earlier date than 1991? What is a person whose operation is unsuccessful supposed to do, according to Stuart-Smith, LJ? Should he say "Oh well, it is just one of those things. I expect the doctor did his best"; or should he take a second opinion just to make sure that the doctor took all reasonable care? Stuart-Smith, LJ had no doubt as to which of these alternatives should be adopted: the latter. Thus, where the patient expected the operation to be successful and it manifestly was not, so that he thereby sustained a major injury, a reasonable man of moderate intelligence such as the husband, if he thought about the matter, would have said that the lack of success was "either just one of those things, a risk of the operation, or something may have gone wrong and there may have been a want of care ... I do not know which, but if I am ever to make a claim, I must find out". He could not simply do nothing and then change his mind and decide to look into the matter 10 years later. *However,* Stuart-Smith, LJ did add that the patient would not be expected to seek advice immediately following his operation: he would need time to overcome the shock, take stock of his grave disability and its consequences and seek advice - 12 to 18 months in the Judge's view (and Evans, LJ and Roch, LJ agreed - the latter, however, pointing out the need not to impute prematurely to plaintiffs the unconscious decision to do nothing and to take no advice,

which might otherwise encourage them to rush off to a different specialist at the first sign of trouble).

(3) Finally, the majority of the Court of Appeal considered the test of reasonableness of seeking medical advice to be purely objective, without taking into account the position, circumstances, character and intelligence of the plaintiff's husband himself. Roch, LJ, while sympathetic, dissented on this point, regarding himself as bound by earlier authority, departed from by the rest, that reasonableness should be assessed in relation to the particular plaintiff in question.

The Court of Appeal, therefore, has set a tough standard. Patients whose operations have not been successful and who know this and that they have suffered a significant injury as a result, have from about 12 to 18 months to find out the cause of their injury and whether it was possibly the result of negligence - after which they have constructive knowledge of the latter and time will run.

It is submitted that whilst it is perfectly reasonable to expect people to ask about the factual cause of their condition (insufficient blood supply to leg), it is not also wholly so to expect them to make inquiries about possible negligent cause (blood restored too late). People tend to be trusting, intimidated or generally reluctant to complain. Furthermore, what is an "injury" for purposes of s.11? Must it be a new ailment, separate from the original - or can it also be the pre-existing, serious condition which simply was not cured through negligence? The latter, surely, in which case the patient must start asking questions about cause and care taken, lest time run out.

If the three-year period passes, the court has a discretion

to extend it, having regard to all the circumstances, including:

- prejudice to plaintiff and defendant;
- reasons for any delays and whether the plaintiff acted promptly on discovering his right of action;
- effects of delay on evidence;
- defendant's conduct; and
- plaintiff's steps to obtain expert advice and its content (s.33).

A plaintiff who issued a writ within the three-year period but failed to proceed with it cannot have the period extended (*Walkely v. Precision Forgings Ltd* [1979] 1 WLR 606).

Dependants claiming following the death of a plaintiff can request an extension under s.33 if the three-year period expired before his death. If he died before the expiry, they are entitled to a new three-year period on his death, for proceedings under Law Reform (Miscellaneous Provisions) Act 1934 and the Fatal Accidents Act 1976.

As to the meaning of "personal injuries" for these purposes, s.38(1) of the 1980 Act defines these as "any disease and any impairment of a person's physical or mental condition". In *Walkin v. South Manchester Health Authority* [1995] 1 WLR 1543, the Court of Appeal held that this would include a claim for an unwanted pregnancy and birth of a child resulting from an allegedly negligently performed sterilization operation on the plaintiff mother, notwithstanding that the plaintiff's action was for the economic cost of caring for and bringing up the child, not merely for pre-natal pain and suffering through the pregnancy (pp.1549, 1553, 1555). It was not, however, the failed sterilization which was the injury, because that in itself did the plaintiff no harm; it was the unwanted conception and resulting bodily effects of pregnancy which amounted to the injury (pp.1550, 1553, 1555). Accordingly, the three years limitation period would run from the date of conception (*ibid.*). Roch, LJ was uncertain whether a claim by a *man* for the financial cost of supporting a child born as a consequence of a failed vasectomy could likewise be so classified as being for personal injuries under the Act - probably not, since neither the man nor the mother, if she wanted the child, would have been injured in any physical sense (pp.1553). Neill, LJ expressed certain doubts over whether date of conception, rather than that of negligent operation, was the proper date to take as that at which the personal injury was suffered: "Take the case of a pianist who receives treatment for a fractured finger. His right to sue is not postponed until he returns to the piano and finds that he cannot play " (p.1555). Although, on the other hand, he seemed more prepared than the others to view a man's claim in respect of costs resulting from a failed vasectomy operation as being for personal injuries - unnecessary to decide in the case itself (p.1555).

3. Hidden ("latent") damage

In an early case, *Cartledge v. Jopling & Sons Ltd* [1963] AC 758, the House of Lords held that the cause of action accrued when an injury could be proved to have caused significant internal damage to the plaintiff, even though he did not know about it until much later. As a result of this hard rule, s.11(4) of the 1980 Act provided, as seen, that the three-year period ran from the date of the plaintiff's knowledge if later than accrual.

4. Buildings: latent damage

In the case of buildings, the position has been as follows:

(a) in *Sparham-Souter v. Town & Country Developments (Essex) Ltd* [1976] QB 858, the Court of Appeal held that the limitation period ran from the date on which the plaintiff discovered or ought reasonably to have discovered the damage; but

(b) the House of Lords declared this to be incorrect in *Pirelli General Cable Works Ltd v. Oscar Faber & Partners* [1983] 2 AC 1: the action accrued and the limitation period ran from the date of physical damage to the building, being

- when the defect caused cracks *et alia*; but
- from the date of defective construction, if the building was doomed from the start by reason of the defect itself.

However, one commentator points out that the second preceding possible time of accrual of a cause of action is now in fact largely superfluous (see Jones, Textbook on Torts, 1993, p.423 *et seq.*), because in *Murphy v. Brentwood District Council* [1990] 2 All ER 908 (see *supra*, ch.5), the House of Lords held that unless the defect in the building causes damage to a different property, there is no cause of action to accrue, *at any time*. In *Murphy*, the Lords referred to the possible exceptions of a defective installation or component part causing damage to the building (though not merely to itself): in this case, (subject to the Latent Damage Act 1986, *infra*) the limitation period would run from the date of physical damage (*Nitrigin Eireann Teoranta v. Inco Alloys Ltd* [1992] 1 All ER 854).

However, in cases after September 18, 1986 which were not already barred on that date, the common law - other than in personal injuries - is replaced by the Latent Damage Act 1986, inserting ss.14A and 14B into the Limitation Act 1980.

Under the Act, the plaintiff has an extended limitation period of six years from the date on which the cause of action accrued or three years from the date of his *knowledge* - that is, in accordance with s.14 (see above, p.710, *et seq.*), from that on which he discovered or ought reasonably to have discovered significant damage - whichever is the later (14A): but in no case can the action be brought more than 15 years from the date of the act constituting negligence (14B) (see *infra*, Appendix Case 7).

These provisions apply too to a case where a defendant is sought to be added, after expiry of the first limitation period, to an action which has already been commenced against initial defendants within the limitation period (see *Busby v. Cooper* (1996) *The Times*, April 15, CA).

5. Minors (plaintiffs under 18 years of age)

Time only starts to run against them when they reach 18 years.

6. Consumer Protection Act 1987

The limitation period is three years from:

- when the damage was suffered; or
- when the requisite knowledge was acquired, if later.

The maximum period is 10 years from when the defendant supplied the product to the market.

7. Concealment

Where the action is for fraud, or the defendant has intentionally concealed the plaintiff's right of action, time will not run until the plaintiff discovers or ought reasonably to have discovered the fraud (1980 Act, s.32(1)) (see too *infra,* Appendix Case 8).

(ix) Contributions Between Tortfeasors

This is governed by the Civil Liability (Contribution) Act 1978.

Where two or more people are jointly responsible towards the plaintiff in respect of the same tort, the plaintiff can sue them both together, or separately, or just one of them for the whole loss - although the loss can only be recovered once by the plaintiff.

Examples include where the two act together in a common purpose, say, where both agree to light a match in order to investigate the smell of gas and this causes an explosion (*Brooke v. Bool* [1928] 2 KB 578), and where an employee is primarily liable and his employer vicariously for his acts.

If the plaintiff releases one of the joint tortfeasors from

liability, this has the effect of releasing the rest - although a mere agreement not to sue does not necessarily also amount to a release (*Watts v. Aldington* (1993) *The Times,* December 16).

If just one of the tortfeasors is sued to judgment, he can, if he wishes, issue third-party proceedings under Rules of the Supreme Court Ord. 16 and join the others to the action brought against him by the plaintiff. Otherwise, he can bring contribution proceedings separately under the 1978 Act if he has been held liable towards the plaintiff. Even if the plaintiff can no longer sue the other tortfeasor, because, for example, the time limitation period has now passed against him, or the plaintiff settled the claim with the other tortfeasor, or he is not subject to English courts' jurisdiction, contribution proceedings themselves may still be brought within two years from the date of the judgment (Limitation Act 1980, s.10).

As to the amount of the contribution, s.2(1) of the 1978 Act says that this shall be such amount:

- as is just and equitable,
- having regard to the extent of the person's responsibility for the damage in question.

The contributor's "responsibility" is judged on a like basis to that of contributory negligence of a plaintiff under the Law Reform (Contributory Negligence) Act 1945 - relative causation and blameworthiness, rather than mere moral responsibility.

In *Birse Construction Ltd v. Haiste Ltd* (1995) *The Times,* December 12, the Court of Appeal held that for one of joint tortfeasors to be liable for a contribution under s.1(1) of the 1978 Act, they had to be liable in respect of the same damage - not where, for example, one was liable for physical damage and the other for financial loss.

Further reading:

Brazier, *Street on Torts*, 9th ed, 1993 (Butterworth & Co., London): ch.15.

Fleming, J.G., *The Law of Torts*, 8th ed, 1992 (The Law Book Company, Sydney): chs.11-13.

Hepple, B.A. and Matthews, M.H., *Tort: Cases and Materials*, 4th ed, 1991 (Butterworth & Co., London): ch.6.

Heuston, R.F.V. and Buckley, R.A., *Salmond and Heuston on The Law of Torts*, 20th ed, 1992 (Sweet & Maxwell, London): ch.22.

Howarth, D., *Textbook on Tort*, 1995 (Butterworth & Co., London): ch.15.

Jaffey, "*Volenti Non Fit Injuria*" (1995) 44 *Cambridge Law Journal* 87.

Jones, M.A., *Textbook on Torts*, 4th ed, 1993 (Blackstone, London): ch.14.

Markesinis, B.S. and Deakin, S.F., *Tort Law*, 3rd ed, 1994 (Clarendon Press, Oxford): ch.8.

Rogers, W.V.H., *Winfield and Jolowicz on Tort*, 14th ed, 1994 (Sweet & Maxwell, London): chs.26 and 27.

Stanton, K.M., *The Modern Law of Tort*, 1994 (The Law Book Company, Sydney): ch.5.

Weir, T., *A Casebook on Tort*, 7th ed, 1992 (Sweet & Maxwell, London): ch.5.

PART XV

Chapter 30

Remedies for Torts

The two main remedies available for victims of torts are:

- damages: financial compensation; *and/or*
- injunction: a court order prohibiting future wrongs or continuation of existing.

There are others, for example, abatement of a nuisance (*supra,* ch.23) and self-defence (*supra,* ch.17), although, as forms of self-help, these are not popular with the courts.

By far the most important remedy is *damages*.

Both main types of remedy will now be considered.

1. Damages

(i) General Comments

The essential aim of the law of damages is *restitutio in integrum:* restoration of the plaintiff, financially, as far as possible, to the position he would have been in had the tort not been committed. The principle is one of compensation, not punishment (subject to certain exceptional cases, in which exemplary damages may be awarded). Lord Scarman summed up the rule in *Lim Poh Choo v. Camden and Islington*

Area Health Authority [1980] AC 174, at p.187: "... the principle of the law is that compensation should as nearly as possible put the party who has suffered in the same position as he would have been in if he had not sustained the wrong." This is distinct from contract, where the object is to compensate the plaintiff for his loss of expected benefits under the contract.

Restitutio is not literal of course. The courts cannot replace a severed arm or an amputated leg. They can only attempt to assess the financial needs and opportunities of the plaintiff if he is to be restored to an optimum living condition for his injured state and to be compensated for financial loss. It is in the assessment of such needs that the greatest challenges present themselves to the courts. Who can say what opportunities may be lost to a seriously injured victim of negligence: a brilliant career; marriage to a millionaire; co-ownership of property? What should they be considered to be entitled to: minimum state health provision; the best private medical care which money can buy; cost of cures which may be available in the future, but which do not yet exist? Should the courts take such factors into account in quantifying damages? Medical science is developing so quickly that there is ever a danger that what the law will provide for and the manner of this provision on the one hand, and availability of costly medical help on the other, are moving further and further apart (see Holding, in *Damages for Personal Injuries*, 1993, ed, Holding and Kaye, ch.6).

On a more general level than personal injuries alone, courts may face the difficult task of having to assess the existence and extent of the mere loss of a *chance* as a consequence of negligence - the former being a matter of causation and the latter quantification of damages. For example, in *Stovold v. Barlows* (1995) *The Times,* October 30 (*supra,* p.296), the Court of Appeal had to evaluate the chances that a prospective purchaser would have gone ahead and bought the plaintiff's house had the defendant solicitors not been negligent in failing to send legal documents in time. The court considered the chances that the documents might not have arrived in time in any event or that, even if they had, the prospective purchaser would have preferred to buy a different property, and concluded that the plaintiff had had a 50 per cent chance of making the sale. He should therefore receive 50 per cent of the difference between the price offered by the prospective purchaser and the lower price at which the plaintiff actually sold his house to a third party when the prospective purchaser withdrew. Such was the nature and extent of the chance lost to the plaintiff.

Conversely, if the plaintiff *might have suffered damage* from the defendant's breach of duty of care, but can no longer do so at the date of the trial, the plaintiff recovers nil or only so much as he in fact sustained, lest the plaintiff should otherwise benefit from a damages windfall. So held the Court of Appeal in *Kennedy v. K.B. Van Emden & Co. etc* (1996) *The Times,* April 5, CA, where the plaintiff purchaser of a lease of a flat in 1983 was held to have a valid negligence claim against the solicitor who acted for her, who had failed to advise her that the sum of £49,500 which she had paid for the lease was an unlawful premium under the Rent Act 1977 and that she herself could not lawfully assign the lease for a premium. Subsequently, in 1989 the legislation was amended so as to enable the plaintiff to assign her lease at a premium. In 1990 the plaintiff claimed the £49,500 as damages from the defendant: she had paid for an assignable lease and at the time of purchase in 1983, the assignable value of the lease was in fact nil. As indicated, the Court of Appeal held that damages had to be assessed in the real world and compensation was given for actual loss, not for a loss which might have been but had not in fact been suffered. Damages should not mechanistically be assessed as at the date of breach of duty where, as here, assessment at the date of trial more accurately reflected the overriding compensatory principle. The plaintiff *now* had a fully assignable lease and consequently had lost nothing.

Where damages for libel are concerned, the amount is left to the jury rather than being decided by the Judge. However, the Court of Appeal recently restated the practice relating to such assessments by juries, in *John v. MGN Ltd* (1995) *The Times,* December 14, CA (see above, p.653, *et seq.*). One change is that Judge and legal representatives can now put suggested amounts to the jury (*ibid.*).

(ii) Types of Damages

There are various descriptions which need to be understood.

General and special damages

This is confusing terminology, because there are two different meanings of these expressions:

(1) Presumed and pleaded damage

This is the far less common use for the expressions "general" and "special":

- general: that damage *assumed* to exist in torts not requiring proof of damage, for example, loss of reputation in libel;
- special: damage which has to be *pleaded* and proven in torts which do require damage for the tort to be made out, for example, negligence or nuisance.

(2) Unliquidated and calculable damage

This is the more usual usage:

- general damages: imprecise losses which have to have a notional value attached to them, for example, *pain and suffering* and loss of amenities ("non-pecuniary", ie, non-monetary loss) and prospective loss of earnings ("pecuniary", ie, monetary loss), in personal injury cases (thus both "non-pecuniary" and "pecuniary");
- special damages: losses up to the date of trial, which can be fairly precisely pleaded and calculated, for example, *lost earnings to date,* medical expenses, damaged property and clothes ("pecuniary losses").

In this sense, both general and special damages have to be pleaded if they are to be recovered, and will not be assumed. Calculation of interest on the two types of damage will be different: on general, from the date of the writ; on special, from the date of injury (see Law Com No.225, para.11).

Nominal damages

When a plaintiff wins his case, but has suffered no loss, as, for example, in the case of torts actionable without proof of damage, such as assault, he will be awarded "nominal damages" - a small, nominal sum of money. The purpose is to establish the validity of the plaintiff's claim and defendant's liability in law (*Constantine v. Imperial Hotels Ltd* [1944] KB 693). The danger for such a plaintiff is that *costs* of the case are at the discretion of the court. Normally, costs follow the event, that is to say, they go to the successful party. However, faced with an award of merely nominal damages, the Judge may decide that the action ought never to have been brought and thereupon deny the plaintiff his costs from the other side - or even make him pay the latter's.

Contemptuous damages

These are similar to nominal damages - here, a derisory, small sum is awarded, normally consisting in the smallest coin in the realm. They are used to express the court's displeasure that the action was ever brought on a technicality, usually for libel, notwithstanding that losses were minimal, and, as in the case of nominal damages, the danger for the plaintiff lies in the realm of costs.

Aggravated damages

These may be awarded where, as a result of the defendant's "bloody-mindedness", the plaintiff has suffered additional loss from the manner of the tort's commission: loss of dignity and hurt feelings deliberately brought about by the defendant, therefore, have a price.

Their object remains compensatory, not punishment (*Kralj v. McGrath* [1986] 1 All ER 54). The plaintiff receives extra damages in order to compensate him for the damage added by the defendant to the original injury, whether consisting of hurt feelings or additional physical pain. For example, the defendant writes a defamatory article about the plaintiff in a newspaper - and then, when it emerges that it is untrue, he writes that the plaintiff deserved to be brought down in people's estimation in any event.

It would seem that aggravated damages will not be awarded in personal injury cases, because if the effects of the defendant's behaviour add to pain and suffering, they will be compensated for in any event in the ordinary award of general damages (*AB v. South West Water Services Ltd* [1993] 1 All ER 609).

Evidently though, even a company is considered to have feelings worthy of £10,000 aggravated damages (*Messenger Newspaper Group Ltd v. National Graphical Association* [1984] IRLR 397).

Exemplary (punitive) damages

These additional damages really are awarded in order to punish the defendant for his behaviour (sometimes they are called "punitive damages"), even though the ultimate beneficiary is the plaintiff and not the court which feels so affronted by the defendant's outrageous conduct (and see *Lancashire County Council v. Municipal Mutual Insurance Ltd* (1996) *The Times,* April 8, CA - it is *not* against public policy to insure against vicarious liability for exemplary damages).

In *Rookes v. Barnard* [1964] AC 1129, the House of Lords

was impressed by the need to distinguish between criminal and civil remedies - the latter being the province of the law of tort - and therefore stipulated that exemplary damages would only be awarded, as a matter of exceptional discretion, in the following three cases:

(a) Where a government servant acts in an arbitrary, oppressive or unconstitutional manner - although, in *Broome v. Cassell & Co. Ltd* [1972] AC 1027, the Lords said that "government servant" would not be interpreted narrowly and would therefore include a police officer (for example, making a wrongful arrest), and local government officers, but not large, *non*-governmental bodies such as trade unions and powerful companies. Thus, in *George v. Metropolitan Commissioner of Police* (1984) *The Times,* March 31, the police entered a house and searched it, punching and kicking the plaintiff, who was the mother of the man they wanted to question. They then fabricated a charge. The plaintiff received £6,000 damages for trespass and battery, and exemplary damages of £2,000.

(b) Where the evidence shows that the defendant actually calculated that he would make a profit or other gain from the tort over and above or in return for any damages payable. In *Broome v. Cassell & Co. Ltd,* there was evidence to just such effect and that the defendants knew that their publication was libellous, so that the House of Lords awarded £15,000 ordinary compensatory damages and £25,000 exemplary, because the defendants had probably worked out that their profits would exceed the former.

(c) Where a particular statute expressly permits exemplary damages, for example, some intellectual property legislation.

Awards of exemplary damages are quite rare. Usually they will be restricted to libel and trespass actions and to those against the police. In *AB v. South West Water Services Ltd* [1993] 1 All ER 609, the Court of Appeal refused to allow a claim to be made for exemplary damages, where it was alleged that the defendants had committed the tort of public nuisance by discharging 20 tons of aluminium sulphate into the water system in Camelford, Cornwall, injuring the plaintiffs, and had ignored the plaintiffs' complaints. The categories for exemplary damages were closed.

In deciding on a figure for exemplary damages, the court can take into account factors affecting their punitive quality: for example, the defendant's financial state, the plaintiff's own conduct, and whether the defendant has also been subject to a criminal penalty (in *Archer v. Brown* [1984] 2 All ER 267, Peter Pain, J said a defendant should not be punished twice for the same offence).

Amounts awarded in jury actions (libel, false imprisonment), are, not surprisingly, far higher than exemplary awards made by a Judge alone (trespass). The Court of Appeal recently restated the practice for award and amount of damages - exemplary and compensatory - in defamation cases, in *John v. MGN Ltd* (1995) *The Times*, December 14, CA (see *supra*, p.653): exemplary damages remained exceptional and should never exceed the minimum sum necessary to meet their underlying public purpose that the defendant should be punished, that tort should be shown not to pay and that other persons are deterred from similar acts (p.658).

(iii) Quantification of Damages Distinguished from Causation in Negligence

In ch.7 preceding (p.293, *et seq*), it was seen that where a plaintiff's negligence action is based on a claim that as a result of the defendant's behaviour the plaintiff lost a *chance* of making a gain, the plaintiff must first satisfy the court, as a matter of *causation,* on a balance of probabilities, that a real and substantial chance of gain existed, not a mere speculative possibility, after which, as a matter of *quantification* of damages, the court will make a more precise and percentage assessment of the likelihood of that occurrence but for the defendant's intervention, as part of the process of valuation of the lost chance (see *Allied Maples Group Ltd v. Simmons & Simmons* [1995] 1 WLR 1602, CA).

(iv) Nature of the Damages Calculation in Personal Injuries Cases

1. General

Under English law, there is a single assessment of damages at the time of the action, based upon the plaintiff's existing and prospective needs, viewed as at that time: and damages are awarded in the form of a single lump sum.

This has two main consequences in personal injuries cases:

(a) First, if the injury gets worse later on, the plaintiff cannot come back for more (unless further damage is distinct, rather than progressive). This was decided very early on in the case of *Fetter v. Beal* (1701) 1 Ld Raym 339, where the plaintiff won damages from the defendant for trespass to the person, and subsequently sought further damages when another piece of his head fell off. He failed.

(b) Secondly, as the award is in the form of a single lump sum, courts have no power to order periodical payments, variable to take account of any changes in the plaintiff's circumstances (originally, juries decided civil cases and could not be recalled). This makes things very difficult for courts, particularly in personal injuries cases, in which they have to try to estimate what a plaintiff's future losses will be: how will his condition develop or deteriorate; what medical and other assistance might be needed; what revolutionary cures might be just around the corner; what chance might there be that during the plaintiff's life span a cure or a treatment as yet completely undreamt of might be found; what in fact is the plaintiff's life expectancy?

Thus, in *Lim Poh Choo v. Camden & Islington Area Health Authority* [1980] AC 174, at p.183, Lord Scarman said: "... knowledge of the future being denied to mankind, so much of the award as is to be attributed to future loss and suffering will almost surely be wrong. There is really only one certainty: the future will prove the award to be either too high or too low." (Significantly, in the non-personal-injuries case of *Deeny v. Gooda Walker Ltd (In Liquidation)* [1995] 1 WLR 1207, Phillips, J preferred to postpone damages towards the plaintiff "Lloyd's Names" under R.S.C. Ord. 33, rr.3 and 4 in respect of their losses from *future* claims for payment against them, in their negligence actions against defendant managing agents and underwriting agents, *inter alia* out of fairness to the defendants, pp.1214-1216).

Furthermore, to make things worse for a plaintiff, prospective losses, including future earnings, will be reduced by what is called "the multiplier": this is a mathematical formula to decrease the amount of the lump sum award according to *inter alia* what may be an unrealistically low life expectancy figure of the victim during which he will require support (so that his relatives do not receive a windfall on his death, the award must be exhausted by that time) and to take account of the varied contingencies of life - such as unemployment or failed career - and his early receipt of future losses.

Supporters of the existing system argue that there is a need for finality of awards so that defendants are freed to get on with their lives. Furthermore, the English adversarial procedure is not suited to a periodical payment-with-reviews system, and the latter would be too expensive for defendants and their insurers (see Law Commission Consultation Paper No.125 "Structured Settlements and Interim and Provisional Damages", 1992, and subsequent Report No.224, 1994, for an examination of advantages and disadvantages of lump sum awards).

Opponents state that the present practice leads to injustice and increases the burden on the state. Awards of a million pounds may seem large; but once the cost of special-needs housing is taken into account and of carers for the rest of the plaintiff's life, and of varying rates of tax on investments together with inflation, it is rarely likely to be enough, and when it has been spent, the plaintiff can then only rely on the social welfare provision of the state.

In the 1970s the Pearson Commission (*Royal Commission on Civil Liability and Compensation for Personal Injury,* Cmnd 7054, 1978) recommended a system of periodical payments, subject to reviews, where, for example, the victim subsequently loses his job, or finds one, or his condition deteriorates. But, with the change of government in 1979 and the new political atmosphere of self-sufficiency and individualism, the proposal was never to see the light of day.

Thus, the following data regarding personal injuries at the present day, supplied by the legal anthropologist Fred Holding (see Holding and Kaye, ed, *Damages for Personal Injuries,* 1993, pp.107, *et. seq.*), may usefully be considered:

The majority of seriously injured spinal patients are young men aged between 18 and 25.

In, for example, Germany, it has been estimated that there are about half a million personal injuries each year.

The projected life span of a seriously ill spinal patient was some 12 hours at the death of Lord Nelson at the battle of Trafalgar in 1805 - 12 days at the time of the First World War - two to three years following the Second World War - 10 to 12 years in the 1970s, and in recent times, a full life span - that is, for an 18-year-old, 50 years.

During the new 50-year life span, the victim is likely to see his doctor every month, possibly every week, in order to stay alive.

Throughout the same period, he may see his lawyer ...

just once.

If his lump sum award runs out, he has the United Kingdom's social welfare system to fall back on. This was set up in the mid-1940s, when it was correctly assumed that seriously injured people would die within a short time and so would not remain a burden to the state for very long. The words of Lord Lloyd in the House of Lords in *Page v. Smith* [1995] 2 All ER 736, p.758, in the context of making reference to developments in the treatment of psychiatric illness come to mind: "As medical science advances, it is important that the law should not be seen to limp too far behind ..."

To be sure, certain reforms have been brought about.

(a) Under s.32A of the Supreme Court Act 1981 and Rules of the Supreme Court Ord.37, rr.7-10, since 1985 a court is able to award *provisional damages* in personal injury cases where there is held to be a chance that a specified, identified serious form of deterioration in the plaintiff's condition may come about:

- if this happens, the plaintiff makes a further claim for additional damages;
- but in the meantime, he receives a provisional lump sum, calculated on the basis that the deterioration will not occur (in *Willson v. Ministry of Defence* [1991] 1 All ER 638, the prospect that arthritis might later develop from an ankle injury was held not to be a new event, but merely a progression of the same condition, and so not within the scope of provisional damages).

(b) Under Rules of the Supreme Court, Ord.29, a plaintiff with urgent financial needs can be awarded *interim damages* pending trial of the action, but this is only possible where:

- the defendant has either admitted liability, or the plaintiff has obtained judgment for damages to be assessed, or the court is satisfied that the defendant will be held liable at trial for substantial damages; and
- the defendant is a person of substantial means, insured or a public authority.

If the plaintiff subsequently wins higher damages at trial, he receives the excess; if lower, he must pay back the excess. If desirable, the court has the power under Rules of the Supreme Court, Ord.33, r.4 and County Court Rules, Ord.13, r.2 to order separate trials of liability and quantum, the first as a prelude to interim payments, where the real issue is quantum rather than liability (plaintiffs should beware, however, that mere *admissions* of liability may subsequently be withdrawn by defendants - see *Gale v. Superdrug Stores plc* (1996) *The Times*, May 2, CA).

In *Stringman v. McArdle* (1993) *The Times*, November 19, CA, the Court of Appeal held that provided that the conditions for making an order for interim payment of damages in Order 29 were satisfied, the court should then make an award of such amount as it thought just, not exceeding a reasonable proportion of the expected final damages - *irrespective of how* the plaintiff intended to spend the money and of whether the court considered such use to be wrong or extravagant. The latter was not a material factor for exercise of the discretion under the rule. Here, the plaintiff had been severely injured when crossing the road with the traffic lights in her favour and had obtained judgment on liability (five per cent contributory negligence) with damages to be assessed. The Judge at first instance had rejected the plaintiff's application for an interim award of damages to convert a house to her special needs without further delay, on the ground that the conversion plans were too elaborate and that an excessive amount of the award would be spent on the house, leaving insufficient for future care. As seen, the Court of Appeal held that it was incorrect for the Judge to have allowed these matters to affect the court's decision on interim payment.

(c) A recent development from America, judicially approved for the first time in England in *Kelly v. Dawes* (1990) *The Times,* September 27, is the "structured settlement", representing an attempt by lawyers and accountants to overcome the problems caused by lack of provision for periodical payments (see Law Com No.225, ch.12). Very simply, the plaintiff and the defendant's insurer reach agreement based on a lump sum: part of this can be paid immediately to the plaintiff for past and current needs, and the rest is used by the defendant (or rather, his insurer) to purchase an annuity from another insurance company - an income - for the remainder of the plaintiff's life-time, held for the plaintiff and structured so as to meet foreseen needs. The crucial element is that the tax authorities (United Kingdom Inland Revenue) have agreed with the Association of British Insurers that the payments will be treated as return of *capital* to the defendant insurer and consequently are not to be taxed as *income,* which means that the defendant insurer is able to claim back the tax deducted from the annuity at basic rate and pay it to the plaintiff for the rest of his life, as index-linked periodical payments (if tax rates and consequent deductions go up, so does the payment). The latter is the "structured" nature of the back-to-back settlement and the precise terms of payment can be specified, as must any circumstances of future variation.

There are, however, limitations upon the effectiveness of these schemes: at present, courts cannot order them and it is for parties to agree out of court (although, frequently, courts will refuse to approve a settlement, unless structuring has first been considered); the basis of the settlement is still the original, single lump sum amount, calculated according to its "multiplier" figure; the defendants will charge a discount for their agreement (in addition to the multiplier), sometimes as much as 20 per cent; and these settlements may be quite vulnerable in times of low interest rates. Nevertheless, their usefulness is undoubted, and the only immediate loser is the taxpayer deprived of the revenue - although this is balanced by the reduced need of the plaintiff to call upon the social welfare provision of the state.

(d) Conditional fees may be charged on a "no win, no fee" basis in *inter alia* personal injuries actions, as from July 5, 1995, under s.58 of the Courts and Legal Services Act 1990 (see J. Levin, Conditional Fees: The New Law (1996) *Personal Injury* 35).

Various problems arising from the type of lump sum damages award available in English courts having thus been considered, it is now appropriate to look in greater detail at some of the actual factors involved in the assessment of damages for personal injuries, which are today probably the most important of all claims in tort.

The vast majority of victims of personal injuries do not sue. They simply want to get better. They are not interested in consulting lawyers. They think, rightly, that they cannot afford them. All they want to do is to forget it and get on with their lives. If it were otherwise, courts could not cope (see Law Com No.225, paras.7 and 10).

Of those who do go to law, most settle out of court and for a relatively low figure. The advantages are predominantly with the defendant insurance companies: they have their specialist teams of personal injuries lawyers; the plaintiff's eventual award may be lost to costs if he decides to go ahead and refuses an offer to settle which ultimately is not exceeded by the award; and his financial needs on discharge from hospital into a lonely, hostile world will be acute. Invariably, he will take whatever low figure is on offer and be thankful for it. Where a claim does not exceed £1,000, it will automatically be referred to arbitration by a district Judge, in the absence of exceptional complexity, under County Court Rules Ord.19, r.3, and recovery of costs in such arbitrated claims is limited (see *Afzal v. Ford Motor Co. Ltd* [1994] 4 All ER 720, CA).

If a case proceeds to judgment, however, courts must make calculations of past and future losses.

As seen, these are divided into special and general damages - otherwise known as *pecuniary losses up to trial* and unquantified *non-pecuniary losses up to and following trial and pecuniary losses following trial.*

2. *Special damages*

i. Actual loss of earnings

This is the plaintiff's actual lost salary, after deduction of tax and national insurance (*British Transport Commission v. Gourley* [1956] AC 185). Increases including promotion and increments will be added, but damages are reduced by any sick pay received.

ii. Medical costs

The principle is that the plaintiff can recover his *reasonable* expenses. Subject to certain statutory provisions, reasonableness is a question of fact. Costs covered will include medicines, hospital, travel, nursing home, nursing care assistants, domestic help, care by spouse or relatives, where and to the extent considered reasonable.

Statutory provisions in question are:

(a) *Law Reform (Personal Injuries) Act 1948, s.2(4).* This provides that availability of free national health treatment is to be disregarded in assessing what is reasonable. So, the plaintiff can have private medical treatment and recover for it. If he decides to go to an ordinary hospital, however, he cannot have the money's worth of private treatment. Many victims, of course, not advised of their rights, automatically use the free national health. Naturally, it is in the government's interests to save money by encouraging and facilitating private medical treatment.

(b) *Administration of Justice Act 1982, s.5.* This says that where the plaintiff is maintained wholly or partly at public expense in a hospital, nursing home or similar institution, a deduction should be made from his damages in respect of lost earnings, in order to take account of his savings in domestic costs; and in the *Lim Poh Choo* case, this was effectively extended to deductions from awards made for private medical care.

For the rest, the criterion is reasonableness in the eyes of the court.

iii. Reasonable accommodation and facilities

The plaintiff can purchase a special home or vehicle or adapt his existing property in order to take account of his injuries if reasonable: although, so that he will not benefit excessively, there is a deduction in damages to take account of the added capital value of cars or houses on future sale (*Roberts v. Johnstone* [1988] 3 WLR 1247). Therefore, facilities such as wheelchairs, lifts and supports are included. In *Povey v. The Governors of Rydal School* [1980] 1 All ER 841, the court made an award of £8,400 for a hydraulic lift to enable the plaintiff to move his wheelchair in and out of a car.

Depending upon reasonableness, he can have nursing at home or in an institution (*Shearman v. Folland* [1950] 2 KB 43). However, in *Cunningham v. Harrison* [1973] QB 942, the court held a sum of £6,000 for a housekeeper and two nurses to live with the plaintiff and take care of him to be unreasonably large in 1973.

Travel expenses to and from hospital can be claimed.

iv. Housewives

If unable to perform domestic work because of injuries, compensation is provided for domestic help (*Daly v. General Steam Navigation Co. Ltd* [1981] 1 WLR 120).

v. Third parties assisting the victim

In *Donnelly v. Joyce* [1974] QB 454, the Court of Appeal held that where a relative, friend or other third party (even the tortfeasor himself) gives up his job or incurs other expenses or spends time in order to look after the injured plaintiff, the third party himself has no claim against the defendant, but the plaintiff can ask for the proper and reasonable cost of reimbursing the third party for his losses. There does not have to be a legal obligation towards the third party on the part of the plaintiff. Nor is the plaintiff under a duty to pay such damages received to the third party. So, if a victim is cared for at home, partly by a nurse and partly by his wife, he can claim for both, even if his wife does not normally work. The justification is his need for the care, so that effectively the wife becomes a substitute expenditure, whatever her previous status (although a person is only entitled to be compensated in respect of loss of earnings or costs of employing another to look after a sick child, and not for both - he cannot have damages twice: *Fish v. Wilcox and Gwent Health Authority* (1993) *The Times*, March 4, CA). Where an injured plaintiff received damages in respect of care by a third party, the rule from *Donnelly v. Joyce* was that he was free to do as he wished with the money awarded and was under no obligation to pay it to the third party - including where the carer was a loved one, say, a relative, who provided the care gratuitously. However, in *Hunt v. Severs* [1994] 2 All ER 385, the House of Lords, while confirming that such a claim for damages could be made for care given gratuitously, nevertheless qualified the earlier finding, by stipulating that the sum received had to be held on trust for the carer by the plaintiff - and yet, somewhat controversially, went on also to hold that if the gratuitous carer was the defendant tortfeasor himself (or, as would often be the position, the defendants were his insurers), the defendant would *not* be required to pay such damages, because it would be equivalent to asking the defendant to pay damages to himself, or at least to be held on trust for himself.

vi. Matrimonial difficulties

Many severely injured people experience marital problems. Legal costs of obtaining a divorce may be recovered, but losses on property arrangements arising from the divorce are not (*Pritchard v. J.H. Cobden Ltd* [1987] 1 All ER 300).

3. General Damages

These consist of future pecuniary and past and future non-pecuniary losses.

Future Pecuniary

a. Loss of future earnings

i. Generally on loss of future earnings

The court is required to look into its crystal ball and to try to see what might have happened if the plaintiff had not been injured:

- would he have kept his job?
- would he have been promoted?
- how much longer would he have been likely to live (is there a family tendency to die young)?
- what would future rates of pay, tax and inflation be?

The method used by the courts to calculate on this basis is considered by some to be rather crude and consists of two parts:

(1) The "multiplicand"

This is the plaintiff's annual loss of earnings, taking into account tax and national insurance deductions, but also promotions and increments, at the date of trial: called the *multiplicand* (note, however, the deducted tax and national insurance is not actually paid to the state by the defendant). In addition, he is entitled to be compensated for lost pension rights.

(2) The "multiplier"

The multiplicand is then multiplied by the number of years the multiplicand is likely to continue: the latter figure is called the *multiplier* (see *supra*, p.733).

However, the multiplier is not the *actual* number of years which the plaintiff has left until retirement at the age of 65 - it is that figure, substantially reduced in order to take account of all the uncertainties - "vicissitudes" - of life, including, for example:

- the possibility that the plaintiff may have lost his job or become ill or she might have become pregnant (deduction of 5-10 per cent) (in *Moriarty v. McCarthy* [1978] 2 All ER 213, the multiplier was reduced because it was assumed that the injured young woman would have given up work in any event in order to start a family);
- the fact that the whole sum is received by the plaintiff in advance of his lost working life, the assumption being that the capital will be invested with a net return of 4½ per cent income up to retirement (the truth being that the average person has no investment expertise, and a 4½ per cent return cannot truly be assumed; and
- the principle that the *capital*, as well as income, should be used up on his death, so that his relatives will not receive a windfall.

As a result, the maximum multiplier used is very low - 18 - and this is exceptional, even for young plaintiffs. If the plaintiff is older, it will be considerably less. This figure has been criticized as being based upon life expectancy assessments now completely out-of-date, while, the other danger will be future rises in inflation and tax, which the courts, however, refuse to take into account, as being hopelessly uncertain - similarly with expert actuarial and economic evidence (*Mitchell v. Mulholland (No.2)* [1972] 1 QB 65). In *Auty v. National Coal Board* [1985] 1 All ER 930, Oliver, LJ likened the predictions of actuaries and economists to those of astrologers, p.939; and in *Lim Poh Choo,* Lord Scarman remarked that tort victims were no more entitled to be protected against future inflation than anyone else, which would otherwise be to put them into a "privileged position at the expense of the tortfeasor, and so to impose upon him an excessive burden (p.194). Further, although the lump sum itself is not subject to tax, investment income from it is; yet, in *Hodgson v. Trapp* [1988] 3 All ER 870, the House of Lords refused to allow the multiplier to be increased in order to take account of possibly higher rates of tax on a large income or potential future rises in rates.

ii. Lost years in loss of future earnings: effects on the multiplier

The previous position was that in deciding upon the size of the multiplier, no account was taken of what the plaintiff's earnings would have been in that part of his working life which had been lost as a result of his injuries. For example, he is 30 years of age and now has a life expectancy of only five years; lost earnings between 35 and 65 would not be included, because nothing was of use to a man who was dead: *Oliver v. Ashman* [1962] 2 QB 210.

This was felt to be unfair to the plaintiff's dependants, if he had any, who would lose the opportunity to inherit his lost additional resources. So in *Pickett v. British Rail Engineering Ltd* [1980] AC 136, the House of Lords overruled *Oliver v. Ashman.* The plaintiff can now claim for the *lost years,* less a deduction for what would have been the plaintiff's living expenses in those years (and see Appendix 9).

In the case of young children, courts are reluctant to allow them to claim for lost years. The position is so uncertain: what would their career have been; what would they have earned; what would they have spent? Impossible to say, except perhaps in the case of infant prodigies, such as a young violinist (*Connolly v. Camden & Islington Area Health Authority* [1981] 3 All ER 250). Furthermore, generally in the case of young people, the overall figure for the multiplier will be rather low for these same reasons. The multiplicand itself will probably have to be based on the national average wage (*Croke v. Wiseman* [1982] 1 WLR 71).

iii. Future prospects and earning capacity: effect on the multiplier

Where the plaintiff keeps his job after the injury, the multiplier will nevertheless be increased to take account of his reduced earning capacity, if any, should he one day lose his job and have to find another (*Moeliker v. Reyrolle & Co. Ltd* [1977] 1 All ER 9). The same is true of young people who have not yet become employed, but who may expect to find it more difficult to be so. Obviously, the more highly qualified a young person is, the greater the prospective loss. Conversely, the more precarious his job, the less he needs to be compensated for loss of future prospects.

iv. Deductions

If the plaintiff receives support from sources other than the damages award, the damages may be reduced in order to take account of these other payments. What are they? In particular, which payments are *not* deducted from damages?

a. *Social Security.* Since legislation in 1989, prescribed social security benefits paid to the plaintiff are *not* deducted in assessing his damages - *but* the defendant himself is required to deduct them from the payment he makes to the plaintiff, calculated as the total benefits to be paid to the plaintiff over a period of five years from the date of injury, and the defendant must then pay the deductions to the social security authorities, which issue a certificate of deduction. Payments include statutory sick pay; unemployment benefit; severe disablement allowance; mobility allowance; income support. Not included are child benefit and widow's benefit - these are deducted from the damages award under previous principles. Some payments - for example, small payments not exceeding £2,500 - are expressly exempted from the new system and these become subject not to common law deduction but to earlier legislation permitting the defendant to retain one half of benefits over a five-year period, although these are not then paid over to the government tax authorities.

b. *Redundancy payments.* These are deducted from damages if caused by the injury.

c. *Private insurance.* This is not deducted - why should the defendant benefit from the plaintiff's good sense?

d. *Occupational disability pension.* Not deductible - like insurance.

e. *Charity payments.* Not deducted - donors wanted to help the plaintiff, not the defendant.

f. *Occupational sick pay.* Not deducted if made up of gratuitous payments by the employer - akin to charity. Deductible if payable as a benefit under contract of employment as a partial substitute for earnings.

b. Future medical expenses

Future nursing fees, reasonable sums for relatives undertaking care, medical care including private, travelling expenses - these can be calculated and claimed (but not for care by the defendant himself, see *Hunt v. Severs supra,* p.743). There is no obligation on the plaintiff to apply the award to these purposes however.

c. Future care

Sometimes in serious cases this is the greatest part of the damages, including cost of medical teams, round-the-clock nursing, medical and financial experts, builders, therapists and so forth.

d. Cost of bringing up children

In *Bennar v. Kettering Health Authority* (1988) 138 NLJ Rep 179, a man fathered a child after a vasectomy. He was awarded costs of its upbringing *and* fees for private education because the other children in the family went to private schools.

However, where parents actually want a child, but the child is born handicapped because of hospital negligence, they only receive the *additional* costs of bringing up a handicapped child (*Salih v. Enfield Health Authority* [1991] 3 All ER 400).

e. Housekeeping

If a housewife is disabled by negligence, as a non-earner she cannot claim for lost earnings. However, as the person who looks after the home, she will receive future "losses" based on the cost of domestic help - even if her tasks are in fact now carried out by other members of the family or friends and no one is paid to come in and help (*Daly v. General Steam Navigation Co. Ltd* [1981] 1 WLR 120).

Non-Pecuniary Past and Future Losses

These are as follows:

a. Pain and suffering from injuries

Damages will cover physical and mental pain and suffering - past and future - caused by the injury. Pain of an unwanted pregnancy is included (reduced by any discomfort which would have been caused by a successful abortion or sterilization) as is any anguish caused by knowledge of a reduced life expectancy. In addition, reduction of marriage prospects and consequent loss of companionship through the injuries can also be recovered for (*Hughes v. McKeown* [1985] 3 All ER 284).

However, persons left unconscious by the injury have been held unable to recover for pain and suffering of which they are unaware (*Wise v. Kaye* [1962] 1 QB 638).

Clearly, the calculation of damages on this basis is not very scientific and courts will look at facts and circumstances and follow the precedents on amounts. An appeal will not succeed unless the Judge was incorrect on law or fact or the award was blatantly wrong.

b. Loss of faculties and amenities

This is about loss of skills or enjoyment ability:

- no more career satisfaction;
- no longer able to play tennis or the violin;
- cannot enjoy domestic life; or
- unable to have sexual relations.

Unlike pain and suffering, loss of amenity is compensatable even if the plaintiff is unconscious (*H. West and Son Ltd v. Shepherd* [1964] AC 326): the deprivation is said to be factual or objective and unaffected by the consciousness or otherwise of the plaintiff as to the loss - it is lost, it is a negative (*Lim Poh Choo v. Camden & Islington Area Health Authority* [1980] AC 174). Some have expressed concern that this encourages relatives of people in a vegetative state to keep them alive until the trial, in order to inherit the damages, whereas, if they were allowed to die before trial, all that the relatives would possess, would be a claim as dependants for loss of a breadwinner under the fatal accidents legislation.

The courts calculate a single global sum for loss of amenities and the injury itself, based upon guidelines and precedents as to the range of value of a particular loss: £X for a broken leg, £Y for an eye, and £Z for a hand. There is a certain scope for differentiation: a 17-year-old amateur footballer will get more for a leg than a 55-year-old librarian.

c. Bereavement and loss of amenity of third parties

It should be mentioned that it is possible for people other than the injured victim himself to make a claim for their own suffering or loss of amenity because of injuries to the victim.

Bereavement

Section 3 of the Administration of Justice Act 1982 has the effect that parents of dead children under 18 and spouses can claim damages for bereavement of a fixed sum of £7,500.

A spouse gets the sum whether they liked their dead partner or not. An unmarried co-habitant receives nothing.

In the case of children, for parents to claim bereavement, the child must be under 18 at death, not just at the time of the prior injury. In *Doleman v. Deaking* (1990) *The Independent,* January 30, a 17-year-old boy was knocked down by a negligent motorist as he walked across a pedestrian crossing. He never regained consciousness and died a few days after his eighteenth birthday. His parents received nothing for bereavement.

Loss of Consortium

This head of damages was removed by the 1982 Act. It refers to what was delicately alluded to as a wife's service and society - in the kitchen and bedroom. However, it still appears possible for a spouse to bring such a claim for loss of the marital relationship under general tortious doctrine. In *Hodgson v. Trapp* [1988] 3 All ER 870, a husband was awarded £20,000.

(v) Mitigation of Damage

Once the defendant has committed a tort against the plaintiff, the plaintiff is under a duty to take *reasonable* steps to mitigate - control - his loss: look for another job; seek medical treatment; buy a second-hand replacement for damaged property, if repairs would cost more. He cannot simply stand by and allow losses to increase when these would have been easy to prevent or reduce - although courts will still try not to place too heavy a burden upon plaintiffs in this respect (*Selvanayagam v. University of the West Indies* [1983] 1 All ER 824).

(vi) Damage to Property

1. Property destroyed

The plaintiff receives the market value as at the date of destruction (*Liesbosch Dredger v. SS Edison* [1933] AC 449). In addition, he may claim costs of hiring a replacement or substitute, if reasonable to do so (*Martindale v. Duncan* [1973] 1 WLR 574).

2. Damaged property

Damages are the decrease in value - even if repair costs are greater - and costs of hiring a replacement pending repairs (*O'Grady v. Westminster Scaffolding Ltd* [1962] 2 Lloyd's Rep 238). In the case of land, it may be that repair costs rather than fall in value - even if the former are higher - would be regarded as the true extent of the loss, where the plaintiff intends to remain in occupation rather than sell (*Dodd Properties (Kent) Ltd v. Canterbury City Council* [1980] 1 All

ER 928). The essential test is what steps are commercially reasonable (*Dodd Properties*).

(vii) Interest on Damages

Actions, in particular those for personal injuries, can take years to come to court. In the meantime, the plaintiff is losing the use or interest which he could have gained from the money between the time of the injury and the judgment.

Can he claim interest?

(a) In personal injuries, interest *must* be awarded, but the courts have a negative discretion not to do so in special circumstances, under the Supreme Court Act 1981, s.35A. Interest may be reduced if the plaintiff delayed in conducting proceedings (*Birkett v. Hayes* [1982] 2 All ER 710).

(b) In other cases, courts have a *discretion*.

(c) As for rates:

i. for accrued pecuniary loss - the rate is one half of normal short-term commercial interest rates, from the date of injury to trial (*Jefford v. Gee* [1970] 2 QB 130);
ii. for past and future (indivisible) non-pecuniary loss - only two per cent from *writ* to trial, because the award itself will take account of current inflation;
iii. no interest is given for future pecuniary loss, because the plaintiff has not yet been deprived of its use.

2. Injunctions

A court may grant the remedy of an injunction instead of or in addition to damages for tort where it is just and convenient to do so (Supreme Court Act 1981, s.37). Injunctions are a discretionary remedy. They are intended to prevent the future repetition of the tort, for example, further publication of a defamatory statement, continuation of trespass or economic torts, or even expected future commission. If damages would be adequate, or the harm is minor, or compliance with an injunction would be impracticable (though not merely difficult or expensive) or in need of constant supervision, or if the plaintiff himself is guilty of delay, an injunction can be refused.

Disobedience to an injunction is a "contempt of court" punishable by a fine or imprisonment.

Different types of injunctions are usually distinguished in the following manner:

(i) Prohibitory

This is a negative injunction requiring the defendant to stop committing a tort, such as trespass, nuisance or defamation. Section 50 of the Supreme Court Act 1981 gives courts power to award damages instead. In *Shelfer v. City of London Electric Lighting Company* [1895] 1 Ch 287, the Court of Appeal said that this should only be done if:

- an injunction would be oppressive to the defendant;
- interference with the plaintiff's interests is not great; and
- the damage is calculable in money.

Without these restraints, rich defendants could "buy off" the plaintiff's rights.

(ii) Mandatory

These are harder to obtain. They order the defendant to do something, for example, to remove an obstruction to a right of light.

In *Morris v. Redland Bricks Ltd* [1970] AC 562, it was made clear by the House of Lords that the tortious wrong would have to be very serious before the discretion would be exercised in favour of a mandatory injunction. Thus: (a) damages would not be sufficient, (b) the defendant's behaviour must have been wanton or unreasonable, and (c) the injunction must state precisely what the defendant is required to do.

(iii) Interim

In cases of great urgency, a Judge can grant an interim injunction, provisionally restraining the defendant until the final application is heard.

On an interim application, the Judge will not have to decide that the plaintiff will win his case eventually, merely that:

- there is a serious question to be tried; and
- the balance of convenience between plaintiff and defendant lies in favour of the grant of an interim injunction (*American Cyanamid Co. v. Ethicon Ltd* [1975] AC 396). The balance can only lie with the plaintiff if damages would be inadequate and the plaintiff has given an undertaking to pay damages to the defendant

for the latter's losses from the injunction should the plaintiff eventually lose his case.

(iv) Quia timet

This is an injunction against a threatened tort before it takes place. It will not be granted unless there is a *very strong likelihood* of its *imminent* occurrence (*Redland Bricks Ltd v. Morris, supra*).

3. Self-help Remedies

These are where the law allows parties to take action against commission of a tort without going to court.

They are strictly limited and exceptional (*Burton v. Winters* [1993] 1 WLR 1077): a house owner can use reasonable force to *eject* a trespasser; to *abate* a nuisance; a person who is falsely imprisoned *escapes*; a victim of assault and battery *defends* himself.

4. Effects of Death upon Tort Actions

Two issues arise from the death of a person as a result of a tort:

- does his action against the tortfeasor survive his death;
- do his dependants have any claim against the tortfeasor for loss of the victim's financial support?

(i) Survival of a Cause of Action in Tort

At common law, if a person was negligent, he might actually have found himself to be in a better position legally if he had finished off his victim, because if the latter was killed, his cause of action died with him!

Now, however, under s.1(1) of the Law Reform (Miscellaneous) Provisions Act 1934, causes of action (except defamation and exemplary damages) existing in favour of or against a deceased person survive for or against his estate.

Damages are assessed on the usual bases: pecuniary and non-pecuniary (pain and suffering, loss of amenity) losses *up to death;* but no non-pecuniary or, expressly under the Administration of Justice Act 1982, s.4(2), lost earnings, if death was instantaneous (so only living plaintiffs can claim for "lost years", see *supra,* p.746, which restriction is intended to prevent a windfall to the estate for dependants who could also claim for loss of a breadwinner under the Fatal Accidents Act 1976), leaving only funeral expenses to be claimed - although gains from death, such as insurance, are not deductible.

As a result of *Hicks v. Chief Constable of South Yorkshire* [1992] 2 All ER 65, it would seem that the victim must survive for a certain length of time following the accident if he is to be considered capable of undergoing pain and suffering which can then survive as a claim for the benefit of his estate: for, pain and terror in the final stages of life, associated with the injury and cause of death, are to be regarded as part of the death itself and consequently not as lifetime pain and suffering for which a claim could be made.

In *Hicks,* two sisters were asphyxiated at the Hillsborough football stadium disaster, and the House of Lords held that death had been too rapid for the pre-death suffering to be taken into account. Parker, LJ said (at p.694) in the judgment of the Court of Appeal ([1992] 1 All ER 690) which was upheld by the House of Lords: "The last few moments of mental agony and pain are in reality part of the death itself, for which no action lies under the 1934 Act."

The parents would be entitled to £7,500 bereavement damages for the sister under 18 years, and reasonable funeral expenses.

(ii) Claims for Loss of Dependency on the Death of a Financial Provider

1. Ability of dependants to claim

It was in 1846 at a time of great increase in accidents due to the industrial revolution in Britain that provision was first made for widows and children to claim compensation for the death of a "breadwinner" through tort - that is, the husband and father who was their financial support.

The current legislation is the Fatal Accidents Act 1976, under which:

(a) the dependant can claim only if the deceased himself or herself would have had a cause of action had he or she lived; and

(b) this means that if the defendant would have had a defence against the deceased or the deceased was contributorily negligent, fatal accident damages towards the dependants will correspondingly be excluded or reduced.

2. *Identity of dependants*

These are listed in the legislation (s.1) and have gradually been extended over the years as social attitudes towards the nature of a "family" have developed.

Dependants for fatal accidents include:

- spouses and former spouses;
- people living as husband and wife at death and for the last two years;
- parents;
- children and step-children, adopted and illegitimate;
- brothers and sisters, uncles and aunts;
- grandparents and grandchildren;
- all by marriage or blood

provided that the claimant was in fact financially dependant.

The action will usually be brought on behalf of dependants by the personal representatives of the deceased. If this is not carried out within six months of death, a dependant can do so instead (s.2). There will be one award under s.2(3), apportioned proportionately between dependants under s.3, usually the surviving spouse receiving more than children, and younger children receiving more than older, whose dependency period has less to run.

3. *Damages*

The following can be claimed under the 1976 Act:

i. *Bereavement*. Spouses, or parents of deceased children under 18 (only the mother, if illegitimate), can claim a fixed sum of £7,500 (s.1A).

Extent of grief, if any, need not be proven.

ii. *Funeral expenses.* Reimbursement of dependants for actual funeral costs is provided for.

iii. *Loss of future financial support.* The object of damages is to provide the dependants with a lump sum of capital, which can be invested so as to substitute for future financial support which the deceased person would have bestowed during the period of dependency.

Therefore, the calculation process is similar to that applied to assess future pecuniary losses to an injured plaintiff himself:

(a) the multiplicand is the deceased's net annual earnings after deducting tax, national insurance, and his personal living expenses (usually assumed to be 33 per cent if no children, 25 per cent if there are children); and
(b) the multiplicand is then multiplied by the multiplier.

The multiplier is calculated:

- as at death, not trial (contrast with live plaintiff

victims), because uncertainty as to what the future might have been starts at death in dependency claims (*Cookson v. Knowles* [1978] 2 All ER 604), whereas in the case of an injured plaintiff himself, his lost earnings between injury and trial are known (*Graham v. Dodds* [1983] 2 All ER 953); and

- taking account of the deceased's former life-expectancy and future prospects in the usual way; and of
- the dependant's own prospects, so that, for example, in the case of children, their dependency is unlikely to be considered to be expected to last beyond prospective full-time education (as to whether the latter will include further education beyond secondary school, the court must make a judgment). As usual too, are they likely to die young; to become ill; to be unable to work?

The court must make a reasonable assessment of what would have been the likely level and length of future support, and fix the amount of the multiplier accordingly. Thus, in *Corbett v. Barking Havering and Brentwood Health Authority* [1991] 1 All ER 498, at pp.508-9, the Court of Appeal stated that the following should be considered in fixing the amount: (1) probability that the breadwinner would have lived on; (2) life-expectancy of dependants; (3) the prospects of the breadwinner, good and bad; (4) prospective changes in needs of dependant; (5) discount for (i) immediate receipt of lump sum support and (ii) for the requirement that the lump sum should not last beyond dependency.

Specifically, the following factors may be of relevance:

a. Surviving spouse's remarriage prospects

In assessing future needs of a dependant, courts used to take into account a widow's prospects of remarriage. This would prove embarrassing and insensitive, with women being cross-examined about their personal lives and - not to put too fine a point on it - Judges forming a view as to the attractiveness or otherwise of an applicant. Consequently, s.3(3) of the 1976 Act now prohibits courts from inquiring into *widows'* remarriage prospects in calculating fatal accident damages: even if the widow has already remarried, this is to be ignored, however wealthy the new husband. Naturally, there has been criticism of this effect. Nevertheless, remarriage prospects are still taken into account:

- in the case of widows, where it is the children who are claiming for lost dependency; or
- where a widower, former spouse or co-habitant is the claimant (co-habitants with no legal rights of support are usually rewarded with a lower multiplier).

Furthermore, likelihood that the plaintiff dependant and the deceased would have divorced may reduce the multiplier, as in *Martin v. Owen* (1992) *The Times,* May 21, in which the figure was lowered from 15 to 11, because the marriage had only gone on for a year and the plaintiff had committed adultery on two occasions.

b. Prospective support

Even if support had not begun at the time of death, courts

can take account of reasonable expectations. For example, in *Taff Vale Railway Co. v. Jenkins* [1913] AC 1, the deceased was a 16-year-old trainee dressmaker and her parents were able to recover on the basis that when she would have shortly finished her apprenticeship, she would have been likely to help them financially. However, in the case of young children, prospects that they would have provided support for their parents had they lived are likely to be regarded as too uncertain (*Barnett v. Cohen* [1921] 2 KB 461).

c. Nature of prospective losses

Losses need not be purely financial: they can alternatively be money's worth. For example:

- a deceased mother's care of home and family, although, in *Stanley v. Saddique* [1991] 1 All ER 529, a child's damages were reduced because the deceased mother had not cared for him very well; in *Watson v. Wilmott* [1991] 1 All ER 473, the court held that damages should represent the difference in level of care provided by a child's adoptive parents when his own had died; however, if the child is better off without his parents, such an "advantage" from their deaths must be disregarded under s.4, 1976 Act (see *infra*); and
- loss of a mother to a child will be assessed as the commercial cost of hiring a full-time nanny, reducing as the child grows up (*Corbett v. Barking, supra*): this will be reduced if the mother worked, but otherwise increased to take account of the fact that parenthood is a 24-hour task.

Losses claimed must derive from lost *family* support - lost *business* opportunities from the death cannot be claimed. Thus, in *Burgess v. Florence Nightingale Hospital for Gentlewomen* [1955] 1 QB 349, a surviving husband was unable to recover for the loss of his wife's services as his professional dancing partner.

d. Deductions

Deductions from damages are not made in order to take account of benefits to the dependants which have, may or will accrue as a consequence of the death (s.4). This includes pensions, insurance, inheritance, social security - and non-financial benefits, such as a *better* family environment than a claimant child had before his mother's death (*Stanley v. Saddique* - although, in *Hayden v. Hayden* [1992] 4 All ER 681, a surviving father's care of the plaintiff child after the wife's death was held by a majority of the Court of Appeal to fall outside s.4, because a father had to care for his child in all events and so this was not as a consequence of the mother's death; and any benefits from adoption subsequent to parents' deaths are also not excluded from being taken into account as a deduction: *Watson v. Wilmott, supra.*

e. Interest

Once an award has been calculated, interest is granted on pre-trial damages at the usual rate for such pecuniary loss in personal injuries actions (*supra,* p.754).

5. Possible Reforms

The Law Commission has published a number of Reports and Consultation Papers on damages in recent times.

Amongst these was Law Commission Consultation Paper No.125 of 1992 on Structured Settlements and Interim and Provisional Damages.

In brief, the Commission's provisional conclusions, after a useful general discussion of advantages and disadvantages of lump sums and of the multiplier/multiplicand method of assessment of damages (paras.2.1-2.19), included the following:

(a) Actuarial evidence of financial needs and resources should have greater judicial recognition than at present - more sophisticated methods of predicting future interest rates and planning for interest rate movements were required (para.2.21).

(b) Damages for loss of earnings should continue to be paid net of tax in order not to overcompensate plaintiffs (para.2.39).

(c) Problems over failure to take account of future rates of tax or inflation in deciding upon the size of awards should be dealt with through greater recognition of actuarial evidence recommended (paras.2.40-2.42).

(d) The Consultation Paper then considers a number of matters relating to structured settlements, eg, the nature of the discount sought by defendants on the lump sum; taxation issues; the extension of tax advantages to where a court orders a structure and parties consent, rather than just where parties first reach agreement and discontinue legal proceedings; reviewability of the settlement where the plaintiff's medical injury deteriorates; position of legal advisers and accountants in the negotiations; judicial imposition of structured settlements (paras.3.1-3.97).

(e) Availability of interim awards on the basis of needs discretion should not be altered, unless it were to appear that the discretion were being exercised ungenerously (para.4.4). However, there may be a case for simplifying procedures in order to encourage solicitors to apply (para.4.7).

(f) Provisional damages should not be extended so as to include a gradual deterioration and progression in the plaintiff's condition, as an alternative to a serious clear-cut event (para.5.6 - see further, paras.5.7-5.21).

Another Law Commission publication was Consultation Paper No.140 called "Damages for Personal Injury: Non-Pecuniary Loss", published at the end of 1995.

Its intention was to examine whether levels of damages for pain and suffering were satisfactory or whether they had failed to keep pace with the inflation of the 1960s and 1970s.

The following is a brief summary of the Law Commission's recommendations and consultation issues.

(1) Damages for pain and suffering and loss of amenities should continue, because of the "importance of recognizing, by means of an award of damages, the fact that actionable

personal injury has very real *personal*, as well as financial, consequences for the individual concerned" (para.4.5). The Canadian "functional" approach toward such damages for non-pecuniary loss, whereby the plaintiff only receives damages for the cost of providing reasonable substitute pleasure was rejected *inter alia* as converting the non-pecuniary consequences into a form of pecuniary loss: "... a person who has lost her sight because of the defendant's wrong may be provided with the best hi-fi equipment and all the CDs she could possibly want ... but that cannot realistically be regarded as a true substitute for restoration of her sight" (para.4.9).

(2) A plaintiff who is permanently unconscious, possibly in a vegetative state, receives nothing for pain and suffering, but damages at the top of the scale for loss of amenities (*supra*, p.751). Should the latter be so? The Law Commission recognized that if a plaintiff was so badly injured that he was incapable of suffering, it was "strongly arguable that, just as if the plaintiff had been instantly killed, the plaintiff should be regarded as incurring no non-pecuniary loss at all ... that, in other words, all non-pecuniary loss should be assessed subjectively (through the plaintiff's awareness of it) and not objectively (irrespective of the plaintiff's unawareness of it)" (para.4.14). It decided to ask for views on the matter - and on the related, though not identical, question of whether conscious but severely brain-damaged plaintiffs with little appreciation of their position should also continue to be permitted to recover for non-pecuniary loss (paras.4.21 and 4.22).

(3) The Law Commission's provisional view, subject to consultees' responses, was against imposing a minimum

value threshold for recovery of non-pecuniary loss in small claims, because, *inter alia*, the way to reduce costs was rather through procedural reforms, plaintiffs might try to inflate or to prolong their symptoms in order to cross the threshold, and if there were no pecuniary losses, a plaintiff would receive no remedy at all if beneath the threshold (paras.4.25 and 4.26).

(4) The Law Commission further posed a whole series of questions concerning the adequacy of existing levels of damages, including *inter alia* the following: were they too high or too low, and if the latter, how should they be raised; was there agreement that awards had failed to keep pace with inflation over the last 30 years; should the existing judicial tariff of awards, with its upper and lower fixed limits and discretionary factors in-between, be retained, or was it better replaced by a new Compensation Advisory Board, with medical scoring systems and computerized assistance (paras.4.27-4.81)?

(5) Assessment of compensatory damages for personal injuries should always be a matter for the Judge and never left to a jury (generally, or where a jury in fact actually sits, namely in malicious prosecution or false imprisonment cases, leading to personal injuries): "Juries do not have the benefit of knowledge of the scale of values that has been developed and the inevitable consequence is unacceptable inconsistency with awards in other cases" (para.4.83). The Law Commission also - in fact prophetically (see *supra*, p.653 *et seq.*, *John v. MGN Ltd*) - recommended that in order to reduce the disparity between levels of personal injury awards and those in defamation cases, Judges in the latter should have the power to direct the jury as to comparative

personal injury amounts for non-pecuniary loss (para.4.103).

(6) The Law Commission reached the provisional view that interest should continue to be awarded on damages for non-pecuniary loss in personal injury actions, since to award no interest at all would be to undercompensate the plaintiff and there was also "the important pragmatic point that an award of interest is one of the few incentives given to defendants either to settle the action or to make efforts to bring the proceedings to trial as quickly as possible" (para.4.110).

However, should interest on non-pecuniary loss in future be confined to past such loss (as in the case of pecuniary) (see *supra,* p.754)? In soliciting views, the Law Commission noted an earlier opinion that "it would be too difficult and very artificial to try to separate the plaintiff's pain and suffering and loss of amenity into that endured in the past and that to be endured in the future and that this ought not therefore to be attempted" (para.4.111). However, further questions arose: generally (and *a fortiori* if future non-pecuniary damages were not to be subject to interest) was the current two per cent rate of interest sufficient (para.4.119); and should interest on damages for non-pecuniary loss be payable from the date of the accident rather than from the date of service of the writ (para.4.114) (see *supra,* p.754)?

(7) With regard to claims for damages for non-pecuniary loss (*supra,* p.750), the Law Commission held the provisional view that these should continue to survive for the benefit of a deceased victim's estate, as being fairer to injured persons and their families and not unfair to defendants, since "survival confers no new rights, but instead simply

permits subsisting rights to survive for the benefit of the deceased's estate" (paras.4.131 and 4.132) - and furthermore, the survival of such claims ought not to be limited to where the deceased commenced the action while alive, because it could encourage premature litigation and discourage the negotiated settlement of claims (para.4.137).

In addition to the preceding, readers are also referred to Law Commission Report No.225 of 1995, entitled *Personal Injury Compensation: How Much is Enough? A Study of the Compensation Experiences of Victims of Personal Injury.* The Law Commission's empirical study presents the results of a large scale survey of adequacy and effectiveness of damages for personal injuries - "the most comprehensive attempt to date to investigate the situation of compensated victims *some time after* the receipt of their compensation and to provide assessments of the adequacy of the damages received in the light of experience" (para.1) ... "qualitative data about the impact of accidental injury, whether minor or catastrophic, on the day-to-day existence of those who have been through the legal system and succeeded in gaining compensation for the injuries they have suffered" (para.12).

The Report lists some of its most important findings, including that:

- four out of five victims still experienced pain at the time of their interview and two in five were in constant pain;
- a high proportion of victims did not return to work at all after their accident or returned for a time but were forced to leave owing to the continuing effects

of the injuries;
- a significant burden of unpaid care was borne by parents, spouses and friends of the victims;
- whilst most victims were initially satisfied with their settlements for what seemed a substantial amount of money, their satisfaction drained away when the reality of long-term ill-effects and reduced capacity for work came to bite;
- a high proportion of those who eventually returned to a different job received much lower average earnings than reported in the job they had prior to the accident;
- availability of independent financial advice to victims was patchy, and although victims were not extravagant, nonetheless they may have made choices on expenditure which eventually they came to regret (para.14 and ch.14).

Ominously, the survey also found that the majority of victims had to wait a long time to receive their damages (para.15). It elaborated:

> "Although some degree of delay is unavoidable while the parties wait for the medical condition of the plaintiff to reach a plateau, a substantial proportion of cases, both large and small, remain unsettled four years after the date of the accident. There are a number of significant ramifications arising from such delay. During the litigation process the victim and the victim's family face a prolonged period of financial difficulty during which debts accumulate, savings are reduced and legal costs increase. These lengthy periods of financial hardship, in

addition to physical distress, affect the degree of satisfaction with damages and attitudes to adequacy. The stress of litigation and apprehension about the future may impede recovery, which has an impact on the probability that accident victims will eventually return to the workforce. Delay in receiving damages also influences decisions about the use of money as accident victims seek to make up for the material comforts that they have lacked in the years while waiting for their case to be settled" (para.15).

Finally, note Lord Woolf, MR's civil justice reform proposals in *Access to Justice* (see *infra*, Appendix Case 11).

Further reading:

Brazier, *Street on Torts*, 9th ed, 1993 (Butterworth & Co., London): chs.28, 29 and 30.

Fleming, J.G., *The Law of Torts*, 8th ed, 1992 (The Law Book Company, Sydney): ch.10.

Hepple, B.A. and Matthews, M.H., *Tort: Cases and Materials*, 4th ed, 1991 (Butterworth & Co., London): chs.8 and 9.

Heuston, R.F.V. and Buckley, R.A., *Salmond and Heuston on The Law of Torts*, 20th ed, 1992 (Sweet & Maxwell, London): chs.23, 24, 25 and 26.

Howarth, D., *Textbook on Tort*, 1995 (Butterworth & Co., London): ch.13.

Jones, M.A., *Textbook on Torts*, 4th ed, 1993 (Blackstone, London): ch.15.

Levin, Conditional Fees: The New Law (1996) Personal Injury 35.

Levin, Solicitors Acting Speculatively and Pro Bono (1996) 15 Civil Justice Quarterly 44.

Markesinis, B.S. and Deakin, S.F., *Tort Law*, 3rd ed, 1994 (Clarendon Press, Oxford): ch.8.

Rogers, W.V.H., *Winfield and Jolowicz on Tort*, 14th ed, 1994 (Sweet & Maxwell, London): chs.23 and 24.

Stanton, K.M, *The Modern Law of Tort*, 1994 (The Law Book Company, Sydney): chs.7 and 12.

Weir, T., *A Casebook on Tort*, 7th ed, 1992 (Sweet & Maxwell, London): ch.17.

Part XVI

Chapter 31

Conclusions

Much has happened in the English law of torts in recent times. This is partly due to the vision, character and responsiveness of a group of reforming Judges, conforming to the traditions of the common law, and partly also to the changing socio-political climate within the United Kingdom after nearly two decades of Conservative government amidst some of the greatest shifts in the world's geo-political structures. Perceptions will differ, but one view of the period would be that of some governmental skill and determination to generate growth and prosperity and thereafter to sustain the economic and social fabric against a backdrop of world recession, while at times, however, seeming almost to lack the, admittedly possibly irreconcilable, capacity for distribution of gains at least with an appearance of fairness without also risking jeopardy to conditions of economic success themselves. It may be no surprise, therefore, that more affluent members of society, which, it has to be said, will include Judges and high-earning, high-profile members of the legal profession, will be included amongst those who seek to achieve a far greater degree of justice on the micro-juridical/societal level - and commendable this is. There are problems, however, with some of their responses. On the social and political level, whereas the reformers' own relatively substantial financial affluence remains largely unaffected by their schemes, the settled expectations, interests and financial liabilities of the vast majority of the population may at times seem rather more threatened by their postures; and, on the legal plain, noble efforts to give effect to justice may not always meet with the strict requirements of analytical purity under the common law system and it is then left to poor academics to present and to clarify the law. Thus are works such as the present unworthy contribution brought into existence.

Some of the most noteworthy developments chronicled in this book include the judicial recognition of equivalence of psychiatric illness in *Page v. Smith,* accompanied by the Law Commission's Consultation Paper No.137 "Liability for Psychiatric Illness"; the possibility of development of a separate tort of causing a plaintiff to suffer physical injury or psychiatric illness through intentional or reckless conduct (outside trespass to the person, through being *indirect* harm), on the basis of the old case of *Wilkinson v. Downton* [1897] 2 QB 57 (commented on by R. Townshend-Smith, Senior Lecturer in Law at the University of Wales Swansea, in "Harassment as a Tort in English and American Law: the Boundaries of *Wilkinson v. Downton*", in (1995) 24 Anglo-American Law Review 299); not wholly unrelated High Court recovery of damages for stress at work in *Walker v. Northumberland County Council* (subsequently settled); the closing down of recovery for pure economic loss from acts in *Murphy v. Brentwood District Council,* but its incremental development from *Hedley Byrne & Co. Ltd v. Heller & Partners,* on the rather nebulous basis of "proximity of relations between plaintiff and defendant", as constituted by assumption of responsibility and reliance, in a number of situations in *Spring v. Guardian Assurance plc, Henderson v. Merrett Syndicates Ltd* and *White v. Jones*; the restatement of duty of care in public body discretion and breach of statutory duty in *X (Minors) v. Bedfordshire County Council, etc*; confirmation of the reasonable foreseeability requirement in cases of nuisance and *Rylands v. Fletcher* in *Cambridge Water Co. Ltd v. Eastern Counties Leather plc*; and the revolutionary changes of practice for the award of libel damages in *John v. MGN Ltd*, now accompanied by a Defamation Bill making its way through Parliament, which attempts to simplify procedures and encourage early settlement of disputes.

Then, of course, there is ... personal injuries.

The current preoccupation is to satisfy each of the criteria of a successful compensatory system within the overall requirements of a just and effective administration of justice.

Plaintiffs should receive the most favourable provision from the community of which they are part; defendants should not be unduly oppressed; risk may be spread, but not so far as to remove the deterrent effects of personal tort liability.

Injuries and motor cars take central place in the discussion.

No-fault liability financed by ... a tax on petrol, liability or first-party insurance, the national lottery?

The problem with taxation sourcing of catastrophic disability finance is the rationale: why negligence disability and not also natural impediments; why not education; why not general health provision?

With insurance, the arguments are familiar: lack of deterrence upon defendants, who are made secure in the knowledge of their liability cover; lower levels of awards, standardized away from individual needs; higher premiums, albeit reduced by savings on liability defence.

The national lottery? Opera houses and rugby stadia seem to have staked their claims - is anything left for the disabled?

Should the burden simply be allowed to remain on defendants and their insurers as at present? Not unless there are significant further procedural improvements to build upon the existing reforms of split trials and interim or provisional damages: penalties on insurers for late settlement and presumption of recoverability of costs in a plaintiff's favour notwithstanding payment into court might be a reasonable start. So too, the Law Commission, in its Consultation Paper No.140 on "Damages for Personal Injury: Non-Pecuniary Loss" (*supra*, ch.30) provisionally concludes that damages for non-pecuniary loss, at least in respect of very serious injuries, have not kept pace with inflation over the last 25 to 30 years (paras.4.50 and 4.51); while, again, in its previous Consultation Paper No.125 on "Structured Settlements and Interim and Provisional Damages", the Commission critically reviewed the adequacy of the existing system of lump sums and multipliers (see paras.2.1-2.19).

Procedural reforms are much in vogue at the present time and specialist personal injuries tribunals or a damages commission (or "Compensation Advisory Board", see Law Commission Consultation Paper No.140, para.4.72) are not an impossibility - the main difficulty being that any such major institutional innovations must enjoy the confidence and support of both plaintiffs and defendants and not merely of one side if they are to prove effective, *a fortiori* if arbitration arrangements are to be voluntary (see too now Lord Woolf, MR's *Access to Justice, infra,* Appendix).

These and other matters concerning long-term financing of care for the severely disabled are prominent on the reforming agenda for forthcoming years and the appropriate remedial role of the law of tort will be a central element in the discussion. For some time now, the prominent political message in the United Kingdom has been that we are to be considered as citizens rather than as members of society. Let it, therefore, be recalled that "citizen" derives from the Latin *civis* - of which the collectivism is "civilization". A personal injuries régime should be no less than *civilized.*

For the present, it remains to report that the author's own, personal gain from the particular exercise of preparing this work has been to discover why the law of tort remains such a popular and appealing subject: it is simply that it is so much less complicated than private international law.

APPENDIX ON RECENT CASE LAW

1. Negligence. Nervous shock - danger to property (ch.5, p.69). *Dobson v. North Tyneside Health Authority* (1996) *The Times,* July 15, CA

According to the Court of Appeal in *Dobson v. North Tyneside Health Authority,* citing *Williams v. Williams* (1880) 20 Ch D 659, 662-3, there is no property in a corpse such as would support an action for torts of conversion or wrongful interference with goods or a duty of care in negligence. In *Dobson* itself, the plaintiff next-of-kin wished to sue the defendant health authority for damages for disposing of a deceased's brain following an autopsy. The plaintiffs had wanted possession of the brain as evidence in their action against the defendants for negligent treatment of the deceased. However, Peter Gibson, LJ did qualify the general principle by adding that there *could* be a legal right to possession of a corpse if (a) plaintiffs were acting in the capacity of administrators, having a duty of burial, or (b) if the body had been stuffed or preserved for science or in a museum (which would not include temporary storage after autopsy).

It should be added nevertheless that even if the "property" in the corpse were, technically, not *owned* by the relatives suffering nervous shock in the situation in the text, policy would surely suggest that such a fine distinction ought nonetheless to be disregarded in application of principles of recovery!

2. Negligence. Duty of care - public policy immunity of the police (ch.5, p.225). *Silcott v. Commissioner of Police of the Metropolis* (1996) *The Times,* July 9, CA

The plaintiff was convicted of the murder of a policeman during a riot and sentenced to life imprisonment. Five years later the conviction was quashed on the ground that it was unsafe and unsound. The plaintiff sued the police for tortious damages, including for malicious prosecution, alleging that the notes of an interview with him were forgeries. The police raised the defence of public policy immunity from suit.

The Court of Appeal upheld police immunity. The plaintiff's argument that there was a difference between, on the one hand, false evidence given by a police officer himself - conceded to be subject to immunity - and, on the other hand, as here, interference with the preparation of evidence - not also to benefit from the immunity - was rejected by the court. Simon Brown, LJ considered that the immunity covered all such conduct which could fairly be said to be part of the investigatory and preparatory process. The alleged forgeries, however, could lead to criminal proceedings for perjury or for perverting the course of justice.

3. Duty of Care and Standard of Care in Negligence (see *supra,* ch.5, pp.217 and 232)

A third High Court decision, this time by Rougier J, in *John Munroe (Acrylics) Ltd v. London Fire and Civil Defence Authority and Others* (1996) *The Times,* May 22, subsequently added to the developing case law some two weeks after *Capital and Counties plc v. Hampshire County Council*. The line taken by Rougier, J was against *Capital and Counties* and consistent with *Church of Jesus Christ of Latter-Day Saints (Great Britain) v. Yorkshire Fire and Civil Defence Authority* - that is to say, no duty of care in negligence upon the defendant fire brigade. However, in the latter, it will be recalled, the fire brigade's "immunity" had been held to be based upon (i) public policy and (ii) the finding that, although there was sufficient *proximity of relationship* between plaintiff and defendant, nevertheless, it would not be fair, just and reasonable to impose a duty at common law upon the fire brigade according to the *Caparo Industries plc v. Dickman* three-stage test of duty of care in negligence. Not so in *John Munroe (Acrylics) Ltd* where the decision against duty of care was based upon (i) public policy and (ii) *absence of a sufficient relationship of proximity* within *Caparo* between the owners of property and fire brigades to respond to a call for assistance!

Public policy

Reasons from the authorities against the duty in the case of the *police* were cited by way of analogy: no extra standard would be achieved in practice; defensive firefighting; superiority of local inquiries into efficiency of fire services; collective welfare role of fire brigade; floodgates arguments.

The report of the Judge's findings goes on, revealingly as to modern incremental judicial attitudes: "It was a truism to say that we lived in an age of compensation. There seemed to be a growing belief that every misfortune, in pecuniary terms at least, had to be laid at someone else's door, and after every mishap, every tragedy, the cupped palms were outstretched for the solace of monetary compensation ... Fire brigades were often reacting to situations created by the hand of God or that of a lunatic or a criminal. Pecuniary compensation was notoriously difficult to obtain from such persons, particularly the first ... The consequence was that the party suffering damage would be eager to fix his canon against a defendant who would be in a position to meet a claim. The money to meet successful claims would have to be subscribed by the general public." Consequently, Rougier, J believed, the countervailing arguments in favour of the imposition of a duty on the ground of public policy had nothing like the weight of the case against so doing.

No relationship of proximity

The apparent discrepancy between this basis for lack of duty of care upon the fire brigade in *John Munroe (Acrylics) Ltd* and that in *Church of Jesus Christ* where proximity was held to exist, but no fair, just and reasonable duty also to do so, was indicated above. What is here considered to be the *artificiality* of the distinction between "proximity" and "fair, just and reasonable" under stages two and three of the orthodox three-stage test in *Caparo,* has previously been referred to (see *supra* Preface and ch.5 - in fairness to Rougier, J, it seems from the report that it was the parties themselves who agreed upon adoption of the three-stage test to decide the case). However, the test represents the law and it may be possible to distinguish *John Munroe* and *Church of Jesus Christ* on their facts. In the latter, it will be recalled, the complaint concerned the defendant fire brigade's performance in fighting the fire - or at least in carrying out inspections and in installing the necessary equipment to do so beforehand. To that extent, therefore, there was some kind of relationship, which might be said to be proximate, between the plaintiff property owners and defendant fire brigade. In *John Munroe (Acrylics) Ltd,* on the other hand, the defendant fire brigade responded to an emergency call from the plaintiff property owners but did not engage in fighting a fire which they incorrectly concluded had burnt itself out. Rougier, J, citing the analogous position of the police in *Alexandrou v. Oxford* [1993] 4 All ER 328, seemed to treat the case - as in *Church of Jesus Christ,* against a background of no personal action for breach of statutory duty under the Fire Services Act 1947 - as one of *failure to respond properly* to an emergency call. According to the Judge, applying the incremental approach in *Caparo* and endorsing the retreat from the wider approach in *Anns v. Merton London Borough Council* [1978] AC 728, there was not a sufficient relationship of proximity between owners of property and the fire brigade which was sufficient to impose a duty of care upon the latter *to respond* to a call for help; and seemingly, even if the fire service did respond, as in *John Munroe (Acrylics) Ltd,* until - at least - they actually started *fighting the fire,* proximity was still absent: "Before the necessary proximity could be established something more, a special ingredient, had to be shown to demonstrate that besides the mere performance of their public duty the fire brigade, or other emergency services, undertook a personal responsibility to some individual during the course of their activity". It must be said, however, that - through no fault of Rougier, J who was hamstrung by the deficiencies of the *Caparo* three-stage test which the parties wished him to apply - the idea of a distinction between these facts and those in *Church of Jesus Christ* is difficult to sustain, as is the conception that, if proximity be the test, there exists no proximity between a fire brigade and property owner unless either the fire brigade has established some prior "relationship" with the property owner, as in *Church of Jesus Christ,* or until the fire brigade actually starts fighting the fire or even later in the course of doing so when it undertakes some special activity. Furthermore, if such distinctions are to be made, *proximity* is not the appropriate method. It is far better simply to say, incrementally, that in these situations in both *Church of Jesus Christ* and *John Munroe (Acrylics) Ltd,* it is both contrary to public policy and in any event not *fair, just and reasonable* to impose a duty of care in negligence upon the fire brigade.

At least, however, one thing is becoming clearer at the end of it all: whatever the basis of the "immunity" - be this public policy or lack of proximity or absence of fair, just and reasonable grounds for liability or low standard of care expected - the balance seems to be tilting away from fire brigade negligence duty of care in the course of its operations.

The eventual decision of Judge Havery, QC in the High Court in *Capital and Counties plc* to order the defendant fire brigade to pay £16 million damages and £2 million costs attracted front-page headlines in the national press (see *The Times* (1996) June 8). A local authority official was quoted as declaring: "This is a dangerous precedent. It will affect the judgment of officers about whether to send their men into a fire. Judges sitting on benches have no idea what it means to go into a blazing building and take life-and-death decisions while facing death themselves." Apparently, the defendants intend to appeal against the Judge's ruling.

4. Negligence. Damage - causation (ch.7). *South Australia Asset Management Corporation v. York Montague Ltd* (1996) *The Times,* June 24, HL

The plaintiff lenders of money on mortgage sued the defendant valuers of the property for damages caused by the defendants' negligent overvaluation, including that attributable to a substantial fall in the market value by the date upon which the borrowers defaulted.

The House of Lords unanimously held that damages should be limited to the difference between the defendants' incorrect valuation and the lower true value of the property at the date of valuation. They would not also include the further fall in value at the date of the borrowers' default.

Lord Hoffmann appeared to distinguish between where, on the one hand, as here, incorrect advice was given by a defendant which enabled the plaintiff to make a decision himself upon a particular course of action, and, on the other hand, advice on a course of action itself. In the former case, it did not seem fair that the defendant should be liable for all consequences of the incorrect advice when this was merely one factor taken into account by the plaintiff in reaching his decision. If a doctor were to pronounce a climber's knee to be fit and the climber then went and scaled a mountain from which he fell for reasons unconnected with the knee, the doctor would not be liable just because the climber would not have gone up the mountain if the diagnosis of the knee had been correct. Similarly therefore, perhaps the plaintiffs would not have lent the money on the same terms or at all had the valuation been accurate. But, having done so, they could not thereafter hold the defendants liable for all further consequences of the advance which they had decided to make.

The report suggests that Lord Hoffmann used the language of *all* of (scope of) duty of care, causation and remoteness of damage as the basis for his decision.

At first glance, of these, remoteness seems the best bet.

However, there is quite a strong argument for the judgment to be treated as one on causation. If negligent advice is given, which then leads to a course of action on the part of the plaintiff which might be harmless or harmful - the latter in the event - the negligent advice may have "caused" the *course of action*, yet not also the subsequent damage, since the course of action would merely have been the *occasion for the loss,* not itself the inevitable *causa causans* thereof. In effect, the course of action - climbing the mountain, or making the mortgage advance, as the case may be - was *novus actus interveniens* breaking any alleged chain of causation between original negligence and the harmful event claimed for.

5. Types of Public Nuisance (see *supra*, ch.23, pp.560 and 561)

In the *criminal* nuisance case of *R. v. Johnson (Anthony Thomas)* (1996) *The Times,* May 22, CA, the appellant made hundreds of obscene telephone calls to at least 13 different women in the South Cumbria area over a period of 5½ years. The defence argued that although the calls might be a private nuisance to an individual recipient, it was wrong to lump them all together and to find the cumulative effect to be a *public* nuisance.

However, the Court of Appeal, Criminal Division, disagreed. Referring to the words of Romer, LJ in *Attorney-General v. P.Y.A. Quaries Ltd* [1957] 2 QB 169, 184, 191 that any nuisance was public if it materially affected the reasonable comfort and convenience of a class of Her Majesty's subjects and to those of Denning, LJ who said that a public nuisance was so widespread in its range or so indiscriminate in its effect that it would not be reasonable to expect one person to take proceedings on his own responsibility to put a stop to it, but that it should be taken on the responsibility of the community at large, Tucker, J expressed the court's view that it was permissible and necessary to consider the cumulative effect of the calls in the area. On so doing, the court found that it was conduct which materially affected the reasonable comfort and convenience of a class of Her Majesty's subjects and was a nuisance so widespread in its range or indiscriminate in its effect that it would not be reasonable to expect one person to take proceedings on her own responsibility. The conclusion was not affected by the fact that the calls were not picked at random and that the appellant had first met the recipients socially or through work. As to whether the scale and amount of the calls was sufficient to constitute a public nuisance, that was a question of fact (for the jury in a criminal case).

Interestingly, therefore, the *class* of subjects affected by public nuisance is in fact potentially nationwide in the case of telephone obscenities.

6. Defamation: mere repetition no defence (*supra,* ch.26, p.614)

In *Stern v. Piper and Others* (1996) *The Times,* May 30, CA, the defendant newspaper's report about the plaintiff concerned an allegation of his failure to honour debts of more than £3 million, which had been made in a sworn affidavit for the purposes of legal proceedings being brought against the plaintiff, a discharged bankrupt. The Court of Appeal held that it was no defence to a defamation action for the defendant to prove that he was merely repeating what he had been told (following *Lewis v. Daily Telegraph Ltd* [1964] AC 234).

Further, since the defence of "privilege" applied to reports of legal proceedings conducted and to documents produced in open court, it was only fair that, in the absence of such publicity, *both* sides' allegations should be reported, fairly and accurately, and not just one side's. If the repetition rule were able to be avoided in such cases, much of the law of privilege could be rendered otiose.

7. Defences. Limitation of actions and accrual of the cause of action for the purposes of Limitation Act 1980, s.14A (ch.29). ***Hamlin v. Edwin Evans (a Firm)*** **(1996)** ***The Times,*** **July 15. CA**

The plaintiffs claimed for two forms of damage arising from a negligent house survey: *i.* dry rot and *ii.* structural defects. The dry rot was discovered two years after the survey and was settled for a relatively minor sum of money. The larger, structural defects become apparent after a further six years. The Court of Appeal held that where the tort complained of was negligence committed in a single report, there was only one single and indivisible cause of action: negligence in the making of the report. Therefore, the cause of action accrued for s.14A of the Limitation Act 1980, inserted by the Latent Damage Act 1986, when the first damage - here, dry rot - came to light, and not also when other damage - structural defects - subsequently appeared. Consequently, the claim for structural defects was now out of time. "It was in the nature of any system of limitation of actions that it might at times work arbitrarily or even harshly" (*per* Waite, LJ).

8. Defences. Limitation of actions - Limitation Act 1980, s.32A (ch.29). ***C v. Mirror Group Newspapers*** **(1996)** ***The Times,*** **July 15, CA**

In March 1988, the defendant newspaper published an untrue statement about the plaintiff which had been made, but subsequently withdrawn, by the plaintiff's ex-husband, alleging membership of a drugs gang. The plaintiff and her ex-husband had been involved in a child custody contest. The defendant claimed that it had the defence of qualified privilege: it was merely reporting what the ex-husband had stated in court. In August 1993, however, the Judge in the custody case wrote to the plaintiff stating that so far as could be recalled the ex-husband had said nothing about drugs in the course of the court proceedings. In March 1994 the plaintiff issued her writ for defamation. Section 32A of the Limitation Act 1980 provides that where a defamation plaintiff had not brought a claim within three years because all or any of the "facts relevant to that cause of action" did not become known to the plaintiff until after expiration of that period, the court may extend it for one year from the date of knowledge. The plaintiff argued that the date of her knowledge of relevant facts was 1993 when the Judge wrote to her, not 1988 when she found out about the defendant newspaper article.

The Court of Appeal disagreed. *Facts relevant to the cause of action* in s.32A meant only such facts as established existence of the cause of action, to be pleaded in the statement of claim, not also those facts - here, the Judge's revelation - which might rebut a defence (of qualified privilege) to the libel claim.

9. Remedies. "Lost years" - calculation of damages (ch.30, p.746). *Phipps v. Brooks Dry Cleaning Services Ltd* (1996) *The Times,* July 18, CA

Damages for lost years were to be reduced by the victim's

estimated living expenses for that period. The victim's common expenses with his spouse would be taken as being a proportionate 50 per cent thereof. With regard to losses from what would have been the victim's "do-it-yourself" activities in those years, this would solely be taken into account as loss of amenity, and not also as the lost value of the end product of those activities.

10. Negligence. Duty of Care - omissions; public policy; breach of statutory duty (ch.5, pp.211 and 214). ***Stovin v. Wise, Norfolk County Council (Third Party)*** **(1996)** ***The Times,*** **July 26, HL**

House of Lords overturns Court of Appeal by majority of three to two, and holds: no common law duty of care upon a public body from a statutory power on the facts.

11. Remedies. Personal injuries - damages (ch.30)

"*Access to Justice*", Lord Woolf, MR's proposals to reform the civil justice system in England and Wales, published on July 26, 1996. See, in particular, *plaintiffs' offers to settle.*

Index